HUMAN VARIATION AND ORIGINS

Readings from
SCIENTIFIC AMERICAN

HUMAN VARIATION AND ORIGINS

An introduction to human biology and evolution

WITH INTRODUCTIONS BY *W. S. Laughlin and R. H. Osborne*
UNIVERSITY OF WISCONSIN, MADISON

W. H. Freeman and Company SAN FRANCISCO AND LONDON

Each of the SCIENTIFIC AMERICAN articles in *Human Variation and Origins* is available as a separate Offprint at twenty cents each. For a complete listing of approximately 550 articles now available as Offprints, write to W. H. Freeman and Company, 660 Market Street, San Francisco, California 94104.

Printed in the United States of America.

Library of Congress Catalog Card Number: 67-22256

PREFACE

The human species has been remarkably successful in maintaining a high degree of diversity and, simultaneously, its identity as a single species. This diversity is seen in the growth of the individual, in the differences between individuals within the same population, and in the differences between populations. Man has adapted to many different ecological zones and is now the most widespread of any primate species. Whether we phrase the objective of physical anthropology (human biology) as the study of human variation, human adaptability, or human evolution, our first focus is necessarily upon the genetics, growth, and ecology of living and recent populations.

The authors are concerned with exploring the multiple bases for human variation—the interactions of genetic and environmental factors, and of processes and conditions—which human populations recombine in many ways to create their biologically and culturally perpetuating communities.

Contemporary variation provides the yardstick for measuring differences between early fossil forms, because, in the study of these forms, sample size and restriction to osseous remains prevent the observation of longitudinal growth, genetics, or behavior that is essential to understanding population dynamics.

The future of our species depends upon a precise understanding of the basis of variation. No one population has a monopoly on the genetic basis of variation or the adaptive systems related to it. Populations differ in the frequency of various traits, the presence or absence of traits, and the genetic basis of some of the same traits; in size, proportions, physiological adaptation, and therefore in growth rates; in densities, breeding structure, and their cultural systems for programming children; and in the major environmental stresses to which they are exposed—nutrition, disease, and climate.

Each population is a valuable laboratory experiment in human adaptability: thus all human populations, whether demes, defect isolates, corporate breeding populations, or continental races, are worth study. Our concern lies with mechanisms and processes, with principles and methods of analysis, as well as with documented population history, as the means to understanding the basis for human variation.

We are especially indebted to Professor Hansjürgen Müller-Beck, Dr. Verner Alexandersen, and Mrs. Mary Wakeman for their scientific and editorial assistance. Mrs. Carol Knott has been associated with the course we offer and has also rendered valuable service. "We thank Dr. Leonard Freedman, University of Wisconsin, for participating in the preliminary edition of this reader for which he was co-editor and for discussions and assistance in arrangement and selection of the articles for the present edition." Future editions will benefit from the observations of students as well as teachers and researchers, and we will welcome such observations.

W. S. LAUGHLIN, R. H. OSBORNE

CONTENTS

IV. INTERPOPULATION VARIATION

Note on cross-references: Cross-references within the articles are of three kinds. A reference to an article included in this book is noted by the title of the article and the page on which it begins; a reference to an article that is available as an offprint but is not included here is noted by the article's title and offprint number; a reference to a SCIENTIFIC AMERICAN article that is not available as an offprint is noted by the title of the article and the month and year of its publication.

HUMAN VARIATION AND ORIGINS

PART I
PROCESSES AND
HISTORY

Introduction: The development of
concepts in the study of human variation

Human beings are of many different shapes and sizes. This homely statement inadequately expresses the fact that they vary in age, sex, race, nutritional condition, disease, family line, blood groups, pigmentation, in response to daily variations in barometric pressure, and in such an infinite number of other ways that no two individuals, including "identical twins," are ever identical. Yet, the variation in human beings is by no means random or capricious, but rather it is clustered and organized in several respects. As a consequence it can be systematically and scientifically studied. The geographical distribution of variation is the most obviously clustered: although one of every six children born in the world may be Chinese, not one of every six born in New York or London is Chinese. As children grow, the annual additions to their stature and physiological maturation vary greatly, but the continuity and regularity permits the identification of the same person at different ages and even some predictions of adult size and form. Parents may produce children who appear dissimilar to each other and to their parents, but there is a limit to this variation and there are rules governing the inheritance of particular traits. Siblings can reliably be distinguished from children to whom they are unrelated. We discover other forms of variation, including differences in skull shape and size, as we move backward in the history of our species. Still another kind of variation is that of reproductive variability: that is, certain matings produce more children than do others. This variation, differential reproduction, is the basis of evolution.

Variation is a useful theme for reviewing both the complex history of the study of man and man's evolutionary history. In pre-Darwinian times (before 1859) little was known of the sources of variation or of its transmission. Correlatively, little was known of the range of variation in human morphology, either within populations or between populations. The boundaries of the human species were obscure, and many "exotic" races (exotic to Europeans) were thought to be semihuman beings that were intermediate between "man" and the apes. Although animal breeders had built up a large body of practical information that significantly contributed to the later development of genetics and evolutionary theory, there was no systematic science of heredity. Individual variations were considered accidental or even pathological departures from a preordained type—an admission that nature did not always hit the mark that it aimed for. Variations between groups were thought to reflect the difference between "lower" and "higher" types, rather than racial variations within one highly variable species. In the years since, scientists of many disciplines have investigated regularities in the production of variation, and have tried to interpret atypical variants in chromosomes, blood, fossil man, exotic racial types, nonhuman primates similar to humans, and abnormal individuals. Publication dates of such studies may be misleading because they neither indicate the period of intellectual gestation nor give proof of parentage. Nevertheless, the history of genetical and evolutionary theory is well documented, owing in part to recent systematic studies and to historians of science.

Historical problems in recognizing man

The elucidation of both the pattern of human evolution and the explanatory processes depended in part upon recognition of the object of study. Until 1859, man was not generally considered an animal who had enjoyed a long period of evolution, and, as a consequence, his similarities and dissimilarities with other animals were not evaluated. Although today an adequate definition of a human being may seem a modest achievement scarcely worth two centuries of scholarly inquiry, the problem of distinguishing humans from all other forms has actually been a central problem in the study of variation.

The inability to distinguish humans from nonhumans has cost many thousands of lives and has resulted in the extermination of entire groups of humans. At present, we can recognize all contemporary human beings and exclude from this elect category all nonhumans. Our ability to make this distinction is of fairly recent origin, and it still does not obtain for the most early emerging forms of man.

There have been five major problem groups in the overall task of defining man. Some of these groups were excluded from the human category when they should have been included, others were included that should not have been. The problem groups are (1) the larger anthropoid apes (gorillas, chimpanzees, and orangutans), (2) newly discovered races of man, (3) fossil man, (4) microcephals and other pathological forms, (5) the most well-known ape-men from Africa, the Australopithecines.

Anthropoid apes and man have occupied common taxonomic territory with alarming frequency. Apes have been mistaken for humans, and humans for apes. Not until 1699 did a qualified researcher dissect an ape with the purpose of determining, by actual and detailed comparison of its similarities and dissimilarities to humans, whether it was in fact an ape or a human. Edward Tyson dissected a young chimpanzee and correctly concluded that it was not a human —neither pygmy nor other. Tyson's study, *Orang-Outang Sive Homo Sylvestris; Or, the Anatomy of a Pygmie compared with that of a Monkey, an Ape, and a Man,* did not become a bestseller. Its effect was slight, and its publication date does not mark the birth of our ability to delimit the human species. In the eighteenth century, Linnaeus, to whom we owe our binomial system of nomenclature, wrestled with the problem of "tailed men" and apes, and lost the match. He included some anthropoid apes in his roster, noting that there has yet to be found the surveyor of nature who can draw a line between apes and man. Indeed, Tyson's monumental study had little more effect on humans than it had on apes.

Newly discovered races of man, many of which were first reported to European audiences by explorers of the fifteenth and sixteenth centuries, were frequently, if not invariably, placed in a nonhuman or quasihuman category. "Brutal Hottentot" and "stupid Lapp" were common appellations for these kinds of peoples, who were suspected of not possessing full powers of human speech. Tasmanians, Ainu, Bushmen, and many populations of American Indians were placed in a suspense account or else placed in subordinate positions in the "Great Chain of Being." The practice of comparing "higher" races, "lower" races, and anthropoid apes unfortunately persists today (Nott and Gliddon, 1854; Montagu, 1933, pp. 331–332; Hoebel, 1966, p. 225). Although this practice may be considered socially beneficial it keeps alive the idea that such comparisons have scientific merit (Washburn, 1946, pp. 371–372). The separation of man and apes from a common ancestry occurred some thirteen to twenty million years ago. The comparison of racial subdivisions within one species, with samples of other genera for hierarchical arguments, is comparable to comparing different races of seagulls with crocodiles in order to find which race is most closely related to a common ancestor.

Fossil men were considered by many to be nonhuman or pathological. The early treatment of fossil men illustrates the fact that identifications are not self-evident but depend upon the sophistication of the observer. The first recognized Neanderthal cranium, found in 1856, was identified by one authority as an Irishman, by another as a Russian Cossack, and by a third as a clearly pathological individual. Two crania found earlier, in 1829 and 1848, went unrecognized until long after Darwin's time. *Pithecanthropus erectus*, the middle Pleistocene man discovered by Dubois in Java in 1890, fared little better than Neanderthal man. Of nineteen authorities polled in 1895, five considered the specimen an ape, seven, a human, and seven, an intermediate. Our knowledge has grown so rapidly that fossil men found today have every chance of being admitted to membership in our genus if not in our species. The border area has been moved back to the beginning of the Pleistocene epoch, at which the problem of speciation is genuinely in question.

Microcephalic and other pathological forms constituted still another large problem in human classification. Most microcephals, who characteristically have small brain cases but faces of normal size and are usually below average stature and intelligence, were classified between the apes and man to provide an example of return to the ancestral human line (Eiseley, 1954). Their inability to speak confirmed the diagnosis of intermediacy between ancestral apes and normal modern man. The idea that past stages or races of man were of lower intelligence than modern man and that pathological individuals are representative of such stages is a recurrent theme and one that appears in popular form. Only a generation ago microcephals were employed in sideshows as "The Last of the Aztecs." Their impromptu phonations, following a prod from the manager, were said to be Aztec speech, for which there were no other surviving communicants. Indian blankets and head feathers added plausibility to the roles in which these persons were inhumanly cast. Pathological variation is no longer used as an explanation of fossil specimens and no scientist has recently suggested an entire phase in human history composed of humans that today are represented by pathological persons.

The last major challenge to the recognition of variation in human morphology came with the unanticipated discovery of the Australopithecines (South African Man-apes) in 1924 by Raymond Dart. Preconceived "missing links" had been envisioned as forms that were midway between existing anthropoid apes and humans. These lower Pleistocene forms, however, showed differentiation in different parts of the body, rather than a total primitiveness. They were fully erect and bipedal like man, but they had much smaller cranial capacities. An important fact was established for the first time—that erect posture preceded the great expansion of the brain. This in turn provided tangible evidence illustrating the basic principle that different parts of the body have evolved at different rates. More recent discoveries of these forms at Olduvai in East Africa and in Southeast Asia suggest an important division between a larger form with crested head and very large chewing apparatus, and a smaller, more gracile form. Whether either of these forms used or manufactured tools is not yet demonstrated.

Extinction and continuity

To keep pace with the descriptions of new discoveries from the lower Pleistocene it is now necessary to read current periodicals (see list of literature cited). These periodicals are essential also for an awareness of the most recent estimates of dates; for example, current estimates indicate that lower Pleistocene began at least 1,750,000 years ago. A continuing problem, for which no single discovery can provide a satisfactory solution, is that of extinction. Owing to gaps in the fossil record it is not possible to demonstrate continuity from one phase of human history to the next; it must be inferred. Extinction is a general biological problem that is neatly focused in the disappearance of Neanderthal man. The appearance of modern man can now be traced to about 40,000 years ago. Whether Neanderthal man, who occupied a large part of western Eurasia, became extinct for natural causes, was killed, or was replaced by modern man, or whether modern man evolved, rapidly, from Neanderthal man, remains as much a question today as it was in the nineteenth century. An increasing knowledge of processes, or of genetic agencies, has contributed little more to the answer than an increased panel of plausible explanations from which a decisive choice cannot yet be made. Norman D. Newell explores some of these possibilities in the fourth article of this section, "Crises in the History of Life." Our increased ability to recognize variations in the human form, and to assign a new specimen correctly to a classificatory category, does not extend to various remote areas of population history.

The great chain of being and its missing links

A common view of man's position in nature—a static preevolutionary view —was that of a vertical chain extending from the highest form through those progressively lower. Each species or kind of organism, immutable in form and unchanging in its position in the chain, formed a link. Because of the concept of variation of archetypal forms in which individual specimens were considered imperfect but representative copies of a supernal model, many of the "links" comprised individuals or types rather than populations. A major task of the eighteenth- and nineteenth-century naturalist was that of taking an inventory of nature, that is, locating and describing all the links in this great chain from Englishmen, lions, and warthogs down to clams and polyps. Where continuity did not appear to prevail, where one link was not separated from the next by the least possible difference, a link was obviously missing—and thus a household expression came into being.

The idea of the Great Chain of Being was based on three premises: (1) The world was as full as it could possibly be of every diverse form that could possibly exist; all possible niches were occupied. (2) Continuity between existing forms was reflected in a gradual transition from inanimate to animate forms, from plants to animals, and between groups of animals. Animals were classed into those of land, air, and water, but because particular groups were intermediate between these, an overall continuity was maintained. Thus, seals were intermediate between marine and land forms; bats, between animals that live on the ground and those that fly. Aristotle noted the ape as an intermediate form between quadrupedal and bipedal mammals, man being the only bipedal form. P. T. Barnum recognized the value of supplying missing links. He displayed the duck-billed platypus of Australia (Ornithornynchus) as the connecting link between the seal and the duck. He named the flying fish as the obvious link between birds and fish, and tossed in a mermaid for good measure (Lovejoy, 1936). (3) The third premise—that of hierarchy or unilinear gradation—was combined with the first two premises of fullness and continuity to create the grand world view of an ascending chain of perfection, of which each link was separated from the next by the least possible degree of difference. Thus, the idea of "higher" and "lower" was applied not only to vastly different forms, but to extremely similar forms. Bushmen and Englishmen could not occupy the same level, nor could any two or more other varieties of man. The habit of hierarchical arrangement has had an unfortuante influence in the assessment of variation within the human species. It is inapplicable and should be dismissed.

Conceptual changes between the eighteenth and twentieth centuries

1859

UNITS

Before	After
Types—original, immutable, and static.	Breeding populations—variable and changing.

VARIATION

Deviations from type— accidental, anomalous, or pathological.	Genetic variation is basis for change and adaptation by natural selection (differential reproduction).

INHERITANCE

Blending inheritance.	Particulate inheritance (Mendelian genetics).

RELATIONSHIP OF UNITS

Types arrayed hierarchically on a unilinear scale of perfection, that is, "Great Chain of Being."	Variable populations, diverging multidimensionally.

TIME DEPTH

Recent creation of world.	Geological eras in millions of years.

The development of time depth and of methods of analysis that led to the enunciation of causative processes is critical to the history of our study. Statistical analysis is essential to genetical analysis, and, interestingly, it was important also in the arrangement of the epochs of the Cenozoic era.

Just as the concept of the "missing link" is meaningless without the larger parental concept of the Great Chain of Being, the names and sequence of the Cenozoic epochs, the Eocene, Oligocene, Miocene, Pliocene and Pleistocene, are irrelevant without the methodology of the intellectual framework that brought them into being. This framework has been authoritatively supplied by a major contributor to statistical analysis, Ronald Fisher (1953). Fisher suggested that statistical science was the particular aspect of human progress that gave the twentieth century its special character, and that the period of "inconspicuous gestation" extended through most of the nineteenth century. The first example chosen by Fisher to document this contribution is directly relevant to Lyell. Lyell faced the problem of arranging the rocks of the Tertiary period into their proper sequence, as had previously been done for the Primary and Secondary periods. However, because the available rocks or formations of the Tertiary occurred in nonoverlapping patches, often widely separated, the actual superposition of one stratum upon another could not be employed. Lyell solved this problem by means of a statistical argument.

In collaboration with the French conchologist M. Deshayes, Lyell tabled the frequencies of the fossil species of shells found in each of five groups of strata, thereby constructing a Life Table which showed what percentage of fossil species were living today, with the fifth group—the strata of today—having 100 percent. Those strata with only 3 or 4 percent of living species he named Eocene, "the dawn of the recent;" those with 18 percent he named the Miocene, "minority recent," and correctly inferred that this epoch came later in time than the preceding epoch with its smaller proportion of modern species. Those strata with 40 percent were named Pliocene (majority recent), and the obviously later strata, with 96 percent of surviving species, were named Pleistocene (mostly recent). This statistical approach was eminently successful; it was accepted and the order of epochs was firmly established. Absolute methods of dating have confirmed this sequence.

Lamentably, the appendix, which in his third volume occupies 56 pages, and in which he provides the details of classification and his calculations, survived only two years. "His designations of the Tertiary formations remain as records of a forgotten past, like the fossils themselves, less intelligible to the geological students than the casts of sea shells they extract from the rocks" (Fisher, 1953).

The idea of evolution and the explanations for evolutionary changes have many historical roots—in geology, paleontology, anatomy, archaeology, primatology, anthropology, genetics, and many other fields of research that were important in the nineteenth century. One influential area of scholarly research that has clearly made a recognized contribution to evolution is that of linguistic science. Recognition of the unity of the Indo-European languages, attributed to Sir William Jones, 1784, provided a model for divergence from a common ancestor (Darlington and Mather, 1952, p. 360; a full discussion is presented in J. Greenberg, 1959). The linguists confronted a problem parallel to that of the biologists, that of language and dialect. Dialects, like races, were found to be open systems, and borrowing could occur between them. Languages, like species, were closed systems, between which little or no overlapping existed. The boundaries of dialects were more difficult to locate than those of the language. The linguists had certain advantages that the natural scientists had lacked, and they made good use of them. Languages ancestral to existing groups of genetically related languages served as paleontological fossils. Sanskrit, Greek, and English were demonstrably related. Because early forms of some languages—Sanskrit, Greek, and Latin—were recorded, and because modern descendants of these were still spoken, it was possible to trace the history of words, and more important, the history of phonemic elements and grammatical rules.

In addition to the accessibility of extinct languages, another advantage of linguistic materials was their rapid rate of change. Changes in pronunciation and in words take place within one person's lifetime, and the changes that take place in the course of three generations are noteworthy. One of the principal objections to biological evolution, or to the transformation of species, was simply that it had never been observed. The prevailing concept that species were fixed types appeared unassailable, for new species did not appear. Therefore, the linguistic analogy served a timely purpose in the eighteenth century, as well as in subsequent periods. Lyell compared languages with biological species in 1863, and Darwin, in *The Descent of Man*, notes that different languages and distinct species have both developed gradually. The lives and achievements of these founders of modern scientific thought are related in this section in the two articles by Loren C. Eiseley, "Charles Lyell" and "Charles Darwin."

It is useful to recall, as Greenberg has noted, that the concept of evolution as "transformism" is distinguishable from the concept of evolution as "advance" or "progress." The fact that evolution had been the gradual transformation of descendant species from antecedent species was established primarily by osteological evidence. Evolution could be considered to be advance in one sense: earlier forms had been less complex, less internally differentiated, and less efficiently adapted. The principle of natural selection rendered intelligible the paleontological record of earlier and simpler forms and provided an explanation of the temporal advance that is applicable both to contemporary diversity between races and species, and to the historical sequence of extinct forms.

Genetic processes   The rediscovery of Mendelian genetics by independent researchers in 1900, and the simultaneous discovery of the human blood groups by Landsteiner caused a new analytical impulse, which vitalized the study of human variation. The concepts of particulate inheritance, segregation, and recombination assumed an increasingly sophisticated form. Thus, although the year 1900, like 1859, is a significant date in the history of genetics and evolution, the various strands of development in genetics, mathematical genetics, and genetics of populations had complex undercurrents that cannot be assigned precise dates of origin.

The formulation of the mathematical basis for genetic equilibrium by Hardy and Weinberg in 1908 was one of the major roots of the development of popular genetics. The study of genetic mechanisms, the mathematical approach to genetics, and the genetics of real populations all developed simultaneously and cannot be placed in a sequence, although the florescence of population genetics has been more recent than that of individual or basic genetics. (Mayr, 1959; Wright, 1960). These genetic mechanisms are discussed in the first article in this section, "The Genetic Basis of Evolution" by Theodosius Dobzhansky. Nineteen years after the discovery of the blood groups by Landsteiner, population differences were demonstrated by the Hirszfelds. At about the same time it was shown that there were high frequencies of blood group B in populations of central Asia and northern India; the occurrence of this blood group decreases in populations west of these areas, reaching its lowest point in the peoples of western Europe. This discovery subsequently supplied excellent material for population genetics as well as enormous factual and theoretical information on the distribution of the human blood groups—material especially useful for microevolutionary studies with a known genetic basis.

Genetic analysis requires the analysis of fertile crosses. By definition these cannot take place across species boundaries, or can do so only infrequently. Consequently, the study of fossil man and the study of nonhuman primates are dependent on inferences based upon genetic analyses of populations within species. Fortunately the human species is large and diverse, and its various divisions can produce fertile crosses whenever the opportunity arises.

Literature cited   Darlington, C. D., and K. Mather. 1952. *The Elements of Genetics.* 3rd ed. New York, Macmillan.

Eiseley, Loren. 1954. The Reception of the First Missing Links. *Pro. Am. Phil. Soc.,* Vol. 98, No. 6, pp. 453–465.

———, 1958. *Darwin's Century.* New York, Doubleday.

Fisher, Ronald. 1954. The Expansion of Statistics. *Am. Scientist,* Vol. 42, No. 2, pp. 275–282, 293.

Greenberg, Joseph. 1959. Language and Evolution. In Betty J. Meggers, ed., *Evolution and Anthropology: A Centennial Appraisal.* Washington, D.C., The Anthropological Society of Washington, pp. 61–75.

Hoebel, E. Adamson. 1966. *Anthropology: The Study of Man.* 3rd ed. New York, McGraw-Hill.

Lovejoy, Arthur O. 1936. *The Great Chain of Being*. Cambridge, Harvard University Press.

Mayr, Ernst. 1959. Where Are We? *Cold Spring Harbor Symp. Quant. Biol.* Vol. 29, pp. 1–14.

Montagu, M. F. Ashley. 1933. The Anthropological Significance of the Pterion in Primates. *Am. J. Phys. Anthro.*, Vol. 18, No. 2, pp. 159–336.

Nott, J. C., and George R. Gliddon. 1854. *Types of Mankind*. Philadelphia, Lippincott, Grambo, & Co.

Washburn, S. L. 1946. Thinking About Race. In *Smithsonian Report for 1945*. Washington, D.C., pp. 363–378.

Wright, Sewall. 1960. Genetics and Twentieth Century Darwinism. A Review and Discussion. *Am. J. of Hum. Genet.*, Vol. 12, No. 2, pp. 365–372.

1

The Genetic Basis of Evolution

THEODOSIUS DOBZHANSKY
January 1950

THE living beings on our planet come in an incredibly rich diversity of forms. Biologists have identified about a million species of animals and some 267,000 species of plants, and the number of species actually in existence may be more than twice as large as the number known. In addition the earth has been inhabited in the past by huge numbers of other species that are now extinct, though some are preserved as fossils. The organisms of the earth range in size from viruses so minute that they are barely visible in electron microscopes to giants like elephants and sequoia trees. In appearance, body structure and ways of life they exhibit an endlessly fascinating variety.

What is the meaning of this bewildering diversity? Superficially considered, it may seem to reflect nothing more than the whims of some playful deity, but one soon finds that it is not fortuitous. The more one studies living beings the more one is impressed by the wonderfully effective adjustment of their multifarious body structures and functions to their varying ways of life. From the simplest to the most complex, all organisms are constructed to function efficiently in the environments in which they live. The body of a green plant can build itself from food consisting merely of water, certain gases in the air and some mineral salts taken from the soil. A fish is a highly efficient machine for exploiting the organic food resources of water, and a bird is built to get the most from its air en-

vironment. The human body is a complex, finely coordinated machine of marvelously precise engineering, and through the inventive abilities of his brain man is able to control his environment. Every species, even the most humble, occupies a certain place in the economy of nature, a certain adaptive niche which it exploits to stay alive.

The diversity and adaptedness of living beings were so difficult to explain that during most of his history man took the easy way out of assuming that every species was created by God, who contrived the body structures and functions of each kind of organism to fit it to a predestined place in nature. This idea has now been generally replaced by the less easy but intellectually more satisfying explanation that the living things we see around us were not always what they are now, but evolved gradually from very different-looking ancestors; that these ancestors were in general less complex, less perfect and less diversified than the organisms now living; that the evolutionary process is still under way, and that its causes can therefore be studied by observation and experiment in the field and in the laboratory.

The origins and development of this theory, and the facts that finally convinced most people of its truth beyond reasonable doubt, are too long a story to be presented here. After Charles Darwin published his convincing exposition and proof of the theory of evolution in 1859, two main currents developed in evolu-

tionary thought. Like any historical process, organic evolution may be studied in two ways. One may attempt to infer the general features and the direction of the process from comparative studies of the sequence of events in the past; this is the method of paleontologists, comparative anatomists and others. Or one may attempt to reconstruct the causes of evolution, primarily through a study of the causes and mechanisms that operate in the world at present; this approach, which uses experimental rather than observational methods, is that of the geneticist and the ecologist. This article will consider what has been learned about the causes of organic evolution through the second approach.

Darwin attempted to describe the causes of evolution in his theory of natural selection. The work of later biologists has borne out most of his basic contentions. Nevertheless, the modern theory of evolution, developed by a century of new discoveries in biology, differs greatly from Darwin's. His theory has not been overthrown; it has evolved. The authorship of the modern theory can be credited to no single person. Next to Darwin, Gregor Mendel of Austria, who first stated the laws of heredity, made the greatest contribution. Within the past two decades the study of evolutionary genetics has developed very rapidly on the basis of the work of Thomas Hunt Morgan and Hermann J. Muller of the U. S. In these developments the principal contributors have been C. D.

CONTROLLED ENVIRONMENT for the study of fruit-fly populations is a glass-covered box. In bottom of the box are cups of food that are filled in rotation to keep food a constant factor in environment.

Darlington, R. A. Fisher, J. B. S. Haldane, J. S. Huxley and R. Mather in England; B. Rensch and N. W. Timofeeff-Ressovsky in Germany; S. S. Chetverikov, N. P. Dubinin and I. I. Schmalhausen in the U.S.S.R.; E. Mayr, J. T. Patterson, C. G. Simpson, G. L. Stebbins and Sewall Wright in the U. S., and some others.

Evolution in the Laboratory

Evolution is generally so slow a process that during the few centuries of recorded observations man has been able to detect very few evolutionary changes among animals and plants in their natural habitats. Darwin had to deduce the theory of evolution mostly from indirect evidence, for he had no means of observing the process in action. Today, however, we can study and even produce evolutionary changes at will in the laboratory. The experimental subjects of these studies are bacteria and other low forms of life which come to birth, mature and yield a new generation within a matter of minutes or hours, instead of months or years as in most higher beings. Like a greatly speeded-up motion picture, these observations compress into a few days evolutionary events that would take thousands of years in the higher animals.

One of the most useful bacteria for this study is an organism that grows, usually harmlessly, in the intestines of practically every human being: *Escherichia coli,* or colon bacteria. These organisms can easily be cultured on a nutritive broth or nutritive agar. At about 98 degrees Fahrenheit, bacterial cells placed in a fresh culture medium divide about every 20 minutes. Their numbers increase rapidly until the nutrients in the culture medium are exhausted; a single cell may yield billions of progeny in a day. If a few cells are placed on a plate covered with nutritive agar, each cell by the end of the day produces a whitish speck representing a colony of its offspring.

Now most colon bacteria are easily killed by the antibiotic drug streptomycin. It takes only a tiny amount of streptomycin, 25 milligrams in a liter of a nutrient medium, to stop the growth of the bacteria. Recently, however, the geneticist Milislav Demerec and his collaborators at the Carnegie Institution in Cold Spring Harbor, N. Y., have shown that if several billion colon bacteria are placed on the streptomycin-containing medium, a few cells will survive and form colonies on the plate. The offspring of these hardy survivors are able to multiply freely on a medium containing streptomycin. A mutation has evidently taken place in the bacteria; they have now become resistant to the streptomycin that was poisonous to their sensitive ancestors.

How do the bacteria acquire their

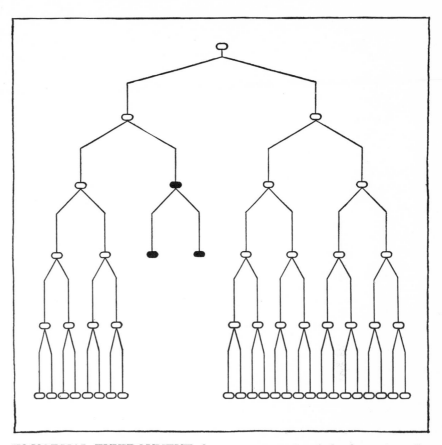

IN NORMAL ENVIRONMENT the common strain of the bacterium *Escherichia coli* (*white bacteria*) multiplies. A mutant strain resistant to streptomycin (*black bacteria*) remains rare because the mutation is not useful.

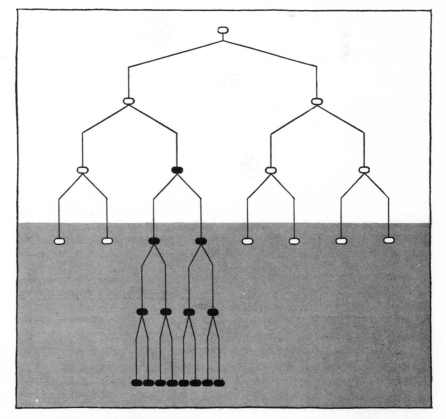

IN CHANGED ENVIRONMENT produced by the addition of streptomycin (*gray area*) the streptomycin-resistant strain is better adapted than the common strain. The mutant strain then multiplies and the common one dies.

resistance? Is the mutation caused by their exposure to streptomycin? Demerec has shown by experimental tests that this is not so; in any large culture a few resistant mutants appear even when the culture has not been exposed to streptomycin. Some cells in the culture undergo mutations from sensitivity to resistance regardless of the presence or absence of streptomycin in the medium. Demerec found that the frequency of mutation was about one per billion; i.e., one cell in a billion becomes resistant in every generation. Streptomycin does not induce the mutations; its role in the production of resistant strains is merely that of a selecting agent. When streptomycin is added to the culture, all the normal sensitive cells are killed, and only the few resistant mutants that happened to be present before the streptomycin was added survive and reproduce. Evolutionary changes are controlled by the environment, but the control is indirect, through the agency of natural or artificial selection.

What governs the selection? If resistant bacteria arise in the absence of streptomycin, why do sensitive forms predominate in all normal cultures; why has not the whole species of colon bacteria become resistant? The answer is that the mutants resistant to streptomycin are at a disadvantage on media free from this drug. Indeed, Demerec has discovered the remarkable fact that about 60 per cent of the bacterial strains derived from streptomycin-resistant mutants become dependent on streptomycin; they are unable to grow on media free from it!

On the other hand one can reverse the process and obtain strains of bacteria that can live without streptomycin from cultures predominantly dependent on the drug. If some billions of dependent bacteria are plated on nutrient media free of the drug, all dependent cells cease to multiply and only the few mutants independent of the drug reproduce and form colonies. Demerec estimates the frequency of this "reverse" mutation at about 37 per billion cells in each generation.

Evolutionary changes of the type described in colon bacteria have been found in recent years in many other bacterial species. The increasing use of antibiotic drugs in medical practice has made such changes a matter of considerable concern in public health. As penicillin, for example, is used on a large scale against bacterial infections, the strains of bacteria that are resistant to penicillin survive and multiply, and the probability that they will infect new victims is increased. The mass application of antibiotic drugs may lead in the long run to increased incidence of cases refractory to treatment. Indications exist that this has already happened in some instances: in certain cities penicillin-resistant gonorrhea has become more frequent than it was.

The same type of evolutionary change has also been noted in some larger organisms. A good example is the case of DDT and the common housefly, Musca domestica. DDT was a remarkably effective poison for houseflies when first introduced less than 10 years ago. But already reports have come from places as widely separated as New Hampshire, New York, Florida, Texas, Italy and Sweden that DDT sprays in certain localities have lost their effectiveness. What has happened, of course, is that strains of houseflies relatively resistant to DDT have become established in these localities. Man has unwittingly become an agent of a selection process which has led to evolutionary changes in housefly populations. Similar changes are known to have occurred in other insects; e.g., in some orchards of California where hydrocyanic gas has long been used as a fumigant to control scale insects that prey on citrus fruits, strains of these insects that are resistant to hydrocyanic gas have developed.

Obviously evolutionary selection can take place only if nature provides a supply of mutants to choose from. Thus no bacteria will survive to start a new strain resistant to streptomycin in a culture in which no resistant mutant cells were present in the first place, and housefly races resistant to DDT have not appeared everywhere that DDT is used. Adaptive changes are not mechanically forced upon the organism by the environment. Many species of past geological epochs died out because they did not have a supply of mutants which fitted changing environments. The process of mutation furnishes the raw materials from which evolutionary changes are built.

Mutations

Mutations arise from time to time in all organisms, from viruses to man. Perhaps the best organism for the study of mutations is the now-famous fruit fly, Drosophila. It can be bred easily and rapidly in laboratories, and it has a large number of bodily traits and functions that are easy to observe. Mutations affect the color of its eyes and body, the size and shape of the body and of its parts, its internal anatomical structures, its fecundity, its rate of growth, its behavior, and so on. Some mutations produce differences so minute that they can be detected only by careful measurements; others are easily seen even by beginners; still others produce changes so drastic that death occurs before the development is completed. The latter are called lethal mutations.

The frequency of any specific mutation is usually low. We have seen that in colon bacteria a mutation to resistance to streptomycin occurs in only about one cell per billion in every generation, and the reverse mutation to independence of streptomycin is about 37 times more frequent. In Drosophila and in the corn plant mutations have been found to range in frequency from one in 100,000 to one in a million per generation. In man, according to estimates by Haldane in England and James Neel in the U. S., mutations that produce certain hereditary diseases, such as hemophilia and Cooley's anemia, arise in one in 2,500 to one in 100,000 sex cells in each generation. From this it may appear that man is more mutable than flies and bacteria, but it should be remembered that a generation in man takes some 25 years, in flies two weeks, and in bacteria 25 minutes. The frequency of mutations per unit of time is actually greater in bacteria than in man.

A single organism may of course produce several mutations, affecting different features of the body. How frequent are all mutations combined? For technical reasons, this is difficult to determine; for example, most mutants produce small changes that are not detected unless especially looked for. In Drosophila it is estimated that new mutants affecting one part of the body or another are present in between one and 10 per cent of the sex cells in every generation.

In all organisms the majority of mutations are more or less harmful. This may seem a very serious objection against the theory which regards them as the mainspring of evolution. If mutations produce incapacitating changes, how can adaptive evolution be compounded of them? The answer is: a mutation that is harmful in the environment in which the species or race lives may become useful, even essential, if the environment changes. Actually it would be strange if we found mutations that improve the adaptation of the organism in the environment in which it normally lives. Every kind of mutation that we observe has occurred numerous times under natural conditions, and the useful ones have become incorporated into what we call the "normal" constitution of the species. But when the environment changes, some of the previously rejected mutations become advantageous and produce an evolutionary change in the species. The writer and B. A. Spassky have carried out certain experiments in which we intentionally disturbed the harmony between an artificial environment and the fruit flies living in it. At first the change in environment killed most of the flies, but during 50 consecutive generations most strains showed a gradual improvement of viability, evidently owing to the environment's selection of the better-adapted variants.

This is not to say that every mutation will be found useful in some environment somewhere. It would be difficult to imagine environments in which such human mutants as hemophilia or the absence of hands and feet might be useful. Most mutants that arise in any species are, in effect, degenerative changes; but some, perhaps a small minority, may be beneficial in some environments. If the environment were forever constant, a species might conceivably reach a summit of adaptedness and ultimately suppress the mutation process. But the environment is never constant; it varies not only from place to place but from time to time. If no mutations occur in a species, it can no longer become adapted to changes and is headed for eventual extinction. Mutation is the price that organisms pay for survival. They do not possess a miraculous ability to produce only useful mutations where and when needed. Mutations arise at random, regardless of whether they will be useful at the moment, or ever; nevertheless, they make the species rich in adaptive possibilities.

The Genes

To understand the nature of the mutation process we must inquire into the nature of heredity. A man begins his individual existence when an egg cell is fertilized by a spermatozoon. From an egg cell weighing only about a 20-millionth of an ounce, he grows to an average weight at maturity of some 150 pounds—a 48-billionfold increase. The material for this stupendous increase in mass evidently comes from the food consumed, first by the mother and then by the individual himself. But the food becomes a constituent part of the body only after it is digested and assimilated, *i.e.*, transformed into a likeness of the assimilating body. This body, in turn, is a likeness of the bodies of the individual's ancestors. Heredity is, then, a process whereby the organism reproduces itself in its progeny from food materials taken in from the environment. In short, heredity is self-reproduction.

The units of self-reproduction are called genes. The genes are borne chiefly in chromosomes of the cell nucleus, but certain types of genes called plasmagenes are present in the cytoplasm, the part of the cell outside the nucleus. The chemical details of the process of self-reproduction are unknown. Apparently a gene enters into some set of chemical reactions with materials in its surroundings; the outcome of these reactions is the appearance of two genes in the place of one. In other words, a gene synthesizes a copy of itself from nongenic materials. The genes are considered to be stable because the copy is a true likeness of the original in the overwhelming majority of cases; but occasionally the copying process is faulty, and the new gene that emerges differs from its model. This is a mutation. We can increase the frequency of mutations in experimental animals by treating the genes with X-rays, ultraviolet rays, high temperature or certain chemical substances.

Can a gene be changed by the environment? Assuredly it can. But the important point is the kind of change produced. The change that is easiest to make is to treat the gene with poisons or heat in such a way that it no longer reproduces itself. But a gene that cannot produce a copy of itself from other materials is no longer a gene; it is dead. A mutation is a change of a very special kind: the altered gene can reproduce itself, and the copy produced is like the changed structure, not like the original. Changes of this kind are relatively rare. Their rarity is not due to any imperviousness of the genes to influences of the environment, for genic materials are probably the most active chemical constituents of the body; it is due to the fact that genes are by nature self-reproducing, and only the rare changes that preserve the genes' ability to reproduce can effect a lasting alteration of the organism.

Changes in heredity should not be confused, as they often are, with changes in the manifestations of heredity. Such expressions as "gene for eye color" or "inheritance of musical ability" are figures of speech. The sex cells that transmit heredity have no eyes and no musical ability. What genes determine are patterns of development which result in the emergence of eyes of a certain color and of individuals with some musical abilities. When genes reproduce themselves from different food materials and in different environments, they engender the development of different "characters" or "traits" in the body. The outcome of the development is influenced both by heredity and by environment.

In the popular imagination, heredity is transmitted from parents to offspring through "blood." The heredity of a child is supposed to be a kind of alloy or solution, resulting from the mixture of the paternal and maternal "bloods." This blood theory became scientifically untenable as long ago as Mendel's discovery of the laws of heredity in 1865. Heredity is transmitted not through miscible bloods but through genes. When different variants of a gene are brought together in a single organism, a hybrid, they do not fuse or contaminate one another; the genes keep their integrity and separate when the hybrid forms sex cells.

Genetics and Mathematics

Although the number of genes in a single organism is not known with precision, it is certainly in the thousands, at least in the higher organisms. For Drosophila, 5,000 to 12,000 seems a reasonable estimate, and for man the figure is, if anything, higher. Since most or all genes suffer mutational changes from time to time, populations of virtually every species must contain mutant variants of many genes. For example, in the human species there are variations in the skin, hair and eye colors, in the shape and distribution of hair, in the form of the head, nose and lips, in stature, in body proportions, in the chemical composition of the blood, in psychological traits, and so on. Each of these traits is influenced by several or by many genes. To be conservative, let us assume that the human species has only 1,000 genes and that each gene has only two variants. Even on this conservative basis, Mendelian segregation and recombination would be capable of producing 2^{1000} different gene combinations in human beings.

The number 2^{1000} is easy to write but is utterly beyond comprehension. Compared with it, the total number of electrons and protons estimated by physicists to exist in the universe is negligibly small! It means that except in the case of identical twins no two persons now living, dead, or to live in the future are at all likely to carry the same complement of genes. Dogs, mice and flies are as individual and unrepeatable as men are. The mechanism of sexual reproduction, of which the recombination of genes is a part, creates ever new genetic constitutions on a prodigious scale.

One might object that the number of possible combinations does not greatly matter; after all, they will still be combinations of the same thousand gene variants, and the way they are combined is not significant. Actually it is: the same gene may have different effects in combinations with different genes. Thus Timofeeff-Ressovsky showed that two mutants in Drosophila, each of which reduced the viability of the fly when it was present alone, were harmless when combined in the same individual by hybridization. Natural selection tests the fitness in certain environments not of single genes but of constellations of genes present in living individuals.

Sexual reproduction generates, therefore, an immense diversity of genetic constitutions, some of which, perhaps a small minority, may prove well attuned to the demands of certain environments. The biological function of sexual reproduction consists in providing a highly efficient trial-and-error mechanism for the operation of natural selection. It is a reasonable conjecture that sex became established as the prevalent method of reproduction because it gave organisms the greatest potentialities for adaptive and progressive evolution.

Let us try to imagine a world providing a completely uniform environment. Suppose that the surface of our planet were absolutely flat, covered everywhere with the same soil; that instead of summer and winter seasons we had eternally constant temperature and humidity; that instead of the existing diversity of foods there was only one kind of energy-yielding substance to serve as nourishment. The Russian biologist Gause has pointed out that only a single kind of organism could inhabit such a tedious world. If two or more kinds appeared in it, the most efficient form would gradually crowd out and finally eliminate the less efficient ones, remaining the sole inhabitant. In the world of reality, however, the environment changes at every step. Oceans, plains, hills, mountain ranges, regions where summer heat alternates with winter cold, lands that are permanently warm, dry deserts, humid jungles —these diverse environments have engendered a multitude of responses by protoplasm and a vast proliferation of distinct species of life through the evolutionary process.

Some Adaptations

Many animal and plant species are polymorphic, *i.e.*, represented in nature by two or more clearly distinguishable kinds of individuals. For example, some individuals of the ladybird beetle *Adalia bipunctata* are red with black spots while others are black with red spots. The color difference is hereditary, the black color behaving as a Mendelian dominant and red as a recessive. The red and black forms live side by side and interbreed freely. Timofeeff-Ressovsky observed that near Berlin, Germany, the black form predominates from spring to autumn, and the red form is more numerous during the winter. What is the origin of these changes? It is quite improbable that the genes for color are transformed by the seasonal variations in temperature; that would mean epidemics of directed mutations on a scale never observed. A much more plausible view is that the changes are produced by natural selection. The black form is, for some reason, more successful than the red in survival and reproduction during summer, but the red is superior to the black under winter conditions. Since the beetles produce several generations during a single season, the species undergoes cyclic changes in its genetic composition in response to the seasonal alterations in the environment. This hypothesis was confirmed by the discovery that black individuals are more frequent among the beetles that die during the rigors of winter than among those that survive.

The writer has observed seasonal changes in some localities in California in the fly *Drosophila pseudoobscura*. Flies of this species in nature are rather uniform in coloration and other external traits, but they are very variable in the structure of their chromosomes, which can be seen in microscopic preparations. In the locality called Piñon Flats, on Mount San Jacinto in southern Califor-

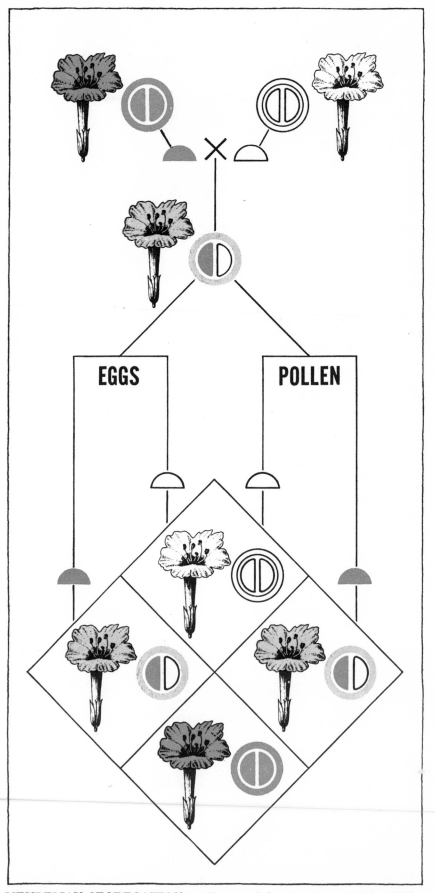

MENDELIAN SEGREGATION is illustrated by the four o'clock (*Mirabilis jalapa*). The genes of red and white flowers combine in a pink hybrid. Genes are segregated in the cross-fertilized descendants of pink flowers.

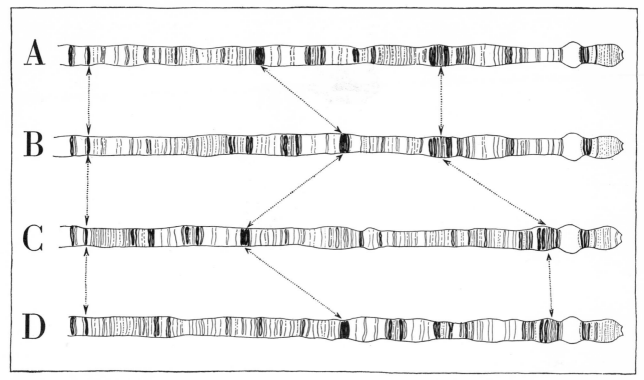

FOUR VARIETIES of the species *Drosophila pseudoobscura* are revealed by differences in the structure of their chromosomes. Under the microscope similar markings may be observed at different locations (*arrows*).

nia, the fruit-fly population has four common types of chromosome structure, which we may, for simplicity, designate as types A, B, C and D. From 1939 to 1946, samples of flies were taken from this population in various months of the year, and the chromosomes of these flies were examined. The relative frequencies of the chromosomal types, expressed in percentages of the total, varied with the seasons as follows:

Month	A	B	C	D
March	52	18	23	7
April	40	28	28	4
May	34	29	31	6
June	28	28	39	5
July	42	22	31	5
Aug.	42	28	26	4
Sept.	48	23	26	3
Oct.-Dec.	50	26	20	4

Thus type A was common in winter but declined in the spring, while type C waxed in the spring and waned in summer. Evidently flies carrying chromosomes of type C are somehow better adapted than type A to the spring climate; hence from March to June, type A decreases and type C increases in frequency. Contrariwise, in the summer type A is superior to type C. Types B and D show little consistent seasonal variation.

Similar changes can be observed under controlled laboratory conditions. Populations of Drosophila flies were kept in a very simple apparatus consisting of a wood and glass box, with openings in the bottom for replenishing the nutrient medium on which the flies lived—a kind of pudding made of Cream of Wheat, molasses and yeast. A mixture of flies of which 33 per cent were type A and 67 per cent type C was introduced into the apparatus and left to multiply freely, up to the limit imposed by the quantity of food given. If one of the types was better adapted to the environment than the other, it was to be expected that the better-adapted type would increase and the other decrease in relative numbers. This is exactly what happened. During the first six months the type A flies rose from 33 to 77 per cent of the population, and type C fell from 67 to 23 per cent. But then came an unexpected leveling off: during the next seven months there was no further change in the relative proportions of the flies, the frequencies of types A and C oscillating around 75 and 25 per cent respectively.

If type A was better than type C under the conditions of the experiment, why were not the flies with C chromosomes crowded out completely by the carriers of A? Sewall Wright of the University of Chicago solved the puzzle by mathematical analysis. The flies of these types interbreed freely, in natural as well as in experimental populations. The populations therefore consist of three kinds of individuals: 1) those that obtained chromosome A from father as well as from mother, and thus carry two A chromosomes (AA); 2) those with two C chromosomes (CC); 3) those that re- ceived chromosomes of different types from their parents (AC). The mixed type, AC, possesses the highest adaptive value; it has what is called "hybrid vigor." As for the pure types, under the conditions that obtain in nature AA is superior to CC in the summer. Natural selection then increases the frequency of A chromosomes in the population and diminishes the C chromosomes. In the spring, when CC is better than AA, the reverse is true. But note now that in a population of mixed types neither the A nor the C chromosomes can ever be entirely eliminated from the population, even if the flies are kept in a constant environment where type AA is definitely superior to type CC. This, of course, is highly favorable to the flies as a species, for the loss of one of the chromosome types, though it might be temporarily advantageous, would be prejudicial in the long run, when conditions favoring the lost type would return. Thus a polymorphic population is better able than a uniform one to adjust itself to environmental changes and to exploit a variety of habitats.

Races

Populations of the same species which inhabit different environments become genetically different. This is what a geneticist means when he speaks of races. Races are populations within a species that differ in the frequencies of some genes. According to the old concept of race, which is based on the notion that

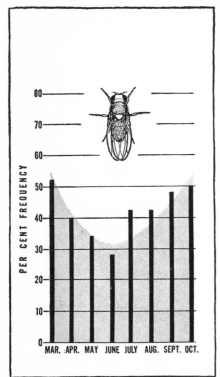
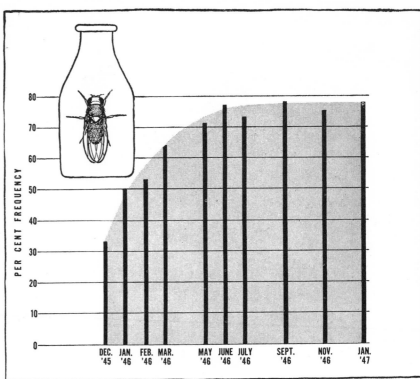

NUMBER OF FLIES of one chromosomal type varies in nature (*left*) and in the laboratory. In seasonal environ-ment of nature the type increases and decreases regular-ly; in constant environment of laboratory it levels off.

heredity is transmitted through "blood" and which still prevails among those ignorant of modern biology, the hereditary endowment of an isolated population would become more and more uniform with each generation, provided there was no interbreeding with other tribes or populations. The tribe would eventually become a "pure" race, all members of which would be genetically uniform. Scientists misled by this notion used to think that at some time in the past the human species consisted of an unspecified number of "pure" races, and that intermarriage between them gave rise to the present "mixed" populations.

In reality, "pure" races never existed, nor can they possibly exist in any species, such as man, that reproduces by sexual combination. We have seen that all human beings except identical twins differ in heredity. In widely differing climatic environments the genetic differences may be substantial. Thus populations native in central Africa have much higher frequencies of genes that produce dark skin than do European populations. The frequency of the gene for blue eye color progressively diminishes southward from Scandinavia through central Europe to the Mediterranean and Africa. Nonetheless some blue-eyed individuals occur in the Mediterranean region and even in Africa, and some brown-eyed ones in Norway and Sweden.

It is important to keep in mind that races are populations, not individuals. Race differences are relative and not absolute, since only in very remote races

do all members of one population possess a set of genes that is lacking in all members of another population. It is often difficult to tell how many races exist in a species. For example, some anthropologists recognize only two human races while others list more than 100. The difficulty is to know where to draw the line. If, for example, the Norwegians are a "Nordic race" and the southern Italians a "Mediterranean race," to what race do the inhabitants of Denmark, northern Germany, southern Germany, Switzerland and northern Italy belong? The frequencies of most differentiating traits change rather gradually from Norway to southern Italy. Calling the intermediate populations separate races may be technically correct, but this confuses the race classification even more, because nowhere can sharp lines of demarcation between these "races" be drawn. It is quite arbitrary whether we recognize 2, 4, 10, or more than 100 races—or finally refuse to make any rigid racial labels at all.

The differences between human races are, after all, rather small, since the geographic separation between them is nowhere very marked. When a species is distributed over diversified territories, the process of adaptation to the different environments leads to the gradual accumulation of more numerous and biologically more and more important differences between races. The races gradually diverge. There is, of course, nothing fatal about this divergence, and under some circumstances the divergence may

stop or even be turned into convergence. This is particularly true of the human species. The human races were somewhat more sharply separated in the past than they are today. Although the species inhabits almost every variety of environment on earth, the development of communications and the increase of mobility, especially in modern times, has led to much intermarriage and to some genetic convergence of the human races.

The diverging races become more and more distinct with time, and the process of divergence may finally culminate in transformation of races into species. Although the splitting of species is a gradual process, and it is often impossible to tell exactly when races cease to be races and become species, there exist some important differences between race and species which make the process of species formation one of the most important biological processes. Indeed, Darwin called his chief work *The Origin of Species.*

Races of sexually reproducing organisms are fully capable of intercrossing; they maintain their distinction as races only by geographical isolation. As a rule in most organisms no more than a single race of any one species inhabits the same territory. If representatives of two or more races come to live in the same territory, they interbreed, exchange genes, and eventually become fused into a single population. The human species, however, is an exception. Marriages are influenced by linguistic, religious, social, economic and other cultural factors.

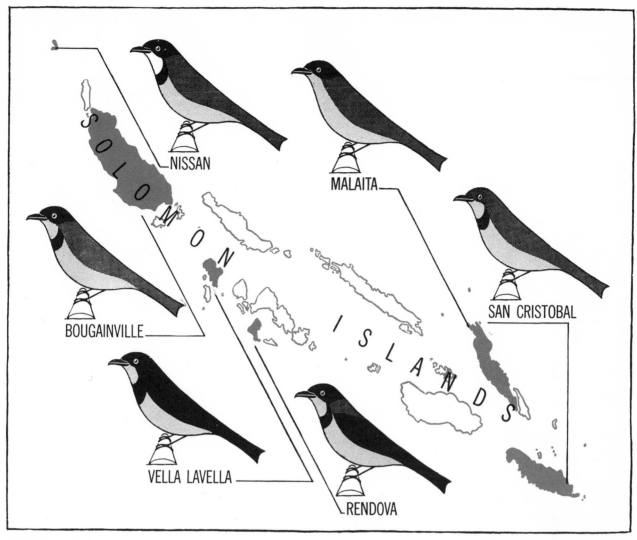

CONCEPT OF RACE is illustrated by the varieties of the golden whistler (*Pachycephala pectoralis*) of the Solomon Islands. The races are kept distinct principally by geographical isolation. They differ in their black and white and colored markings. Dark gray areas are symbol for green markings; light gray for yellow.

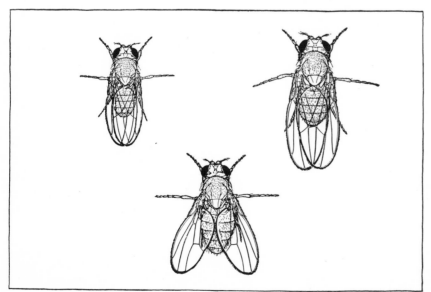

SPECIES OF DROSOPHILA and some other organisms tend to remain separate because their hybrid offspring are often weak and sterile. At left is *D. pseudoobscura*; at right *D. miranda*. Their hybrid descendant is at bottom.

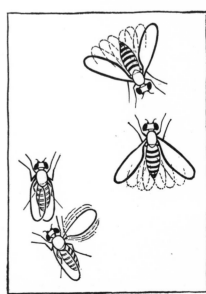

RITUALS OF MATING in *D. nebulosa* (*top*) and *D. willistoni* are example of factor that separates species.

Hence cultural isolation may keep populations apart for a time and slow down the exchange of genes even though the populations live in the same country. Nevertheless, the biological relationship proves stronger than cultural isolation, and interbreeding is everywhere in the process of breaking down such barriers. Unrestricted interbreeding would not mean, as often supposed, that all people would become alike. Mankind would continue to include at least as great a diversity of hereditary endowments as it contains today. However, the same types could be found anywhere in the world, and races as more or less discrete populations would cease to exist.

The Isolationism of Species

Species, on the contrary, can live in the same territory without losing their identity. F. Lutz of the American Museum of Natural History found 1,402 species of insects in the 75-by-200-foot yard of his home in a New Jersey suburb. This does not mean that representatives of distinct species never cross. Closely related species occasionally do interbreed in nature, especially among plants, but these cases are so rare that the discovery of one usually merits a note in a scientific journal.

The reason distinct species do not interbreed is that they are more or less completely kept apart by isolating mechanisms connected with reproduction, which exist in great variety. For example, the botanist Carl C. Epling of the University of California found that two species of sage which are common in southern California are generally separated by ecological factors, one preferring a dry site, the other a more humid one. When the two sages do grow side by side, they occasionally produce hybrids. The hybrids are quite vigorous, but their seed set amounts to less than two per cent of normal; i.e., they are partially sterile. Hybrid sterility is a very common and effective isolating mechanism. A classic example is the mule, hybrid of the horse and donkey. Male mules are always sterile, females usually so. There are, however, some species, notably certain ducks, that produce quite fertile hybrids, not in nature but in captivity.

Two species of Drosophila, *pseudoobscura* and *persimilis*, are so close together biologically that they cannot be distinguished by inspection of their external characteristics. They differ, however, in the structure of their chromosomes and in many physiological traits. If a mixed group of females of the two species is exposed to a group of males of one species, copulations occur much more frequently between members of the same species than between those of different species, though some of the latter do take place. Among plants, the flowers of related species may differ so much in structure that they cannot be pollinated by the same insects, or they may have such differences in smell, color and shape that they attract different insects. Finally, even when cross-copulation or cross-pollination can occur, the union may fail to result in fertilization or may produce offspring that cannot live. Often several isolating mechanisms, no one of which is effective separately, combine to prevent interbreeding. In the case of the two fruit-fly species, at least three such mechanisms are at work: 1) the above-mentioned disposition to mate only with their own kind, even when they are together; 2) different preferences in climate, one preferring warmer and drier places than the other; 3) the fact that when they do interbreed the hybrid males that result are completely sterile and the hybrid females, though fertile, produce offspring that are poorly viable. There is good evidence that no gene exchange occurs between these species in nature.

The fact that distinct species can coexist in the same territory, while races generally cannot, is highly significant. It permits the formation of communities of diversified living beings which exploit the variety of habitats present in a territory more fully than any single species, no matter how polymorphic, could. It is responsible for the richness and colorfulness of life that is so impressive to biologists and non-biologists alike.

Evolution v. Predestination

Our discussion of the essentials of the modern theory of evolution may be concluded with a consideration of the objections raised against it. The most serious objection is that since mutations occur by "chance" and are undirected, and since selection is a "blind" force, it is difficult to see how mutation and selection can add up to the formation of such complex and beautifully balanced organs as, for example, the human eye. This, say critics of the theory, is like believing that a monkey pounding a typewriter might accidentally type out Dante's *Divine Comedy*. Some biologists have preferred to suppose that evolution is directed by an "inner urge toward perfection," or by a "combining power which amounts to intentionality," or by "telefinalism" or the like. The fatal weakness of these alternative "explanations" of evolution is that they do not explain anything. To say that evolution is directed by an urge, a combining power, or a telefinalism is like saying that a railroad engine is moved by a "locomotive power."

The objection that the modern theory of evolution makes undue demands on chance is based on a failure to appreciate the historical character of the evolutionary process. It would indeed strain credulity to suppose that a lucky sudden combination of chance mutations produced the eye in all its perfection. But the eye did not appear suddenly in the offspring of an eyeless creature; it is the result of an evolutionary development that took many millions of years. Along the way the evolving rudiments of the eye passed through innumerable stages, all of which were useful to their possessors, and therefore all adjusted to the demands of the environment by natural selection. Amphioxus, the primitive fish-like darling of comparative anatomists, has no eyes, but it has certain pigment cells in its brain by means of which it perceives light. Such pigment cells may have been the starting point of the development of eyes in our ancestors.

We have seen that the "combining power" of the sexual process is staggering, that on the most conservative estimate the number of possible gene combinations in the human species alone is far greater than that of the electrons and protons in the universe. When life developed sex, it acquired a trial-and-error mechanism of prodigious efficiency. This mechanism is not called upon to produce a completely new creature in one spectacular burst of creation; it is sufficient that it produces slight changes that improve the organism's chances of survival or reproduction in some habitat. In terms of the monkey-and-typewriter analogy, the theory does not require that the monkey sit down and compose the *Divine Comedy* from beginning to end by a lucky series of hits. All we need is that the monkey occasionally form a single word, or a single line; over the course of eons of time the environment shapes this growing text into the eventual masterpiece. Mutations occur by "chance" only in the sense that they appear regardless of their usefulness at the time and place of their origin. It should be kept in mind that the structure of a gene, like that of the whole organism, is the outcome of a long evolutionary development; the ways in which the genes can mutate are, consequently, by no means indeterminate.

Theories that ascribe evolution to "urges" and "telefinalisms" imply that there is some kind of predestination about the whole business, that evolution has produced nothing more than was potentially present at the beginning of life. The modern evolutionists believe that, on the contrary, evolution is a creative response of the living matter to the challenges of the environment. The role of the environment is to provide opportunities for biological inventions. Evolution is due neither to chance nor to design; it is due to a natural creative process.

Charles Lyell

LOREN C. EISELEY
August 1959

"I feel as if my books," Charles Darwin once confessed, "came half out of Sir Charles Lyell's brain." The great biologist was admitting to no more than the simple truth. Sir Charles Lyell, who remained until late in his career a reluctant evolutionist, was paradoxically the ground-breaker for the triumph of the *Origin of Species*.

Lyell is remembered chiefly as a founder of modern historical geology. But he was also a biologist whose studies form the backbone of the achievement of Darwin and Alfred Russel Wallace. In his day he addressed tabernacles in both England and America full of people eager to hear the world-shaking views of the new geology. Today the man in the street has forgotten him. By a curious twist of history, Darwin replaced Lyell as a popular idol. Yet this gaunt-faced man who ended his days in near-blindness was one of the greatest scientists in a century of distinguished men.

A generation before Darwin he took a world of cataclysms, supernatural violence and mystery, and made of it something plain, expected and natural. If today we look upon our planet as familiar even when its bowels shake and its volcanoes grumble, it is because Lyell taught us long ago the simple powers in the earth.

It was as though we had been unable to see the earth until we observed it through the eyes of Lyell. Ralph Waldo Emerson wrote at mid-century: "Geology, a science of forty or fifty summers, has had the effect to throw an air of novelty and mushroom speed over entire history. The oldest empires—what we called venerable antiquity—now that we have true measures of duration, show like creations of yesterday. . . . The old six thousand years of chronology becomes a kitchen clock."

To Darwin and Wallace, Lyell gave the gift of time. Without that gift there would have been no *Origin of Species*. Geologic time is now so commonplace that the public forgets it once had to be fought for with something of the vigor that was later to be transferred to the evolutionary debates of the 1860's.

Lyell was, in modern terms, both zoologist and geologist. Indeed, he defined geology as that science "which investigates the successive changes that have taken place in the organic and inorganic kingdoms of nature." Today the splitting-up of science into numerous special disciplines has left Lyell one of the founders of historical geology. The world has tended to forget that he also wrote extensively upon zoological subjects, and that he exerted, as an older friend and influential scholar, a profound effect upon the career of Charles Darwin. "Lyell," remarked the great U. S. evolutionist Asa Gray in the year of Darwin's death "is as much the father of the new mode of thought which now prevails as is Darwin."

Yet in the first years of evolutionary controversy, beginning with Jean Baptiste de Lamarck and extending into the time of Robert Chambers and Charles Darwin, Lyell found himself popularly arrayed with the resistance to evolution. He was not to alter his public position until the autumn of his life. To us it may seem an almost willful rejection of the new age of science. Oddly enough we are wrong. Reading history backward is almost worse than not reading history at all. One must live both in a given time and beyond it to appreciate at once its complexities and its half-veiled insights.

Lyell's rejection of evolution was one of the first rational products of the new geology. A hint as to the nature of the situation is to be found in a passage in Lyell's *The Antiquity of Man*, published in 1863. The issue, to our modern eyes, is obscured by the terms in which it was argued. Lyell wrote: "It may be thought almost paradoxical that writers who are most in favor of transmutation (Mr. C. Darwin and Dr. J. Hooker, for example) are nevertheless among those who are most cautious, and one would say timid, in their mode of espousing the doctrine of progression; while on the other hand, the most zealous advocates of progress are, oftener than not, very vehement opponents of transmutation. We might have expected a contrary leaning on the part of both."

It is in the words "transmutation" and "progression," now unfamiliar, that the key to this mystery lies. When we come to know their significance, we will have learned that the road to the acceptance of evolution had unexpected turnings which, as we look backward, seem to have vanished, but which were real enough to the men of the 19th century. Before we can understand Lyell's position, this queer order of events has to be explored and comprehended.

Charles Lyell was born, the first of 10 children, to well-to-do parents in Scotland in 1797. His father possessed a strong interest in natural history and may have helped unconsciously to guide his son's interests in that direction. As Charles Darwin and Alfred Russel Wallace were later to do, the young Lyell collected insects in his boyhood. Absent-minded but versatile, tree-climber and chess player, he matriculated at Exeter College, Oxford, in 1816. Having early stumbled upon a copy of Robert Bakewell's *Introduction to Geology* in his father's library, he sought out Dean Buckland's geological lectures at Oxford, and from then on was a haunter of chalk pits, rock quarries, caves and river terraces.

In 1818 he made the usual continental tour with his parents and sisters. The slow carriage travel of that day promoted leisurely observation, and Charles made the most of it. He saw the red snow and glaciers of the high Alps as well as the treasures that lie open to the observant in the flints of the common road. Lyell had not as yet settled upon a career in geology. He was destined for the law, and shortly after his graduation from Oxford he came to London to prepare himself for the bar.

Even in London, however, Lyell was soon elected a Fellow of the Geological Society and joined the Linnean Society. Two handicaps tended to retard his legal career. His eyes were weak and troublesome, and he suffered from a slight speech difficulty, with which he was to contend bravely in his years as a lecturer on the natural sciences. When he was called to the bar in 1825 he was already contributing articles on scientific subjects to the *Quarterly Review*.

It has sometimes been intimated that Charles Lyell was "only an armchair geologist," that he was scientifically timid, a rich man's son who happened to dabble his way to success in a new science. But in those days there was little in the way of public support for science. Even the great schools were still largely concentrated upon the classical education of gentlemen. Only the man of independent means, like Lyell or Darwin, could afford to indulge his interest in science. With occasional struggling exceptions such as Wallace, it was the amateur who laid the foundations of the science of today. The whole philosophy of modern biology was established by such a "dabbler" as Charles Darwin, who never at any time held a professional position in the field. Charles Lyell and his great precursor, the Scotsman James Hutton, similarly laid the foundations of modern geology without claiming much in the way of formal institutional connections. Important though institutional and government support has come to be, it has led to a certain latent snobbery in professional circles. The amateur has had his day. But his was the sunrise of science, and it was a sunrise it ill becomes us to forget.

The charge that Lyell was an armchair worker will not stand against the facts. But even if the accusation held, the whole question would turn on what came out of the armchair. In actuality Lyell in his younger years made numerous trips to the continent to examine the evidence of geology at firsthand. Later, in the 1840's, he visited America, where he made similar ventures into the field, even though he was by then lecturing to thousands. As his biographer T. G. Bonney remarks: "Whenever there was hope of securing any geological information or of seeing some remarkable aspect of nature, Lyell was almost insensible either to heat or to fatigue." It is hard to see how a man suffering from bad eyes could have done more.

In support of the charge of scientific timidity, it is observed that Lyell opposed himself for many years to evolutionary views; it is said that his public and his private statements upon this score were vacillating. "How could Sir Charles Lyell," wrote one of Darwin's contemporaries, "for thirty years read, write and think on the subject of species and their succession, and yet constantly look down the wrong road?" From the vantage point of a hundred years this question can be answered. A whole new theory of life and time is not built by one man, however able. It is the product of multitudinous minds, and as a consequence it is also compounded of the compromises and hesitations of those same minds. Later, when the new world view comes to be ascribed, as it generally is, to a single individual such as Darwin the precursors of the discoverer begin to seem incredibly slow-witted.

Whatever men may think on this score, however, the record shows that

LYELL was born in Scotland in 1797 and died in 1875. He prepared for a legal career, but turned to geology. This photograph is in *Portraits of Men of Eminence*, published in 1863.

Lyell was a man of intellectual courage. He entered the geological domain when it was a weird, half-lit landscape of gigantic convulsions, floods and supernatural creations and extinctions of life. Distinguished men had lent the power of their names to these theological fantasies. Of the young Lyell, the "timid" Lyell who later strained Darwin's patience, a contemporary geologist wrote: "He stood up as a reformer, a radical reformer, denouncing all the old notions about paroxysms and solving every geological question by reference to the action of constant and existing physical causes. Never had a revolutionist harder work to get a sober hearing, or less prospect of overturning the works and conclusions of other men."

Geology at the beginning of the 19th century was known to many in England as a dangerous science. As such it both attracted and repelled the public. A body of fact and interpretation had arisen that could only be kept in accord with the Scriptural interpretation of earth's history by the exercise of considerable ingenuity. Theological authority was strong, and there was the greatest pressure upon geologists to avoid direct conflict with the church. Moreover, some of the early geologists were primarily theologians themselves, and were understandably anxious to reconcile geology with their religious beliefs. By degrees there had thus arisen a widely accepted view of geological history known as catastrophism.

This orthodox geological creed was an uneasy amalgam of the new scientific facts seen in the flickering, unreal light of mythological and romantic fantasy. Unlike the slow evolutionary successions that we recognize today, the record of geology was held to contain sudden catastrophic breaks. Mountain ranges were thought to be heaved up overnight; gigantic tidal waves, floods, paroxysms of the earth's crust were thought to mark the end of periods of calm. At such hours life vanished only to be restored through renewed divine creation, taking in the new period a more advanced form, and pointing steadily on toward the eventual emergence of man. It may thus be observed that the students of catastrophism had become aware of organic change in the rocks, but they saw the planet as having been molded by forces seemingly more powerful than those at work in the present day, and thus by implication supernatural.

Awareness of a succession of lifeforms in the strata of the earth had been slowly increasing since the close of the 18th century. Furthermore, it was seen that these extinct forms of life showed an increasing complexity as one approached the present. Since the record of the land vertebrates is particularly incomplete and broken, there arose the idea that, instead of a genuine continuity of life from age to age, the breaks in the geological record were real breaks. There had been a genuine interruption between the life of one age and that of another; each geological period had its own flora and fauna largely distinct from that which preceded and followed it. The slow, grand progression of life was seen as through a jerky, discontinuous, ill-run motion picture.

Men still did not understand the real age of the earth, nor the fact that the

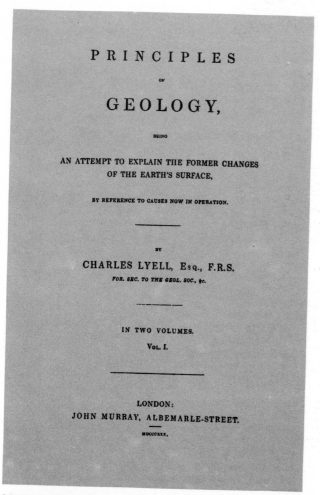

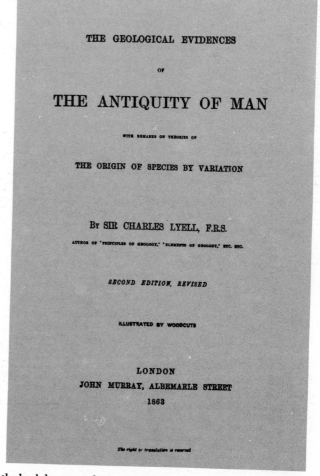

LYELL'S PRINCIPAL WORK was *Principles of Geology*, published in 1830. Although the title page reproduced at left states that the book has two volumes, Lyell later wrote a third. At right is the title page of *The Antiquity of Man*, which was published in 1863.

EARTH'S CRUST is depicted in Lyell's *Elements of Geology*. It is captioned: "Ideal section of . . . the Earth's crust explaining the theory of the . . . origin of the four great clafses of rocks." The classes were: aqueous (**A**), volcanic (**B**), metamorphic (**C**) and plutonic (**D**).

breaks they found in the records of the rocks were not world-wide, but rather only local discontinuities. The imperfections of the geological record, or the passages between the discontinuities, could only be learned through the piling-up of empirical evidence, a task that had only begun.

The catastrophic school had a powerful religious appeal. It retained both the creative excess and fury of an Old Testament Jehovah. "At succeeding periods," wrote Adam Sedgwick, one of Darwin's geological teachers at Cambridge, "new tribes of beings were called into existence, not merely as the progeny of those that had appeared before them, but as new and living proofs of creative interference; and though formed on the same plan, and bearing the same marks of wise contrivance, oftentimes unlike those creatures which preceded them, as if they had been matured in a different portion of the universe and cast upon the earth by the collision of another planet."

People thought in terms of a geotheological drama, a prologue to the emergence of man on the planet, after which no further organic developments were contemplated. The theory predicated a finished world which, in some eyes at least, could be compressed into the figurative week of the Book of Genesis. "Never," commented Lyell, "was there a dogma more calculated to foster indolence, and to blunt the keen edge of curiosity, than this assumption of the discordance between the former and the existing causes of change."

In this half-supernatural atmosphere Sir Charles Lyell in 1830 published the first volume of his *Principles of Geology*. Like most great ideas it was not totally original with its author. But to Sir Charles belongs the unquestioned credit of documenting a then unpalatable truth so effectively and formidably that it could no longer be ignored. In this respect again his career supplies a surprising parallel to that of Darwin. For Darwin too, at a later time, was the resurrector and documenter of forgotten and ill-used truths.

Lyell's principal precursor, James Hutton, died in intellectual eclipse in 1797, the very year that saw the birth of the man who was to revive his views—so tenuous and yet so persistent is the slow growth of scientific ideas. In the 1780's Hutton made the first organized and comprehensive attempt to demonstrate that the forces that had shaped the planet—its mountains, boulders and continents—are the same forces that can be observed in action around us today. Hutton had an ear for the work of raindrops, an eye for frost crystals splitting stones, a feel for the leaf fall of innumerable autumns. Wind and frost and running water, given time enough, can erode continents, ran his argument. Peering into the depths of the past, he could see "no vestige of a beginning, no prospect of an end."

Hutton, though not the first to suspect the earth's antiquity, nor the work that perfectly natural forces can perform, was the first to write learnedly and extensively upon the subject. His work fell, however, into undeserved neglect. He was criticized as irreligious. In England, particularly in the conservative reaction following the French Revolution, the catastrophism theory, with its grander scenery and stage effects, had a more popular appeal. The world of Hutton by

contrast was an unfinished world still unrolling into an indeterminate future. Its time depths were immeasurable, and the public had recoiled from its first glimpses into that abyss.

Yet this was the domain, and this the philosophy, upon which Sir Charles Lyell was to force his colleagues to take a long second look. He was a more eloquent and able writer than Hutton. But beyond this he had the advantage of almost 50 years of additional data, including his own personal study of the continental deposits. "Lyell," remarks one of his contemporaries, "was deficient of power in oral discourse, and was opposed by men who were his equals in knowledge, his superiors in the free delivery of their opinions. But in resolute combats, yielding not an inch to his adversaries, he slowly advanced upon the ground they abandoned, and became a conqueror without ever being acknowledged as a leader."

By degrees the idea of gradual change (uniformitarianism, as it came to be called) succeeded the picture of world-wide catastrophes. Supposition and quasi-theological imaginings gave place to a recognition of the work of natural forces still active and available for study in the world about us. The disjoined periods of the catastrophists began to be seen as one continuous world extending into a past of awe-inspiring dimensions. The uniformitarian school began to dominate the geological horizon. With the success of the *Principles* Lyell became one of two or three leading figures in English natural science until the peak of Darwin's fame was achieved with the publication of the *Origin of Species* in 1859. It is no wonder that the young Darwin, just returned from the voyage of the *Beagle* in 1836, gravitated so quickly to Lyell. It was Lyell's revision of geology that was to make Darwin's triumph possible.

Sir Charles Lyell had been raised in a more orthodox home than Charles Darwin. In fact, he was to confess in after-years that it cost him a severe struggle to renounce his old beliefs. Nevertheless, in reviving the conception of limitless time, and in abandoning the notion of world-wide breaks in the geological record as urged by the catastrophists, Lyell was inevitably forced to confront the problem of life itself in all its varied appearances. His great predecessor, Hutton, had been largely able to avoid the issue because of the lack of paleontological information. In Lyell's time, however, the questions pressed for answer.

The catastrophist doctrine had given birth to a kind of romantic evolutionism to explain the increasing complexity of life. This was the doctrine of "progression" which Lyell opposed in many of his writings from the time of the *Principles* onward. Progressionism was the product of the new paleontology which had discovered differences among the life-forms of successive geological eras. The theory can be said to have borrowed from Lamarck the conception of a necessary advance in the complexity of life as we ascend through the geological strata to the present. Instead of establishing biological continuity (the actual physical relationship between one set of forms and their descendants) the progressionists sought to show only a continuity or an organic plan in the mind of God between one age and another. There was, in other words, no phylogenetic relationship on the material plane between the animals of one era and those of a succeeding one.

Progressionism thus implied a kind of miraculous spiritual evolution which ceases only when the human level has been attained. The idea is confusing to the modern thinker because he tends to read back into this literature true evolutionary connotations that frequently were not intended by these early writers. The doctrine is interesting as a sign of the compromises being sought between an advancing science and a still-powerful religious orthodoxy.

"I shall adopt a different course," the young.Lyell had written when he was contending for the uniformitarian view in geology. "We are not authorized in the infancy of our science to recur to extraordinary agents." The same point of view led him, in company with T. H. Huxley, Joseph Hooker and, later, Darwin, to reject the claims of progressionism. All of these men, Lyell foremost among them, were uniformitarians in geology. They believed in the play of purely natural forces upon the earth. They refused or were reluctant to accept the notion of divine interposition of creative power at various stages of the geological record. They felt in their bones that there must be a natural explanation for organic as well as geological change, but the method was not easily to be had. Since Lyell was the immediate parent of the new geology, and since he was committed to natural processes, he was continually embarrassed by those who said: "You cannot show how nor why life has altered. Why then should we not believe that geological changes are equally the product of mysterious and unknown forces?"

We are now at the crux of the reason why Lyell was dubious about notions of

"transmutation"—the term then reserved for ideas implying true physical connection among the successions of species or, as we would say, "evolution" from one form to another. Lyell's attitude toward evolution was influenced by the antipathy that he felt toward progression, toward the unexplainable. In bracketing the two together he in effect was indicating the need of a scientific explanation of organic change, if change indeed was demonstrable.

Beginning with the *Principles of Geology*, in which the second volume and part of the third are devoted to

biological matters, Lyell had sought to examine the biological realm with an eye to answering the challenge of the catastrophist progressionists. As a consequence he came close to, but missed the significance of, the natural-selection hypothesis which was to establish the fame of Charles Darwin. It was here that he took the wrong turning that led him away from evolution. Yet ironically enough, though Lyell failed to comprehend the creative importance of natural selection, he did not miss its existence. In fact, through a strange series of circumstances just discovered in the literature, it is likely that he was fundamentally in-

PERIODS.		Character of Formations.	Localities of the different Formations.
I. Recent.		Marine.	Coral formations of Pacific. Delta of Po, Ganges, &c.
		Freshwater.	Modern deposits in Lake Superior—Lake of Geneva—Marl lakes of Scotland—Italian travertin, &c.
		Volcanic.	Jorullo — Monte Nuovo — Modern lavas of Iceland, Etna, Vesuvius, &c.
II. Tertiary.	1. Newer Pliocene.	Marine.	Strata of the Val di Noto in Sicily. Ischia, Morea? Uddevalla.
		Freshwater.	Valley of the Elsa around Colle in Tuscany.
		Volcanic.	Older parts of Vesuvius, Etna, and Ischia—Volcanic rocks of the Val di Noto in Sicily.
	2. Older Pliocene.	Marine.	Northern Subapennine formations, as at Parma, Asti, Sienna, Perpignan, Nice—English Crag.
		Freshwater.	Alternating with marine beds near the town of Sienna.
		Volcanic.	Volcanos of Tuscany and Campagna di Roma.
	3. Miocene.	Marine.	Strata of Touraine, Bordeaux, Valley of the Bormida, and the Superga near Turin—Basin of Vienna.
		Freshwater.	Alternating with marine at Saucats, twelve miles south of Bordeaux.
		Volcanic.	Hungarian and Transylvanian volcanic rocks. Part of the volcanos of Auvergne, Cantal, and Velay?
	4. Eocene.	Marine.	Paris and London Basins.
		Freshwater.	Alternating with marine in Paris basin—Isle of Wight—purely lacustrine in Auvergne, Cantal, and Velay.
		Volcanic.	Oldest part of volcanic rocks of Auvergne.

Synoptical Table of Recent and Tertiary Formations.

ROCK FORMATIONS of Recent and Tertiary periods were tabulated in first volume of *Principles of Geology*. Such tabulations showed the continuity of formations over a large area. Before the rise of historical geology local breaks in the continuity of rock formations had been taken as evidence that the history of the earth was a series of catastrophic events.

strumental in presenting Darwin with the key to the new biology. He was so concerned, however, to array the evidence against the doctrine of progression that he missed the support that the same evidence gave for a rational explanation of the origin of species.

Against the progressionists' idea of mass extinction at each break in the geological record he cited the imperfections in that record. "There must," he contended, "be a perpetual dying out of animals and plants, not suddenly and by whole groups at once, but one after another." Although not solving the problem of the emergence of new forms of life, Lyell by arguing for geological continuity was bringing the question of extinction and of the origin of new species within the domain of scientific investigation.

He countered the progressionist hypothesis with a short-lived "nonprogressionism" in which he argued that the discovery of higher forms of life in older strata would demonstrate that the progressionist doctrine was based solely upon the fallible geological record. This retreat from straight evolution on the part of Lyell was somewhat wavering, but it continued into the 1850's. There is no doubt that it was an attempt philosophically to evade a problem which threatened to interpose into his system something miraculous and unexplainable that savored of the catastrophist doctrines he had struggled for so long to defeat. Only with the triumph of Darwin would a uniformitarian, a "naturalistic," explanation for the mutability of life be available to the uniformitarian followers of Lyell. It was only then that Huxley, Hooker and finally Lyell himself became converts to evolution, at a time when it was still being resisted by such men as Sir Richard Owen and Louis Agassiz—old-style catastrophists and progressionists who at first glance one might think would have eagerly embraced the new doctrine of genuine physical evolution.

Although the question has been obscured by hazy difficulties of terminology, Sir Charles Lyell had already described before Darwin the struggle for existence and, up to a certain point, natural selection. He had not, however, visualized its creative aspect. Lyell made the first systematic attempt to treat the factors affecting the extinction of species and the effects of climatic change upon animal life throughout the long course of ages. "Every species," Lyell contended, "which has spread itself from a small point over a wide area must have marked its progress by

the diminution or the entire extirpation of some other, and must maintain its ground by a successful struggle against the encroachments of other plants and animals." He goes on to speak of "the tendency of population to increase in a limited district beyond the means of subsistence." Nor was Lyell unaware of plant and animal variation, although he believed such variation to be limited. "The best-authenticated examples of the extent to which species can be made to vary may be looked for in the history of domesticated animals and cultivated plants," he wrote, long before Darwin's investigations.

But Lyell did more than this. In the *Principles of Geology* he marshaled a powerful attack on the possibility that new evolutionary forms might be able thus to maintain or perfect themselves. Lyell advanced what he called his principle of "preoccupancy." In essence this principle simply assumes that creatures or plants already well fitted for occupying a given ecological zone will keep any other forms from establishing themselves in the new habitat, even assuming that the competitors are capable of evolving. "It is idle," said Lyell, "to dispute about the abstract possibility of the conversion of one species into another, when there are known causes so much more active in their nature which must always intervene and prevent the actual accomplishment of such conversions." Using a number of present-day examples Lyell sought to show that local alterations, say that from marsh to dry land, or fresh to brackish water, would never permit of slow organic change, because long before the organisms of the older environment could alter they would die out in competition with already adapted forms intruding to take advantage of the new conditions.

Lyell, in other words, could see how time and changing conditions might alter the percentages of living forms in given localities or change the whole nature of a flora. He understood that "the successive destruction of species must now be part of the regular and constant order of nature." What he still failed to grasp was that he was observing the cutting edge of the natural-selection process in terms of its normal, short-time effects. The struggle in nature that had so impressed him he had seen, if anything, too vividly. There was left no refuge, no nursing ground, by which the new could come into existence. The already created, the already fit, dominated every niche and corner of the living world. Lyell understood ecology before Dar-

win. He saw the web of life, but he saw it so tightly drawn that nothing new could emerge from it. As geographical or climatic conditions altered in the course of geological time, already existing forms moved from one area to another; he could see no evidence for a mechanism to explain the emergence of new forms.

His vision of the history of life was not wrong; it was simply incomplete. Lyell himself realized the complexities of the problem that beset him: There was a going-out without an equivalent coming-in, an attrition without a compensating creation.

"The reader will immediately perceive," Lyell wrote, "that amidst the vicissitudes of the earth's surface, species cannot be immortal, but must perish one after the other, like the individuals which compose them. There is no possibility of escaping this conclusion without resorting to some hypothesis as violent as that of Lamarck." Drawing back from this gulf, Lyell returns again and again to nonprogressionism. Nevertheless, like many naturalists of his day, he was willing to recognize "a capacity in all species to accommodate themselves, to a certain extent, to a change of external circumstances, this extent varying greatly, according to the species." Lyell recognized minor varietal differences of a seemingly genetic character in some animals. Beyond this he did not venture.

The term natural selection, introduced by Darwin and now everywhere regarded as the leading mechanism in evolutionary change, has a peculiar history. Under other names it was known earlier within the century, but this is little realized. Darwin introduced the principle to his readers under a new term and with new implications so that it has been widely assumed that it originated in his mind. One might say, without minimizing Darwin's achievement, that this widespread impression is not quite accurate. Charles Darwin in reality took a previously recognized biological device and gave it a new and quite different interpretation. In doing so he opened the doorway to unlimited organic change and provided that empirical evolutionary mechanism which had driven Lyell and other objective scientists away from the progressionists, even though the latter had been correct, in a general sense, about the ascending complexity of life. Darwin's achievement was an apt illustration of what can sometimes be done with old principles when someone looks at them in a new way and sees some unexpected possibility within them. Darwin altered our whole conception of the nature of the world in which we live. He did so by making use of a principle already known to Charles Lyell and one other man, a young zoologist by the name of Edward Blyth. Essentially it was the principle that Lyell advanced against the evolutionary arguments of Lamarck in the 1830's.

"Of all forms of mental activity," the historian Herbert Butterfield once wrote, "the most difficult to induce is the act of handling the same bundle of data as before, but placing them in a new system of relations with one another by giving them a different framework, all of which virtually means putting on a different kind of thinking cap for the moment." This is precisely what Charles Darwin did when he took the older conception of natural selection and by altering it a hairbreadth created that region of perpetual change, of toothed birds, footless serpents and upright walking apes in which we find ourselves. Yet difficult as Darwin's feat proved to be, he received a hint, a nudge as it were, which began with Lyell, was elaborated by young Edward Blyth and from him was apparently transferred to Darwin. No clearer sequence in the evolution of ideas can be perceived anywhere in the domain of science.

Edward Blyth was a man of 25 when he read Lyell and, impressed by his ideas, carried them a little further. In the British *Magazine of Natural History* in 1835 and again in 1837, the very year that Darwin opened his first notebook upon the species question, Blyth discussed what today we would call both natural and sexual selection.

"Among animals which procure their food by means of their agility, strength or delicacy of sense, the one best organized must always obtain the greatest quantity; and must, therefore, become physically the strongest and be thus enabled, by routing its opponents, to transmit its superior qualities to a greater number of offspring. The same law, therefore, which was intended by Providence to keep up the typical qualities of a species can be easily converted by man, into a means of raising different varieties."

This idea young Blyth referred to as his "localizing principle." Like Lyell he saw the conservative aspect of selection, but he saw it more clearly. He actually discussed its genetic aspects. As the above quotation indicates, however, he interpreted natural selection as a providential device eliminating the variant

and unfit and holding each organism to its divinely appointed place in nature. Nevertheless in the course of his speculations he draws up short before a startling thought. "A variety of important considerations here crowd upon the mind," he confesses, "foremost of which is the enquiry, that, as man, by removing species from their appropriate haunts, superinduces changes on their physical constitution and adaptations, to what extent may not the same take place in wild nature, so that, in a few generations distinctive characters may be acquired, such as are recognized as indicative of specific diversity. . . ? May not then a large proportion of what are considered species have descended from a common

parentage?"

The great question had been asked again, but this time more definitively, more perspicaciously, than it had ever been asked before. Sadly, timidly young Blyth in the end rejects his own question: Like Lyell, from whom he had drawn much, he found the new world he had glimpsed too dim, too distant, too awe-inspiringly new to be quite real. One rubbed one's eyes and it was gone. The safe, constricted world of the English hedgerows remained—the world in which everything held its place.

But the year was 1837. Charles Darwin was home from the Galápagos, home from the five-year voyage of the *Beagle*, home with turtles and coral,

CATASTROPHIC VIEW of the earth's history is reflected in this engraving by Albrecht Dürer. The engraving illustrates the passage in the Bible (*The Revelations of Saint John the Divine*, Chapter 6, Verse 13) beginning: "And the stars of heaven fell unto the earth. . . ."

bird beaks and pampas thistles in his head. He read the *Magazine of Natural History* consistently in this time. We know it from recently discovered evidence. In fact, Darwin, in a somewhat cryptic early letter, tells us so: "In such foreign periodicals as I have seen, there are no such papers as White or Waterton, or some few other naturalists in Loudon's and Charlesworth's Journal would have written; and a great loss it has always appeared to me." Loudon's and Charlesworth's Journal is the *Magazine of Natural History*. There, to lie undiscovered for a century, reposed the hint that seemingly started Darwin along the road to the *Origin*. There at last is the reason for the sudden burgeoning of his ideas after the return from the voyage. Interior evidence in Darwin's early essays strongly suggests the relationship.

Later on in the century the two men became friends. As to whether Edward Blyth ever saw or grasped the connection between his youthful thoughts and the intellectual revolution that came in 1859, we do not know. After many years in India, where he devoted himself largely to ornithology, he was invalided home and died in 1873.

Passing from Lyell to Blyth to Darwin, the world faintly glimpsed by a few thinkers before them—that marred, imperfect and yet forever changing world which brings equally into being butterflies and men—dawns fully in our minds. If there is revealed to us the dark shadow of tooth and club by which we have arisen, we are taught also the utter novelty of life, its unguessed potentialities. The lost Eden which, as Francis Bacon had dreamed, might be repossessed by knowledge lies ahead of us, but it waits upon moral powers that may be as necessary to man as learning.

"Man is an ape and a beast," writes the pessimist. The true evolutionist will only say: "Man is a changeling. He is making himself blindly now, and dragging the dead past forward like a snake's cast-off skin whose fragments still bind him. He is a very young creature, a tick on Emerson's kitchen clock. Do not define him. Let the clock tick once more. Then we will know."

Already in Sir Charles Lyell's mind man's next hour was striking. As one surveys the long record of his life, as one sees his influence upon Edward Blyth, upon Darwin and upon Alfred Russel Wallace, as well as upon many other aspiring workers, one comes to recognize that to a major degree he set the scientific tone of the Victorian age. He brought to bear upon scientific thought and speculation a mind trained to the value of legal evidence. He was, on the whole, dispassionate, clear-headed and objective. By precept and example he transmitted that heritage to Darwin. He emphasized synthesis and logical generalization from facts. Both men eschewed small works and both amassed great bodies of material to carry their points. Lyell warned Darwin away from petty scientific bickering as a waste of time and nerves. At almost every step of Darwin's youthful career Lyell was an indefatigable guide and counselor. Then at that critical hour when Darwin was appalled by the reception of the news of Wallace's independent discovery of natural selection, it was Lyell and Hooker who counseled the simultaneous publication of the papers of both men.

Darwin and Wallace were Lyell's intellectual children. Both would have failed to be what they were without the *Principles of Geology* to guide them. In science there is no such thing as total independence from one's forerunners. It is an illusion we sometimes like to foster, but it does not bear close examination. Even our boasted discoveries are often in reality a construct of many minds. We are fortunate if we sometimes succeed in fitting the last brick into such an edifice. Lyell himself knew this and tasted its irony.

He died in 1875 at the end of a long, outwardly uneventful life spent largely in the company of a beautiful, gracious and intelligent woman. After his wife's death in 1873 the light began to pass away from Lyell; he did not long survive her. A few years before, he had written to Ernst Haeckel: "Most of the zoologists forget that anything was written between the time of Lamarck and the publication of our friend's *Origin of Species*."

Much indeed had been forgotten. In this little sigh of regret Lyell was even then resigning his hold upon the public which had once idolized him. To the true historian of science, however, he remains the kingmaker whose giant progeny, whether acknowledging their master by direct word or through the lines of their books, continue today to influence those who have never heard his name.

Of Charles Lyell, Darwin himself said what is so often remarked in our day of Darwin: "The great merit of the *Principles* was that it altered the whole tone of one's mind and, therefore, that when seeing a thing never seen by Lyell, one yet saw it partially through his eyes."

Charles Darwin

LOREN C. EISELEY

February 1956

In the autumn of 1831 the past and the future met and dined in London—in the guise of two young men who little realized where the years ahead would take them. One, Robert Fitzroy, was a sea captain who at 26 had already charted the remote, sea-beaten edges of the world and now proposed another long voyage. A religious man with a strong animosity toward the new-fangled geology, Captain Fitzroy wanted a naturalist who would share his experience of wild lands and refute those who used rocks to promote heretical whisperings. The young man who faced him across the table hesitated. Charles Darwin, four years Fitzroy's junior, was a gentleman idler after hounds who had failed at medicine and whose family, in desperation, hoped he might still succeed as a country parson. His mind shifted uncertainly from fox hunting in Shropshire to the thought of shooting llamas in South America. Did he really want to go? While he fumbled for a decision and the future hung irresolute, Captain Fitzroy took command.

"Fitzroy," wrote Darwin later to his sister Susan, "says the stormy sea is exaggerated; that if I do not choose to remain with them, I can at any time get home to England; and that if I like, I shall be left in some healthy, safe and nice country; that I shall always have assistance; that he has many books, all instruments, guns, at my service. . . . There is indeed a tide in the affairs of men, and I have experienced it. Dearest Susan, Goodbye."

They sailed from Devonport December 27, 1831, in H.M.S. *Beagle*, a 10-gun brig. Their plan was to survey the South American coastline and to carry a string of chronometrical measurements around the world. The voyage almost ended before it began, for they at once encountered a violent storm. "The sea ran very high," young Darwin recorded in his diary, "and the vessel pitched bows under and suffered most dreadfully; such a night I never passed, on every side nothing but misery; such a whistling of the wind and roar of the sea, the hoarse screams of the officers and shouts of the men, made a concert that I shall not soon forget." Captain Fitzroy and his officers held the ship on the sea by the grace of God and the cat-o'-nine-tails. With an almost irrational stubbornness Darwin decided, in spite of his uncomfortable discovery of his susceptibility to seasickness, that "I did right to accept the offer." When the *Beagle* was buffeted back into Plymouth Harbor, Darwin did not resign. His mind was made up. "If it is desirable to see the world," he wrote in his journal, "what a rare and excellent opportunity this is. Perhaps I may have the same opportunity of drilling my mind that I threw away at Cambridge."

So began the journey in which a great mind untouched by an old-fashioned classical education was to feed its hunger upon rocks and broken bits of bone at the world's end, and eventually was to shape from such diverse things as bird beaks and the fused wing-cases of island beetles a theory that would shake the foundations of scientific thought in all the countries of the earth.

The Intellectual Setting

The intellectual climate from which Darwin set forth on his historic voyage was predominantly conservative. Insular England had been horrified by the excesses of the French Revolution and was extremely wary of emerging new ideas which it attributed to "French atheists." Religious dogma still held its powerful influence over natural science. True, the 17th-century notion that the world had been created in 4004 B.C. was beginning to weaken in the face of naturalists' studies of the rocks and their succession of life forms. But the conception of a truly ancient and evolving planet was still unformed. No one could dream that the age of the earth was as vast as we now know it to be. And the notion of a continuity of events—of one animal changing by degrees into another—seemed to fly in the face not only of religious beliefs but also of common sense. Many of the greatest biologists of the time—men like Louis Agassiz and Richard Owen—tended to the belief that the successive forms of life in the geological record were all separate creations, some of which had simply been extinguished by historic accidents.

Yet Darwin did not compose the theory of evolution out of thin air. Like so many great scientific generalizations, the theory with which his name is associated had already had premonitory beginnings. All of the elements which were to enter into the theory were in men's minds and were being widely discussed during Darwin's college years. His own grandfather, Erasmus Darwin, who died seven years before Charles was born, had boldly proposed a theory of the "transmutation" of living forms. Jean Baptiste Lamarck had glimpsed a vision of evolutionary continuity. And Sir Charles Lyell—later to be Darwin's lifelong confidant—had opened the way for the evolutionary point of view by demonstrating that the planet must be very old—old enough to allow extremely slow organic change. Lyell dismissed the notion of catastrophic extinction of animal forms on a world-wide scale as impossible, and he made plain that natural forces—the work of wind and frost and water—were sufficient to explain most of the phenomena found in the rocks, provided these forces were seen as operating over enormous periods. Without Lyell's gift of time in immense quantities, Darwin would not have been able to devise the theory of natural selection.

If all the essential elements of the Darwinian scheme of nature were known prior to Darwin, why is he accorded so important a place in biological history? The answer is simple: Almost every great scientific generalization is a supreme act of creative synthesis. There comes a time when an accumulation of smaller discoveries and observations can be combined in some great and comprehensive view of nature. At this point the need is not so much for increased numbers of facts as for a mind of great insight capable of taking the assembled information and rendering it intelligible. Such a synthesis represents the scientific mind at its highest point of achievement. The stature of the discoverer is not diminished by the fact that he has slid into place the last piece of a tremendous puzzle on which many others have worked. To finish the task he must see correctly over a vast and diverse array of data.

Still it must be recognized that Darwin came at a fortunate time. The fact that another man, Alfred Russel Wallace, conceived the Darwinian theory independently before Darwin published it shows clearly that the principle which came to be called natural selection was in the air—was in a sense demanding to be born. Darwin himself pointed out in his autobiography that "innumerable well-observed facts were stored in the minds of naturalists ready to take their proper places as soon as any theory which would receive them was sufficiently explained."

The Voyage

Darwin, then, set out on his voyage with a mind both inquisitive to see and receptive to what he saw. No detail was too small to be fascinating and provocative. Sailing down the South American coast, he notes the octopus changing its color angrily in the waters of a cove. In the dry arroyos of the pampas he observes great bones and shrewdly seeks to relate them to animals of the present. The local inhabitants insist that the fossil bones grew after death, and also that certain rivers have the power of "changing small bones into large." Everywhere men wonder, but they are deceived through their thirst for easy explanations. Darwin, by contrast, is a working dreamer. He rides, climbs, spends long

days on the Indian-haunted pampas in constant peril of his life. Asking at a house whether robbers are numerous, he receives the cryptic reply: "The thistles are not up yet." The huge thistles, high as a horse's back at their full growth, provide ecological cover for bandits. Darwin notes the fact and rides on. The thistles are overrunning the pampas; the whole aspect of the vegetation is altering under the impact of man. Wild dogs howl in the brakes; the common cat, run wild, has grown large and fierce. All is struggle, mutability, change. Staring into the face of an evil relative of the rattlesnake, he observes a fact "which appears to me very curious and instructive, as showing how every character, even though it may be in some degree independent of structure . . . has a tendency to vary by slow degrees."

He pays great attention to strange animals existing in difficult environ-

ments. A queer little toad with a scarlet belly he whimsically nicknames *diabolicus* because it is "a fit toad to preach in the ear of Eve." He notes it lives among sand dunes under the burning sun, and unlike its brethren, cannot swim. From toads to grasshoppers, from pebbles to mountain ranges, nothing escapes his attention. The wearing away of stone, the downstream travel of rock fragments and boulders, the great crevices and upthrusts of the Andes, an earthquake—all confirm the dynamic character of the earth and its great age.

Captain Fitzroy by now is anxious to voyage on. The sails are set. With the towering Andes on their right flank they run north for the Galápagos Islands, lying directly on the Equator 600 miles off the west coast of South America. A one-time refuge of buccaneers, these islands are essentially chimneys of burned-out volcanoes. Darwin remarks that they

PHOTOGRAPHIC PORTRAIT of Darwin was made some years after the appearance of *Origin of Species*. It is from the collection of George Eastman House in Rochester, N. Y.

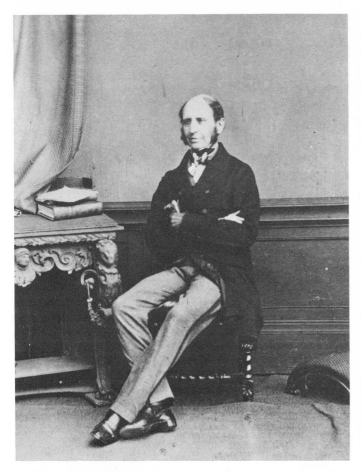

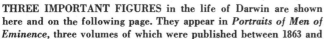

THREE IMPORTANT FIGURES in the life of Darwin are shown here and on the following page. They appear in *Portraits of Men of Eminence*, three volumes of which were published between 1863 and 1865. This book is also from George Eastman House. At left is Robert Fitzroy, Captain of the *Beagle*; at right, Charles Lyell, the geologist who was Darwin's lifelong confidant.

remind him of huge iron foundries surrounded by piles of waste. "A little world in itself," he marvels, "with inhabitants such as are found nowhere else." Giant armored tortoises clank through the undergrowth like prehistoric monsters, feeding upon the cacti. Birds in this tiny Eden do not fear men: "One day a mocking bird alighted on the edge of a pitcher which I held in my hand. It began very quietly to sip the water, and allowed me to lift it with the vessel from the ground." Big sea lizards three feet long drowse on the beaches, and feed, fantastically, upon the seaweed. Surveying these "imps of darkness, black as the porous rocks over which they crawl," Darwin is led to comment that "there is no other quarter of the world, where this order replaces the herbivorous mammalia in so extraordinary a manner."

Yet only by degrees did Darwin awake to the ·fact that he had stumbled by chance into one of the most marvelous evolutionary laboratories on the planet. Here in the Galápagos was a wealth of variations from island to island—among the big tortoises, among plants and es-pecially among the famous finches with remarkably diverse beaks. Dwellers on the islands, notably Vice Governor Lawson, called Darwin's attention to these strange variations, but as he confessed later, with typical Darwinian lack of pretense, "I did not for some time pay sufficient attention to this statement." Whether his visit to the Galápagos was the single event that mainly led Darwin to the central conceptions of his evolutionary mechanism—hereditary change within the organism coupled with external selective factors which might cause plants and animals a few miles apart in the same climate to diverge—is a moot point upon which Darwin himself in later years shed no clear light. Perhaps, like many great men, nagged long after the event for a precise account of the dawn of a great discovery, Darwin no longer clearly remembered the beginning of the intellectual journey which had paralleled so dramatically his passage on the seven seas. Perhaps there had never been a clear beginning at all—only a slowly widening comprehension until what had been seen at first mistily and through a veil grew magnified and clear.

The Invalid and the Book

The paths to greatness are tricky and diverse. Sometimes a man's weaknesses have as much to do with his rise as his virtues. In Darwin's case it proved to be a unique combination of both. He had gathered his material by a courageous and indefatigable pursuit of knowledge that took him through the long vicissitudes of a voyage around the world. But his great work was written in sickness and seclusion. When Darwin reached home after the voyage of the *Beagle*, he was an ailing man, and he remained so to the end of his life. Today we know that this illness was in some degree psychosomatic, that he was anxiety-ridden, subject to mysterious headaches and nausea. Shortly after his voyage Darwin married his cousin Emma Wedgwood, granddaughter of the founder of the great pottery works, and isolated himself and his family in a little village in Kent. He avoided travel like the plague,

THE THIRD IMPORTANT FIGURE, shown above, is Thomas Huxley, who defended Darwin in debate.

save for brief trips to watering places for his health. His seclusion became his strength and protected him; his very fears and doubts of himself resulted in the organization of that enormous battery of facts which documented the theory of evolution as it had never been documented before.

Let us examine the way in which Darwin developed his great theory. The nature of his observations has already been indicated—the bird beaks, the recognition of variation and so on. But it is an easier thing to perceive that evolution has come about than to identify the mechanism involved in it. For a long time this problem frustrated Darwin. He was not satisfied with vague references to climatic influence or the inheritance of acquired characters. Finally he reached the conclusion that since variation in individual characteristics existed among the members of any species, selection of some individuals and elimination of others must be the key to organic change.

This idea he got from the common recognition of the importance of selective breeding in the improvement of domestic plants and livestock. He still did not understand, however, what selective force could be at work in wild nature. Then in 1838 he chanced to read Thomas Malthus, and the solution came to him.

Malthus had written in 1798 a widely population study in which he pointe that the human population tende increase faster than its food supply, cipitating in consequence a struggl existence.

Darwin applied this principle to whole world of organic life and argued the struggle for existence under char environmental conditions was wha duced alterations in the physical struc of organisms. In other words, fo tous and random variations occurr living things. The struggle for life petuated advantageous variation means of heredity. The weak and were eliminated and those with the heredity for any given environment "selected" to be the parents of the generation. Since neither life nor cli nor geology ever ceased changing, lution was perpetual. No organ a animal was ever in complete equili with its surroundings.

This, briefly stated, is the crux Darwinian argument. Facts which been known before Darwin but ha been recognized as parts of a scheme—variation, inheritance of tion, selective breeding of dor plants and animals, the struggle fe istence—all suddenly fell into pla "natural selection," as "Darwinisn

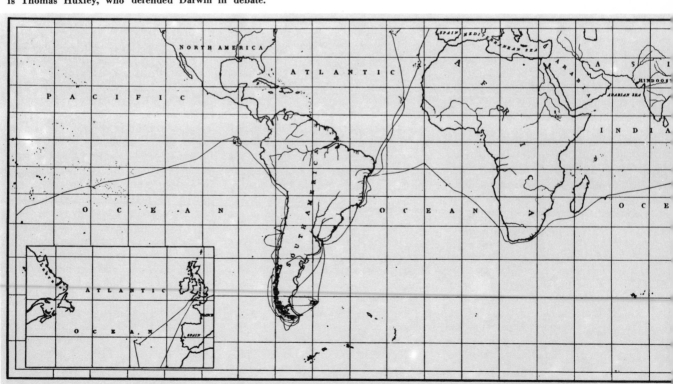

VOYAGE OF THE BEAGLE is traced in this map from Fitzroy's *Narrative of the Surveying Voyage of His Majesty's Ships Adven-* *ture and Beagle*. The *Beagle*'s course on her departure from and return to England is at lower left. The ship made frequent stops at

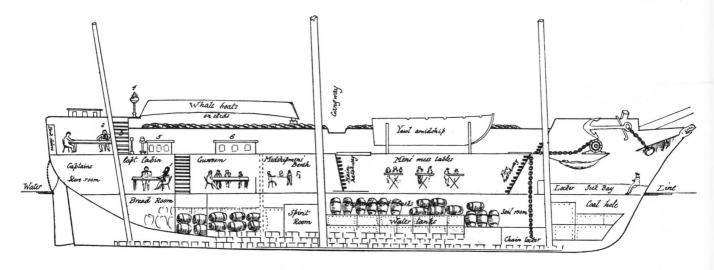

H. M. S. BEAGLE was drawn in cross section many years after the voyage by Philip Gidley King, who accompanied Darwin when he was ashore during the voyage. Darwin is shown in two places: the captain's cabin (*small figure 1 at upper left*) and poop cabin (*2*).

Procrastination

While he developed his theory and marshaled his data, Darwin remained in seclusion and retreat, hoarding the secret of his discovery. For 22 years after the *Beagle*'s return he published not one word beyond the bare journal of his trip (later titled *A Naturalist's Voyage around the World*) and technical monographs on his observations.

Let us not be misled, however, by

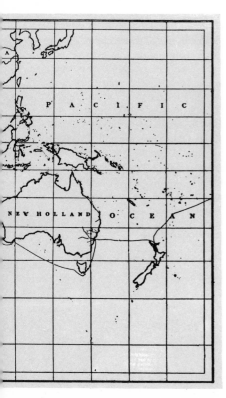

oceanic islands. The Galápagos Islands are on the Equator to the west of South America.

Darwin's seclusiveness and illness. No more lovable or sweet-tempered invalid ever lived. Visitors, however beloved, always aggravated his illness, but instead of the surly misanthropy which afflicts most people under similar circumstances, the result in Darwin's case was merely nights of sleeplessness. Throughout the long night hours his restless mind went on working with deep concentration; more than once, walking alone in the dark hours of winter, he met the foxes trotting home at dawn.

Darwin's gardener is said to have responded once to a visitor who inquired about his master's health: "Poor man, he just stands and stares at a yellow flower for minutes at a time. He would be better off with something to do." Darwin's work was of an intangible nature which eluded people around him. Much of it consisted in just such standing and staring as his gardener reported. It was a kind of magic at which he excelled. On a visit to the Isle of Wight he watched thistle seed wafted about on offshore winds and formulated theories of plant dispersal. Sometimes he engaged in activities which his good wife must surely have struggled to keep from reaching the neighbors. When a friend sent him a half ounce of locust dung from Africa, Darwin triumphantly grew seven plants from the specimen. "There is no error," he assured Lyell, "for I dissected the seeds out of the middle of the pellets." To discover how plant seeds traveled, Darwin would go all the way down a grasshopper's gullet, or worse, without embarrassment. His eldest son Francis spoke amusedly of his father's botanical experiments: "I think he personified each seed as a small demon trying to elude him by getting into the wrong heap, or jumping away all together; and this gave to the work the excitement of a game."

The point of his game Darwin kept largely to himself, waiting until it should be completely finished. He piled up vast stores of data and dreamed of presenting his evolution theory in a definitive, monumental book, so large that it would certainly have fallen dead and unreadable from the press. In the meantime, Robert Chambers, a bookseller and journalist, wrote and brought out anonymously a modified version of Lamarckian evolution, under the title *Vestiges of the Natural History of Creation*. Amateurish in some degree, the book drew savage onslaughts from the critics, including Thomas Huxley, but it caught the public fancy and was widely read. It passed through numerous editions both in England and America—evidence that *sub rosa* there was a good deal more interest on the part of the public in the "development hypothesis," as evolution was then called, than the fulminations of critics would have suggested.

Throughout this period Darwin remained stonily silent. Many explanations of his silence have been ventured by his biographers: that he was busy accumulating materials; that he did not wish to affront Fitzroy; that the attack on the *Vestiges* had intimidated him; that he thought it wise not to write upon so controversial a subject until he had first acquired a reputation as a professional naturalist of the first rank. Primarily, however, the basic reason lay in his personality—a nature reluctant to face the storm that publication would bring about his ears. It was pleasanter to procrastinate, to talk of the secret to a few chosen companions such as Lyell

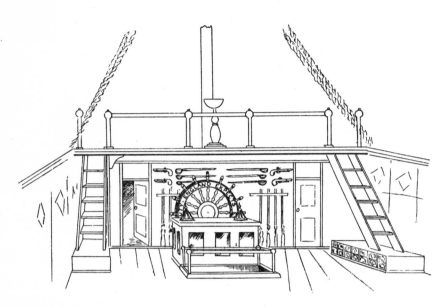

QUARTER-DECK of the *Beagle* is depicted in this drawing by King. In the center is the wheel, the circumference of which is inscribed: "England expects every man to do his duty."

and the great botanist Joseph Hooker.

The Darwin family had been well-to-do since the time of grandfather Erasmus. Charles was independent, in a position to devote all his energies to research and under no academic pressure to publish in haste.

"You will be anticipated," Lyell warned him. "You had better publish." That was in the spring of 1856. Darwin promised, but again delayed. We know that he left instructions for his wife to see to the publication of his notes in the event of his death. It was almost as if present fame or notoriety were more than he could bear. At all events he continued to delay, and this situation might very well have continued to the end of his life, had not Lyell's warning suddenly come true and broken his pleasant dream.

Alfred Russel Wallace, a comparatively unknown, youthful naturalist, had divined Darwin's great secret in a moment of fever-ridden insight while on a collecting trip in Indonesia. He, too, had put together the pieces and gained a clear conception of the scheme of evolution. Ironically enough, it was to Darwin, in all innocence, that he sent his manuscript for criticism in June of 1858. He sensed in Darwin a sympathetic and traveled listener.

Darwin was understandably shaken.

The work which had been so close to his heart, the dream to which he had devoted 20 years, was a private secret no longer. A newcomer threatened his priority. Yet Darwin, wanting to do what was decent and ethical, had been placed in an awkward position by the communication. His first impulse was to withdraw totally in favor of Wallace. "I would far rather burn my whole book," he insisted, "than that he or any other man should think that I had behaved in a paltry spirit." It is fortunate for science that before pursuing this quixotic course Darwin turned to his friends Lyell and Hooker, who knew the many years he had been laboring upon his *magnum opus*. The two distinguished scientists arranged for the delivery of a short summary by Darwin to accompany Wallace's paper before the Linnaean Society. Thus the theory of the two men was announced simultaneously.

Publication

The papers drew little comment at the meeting but set in motion a mild undercurrent of excitement. Darwin, though upset by the death of his son Charles, went to work to explain his views more fully in a book. Ironically he called it *An Abstract of an Essay on the Origin of Species* and insisted it would be only a kind of preview of a much larger work. Anxiety and devotion to his great hoard of data still possessed him. He did not like to put all his hopes in this volume, which must now be written at top speed. He bolstered himself by references to the "real" book—that Utopian volume in which all that could not be made clear in his abstract would be clarified.

His timidity and his fears were totally groundless. When the *Origin of Species* (the title distilled by his astute publisher from Darwin's cumbersome and half-hearted one) was published in the fall of 1859, the first edition was sold in a single day. The book which Darwin had so apologetically bowed into existence was, of course, soon to be recognized as one of the great books of all time. It would not be long before its author would sigh happily and think no more of that huge, ideal volume which he had imagined would be necessary to convince the public. The public and his brother scientists would find the *Origin* quite heavy going enough. His book to end all books would never be written. It did not need to be. The world of science in the end could only agree with the sharp-minded Huxley, whose immediate reaction upon reading the *Origin* was: "How extremely stupid not to have thought of that!" And so it frequently seems in science, once the great synthesizer has done his work. The ideas were not new, but the synthesis was. Men would never again look upon the world in the same manner as before.

No great philosophic conception ever entered the world more fortunately. Though it is customary to emphasize the religious and scientific storm the book aroused—epitomized by the famous debate at Oxford between Bishop Wilberforce and Thomas Huxley—the truth is that Darwinism found relatively easy acceptance among scientists and most of the public. The way had been prepared by the long labors of Lyell and the wide popularity of Chambers' book, the *Vestiges*. Moreover, Darwin had won the support of the great Hooker and of Huxley, the most formidable scientific debater of all time. Lyell, though more cautious, helped to publicize Darwin and at no time attacked him. Asa Gray, one of America's leading botanists, came to his defense. His codiscoverer, Wallace, as generous-hearted as Darwin, himself advanced the word "Darwinism" for Darwin's theory, and minimized his own part in the elaboration of the theory as "one week to 20 years."

This sturdy band of converts assumed

the defense of Darwin before the public, while Charles remained aloof. Sequestered in his estate at Down, he calmly answered letters and listened, but not too much, to the tumult over the horizon. "It is something unintelligible to me how anyone can argue in public like orators do," he confessed to Hooker, though he was deeply grateful for the verbal swordplay of his cohorts. Hewett Watson, another botanist of note, wrote to him shortly after the publication of the *Origin:* "Your leading idea will assuredly become recognized as an established truth in science, *i.e.,* 'Natural Selection.' It has the characteristics of all great natural truths, clarifying what was obscure, simplifying what was intricate, adding greatly to previous knowledge. You are the greatest revolutionist in natural history of this century, if not of all centuries."

Watson's statement was clairvoyant. Not a line of his appraisal would need to be altered today. Within 10 years the

Origin and its author were known all over the globe, and evolution had become the guiding motif in all biological studies.

Summing up the achievement of this book, we may say today, first, that Darwin had proved the reality of evolutionary change beyond any reasonable doubt, and secondly, that he had demonstrated, in natural selection, a principle capable of wide, if not universal, application. Natural selection dispelled the confusions that had been introduced into biology by the notion of individual creation of species. The lad who in 1832 had noted with excited interest "that there are three sorts of birds which use their wings for more purposes than flying; the Steamer [duck] as paddles, the Penguin as fins, and the Ostrich (*Rhea*) spreads its plumes like sails" now had his answer—"descent with modification." "If you go any considerable lengths in the admission of modification," warned Darwin, "I can see no possible means of

drawing the line, and saying here you must stop." Rung by rung, was his plain implication, one was forced to descend down the full length of life's mysterious ladder until one stood in the brewing vats where the thing was made. And similarly, rung by rung, from mudfish to reptile and mammal, the process ascended to man.

A Small Place for Man

Darwin had cautiously avoided direct references to man in the *Origin of Species.* But 12 years later, after its triumph was assured, he published a study of human evolution entitled *The Descent of Man.* He had been preceded in this field by Huxley's *Evidences as to Man's Place in Nature* (1863). Huxley's brief work was written with wonderful clarity and directness. By contrast, the *Descent of Man* has some of the labored and inchoate quality of Darwin's overfull folios of data. It is contradictory in spots, as

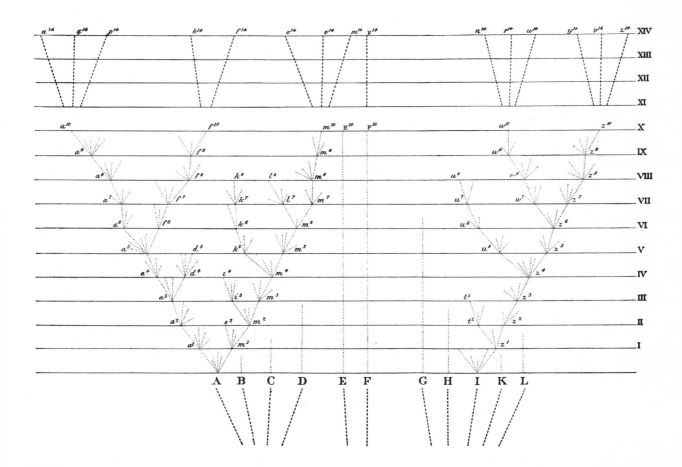

NATURAL SELECTION through the divergence of characters is illustrated in *Origin of Species.* The capital letters at the bottom of the illustration represent different species of the same genus. Each horizontal line, labeled with a Roman numeral at the right, represents 1,000 or more generations. Darwin believed that some of the original species, such as A, would diverge more than others. After many generations they would give rise to new varieties, such as a^1 and m^1. These new varieties would diverge in turn. After thousands of generations the new varieties would give rise to entirely new species, such as a^{14}, q^{14}, p^{14} and so on. The original species would meantime have died out. Darwin thought that only some species of the original genus would diverge sufficiently to give rise to new species. Some of the species, such as F, would remain much the same. Others, such as B, C and D, would die out.

though the author simply poured his notes together and never fully read the completed manuscript to make sure it was an organic whole.

One of its defects is Darwin's failure to distinguish consistently between biological inheritance and cultural influences upon the behavior and evolution of human beings. In this, of course, Darwin was making a mistake common to biologists of the time. Anthropology was then in its infancy. In the biological realm, the *Descent of Man* did make plain in a general way that man was related to the rest of the primate order, though the precise relationship was left ambiguous. After all, we must remember that no one had yet unearthed any clear fossils of early man. A student of evolution had to content himself largely with tracing morphological similarities between living man and the great apes. This left considerable room for speculation as to the precise nature of the human ancestors. It is not surprising that they were occasionally visualized as gorilloid beasts with huge canine teeth, nor that Darwin wavered between this and gentler interpretations.

An honest biographer must record the fact that man was not Darwin's best subject. In the words of a 19th-century critic, his "was a world of insects and pigeons, apes and curious plants, but man as he exists, had no place in it." Allowing for the hyperbole of this religious opponent, it is nonetheless probable that Darwin did derive more sheer delight from writing his book on earthworms than from any amount of contemplation of a creature who could talk back and who was apt stubbornly to hold ill-founded opinions. In any case, no man afflicted with a weak stomach and insomnia has any business investigating his own kind. At least it is best to wait until they have undergone the petrification incident to becoming part of a geological stratum.

Darwin knew this. He had fled London to work in peace. When he dealt with the timid gropings of climbing plants, the intricacies of orchids or the calculated malice of the carnivorous sundew, he was not bedeviled by metaphysicians, by talk of ethics, morals or the nature of religion. Darwin did not wish to leave man an exception to his system, but he was content to consider man simply as a part of that vast, sprawling, endlessly ramifying ferment called "life." The rest of him could be left to the philosophers. "I have often," he once complained to a friend, "been made wroth (even by Lyell) at the confidence with which people speak of the intro-

duction of man, as if they had seen him walk on the stage and as if in a geological sense it was more important than the entry of any other mammifer."

Darwin's fame as the author of the theory of evolution has tended to obscure the fact that he was, without doubt, one of the great field naturalists of all time. His capacity to see deep problems in simple objects is nowhere better illustrated than in his study of movement in plants, published some two years before his death. He subjected twining plants, previously little studied, to a series of ingenious investigations of pioneer importance in experimental botany. Perhaps Darwin's intuitive comparison of plants to animals accounted for much of his success in this field. There is an entertaining story that illustrates how much more perceptive than his contemporaries he was here. To Huxley and another visitor, Darwin was trying to explain the remarkable behavior of *Drosera*, the sundew plant, which catches insects with grasping, sticky hairs. The two visitors listened to Darwin as one might listen politely to a friend who is slightly "touched." But as they watched the plant, their tolerant poise suddenly vanished and Huxley cried out in amazement: "Look, it *is* moving!"

The Islands

As one surveys the long and tangled course that led to Darwin's great discovery, one cannot but be struck by the part played in it by oceanic islands. It is a part little considered by the general public today. The word "evolution" is commonly supposed to stand for something that occurred in the past, something involving fossil apes and dinosaurs, something pecked out of the rocks of eroding mountains—a history of the world largely demonstrated and proved by the bone hunter. Yet, paradoxically, in Darwin's time it was this very history that most cogently challenged the evolutionary point of view. Paleontology was not nearly so extensively developed as today, and the record was notable mainly for its gaps. "Where are the links?" the critics used to rail at Darwin. "Where are the links between man and ape—between your lost land animal and the whale? Show us the fossils; prove your case." Darwin could only repeat: "This is the most obvious and gravest objection which can be urged against my theory. The explanation lies, as I believe, in the extreme imperfection of the geological record." The evidence for the continuity of life must be found else-

where. And it was the oceanic islands that finally supplied the clue.

Until Darwin turned his attention to them, it appears to have been generally assumed that island plants and animals were simply marooned evidences of a past connection with the nearest continent. Darwin, however, noted that whole classes of continental life were absent from the islands; that certain plants which were herbaceous (nonwoody) on the mainland had developed into trees on the islands; that island animals often differed from their counterparts on the mainland.

Above all, the fantastically varied finches of the Galápagos particularly amazed and puzzled him. The finches diverged mainly in their beaks. There were parrot-beaks, curved beaks for probing flowers, straight beaks, small beaks—beaks for every conceivable purpose. These beak variations existed nowhere but on the islands; they must have evolved there. Darwin had early observed: "One might really fancy that, from an original paucity of birds in this archipelago, one species had been taken and modified for different ends." The birds had become transformed, through the struggle for existence on their little islets, into a series of types suited to particular environmental niches where, properly adapted, they could obtain food and survive. As the ornithologist David Lack has remarked: "Darwin's finches form a little world of their own, but one which intimately reflects the world as a whole" [see "Darwin's Finches," by David Lack; SCIENTIFIC AMERICAN Offprint #22].

Darwin's recognition of the significance of this miniature world, where the forces operating to create new beings could be plainly seen, was indispensable to his discovery of the origin of species. The island worlds reduced the confusion of continental life to more simple proportions; one could separate the factors involved with greater success. Over and over Darwin emphasized the importance of islands in his thinking. Nothing would aid natural history more, he contended to Lyell, "than careful collecting and investigating of *all the productions* of the most isolated islands. . . . Every sea shell and insect and plant is of value from such spots."

Darwin was born in precisely the right age even in terms of the great scientific voyages. A little earlier the story the islands had to tell could not have been read; a little later much of it began to be erased. Today all over the globe the populations of these little worlds are vanishing, many without ever having

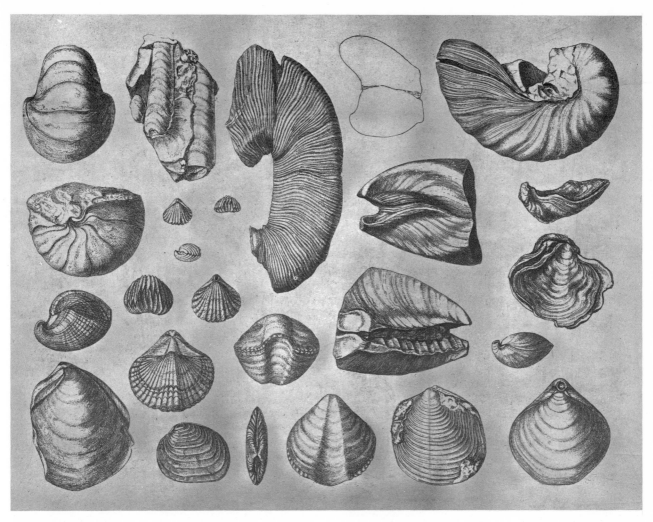

FOSSIL SHELLS were depicted in this engraving from Darwin's *Geological Observations on the Volcanic Islands and Parts of South* *America Visited during the Voyage of H. M. S. Beagle.* This was a technical work published by Darwin before *Origin of Species.*

been seriously investigated. Man, breaking into their isolation, has brought with him cats, rats, pigs, goats, weeds and insects from the continents. In the face of these hardier, tougher, more aggressive competitors, the island faunas—the rare, the antique, the strange, the beautiful— are vanishing without a trace. The giant Galápagos tortoises are almost extinct, as is the land lizard with which Darwin played. Some of the odd little finches and rare plants have gone or will go. On the island of Madagascar our own remote relatives, the lemurs, which have radiated into many curious forms, are now being exterminated through the destruction of the forests. Even that continental island Australia is suffering from the decimation wrought by man. The Robinson Crusoe worlds where

small castaways could create existences idyllically remote from the ravening slaughter of man and his associates are about to pass away forever. Every such spot is now a potential air base where the cries of birds are drowned in the roar of jets, and the crevices once frequented by bird life are flattened into the long runways of the bombers. All this would not have surprised Darwin, one would guess.

Of Darwin's final thoughts in the last hours of his life in 1882, when he struggled with a weakening heart, no record remains. One cannot but wonder whether this man who had no faith in Paradise may not have seen rising on his dying sight the pounding surf and black slag heaps of the Galápagos, those islands called by Fitzroy "a fit shore for Pande-

monium." None would ever see them again as Darwin had seen them—smoldering sullenly under the equatorial sun and crawling with uncertain black reptiles lost from some earlier creation. Once he had cried out suddenly in anguish: "What a book a devil's chaplain might write on the clumsy, wasteful, blundering, low and horribly cruel works of nature!" He never spoke or wrote in quite that way again. It was more characteristic of his mind to dwell on such memories as that Eden-like bird drinking softly from the pitcher held in his hand. When the end came, he remarked with simple dignity, "I am not in the least afraid of death."

It was in that spirit he had ventured upon a great voyage in his youth. It would suffice him for one more journey.

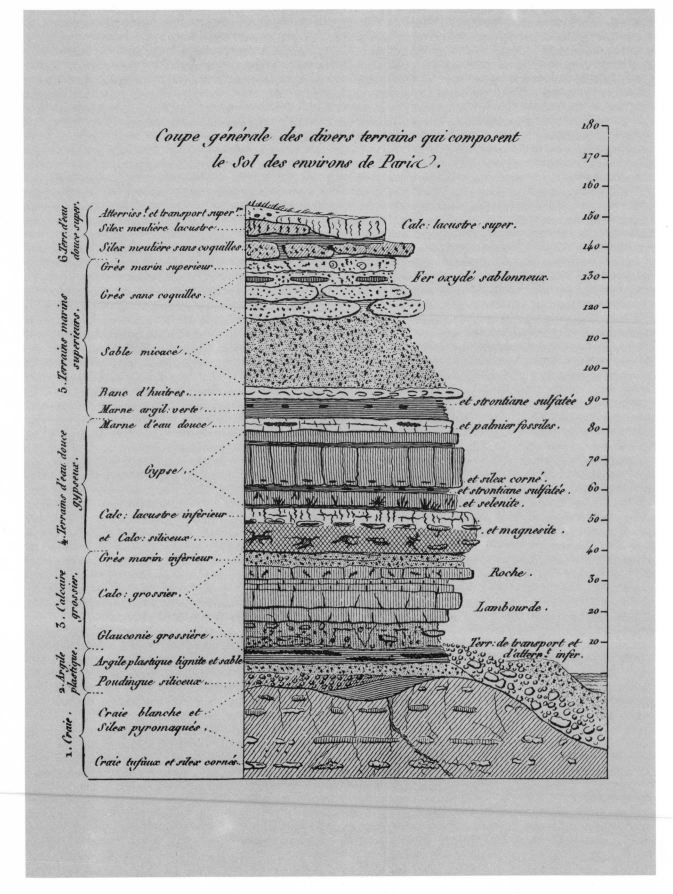

Coupe générale des divers terrains qui composent le Sol des environs de Paris.

6. Terr. d'eau douce super.
Atterriss.^t et transport super.^r
Silex meulière lacustre
Silex meulière sans coquilles
Calc: lacustre super.

5. Terrains marins superieurs.
Grès marin superieur
Grès sans coquilles
Fer oxydé sablonneux.
Sable micacé
Banc d'huîtres
et strontiane sulfatée.
Marne argil. verte
Marne d'eau douce
et palmier fossiles.

4. Terrains d'eau douce gypseux.
Gypse
et silex corné.
et strontiane sulfatée.
et selenite.
Calc: lacustre inferieur
et Calc: siliceux
et magnesite.

3. Calcaire grossier.
Grès marin inferieur
Calc: grossier.
Roche.
Lambourde.
Glauconie grossière
Terr: de transport et d'attert inferieur.

2. Argile plastique.
Argile plastique lignite et sable
Poudingue siliceux

1. Craie.
Craie blanche et Silex pyromaqués
Craie tufiaux et silex cornés.

"EVIDENCE" FOR CATASTROPHISM was adduced by the French naturalist Baron Georges Cuvier from his study of the Paris basin. He and Alexandre Brongniart published this diagram in 1822. Cuvier believed that the abrupt changes in the strata bespoke the occurrence of cataclysms. Although his observations were accurate, his conclusions are no longer generally accepted.

Crises in the History of Life

NORMAN D. NEWELL

February 1963

The stream of life on earth has been continuous since it originated some three or four billion years ago. Yet the fossil record of past life is not a simple chronology of uniformly evolving organisms. The record is prevailingly one of erratic, often abrupt changes in environment, varying rates of evolution, extermination and repopulation. Dissimilar biotas replace one another in a kind of relay. Mass extinction, rapid migration and consequent disruption of biological equilibrium on both a local and a world-wide scale have accompanied continual environmental changes.

The main books and chapters of earth history—the eras, periods and epochs— were dominated for tens or even hundreds of millions of years by characteristic groups of animals and plants. Then, after ages of orderly evolution and biological success, many of the groups suddenly died out. The cause of these mass extinctions is still very much in doubt and constitutes a major problem of evolutionary history.

The striking episodes of disappearance and replacement of successive biotas in the layered fossil record were termed revolutions by Baron Georges Cuvier, the great French naturalist of the late 18th and early 19th centuries. Noting that these episodes generally correspond to unconformities, that is, gaps in the strata due to erosion, Cuvier attributed them to sudden and violent catastrophes. This view grew out of his study of the sequence of strata in the region of Paris. The historic diagram on the opposite page was drawn by Cuvier nearly 150 years ago. It represents a simple alternation of fossil-bearing rocks of marine and nonmarine origin, with many erosional breaks and marked interruptions in the sequence of fossils.

The objection to Cuvier's catastrophism is not merely that he ascribed events in earth history to cataclysms; many normal geological processes are at times cataclysmic. The objection is that he dismissed known processes and appealed to fantasy to explain natural phenomena. He believed that "the march of nature is changed and not one of her present agents could have sufficed to have effected her ancient works." This hypothesis, like so many others about extinction, is not amenable to scientific test and is hence of limited value. In fairness to Cuvier, however, one must recall that in his day it was widely believed that the earth was only a few thousand years old. Cuvier correctly perceived that normal geological processes could not have produced the earth as we know it in such a short time.

Now that we have learned that the earth is at least five or six billion years old, the necessity for invoking Cuverian catastrophes to explain geological history would seem to have disappeared. Nevertheless, a few writers such as Immanuel Velikovsky, the author of *Worlds in Collision*, and Charles H. Hapgood, the author of *The Earth's Shifting Crust*, continue to propose imaginary catastrophes on the basis of little or no historical evidence. Although it is well established that the earth's crust has shifted and that climates have changed, these changes almost certainly were more gradual than Hapgood suggests. Most geologists, following the "uniformitarian" point of view expounded in the 18th century by James Hutton and in the 19th by Charles Lyell, are satisfied that observable natural processes are quite adequate to explain the history of the earth. They agree, however, that these processes must have varied greatly in rate.

Charles Darwin, siding with Hutton and Lyell, also rejected catastrophism as an explanation for the abrupt changes in the fossil record. He attributed such changes to migrations of living organisms, to alterations of the local environment during the deposition of strata and to unconformities caused by erosion. Other important factors that are now given more attention than they were in Darwin's day are the mass extinction of organisms, acceleration of the rate of evolution and the thinning of strata due to extremely slow deposition.

The Record of Mass Extinctions

If we may judge from the fossil record, eventual extinction seems to be the lot of all organisms. Roughly 2,500 families of animals with an average longevity of somewhat less than 75 million years have left a fossil record. Of these, about a third are still living. Although a few families became extinct by evolving into new families, a majority dropped out of sight without descendants.

In spite of the high incidence of extinction, there has been a persistent gain in the diversity of living forms: new forms have appeared more rapidly than old forms have died out. Evidently organisms have discovered an increasing number of ecological niches to fill, and by modifying the environment they have produced ecological systems of great complexity, thereby making available still more niches. In fact, as I shall develop later, the interdependence of living organisms, involving complex chains of food supply, may provide an important key to the understanding of how relatively small changes in the environment could have triggered mass extinctions.

The fossil record of animals tells more about extinction than the fossil record of plants does. It has long been known

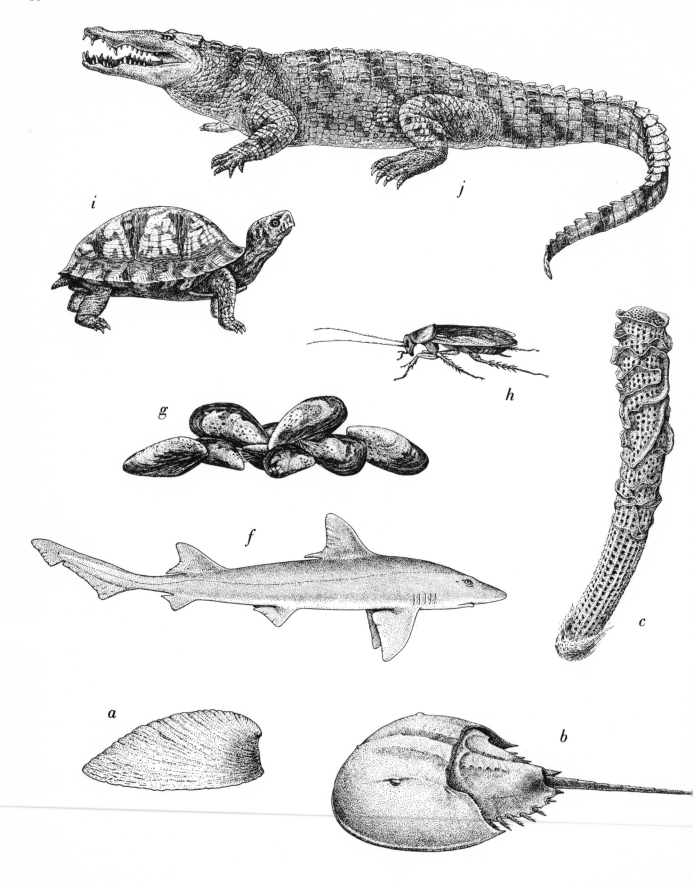

GALLERY OF HARDY ANIMALS contains living representatives of 11 groups that have weathered repeated crises in evolutionary history. Four of the groups can be traced back to the Cambrian period: the mollusk *Neopilina* (*a*), the horseshoe crab (*b*), the Venus's-flower-basket, *Euplectella* (*c*) and the brachiopod *Lingula* (*d*). One animal represents a group that goes back to the Ordovician period: the ostracode *Bairdia* (*e*). Two arose in the Devonian period: the shark (*f*) and the mussel (*g*). The cockroach

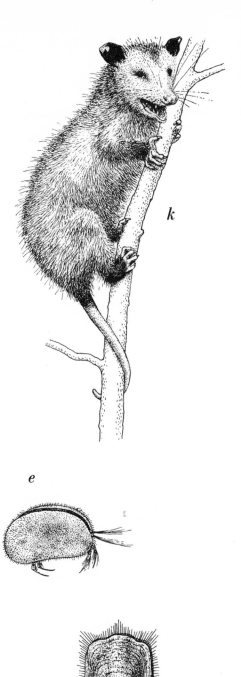

that the major floral changes have not coincided with the major faunal ones. Each of the three successive principal land floras—the ferns and mosses, the gymnosperms and angiosperms—were ushered in by a short episode of rapid evolution followed by a long period of stability. The illustration on page 41 shows that once a major group of plants became established it continued for millions of years. Many groups of higher plants are seemingly immortal. Since green plants are the primary producers in the over-all ecosystem and animals are the consumers, it can hardly be doubted that the great developments in the plant kingdom affected animal evolution, but the history of this relation is not yet understood.

Successive episodes of mass extinction among animals—particularly the marine invertebrates, which are among the most abundant fossils—provide world-wide stratigraphic reference points that the paleontologist calls datums. Many of the datums have come to be adopted as boundaries of the main divisions of geologic time, but there remains some uncertainty whether the epochs of extinction constitute moments in geologic time or intervals of significant duration. In other words, did extinction occur over hundreds, thousands or millions of years? The question has been answered in many ways, but it still remains an outstanding problem.

A good example of mass extinction is provided by the abrupt disappearance of nearly two-thirds of the existing families of trilobites at the close of the Cambrian period. Before the mass extinction of these marine arthropods, which are distantly related to modern crustaceans, there were some 60 families of them. The abrupt disappearance of so many major groups of trilobites at one time has served as a convenient marker for defining the upper, or most recent, limit of the Cambrian period [see illustration on page 42].

Similar episodes of extinction characterize the history of every major group and most minor groups of animals that have left a good fossil record. It is striking that times of widespread extinction generally affected many quite unrelated groups in separate habitats. The parallelism of extinction between some of the aquatic and terrestrial groups is particularly remarkable [see illustration on page 44].

One cannot doubt that there were critical times in the history of animals. Widespread extinctions and consequent revolutionary changes in the course of

animal life occurred roughly at the end of the Cambrian; Ordovician, Devonian, Permian, Triassic and Cretaceous periods. Hundreds of minor episodes of extinction occurred on a more limited scale at the level of species and genera throughout geologic time, but here we shall restrict our attention to a few of the more outstanding mass extinctions.

At or near the close of the Permian period nearly half of the known families of animals throughout the world disappeared. The German paleontologist Otto Schindewolf notes that 24 orders and superfamilies also dropped out at this point. At no other time in history, save possibly the close of the Cambrian, has the animal world been so decimated. Recovery to something like the normal variety was not achieved until late in the Triassic period, 15 or 20 million years later.

Extinctions were taking place throughout Permian time and a number of major groups dropped out well before the end of the period, but many more survived to go out together, climaxing one of the greatest of all episodes of mass extinction affecting both land and marine animals. It was in the sea, however, that the decimation of animals was particularly dramatic. One great group of animals that disappeared at this time was the fusulinids, complex protozoans that ranged from microscopic sizes to two or three inches in length. They had populated the shallow seas of the world for 80 million years; their shells, piling up on the ocean floor, had formed vast deposits of limestone. The spiny productid brachiopods, likewise plentiful in the late Paleozoic seas, also vanished without descendants. These and many other groups dropped suddenly from a state of dominance to one of oblivion.

By the close of the Permian period 75 per cent of amphibian families and more than 80 per cent of the reptile families had also disappeared. The main suborders of these animals nonetheless survived the Permian to carry over into the Triassic.

The mass extinction on land and sea at the close of the Triassic period was almost equally significant. Primitive reptiles and amphibians that had dominated the land dropped out and were replaced by the early dinosaurs that had appeared and become widespread before the close of the period. It is tempting to conclude that competition with the more successful dinosaurs was an important factor in the disappearance of these early land animals, but what bearing could this have had on the equally impressive and

(h) goes back to the Pennsylvanian period. Two arose in the late Triassic: the turtle (i) and the crocodile (j). The opossum (k) appeared during the Cretaceous period.

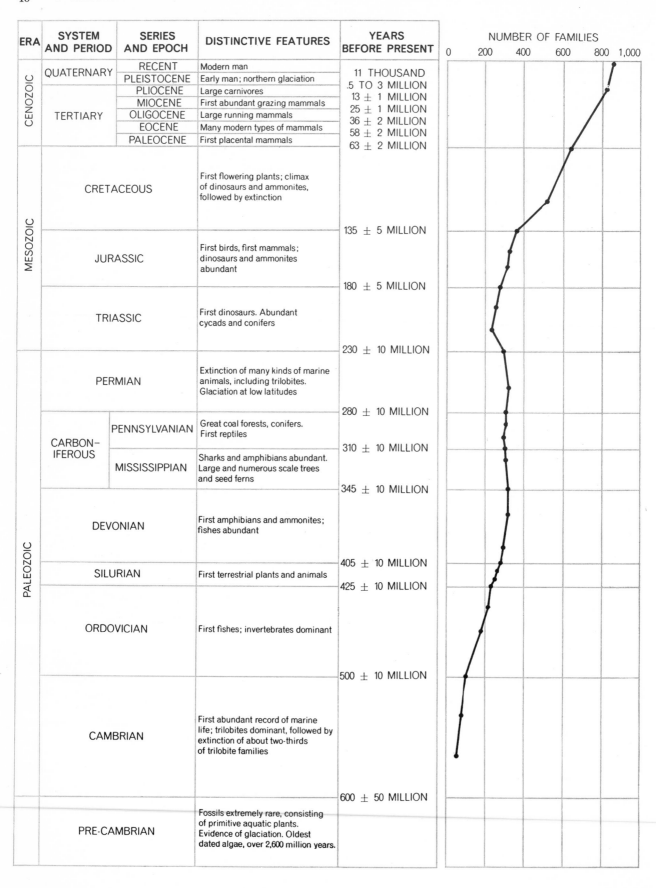

ERA	SYSTEM AND PERIOD	SERIES AND EPOCH		DISTINCTIVE FEATURES	YEARS BEFORE PRESENT
CENOZOIC	QUATERNARY	RECENT		Modern man	11 THOUSAND
		PLEISTOCENE		Early man; northern glaciation	.5 TO 3 MILLION
	TERTIARY	PLIOCENE		Large carnivores	13 ± 1 MILLION
		MIOCENE		First abundant grazing mammals	25 ± 1 MILLION
		OLIGOCENE		Large running mammals	36 ± 2 MILLION
		EOCENE		Many modern types of mammals	58 ± 2 MILLION
		PALEOCENE		First placental mammals	63 ± 2 MILLION
MESOZOIC	CRETACEOUS			First flowering plants; climax of dinosaurs and ammonites, followed by extinction	
	JURASSIC			First birds, first mammals; dinosaurs and ammonites abundant	135 ± 5 MILLION
	TRIASSIC			First dinosaurs. Abundant cycads and conifers	180 ± 5 MILLION
PALEOZOIC	PERMIAN			Extinction of many kinds of marine animals, including trilobites. Glaciation at low latitudes	230 ± 10 MILLION
	CARBON–IFEROUS	PENNSYLVANIAN		Great coal forests, conifers. First reptiles	280 ± 10 MILLION
		MISSISSIPPIAN		Sharks and amphibians abundant. Large and numerous scale trees and seed ferns	310 ± 10 MILLION
	DEVONIAN			First amphibians and ammonites; fishes abundant	345 ± 10 MILLION
	SILURIAN			First terrestrial plants and animals	405 ± 10 MILLION
	ORDOVICIAN			First fishes; invertebrates dominant	425 ± 10 MILLION
	CAMBRIAN			First abundant record of marine life; trilobites dominant, followed by extinction of about two-thirds of trilobite families	500 ± 10 MILLION
	PRE-CAMBRIAN			Fossils extremely rare, consisting of primitive aquatic plants. Evidence of glaciation. Oldest dated algae, over 2,600 million years.	600 ± 50 MILLION

GEOLOGICAL AGES can be dated by comparing relative amounts of radioactive elements remaining in samples of rock obtained from different stratigraphic levels. The expanding curve at the right indicates how the number of major families of fossil animals increased through geologic time. The sharp decline after the Permian reflects the most dramatic of several mass extinctions.

simultaneous decline in the sea of the ammonite mollusks? Late in the Triassic there were still 25 families of widely ranging ammonites. All but one became extinct at the end of the period and that one gave rise to the scores of families of Jurassic and Cretaceous time.

The late Cretaceous extinctions eliminated about a quarter of all the known families of animals, but as usual the plants were little affected. The beginning of a decline in several groups is discernible near the middle of the period, some 30 million years before the mass extinction at the close of the Cretaceous. The significant point is that many characteristic groups—dinosaurs, marine reptiles, flying reptiles, ammonites, bottom-dwelling aquatic mollusks and certain kinds of extinct marine plankton—were represented by several world-wide families until the close of the period. Schindewolf has cited 16 superfamilies and orders that now became extinct. Many world-wide genera of invertebrates and most of the known species of the youngest Cretaceous period drop out near or at the boundary between the Cretaceous and the overlying Paleocene rocks. On the other hand, many families of bottom-dwelling sea organisms, fishes and nautiloid cephalopods survived with only minor evolutionary modifications. This is also true of primitive mammals, turtles, crocodiles and most of the plants of the time.

In general the groups that survived each of the great episodes of mass extinction were conservative in their evolution. As a result they were probably able to withstand greater changes in environment than could those groups that disappeared, thus conforming to the well-known principle of "survival of the unspecialized," recognized by Darwin. But there were many exceptions and it does not follow that the groups that disappeared became extinct simply because they were highly specialized. Many were no more specialized than some groups that survived.

The Cretaceous period was remarkable for a uniform and world-wide distribution of many hundreds of distinctive groups of animals and plants, which was probably a direct result of low-lying lands, widespread seas, surprisingly uniform climate and an abundance of migration routes. Just at the top of the Cretaceous sequence the characteristic fauna is abruptly replaced by another, which is distinguished not so much by radically new kinds of animals as by the elimination of innumerable major groups that had characterized the late Cre-

taceous. The geological record is somewhat obscure at the close of the Cretaceous, but most investigators agree that there was a widespread break in sedimentation, indicating a brief but general withdrawal of shallow seas from the area of the continents.

Extinctions in the Human Epoch

At the close of the Tertiary period, which immediately preceded the Quaternary in which we live, new land connections were formed between North America and neighboring continents. The horse and camel, which had evolved in North America through Tertiary time, quickly crossed into Siberia and spread throughout Eurasia and Africa. Crossing the newly formed Isthmus of Panama at about the same time, many North American animals entered South America. From Asia the mammoth, bison, bear and large deer entered North America, while from the south came ground sloths and other mammals that had originated and evolved in South America. Widespread migration and concurrent episodes of mass extinction appear to mark the close of the Pliocene (some two or three million years ago) and the middle of the Pleistocene in both North America and

Eurasia. Another mass extinction, particularly notable in North America, occurred at the very close of the last extensive glaciation, but this time it apparently was not outstandingly marked by intercontinental migrations. Surprisingly, none of the extinctions coincided with glacial advances.

It is characteristic of the fossil record that immigrant faunas tend to replace the old native faunas. In some cases newly arrived or newly evolved families replaced old families quite rapidly, in less than a few million years. In other cases the replacement has been a protracted process, spreading over tens of millions or even hundreds of millions of years. We cannot, of course, know the exact nature of competition between bygone groups, but when they occupied the same habitat and were broadly overlapping in their ecological requirements, it can be assumed that they were in fact competitors for essential resources. The selective advantage of one competing stock over another may be so slight that a vast amount of time is required to decide the outcome.

At the time of the maximum extent of the continental glaciers some 11,000 years ago the ice-free land areas of the Northern Hemisphere supported a rich

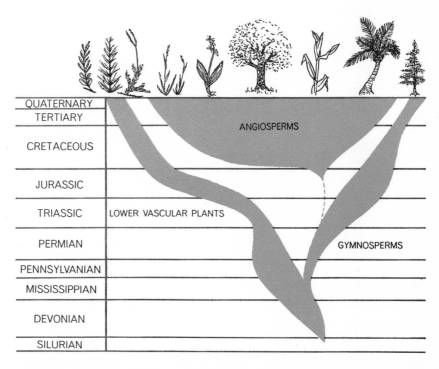

HISTORY OF LAND PLANTS shows the spectacular rise of angiosperms in the last 135 million years. The bands are roughly proportional to the number of genera of plants in each group. Angiosperms are flowering plants, a group that includes all the common trees (except conifers), grasses and vegetables. Lower vascular plants include club mosses, quillworts and horsetails. The most familiar gymnosperms (naked-seed plants) are the conifers, or evergreens. The diagram is based on one prepared by Erling Dorf of Princeton University.

and varied fauna of large mammals comparable to that which now occupies Africa south of the Sahara. Many of the species of bears, horses, elks, beavers and elephants were larger than any of their relatives living today. As recently as 8,000 years ago the horse, elephant and camel families roamed all the continents but Australia and Antarctica. Since that time these and many other families have retreated into small regions confined to one or two continents.

In North America a few species dropped out at the height of the last glaciation, but the tempo of extinction stepped up rapidly between about 12,000 and 6,000 years ago, with a maximum rate around 8,000 years ago, when the climate had become milder and the glaciers were shrinking [*see illustration on page 48*]. A comparable, but possibly more gradual, loss of large mammals occurred at about the same time in Asia and Australia, but not in Africa. Many of the large herbivores and carnivores had been virtually world-wide through a great range in climate, only to become extinct within a few hundred years. Other organisms were generally unaffected by this episode of extinction.

On the basis of a limited series of radiocarbon dates Paul S. Martin of the University of Arizona has concluded that now extinct large mammals of North America began to disappear first in Alaska and Mexico, followed by those in the Great Plains. Somewhat questionable datings suggest that the last survivors may have lived in Florida only 2,000 to 4,000 years ago. Quite recently, therefore, roughly three-quarters of the North American herbivores disappeared, and most of the ecological niches that were vacated have not been filled by other species.

Glaciation evidently was not a significant agent in these extinctions. In the first place, they were concentrated during the final melting and retreat of the continental glaciers after the entire biota had successfully weathered a number of glacial and interglacial cycles. Second, the glacial climate certainly did not reach low latitudes, except in mountainous areas, and it is probable that the climate over large parts of the tropics was not very different from that of today.

Studies of fossil pollen and spores in many parts of the world show that the melting of the continental glaciers was accompanied by a change from a rainy climate to a somewhat drier one with higher mean temperatures. As a result of these changes forests in many parts of the world retreated and were replaced by deserts and steppes. The changes, however, probably were not universal or severe enough to result in the elimination of any major habitat.

A number of investigators have proposed that the large mammals may have been hunted out of existence by prehistoric man, who may have used fire as a weapon. They point out that the mass extinctions coincided with the rapid growth of agriculture. Before this stage in human history a decrease in game supply would have been matched by a decrease in human populations, since man could not have destroyed a major food source without destroying himself.

In Africa and Eurasia, where man had lived in association with game animals throughout the Pleistocene, extinctions were not so conspicuously concentrated in the last part of the epoch. There was ample opportunity in the Old World for animals to become adapted to man through hundreds of thousands of years of coexistence. In the Americas and

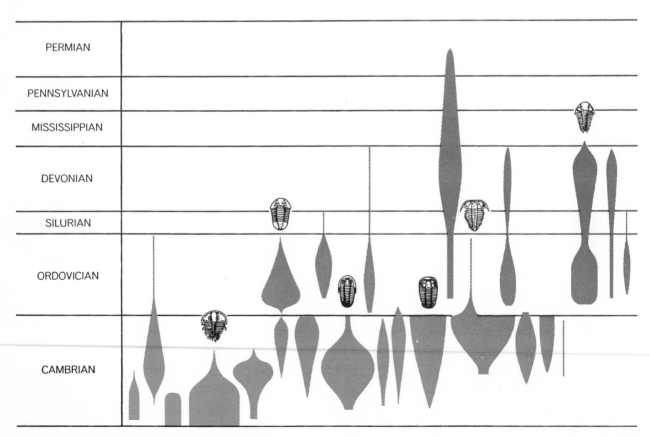

MASS EXTINCTION OF TRILOBITES, primitive arthropods, occurred at the close of the Cambrian period about 500 million years ago. During the Cambrian period hundreds of kinds of trilobites populated the shallow seas of the world. The chart depicts 15 superfamilies of Cambrian trilobites; the width of the shapes is roughly proportional to the number of members in each superfamily. Final extinction took place in the Permian. The chart is based on the work of H. B. Whittington of Harvard University.

Australia, where man was a comparative newcomer, the animals may have proved easy prey for the hunter.

We shall probably never know exactly what happened to the large mammals of the late Pleistocene, but their demise did coincide closely with the expansion of ancient man and with an abrupt change from a cool and moist to a warm and dry climate over much of the world. Possibly both of these factors contributed to this episode of mass extinction. We can only guess.

The Modern Crisis

Geological history cannot be observed but must be deduced from studies of stratigraphic sequences of rocks and fossils interpreted in the context of processes now operating on earth. It is helpful, therefore, to analyze some recent extinctions to find clues to the general causes of extinction.

We are now witnessing the disastrous effects on organic nature of the explosive spread of the human species and the concurrent development of an efficient technology of destruction. The human demand for space increases, hunting techniques are improved, new poisons are used and remote areas that had long served as havens for wildlife are now easily penetrated by hunter, fisherman, lumberman and farmer.

Studies of recent mammal extinctions show that man has been either directly or indirectly responsible for the disappearance, or near disappearance, of more than 450 species of animals. Without man's intervention there would have been few, if any, extinctions of birds or mammals within the past 2,000 years. The heaviest toll has been taken in the West Indies and the islands of the Pacific and Indian oceans, where about 70 species of birds have become extinct in the past few hundred years. On the continents the birds have fared somewhat better. In the same period five species of birds have disappeared from North America, three from Australia and one from Asia. Conservationists fear, however, that more North American birds will become extinct in the next 50 years than have in the past 5,000 years.

The savannas of Africa were remarkable until recently for a wealth of large mammals comparable only to the rich Tertiary and Pleistocene faunas of North America. In South Africa stock farming, road building, the fencing of grazing lands and indiscriminate hunting had wiped out the wild populations of large grazing mammals by the beginning of the 20th century. The depletion of ani-

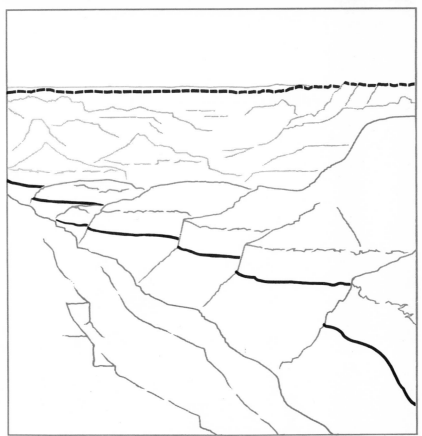

PALEONTOLOGICAL BOUNDARIES are clearly visible in this photograph of the Grand Canyon. The diagram below identifies the stratigraphic boundary between the Cambrian and Ordovician periods (*solid line*) and the top of the Permian rocks (*broken line*). These are world-wide paleontological division points, easily identified by marine fossils.

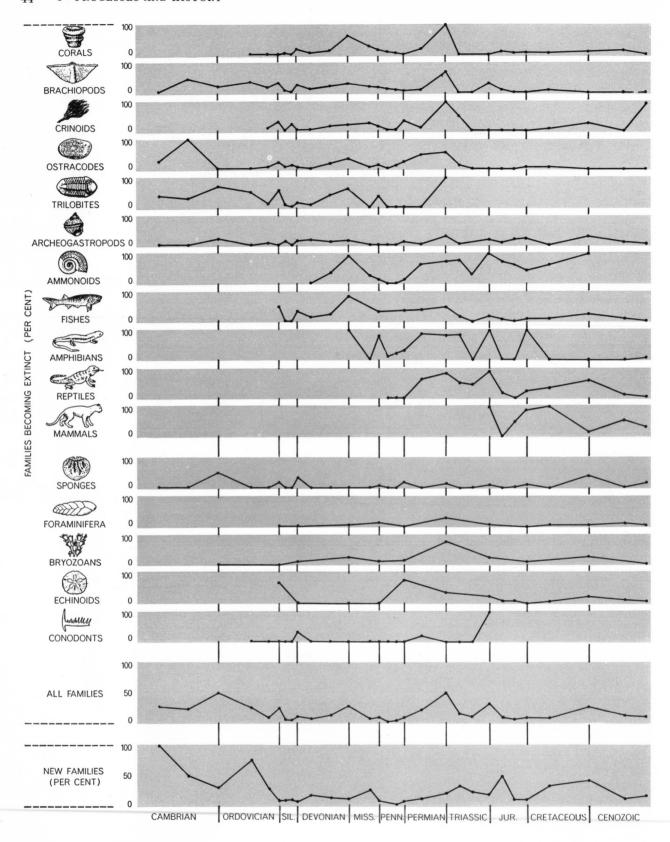

RECORD OF ANIMAL EXTINCTIONS makes it quite clear that the history of animals has been punctuated by repeated crises. The top panel of curves plots the ups and downs of 11 groups of animals from Cambrian times to the present. Massive extinctions took place at the close of the Ordovician, Devonian and Permian periods. The second panel shows the history of five other groups for which the evidence is less complete. (Curves are extrapolated between dots.) The next to bottom curve depicts the sum of extinctions for all the fossil groups plotted above (plus bivalves and caenogastropods). The bottom curve shows the per cent of new families in the main fossil groups. It indicates that periods of extinction were usually followed by an upsurge in evolutionary activity.

mals has now spread to Equatorial Africa as a result of poaching in and around the game reserves and the practice of eradicating game as a method of controlling human and animal epidemics. Within the past two decades it has become possible to travel for hundreds of miles across African grasslands without seeing any of the large mammals for which the continent is noted. To make matters worse, the great reserves that were set aside for the preservation of African wildlife are now threatened by political upheavals.

As a factor in extinction, man's predatory habits are supplemented by his destruction of habitats. Deforestation, cultivation, land drainage, water pollution, wholesale use of insecticides, the building of roads and fences—all are causing fragmentation and reduction in range of wild populations with resulting loss of environmental and genetic resources. These changes eventually are fatal to populations just able to maintain themselves under normal conditions. A few species have been able to take advantage of the new environments created by man, but for the most part the changes have been damaging.

Reduction of geographic range is prejudicial to a species in somewhat the same way as overpopulation. It places an increasing demand on diminishing environmental resources. Furthermore, the gene pool suffers loss of variability by reduction in the number of local breeding groups. These are deleterious changes, which can be disastrous to species that have narrow tolerances for one or more environmental factors. No organism is stronger than the weakest link in its ecological chain.

Man's direct attack on the organic world is reinforced by a host of competing and pathogenic organisms that he intentionally or unwittingly introduces to relatively defenseless native communities. Charles S. Elton of the University of Oxford has documented scores of examples of the catastrophic effects on established communities of man-sponsored invasions by pathogenic and other organisms. The scale of these ecological disturbances is world-wide; indeed, there are few unmodified faunas and floras now surviving.

The ill-advised introduction of predators such as foxes, cats, dogs, mongooses and rats into island communities has been particularly disastrous; many extinctions can be traced directly to this cause. Grazing and browsing domestic animals have destroyed or modified vegetation patterns. The introduction of

European mammals into Australia has been a primary factor in the rapid decimation of the native marsupials, which cannot compete successfully with placental mammals.

An illustration of invasion by a pathogenic organism is provided by an epidemic that in half a century has nearly wiped out the American sweet chestnut tree. The fungus infection responsible for this tragedy was accidentally intro-

duced from China on nursery plants. The European chestnut, also susceptible to the fungus, is now suffering rapid decline, but the Chinese chestnut, which evolved in association with the blight, is comparatively immune.

Another example is provided by the marine eelgrass *Zostera*, which gives food and shelter to a host of invertebrates and fishes and forms a protective blanket over muddy bottoms. It is the

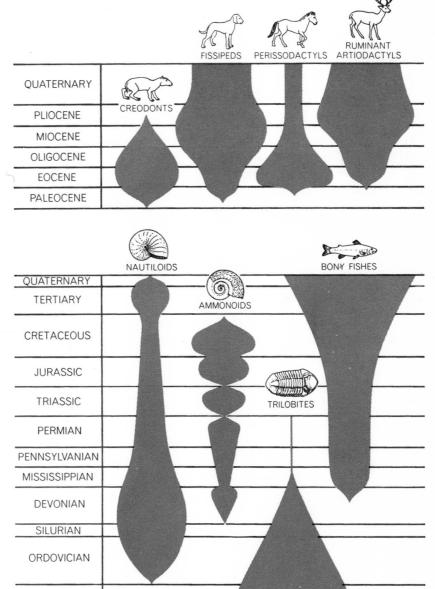

ECOLOGICAL REPLACEMENT appears to be a characteristic feature of evolution. The top diagram shows the breadth of family representation among four main groups of mammals over the last 60-odd million years. The bottom diagram shows a similar waxing and waning among four groups of marine swimmers, dating back to the earliest fossil records. The ammonoid group suffered near extinction twice before finally expiring. The diagrams are based on the work of George Gaylord Simpson of Harvard University and the author.

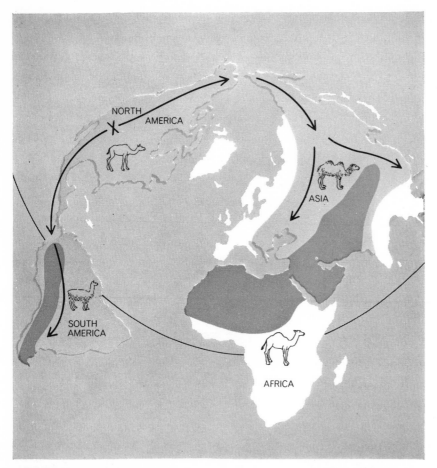

DISPERSAL OF CAMEL FAMILY from its origin (X) took place during Pleistocene times. Area in light color shows the maximum distribution of the family; dark color shows present distribution. This map is based on one in *Life: An Introduction to Biology*, by Simpson, C. S. Pittendrigh and L. H. Tiffany, published by Harcourt, Brace and Company.

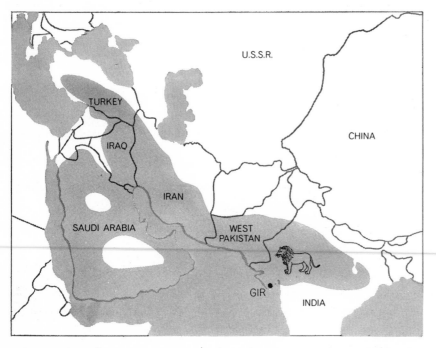

DISTRIBUTION OF ASIATIC LION has contracted dramatically just since 1800, when it roamed over large areas (*shown in color*) of the Middle East, Pakistan and India. Today the Asiatic lion is found wild only in Gir, a small game preserve in western India.

most characteristic member of a distinctive community that includes many plant and animal species. In the 1930's the eelgrass was attacked by a virus and was almost wiped out along the Atlantic shores of North America and Europe. Many animals and plants not directly attacked nevertheless disappeared for a time and the community was greatly altered. Resistant strains of *Zostera* fortunately escaped destruction and have slowly repopulated much of the former area. Eelgrass is a key member of a complex ecological community, and one can see that if it had not survived, many dependent organisms would have been placed in jeopardy and some might have been destroyed.

This cursory glance at recent extinctions indicates that excessive predation, destruction of habitat and invasion of established communities by man and his domestic animals have been primary causes of extinctions within historical time. The resulting disturbances of community equilibrium and shock waves of readjustment have produced ecological explosions with far-reaching effects.

The Causes of Mass Extinctions

It is now generally understood that organisms must be adapted to their environment in order to survive. As environmental changes gradually pass the limits of tolerance of a species, that species must evolve to cope with the new conditions or it will die. This is established by experiment and observation. Extinction, therefore, is not simply a result of environmental change but is also a consequence of failure of the evolutionary process to keep pace with changing conditions in the physical and biological environment. Extinction is an evolutionary as well as an ecological problem.

There has been much speculation about the causes of mass extinction; hypotheses have ranged from worldwide cataclysms to some kind of exhaustion of the germ plasm—a sort of evolutionary fatigue. Geology does not provide support for the postulated cataclysms and biology has failed to discover any compelling evidence that evolution is an effect of biological drive, or that extinction is a result of its failure. Hypotheses of extinction based on supposed racial old age or overspecialization, so popular among paleontologists a few generations ago and still echoed occasionally, have been generally abandoned for lack of evidence.

Of the many hypotheses advanced to explain mass extinctions, most are un-

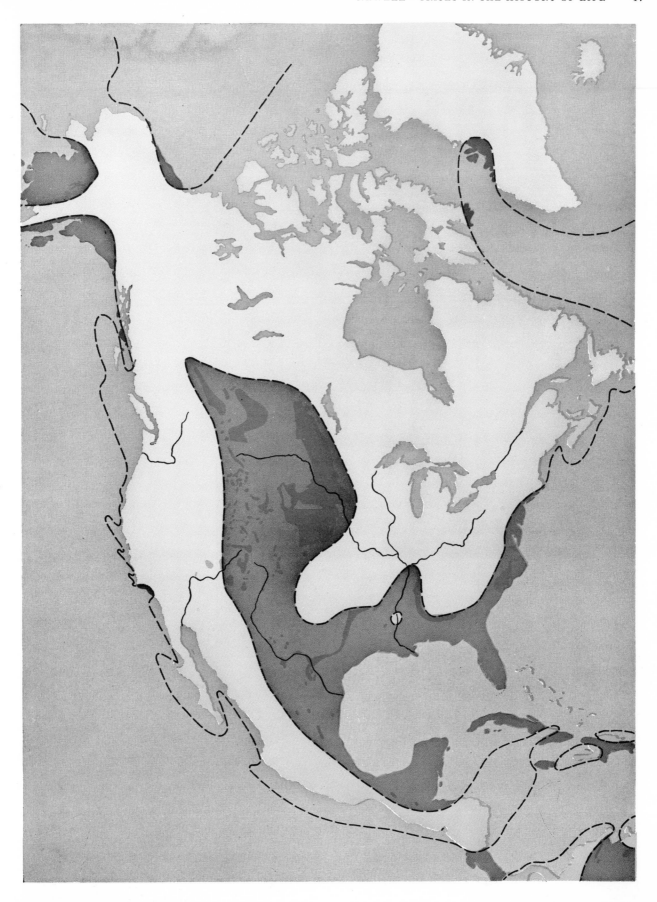

LATE CRETACEOUS SEA covered large portions of Central and North America (*dark gray*). Fossil-bearing rocks laid down at that time, and now visible at the surface of the earth, are shown in dark color. The approximate outline of North America in the Cretaceous period is represented by the broken line. The map is based on the work of the late Charles Schuchert of Yale University.

MASTODON
COLUMBIAN MAMMOTH
DIRE WOLF
CAMEL
HORSE
GIANT ARMADILLO
BISON OCCIDENTALIS
BISON ANTIQUUS
GIANT GROUND SLOTH
GROUND SLOTH
EXTINCT TAPIR
WOOLLY MAMMOTH
IMPERIAL MAMMOTH
DWARF ELEPHANT
EXTINCT PECCARY
SABER-TOOTHED CAT

14,000   13,000   12,000   11,000   10,000   9,000   8,000   7,000   6,000
YEARS BEFORE PRESENT

satisfactory because they lack testable corollaries and are designed to explain only one episode of extinction. For example, the extinction of the dinosaurs at the end of the Cretaceous period has been attributed to a great increase in atmospheric oxygen and alternatively to the explosive evolution of pathogenic fungi, both thought to be by-products of the dramatic spread of the flowering plants during late Cretaceous time.

The possibility that pathogenic fungi may have helped to destroy the dinosaurs was a recent suggestion of my own. I was aware, of course, that it would not be a very useful suggestion unless a way could be found to test it. I was also aware that disease is one of the most popular hypotheses for explaining mass extinctions. Unfortunately for such hypotheses, pathogenic organisms normally attack only one species or at most a few related species. This has been interpreted as an indication of a long antecedent history of coadaptation during which parasite and host have become mutually adjusted. According to this theory parasites that produce pathological reactions are not well adapted to the host. On first contact the pathogenic organism might destroy large numbers of the host species; it is even possible that extinction of a species might follow a pandemic, but there is no record that this has happened in historical times to any numerous and cosmopolitan group of species.

It is well to keep in mind that living populations studied by biologists generally are large, successful groups in which the normal range of variation provides tolerance for all the usual exigencies, and some unusual ones. It is for this reason that the eelgrass was not extinguished by the epidemic of the 1930's and that the human race was not eliminated by the influenza pandemic following World War I. Although a succession of closely spaced disasters of various kinds might have brought about extinction, the particular virus strains responsible for these diseases did not directly attack associated species.

Another suggestion, more ingenious

than most, is that mass extinctions were caused by bursts of high-energy radiation from a nearby supernova. Presumably the radiation could have had a dramatic impact on living organisms without altering the climate in a way that would show up in the geological record. This hypothesis, however, fails to account for the patterns of extinction actually observed. It would appear that radiation would affect terrestrial organisms more than aquatic organisms, yet there were times when most of the extinctions were in the sea. Land plants, which would be more exposed to the radiation and are more sensitive to it, were little affected by the changes that led to the animal extinctions at the close of the Permian and Cretaceous periods.

Another imaginative suggestion has been made recently by M. J. Salmi of the Geological Survey of Finland and Preston E. Cloud, Jr., of the University of Minnesota. They have pointed out that excessive amounts or deficiencies of certain metallic trace elements, such as copper and cobalt, are deleterious to organisms and may have caused past extinctions. This interesting hypothesis, as applied to marine organisms, depends on the questionable assumption that deficiencies of these substances have occurred in the ocean, or that a lethal concentration of metallic ions might have diffused throughout the oceans of the world more rapidly than the substances could be concentrated and removed from circulation by organisms and various common chemical sequestering agents. To account for the disappearance of land animals it is necessary to postulate further that the harmful elements were broadcast in quantity widely over the earth, perhaps as a result of a great volcanic eruption. This is not inconceivable; there have probably been significant variations of trace elements in time and place. But it seems unlikely that such variations sufficed to produce worldwide biological effects.

Perhaps the most popular of all hypotheses to explain mass extinctions is that they resulted from sharp changes in climate. There is no question that large-scale climatic changes have taken place many times in the past. During much of geologic time shallow seas covered large areas of the continents; climates were consequently milder and less differentiated than they are now. There were also several brief episodes of continental glaciation at low latitudes, but it appears that mass extinctions did not coincide with ice ages.

It is noteworthy that fossil plants,

which are good indicators of past climatic conditions, do not reveal catastrophic changes in climate at the close of the Permian, Triassic and Cretaceous periods, or at other times coincident with mass extinctions in the animal kingdom. On theoretical grounds it seems improbable that any major climatic zone of the past has disappeared from the earth. For example, climates not unlike those of the Cretaceous period probably have existed continuously at low latitudes until the present time. On the other hand, it is certain that there have been great changes in distribution of climatic zones. Severe shrinkage of a given climatic belt might adversely affect many of the contained species. Climatic changes almost certainly have contributed to animal extinctions by destruction of local habitats and by inducing wholesale migrations, but the times of greatest extinction commonly do not clearly correspond to times of great climatic stress.

Finally, we must consider the evidence that so greatly impressed Cuvier and many geologists. They were struck by the frequent association between the last occurrence of extinct animals and unconformities, or erosional breaks, in the geological record. Cuvier himself believed that the unconformities and the mass extinctions went hand in hand, that both were products of geologic revolutions, such as might be caused by paroxysms of mountain building. The idea still influences some modern thought on the subject.

It is evident that mountains do strongly influence the environment. They can alter the climate, soils, water supply and vegetation over adjacent areas, but it is doubtful that the mountains of past ages played dominant roles in the evolutionary history of marine and lowland organisms, which constitute most of the fossil record. Most damaging to the hypothesis that crustal upheavals played a major role in extinctions is the fact that the great crises in the history of life did not correspond closely in time with the origins of the great mountain systems. Actually the most dramatic episodes of mass extinction took place during times of general crustal quiet in the continental areas. Evidently other factors were involved.

Fluctuations of Sea Level

If mass extinctions were not brought about by changes in atmospheric oxygen, by disease, by cosmic radiation, by trace-element poisoning, by climatic changes or by violent upheavals of the

ICE-AGE MAMMALS provided North America with a fauna of large herbivores comparable to that existing in certain parts of Africa today. Most of them survived a series of glacial periods only to become extinct about 8,000 years ago, when the last glaciers were shrinking. The chart is based on a study by Jim J. Hester of the Museum of New Mexico in Santa Fe.

earth's crust, where is one to look for a satisfactory—and testable—hypothesis?

The explanation I have come to favor, and which has found acceptance among many students of the paleontological record, rests on fluctuations of sea level. Evidence has been accumulating to show an intimate relation between many fossil zones and major advances and retreats of the seas across the continents. It is clear that diastrophism, or reshaping, of the ocean basins can produce universal changes in sea level. The evidence of long continued sinking of the sea floor under Pacific atolls and guyots (flat-topped submarine mountains) and the present high stand of the continents indicate that the Pacific basin has been subsiding differentially with respect to the land at least since Cretaceous time.

During much of Paleozoic and Mesozoic time, spanning some 540 million years, the land surfaces were much lower than they are today. An appreciable rise in sea level was sufficient to flood large areas; a drop of a few feet caused equally large areas to emerge, producing major environmental changes. At least 30 major and hundreds of minor oscillations of sea level have occurred in the past 600 million years of geologic time.

Repeated expansion and contraction of many habitats in response to alternate flooding and draining of vast areas of the continents unquestionably created profound ecological disturbances among offshore and lowland communities, and repercussions of these changes probably extended to communities deep inland and far out to sea. Intermittent draining of the continents, such as occurred at the close of many of the geologic epochs and periods, greatly reduced or eliminated the shallow inland seas that pro-

vided most of the fossil record of marine life. Many organisms adapted to the special estuarine conditions of these seas evidently could not survive along the more exposed ocean margins during times of emergence and they had disappeared when the seas returned to the continents. There is now considerable evidence that evolutionary diversification was greatest during times of maximum flooding of the continents, when the number of habitats was relatively large. Conversely, extinction and natural selection were most intense during major withdrawals of the sea.

It is well known that the sea-level oscillations of the Pleistocene epoch caused by waxing and waning of the continental glaciers did not produce numerous extinctions among shallow-water marine communities, but the situation was quite unlike that which prevailed during much of geological history. By Pleistocene times the continents stood high above sea level and the warm interior seas had long since disappeared. As a result the Pleistocene oscillations did not produce vast geographic and climatic changes. Furthermore, they were of short duration compared with major sea-level oscillations of earlier times.

Importance of Key Species

It might be argued that nothing less than the complete destruction of a habitat would be required to eliminate a world-wide community of organisms. This, however, may not be necessary. After thousands of years of mutual accommodation, the various organisms of a biological community acquire a high order of compatibility until a nearly steady state is achieved. Each species

plays its own role in the life of the community, supplying shelter, food, chemical conditioners or some other resource in kind and amount needed by its neighbors. Consequently any changes involving evolution or extinction of species, or the successful entrance of new elements into the community, will affect the associated organisms in varying degrees and result in a wave of adjustments.

The strength of the bonds of interdependence, of course, varies with species, but the health and welfare of a community commonly depend on a comparatively small number of key species low in the community pyramid; the extinction of any of these is sure to affect adversely many others. Reduction and fragmentation of some major habitats, accompanied by moderate changes in climate and resulting shrinkage of populations, may have resulted in extinction of key species not necessarily represented in the fossil record. Disappearance of any species low in the pyramid of community organization, as, for example, a primary food plant, could lead directly to the extinction of many ecologically dependent species higher in the scale. Because of this interdependence of organisms a wave of extinction originating in a shrinking coastal habitat might extend to more distant habitats of the continental interior and to the waters of the open sea.

This theory, in its essence long favored by geologists but still to be fully developed, provides an explanation of the common, although not invariable, parallelism between times of widespread emergence of the continents from the seas and episodes of mass extinction that closed many of the chapters of geological history.

PART II
INTRAINDIVIDUAL VARIATION

Introduction: Structure and function

An appreciation of the remarkable acceleration in the accumulation of knowledge of structure and function in living material that has taken place in the last few decades, as well as an awareness of all that is still to be learned, can be gained by a brief overview of the history of biological discovery. Science began in the mid-sixteenth century with Francis Bacon's formulations on direct observation and experimentation. Nearly one hundred years later, Robert Hooke's observation through a microscope of the cells in a simple piece of cork began the scientific study of the structure of living organisms. But it was two more centuries before Schleiden, Schwann, and Virchow established the cell as a unit of structure, and cell division as the basic mechanism by which living organisms develop. The structure and function of the cell is described in "The Living Cell" by Jean Brachet.

Mendel's careful experimentation between 1858 and 1865 made it possible for him to explain the 1822 observations of Gross and Seton on inheritance in garden peas; the principles that he originated were independently rediscovered in 1900 by de Vries and Correns (Castle, 1951; Stern and Sherwood, 1966). Within two years of this rediscovery, Sutton, in 1902, formulated the chromosome theory, which recognized that the behavior of the chromosomes at reproduction provides the physical basis for Mendel's laws of heredity, thereby bringing the observations and experiments of Schleiden, Schwann and Virchow together with those of Mendel. R. G. Edwards describes the earliest stages of human development in his article "The Mammalian Eggs in the Laboratory." By 1911, Morgan had established the principles of linkage and crossing-over between homologous chromosomes, and in 1913 Sturtevant had begun the construction of chromosome maps; these developments were important milestones in understanding the structure of chromosomes and applying genetics to the experimental solution of many biological problems. The principles of Mendelian genetics were extended to continuous variation by Bateson in 1914 and Fisher in 1918 (Sturtevant, 1951), and experiments for partitioning heredity-environment interaction were introduced by Wright in 1920. Darwin had presented the theory of natural selection in 1859, but it wasn't until the work of Bateson, Fisher, and Wright that genetic explanations became possible. Similarly, Pearson and Hardy had laid the foundation of population genetics in 1904 and 1908, but population genetics did not develop as a biological sub-science until Fisher's *The Genetical Theory of Natural Selection* was published in 1929, and Wright's paper, "Evolution in Mendelian Populations," appeared in 1931. Within the succeeding twenty years genetics completely dominated evolutionary thought, and brought about important changes in medicine, dentistry, and agriculture, as well as in theoretical areas of the life sciences.

The direct investigation of hereditary material was begun in 1928 by Kassel and Griffith, and the nucleic acids DNA and RNA were named by Levene in 1931. It was not until 1953 that an explanation of the molecular structure of the chromosomes was presented by Watson and Crick. The manner in which this structure relates to mutation theory is described by Crick in "The Genetic Code." This explanation united genetics, the meeting ground of all the Biological Sciences, to biochemistry and biophysics.

Tissues and organ systems

Experimentation can most effectively supplement and advance observation at the molecular and cellular levels, at which there are comparatively few contributing variables. Because of the larger numbers of variables at higher levels of organization, more complex experimental procedures are needed for testing and extending even the most sophisticated observations. Consequently, at the next level of organization, where cells form tissues and organs, our information is less definitive, as C. H. Waddington points out in his article "How Do Cells Differentiate." Yet it is the complex tissue and organ systems that establish the higher organism's structural and functional relationship to his environment. In "The Skin" William Montagna shows both the complexity of these systems and their importance to a living organism's relationship to his environment.

Early in embryonic development, cells are committed to the construction of the skin and its various derivatives, and many of the specialized structures are formed in the third, fourth, and fifth months after conception. In man, some of these regress or disappear before birth; others develop only at puberty. It is by this sequence of regression and development that the characteristic human skin and its derivatives come into being. The two sexes, individual members of both sexes, and populations differ in anatomical distribution, quantitative and even qualitative nature of pigments, hair follicles, the hair produced by these follicles, and the numbers and distribution of sebaceous and sweat glands. The ways in which these differences occur are patterned upon the embryological and pubertal appearances and involutions of these elements. All of these observed variances are probably mediated by complex genetic and environmental interaction mechanisms. The functional relationships of some of these structures, such as the mammary glands, are clear; certain functions of the other structures, such as the role of the eccrine glands in temperature control, are also known, but the functions of some structures can only be guessed at.

Certain kinds of experimentation can be conducted in the search for answers to these unknowns. For example, the sweating responses under different conditions of temperature and stress can be compared, and inferences can be drawn from comparisons of different genetic populations within the single living species of mankind. However, no actual evidence about the evolutionary or adaptive changes of the skin and its derivatives is obtainable; similar limitations pertain to most of the other tissues. Only the osseous skeleton can provide empirical evidence for evolutionary change because it alone is preserved through geological time.

Skeleton   The human skeleton represents a series of evolutionary solutions to a series of biological problems. The ways in which these problems—problems of locomotion, metabolism, growth, protection of vital organs, and many others—have been solved are firmly recorded directly in the tissue, structure, and form of the skeleton. Some problems were solved in the distant past and the solutions are not essentially different in various mammalian groups. The fundamental division of a long bone, such as the femur of the thigh, into a shaft (diaphysis) and two caps or joint surfaces at either end (epiphyses) is common to most mammals. The upper leg can therefore grow in length, primarily at the point of junction of the diaphysis and epiphysis, while it remains functionally articulated to the pelvis above and the lower leg below. Other basic characteristics of bone are also common to large groups of distantly related mammals. The differentiation of bone into a compact outer (cortical) layer and a cancellous or spongy internal portion is ubiquitous. The form of the skeleton in each species, however, differs considerably; it will correspond largely to the method of locomotion. The important processes of red cell manufacture (hematopoiesis) can proceed wherever there is cancellous bone, as in the crest of the pelvis, the sternum, the insides of the long bones, and the spongy middle table (diploe) of the cranial vault; the basic functions of bone as a tissue are not necessarily related to external form.

Although all mammals have a similar type of pelvic girdle (composed of two innominate bones and one sacrum), only in humans has the form of the pelvis been so reorganized as to be suitable for habitually erect posture. Thus, humans have a sciatic notch in the iliac portion of the innominate bone, a feature that appeared only with the rise of the human species and is unique to it, including one extinct fossil genus (*Australopithecus robustus*: Paranthropus or Zinjanthropus). The reorganization of the pelvis and a related complex of structures is extremely important in human evolution and represents a large part of our solution to a locomotor problem, as John Napier points out in "The Antiquity of Human Walking." The remarkable differences between a human skeleton and the skeleton of even such a close relative as the chimpanzee call attention to the way in which bone (a tissue) and bones (organs) have been remodeled in the course of evolution. The reorganizations and processes that take place in the growth of each individual, and that are constantly taking place at the cellular level, are of equal interest and crucial significance.

Because most skeletons we see have been cleaned of all their associated tissues, deprived of their blood supply, and perhaps even bleached for display purposes, we automatically tend to think of bone as hard and inert, significant for the structural strength it lends the body and for its variation in form between different races and species. The fact that bone is a highly dynamic tissue becomes evident upon recollection of common events: fractured bones heal, even in very old people; bone increases in size, both with normal growth and with exercise; bone grows out in such new forms as arthritic spurs and may even fuse at joints in osteoarthritis; bone decalcifies and loses its internal structure (changes in the trabeculae of spongy bone) with inactivity—such as that imposed by prolonged bed rest—or with the weightlessness experienced by astronauts; true bone develops from various precursors, including both membrane and cartilaginous tissues. Bone responds to diseases in a variety of ways. In hyperostosis cranii the diploe enlarges in an effort to produce more red cells because of an anemia; in acromegaly, a disease affecting the anterior pituitary, certain parts of the skeleton—especially the distal portions, such as the fingers, the browridges, and the mandible—are stimulated to grow. The administration of growth hormone can regulate and stimulate growth in such a way to contribute to the total stature of a person whose epiphyses are not yet closed. The ability of bone to take on new form is illustrated in orthodontic treatment, in which teeth are moved about and the bone accommodates, or in which the mandible is actually resectioned and lengthened. The fact that bone has a memory and repeats an imposed form is demonstrated by the retention of a permanently deformed skull in those persons whose heads have been bound in a cradleboard. Many groups of American Indians placed the infant in a cradleboard and secured a wood headpiece which flattened the frontal area while the base of the cradleboard flattened the back of the head. Other Indian groups simply wrapped a rope about the infant's head. With either method, the form remained throughout the lifetime of the person, new bone constantly reduplicating the artificially imposed form.

A major component of bone is collagen, a protein, which has a crystalline structure. The crystals are small, but with relatively large surface areas, and together they present about 160 acres of surface area. As a building material bone is unique in being equally resistant to tension and to compression. This characteristic is obviously related to its structure, but it also has relevance to the composition of bone because mechanical stresses—compression and tension—set up an electrical current (Piezoelectric effect) in the collagen fibers and hydroxyapatite crystals, which may pick up ions passing by and thus contribute to the growth of bone. Knowledge of the complex relations of physical stress and the biochemistry of bone are basic to understanding the cellular and other structural aspects of bone, as discussed by C. Andrew L. Bassett in "Electrical Effects in Bone." Bone grows or resorbs in response to signals that are not yet completely elucidated. The calcium hydroxyapatite of the crystalline structure is important also to the relative dating of fossil bones. The hydroxyapatite is slowly converted to fluorapatite by the uptake of fluorine present in surrounding ground water. All bones in a single deposit may be expected to have absorbed approximately similar amounts of fluorine. If the amounts of fluorine vary, either those bones with markedly larger amounts than other bones have been in that deposit for a longer period of time, or all the bones in the deposit may not have come from the same place—some may be intrusive.

Microscopic age changes in human cortical bone are sufficiently regular to permit a useful assignment of age at death for dried skeletons such as those found archaeologically. The number of osteons (Haversian systems), the fragments of old osteons, the percentage of circumferential lamellar bone, and the number or non-Haversian canals all vary with age. The number of fragments of old osteons increases with age to provide an especially prominent and quantifiable age characteristic (Kerley, 1965).

Important nutritional and disease effects as well as subtle normal growth changes can be seen in bone by measuring its mineral content (Cameron and Sorenson, 1963) by means of a radioactive photon source, iodine-125, which provides a monochromatic beam of very low radioactivity and can therefore be used to scan bone in the living person at frequent intervals. Use of Iodine is preferable to that of X-ray because it is more sensitive as well as much less radioactive.

Teeth are especially useful for studies of growth, genetics, population variation, and evolution. Whether we begin with an interest in the characteristics of teeth as such, or whether our primary interest is in growth processes or in genetic processes, such as the effects of inbreeding, dental and supporting tissues are ideal materials to work with.

Although the mode of inheritance of many or most dental variations is not yet known, they are clearly under close genetic control. Because the eruption of both the deciduous (milk teeth) and the permanent teeth is fairly regular, study of the teeth provides a semi-independent method of assessing growth. The first lower molar of the permanent series erupts so closely to the age of six that it has become known as the six-year molar. Nutritional deprivation may be registered on the enamel surfaces of teeth, so that pitting or defective development of the enamel may reflect the approximate time of the deprivation.

Structural similarities accompanied by behavioral or functional similarities in unrelated or only distantly related forms provide useful evidence for analyzing complexes of related traits and for identifying their functional significance. A basic example is that of the locomotor habit of brachiation occurring in three closely related South American monkeys, and in the anthropoid apes of Africa and Asia, who are less closely related to each other. Brachiation is the locomotor habit of progression through trees by swinging by the arms. It is most skillfully executed by the gibbons, siamangs, and orangutans of southeast Asia. Of these the small gibbon and siamang are the most rapid and agile brachiators. The African chimpanzees and gorillas are less skillful; the adult gorilla brachiates very little. The most versatile brachiators, those who spend much time traveling in the forest canopy, have relatively long arms, especially forearms, and narrow hands with long, flexed fingers and a reduced or absent external thumb; the chest is relatively broad and the lumbar region (the low back) is short.

Although the New World primates have been separated from Old World primates for more than 30,000,000 years, the same general structural complex is found in both, as is the essential locomotor behavior related to it. It is entirely possible that the habit of brachiation evolved separately in at least three geographic regions—southeast Asia, Africa, and South America—although the differences between anthropoid apes and the South American spider monkeys (*Ateles, Lagothrix,* and *Brachyteles*) are multitudinous. The differences are serological, chromosomal, dental, dermal, and of other kinds, the most obvious being the large and functional prehensile tail of the New World brachiators.

In order to appreciate the essential elements of some complexes of traits, and in order to identify others that are nonessential or even irrelevant, observational studies of behavior are indispensable. The approximation of the chest cage and the iliac crest—that is, the short lumbar region—has recurred in at least three separate evolutionary trials, and tails, although they are used by five groups of South American monkeys, including the three forms that brachiate, are not essential to the basic complex.

An excellent analysis of human walking, with its emphasis upon an habitual and efficient stride, is provided by John Napier in "The Antiquity of Human Walking." His suggestion that the gait of *Australopithecus* was physiologically inefficient and that long-distance bipedal travel was probably impossible has much significance for interpreting the early evolution of man. True man, *Homo erectus,* did have efficient bipedal abilities and was geographically widespread. Clearly the interpretation of fossil remains depends upon a sound knowledge of modern morphology and its functional implications.

Teeth are found in all mammals—except in a few forms, such as some edentates and sea cows—and within species of primates and often between species, they have little functional relation to their dietary uses. Although teeth and their supporting tissues are critical to their owner, and oral health and functioning teeth are basic to his biological welfare, the teeth can vary greatly in size, proportions, fissural patterns, and cusp numbers, quite independently of extremely different diets. Human beings can prosper on a high protein diet (Eskimos), or on a high cereal diet (agricultural peoples); they can rend meat from bones or eat vegetable mush with equal facility. The fissural patterns, which are of much phylogenetic interest, are erased by attrition early in life among primitive peoples, whether they subsist on a hunting and collecting diet or on an agricultural diet. Teeth and dietary habit are somewhat indirectly related to posture and muscle complexes in that large teeth and jaws, such as those of a gorilla, are accompanied by large chewing muscles. If the size of the braincase is relatively small the chewing muscles attach to a bony septum on top of the cranium (sagittal crest). This bony crest provides the necessary area for the attachment of the large chewing muscles. But such a head is poorly balanced. The neck muscles of the gorilla are very large, and these are functionally correlated with a large crest running across the rear portion of the cranium (occipital crest) to which they attach, and also with large projecting processes on the vertebrae (spinous processes). Therefore, although there are many interesting correlations between the teeth, jaw size, crests for the attachment of muscles on the cranium, long spinous processes, and posture and locomotion generally, which can be noted, the correlation between the form of the teeth and posture is neither functional nor essential.

Another way in which morphological structures are organized is seen in the genetic basis of the dental features of the Mongoloid dental complex, or master pattern (Moorrees, 1957; Hanihara, 1966). Several traits of the dentition appear with high frequency in Mongoloid groups, such as Japanese, Eskimos, Aleuts, and American Indians. These traits include a marked shovel shape of the upper incisors, relatively small differences in mesiodistal crown diameters between the upper central and lateral incisors, a very low frequency of Carabelli's cusp (an extra cusp on the lingual surface of the maxillary molars), and various other features which are seen in the deciduous dentition. That such characters constitute a complex is demonstrated by the fact that they tend to occur together in groups that have had relatively separate biological histories. The exact mode of inheritance of many of these traits is not known, but that they are inherited is demonstrable. They do not form a functional complex, in the sense that the traits associated with erect posture or brachiation do, nor are they as unrelated as are traits derived from different embryonic tissues. They are genetically coadapted to the extent that they persist from generation to generation. Yet, it has never been demonstrated that an incisor tooth with a scooped-out hollow on its lingual surface (shovel-shaped) is related to reproductive success, diet, or any external environmental pressure.

There is a correspondence among (1) the genetic control of tooth size, established by twin study methods (Osborne, Horowitz, and De George, 1958), (2) field or regional variation in teeth of different series (Dahlberg, 1951), (3) racial variation in teeth, (4) the developmental history of teeth in the individual (Schour, 1955), and (5) the evolutionary history of teeth. The corresponding complex of analytical methods helps us to understand in retrospect why the dentition, like other parts of the body, does not contain one uniform phase of evolutionary development at any one time.

The incisors and canine teeth are under genetic control for size, and at the same time each of these teeth has a degree of genetic independence. Of these three teeth, the canines display the least variance, they are the teeth with the largest roots in the human dentition, and the range of their evolutionary history is fairly well known. Of the two maxillary incisors the lateral incisor is the most variable in form, size, and absence or presence. Such racial variations as the Mongoloid dental complex, with its broad median and broad lateral incisors, illustrates the way in which these two teeth have evolved. European dentitions show a different genetic pattern in the marked reduction of the lateral incisors, with many other variations affecting them as well. The teeth of *Australopithecus robustus* (Zinjanthropus and Paranthropus) show how the entire field of canines and incisors may act as a unit with marked reduction in size while the cheek teeth (premolars and molars) are of quite large size.

The analysis of structure and function is a constant endeavor to move from correlations to causes and processes, to developmental etiologies, and to multiple forms of significance. Armchair speculation is a poor substitute for observation, experiment, and rigorous comparative studies.

Growth   The manner in which one individual differs from another in any observable or measurable feature, or the ways in which the osseous skeletons of living members of the human species differ from those of ancestral forms or other primates, are the results of differences in pattern or rate of growth. An understanding of growth is, therefore, critical to our understanding of human variation, normal and pathological.

Animal growth experiments provide many important insights into growth and development. But because we cannot experiment directly with man, knowledge of growth as it occurs in man depends primarily upon observation. George W. Gray describes such observations of physiological and psychological development in "Human Growth." Deductive reasoning from carefully designed observations, most particularly those obtained under conditions that approximate experimental situations, can provide valuable information about characteristics of growth that are peculiar to man. Comparisons of the different patterns of growth between males and females, and between twins and siblings; observations of growth patterns in known genetic abnormalities, and in racial hybrids; studies of secular changes in growth, growth changes among immigrants, and the effect of specific environmental conditions—temperature, altitude, famine, protein deficiencies, and so on—can all yield the equivalents of experimental data.

Growth begins at conception. At the beginning there is a rapid increase in cell number with only a small increase in the total volume of the developing organism. After implantation volume increases rapidly by cell multiplication, and growth rates are the most rapid during the prenatal period. After birth, growth results largely from an increase in the size of the cells, rather than from an increase in cell number. As growth progresses, the increase of certain tissues predominates at one stage, and that of other tissues at another stage, so that body composition and proportion change with age (Israelsohn, 1960). The rate of change of a given component and the length of time a specific growth rate is sustained differs between the sexes, between individuals, between subgroups of a species, and between species, resulting in differences in various components and dimensions. Differences in the rate of height growth between the sexes provide an illustration (Figure 1). The legs, one of the components of height, grow more rapidly than the trunk during the prepubertal period. As seen in Figure 1, boys have a longer prepubertal growth period than do girls, and consequently, boys have relatively longer legs than do girls.

In Figure 2, the similarity of growth pattern for genetically identical twin girls can be seen. Also to be seen in the lower part of the figure, are the effects

Figure 1 (left). Adolescent spurt in height growth for girls and boys. The curves are from subjects who have their peak velocities during the modal years 12–13 for girls, and 14–15 for boys. Actual mean increments, each plotted at the center of its half-year period. [From Tanner, 1961.]

Figure 2 (right). Growth in height of identical twin girls, showing seasonal effect on rate of growth. [From Tanner, 1961.]

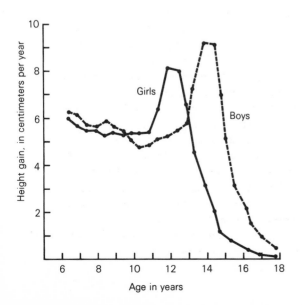

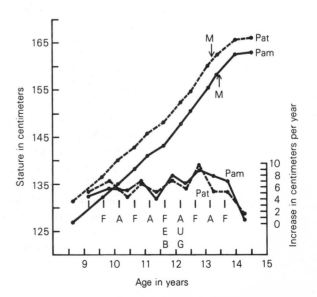

Table 1. Mean difference in months of age at menarche of related and unrelated women. [From Tanner, 1961.]

Relationship	From Petri (1935)		From Tisserand-Perrier (1953)	
	No. pairs	Diff. months	No. pairs	Diff. months
Identical twins	51	2.8±0.33	46	2.2
Nonidentical twins	47	12.0±1.62	39	8.2
Sisters	145	12.9		
Unrelated women	120	18.6		

of the season upon growth and the similarity of response for the two genetically identical individuals. A convenient indicator of physical and physiological development is the age of menarche. Table 1 presents data from two different studies indicating the importance of the genetic control of menarche. Menarche is also affected by environmental conditions, such as adequacy of nutrition, altitude, and climate. Few, if any, parameters of growth are not affected by both genetic and environmental factors, and often simultaneously.

One of the most interesting growth phenomena is secular change, or change through time (Boyne, 1960). People are taller today than they were 100 or even 50 years ago. This stature increase can be accounted for largely by an acceleration of growth during the prepubertal period. The secular change in this period of growth is greater than that in adult stature, and in males adult stature is now achieved by the age of 18, rather than by the age of 22 or 23, as it was 100 years ago. Associated with this is a secular change in menarche; puberty now occurs at an earlier average age than it did even one generation ago.

Growth patterns are of great evolutionary significance, not only because of their effect upon bodily proportions, but because of their relationship to behavioral and cultural phenomena as well. The graph shown in Figure 3 compares the lengths of developmental periods for man and other primates.

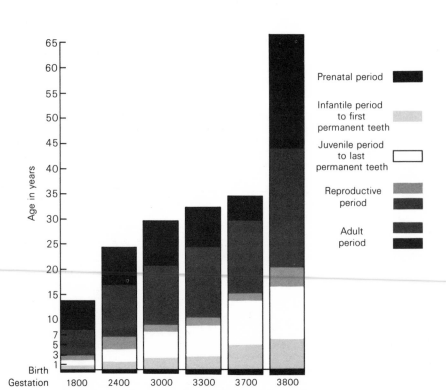

Figure 3. Diagrammatic representation of the approximate durations of some periods of life in primates. The column for early man represents merely the most likely conditions. [After Schultz, 1960.]

The most unique feature of primate growth, the prolongation of time from weaning to puberty, is most exaggerated for man, and may bear importantly upon some of the other characteristics in which man differs from other primates.

The long infantile and juvenile period means a longer period of dependency upon the parent. This provides a longer period for transmission of learned behavior before either the individual is able to fend for itself, or it is forced to do so as a consequence of sexual maturation and thereby sexual competition with the parent. This biological characteristic of man must have been an important contributor to the elaboration and transmission of culture.

Literature cited   Boyne, A. W. 1960. Secular Changes in the Stature of Adults and the Growth of Children, with Special Reference to Changes in Intelligence of 11-year-olds. In J. M. Tanner, ed., *Human Growth*. New York, Pergamon Press.

Cameron, John R., and James Sorenson. 1963. Measurement of Bone Mineral In Vivo: An Improved Method. *Science*, Vol. 142, No. 3589, pp. 230–232.

Castle, W. E. 1951. The Beginnings of Mendelism in America. In L. C. Dunn, ed., *Genetics in the 20th Century*. New York, Macmillan.

Dahlberg, Albert A. 1951. The Dentition of the American Indian. In W. S. Laughlin, ed., *Papers on the Physical Anthropology of the American Indian*. New York, The Viking Fund, Inc.

Fisher, R. A. 1958. *The Genetical Theory of Natural Selection*. 2nd revised edition. New York, Dover Publications, Inc.

Hanihara, Kazuro. 1966. "Mongoloid Dental Complex in the Deciduous Dentition," *Zinruigaku Zassi (Anthropol. Soc. of Nippon)*, Vol. 74, No. 749.

Hardy, G. H. 1908. Mendelian Proportions in a Mixed Population. *Science*, Vol. 28, pp. 49–50.

Israelsohn, Wilma J. 1960. Description and Modes of Analysis of Human Growth. In J. M. Tanner, ed., *Human Growth*. New York, Pergamon Press.

Kerley, Ellis R. 1965. The Microscopic Determination of Age in Human Bone. *Am. J. Phys. Anthro.*, Vol. 23, No. 2, pp. 149–163.

Moorrees, C. F. A. 1957. *The Aleut Dentition: A Correlative Study of the Dental Characteristics in an Eskimoid People*. Cambridge, Massachusetts, Harvard University Press.

Osborne, Richard H., Sidney L. Horowitz, and Frances V. De George. 1958. Genetic Variation in Tooth Dimensions. A Twin Study of the Permanent Anterior Teeth. *Am. J. Hum. Genet.*, Vol. 10, No. 3, pp. 350–356.

Pearson, K. 1904. On a Generalized Theory of Alternative Inheritance with Special References to Mendel's Laws. *Phil. Trans: Roy. Soc.*, Vol. 203, pp. 53–86.

Schultz, A. H. 1960. Age Changes in Primates and Their Modification in Man. In J. M. Tanner, ed., *Human Growth*. New York, Pergamon Press.

Schour, I. 1955. In B. H. Willier, P. A. Weiss, and V. Hamburger, eds., *Analysis of Development*. Philadelphia, W. B. Saunders.

Stern, C., and E. R. Sherwood. 1966. *The Origin of Genetics, A Mendel Source Book*. San Francisco, W. H. Freeman and Company.

Sturtevant, A. H. 1951. The Relation of Genes and Chromosomes. In L. C. Dunn, ed., *Genetics in the 20th Century*. New York, Macmillan.

Tanner, J. M. 1961. *Growth at Adolescence*. 2nd ed. Oxford, Blackwell Science Publications.

Wright, S. 1920. The Relative Importance of Heredity and Environment in Determining the Piebald Pattern of Guinea Pigs. *Proc. Nat. Acad. Sci.*, Vol. 6, No. 1920, pp. 320–332.

Wright, Sewall. 1931. Evolution in Mendelian Populations. *Genetics*, Vol. 16, pp. 97–159.

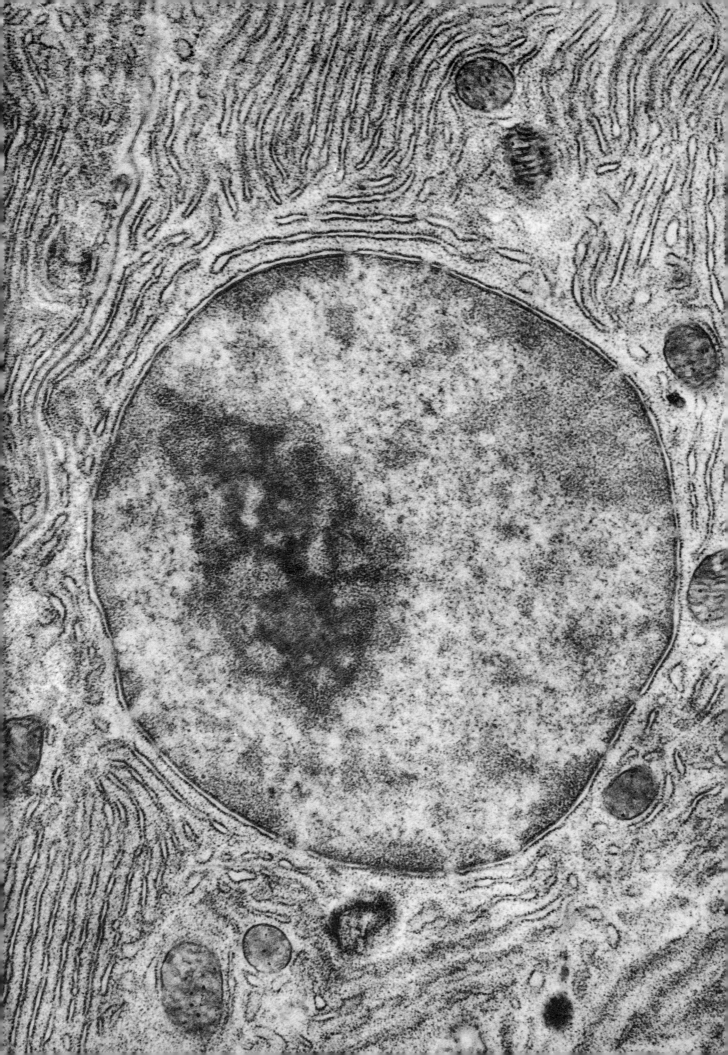

5

The Living Cell

JEAN BRACHET
September 1961

The living cell is the fundamental unit of which all living organisms are made. To a reader who finds this a commonplace, it may come as a surprise that the recognition of the cell dates back only a little more than 100 years. The botanist Matthias Jakob Schleiden and the zoologist Theodor Schwann first propounded the cell theory in 1839 out of their parallel and independent studies of the tissues of plants and animals. Not long after, in 1859, Rudolf Virchow confirmed the cell's unique role as the vessel of "living matter" when he showed that all cells necessarily derive from pre-existing cells: *omnis cellula e cellula*. Since cells are concrete objects and can easily be observed, the experimental investigation of cells thereafter displaced philosophical speculations about the problem of "life" and the uncertain scientific studies that had pursued such vague concepts as "protoplasm."

In the century that followed investiga-

tors of the cell approached their subject from two fundamentally different directions. Cell biologists, equipped with increasingly powerful microscopes, proceeded to develop the microscopic and submicroscopic anatomy of the intact cell. Beginning with a picture of the cell as a structure composed of an external membrane, a jelly-like blob of material called cytoplasm and a central nucleus, they have shown that this structure is richly differentiated into organelles adapted to carry on the diverse processes of life. With the aid of the electron microscope they have begun to discern the molecular working parts of the system. Here, in recent years, their work has converged with that of the biochemists, whose studies begin with the ruthless disruption of the delicate structure of the cell. By observing the chemical activity of materials collected in this way, biochemists have traced some of the pathways by which the cell carries out the biochemical reactions that underlie

the processes of life, including those responsible for manufacturing the substance of the cell itself.

It is the present intersection of the two lines of study that enables an attempt at a synthesis of what is known of the structure and function of the living cell. The cell biologist now seeks to explain in molecular terms what he sees with the aid of his instruments; he has become a molecular biologist. The biochemist has become a biochemical cytologist, interested equally in the structure of the cell and in the biochemical activity in which it is engaged. As the reader will see, the mysteries of cell structure and function cannot be resolved by the exercise of either morphological or biochemical techniques alone. If the research is to be successful, the approach must be made from both sides at once. But the understanding of life phenomena that flows from investigation of the cell has already fully ratified the judgment of the 19th-century biologists who perceived that living matter is divided into cells, just as molecules are made of atoms.

A description of the functional anatomy of the living cell must begin with the statement that there is no such thing as a typical cell. Single-celled organisms of many different kinds abound, and the cells of brain and muscle tissue are as different in morphology as they are in function. But for all their variety they are cells, and so they all have a cell membrane, a cytoplasm containing various

NUCLEUS OF THE LIVING CELL is the large round object in the center of the electron micrograph on the opposite page. The membrane around the nucleus is interrupted by pores through which the nucleus possibly communicates with the surrounding cytoplasm. The smaller round objects in the cytoplasm are mitochondria; the long, thin structures are the endoplasmic reticulum; the dark dots lining the reticulum are ribosomes. Actually the micrograph shows not a living cell but a dead cell: the cell has been fixed with a compound of the heavy metal osmium, immersed in a liquid plastic that is then made to solidify and finally sliced with a glass knife. The electron beam of the microscope mainly detects the atoms of osmium, distributed according to the affinity of the fixing compound for various cell constituents. The micrograph was made by Don W. Fawcett of the Harvard Medical School. The enlargement is 28,400 diameters. The cell itself is from the pancreas of a bat.

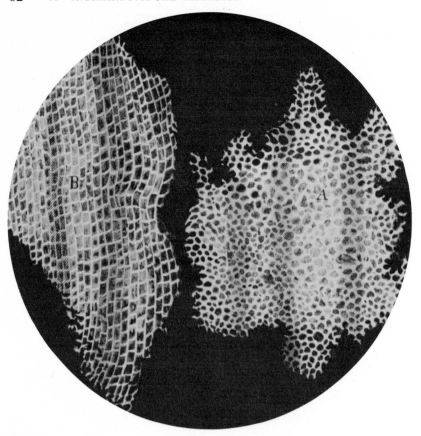

DRAWING OF CELLS in cork was published by Robert Hooke in 1665. Hooke called them cells, but the fact that all organisms are made of cells was not recognized until 19th century.

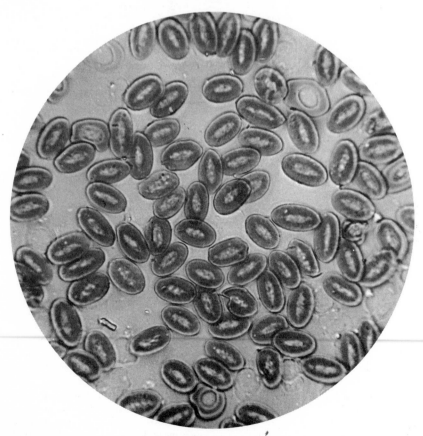

PHOTOMICROGRAPH OF CELLS in the blood of a pigeon was made by J. J. Woodward, a U.S. Army surgeon, in 1871. Woodward had made the first cell photomicrograph in 1866.

organelles and a central nucleus. In addition to having a definite structure, cells have a number of interesting functional capacities in common.

They are able, in the first place, to harness and transform energy, starting with the primary transformation by green-plant cells of the energy of sunlight into the energy of the chemical bond. Various specialized cells can convert chemical-bond energy into electrical and mechanical energy and even into visible light again. But the capacity to transform energy is essential in all cells for maintaining the constancy of their internal environment and the integrity of their structure [see "How Cells Transform Energy," Offprint #91].

The interior of the cell is distinguished from the outer world by the presence of very large and highly complex molecules. In fact, whenever such molecules turn up in the nonliving environment, one can be sure they are the remnants of dead cells. On the primitive earth, life must have had its origin in the spontaneous synthesis of complicated macromolecules at the expense of smaller molecules. Under present-day conditions, the capacity to synthesize large molecules from simpler substances remains one of the supremely distinguishing capacities of cells.

Among these macromolecules are proteins. In addition to making up a major portion of the "solid" substance of cells, many proteins (enzymes) have catalytic properties; that is, they are capable of greatly accelerating the speed of chemical reactions inside the cell, particularly those involved in the transformation of energy. The synthesis of proteins from the simpler units of the 20-odd amino acids goes forward under the regulation of deoxyribonucleic acid (DNA) and ribonucleic acid (RNA), by far the most highly structured of all the macromolecules in the cell [see "How Cells Make Molecules," Offprint #92]. In recent years and months investigators have shown that DNA, localized in the nucleus of the cell, presides at the synthesis of RNA, which is found in both the nucleus and the cytoplasm. The RNA in turn arranges the amino acids in proper sequence for linkage into protein chains. The DNA and the RNA may be compared to the architect and contractor who collaborate on the construction of a nice-looking house from a heap of bricks, stones and tiles.

At one or another stage of life every cell has divided: a mother cell has grown

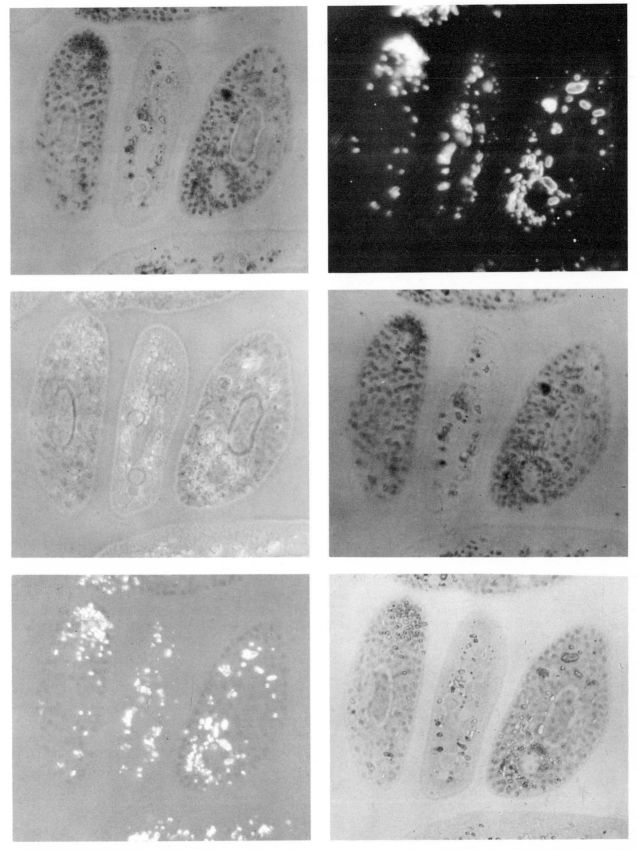

VARIOUS KINDS OF LIGHT MICROSCOPY are used to photograph the same three paramecia. The photomicrograph at top left was made with a conventional light microscope and bright-field illumination; the one at top right, with dark-field illumination. The photomicrograph at middle left was made with a phase microscope at low contrast; the one at middle right, with a phase microscope at high contrast. The photomicrograph at bottom left was made with a polarized-light microscope; the one at bottom right, with an interference microscope of the AO-Baker type. The bright spots that appear in some of the photomicrographs are small crystals that are normally present in paramecia. All the micrographs were made by Oscar W. Richards of the American Optical Company.

and given rise to two daughter cells, according to the delicate process described by Daniel Mazia [see "How Cells Divide," Offprint #93]. Before the turn of the century biologists had observed that the crucial event in this process was the equal division of bodies in the nucleus that accepted a certain colored dye and so were called chromosomes. It was correctly surmised that the chromosomes are the agents of heredity; in their precise self-replication and division they convey to the daughter cells all the capacities of the mother cell. Contemporary biochemistry has now shown that the principal constituent of the chromosomes is DNA, and an important aim of the molecular biologist today is to discover how the genetic information is encoded in the structure of this macromolecule.

The capacity for generative reproduction is not confined exclusively to the living cell. There are in the present world macromolecules called viruses that contain nucleic acids and proteins of great complexity and specificity. When they penetrate into suitable cells, they multiply just as cells do, but at the expense of the cell. They have a heredity, since they breed true when they replicate themselves, and they synthesize

their own proteins. But, lacking the full anatomical endowment of the cell, they are unable to generate the energy required for their multiplication. Viruses are thus obligatory parasites of cells and take over the enzyme system of the infected cell in order to supply the energy they need. The cell must, however, furnish exactly the right complement of enzymes. This is why tobacco mosaic virus, for example, will not multiply in human cells and so is harmless to human beings.

Such single-celled organisms as bacteria, having the capacity to make their own enzymes and so to generate the energy required for their growth and multiplication, can live and multiply in a much simpler medium than that provided by the interior of a living cell. They are, therefore, not obligatory parasites. From the viewpoint of anatomy, however, bacteria are much simpler than cells, and the various bacteria are distributed over the range of complexity from the virus upward to the cell.

In addition to the capacity for energy transformation, biosynthesis and reproduction by self-replication and division, the cells of higher organisms possess other capacities that fit them for

the concerted community life that is the life of the organism. From the single-celled fertilized egg the multicelled organism arises not only by the division of the daughter cells but also by their concurrent differentiation into the specialized cells that form various tissues. In many cases when a cell has become differentiated and specialized, it does not divide any more; there is a kind of antagonism between differentiation and growth by cell division.

In the adult organism the capacity for reproduction and perpetuation of the species is left to the eggs and spermatozoa. These gametes, like all other cells in the body, have arisen by cell division from the fertilized egg, followed by differentiation. Cell division remains, however, a frequent event in the adult organism wherever cells continuously wear out and degenerate, as they do in the skin, the intestine and in the bone marrow from which the blood cells arise.

During embryonic development the differentiating cells display a capacity for recognition of others of their own kind. Cells that belong to the same family and resemble one another tend to cluster together, forming a tissue from which cells of all other kinds are excluded. In this mutual association and rejection of cells the cell membrane appears to play a decisive role. The membrane is also one of the principal cell components involved in the function of the muscle cells that endow the organism with the power of movement, of the nerve cells that provide communication lines to integrate the activity of the organism and of the sensory cells that receive stimuli from without and within.

Although there is no typical cell, one may usefully put together a composite cell for the purpose of charting the anatomical features that are shared in varying degrees by all cells. Such a cell, based largely upon what is seen in electron micrographs, is presented on the opposite page; comparison of this cell with the corresponding cell drawn from photomicrographs made by Edmund B. Wilson of Columbia University in 1922 suggests the rapid advances that have been brought about by the electron microscope.

Even the cell membrane, which is only 100 angstrom units thick (one angstrom unit is one ten-millionth of a millimeter) and appears as little more than a boundary in the light microscope, is shown by the electron microscope to have a structure. It is true that electron micrographs have not yet revealed much

DIAGRAM OF A TYPICAL CELL (although there is no such thing as a typical cell) is based on what is seen in the conventional light microscope. Diagram is based on one that appears in 1922 edition of Edmund B. Wilson's *The Cell in Development and Inheritance.*

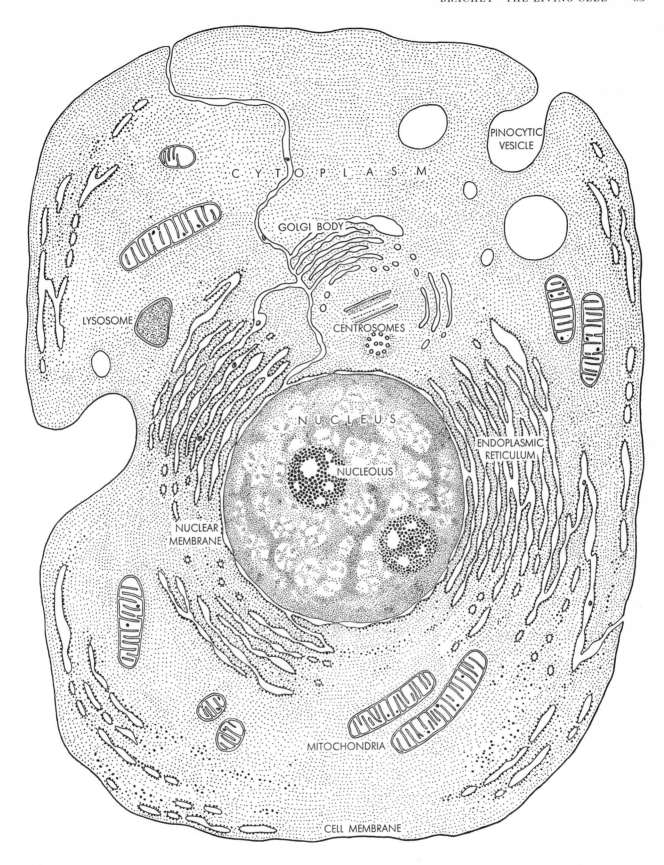

MODERN DIAGRAM OF A TYPICAL CELL is based on what is seen in electron micrographs such as the one reproduced on page 60. The mitochondria are the sites of the oxidative reactions that provide the cell with energy. The dots that line the endoplasmic reticulum are ribosomes: the sites of protein synthesis. In cell division the pair of centrosomes, one shown in longitudinal section (*rods*), other in cross section (*circles*), part to form poles of apparatus that separates two duplicate sets of chromosomes.

about this structure. On the other hand, such complexity as is shown clearly accords with what is known about the functional properties of the membrane. In red blood cells and nerve cells, for example, the membrane distinguishes between sodium and potassium ions although these ions are alike in size and electrical charge. The membrane helps potassium ions get into the cell and opposes more than a mere permeability barrier to sodium ions; that is, it is capable of "active transport." The membrane also brings large molecules and macroscopic bodies into the interior of the cell by mechanical ingestion [see "How Things Get Into Cells," Offprint #96].

Beyond the membrane, in the cytoplasm, the electron microscope has resolved the fine structure of organelles that appear as mere granules in the light microscope. Principal among them are the chloroplasts of green-plant cells and the mitochondria that appear in both animal and plant cells. These are the "power plants" of all life on earth. Each is adapted to its function by an appro-

priate fine structure, the former to capturing the energy of sunlight by photosynthesis, the latter to extracting energy from the chemical bonds in the nutrients of the cell by oxidation and respiration. From each of these power plants the yield of energy is made available to the energy-consuming processes of the cell, neatly packaged in the phosphate bonds of the compound adenosine triphosphate (ATP).

The electron microscope clearly distinguishes between the mitochondrion, with its highly organized fine structure, and another associated body of about the same size: the lysosome. As Christian de Duve of the Catholic University of Louvain has shown, the lysosome contains the digestive enzymes that break down large molecules, such as those of fats, proteins and nucleic acids, into smaller constituents that can be oxidized by the oxidative enzymes of the mitochondria. De Duve postulates that the lysosome represents a defense mechanism; the lysosomal membrane isolates the digestive enzymes from the rest of the cytoplasm. Rupture of the membrane

and release of the accumulated enzymes lead quickly to the lysis (dissolution) of the cell.

The cytoplasm contains many other visible inclusions of less widespread occurrence among cells. Particularly interesting are the centrosomes and kinetosomes. The centrosomes, or centrioles, become plainly visible under the light microscope only when the cell approaches the hour of division, in which these bodies play a commanding role as the poles of the spindle apparatus that divides the chromosomes. The kinetosomes, on the other hand, are found only in those cells which are equipped with cilia or flagella for motility; at the base of each cilium or flagellum appears a kinetosome. Both of these organelles have the special property of self-replication. Each pair of centrosomes gives rise to another when cells divide; a kinetosome duplicates itself each time a new cilium forms on the cell surface. Long ago certain cytologists advanced the idea that these two organelles have much the same structure, even though their functions are so different. The electron

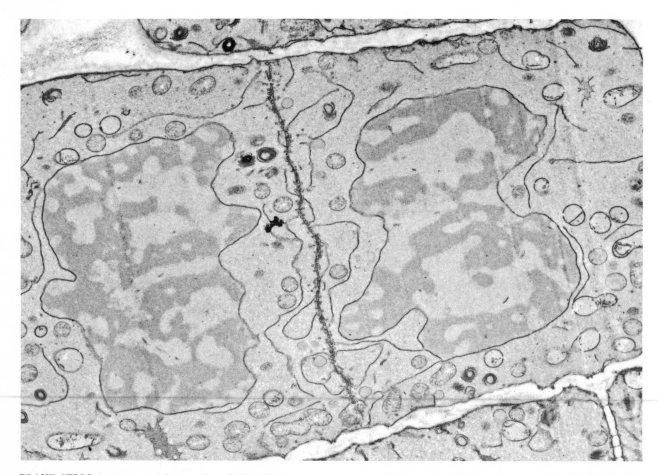

PLANT CELLS (onion root tip) are enlarged 6,700 diameters in this electron micrograph made by K. R. Porter of the Rockefeller Institute. The thin, dark line running from top to bottom of the micrograph shows the membrane between two cells shortly after the cells have divided. The large, irregularly shaped bodies to the left and right of the membrane are the nuclei of the two cells.

microscope has confirmed this suggestion. Each is a cylinder made up of 11 fibers, with two in the center and the other nine on the outside. This is the universal structure of all cilia and of flagella as well. The reason for the structure remains unknown, but it is undoubtedly related to the contractility of the cilia and flagella. It may be that the same "monomolecular muscle" principle underlies the action of the kinetosome and centrosome in their quite diverse functions.

The electron microscope has confirmed another surmise of earlier cytologists: that the cytoplasm has an invisible organization, a "cytoskeleton." Most cells show complicated systems of internal membranes not visible in the ordinary light microscope. Some of these membranes are smooth; others are rough, having tiny granules attached to one surface. The degree to which the membrane systems are developed varies from cell to cell, being rather simple in amoebae and highly articulated and roughened with granules in cells that

specialize in the production of proteins, such as those of the liver and pancreas.

Electron microscopists differ in their interpretation of these images. The generally accepted view is that of K. R. Porter of the Rockefeller Institute, who has given the membrane system its name, the endoplasmic reticulum; through the network of canaliculi formed by the membrane, substances are supposed to move from the outer membrane of the cell to the membrane of the nucleus. Some investigators hold that the internal membrane is continuous with the external membrane, furnishing a vastly increased and deeply invaginated surface area for communication with the fluid in which the cell is bathed, If the membrane does indeed have such vital functions, then it is likely that the cell is equipped with a factory for the continuous production of new membrane. This might be the role, as George E. Palade of the Rockefeller Institute has recently suggested, of the enigmatic Golgi bodies, first noted by the Italian cytologist Camillo Golgi at the end of the last century. The electron micro-

scope reveals that the Golgi bodies are made of smooth membrane, often continuous with that of the endoplasmic reticulum.

There is no doubt about the nature of the granules, which appear consistently on the "inner" surface of the membrane. They appear particularly in cells that produce large amounts of protein. As Torbjörn O. Caspersson and I showed some 20 years ago, such cells possess a high RNA content. Recent studies have revealed that the granules are exceedingly rich in RNA and correspondingly active in protein synthesis. For this reason the granules are now called ribosomes.

The membrane that surrounds the cell nucleus forms the interior boundary of the cytoplasm. There is still much speculation about what the electron microscope shows of this membrane. It appears as a double membrane with annuli, or holes, in the outer layer, open to the cytoplasm. To some investigators these annuli represent pores through which large molecules may move in either direction. Since the outer layer is often in close contact with the endoplasmic reticulum, it is also argued that the nuclear membrane participates in the formation of the reticulum membrane. Another possibility is that fluids percolating through the canaliculi of the endoplasmic reticulum are allowed to accumulate between the two layers of nuclear membrane.

Inside the nucleus are the all-important filaments of chromatin, in which the cell's complement of DNA is entirely localized. When the cell is in the "resting" state, that is, engaged in the processes of growth between divisions, the chromatin is diffusely distributed in the nucleus. The DNA thus makes maximum surface contact with other material in the nucleus from which it presumably pieces together the molecules of RNA and replicates itself. In preparation for division the chromatin coils up tightly to form the chromosomes, always a fixed number in each cell, to be distributed equally to each daughter cell.

Much less elusive than the chromatin are the nucleoli; these spherical bodies are easily resolved inside the nucleus with an ordinary light microscope. Under the electron microscope they are seen to be packed with tiny granules similar to the ribosomes of the cytoplasm. In fact, the nucleoli are rich in RNA and appear to be active centers of protein and RNA synthesis. Finally, to complete this functional anatomy of the

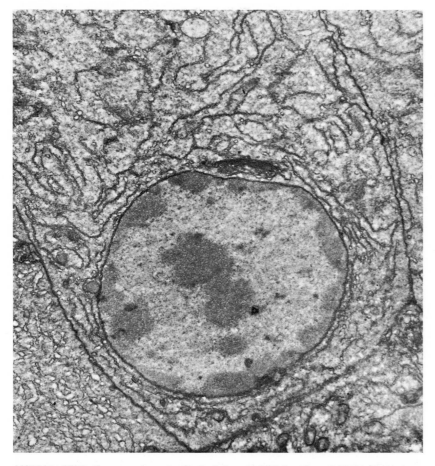

ANIMAL CELL (hepato-pancreatic gland of the crayfish) is enlarged 12,500 diameters in electron micrograph by George B. Chapman of the Cornell University Medical College. The large round object is the nucleus; the smaller dark region just above it is the Golgi body.

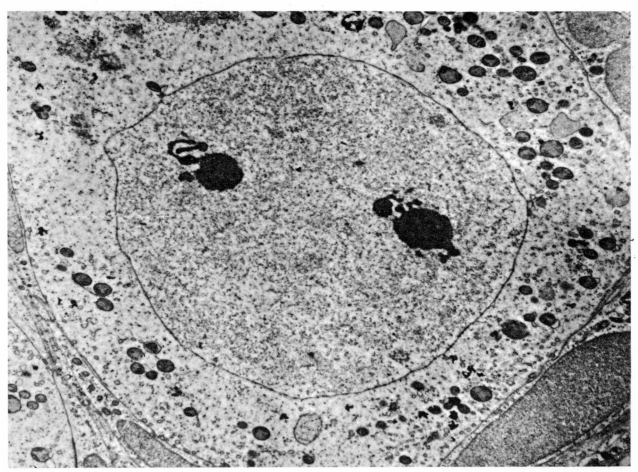

EGG CELL of rabbit is enlarged 7,500 diameters. The large round object is the nucleus; the two prominent dark bodies within it are nucleoli. Electron micrograph was made by Joan Blanchette of Columbia University College of Physicians and Surgeons.

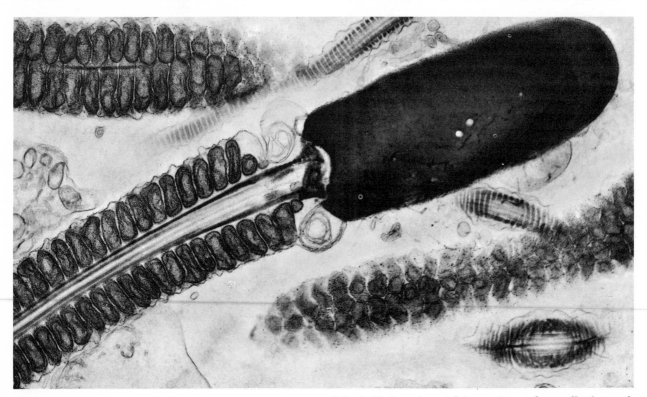

SPERM CELL of a bat is enlarged 21,500 diameters in electron micrograph by Fawcett and Susumu Ito of the Harvard Medical School. Nucleus (*top right*) constitutes almost all of sperm's head; arranged behind head are numerous mitochondria (*left*).

cell, it should be added that the chromatin and nucleoli are bathed together in the amorphous, proteinaceous matrix of the nuclear sap.

A remarkable history in the development of instruments and technique has gone into the drawing of the present portrait of the cell. The ordinary light microscope remains an essential tool. But its use in exploring the interior of the cell usually requires killing the cell and staining it with various dyes that selectively show the cell's major structures. To see these structures in action in the living cell, microscopists have developed a range of instruments—including phase, interference, polarizing and fluorescence microscopes—that manipulate light in various ways. In recent years the electron microscope, as the reader has gathered from this article, has become the major tool of the cytologist. But this instrument has a serious limitation in that it requires elaborate preparation and fixation of the specimen, which must inevitably confuse the true picture with distortions and artifacts. Progress is being made, however, toward the goal of resolving under the same high magnification the structure of the living cell.

Biochemistry has had an equally remarkable history of technical development. Centrifuges of ever higher rotation speed have made it possible to separate finer fractions of the cell's contents. These are divided and subdivided in turn by chromatography and electrophoresis. The classical techniques have been variously adapted to the analysis of quantities and volumes 1,000 times smaller than the standard of older micromethods; investigators can now measure the respiration or the enzyme content of a few amoebae or sea-urchin eggs. Finally, autoradiography, employing radioactive tracer elements, allows the worker to observe at subcellular dimensions the dynamic processes in the intact living cell.

The achievements and prospects that have been generated by the convergence of these two major movements in the life sciences furnish the subject of the articles that follow. To conclude this discussion it will be useful to consider how the two approaches have been employed to illuminate a single question: the role of the nucleus in the economy of the cell.

A simple experiment shows, first of all, that removal of the nucleus in a unicellular organism does not bring about the immediate death of the cytoplasm. The nucleate and enucleate

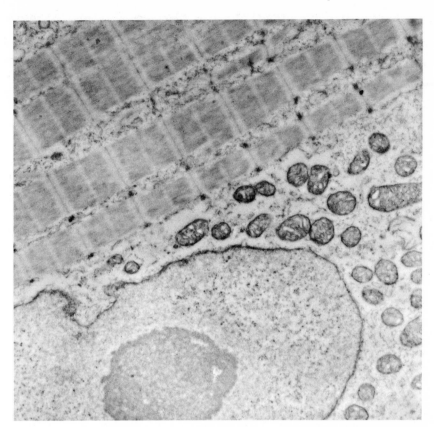

PART OF MUSCLE CELL of a salamander is enlarged 19,500 diameters in electron micrograph by George D. Pappas and Philip W. Brandt of Columbia College of Physicians and Surgeons. The nucleus is at bottom; around it are mitochondria. At top are muscle fibers.

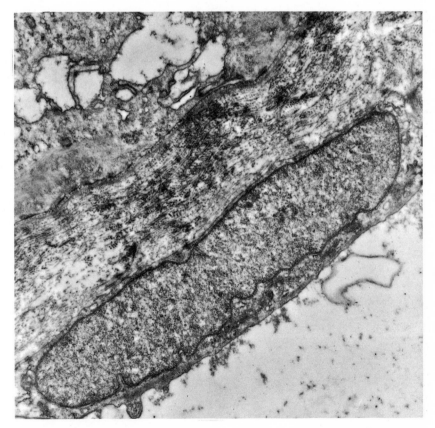

PART OF CONNECTIVE-TISSUE CELL of a tadpole is enlarged 14,500 diameters in electron micrograph by Chapman. Nucleus is oblong object; above it are fibrils of collagen.

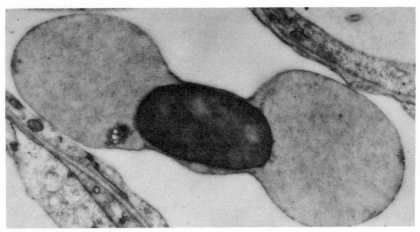

RED BLOOD CELL of a fish is enlarged 8,000 diameters in electron micrograph by Fawcett. Large dark body in center is nucleus. The mature red cells of mammals have no nuclei.

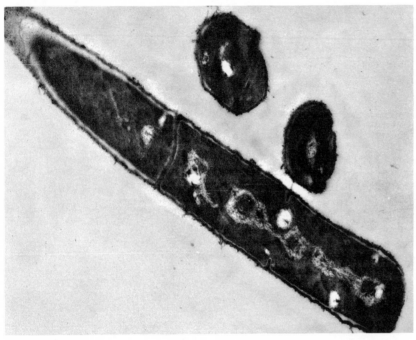

BACTERIUM *Bacillus cereus* (*long object*) is enlarged 30,000 diameters in electron micrograph by Chapman and by James Hillier of RCA Laboratories. Bacillus has several nuclei.

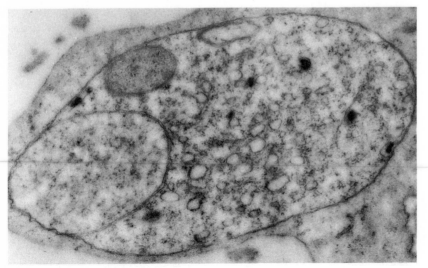

PROTOZOON *Plasmodium berghei* is enlarged 21,000 diameters in electron micrograph by Maria A. Rudzinska of the Rockefeller Institute. The nucleus is the large body at lower left.

halves of amoebae, if kept fasting, attain the same survival time of about two weeks; the cilia of an enucleate protozoon such as the paramecium continue to beat for a few days; the enucleate fragments of the unicellular giant alga *Acetabularia* may survive several months and are even capable of an appreciable amount of regeneration. Many of the basic activities of the cell, including growth and differentiation in the case of *Acetabularia,* can therefore proceed in the total absence of the genes and DNA. In fact, the enucleate pieces of *Acetabularia* are perfectly capable of making proteins, including specific enzymes, although enzyme synthesis is known to be genetically controlled. These synthetic activities, however, die out after a time. One must conclude that the nucleus produces something that is not DNA but which is formed under the influence of DNA and is transferred from the nucleus to the cytoplasm, where it is slowly used up. From such experiments—employing the combined techniques of cell biology and biochemistry—a number of fundamental conclusions emerge.

First, the nucleus is to be considered as the main center for the synthesis of nucleic acid (both DNA and RNA). Second, this nuclear RNA (or part thereof) goes over to the cytoplasm, playing the role of a messenger and transferring genetic information from DNA to the cytoplasm. Finally, the experiments show that the cytoplasm and in particular the ribosomes are the main site for the synthesis of specific proteins such as the enzymes. It should be added that the possibility of independent RNA synthesis in the cytoplasm is not ruled out and that such synthesis can, under suitable conditions, be demonstrated in enucleate fragments of *Acetabularia.* From this brief description of recently observed facts it is clear that the cell is not only a morphological but also a physiological unit.

Perhaps the reader will wonder how such knowledge of this unit helps to answer questions under the more general headings of "life" and "living." All one can venture to say is that the results of investigation invariably point in the same direction: Life, in the case of the cell and its constituents, is more a quantitative than an "all or none" concept. This dissection of cells into their constituents does not, therefore, throw much light on the questions posed by philosophy. But without this dissection, without experimentation, we would know next to nothing about the cell. And, after all, the cell is the fundamental unit of life.

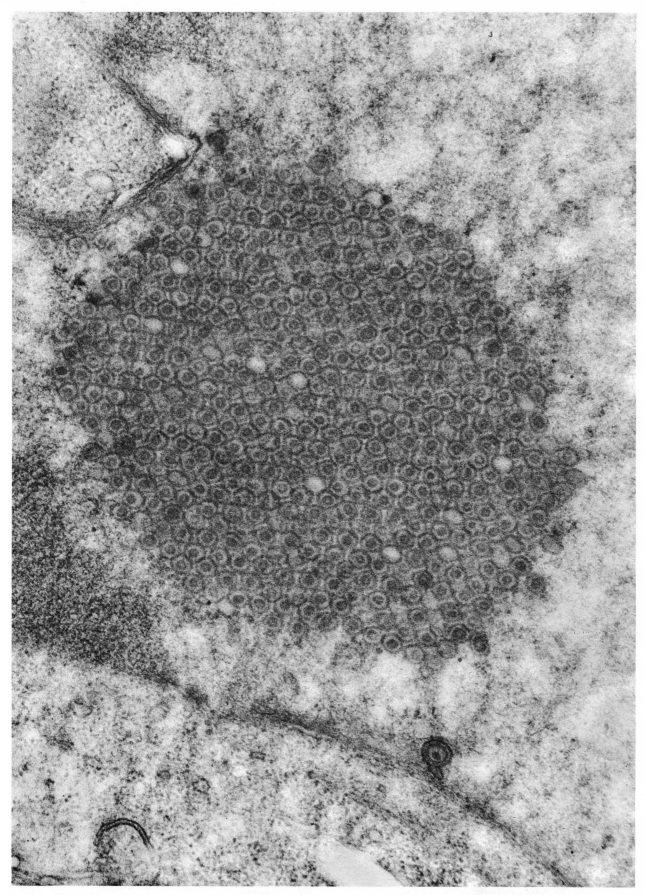

PARTICLES OF VIRUS *Herpes simplex* form a crystal within the nucleus of a cell. This electron micrograph, which enlarges the particles 73,000 diameters, was made by Councilman Morgan of the Columbia College of Physicians and Surgeons. Although viruses are exceptions to the rule that all living things are cells or are made of cells, they can reproduce only when they are inside cells.

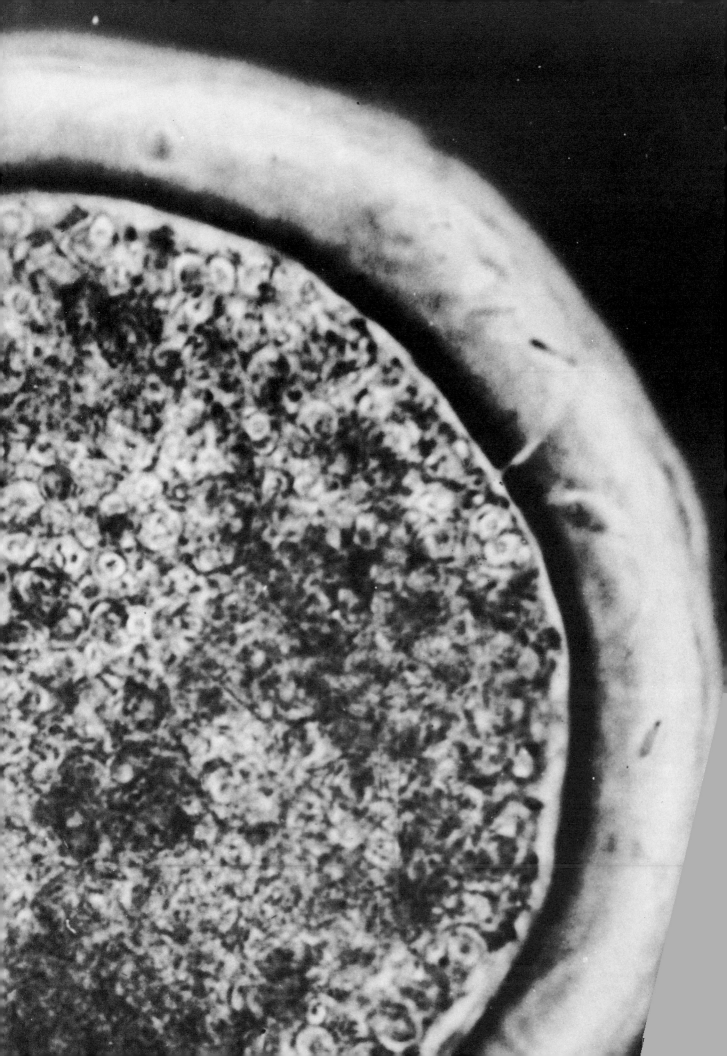

Mammalian Eggs in the Laboratory

R. G. EDWARDS
August 1966

Much of what is known about animal reproduction has been learned from such organisms as the sea urchin and the chicken. This is partly because the eggs of these organisms are readily accessible to observation during such crucial stages of the reproductive process as fertilization and embryonic development. During the past quarter-century the eggs of certain mammals—rodents, rabbits and some farm animals—have become more accessible to study. This increasing availability of mammalian eggs arises largely from advances in knowledge of how ovulation is controlled by hormones. The eggs of man and other primates, however, are still secured very rarely. It has long been recognized by workers in the field that, if a significant number of viable mammalian eggs were available on a regular basis, a host of questions about the early stages of mammalian reproduction would be open to investigation.

Experiments that my colleagues and I have conducted at the University of Cambridge and Johns Hopkins University indicate that such a situation may soon obtain. So far the experiments have been concerned mainly with oocytes, which are immature eggs. In most mammalian species, including man, the female has her full comple-

ment of oocytes when she is born. The development of the oocytes into mature eggs ready for fertilization is a long process that goes through many stages. Our experiments have involved removing oocytes from the ovaries of various mammals and stimulating them to proceed to maturity. We have also worked with some human oocytes removed surgically from women for medical reasons. Our experiments have included the fertilization of some of the animal eggs brought to maturity in vitro and attempts to fertilize the human oocytes. In discussing these experiments it will be useful to begin by describing briefly two of the key processes in the reproduction of mammals and other higher organisms: mitosis and meiosis [*see illustration on page 75*].

Mitosis is the name for the processes that take place in most cells (both plant and animal) when the cells reproduce by dividing. The events of mitosis are usually regarded as occurring in four more or less distinct phases: prophase, metaphase, anaphase and telophase. The process can be described simply for a hypothetical organism in which each cell contains four chromosomes: the bodies that carry the cell's genetic information. Two of the chromosomes, say a long one and a short one, were inherited from the mother and two from the father. The two long chromosomes are similar to each other, as are the two short chromosomes. When the members of each pair are matched in this way, they are called homologous chromosomes; the four-chromosome cell would have two pairs of homologous chromosomes. At the beginning of mitosis each chromosome has divided into two strands, which are held together by a central body called the centromere.

In prophase the chromosomes begin to shorten and thicken, and the remarkable structure called the mitotic spindle starts to form. The spindle consists of fibers in an array resembling the meridian lines of a globe that has been stretched at the poles. In metaphase the centromeres migrate to the equator of the spindle. In anaphase the centromeres divide, and the two daughter centromeres resulting from each division move toward opposite poles of the spindle, pulling their chromosome strands with them. In telophase the separation is complete; the cell divides into two daughter cells, each with a nucleus containing four chromosomes and thus the same complement of genetic information that was contained in the original cell. This completes mitosis; until one of the new cells itself begins mitosis it is said to be in interphase. Toward the end of interphase the chromosomes again divide into two strands.

Meiosis is a special form of mitosis that occurs in the cells that give rise to sperm and eggs. Before the process begins, these cells, like others in the body, are diploid: they have a normal complement of chromosomes. Since mammalian reproduction involves the union of a spermatozoon and an egg, the cells of the offspring would have a double complement of chromosomes if there were not some mechanism by which the spermatozoon and the egg became haploid, meaning that the chromosome complement of each was reduced by half. That mechanism is meiosis. It occurs in two cell divisions, known as meiosis I and meiosis II [*see top illustration on pages 76 and 77*].

The prophase of meiosis I is highly specialized and occupies a comparatively long period of time. For these reasons it is subdivided into five stages: lep-

PIG EGG was matured in culture and fertilized in the animal. In the photomicrograph on the opposite page a segment of the egg and the zona pellucida, or outer membrane, appears at an enlargement of 1,400 diameters. The small, dark objects in the zona pellucida are sperm heads; the lighter curved lines are trails made by spermatozoa as they penetrated the zona pellucida. Penetration by such a large number of spermatozoa is an unusual condition that appeared in initial experiments with cultured eggs.

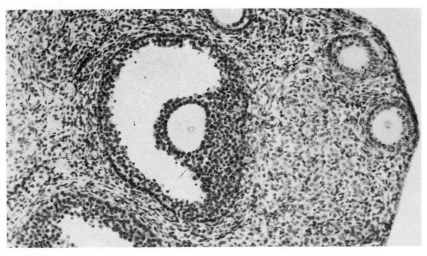

MOUSE OVARY in cross section is enlarged 200 diameters. The light circular areas are oocytes, or immature eggs, enveloped by follicles, which are composed of granulosa cells. The large, light, semicircular area at left center is the antrum, or cavity, of a Graafian follicle; when a follicle has developed to that stage, the oocyte is ready for ovulation.

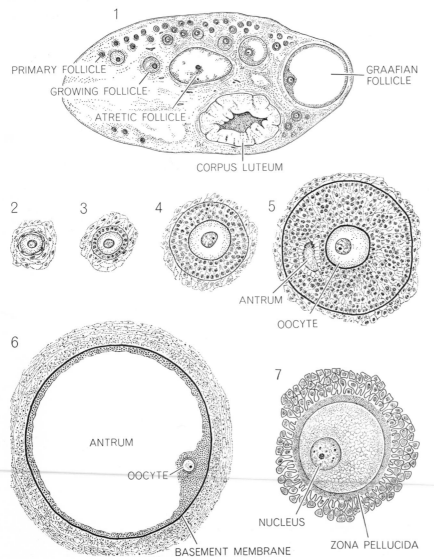

MATURATION OF OOCYTES occurs continually. At top is an ovary with several follicles containing oocytes at various stages of development. At center four stages in the maturation of a follicle are shown. At bottom are a fully grown Graafian follicle (6) and a mature egg (7).

totene, zygotene, pachytene, diplotene and diakinesis. Each relates to the activities of the chromosomes. Essentially what happens in meiosis, as distinct from mitosis, is that the homologous chromosomes pair up and duplicate. At metaphase the homologous pairs line up on the spindle. In anaphase one member of each pair, without splitting, goes to each pole. Thus after the cell divides at telophase each daughter cell has only one member of each pair of homologous chromosomes.

In meiosis II there is no further duplication of chromosomes. The twin-strand chromosomes simply line up on the spindle and separate. When the two cells that resulted from meiosis I divide in meiosis II, each of the four resulting cells has only half the original number of chromosomes. In the case of our hypothetical four-chromosome cell the result of meiosis would be four cells with two chromosomes each. By this process sperm and eggs are made haploid; when they unite through fertilization and begin the mitotic divisions known as cleavage (the first steps in the growth of an embryo), all the resulting cells are diploid.

Let us now examine the normal maturation of a mammalian oocyte. It undergoes the first four stages of the first meiotic division in the ovary of the fetus. In other words, before a female mammal is born her oocytes have completed the leptotene, zygotene and pachytene stages and are well into the diplotene stage. Meiosis halts, however, late in the diplotene stage. At this point a nucleus, called the germinal vesicle, forms in the oocyte.

These developments coincide with the envelopment of the oocyte by an array of cells known as granulosa cells. These gradually form the follicle in which the oocyte will remain enclosed until ovulation. This situation—in which the oocyte is in an arrested state of meiosis, contains a nucleus and is enveloped in a follicle—prevails at the birth of the female and persists during growth to adulthood. During the entire span of this time (up to some 40 years in the human species) the homologous chromosomes remain paired in the germinal vesicle. To many biologists this long period is known as the dictyate stage of oocyte development; others call it the dictyotene stage or the diffuse diplotene stage.

Near puberty many of the oocytes undergo atresia: they degenerate and are resorbed. This process results in a large reduction in the number of oocytes. Those that remain resume their progress toward maturity in the adult ovary. With the onset of puberty, follicles mature in groups during each sexual cycle. The follicles grow by a rapid increase in the number of granulosa and other cells. The oocyte also increases in size, usually before the follicle shows much enlargement; for the time being, however, the oocyte remains in the dictyate stage.

The later stages of follicular growth are characterized by the formation of a cavity, the antrum, in the granulosa layer; the structure is now known as a Graafian follicle. At this stage the follicle is responsive to the hormone called FSH (for follicle-stimulating hormone). FSH is secreted by the anterior part of the pituitary gland during the early part of the sexual cycle and stimulates the final enlargement of the Graafian follicle.

Now the Graafian follicle becomes sensitive to a second pituitary hormone, luteinizing hormone (LH), which has a dual action: it stimulates the oocyte to resume meiosis and it initiates changes in the follicle that lead to ovulation. Under the influence of LH the oocyte completes its first meiotic division, progressing through diakinesis, metaphase, anaphase and telophase. The daughter cells that result from this division are far from identical. One of them, the secondary oocyte, receives a disproportionate share of the original cell's cytoplasm; hence the other, the first polar body, is much smaller.

The second meiotic division begins as soon as the first ends. It reaches metaphase within minutes. Except in a few mammalian species ovulation occurs while the oocyte is in metaphase II.

In the process of ovulation the Graafian follicle fills with fluid, moves toward the surface of the ovary and erupts, releasing the oocyte. The cells of the ruptured follicle are converted to a new structure, the corpus luteum. This is the structure that produces the hormone progesterone, which conditions the walls of the uterus for the development of the fertilized egg.

At this stage meiosis is still not complete. It awaits fertilization in the fallopian tubes. Only when the fertilizing spermatozoon enters the egg is meiosis II ended by the extrusion of the second polar body. The entire process—the first stages of which took place in the fetal ovary, the middle stages in the adult ovary and the final stages in the fallopian tubes after fertilization—is now complete.

In this account of the maturation of a single oocyte the reader may well have lost sight of the setting in which these developments occur. It has been estimated that there are some 500,000 oocytes in the female human fetus, a number vastly exceeding the reproductive needs of the female. Indeed, many mammals shed only one egg during each ovulation. Others—for example mice, rabbits and pigs—produce several eggs in one ovulation, but the number is still tiny in relation to the original population of oocytes. During each sexual cycle FSH stimulates the development of many follicles, but only a few of them progress as far as ovulation. Most of them degenerate, although the oocytes in some of these atretic follicles can complete meiosis as far as metaphase II.

Atresia evidently begins when the amount of FSH becomes insufficient to maintain the growth of all the follicles developing during the female cycle, because if extra FSH is provided by injection, large numbers of follicles continue their growth. In response to LH they will proceed to ovulation.

Treatment with FSH and LH will thus induce the ovulation of large numbers of eggs—several in man, as many as 70 in mice: These eggs can be fertilized, although for many years they were regarded as being somewhat abnormal because a large proportion of the embryos to which they gave rise died during pregnancy. It is now known, primarily from evidence in mice, that such embryos are perfectly capable of normal development provided that the uterus is not overcrowded.

With FSH and LH an experimenter can therefore obtain oocytes from many or all of the Graafian follicles developing during a particular cycle. The method can, however, be laborious and

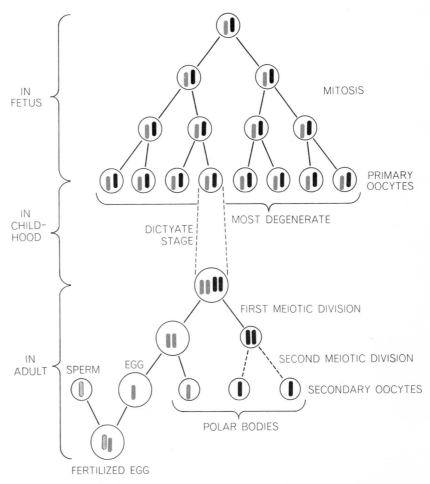

EVOLUTION OF AN EGG is traced through the processes of mitosis and meiosis. The original cell (*top*) is diploid: it has a set of chromosomes from the father (*color*) and one from the mother (*black*). This arrangement is repeated in the daughter cells that result from mitotic divisions to produce oocytes. In meiosis successive divisions produce an egg that is haploid: it has half the normal complement of chromosomes. When the egg and a sperm join to produce fertilization, the resulting cells of the growing embryo are again diploid.

FIRST MEIOTIC DIVISION

PROPHASE

1

LEPTOTENE

2

ZYGOTENE

3

PACHYTENE

4

DIPLOTENE

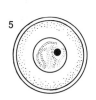

5

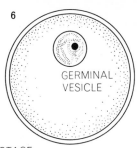

6

GERMINAL VESICLE

———— IN FETUS ————————→ ←———— DICTYATE STAGE IN CHILDHOOD ————

SECOND MEIOTIC DIVISION

METAPHASE

11

FIRST POLAR BODY

ANAPHASE

12

SPERM

TELOPHASE

13

14

SECOND POLAR BODY

OVULATION

——IN ADULT OVARY——→ ←———— FERTILIZATION IN FALLOPIAN TUBE ————

DURATION OF MEIOSIS can be as long as 40 years in human oocytes. Its prophase has a particularly long duration and several chromosomal events; hence it is subdivided into five stages, beginning with leptotene and ending with diakinesis. Homol-ogous, or similar, chromosomes, one (*black*) from the father and one (*color*) from the mother, are paired during much of the process. Meiosis halts late in the diplotene stage and the germinal vesicle appears. Meiosis is resumed in adulthood under the influ-

uncertain. In many species it requires the detailed recording of the female cycle, and in large animals it calls for organizing surgical operations or slaugh-tering to obtain the eggs from the fal-lopian tubes. For various reasons it is exceedingly difficult in its application to man. Nonetheless, it is clear that a large

supply of oocytes can be tapped in the ovary at any time during the reproduc-tive life of the female.

Once an experimenter removes an oocyte from its follicle he is confronted by two main problems. First, the oocytes (particularly those taken from atretic or underdeveloped follicles) may

be abnormal. Second, the oocytes will have to be stimulated in some way to complete their meiosis to metaphase II so that they will be comparable to eggs ovulated normally.

The problem of abnormality is man-ageable. Oocytes from atretic follicles can usually be recognized quickly and

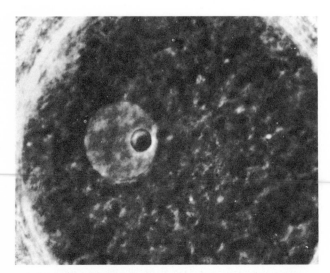

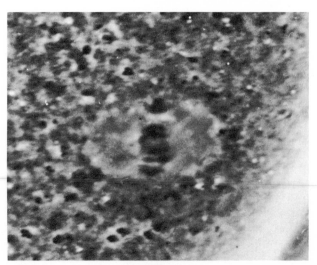

STAGES OF MEIOSIS appear in various oocytes matured in cul-ture. At left is a living monkey oocyte in the dictyate stage; its germinal vesicle, or nucleus (*light circle*), contains a single nucle-olus (*dark circle*). The next photomicrograph shows a living rat oocyte in metaphase I; the light oval area is the spindle, with chro-mosomes on its equator. The third photomicrograph shows a pig

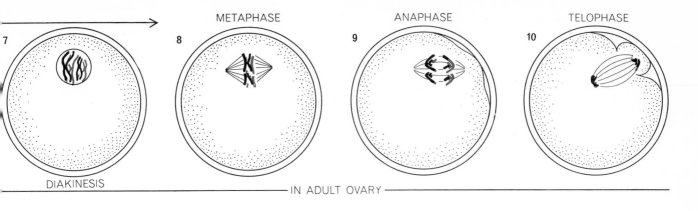

DIAKINESIS   METAPHASE   ANAPHASE   TELOPHASE

—————————————— IN ADULT OVARY ——————————————

MITOSIS

PROPHASE   METAPHASE   TWO-CELL EMBRYO

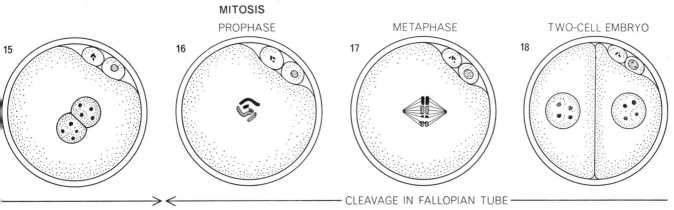

—————————— CLEAVAGE IN FALLOPIAN TUBE ——————————

ence of luteinizing hormone. At the end of meiosis I the cell divides; one of the daughter cells, the secondary oocyte, receives more of the original cell's cytoplasm than the other, the first polar body, and so is larger. Meiosis II begins when the first ends and proceeds quickly to metaphase. At this point ovulation occurs in most mammalian species. The second meiotic division is completed in the fallopian tube after entry of a spermatozoon into the egg. Meiosis thus begins in the fetus and ends long afterward.

excluded from experiments. Underdeveloped follicles either can be recognized or will end up as experimental failures.

An obvious solution to the problem of stimulating oocytes to resume meiosis was to grow them in culture outside the body. A reasonable assumption was that the culture medium would need to contain LH. It turned out, however, that LH was not needed, and the techniques required to induce the resumption of meiosis proved quite simple. Oocytes had only to be removed from the follicles and placed in a standard culture medium for meiosis to recommence in a manner seemingly identical with that in the ovary after stimulation by LH.

These observations were first made in rabbits by Gregory Pincus, now at the Worcester Foundation for Experimental Biology, and his collaborators in 1935. They also made the initial attempts with human oocytes. Our recent work has

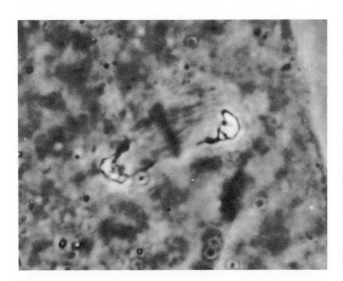

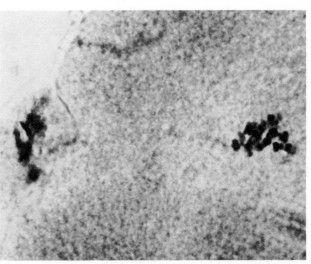

oocyte fixed and stained in telophase I; the dark vertical band is the center of the spindle and the chromosomes have moved to opposite poles. At right is a human oocyte fixed in metaphase II; it has extruded its first polar body (left). The chromosomes are the dark structures. The enlargement of each photomicrograph except the third is about 1,200 diameters; that of the third is 2,000.

shown that their method can be applied successfully to the oocytes of many mammalian species.

We first noted that oocytes from mice, rats and hamsters would recommence meiosis in culture. A clear sign of resumed meiosis is a receding of the germinal vesicle; it becomes indistinct as the chromosomes condense. The germinal vesicles of most oocytes in these species regressed after two hours, and meiosis proceeded from diakinesis to metaphase II within 12 hours. These rates are similar to those in the ovary after LH has done its work.

We then assumed (mistakenly) that the oocytes of mammals other than rodents and rabbits would mature after similar periods in culture. When it became clear that in dog, monkey, baboon and human oocytes the germinal vesicle was still intact after as long as 20 hours in culture, we erroneously concluded that oocytes from species with a prolonged sexual cycle required an extra stimulus for the resumption of meiosis. Therefore we added various plant and animal hormones to the culture. They had no effect whatever. Finally we found that by simply extending the period of culture we could induce between 60 and 80 percent of the oocytes from all the animals with which we worked to resume meiosis. In certain species—cow, sheep, monkey and probably baboon (we have had too few baboon oocytes to be sure)—20 to 24

hours passed before the germinal vesicle regressed.

Obviously we had to ensure that the persistence of the germinal vesicle in certain species for as long as 24 hours in vitro mirrored the events in the ovary after stimulation by LH. It was therefore fortunate that Christopher Polge and Ronald Hunter of the British Agricultural Research Council had made detailed estimates of the pig oocyte's meiotic stages in vivo after the pigs had been injected with LH. These estimates showed that the germinal vesicle persisted for 20 to 24 hours after the injection and that meiosis was then resumed. Polge and I examined cultured oocytes and found that they matured at a rate closely comparable to the rate of maturation in the ovary. This was most encouraging to us. If pig oocytes were maturing normally in vitro, we could reasonably conclude that the same was true of oocytes from other species in which there was a long delay before the germinal vesicle regressed.

In all species most oocytes matured to metaphase II. Some oocytes, however, proceeded to anaphase of the first meiotic division and meiosis then halted. The chromosomes failed to segregate along the spindle. The number of oocytes showing this arrest in anaphase was found to depend on the culture medium used. For the most part we now have mediums in which the number of oocytes that fail to reach metaphase II is very small, although in some spe-

cies—notably the pig and the mouse—we have not fully solved this problem.

A remarkable phenomenon in the culturing of oocytes was that within each species the oocytes matured synchronously, even though they had been taken from females in widely differing stages of the sexual cycle. In other words, it made no difference how near to or far from ovulation an oocyte might have been at the time of removal; once put into the culture medium all the oocytes matured together. As a result of this phenomenon we were able to predict with considerable accuracy the stage of meiosis the oocytes from a particular species of mammal would reach after specific periods in culture. Indeed, by timing the interval between the release of oocytes from their follicles and metaphase II in vitro we can now predict the interval in vivo between the secretion of LH from the pituitary gland and ovulation in cases where this interval is unknown.

Our success with the culturing of oocytes from various experimental and domestic animals presented a major challenge: Would human oocytes respond similarly? After preliminary trials it became abundantly clear they would. In culture the germinal vesicle persisted for 24 hours; the chromosomes condensed at diakinesis between 25 and 28 hours; metaphase I occurred between 26 and 35 hours, and the first polar body was extruded between 36

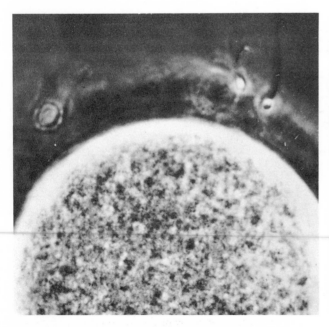 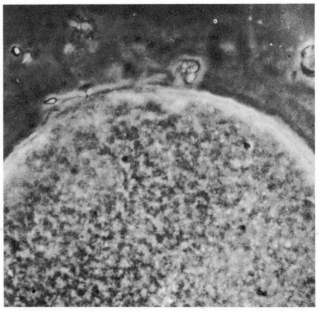

HUMAN EGGS have proved difficult to fertilize in vitro. At left is a human egg with several spermatozoa that have failed to penetrate fully the zona pellucida. In the photomicrograph at right a sperma- tozoon (*top left*) has passed through the zona pellucida and reached the surface of the egg, but that is inconclusive evidence of fertilization. Some eggs showed other inconclusive evidence of fertilization.

and 43 hours. A large majority of the oocytes examined after 43 hours were in metaphase II and had a polar body.

Even though the oocytes were necessarily taken from women who were ill and undergoing surgery and who were at widely differing stages of the menstrual cycle, approximately 80 percent of the oocytes thus obtained resumed maturation in culture and progressed synchronously through meiosis to metaphase II. From our observations we could therefore estimate that the interval in man between the secretion of LH and ovulation during the menstrual cycle is probably 36 to 43 hours. Moreover, the results showed that we could induce large numbers of oocytes to proceed in culture to the stage where fertilization normally occurs.

Our experiments in the culture of oocytes provide some indications of the mechanisms involved in the normal evolution of oocytes in the ovary. There is evidence that cultured oocytes resume their meiosis when the follicular architecture is destroyed by the rupture of a membrane (variously called the basement membrane or membrana propria) as the oocytes are removed from the ovary. This implies that the intact basement membrane plays a role in restraining the maturation of the oocyte. If it does, that would shed light on several phenomena. For example, in some atretic follicles the oocyte resumes meiosis before the complete degeneration of the follicle. Secondly, the basement membrane is associated with the granulosa cells, and the dictyate stage actually begins when the granulosa cells first enfold the oocyte in the ovary. Moreover, there is evidence that the granulosa cells will begin the changes leading to the formation of a corpus luteum when the follicle is ruptured. It would be most interesting to establish that both of the changes induced in the ovary by LH —the resumption of meiosis in the oocyte and the transformation of a Graafian follicle into a corpus luteum—could be set in motion by rupturing the follicular membrane.

Since it is now possible to induce at will any stage of meiosis between diakinesis and metaphase II, the way is open to investigate how and at what stage chromosome abnormalities arise. In recent years it has been clearly established that in man one such abnormality is associated with mongolism. Many mongoloids have 47 chromosomes per cell instead of the normal 46. The extra chromosome is No. 21, that is,

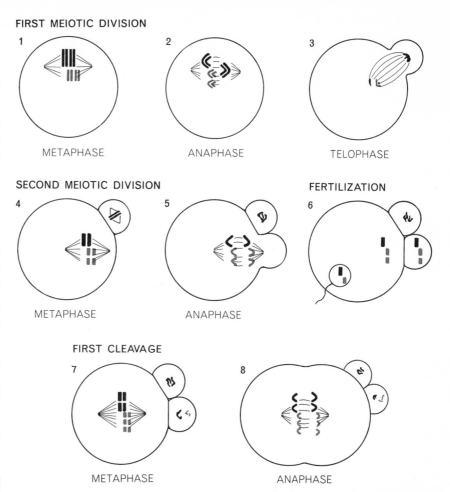

FIRST MEIOTIC DIVISION

1 METAPHASE

2 ANAPHASE

3 TELOPHASE

SECOND MEIOTIC DIVISION

4 METAPHASE

5 ANAPHASE

FERTILIZATION

6

FIRST CLEAVAGE

7 METAPHASE

8 ANAPHASE

ORIGIN of chromosomal abnormalities such as that leading to mongolism can probably be studied by growing eggs in culture and watching the chromosomes. Such abnormalities might arise in several ways; here paired chromosomes (*color*) fail to separate normally during anaphase I and hence move together to one pole of the spindle. Thus their distribution in the egg and first polar body is faulty and could result in abnormalities after fertilization.

there are three homologous No. 21 chromosomes instead of the two usually found. Mongolism occurs much more frequently among the children of older mothers. Evidently the defect arises early in embryonic development, or perhaps during meiosis in the oocyte. The immediate cause might be an infection.

Several explanations have been put forward to explain the mechanism of this and other chromosomal abnormalities. The reader will recall from the description of meiosis that homologous chromosomes are paired at the beginning of the dictyate stage and should remain paired until meiosis is resumed under the influence of LH. If homologous chromosomes were gradually to separate during the dictyate stage so that they were no longer paired when meiosis was resumed, they would move independently along the spindle at anaphase. Their distribution in the egg and first polar body would become a matter of chance. This failure of the

controlled segregation of the chromosomes would inevitably lead to abnormal karyotypes, or arrays of chromosomes, in some embryos.

Another source of abnormalities might be the nucleolus, the structure that contains much of the ribonucleic acid in the nucleus. Nucleoli are formed from nucleolus-organizer regions in certain chromosomes. The five pairs of human chromosomes carrying nucleolus organizers are involved in a high proportion of chromosomal anomalies. Each of these chromosomes can produce a nucleolus, although in the later stages of maturation an oocyte usually has only one nucleolus because of nucleolar fusion. The close relation of these chromosomes with the nucleolus during the prolonged dictyate stage might lead to abnormal segregation at anaphase. In many of the oocytes that we grew in culture we saw several chromosomes— probably those carrying nucleolus organizers—in intimate association with the nucleolus during diakinesis. In other oocytes all the chromosomes appeared to be associated with the nucleolus or to be sticking together.

Having caused oocytes to mature in culture to the point of development at which fertilization occurs, we decided to see if they could be fertilized. Our technique with animal oocytes was to transfer them into the fallopian tubes of females of the same species. The females were then normally mated.

In earlier work on the rabbit M. C. Chang of the Worcester Foundation for Experimental Biology found that as many as 80 percent of cultured oocytes were fertilized when transferred into a doe. The rate of fetal abnormality, however, was high. Only three normal fetuses and 14 that had died during pregnancy were recovered from 81 oocytes transferred in the experiments.

We worked with the pig oocyte, because it matures at a rate similar to that in man and other large mammals. Our initial attempts produced a high incidence of anomalies. For one thing, large numbers of spermatozoa penetrated the egg instead of the normal one or two [see illustration on page 72]. In addition there was considerable fragmentation of the eggs. After we had improved this situation by modifying the culture medium the results of fertilization grew progressively better, although many eggs are still anomalous. This result may be partly due to a fact mentioned earlier: that the pig oocyte has a tendency to halt its development in anaphase I. Apparently our conditions of culture are still insufficient for the pig oocyte. So far we have examined all the eggs immediately after fertilization. Our immediate tasks are to improve the culture mediums and to study the further development of fertilized eggs. We have learned already that we can use fluid from the Graafian follicle itself to culture the oocytes.

Since pig ovaries can be obtained easily and cheaply, pig oocytes can be matured and perhaps fertilized in large numbers. On three occasions we have had some 700 pig oocytes maturing synchronously in vitro; we could have had many more. Such large numbers of oocytes should facilitate investigation of the biochemical aspects of early mammalian development.

Among the questions that might be thus elucidated is the matter of where and when DNA and RNA are synthesized. Some evidence suggests that DNA is synthesized during the interphase of each cleavage division of mammalian eggs; there appear to be no large stores of DNA in the cytoplasm. The type of RNA being synthesized probably varies with the stage of development. Large amounts of RNA are found in fully grown follicular oocytes, although it is not certain when the RNA is synthesized. It would be of interest to characterize the types of RNA in mature oocytes and early embryos. Apparently little, if any, "messenger" RNA or protein is synthesized until the early embryonic stage. An intriguing fact is that the earliest evidence of gene action appears in this stage, as does the genetic inactivation of one of the two "X" chromosomes in female embryos. These events suggest that some delicate genetic mechanism has begun to operate.

If rabbit and pig eggs can be fertilized after maturation in culture, presumably human eggs grown in culture could also be fertilized, although obviously it would not be permissible to implant them in a human recipient. We have therefore attempted to fertilize cultured human eggs in vitro. Here we promptly encountered a problem involving what is called capacitation of the spermatozoa. Capacitation, without which most mammalian eggs cannot be fertilized, is a poorly understood change undergone by spermatozoa in the female reproductive tract. Noncapacitated spermatozoa are unable to penetrate through the zona pellucida: the outer membrane of the egg.

We attempted to overcome this problem by removing the seminal fluid from the spermatozoa, since this fluid is reported to suppress capacitation. Then we added spermatozoa thus treated to 40 oocytes in vitro a few hours before

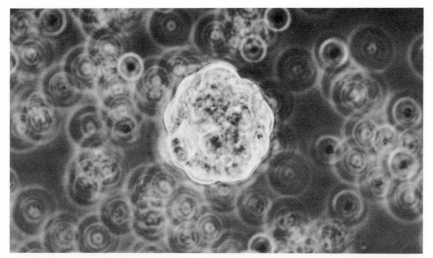

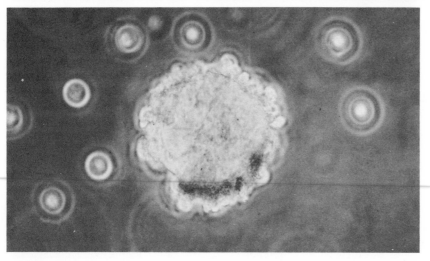

MOUSE EMBRYOS tested for antigens indicate possibilities of the work with eggs. At top is a negative result; red cells fail to adhere to a living embryo. Adherence of red cells to the embryo at bottom is a positive test for an antigen. A distant possibility is detecting female embryos by the presence of sex chromatin in cells excised from living embryos.

the extrusion of the first polar body. Except in rare cases spermatozoa had attached themselves to but not penetrated the zona pellucida 24 to 36 hours later [*see illustration on page 78*]. Three eggs had two or more nuclei, which might have been a sign of fertilization but was inconclusive evidence. These results were similar to those obtained in earlier attempts by Landrum B. Shettles of the Columbia University College of Physicians and Surgeons. It is undoubtedly significant that when we attempted to fertilize rabbit and pig eggs in vitro after their maturation in culture, the result was the same: spermatozoa failed to pass through the zona pellucida, although they did so, often in large numbers, when the oocytes were transferred into a mated recipient.

We accordingly tried to capacitate human spermatozoa. Small pieces of human fallopian tube were added to some cultures, but this brought no increase in fertilization. Next we transferred some oocytes, together with human spermatozoa, into the fallopian tubes of rabbits or monkeys. None of the oocytes were fertilized in the rabbit; those put into monkeys simply disappeared after about 12 hours.

Then we tried placing human spermatozoa in the fallopian tubes or uterus of a rabbit, flushing them out later and adding them to human oocytes in vitro. None of the oocytes were fertilized. Finally, in an attempt to imitate the situation in animals, we took spermatozoa from the uterine cervix of women 10 hours after coitus. The addition of these spermatozoa to human oocytes in vitro produced no fertilization.

So far, then, we have either failed or have at best achieved a very limited success in fertilizing human eggs in vitro. We intend to continue these experiments; the ability to observe cleaving human eggs could be of great medical and scientific value. For example, sterility caused by faulty passage of embryos along the fallopian tube could probably be alleviated by removing oocytes from the ovary, growing and fertilizing them in vitro and then transferring them back into the mother. Another possibility, arising from the number of oocytes that can be obtained from a human ovary (up to 65 in our experiments), is that oocytes and embryos showing anomalies could be eliminated in favor of those developing normally. This achievement might one day permit some choice to be made in the type of offspring born to particular parents.

7

The Genetic Code

F. H. C. CRICK

October 1962

Within the past year important progress has been made in solving the "coding problem." To the biologist this is the problem of how the information carried in the genes of an organism determines the structure of proteins.

Proteins are made from 20 different kinds of small molecule—the amino acids—strung together into long polypeptide chains. Proteins often contain several hundred amino acid units linked together, and in each protein the links are arranged in a specific order that is genetically determined. A protein is therefore like a long sentence in a written language that has 20 letters.

Genes are made of quite different long-chain molecules: the nucleic acids DNA (deoxyribonucleic acid) and, in some small viruses, the closely related RNA (ribonucleic acid). It has recently been found that a special form of RNA, called messenger RNA, carries the genetic message from the gene, which is located in the nucleus of the cell, to the surrounding cytoplasm, where many of the proteins are synthesized [see "Messenger RNA," by Jerard Hurwitz and J. J. Furth; SCIENTIFIC AMERICAN Offprint #119].

The nucleic acids are made by joining up four kinds of nucleotide to form a polynucleotide chain. The chain provides a backbone from which four kinds of side group, known as bases, jut at regular intervals. The order of the bases, however, is not regular, and it is their precise sequence that is believed to carry the genetic message. The coding problem can thus be stated more explicitly as the problem of how the sequence of the four bases in the nucleic acid determines the sequence of the 20 amino acids in the protein.

The problem has two major aspects, one general and one specific. Specifically one would like to know just what sequence of bases codes for each amino acid. Remarkable progress toward this goal was reported early in 1962 by Marshall W. Nirenberg and J. Heinrich Matthaei of the National Institutes of Health and by Severo Ochoa and his colleagues at the New York University School of Medicine. [Editor's note: Brief accounts of this work appeared in "Science and the Citizen" for February and March, 1962. This article was planned as a companion to one by Nirenberg (Offprint #153), which deals with the biochemical aspects of the genetic code.]

The more general aspect of the coding problem, which will be my subject, has to do with the length of the genetic coding units, the way they are arranged in the DNA molecule and the way in which the message is read out. The experiments I shall report were performed at the Medical Research Council Laboratory of Molecular Biology in Cambridge, England. My colleagues were Mrs. Leslie Barnett, Sydney Brenner, Richard J. Watts-Tobin and, more recently, Robert Shulman.

The organism used in our work is the bacteriophage T4, a virus that infects the colon bacillus and subverts the biochemical machinery of the bacillus to make multiple copies of itself. The infective process starts when T4 injects its genetic core, consisting of a long strand of DNA, into the bacillus. In less than 20 minutes the virus DNA causes the manufacture of 100 or so copies of the complete virus particle, consisting of a DNA core and a shell containing at least six distinct protein components. In the process the bacillus is killed and the virus particles spill out. The great value of the T4 virus for genetic experiments is that many generations and billions of individuals can be produced in a short time. Colonies containing mutant individuals can be detected by the appearance of the small circular "plaques" they form on culture plates. Moreover, by the use of suitable cultures it is possible to select a single individual of interest from a population of a billion.

Using the same general technique, Seymour Benzer of Purdue University was able to explore the fine structure of the A and B genes (or cistrons, as he prefers to call them) found at the "rII" locus of the DNA molecule of T4 [see "The Fine Structure of the Gene," by Seymour Benzer; SCIENTIFIC AMERICAN Offprint #120]. He showed that the A and B genes, which are next to each other on the virus chromosome, each consist of some hundreds of distinct sites arranged in linear order. This is exactly what one would expect if each gene is a segment, say 500 or 1,000 bases long, of the very long DNA molecule that forms the virus chromosome [see illustration on following page]. The entire DNA molecule in T4 contains about 200,000 base pairs.

The Usefulness of Mutations

From the work of Benzer and others we know that certain mutations in the A and B region made one or both genes inactive, whereas other mutations were only partially inactivating. It had also been observed that certain mutations were able to suppress the effect of harmful mutations, thereby restoring the function of one or both genes. We suspected that the various—and often puzzling—consequences of different kinds of mutation might provide a key to the nature of the genetic code.

We therefore set out to re-examine the effects of crossing T4 viruses bearing mutations at various sites. By growing two different viruses together in a common culture one can obtain "recombinants" that have some of the properties

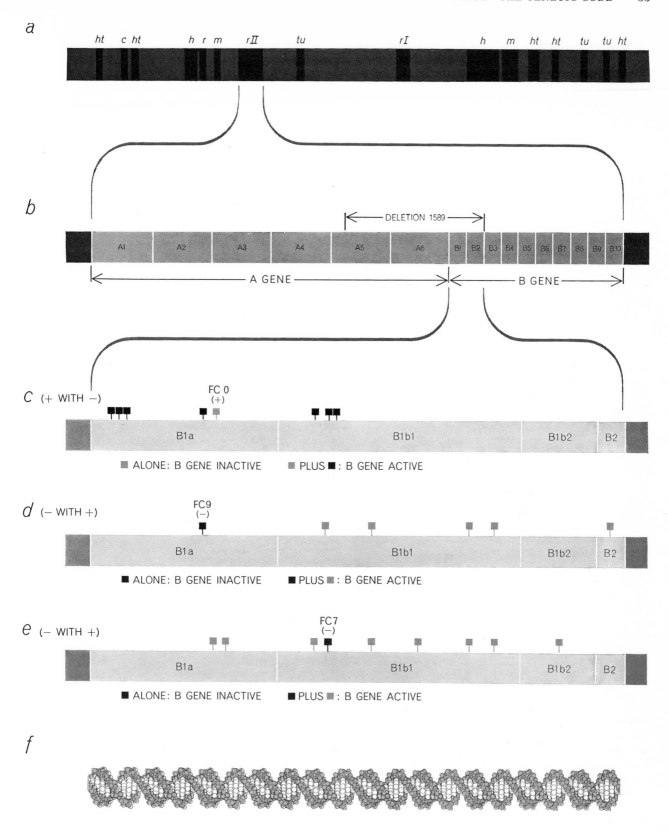

rII REGION OF THE T4 VIRUS represents only a few per cent of the DNA (deoxyribonucleic acid) molecule that carries full instructions for creating the virus. The region consists of two genes, here called A and B. The A gene has been mapped into six major segments, the B gene into 10 (*b*). The experiments reported in this article involve mutations in the first and second segments of the B gene. The B gene is inactivated by any mutation that adds a molecular subunit called a base (*colored square*) or removes one (*black square*). But activity is restored by simultaneous addition and removal of a base, as shown in *c*, *d* and *e*. An explanation for this recovery of activity is illustrated on page 86. The molecular representation of DNA (*f*) is estimated to be approximately in scale with the length of the B1 and B2 segments of the B gene. The two segments contain about 100 base pairs.

of one parent and some of the other. Thus one defect, such as the alteration of a base at a particular point, can be combined with a defect at another point to produce a phage with both defects [*see upper illustration below*]. Alternatively, if a phage has several defects, they can be separated by being crossed with the "wild" type, which by definition has none. In short, by genetic methods one can either combine or separate different mutations, provided that they do not overlap.

Most of the defects we shall be considering are evidently the result of adding or deleting one base or a small group of bases in the DNA molecule and not merely the result of altering one of the bases [*see lower illustration on this page*]. Such additions and deletions can be produced in a random manner with the compounds called acridines, by a process that is not clearly understood. We think they are very small additions or deletions, because the altered gene seems to have lost its function completely; mutations produced by reagents capable of changing one base into another are often partly functional. Moreover, the acridine mutations cannot be reversed by such reagents (and vice versa). But our strongest reason for believing they are additions or deletions is that they can be combined in a way that suggests they have this character.

To understand this we shall have to go back to the genetic code. The simplest sort of code would be one in which a small group of bases stands for one particular acid. This group can scarcely be a pair, since this would yield only 4 × 4, or 16, possibilities, and at least 20 are needed. More likely the shortest code group is a triplet, which would provide 4 × 4 × 4, or 64, possibilities. A small group of bases that codes one amino acid has recently been named a codon.

The first definite coding scheme to be proposed was put forward eight years ago by the physicist George Gamow, now at the University of Colorado. In this code adjacent codons overlap as illustrated on the following page. One consequence of such a code is that only certain amino acids can follow others. Another consequence is that a change in a single base leads to a change in three adjacent amino acids. Evidence gathered since Gamow advanced his ideas makes an overlapping code appear unlikely. In the first place there seems to be no restriction of amino acid sequence in any of the proteins so far examined. It has also been shown that typical mutations change only a single amino acid in the

polypeptide chain of a protein. Although it is theoretically possible that the genetic code may be partly overlapping, it is more likely that adjacent codons do not overlap at all.

Since the backbone of the DNA molecule is completely regular, there is nothing to mark the code off into groups of three bases, or into groups of any other size. To solve this difficulty various ingenious solutions have been proposed. It was thought, for example, that the code might be designed in such a way that if the wrong set of triplets were chosen, the message would always be complete nonsense and no protein would

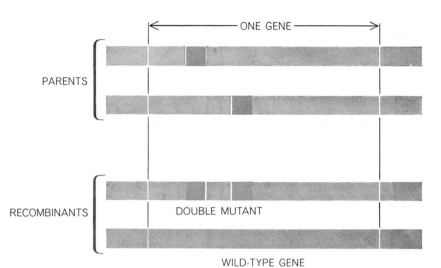

GENETIC RECOMBINATION provides the means for studying mutations. Colored squares represent mutations in the chromosome (DNA molecule) of the T4 virus. Through genetic recombination, the progeny can inherit the defects of both parents or of neither.

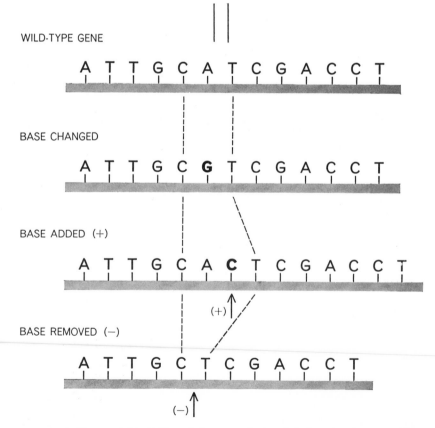

TWO CLASSES OF MUTATION result from introducing defects in the sequence of bases (A, T, G, C) that are attached to the backbone of the DNA molecule. In one class a base is simply changed from one into another, as A into G. In the second class a base is added or removed. Four bases are adenine (A), thymine (T), guanine (G) and cytosine (C).

be produced. But it now looks as if the most obvious solution is the correct one. That is, the message begins at a fixed starting point, probably one end of the gene, and is simply read three bases at a time. Notice that if the reading started at the wrong point, the message would fall into the wrong sets of three and would then be hopelessly incorrect. In fact, it is easy to see that while there is only one correct reading for a triplet code, there are two incorrect ones.

If this idea were right, it would immediately explain why the addition or the deletion of a base in most parts of the gene would make the gene completely nonfunctional, since the reading of the genetic message from that point onward would be totally wrong. Now, although our single mutations were always without function, we found that if we put certain pairs of them together, the gene would work. (In point of fact we picked up many of our functioning double mutations by starting with a nonfunctioning mutation and selecting for the rare second mutation that restored gene activity, but this does not affect our argument.) This enabled us to classify all our mutations as being either plus or minus. We found that by using the following rules we could always predict the

behavior of any pair we put together in the same gene. First, if plus is combined with plus, the combination is nonfunctional. Second, if minus is combined with minus, the result is nonfunctional. Third, if plus is combined with minus, the combination is nonfunctional if the pair is too widely separated and functional if the pair is close together.

The interesting case is the last one. We could produce a gene that functioned, at least to some extent, if we combined a plus mutation with a minus mutation, provided that they were not too far apart.

To make it easier to follow, let us assume that the mutations we called plus really had an extra base at some point and that those we called minus had lost a base. (Proving this to be the case is rather difficult.) One can see that, starting from one end, the message would be read correctly until the extra base was reached; then the reading would get out of phase and the message would be wrong until the missing base was reached, after which the message would come back into phase again. Thus the genetic message would not be wrong over a long stretch but only over the short distance between the plus and the minus. By the same sort of argument one

can see that for a triplet code the combination plus with plus or minus with minus should never work [see illustration on the next page].

We were fortunate to do most of our work with mutations at the left-hand end of the B gene of the rII region. It appears that the function of this part of the gene may not be too important, so that it may not matter if part of the genetic message in the region is incorrect. Even so, if the plus and minus are too far apart, the combination will not work.

Nonsense Triplets

To understand this we must go back once again to the code. There are 64 possible triplets but only 20 amino acids to be coded. Conceivably two or more triplets may stand for each amino acid. On the other hand, it is reasonable to expect that at least one or two triplets may not represent an amino acid at all but have some other meaning, such as "Begin here" or "End here." Although such hypothetical triplets may have a meaning of some sort, they have been named nonsense triplets. We surmised that sometimes the misreading produced in the region lying between a plus and a minus mutation might by chance give rise to a nonsense triplet, in which case the gene might not work.

We investigated a number of plus-with-minus combinations in which the distance between plus and minus was relatively short and found that certain combinations were indeed inactive when we might have expected them to function. Presumably an intervening nonsense triplet was to blame. We also found cases in which a plus followed by a minus worked but a minus followed by a plus did not, even though the two mutations appeared to be at the same sites, although in reverse sequence. As I have indicated, there are two wrong ways to read a message; one arises if the plus is to the left of the minus, the other if the plus is to the right of the minus. In cases where plus with minus gave rise to an active gene but minus with plus did not, even when the mutations evidently occupied the same pairs of sites, we concluded that the intervening misreading produced a nonsense triplet in one case but not in the other. In confirmation of this hypothesis we have been able to modify such nonsense triplets by mutagens that turn one base into another, and we have thereby restored the gene's activity. At the same time we have been able to locate the position of the nonsense triplet.

Recently we have undertaken one

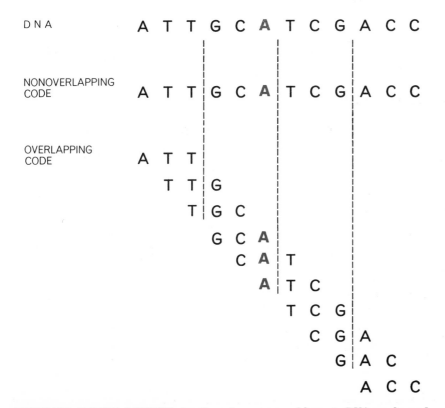

PROPOSED CODING SCHEMES show how the sequence of bases in DNA can be read. In a nonoverlapping code, which is favored by the author, code groups are read in simple sequence. In one type of overlapping code each base appears in three successive groups.

WILD-TYPE GENE

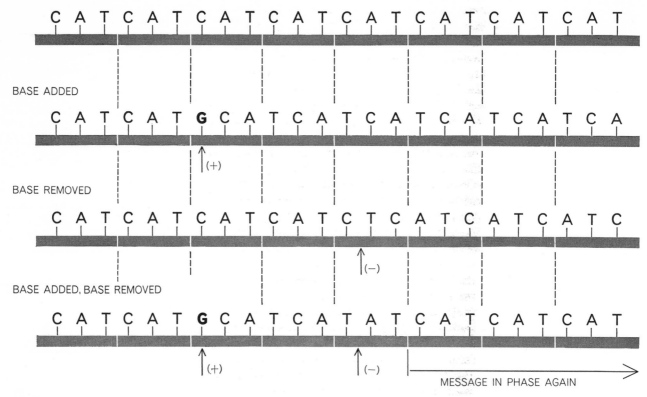

EFFECT OF MUTATIONS that add or remove a base is to shift the reading of the genetic message, assuming that the reading begins at the left-hand end of the gene. The hypothetical message in the wild-type gene is CAT, CAT... Adding a base shifts the reading to TCA, TCA... Removing a base makes it ATC, ATC... Addition and removal of a base puts the message in phase again.

other rather amusing experiment. If a single base were changed in the left-hand end of the B gene, we would expect the gene to remain active, both because this end of the gene seems to be unessential and because the reading of the rest of the message is not shifted. In fact, if the B gene remained active, we would have no way of knowing that a base had been changed. In a few cases, however, we have been able to destroy the activity of the B gene by a base change traceable to the left-hand end of the gene. Presumably the change creates a nonsense triplet. We reasoned that if we could shift the reading so that the message was read in different groups of three, the new reading might not yield a nonsense triplet. We therefore selected a minus and a plus that together allowed the B gene to function, and that were on each side of the presumed nonsense mutation. Sure enough, this combination of three mutants allowed the gene to function [see top illustration on page 88]. In other words, we could abolish the effect of a nonsense triplet by shifting its reading.

All this suggests that the message is read from a fixed point, probably from one end. Here the question arises of how one gene ends and another begins,

since in our picture there is nothing on the backbone of the long DNA molecule to separate them. Yet the two genes A and B are quite distinct. It is possible to measure their function separately, and Benzer has shown that no matter what mutation is put into the A gene, the B function is not affected, provided that the mutation is wholly within the A gene. In the same way changes in the B gene do not affect the function of the A gene.

The Space between the Genes

It therefore seems reasonable to imagine that there is something about the DNA between the two genes that isolates them from each other. This idea can be tested by experiments with a mutant T4 in which part of the rII region is deleted. The mutant, known as T4 1589, has lost a large part of the right end of the A gene and a smaller part of the left end of the B gene. Surprisingly the B gene still shows some function; in fact this is why we believe this part of the B gene is not too important.

Although we describe this mutation as a deletion, since genetic mapping shows that a large piece of the genetic

information in the region is missing, it does not mean that physically there is a gap. It seems more likely that DNA is all one piece but that a stretch of it has been left out. It is only by comparing it with the complete version—the wild type —that one can see a piece of the message is missing.

We have argued that there must be a small region between the genes that separates them. Consequently one would predict that if this segment of the DNA were missing, the two genes would necessarily be joined. It turns out that it is quite easy to test this prediction, since by genetic methods one can construct double mutants. We therefore combined one of our acridine mutations, which in this case was near the beginning of the A gene, with the deletion 1589. Without the deletion present the acridine mutation had no effect on the B function, which showed that the genes were indeed separate. But when 1589 was there as well, the B function was completely destroyed [see top illustration on page 87]. When the genes were joined, a change far away in the A gene knocked out the B gene completely. This strongly suggests that the reading proceeds from one end.

We tried other mutations in the A

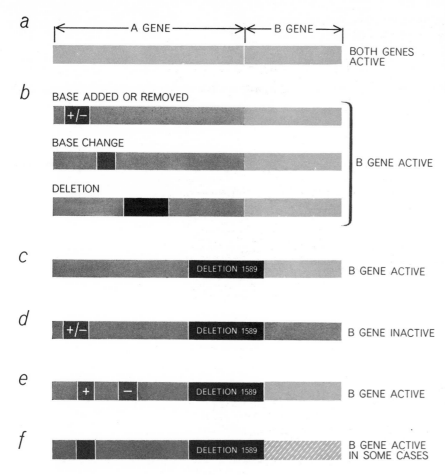

a A GENE — B GENE —
BOTH GENES ACTIVE

b BASE ADDED OR REMOVED
+/−
BASE CHANGE
DELETION
B GENE ACTIVE

c DELETION 1589
B GENE ACTIVE

d +/− DELETION 1589
B GENE INACTIVE

e + − DELETION 1589
B GENE ACTIVE

f DELETION 1589
B GENE ACTIVE IN SOME CASES

DELETION JOINING TWO GENES makes the B gene vulnerable to mutations in the A gene. The messages in two wild-type genes (*a*) are read independently, beginning at the left end of each gene. Regardless of the kind of mutation in A, the B gene remains active (*b*). The deletion known as 1589 inactivates the A gene but leaves the B gene active (*c*). But now alterations in the A gene will often inactivate the B gene, showing that the two genes have been joined in some way and are read as if they were a single gene (*d, e, f*).

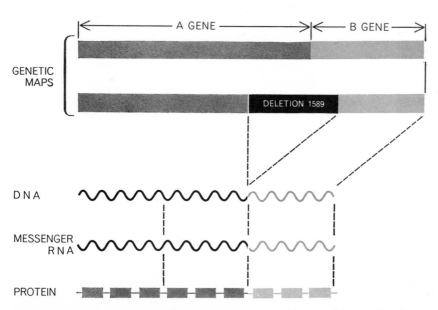

GENETIC MAPS   A GENE — B GENE —
DELETION 1589

DNA

MESSENGER RNA

PROTEIN

PROBABLE EFFECT OF DELETION 1589 is to produce a mixed protein with little or no A-gene activity but substantial B activity. Although the conventional genetic map shows the deletion as a gap, the DNA molecule itself is presumably continuous but shortened. In virus replication the genetic message in DNA is transcribed into a molecule of ribonucleic acid, called messenger RNA. This molecule carries the message to cellular particles known as ribosomes, where protein is synthesized, following instructions coded in the DNA.

gene combined with 1589. All the acridine mutations we tried knocked out the B function, whether they were plus or minus, but a pair of them (plus with minus) still allowed the B gene to work. On the other hand, in the case of the other type of mutation (which we believe is due to the change of a base and not to one being added or subtracted) about half of the mutations allowed the B gene to work and the other half did not. We surmise that the latter are nonsense mutations, and in fact Benzer has recently been using this test as a definition of nonsense.

Of course, we do not know exactly what is happening in biochemical terms. What we suspect is that the two genes, instead of producing two separate pieces of messenger RNA, produce a single piece, and that this in turn produces a protein with a long polypeptide chain, one end of which has the amino acid sequence of part of the presumed A protein and the other end of which has most of the B protein sequence—enough to give some B function to the combined molecule although the A function has been lost. The concept is illustrated schematically at the bottom of this page. Eventually it should be possible to check the prediction experimentally.

How the Message Is Read

So far all the evidence has fitted very well into the general idea that the message is read off in groups of three, starting at one end. We should have got the same results, however, if the message had been read off in groups of four, or indeed in groups of any larger size. To test this we put not just two of our acridine mutations into one gene but three of them. In particular we put in three with the same sign, such as plus with plus with plus, and we put them fairly close together. Taken either singly or in pairs, these mutations will destroy the function of the B gene. But when all three are placed in the same gene, the B function reappears. This is clearly a remarkable result: two blacks will not make a white but three will. Moreover, we have obtained the same result with several different combinations of this type and with several of the type minus with minus with minus.

The explanation, in terms of the ideas described here, is obvious. One plus will put the reading out of phase. A second plus will give the other wrong reading. But if the code is a triplet code, a third plus will bring the message back into phase again, and from then on to the end it will be read correctly. Only between the pluses will the message be wrong [*see illustration below*].

Notice that it does not matter if plus is really one extra base and minus is one fewer; the conclusions would be the same if they were the other way around. In fact, even if some of the plus mutations were indeed a single extra base, others might be two fewer bases; in other words, a plus might really be minus minus. Similarly, some of the minus mutations might actually be plus plus. Even so they would still fit into our scheme.

Although the most likely explanation is that the message is read three bases at a time, this is not completely certain. The reading could be in multiples of three. Suppose, for example, that the message is actually read six bases at a time. In that case the only change needed in our interpretation of the facts is to assume that all our mutants have been changed by an even number of bases. We have some weak experimental evidence that this is unlikely. For instance, we can combine the mutant 1589 (which joins the genes) with medium-sized deletions in the A cistron. Now, if deletions were random in length, we should expect about a third of them to allow the B function to be expressed if the message is indeed read three bases at a time, since those deletions that had lost an exact multiple of three bases should allow the B gene to function. By the same reasoning only a sixth of them should work (when combined with 1589) if the reading proceeds six at a time. Actually we find that the B gene is active in a little more than a third. Taking all the evidence together, however, we find that although three is the most likely coding unit, we cannot completely rule out multiples of three.

There is one other general conclusion we can draw about the genetic code. If we make a rough guess as to the actual

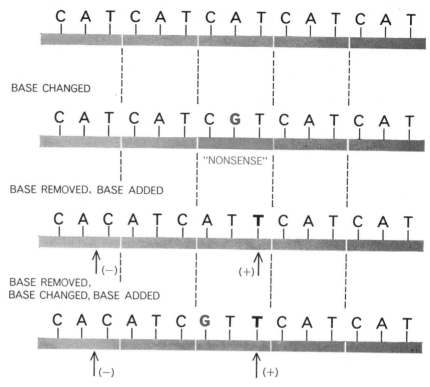

NONSENSE MUTATION is one creating a code group that evidently does not represent any of the 20 amino acids found in proteins. Thus it makes the gene inactive. In this hypothetical case a nonsense triplet, CGT, results when an A in the wild-type gene is changed to G. The nonsense triplet can be eliminated if the reading is shifted to put the G in a different triplet. This is done by recombining the inactive gene with one containing a minus-with-plus combination. In spite of three mutations, the resulting gene is active.

size of the B gene (by comparing it with another gene whose size is known approximately), we can estimate how many bases can lie between a plus with minus combination and still allow the B gene to function. Knowing also the frequency with which nonsense triplets are created in the misread region between the plus and minus, we can get some idea whether there are many such triplets or only a few. Our calculation suggests that nonsense triplets are not too common. It seems, in other words, that most of the 64 possible triplets, or codons, are not nonsense, and therefore they stand for amino acids. This implies that probably more than one codon can stand for one amino acid. In the jargon of the trade, a code in which this is true is "degenerate."

In summary, then, we have arrived at three general conclusions about the genetic code:

1. The message is read in nonover-

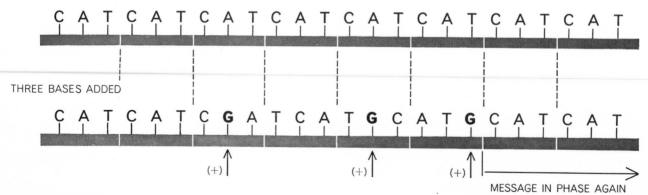

TRIPLE MUTATION in which three bases are added fairly close together spoils the genetic message over a short stretch of the gene but leaves the rest of the message unaffected. The same result can be achieved by the deletion of three neighboring bases.

lapping groups from a fixed point, probably from one end. The starting point determines that the message is read correctly into groups.

2. The message is read in groups of a fixed size that is probably three, although multiples of three are not completely ruled out.

3. There is very little nonsense in the code. Most triplets appear to allow the gene to function and therefore probably represent an amino acid. Thus in general more than one triplet will stand for each amino acid.

It is difficult to see how to get around our first conclusion, provided that the B gene really does code a polypeptide chain, as we have assumed. The second conclusion is also difficult to avoid. The third conclusion, however, is much more indirect and could be wrong.

Finally, we must ask what further evi

dence would really clinch the theory we have presented here. We are continuing to collect genetic data, but I doubt that this will make the story much more convincing. What we need is to obtain a protein, for example one produced by a double mutation of the form plus with minus, and then examine its amino acid sequence. According to conventional theory, because the gene is altered in only two places the amino acid sequences also should differ only in the two corresponding places. According to our theory it should be altered not only at these two places but also at all places in between. In other words, a whole string of amino acids should be changed. There is one protein, the lysozyme of the T4 phage, that is favorable for such an approach, and we hope that before long workers in the U.S. who have been studying phage lysozyme will confirm

our theory in this way.

The same experiment should also be useful for checking the particular code schemes worked out by Nirenberg and Matthaei and by Ochoa and his colleagues. The phage lysozyme made by the wild-type gene should differ over only a short stretch from that made by the plus-with-minus mutant. Over this stretch the amino acid sequence of the two lysozyme variants should correspond to the same sequence of bases on the DNA but should be read in different groups of three.

If this part of the amino acid sequence of both the wild-type and the altered lysozyme could be established, one could check whether or not the codons assigned to the various amino acids did indeed predict similar sequences for that part of the DNA between the base added and the base removed.

How Do Cells Differentiate?

C. H. WADDINGTON
September 1953

How is it that a single fertilized egg, a tiny blob of apparently formless protoplasm, can become a man—with eyes, ears, arms, legs, heart and brain? How from one generalized cell do we get the myriad of different specialized cells that make a human body? This puzzle, differentiation, is of course one of the great questions of biology. The process of differentiation has always seemed particularly mysterious because there are so few phenomena in the non-living world that might give us clues as to how it takes place. In the inanimate realm we do not often come across a situation in which parts of a single mass of material gradually diverge from one another and become completely distinct in character. Yet in all living things, except perhaps the viruses, differentiation is a basic law of nature.

For half a century biologists have been searching for the answers to this question by two main methods of attack: the modern sciences of embryology and genetics. On one hand they have been investigating directly by experiment how the embryo develops, and on the other they have studied how the genes control the processes of development. Let us start with the embryological approach.

The problem was bogged down for a long time in a debate between two theories first described by Aristotle in the fourth century B.C. One school argued that the newly fertilized egg contains all the organs of the animal in miniature, and that these preformed parts merely grow and enlarge to produce the adult. The second view, supported by Aristotle, was that the organs are formed only gradually by interaction among simple parts or constituents of the egg. Aristotle called this process "epigenesis," and epigenetics is still an appropriate name for the embryological approach to the problem.

When modern investigators began to experiment on animal embryos, they seemed to find support for both of the ancient theories. They cut an egg of a simple animal in half, or removed a part of the egg, and let the remaining part develop. In some types of animals, the fragment of egg developed into an adult with certain parts missing, which suggested that the egg contained preformed and rather rigidly localized rudiments of the adult organs. On the other hand, in other cases a complete and normal adult grew from the amputated egg. It was clear that epigenetic interactions must have taken place in these eggs.

The first experimenter to carry out a controlled study of such interactions was the German embryologist Hans Spemann, of the little Black Forest town of Freiburg. He operated on early embryos of the common newt. As the eggs of this animal develop, the first visible structure to appear is a small depression, called the blastopore, which eventually will become the main part of the intes-

PRELUDE TO DIFFERENTIATION is depicted by the early stages in the life of the marine animal Amphioxus. In the first drawing is the fertilized egg. In the second the egg has divided into two cells. In the third the two cells have divided into four. In the fourth

tine. Spemann cut out the region of the blastopore from one egg and grafted it into a second egg in a different position. There it not only continued to develop but influenced the cells surrounding it. They then became the main organs of the embryo, *e.g.*, the central nervous system and the rudiments of the spinal column.

Here was a clear-cut case of exactly the kind of interaction suggested by the epigenetic theory. Spemann called the blastopore region the "organizer" of the embryo. Soon organizers very similar to the one he had discovered in his salamander were found in many other classes of vertebrate animals. Such organizers were found to be responsible for the formation not only of the main embryonic axis but of many secondary organs which arise rather later: the ear, the nose, the lens of the eye, and so on. Sometimes the organizer region is relatively sharply demarcated and precisely localized. In other eggs it may be more diffuse, and the interactions may take place in a graded way, one end of the region being more powerful than the other. But in either case, the development of organs is determined by the interaction between some dominant part of the egg and its more receptive surroundings.

Now an organ has two aspects. It consists in the first place of specific types of tissue, which can come into being only by differentiation of the cells. But further than that, the tissues in an organ are arranged in certain relations to one another that give the organ its characteristic shape. Of course in the last analysis the shape of an organ presumably is an expression of the nature of the tissues composing it, but it is convenient to make a rough distinction between the formation of specific tissues and the

molding of these tissues into organic structures. Most recent work has concentrated on the first of these problems: the nature of the chemical processes by which the embryonic cells become differentiated.

It was natural to suppose at first that the organizer could act only as a living entity. But in 1932 it was discovered that an organizer is able to influence its surroundings even after it has been killed! This discovery was made simultaneously in the newt embryo by a group of German workers including Johannes Holtfreter (who is now at the University of Rochester) and in the chick embryo by myself at Cambridge University. It seemed that we might be on the verge of a critically important advance: that the influence of the organizer on development might be traced to some chemical substance which could be extracted from it. Several groups of workers tried to identify the substance, but their hopes were too optimistic and their picture of the situation too simple. The trouble is not in finding a substance that will act like the organizer in inducing cellular differentiation but that *too many* substances will do just that. Within a year or two Joseph Needham, Jean Brachet and I had proved conclusively that methylene blue, a substance which cannot by any stretch of the imagination be supposed to exist in the normal embryo, will bring about the formation of nerve tissue when injected into the embryo. It seems useless to look for some master substance in the cells which will give us the key to the understanding of differentiation. The place to study differentiation is in the reacting tissue, which actually carries out the differentiation. Only during a certain period of development is this tissue able to react to the organizer stimulus; it is then said

to be "competent." The way to a deeper insight into the nature of development is through a fuller understanding of competence.

It is here that the hereditary genes come into the picture. In all likelihood the competence of the cell for differentiation is a complex state of affairs, involving many different chemical systems. We know that there are many genes in the nucleus of a cell and that each gene controls the formation of one or more of the substances produced as the cell develops. Thus the set of gene-controlled processes must be the system of reactions involved in the state of competence.

The most obvious question to ask is: What is the nature of each individual gene reaction? But, before considering that, there is another point which may be almost as important and is perhaps easier to approach. We are dealing with a complex system of reactions, one starting from each gene, and finishing up with all the numerous constituents of an adult tissue. Do any general features characterize the system as a whole?

There is one important general feature. An adult animal consists of a number of different organs and tissues which are sharply bounded off from one another. The liver does not merge gradually into the pancreas and that into some other organ. Cells develop into one type or the other; they do not form graded intermediates. Further, there is a strong tendency for these normal end-products to be produced even if conditions during development have been somewhat abnormal. We can, for instance, cut pieces out of the embryo or cause other experimental alterations, and the embryo will still produce a normal adult.

This means that development must be

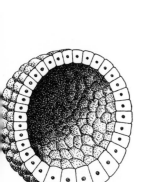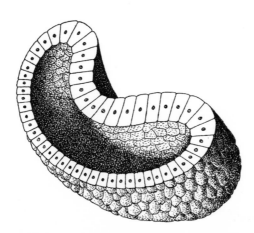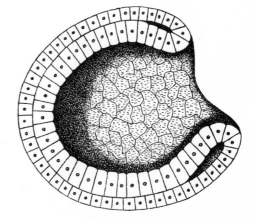

drawing, after more divisions, the cells are marshaled into a hollow ball called the blastula. In the fifth one side of the blastula has begun to turn inward. In the sixth the cells form a cup called the gastrula. The hole at the right of the gastrula is the blastopore.

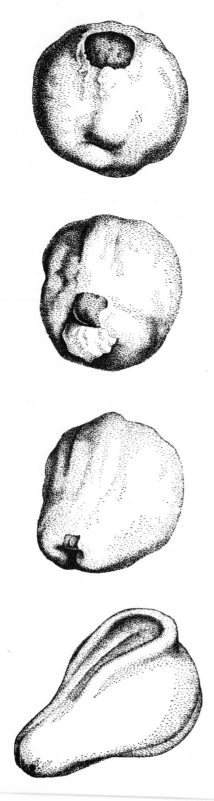

ORGANIZER is demonstrated by grafting a piece of the blastopore region from one newt's embryo into another. In the first drawing the original blastopore is at the bottom; the graft is at the dark spot at the top. In the second and third drawings the graft rolls into the interior of the embryo. In the fourth drawing the horseshoe-shaped structure is the rudiment of the central nervous system induced by the graft. At the bottom right is the nervous system of the original embryo.

organized into a number of distinct systems. One system of processes will bring about the development of, say, the nervous tissue. A different system will produce liver or kidney or some other tissue of the body. Moreover, each system must be stabilized in some way so that it gives its normal end-product even if it has to go by an unusual way to get there.

This shows us the kinds of facts we have to account for. One of the great tasks for embryology in the immediate future is to explore the ways in which systems with properties of this kind can arise. There are several different ways by which we could seek to account for the fact that development is channeled into separate, distinct pathways. For instance, if the product of the reaction itself makes the reaction go faster—that is to say, if the processes are autocatalytic—it is easy to see that once a process has begun to form a particular product, that product will encourage the process to go still further in the same direction, and thus exclude any other possible product. Similarly, if the product of one reaction inhibits the progress of some other reaction, then as soon as the first process gets under way it will tend to prevent the second from occurring. Common sense is enough to offer certain general suggestions of this kind, but we badly need a thorough theoretical study of the various conceivable types of interaction between processes. Beyond that, we need an experimental analysis of developmental processes, aimed at discovering which of the theoretical possibilities are realized in practice.

For the self-regulating feature of the embryo's development, we can find models in the field of engineering: automatic ships' compasses, automatic pilots and other feedback mechanisms for which the name of cybernetics has recently become fashionable. In cell differentiation we must be dealing with chemical cybernetic systems. The properties of biological enzymes should make it possible for such systems to be built up in several different ways, but we still know remarkably little about them. Very probably much of the work required to understand these systems will be done on systems of isolated chemical substances which may at first sight seem to have little or nothing to do with embryology.

I have found it helpful to make a mechanical picture of the set of differentiation systems, each of which leads to one definite end-result and is balanced internally by some sort of cybernetic mechanism. Let us imagine the cells as a group of balls perched on the top of a slope. On this slope we may suppose there is a radiating system of valleys. As each ball rolls down, it must pass into one valley or another. Once it has started down a given valley, its fate (the end-product it will become) is determined, for it will be very unlikely to roll over the intervening hill into another valley, and even if some abnormal condition temporarily pushes it part way up the bank, it will tend, like a bobsled, to slide back to the bottom of its chute and continue its normal course. I have used the name "epigenetic landscape" for this picture of the developing system.

Our other principal task is a detailed study of the chemical processes that go on in a cell as it moves from its embryonic beginnings to its final differentiated state. When it was discovered that many substances could act like the organizer to induce differentiations, most people argued that they must be acting in a secondary way. Suppose that all the cells of the embryo contain some substance which can induce the formation of, for instance, nervous tissue. Suppose further that in most cases this substance is concealed or inactivated, but that it can be liberated by certain types of cell metabolism. Then one would expect that the organizer gets its peculiar properties from its specific metabolism. Following this line of thought, several groups of investigators have measured the metabolism of the organizer against that of other regions of the egg. They have duly found that the organizer has certain special metabolic characteristics, and it is quite clear that these are essentially involved in its developmental activity. For instance, in the eggs of the sea urchin the fundamental developmental system consists of two gradients of activity, one of which is most powerful at the upper end of the egg, the other at the lower end. The thing that varies along these gradients is the intensity of processes of cellular metabolism, and on these variations depends the differentiation of the parts of the egg.

Eggs and embryos are, of course, exceedingly small things, and the technical difficulty of studying the metabolism of parts of the egg is very large indeed. Some subtle types of supersensitive apparatus have been worked out which enable one to operate with minute quantities of material. One of the most refined is the well-known Cartesian diver. This old toy, which apparently has nothing to do with the French philosopher Descartes, after whom it is named, is a tiny vessel of thin glass with an open neck. In this neck a drop of oil is placed and the whole thing is immersed in a flask of water. As the diver sinks below the water surface, the pressure of water from above forces down the oil drop, compresses the air in the vessel into a smaller volume and so makes the glass bubble sink further. It can be made to float at a predetermined level, however, by adjusting the atmospheric pressure on the surface of the water in the flask. If now we have inside the stabilized diver a small piece of tissue which is using up oxygen or giving out carbon dioxide, this will alter the volume of the gas inside the diver and thus affect its buoyancy. This change can be measured by altering the atmospheric pressure until the diver just floats at its original level. The apparatus provides an exceedingly sensitive method of measuring minute changes in gas volume; with it one can measure respirations which involve as little as one millionth of a cubic centimeter of gas.

With such instruments we have acquired in the last few years a large amount of information about the respiration of various parts of the egg and other aspects of metabolism which are technically easy to measure. Unfortunately these processes are not always the kinds that seem most likely to lead to an understanding of cell differentiation. Differentiated cells probably are distinguished from one another principally by their protein constituents. We still know exceedingly little about how proteins are formed, and biochemical investigation of protein production in embryos has not yet made much progress.

Like so many projects in biology, this investigation may turn largely on finding a suitable experimental material. The whole of embryology suffers at present from operating too much in terms of complex entities. Instead of considering the development of nervous tissue or liver tissue, each of which contains many substances, we must be able to investigate the development of some single substance. Again, instead of thinking in terms of transplanting lumps of material from one part of the embryo to the other, we shall have to start experimenting on the constituents of a single cell. We have as yet no good material in which we can follow quantitatively the synthesis of some specific protein and investigate the effect of various conditions on this process.

The genetic study of development is not open to this reproach. In genetics we can easily study one kind of unit involved in development, namely the gene. One of the most important things that has been going on in genetics recently is the attempt to connect individual genes with the specific single substances for whose production they are responsible. In microorganisms such as yeasts or fungi, which have a very simple body and a somewhat simpler biochemical system than more complicated animals, a change in a single gene often produces an obvious alteration in only one chemical constituent. Frequently this constituent is an enzyme, that is to say, one of the biological catalysts on which the functioning of the cell depends. It is probable, indeed, that all genes exert their influence through enzymes, and data from microorganisms suggest that each gene has an effect on a particular enzyme. If this is so, it would be logical to suppose that the gene manufactures the enzyme. It is not by any means certain that the matter is really as simple as all that. There may be several steps between the gene and the enzyme, in which case a number of different substances would be involved. We should then be dealing with a chemical system not very different from the one discussed in connection with the competence of embryonic tissues.

From the point of view of cell differentiation, however, this work in microbiology is not so helpful as one might think. The microorganisms are the very creatures that show the least amount of differentiation. Genes exercise their control, it is generally believed, by interacting in different ways with different regions of the cytoplasm in the egg. In microorganisms there is little or no specialization of different regions of cytoplasm, so we cannot hope to get from them any direct information about this fundamental relationship between genes and cytoplasm.

We have, however, found some valuable indirect clues. It has been known for some time that a strain of yeast growing in a sugar solution will often develop the ability to ferment that type of sugar although it could not do so originally. It forms what is known as an adaptive enzyme for doing so. Biochemists and geneticists have learned that in general a strain of yeast can form an adaptive enzyme to a particular sugar

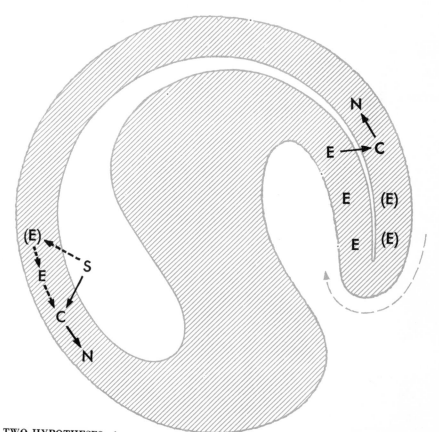

TWO HYPOTHESES of organizer action are illustrated by this cross section of a newt's embryo. At the right is the organizer region. Tissue containing an inducing substance in an inactive form labeled (E) moves into the interior of the embryo. There (E) becomes an active form E, which reacts with the competent tissue C and causes it to become the nervous tissue N. At the left is a diagram showing how a chemical substance S might produce nervous tissue either directly by acting on C or indirectly by causing (E) to be converted into E.

only if it has a hereditary capacity to do so. In other words, the forming of an adaptive enzyme depends on the presence of the appropriate gene. This gene must, however, be activated by the presence of the sugar. The situation is an extraordinary parallel to what we imagine must happen when specific genes are activated in certain cytoplasmic regions of the egg. Since each adaptive enzyme is a specific protein, we have here an opportunity to study quantitatively the physical and chemical factors involved in protein synthesis. Sir Cyril Hinshelwood at Oxford University, Sol Spiegelman at the University of Illinois, Jacques Monod in Paris and others are already pursuing this line of inquiry.

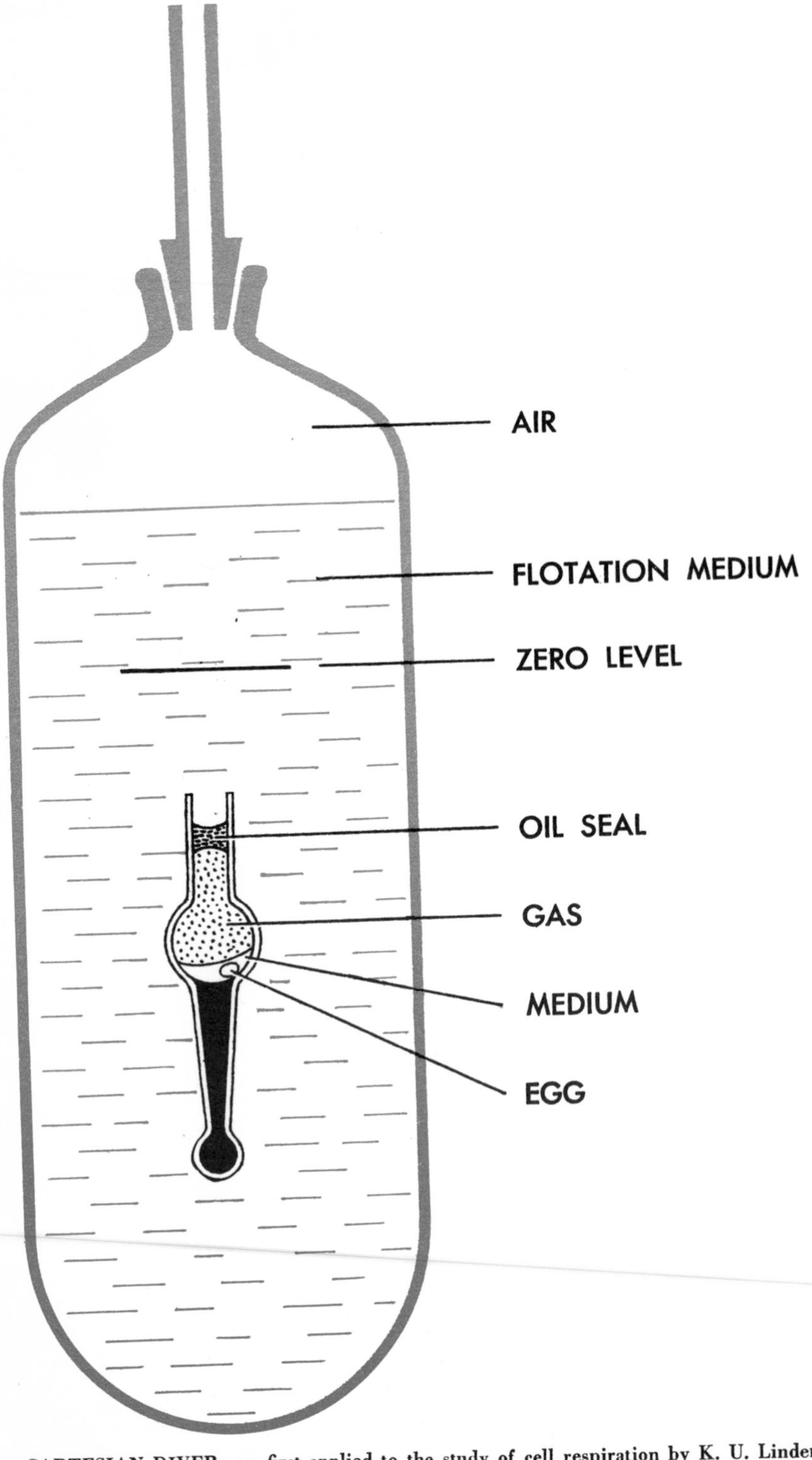

From this protein study has come the stimulating suggestion that between the gene and the final enzyme there may be intermediates which, once formed, can reproduce themselves, for some time at least, even if the gene that produced them is removed. Several authors recently have come to the conclusion, some rather hastily, that they had evidence for the existence of such substances, and they have given them a variety of names—plasmagenes, cytogenes and so on. In several cases further investigation showed either that the evidence was not as good as had been thought or that the suggested plasmagenes were actually foreign virus particles or something of a similar nature. In a certain number of cases, however, there is fairly convincing evidence for the existence of plasmagene-like bodies. One of the best known is found in the little Paramecium. In this single-celled organism the cell develops certain substances which can be recognized by the fact that they stimulate the production of specific antibodies when they are injected into rabbits. The development of each substance is controlled by a corresponding plasmagene. The plasmagenes again are under the control of nuclear genes, and the nucleus itself is influenced by the condition of the cytoplasm of the cell. The cytoplasmic state can be altered by growing the animals at different temperatures or by changing their environment in other ways. Each cytoplasmic condition activates a certain gene to manufacture its corresponding plasmagene, and that in turn produces the final cell constituent.

It seems likely that something similar goes on in embryonic development. The different regions of the egg can be supposed to activate particular groups of genes in the nuclei which enter them; the activated genes then control the differentiation of cells. The first step in this will be the production of immediate gene products which may or may not be endowed with the power of self-reproduction, like plasmagenes. The Belgian embryologist Brachet has argued that certain minute particles which can be discovered in cells, the so-called microsomes, are the actual plasmagenes. These particles, just barely visible under ordinary microscopes, can be separated from the rest of the cell by ultracentrifugation. Brachet supposes that they are the immediate agents of protein syn-

AIR

FLOTATION MEDIUM

ZERO LEVEL

OIL SEAL

GAS

MEDIUM

EGG

CARTESIAN DIVER was first applied to the study of cell respiration by K. U. Linderstrom-Lang at the Carlsberg Laboratories in Copenhagen. Minute quantities of gas absorbed or given off by egg in vessel affect the buoyancy of the diver in the flotation medium.

thesis in the cytoplasm, operating under the ultimate control of the nuclear genes. There is as yet no absolutely convincing proof of this. We badly need to develop techniques for investigating more thoroughly the relation between these microsomes and the nucleus, for instance by isolating the microsomes from one cell and transplanting them into another whose development would normally be different.

The gene-plasmagene and gene-microsome story is the place at which the two sciences of genetics and embryology are coming together most closely. It also introduces the last pair of actors in our account. These are the two nucleic acids, usually known as DNA (desoxyribonucleic acid) and RNA (ribonucleic acid). They are always present in those parts of the cell most deeply involved in the production of new substances, and it seems most probable that nucleic acid of one kind or the other is essential for the production of any protein. There seems to be no doubt that DNA, a constituent of the chromosomes that house the genes, must be in some way closely connected with the genes themselves, which contain protein. RNA always occurs in high concentration in any region of cytoplasm in which rapid synthesis of proteins is proceeding. The microsomes, for instance, contain large quantities of RNA but little or no DNA. According to one present theory, the DNA-containing chromosomes manufacture RNA, which passes out of the nucleus into the cytoplasm and there becomes attached to the microsomes and takes part in the synthesis of the cellular proteins.

Here again we are standing on the challenging frontier of unexplored territory. We may flatter ourselves that we are converging on the secret of differentiation from all sides, but the advances we have made so far do more to reveal the extent of the area still to be explored than to provide satisfying explanations. The older surgical methods of experimental embryology and the general genetical studies have given us some clues as to the over-all nature of the system we are dealing with. But they emphasize, on the one hand, the need for developing a broad picture of it and, on the other, the importance of getting down to concrete chemical detail. Thus every part of the advancing front of knowledge must look for support to every other, and the order of the day all along the line must be to press on.

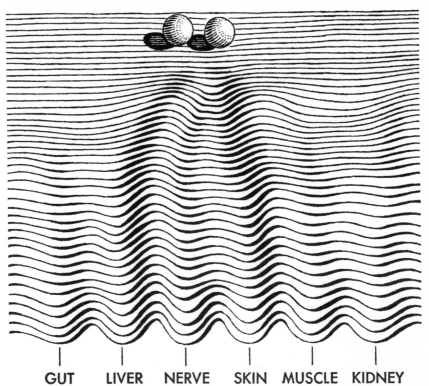

GUT   LIVER   NERVE   SKIN   MUSCLE   KIDNEY

EPIGENETIC LANDSCAPE is an abstract representation of differentiation. The balls roll down the slope into one or another valley leading to a specialized organ of the adult.

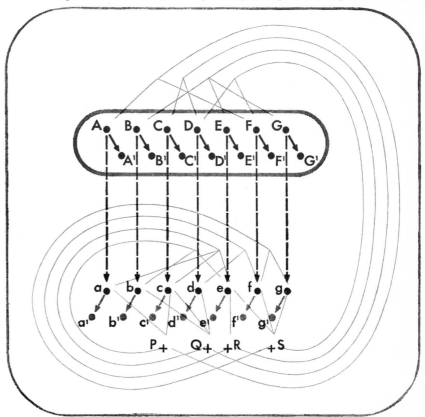

DEVELOPMENTAL SYSTEM within the cell must be an elaborate network of chemical interactions. The genes in the nucleus (A, B, C, etc.) not only form replicas of themselves (A^1, B^1, C^1, etc.) for the next division of the cell but also must produce "immediate gene products" (a, b, c, etc.). These may or may not be "plasmagenes," able to form duplicates of themselves (a^1, b^1, c^1, etc.). They must interact, however, to produce the cell proteins (P, Q, R, etc.). These in turn condition the activities of both the gene products and the genes.

The Skin

WILLIAM MONTAGNA
February 1965

As a naked animal who is apparently becoming progressively more hairless as his evolution advances, man is extraordinarily dependent on the properties of his skin. Skin is a remarkable organ—the largest and by far the most versatile of the body. It is an effective shield against many forms of physical and chemical attack. It holds in the body's fluids and maintains its integrity by keeping out foreign substances and microorganisms. It acts to ward off the harsh ultraviolet rays of the sun. It incorporates mechanisms that cool the body when it is warm and retard the loss of heat when it is cold. It plays a major role in regulating blood pressure and directing the flow of blood. It embodies the sense of touch. It is the principal organ of sexual attraction. It identifies each individual, by shaping the facial and bodily contours as well as by distinctive markings such as fingerprints. The skin crowns all these properties with the ability to regenerate itself and thereby heal wounds. As A. E. Needham of the University of Oxford has remarked, scratches and other minor wounds are so common (probably, at a conservative estimate, averaging one a week per person) that few human beings would survive very long if it were not for the skin's property of self-repair.

We shall survey in this article the highlights of what has been learned about man's skin: its anatomical properties, functions and evolution. The subject has many aspects, because skin is a complex tissue that forms a great variety of structures. In mammals the same tissue that produces the epidermis also differentiates into hair, spines, nails, claws, hooves, scales and horns; in birds it produces feathers, the beak, scales and claws; in reptiles it gives rise to scales, spines and claws. In man the glands of the skin deserve particular attention, because they perform several vital roles.

The skin is composed of two principal layers: (1) the underlying dermis, a thick, fibrous tissue that forms its main bulk, and (2) the epidermis, the thin surface coat, which consists of four or five sheets of cells veneered on one another. The top layer of the epidermis is made up of flattened, dead cells—necessarily dead, because living cells cannot survive exposure to air or water. It is this mantle of dead tissue, called the horny layer, that serves as the principal shield of the body. Thin, flexible and transparent, it is nevertheless a sturdy structure, with its cells held together by "attachment plaques." In protected areas of the body this layer is smooth and very supple; on surfaces that get a good deal of wear, such as the palms of the hands, it is thicker and more rugged.

If you scratch your skin with your fingernails, you will scrape off tiny flakes of the dead surface tissue. The skin of the whole body is continually exfoliated by the wear and tear of rubbing and exposure to the environment. The deeper layers of the epidermis steadily replenish the horny layer, however, by moving up more cells. As the cells ascend toward the surface, they die by degrees as they produce keratin, the fibrous protein that constitutes the bulk of the dead surface structures, not only of the skin proper but also of the hair, nails and other skin growths. Death is the goal of every epidermal cell, and it is achieved in an orderly manner. Like the leaves of autumn, the epidermal cells, having lived for their season, eventually dry out and peel off.

The horny layer they form is a relatively effective barrier against the entry of most foreign substances, but its effectiveness is not complete. Among some of the noxious substances it fails to keep out are metallic nickel and the oleoresins of poison ivy. The skin is so sensitive to nickel that even the comparatively few molecules that are rubbed off on contact may produce a violent reaction with the living tissues if the nickel penetrates the epidermis. The skin's sensitivity to an encounter with the leaves of poison ivy, or even the smoke from its burning leaves, is well known. A thicker horny layer might have made man impervious to all invasions, as it has the elephant, but man would then have had to pay the price of a loss of suppleness and agility. The human skin, all things considered, has achieved a remarkably effective compromise.

To continue with our examination of the skin's surface, we observe that, like a very detailed map, it is heavily marked with topographical features: furrows, ridges, pores, hair follicles, pebbled areas and so on. Each area of the body has its own characteristic topography. Some of the markings have obvious general usefulness. The hands and feet need rough surfaces; if they were perfectly smooth, they could not get a good grip. Some features are clearly the result of long habit in the exercise of certain muscles that pull on the skin; among these are the wrinkles formed by smiling and by knitting the brow. By and large, however, most of the patterns in the skin are strictly genetic. Largely determined by the orientation of the fibers in the dermis and by other anatomical factors, they are peculiar to each individual and therefore serve as a means of personal identification.

Look at the skin of your palm or a finger under a magnifying lens. Its ridges, forming whorls, loops and arch-

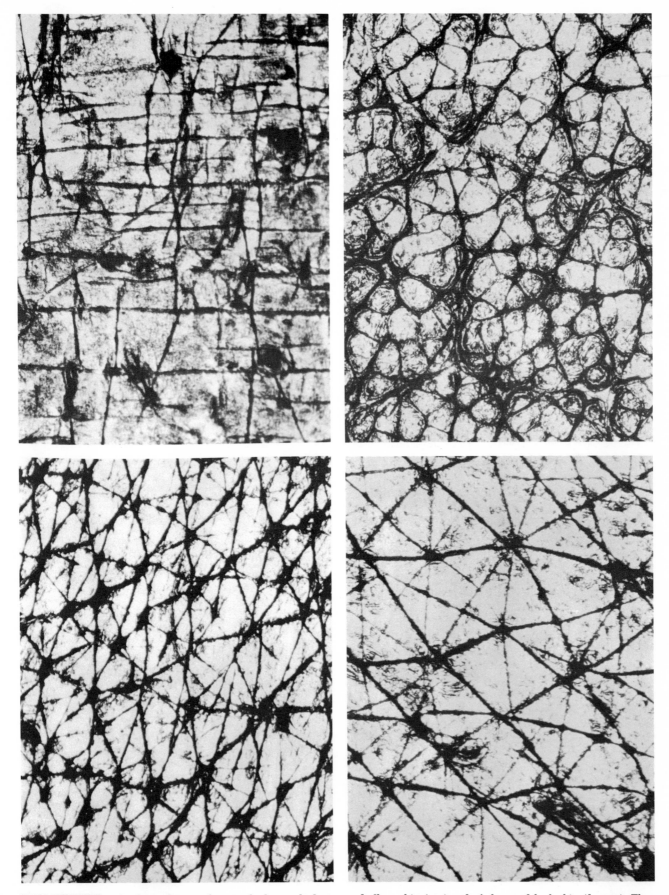

SKIN TEXTURE varies from place to place on the human body, as is evidenced by varying patterns of lines and pores. From left to right, the four illustrations show impressions in plastic of forehead and elbow skin (*top*) and of chest and back skin (*bottom*). The work of H. D. Chim and R. L. Dobson at the University of Oregon Medical School, the impressions are here enlarged 75 diameters.

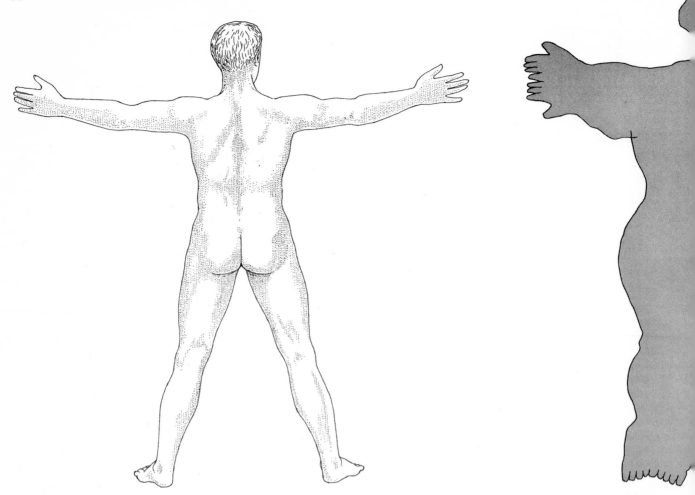

TOTAL SURFACE AREA of the skin, which seems surprisingly large in contrast to the outline of a human figure (*left*), is calcu- lated by adding the areas of a series of cylinders constructed from an average of leg, arm and torso circumferences. A man six feet

es, make up specific pattern designs, called dermatoglyphics. No two individuals, not even identical twins, have exactly the same dermatoglyphics. The patterns are formed before birth; they are laid down in the fetus during the third and fourth months of development. Their congenital origin shows itself in certain graphic ways. For example, women's fingerprints are distinctly different from men's: women have fewer whorls and more arches. In an individual the dermatoglyphics of the right hand show major differences from those of the left, which suggests that handedness may be established during the third or fourth month of fetal life. There are even indications that unusual skin markings may be associated with congenital brain abnormalities, such as mental deficiency and epilepsy [*see bottom illustration on page 102*]. Dermatoglyphic peculiarities have shown up consistently in such individuals; this implies that the factors responsible for the brain abnormalities may have operated during the third and

fourth fetal months, when the skin patterns were being formed.

The development of skin begins very early in the human embryo. The epidermal cells soon differentiate further into the skin's suborgans: hair follicles, nails, sebaceous glands and sweat glands. At about three months, for example, hair follicles start to form on the head, the part of the body that develops first, and as the fetus grows the trunk and limbs also acquire hair follicles. By the time the infant is born it has as many hairs or rudiments of hairs on its body as it will ever have. The common notion that hair does not begin to form on some parts of the body until one matures (for instance, that a boy's cheeks are hairless until he approaches the age of shaving) is incorrect. The hairs are there all the time, although they may not grow noticeably before puberty. Moreover, there is no substantial difference between men and women with respect to the number of hair follicles: a woman has about as many hairs on her body as a man, but

many of them are so small and colorless that they escape notice. Indeed, the same observation holds for the comparison between man and his furrier relatives—the gorilla, the orangutan and the chimpanzee. Man has about the same number of hair follicles as these animals; the difference is simply that most of his are obsolescent and fail to grow much.

Man's skin follows a characteristic life cycle. In infancy and early childhood it is dry, soft, velvety, clear and apparently almost hairless. Because it is so free of blemishes and presumably because it suggests the clear, soft skin of a sexually attractive young woman, baby skin has come to be regarded as the epitome of skin beauty. With adolescence comes an enlargement of the hair follicles and a more active growth of the hair. The sweat glands and sebaceous glands (which produce a fatty secretion) go from a nearly dormant state to full activity. Physiologically speaking, the skin arrives at full bloom with puberty. Its ensuing history, however, is not completely happy, partly

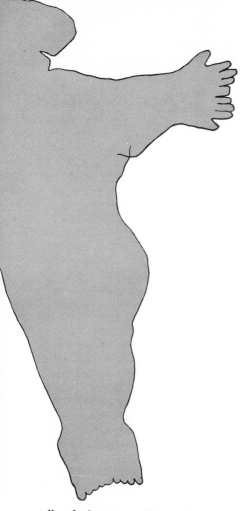

tall and of average weight and body build has about 3,000 square inches of skin area.

because its owner proceeds to subject it to daily abuses.

In the effort to enhance its attractiveness, men and women submit their skin to systematic stretching, scraping, gouging, soaking and burning. In our fastidious society the skin is treated with daily baths, which remove its natural emollients and essential substances. It is doused with powders, poultices, oils and other chemical and physical treatments that may cause varying degrees of irritation. To give it a "healthy" tan, the skin is ritualistically exposed to excessive and injurious doses of sunlight and wind.

That the skin survives these daily torments is a remarkable tribute to its toughness. But age and decades of indignities do, of course, take their toll. Man's most obvious sign of age is the dry, wrinkled, flaccid skin that marks his late years. It is then a tired organ—a relic of what it was in its youth.

From place to place on the body the skin is a study in contrasts. On the eyebrows it is thick, coarse and hairy; on the eyelids, thin and hairless. On the red border of the lips it is completely hairless; on the upper lip, chin and jowl of a man, so hairy that bristles are visible within a few hours after shaving. On the nose, the cheeks and the forehead the skin is oily; on the jowls, dry and greaseless. The rest of the body shows contrasts as striking as those on the face. The skin areas of the chest, the pubic region, the scalp, the abdomen and the soles of the feet are as different from one another, structurally and functionally, as if they belonged to different animals.

A brief examination of a few specific properties of the skin will serve to illustrate how exquisitely it is adapted to its functions. As a wrapping that must accommodate itself to changes in the shape and size of the body, the skin is highly elastic. Pull the skin and it will snap back. Cut out a piece and the detached piece will contract, whereas the skin around the wound will widen the cut by elastically pulling away from it. During pregnancy the skin of the lower trunk of a woman is highly stretched. Afterward, when her body returns to its normal size, the skin makes heroic efforts to regain its former area, but the stretching may leave permanent scars—the light streaks in the skin that commonly appear on the abdomen of a woman who has borne children. Similar streaks appear on the body of a person who has gone through repeated bouts of gaining weight and reducing. Such bouts sometimes leave the fatigued skin sagging in pendulous folds that refuse to shrink back.

Another conspicuous property of the skin is its pigmentation. Evenly scattered deep in the epidermis are the melanocytes, cells that produce the dark pigment melanin. Spider-shaped, with long tentacle-like processes, these cells inject granules of melanin into the surrounding epidermal cells, where the pigment forms a protective awning over each cell nucleus on the side toward the skin surface. The prime function of the pigment is to shield the cells by absorbing the ultraviolet rays of the sun. All human beings, regardless of race, have about the same number of melanocytes; the darker races are distinguished from the lighter ones only by the fact that their melanocytes manufacture more pigment. This protective capacity has evolved in the tropical peoples of the world as an asset with high survival value.

Dense webs of blood vessels course through the skin all over the body.

They transport through the skin a great deal more blood than is needed to nourish the skin itself; this immense circulation performs two important functions for the entire body. First, it acts as a cooling system. The skin's sweat glands pour water onto the skin's surface, and the evaporation of the water cools the blood circulating through the skin. When the outside environment is warm or the body is engaged in strenuous exercise, the blood vessels assist the cooling process by relaxing and allowing a maximum flow of blood through the skin, which accounts for the flushed appearance of the skin at such times. On the other hand, when the environment is cold, the vessels contract rapidly and greatly reduce the blood flow in the skin, thus conserving the internal body heat.

Second, the skin's circulation serves to help regulate the blood pressure. The blood vessels in the skin have sphincter-like passages that can shut off the flow through the capillaries and thereby cause the blood to bypass them so that it flows directly from the small arteries into the veins. This mechanism for speeding the flow acts like a safety valve when the blood pressure rises to a dangerous level.

The skin's extraordinary network of blood vessels is matched by an equally massive network of nerves. Much of this nervous system is concerned with controlling the glands, blood vessels and other organs in the skin. There is also a vast complex of sensory nerve endings. These are particularly prominent in the most naked surfaces of the body: the fingers, palms, soles, lips and even the cornea of the eye, which has no blood vessels. These specialized nerves are sensitive to tactile and thermal stimuli. Without them the human body would be almost as out of touch with the outside world as it would be if it lacked the major sense organs.

The Hair

Hairs are products of the skin that man shares with all the rest of the mammalian order. In many ways hair is a paradoxical growth. For other mammals it serves a wide variety of useful functions, but man is able to dispense with most of them. In fact, in man hair has become largely an ornamental appendage; it seems to survive mainly as a means of sexual attraction.

The most obvious function of a heavy coat of hair for mammals in the natural state is protective insulation against the weather and other hazards of the environment. This is as true in a warm climate as in a cold one: the fur-covered animals of the Tropics are insulated by their hair against the strong sun and heat. Hair, however, is only one of the devices that have evolved among mammals for this purpose. The whale, a completely naked mammal, is adapted to living in polar waters by a thick layer of insulating blubber, capped by a heavy skin with a thick, horny layer. Man's nakedness and his thin skin plain-

ly indicate that he originated in a tropical or temperate environment. His spread into the colder regions of the earth was made possible only by his development of artificial clothing and shelter.

A few special protective functions of hair remain important to the human body. The hairs inside the nostrils slow incoming air currents, trap dust particles, keep out insects and prevent the nasal mucus from pouring down over the lips. The hairs in the outer ear and

around the anogenital orifices act as barriers against the entry of foreign matter and small invaders such as insects. The bushy eyebrows and the eyelashes help to shield the vulnerable eyeballs.

Man also retains some use of the sensory function of hair. Most hair follicles in a mammal's skin have a collar of sensory nerves around them, and the animal therefore senses any slight movement of the hair due to contact with an object. The nerve supply is par-

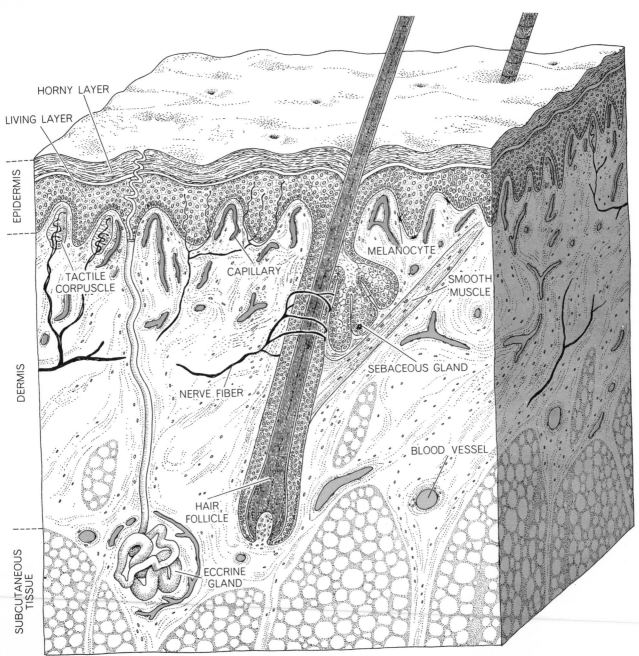

ZONES OF THE SKIN are displayed in an idealized section. The underlying dermis, the thickest part of the organ, is supported by a fat-rich subcutaneous stratum. Intermingled with the cells of the dermis are fine blood vessels (color), tactile and other nerves, the smooth muscles that raise the hair when contracted, and a variety of specialized glands. Above the dermis are the twin levels of the epidermis: a lower zone of living cells capped by a horny layer of dead cells filled with the fibrous protein keratin. Melanocytes, the pigment organs that produce the granules responsible for varying skin colors, lie at the base of the epidermis.

ticularly rich around hair follicles in
certain sensitive regions of the body,
among them the face, the anogenital
areas and certain special areas that
are important to a given animal's activities. A squirrel, for instance, is sen-
sitized in this way on the surface of
the abdomen, so that it feels its way
with its abdominal hairs as it runs along
the bark of a tree. Lemurs, which use
their hands to move about in trees, have
patches of sensory hairs on the inner
surface of their wrists. Nearly all mammals have long, sensitive vibrissae, or
whiskers, around the muzzle; these
hairs communicate their motion directly to nerves and indirectly through
pressure on blood-filled sacs around the
follicles. The whiskers are particularly
well developed in nocturnal animals,
and they attain large size in seals and
walruses. Man, although he lacks the
blood-filled sacs around the follicles,
possesses nerve endings around many
of his hair follicles, particularly those
that surround the mouth.

Obviously, aside from a few special
functions such as the screening of external passages, hair is not really essential to man. It is not so easy to see,
however, what positive advantages may
have been responsible for his evolution
toward nakedness, as compared with
other primates. It has been suggested
that lack of a heavy fur may have had
some adaptive value for running and
hunting in the open savannas, but this
is conjectural. At all events, there is no
doubt that, although man still has as
many hair follicles as his primate cousins, his hair growth is gradually declining, and one of the most obvious indications of this is the increasing preva-
lence of baldness.

Hair Growth

The follicle that produces a hair is
a tube that extends all the way through
the skin and widens into a bulb—the
hair root—at its deep end. When the
hair has attained its characteristic
length, it stops growing (except on the
scalp, where the hair may grow very
long if it is not cut). Having reached its
limit, the hair forms a clublike base and
puts out rootlets that anchor it to the
surrounding follicle. The follicle shrinks
and goes into a resting period. After a
time it forms the germ of a new hair,
which then works its way toward the
surface, loosening the old hair and causing it to be shed. Thus hair growth is a
matter of alternate growing and resting
periods, with new hairs arising period-

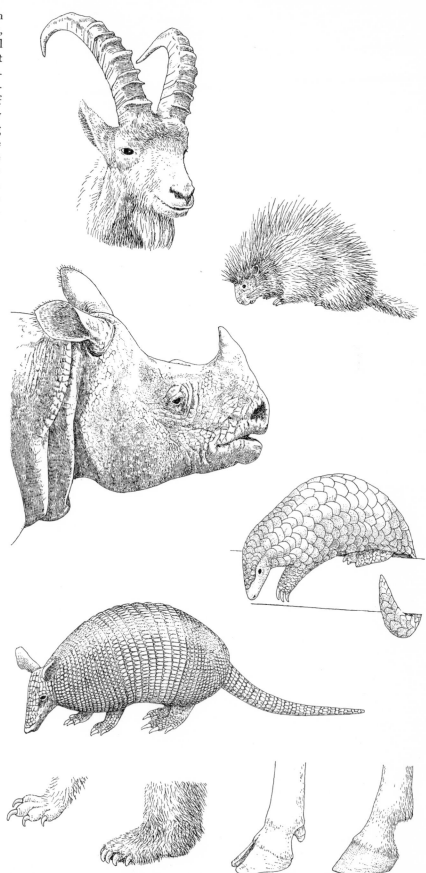

THE VERSATILE SKIN gives rise to a wide variety of superficial structures; among the
mammals these include, from top to bottom, the bold horns of the ibex, the quills of the por-
cupine, the hairy "horn" of the rhinoceros, the scales of the pangolin and the armadillo, and
various claws and hooves. Like all of these, man's hair and nails are special skin structures.

INDIVIDUALITY OF FINGERPRINTS is one of the best-known characteristics of the skin. These thumbprints can be readily told apart, although they are those of identical twins. The same individual quality exists on any skin surface, but the strong pattern of ridges and grooves found on the ventral surfaces of hands and feet are the most easily identified.

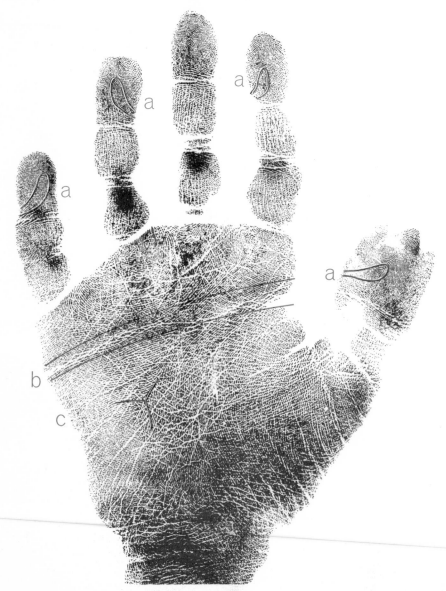

GENETIC BASIS of skin patterns is shown by the existence of similar patterns among un-related individuals with similar chromosomal abnormalities. None of the patterns outlined (*color*) on this palm print of a mongoloid imbecile is abnormal, yet the simultaneous pres-ence of these configurations is a very rare event among normal people. These patterns are ulnar loops on the digits (*a*), the simian crease (*b*) and an off-center axial triradius (*c*). The palm print was made by Irene A. Uchida of the Children's Hospital in Winnipeg, Canada.

ically to displace the old. In many ani-mals this is a seasonal process; the ani-mal sheds nearly all its hair at one time, starting a completely new crop.

The pelt of such an animal makes a good fur piece only if it is taken during the resting period, when the clubbed hairs are firmly attached to the follicles and will remain so after the skin is tanned. In man and some other mam-mals the pattern of growth and shedding is different: in any given area there are always some follicles growing and some resting, so that normally there is no wholesale shedding and the total hair growth remains constant in all seasons of the year.

Human hair grows at the rate of about a third of a millimeter per day. The follicle is at an angle to the skin surface, hence the emerging hair lies over on the skin except when certain muscle fibers attached to the follicle pull on it and cause the hair to stand erect. The same muscle action also forms the mounds known as goose pimples. Thus proverbial references to goose pimples and hair standing on end in moments of fright have a real basis; it will happen when the hormones released by the emotion activate the muscles of the hair follicles.

The individual hairs of man may be round (which causes the hair to be straight), alternately round and oval (which makes the hair wavy) or ribbon-shaped (which makes it kinky). The color of the hair depends on the amount and distribution of melanin in it and on the hair's surface structure, which af-fects the reflection of light. A study of how hair grows helps to explain some of the superstitions about it. One of these is the notion that a traumatic experience may turn the hair gray or white over-night. The idea is incorrect, but it has this much basis: a shock may cause some shedding of fine, normally pig-mented hairs, thereby exposing to great-er prominence the coarser graying hairs, which were already present and are more resistant to stress.

Another common misconception is the one that shaving causes the hair to grow increasingly coarse. It is true that the stubble after shaving feels rough, but the reason is simply that the soft, tapered ends of the hairs have been cut off; the new hairs that will suc-ceed them later will still have soft, tapered ends. Then there are the star-tling stories about corpses that have been observed to grow a beard in the days after death. This phenomenon too has a simple explanation: after the skin of a dead person dries and shrinks it may expose a millimeter or two of hair that was below the surface before death.

From the evolutionary point of view the most interesting aspect of man's hair is the baldness that develops on the top of his head. This baldness is actually an extension of a natural process that occurs in all human beings and begins before birth. In the young fetus the entire head is covered with hairs—the forehead as well as the scalp. After the fifth month the hair follicles on the forehead gradually become involuted and diminish in size. At birth the infant often still has some visible hair on its brow, but the forehead continues to become increasingly naked, and by late childhood it establishes a high, well-defined hairline. (There are, however, freakish cases in which an individual retains a bushy growth of hair on his forehead like that on his scalp.) The same balding process that occurs on the forehead also takes place elsewhere on the body; babies are often visibly hairier at birth than they are later. Thus man's nakedness is the result of a progressive involution of his hair follicles. Although he has as many follicles as other primates, most of them are so small that the hairs they produce are not visible on the surface.

Exactly the same process of involution of follicles is responsible for balding of the scalp, which may begin in young men as early as the twenties. It is curious that this dramatic loss of hair should take place on the scalp, which, unlike other parts of the body, will normally grow hair to almost unlimited length (as much as 12 feet) if the hair is not cut. The explanation lies in the action of androgenic (male) hormones, which paradoxically are responsible not only for the growth of all hair but also, under certain circumstances, for the reduction of the scalp hair. Eunuchs, having a deficiency of androgenic hormones, rarely become bald on top—a fact that was noted by Aristotle, who himself was bald. I should emphasize at this point that once involution of the scalp follicles has taken place no agency will avail to grow a new crop of hair.

Significantly, man is not the only primate that develops baldness. The stump-tailed macaque and the orangutan become virtually bald on the forehead when they mature. The ouakari monkey of South America, starting with a full head of hair in its youth, loses all the hair on its scalp and forehead by the time it reaches adulthood. We hope to learn a great deal about baldness by studying these animals. Whether

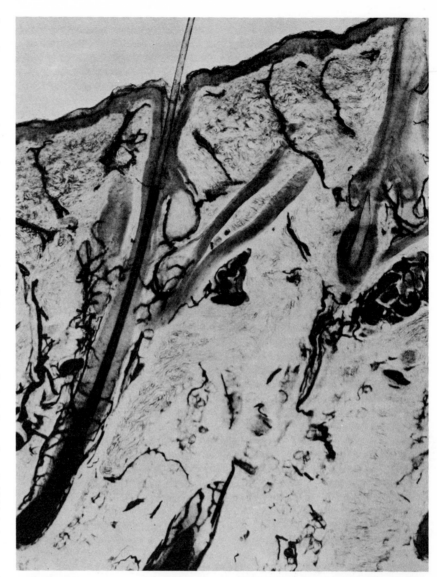

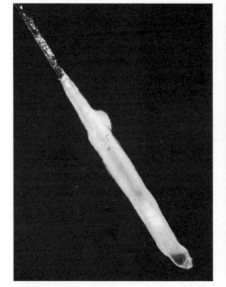 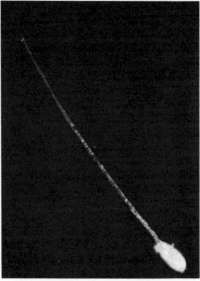

HAIR GROWTH alternates between active and dormant phases. The human hair at the left in the upper photograph is growing; the follicle that produces it is surrounded by many blood vessels. In contrast, the hair at the right is not growing; its follicle is quiescent and shriveled and the base of the hair is clubbed. The lower pair of photographs contrasts an active hair (left) with a dormant one (right). Each hair has been plucked from its follicle.

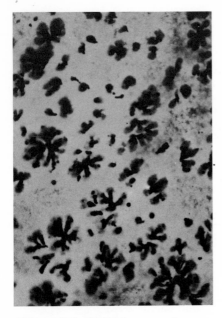 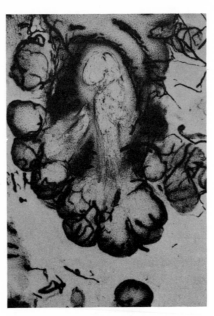

SEBACEOUS GLANDS are not always associated with hair follicles; these photographs show the numerous nests of these glands situated on the inside of the human cheek (*left*) and the abundance of fine blood vessels surrounding one such cheek gland (*right*). Wherever located, the cells of these glands synthesize and accumulate globules of fat (*see below*).

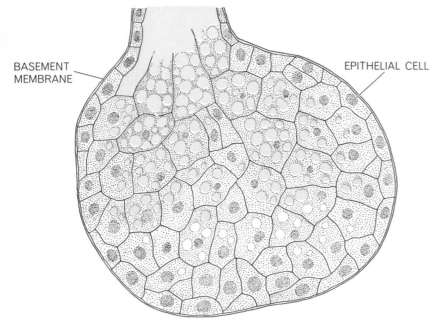

BASEMENT
MEMBRANE

EPITHELIAL CELL

PRODUCTION OF SEBUM, a mixture of fatty acids, triglycerides, waxes and cholesterol, occurs as the sebaceous gland cells become choked with accumulated fat globules (*color*), die and disintegrate. As the sebum accumulates in the gland's duct, capillary traction and the pressure from skin movements bring the semiliquid material to the surface of the skin.

some odorless and some extraordinarily malodorous, some fatty and some watery, some colorless and some strikingly pigmented, perform a wide range of functions, prominent among which is sexual attraction. The skin of man has two main kinds of secretory gland: the sebaceous glands and the sweat glands.

The former produce an odd material called sebum, which is a semiliquid mixture of fatty acids, triglycerides, waxes, cholesterol and cellular debris. The production of sebum is somewhat like the production of the horny layer by the epidermis. The cells of the sebaceous glands synthesize globules of fat, gradually become bloated with the accumulation of these globules and eventually break up. This mélange of dead and decaying cell fragments is the sebum.

Investigators who have studied sebum are at a loss to imagine what useful purpose it may serve. The secretion does not emulsify readily, it is toxic to living tissues, produces skin blemishes and in general seems to do more harm than good. The sebaceous glands themselves offer no clear clues, only a confusion of inconsistencies. Most of them are attached to hair follicles and deposit their sebum on the hairs inside the follicles, but in some areas of the skin the glands are not connected with follicles; there the sebum oozes out on the skin through ducts. The glands are particularly prominent around the nose and mouth, on the inside of the cheeks, on the hairless border of the upper lip, on the forehead, over the cheekbones, on the inside edge of the eyelids (where they are so large that one can easily see them with the naked eye by turning up a lid before a mirror), on parts of the neck and upper torso and on the genital organs. All this suggests that the sebum may play useful roles, although it is hard to see what they are. It does not seem likely that sebum is only a lubricant.

The human body often appears to contain senseless appendages and even to make outright mistakes, but the sebaceous glands are too numerous and active to be dismissed as trivial. Nor do they seem to be mere survivals from earlier stages of evolution in which they were more important to the body; man has a greater number of and more active sebaceous glands than most other mammals and has them in places where they do not appear in other animals.

In spite of a considerable amount of research, very little has been learned about the cause or treatment of acne,

we like it or not, it seems clear that in the long run we shall have to accept the fact that man is becoming increasingly bald and must reconcile himself to the ornamental value of nakedness.

Most of the members of the animal kingdom possess skin glands of one sort or another, which produce a remarkable variety of secretions. Fishes and amphibians secrete slime; toads produce poisons that make them unpalatable to most predators; the duckbill platypus secretes toxic substances from rosettes of glands on its hind legs; most birds have a pair of preen glands over the tail (in chickens and turkeys vulgarly known as "the pope's nose") that secretes a preening ointment that contains precursors of vitamin D. The many varieties of mammalian skin secretions,

for which the sebaceous glands are in some way responsible. Why do these lesions occur particularly in young adolescents? Why do they break out on the face, neck and upper torso but not on the scalp or the anogenital areas, where the sebaceous glands are also large and numerous? The only facts about acne that seem definitely established are that there is a hereditary disposition to it and that it is connected in some way with diet and with the activity of the androgenic hormones. These hormones have a great deal to do with the development and functioning of the sebaceous glands. The glands are large in a newborn infant, become dormant during childhood, begin to enlarge again in early puberty and grow to full bloom in adults. They show a definite relation to the level of androgenic hormones in the individual. The glands are larger and more active in men than in women; they are only poorly developed in eunuchs, and they increase in size and number when a eunuch is treated with androgens.

The Two Kinds of Sweat Gland

In the usage of physiologists the term "sweat glands" lumps together many different organs, most of which have nothing to do with sweating. Some produce scent or musk, others mucoid substances, still others colored secretions. What all the so-called sweat glands have in common is that they are tubular in form and are found only among the mammals.

The glands that actually produce sweat are of two general kinds: the apocrine glands, which are usually associated with hair follicles, and the eccrine glands, which are not. The two types have different origins, structures and functions. Because the eccrine glands predominate in the more advanced primates, some evolutionists have supposed that this type evolved more recently and that the apocrine type is more primitive; actually one of the most primitive of all mammals, the duckbill platypus, has well-developed eccrine glands, and man not only is richer in eccrine glands than any other primate but also has more and better-developed apocrine glands in certain parts of his body. It is not possible to say definitely that either type is more ancient or more primitive than the other.

The apocrine glands secrete the odorous component of sweat. They are primarily scent glands, and they produce their secretions in response to stress or sexual stimulation. Before the deodorant and perfume industries usurped their function of creating a person's body odor, the apocrine glands no doubt played an important role in human society. Aside from their odor-generating property, these glands are quite unnecessary to man. There are clear signs that man's apocrine glands, like his hair, are much less luxuriant than they were in his ancestors.

A human fetus in its fifth month produces rudiments of apocrine sweat glands over almost its entire body. Within a few weeks, however, most of these rudiments disappear, and the human body eventually has well-developed apocrine glands only in the armpits, the navel, the anogenital areas, the nipples and the ears. This seems to be a clear case of ontogeny mirroring phylogeny—the fetus recapitulating

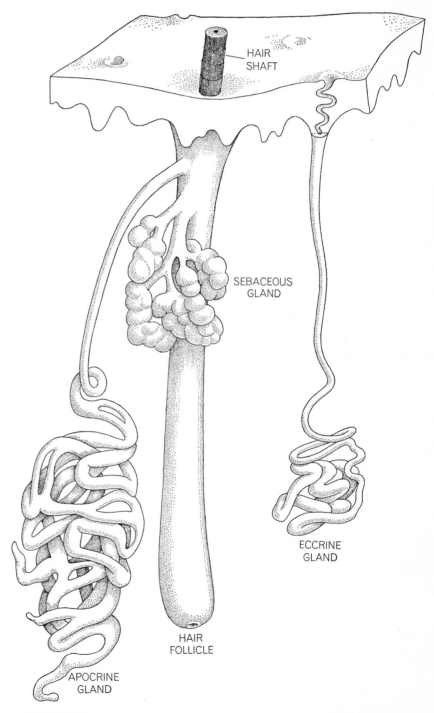

SWEAT GLANDS comprise two major categories: apocrine glands, which secrete a milky, odorous fluid (*left*), and eccrine glands, which secrete water (*right*). The former, together with the sebaceous glands, produce the body's odors; the latter help to regulate body heat.

man's evolutionary history. Oddly, although man no longer has apocrine glands all over his body, in his armpits these glands are larger and more numerous than in all other animals. Man is distinguished from all other mammals by a highly developed axillary organ in his armpits, made up of very large apocrine glands with eccrine glands interspersed among them.

The apocrine secretion is a milky, sticky fluid of varying color—pale gray, whitish, yellow or reddish. Although the glands are large, the amount of their secretion is very small; most of the fluid in the copious sweat of the armpits is supplied by the eccrine glands, which provide the vehicle for the spread of the odorous apocrine substances. The freshly secreted apocrine sweat is actually rather odorless, but it becomes malodorous when its substances are decomposed by the action of bacteria on the skin's surface.

The eccrine glands, the source of most of man's sweat, secrete water, which has two main functions: (1) cooling the body by evaporation and (2) moistening the friction surfaces, such as those of the palms and the soles, which prevents flaking of the horny layer, improves the grip and assists the tactile sensitivity. The glands responsible for the two functions show clear-cut differences, both in their response to stimuli and in their embryonic development. Eccrine glands of the first category produce sweat in response to heat; those in the second category, sweat in response to psychic stimuli. As for development, the eccrine glands on the palms and soles appear in the fetus at the age of three and a half months, whereas those in the rest of the body do not develop until

the fifth month and are the last structures to form. This suggests that the secretions for gripping arrived early in evolution and the cooling secretions may be a recent development.

Cats, dogs and rodents have eccrine glands only in the pads of their paws. Some South American monkeys have a hairless surface on the lower side of the prehensile tail, and this surface is copiously supplied with eccrine glands. So are the knuckles of the gorilla's and the chimpanzee's hands, which they use in walking. In the monkeys and the apes the hairy skin of the body also has a considerable sprinkling of eccrine glands, but it is significant that these are not nearly so active as man's. The skin of a monkey remains dry even on the hottest days. Obviously profuse sweating would be a liability to a furry animal: if its hair were soaked with sweat, the animal would continually be wrapped in a wet and chilling blanket.

For naked man, on the other hand, the array of active sweat glands all over the body skin is a highly useful adaptation. It endows him with an essential cooling system that compensates for his lack of an insulating pelage. Man has millions of eccrine glands on his body, the number varying with individuals and ranging from two million to five million, or an average of about 150 to 340 per square centimeter of skin surface. Some of the individual differences may depend on differences in body size. Some people sweat much more profusely than others, but this is not strictly related to the individual's total number of sweat glands; the difference lies, rather, in the relative activity of the glands.

The human sweating response has

been investigated by means of such experiments as the administration of drugs, spices and other treatments. The results are not very enlightening. Sweating can be evoked by different drugs of apparently opposite chemical properties; individuals often respond differently to a given drug; the drug may produce inconsistent responses even in the same individual. Moreover, sweating is an enigma that amounts to a major biological blunder: it depletes the body not only of water but also of sodium and other essential electrolytes that are carried off with the water.

Perhaps the eccrine glands are still an experiment of nature—demonstrably useful to man but not yet fully refined by the evolutionary process. In view of its indispensability to the human body, sweating is likely to survive, in spite of the determined efforts of antiperspirant technologists.

To sum up, the outstanding features of man's skin are its nakedness and its ability to sweat profusely. His hair is largely ornamental, the only luxuriant growths of his body having no practical value for protecting him from the environment. One of the important mechanisms man has developed as an adaptation to his increasing nakedness is the body-temperature control system regulated by the eccrine sweat glands, which adjust their output of cooling water both to changes in the outside temperature and to the internal heat generated in the body by exercise. All in all, the seemingly delicate skin of man is a remarkably complex and adaptable organ, serving not only as armor against the outside world but also as an important contributor to the body's internal husbandry.

10

Electrical Effects in Bone

C. ANDREW L. BASSETT

October 1965

The most striking characteristics of bone are its solidity and strength. In performing operations on bone the surgeon saws it, drills it, places screws in it, nails it and otherwise treats it like wood. Before the advent of materials such as steel and plastics men used it in a wide variety of tools, weapons and art objects, largely because it was hard and durable. Yet in the living organism bone has another feature that seems the opposite of durability: it is remarkably changeable.

Living bone adapts its structure to changes in mechanical load; like the proverbial twig, as bone is bent, so grows the bone. This property of bone was concisely stated in 1892 by the German anatomist Julius Wolff. In its modern form Wolff's law can be phrased: "The form of the bone being given, the bone elements place or displace themselves in the direction of the functional pressure and increase or decrease their mass to reflect the amount of functional pressure." In other words, bone not only alters its orientation in response to mechanical stress but also gains or loses substance.

How is bone able to achieve these changes? Its capacity is perhaps even more impressive in view of the fact that it is largely composed of hard mineral crystals. Here, however, is a clue to a possible mechanism by which bone shapes itself. Many crystals are piezoelectric; that is, when they are subjected to mechanical stress, they produce an electric current. It seems likely that such electrical effects play an important role in the behavior of bone—even though it now appears that the mineral crystals of bone may be only secondarily involved in them.

Let us consider the behavior of bone in a little more detail. In a child any long bone, such as the thighbone, can be fractured completely and yet can heal even when the two sides of the break are not precisely aligned [*see illustration on page 110*]. After the fracture a mass of reparative tissue grows across the break, setting the stage for osteogenesis: the formation of new bone. The reparative tissue—which may contain cartilage, connective tissue and fibers of new bone—is called a callus. The new bone is formed by specialized cells known as osteoblasts; at the same time it is trimmed and shaped by bone-destroying cells, the osteoclasts. (A third type of cell—the osteocyte—is found inside the bone in the tiny spaces called lacunae, where it serves to maintain normal bone tissue.) After the healed bone has been in use for a year or two, the site of the fracture will probably be impossible to distinguish on an X-ray plate.

The question is: What is the nature of the stimulus that induces the formation and destruction of bone exactly where these processes are needed? Or, to put the question in a more general form, what is the signal for change in bone? A number of laboratories have undertaken to look into the matter, among them our Orthopedic Research Laboratories at the Columbia University College of Physicians and Surgeons and those of E. Fukada at the Institute of Physical and Chemical Research in Tokyo and I. Yasuda at the Second Red Cross Hospital in Kyoto.

A concept basic to such investigations, as it is to many other investigations in modern biology, is that of negative-feedback control. Here the negative-feedback control system consists of (1) a signal from the environment, (2) a transducer to convert the signal into a meaningful biological response and (3) the response itself. Usually the system also involves (4) a second transducer to translate the response into (5) activity that will correct or stop the original environmental signal. This circular feedback system is said to be negative when it damps the effect of an excessive signal, as opposed to enhancing the effect.

It had been known that a negative-feedback system appears to control another activity of bone: supplying calcium to the blood. Franklin C. McLean of the University of Chicago had pointed out that when the level of calcium ions in the blood plasma fell below a certain point, this gave rise to a signal for the parathyroid glands to secrete greater quantities of hormone. The parathyroid hormone activates the osteoclasts to destroy a certain amount of bone and release calcium to the plasma, thereby eliminating the cause of the original signal [see "Bone," By Franklin C. McLean, SCIENTIFIC AMERICAN Offprint #1064].

It now appears that the phenomenon summarized by Wolff's law also represents a negative-feedback system. In this case the environmental signal and the final correcting response were known: a deforming force results in a change in bone structure needed to resist the force. The mechanisms by which one led to the other, however, seemed quite mysterious until the transducers were identified.

The mineral crystals of bone are embedded in an organic matrix; they account for roughly two-thirds of bone by weight. The structure of the bone crystals closely resembles the structure of fluorapatite, a mineral found in rocks. In the bone crystal, however, the positions of the fluorine atoms in fluorapatite are occupied by hydroxyl groups (OH); accordingly the bone crystal is called hydroxyapatite. The organic ma-

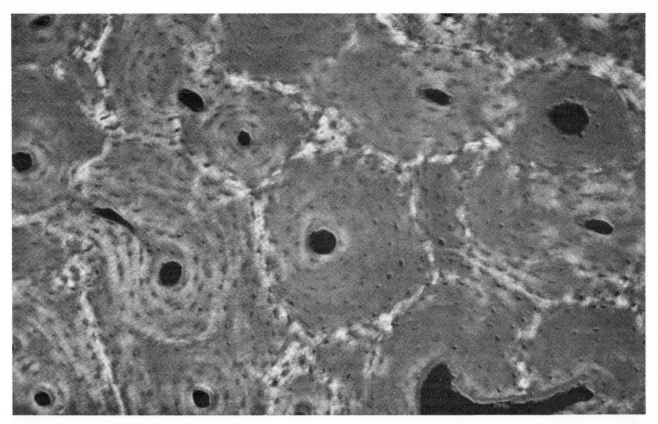

PHOTOMICROGRAPH OF BONE enlarges some 80 diameters the roughly cylindrical units called osteons. Here the osteons are seen end on; each one is represented by a whitish outline. The large dark spot in the middle of each unit is a canal traversed by blood vessels. The smaller dark spots arrayed in circles around the canals are cavities that contain the specialized cells of bone.

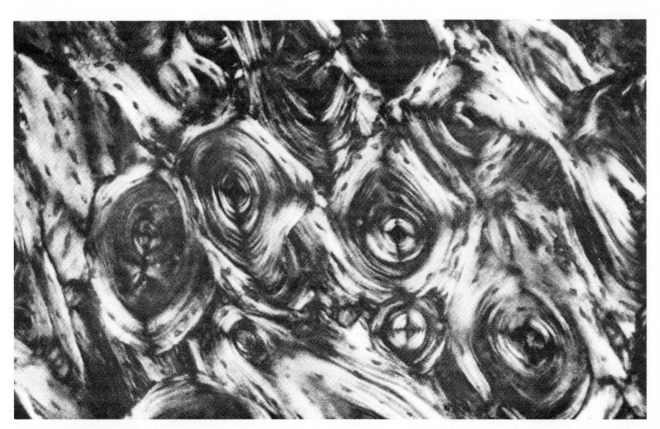

POLARIZED-LIGHT MICROGRAPH made at the same magnification indicates that bone is highly crystalline. This is shown by the rings around each canal and also by the dark cross pattern, which is characteristic of certain crystals viewed in polarized light. The rings are made up of crystals of the mineral hydroxyapatite embedded in a crystalline matrix of the protein collagen. The rings are alternately light and dark because the orientation of the crystalline material changes, alternately passing light and blocking it.

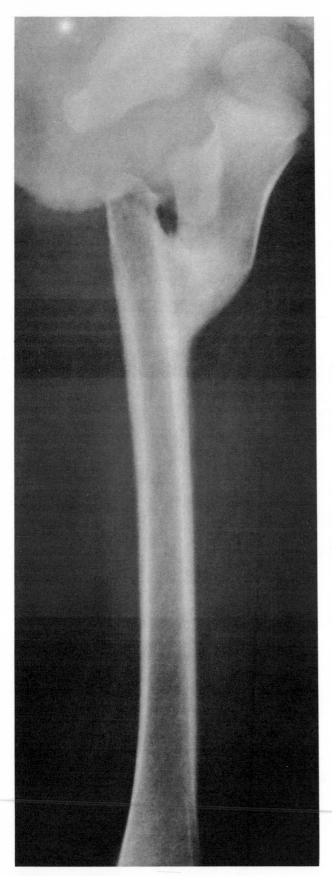

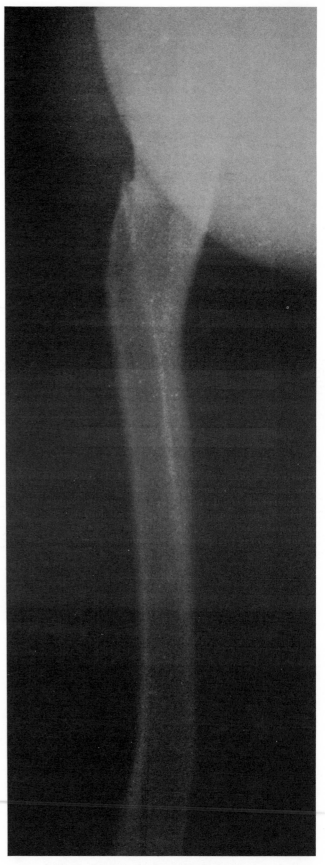

CHANGEABILITY OF BONE is exemplified by the healing of a fracture, depicted in these two X-ray plates. Fractured thighbone of a two-year-old boy appears in plate at left, made in August, 1963, four months after the break occurred. Upper part of bone had been broken off toward right; it was not set, although a cast was placed around the leg to prevent further damage. Callus of connective tissue, cartilage and new bone extends across the fracture gap. In plate at right, made in October, 1964, a year and a half after fracture occurred, the bone has healed and the site of fracture is scarcely apparent. Special cells are trimming the rough edges, and the healed bone is gaining a mass and orientation appropriate to resist normal stresses to which it is exposed.

trix in which the hydroxyapatite is deposited is composed mainly of the protein collagen, and it too is in a crystalline state: its long-chain helical molecules lie side by side in an array that forms a regular hexagonal pattern when it is viewed from the end. Thus bone is made up of at least two crystalline systems.

The fact that bone is so highly crystalline suggested to several investigators that it might be piezoelectric—that it generates an electric current when it is mechanically deformed. In 1953 Yasuda demonstrated that it was indeed piezoelectric; similar observations were made in our laboratory in 1956 and 1957. Later in 1957 Fukada and Yasuda (who were then working together) published a detailed study of bone's piezoelectric properties. They also discovered that dry collagen would develop an electric charge when it was stressed or bent, and this led them to propose that the source of piezoelectricity in bone was collagen.

No evidence has yet been advanced to suggest that hydroxyapatite crystals are primarily involved in the piezoelectricity of bone. There are, however, at least two other systems in bone that may give rise to electric charge. First, the organic matrix in which hydroxyapatite crystals are embedded contains not only collagen but also hyaluronic acid, a long-chain molecule of the class known as mucopolysaccharides; recently it has been found that when certain members of this class of molecules are deformed, a separation of the electric charges in them occurs. Second, work by R. O. Becker at Syracuse University suggests that the interface between collagen and hydroxyapatite is a semiconductor junction of the *p-n* type: a junction between two crystals in which the relative availability of electrons is different. Crystalline collagen tends to have an abundance of electrons; crystals of hydroxyapatite, a lack of them. Bending a *p-n* junction between the two would generate an electric potential. In short, electricity theoretically could be generated in bone in any or all of three ways: a stress on or bending of collagen fibers, a bending of mucopolysaccharide molecules and a stress on the collagen-hydroxyapatite interface.

Becker, together with C. H. Bachman, has analyzed the electrical properties of bone in an effort to determine which of the mechanisms actually operates. His studies indicate that these properties are not simple enough to be ex-

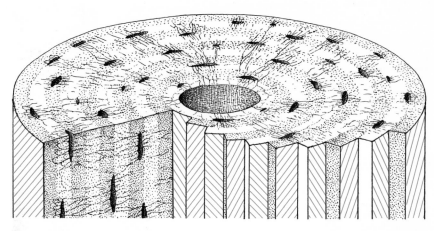

STRUCTURE OF OSTEON is shown in three dimensions. In the middle is the canal that contains the blood vessels; it is connected by much finer canals to cavities that contain osteocytes, the cells that maintain the bone tissue. The concentric layers are composed mainly of hydroxyapatite embedded in variously oriented fibers of collagen (*colored lines*).

plained by the usual piezoelectric effects encountered in one kind of crystal. His view is disputed by, among others, Morris H. Shamos and Leroy S. Lavine of New York University, who believe that collagen alone is probably the main source of stress-induced potentials. The investigations in our laboratory, however, tend to substantiate Becker's view in that they suggest that the source of electricity is a multitude of tiny junctions between collagen and hydroxyapatite.

In a series of experiments designed to clarify the matter, strips of bone of various widths were gradually deformed while the electricity generated in response was measured. At a certain point, known as the plastic range, the bone will not completely spring back from its deformed position. We observed that, until the plastic range was reached, bone strips of all widths generated electricity roughly in direct proportion to the amount of deformation they had undergone. Thereafter the rate of increase of electrical output dropped—most markedly in the thicker specimens, which reach the plastic range after significantly less deformation.

When we chemically removed the hydroxyapatite from the specimens, however, the amount of electricity generated by deformation was much less. This suggests that collagen alone cannot be the main source of electric charge. In this connection it is useful to regard bone as a two-phase material, one phase being hydroxyapatite and the other collagen. (Actually bone is a three-phase material if we include the substances that appear to cement the hydroxyapatite crystals together.) In such materials, a nonbiological example of which is

fiber glass, a strong but brittle substance is embedded in a weaker but more flexible one; the combined substances have a greater strength for their weight than either substance alone [see "Two-Phase Materials," by Games Slayter; SCIENTIFIC AMERICAN, January, 1962]. In bone, of course, hydroxyapatite is the stronger material and collagen the more flexible, and bone's modulus of elasticity lies between that of the mineral and that of the protein. Accordingly collagen probably cannot be flexed enough to give rise to the observed potentials. A significant stress would be likely to develop, however, at the junction between the collagen and the hydroxyapatite when bone is deformed.

Now let us consider the role electrical effects are likely to play in the feedback system that regulates change in bone. Four of the five elements in our generalized negative-feedback system can be identified. The initial environmental signal is a deforming force. It activates a large number of piezoelectric transducers, which generate electric potentials proportional to the applied force. In order to change the architecture of bone so that in time it can resist the force, the potentials must stimulate a second transducer mechanism. If the original force is compressive, that is, if it is directed along the axis of an existing bone structure, the change may involve only an increase in mass; if the force acts at an angle to the axis, giving rise to shear, the modifications will involve realignment. In 1962 Becker and I postulated that electric potentials not only affect the activity of bone cells directly but also influence the pattern in which large molecules such as collagen come together. Our investigations since then have generally confirmed these postulates. We have found that formation of bone in living animals can be influenced by weak, artificially induced direct currents and that the alignment of collagen molecules in solution outside the body can be influenced in much the same way.

When drops of collagen in solution were subjected in our laboratory to a current comparable to that calculated for living bone responding to deformation, in from one to five minutes a band of collagen formed at right angles to the direction of the electric field (and near the negative electrode). The collagen molecules in this band could be made to form fibers by the addition of salts of the appropriate ionic concentration. Once the fibers had formed they remained stationary after the current had been shut off; they were found

to be parallel to one another and perpendicular to the lines of force of the electric field in which they had developed. The bands formed more rapidly when we used an intermittent current rather than a continuous one. Although it was not surprising that the electrically charged molecules of collagen migrated in an electric field, it was most interesting that they moved so rapidly and formed such an orderly pattern under the influence of currents as small as those we were using.

On the basis of these results in vitro it seemed possible that molecules with a net electric charge could migrate and align themselves under the influence of currents of the magnitude found in vivo. Such behavior may have far-reaching biological significance. If the long-chain molecules manufactured by living cells are piezoelectric, they may possess an automatic control mechanism when they

are outside the cell. When they are deformed, they may produce an electric charge that can selectively attract, repel or align charged molecules and ions in their immediate vicinity.

Here the precise nature of the electrical signal produced in living bone is of central importance. For example, if the signal is a wave with positive and negative phases of equal amplitude, an electrically charged molecule would merely move back and forth as the wave passed. There is an exception to this statement: if, as one phase of the wave passes, the molecule is chemically linked with another, it may not be able to move back when the second phase passes. On the other hand, the signal may not be a wave with two equal and opposite phases; one of the two phases may be dominant or there may be only one phase. In that case it would not be necessary to invoke the exception in

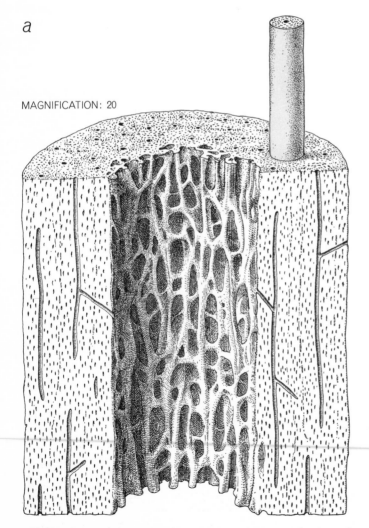

a

MAGNIFICATION: 20

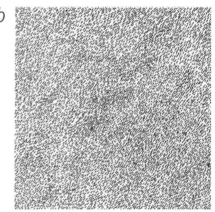

b

MAGNIFICATION: 10,000

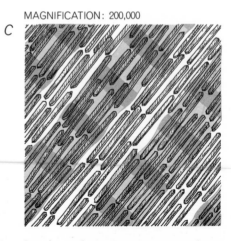

MAGNIFICATION: 200,000

c

FINE STRUCTURE OF BONE is illustrated on three levels of magnification. At left (a) is a section of bone depicted without its inner marrow. Haversian canals oriented on the long axis are the main branches of the circulatory network in bone. One osteon is shown extending from bone to emphasize its unit structure. At top right (b) section of osteon is shown to consist of collagen fibers (*color*) and hydroxyapatite crystals (*gray*). At bottom right (c) juxtaposition of collagen and hydroxyapatite is rendered in detail.

order to show that the signal can move a molecule in one direction to form bone.

What must the electrical signal actually achieve to build bone? The fundamental structural unit of bone is the osteon: a cylinder with a central canal traversed by blood vessels. Around the canal are concentric lamellae, or thin layers, of hydroxyapatite within and around highly organized bundles of collagen fibers; the lamellae are penetrated by smaller canals [*see illustration on opposite page*]. The regularity of this repeating unit implies that its construction involves a very precise control system. Such a system must obviously do more than simply influence molecules to move into position; it must also organize the activity of such cells as the osteoblasts and the osteoclasts. This idea is not farfetched; there appears to be a close relation between the electrical characteristics of the living cell and its external electrical environment.

In our laboratory we have shown that the nature of the electrical pulses obtained from bone varies significantly with the rate, magnitude and duration of its deformation. The orientation of osteons, lamellae, canals or mineralized bundles of collagen with respect to the direction of the applied force can also affect the character of the pulse. Moreover, it is likely that the relative degree of mineralization or hydration in various parts of the bone will affect its electrical behavior. The actual generators of electricity are so small that it is not possible to measure their individual activity; the pulses recorded in these studies must therefore represent the summation of billions of individual events occurring within the specimen under investigation.

Even though these considerations influence such characteristics of the electrical signal as magnitude and decay time, we have found in our laboratory a uniformity in one feature of the pulses obtained by deformation: their polarity. Regions under compression, which tend to be concave, are usually negatively charged; regions under tension, which tend to be convex, are usually positively charged. It is known both clinically and experimentally that a concave region of bone will be built up and a convex region torn down. This observation led to the prediction that electrically negative regions are associated with the building up of bone and the positive regions with its tearing down. With this prediction in mind we

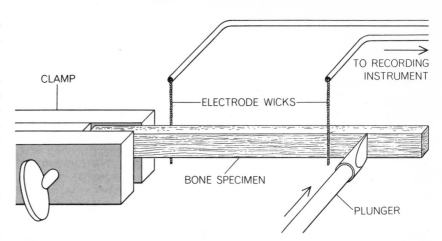

DEFORMATION EXPERIMENT to measure the current produced when bone is bent is diagrammed. A thin, moist strip of bone is placed in an insulated clamp at one end and bent by an insulated plunger at the other. Two electrode wicks are attached to bone, one on each side, an inch apart. Current generated in the bone is recorded on an oscilloscope.

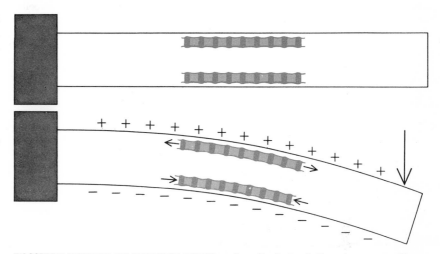

POSSIBLE EFFECT OF DEFORMATION on bone is depicted. In strip at top collagen fibers are represented in normal alignment. Strip at bottom is bent so that collagen fibers stretch on one side, are compressed on the other. As a result shear stresses develop between adjacent strands of collagen and opposite charges build up on opposite sides of the unit.

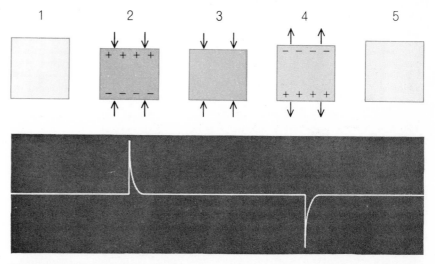

PIEZOELECTRIC EFFECT caused by stress on bone is illustrated. Each rectangle represents a piezoelectric crystal which, when compressed (2), produces an electric charge that tends to "leak" (3). When stress is removed (4), crystal resumes its original shape and charge is reversed. These steps give rise to oscilloscope trace of shape shown at bottom.

observed the effects on living bone of artificially induced continuous direct currents. We implanted a small, painless battery pack in the thigh of each of several dogs so that two platinum electrodes projected into the marrow space. For purposes of experimental control we inserted inactive batteries in some of the dogs; these dogs developed small masses of new bone at the point where each inactive electrode projected into the marrow space. In those dogs carrying active batteries a larger mass of new bone formed only around the negative electrode. Similar results have been reported by Yasuda in Japan. Surprisingly in our experiments there was no erosion of bone around the positive electrode.

How can this partial refutation of our prediction be explained? The dogs were active after the electrodes were inserted, and strong stresses were probably developed in the region of both holes in the bone. Such concentrations of stress might have caused an increased electrical activity of the bone itself that overrode the local effects of the artificial positive electrode. On the other hand, a simple connection between positive charge and bone destruction may not exist. The experiment nonetheless demonstrated that bone growth is enhanced in regions of negative charge. The effect of artificial continuous currents did not, however, establish a conclusive link between stress-induced potentials and the activity of bone cells.

All the evidence so far indicates that the intermittent electrical signals measured on bone surfaces have two phases; that is, the signal first has one polarity and then the other. It thus seems reasonable to ask: Can a cell discriminate between the positive and the negative phases of the signal and act accordingly? Or does it react to the greater or lesser electrical activity produced by greater or lesser stress? Although concrete answers are not yet available, one can put forward a working hypothesis. Such a hypothesis should explain how bone cells can simultaneously specialize as osteoblasts and osteoclasts even when they are only a few thousandths of a millimeter apart.

Generally speaking, to detect a difference in electric potential means to measure the relative availability of electrons or certain ions. One might put forward the hypothesis that bone destruction results when electrical activity is diminished or nonexistent. This line of reasoning can lead in any one of several directions, but here I shall take up only one of them.

Tissues are nourished by the movement of fluids, and bone is no exception. Obviously, however, the movement of fluids through bone presents difficulties. Bone is almost incompressible under normal loads, so that fluids cannot be "massaged" back and forth. The tiny canals in the bone through which the fluids must move account for only 3 percent of the area in a cross section of bone tissue. Furthermore, many of the bone-tending osteocytes are situated at relatively large distances from blood vessels. In view of the inefficiency of this supply line, it might be expected that most osteocytes would be on the brink of starvation for nutrients or oxygen. Under the stimulus of minor, normal deformations of the skeleton, however, an alternating electrical signal could act as a pump to promote the ebb and flow of ions and charged molecules. If such a pumping system exists (and if it does not, the nutrition of bone cells remains a mystery), it may depend on the junctions between hydroxyapatite and collagen. There are approximately a billion of these possible generators of electricity around each osteocyte.

If the generation of current were increased above normal levels in a given region, cells in the region might be activated to produce bone and stabilize the region. Conversely, diminished electrical activity might result in the death of osteocytes by starvation. It should be emphasized that the potentials generated by stress apparently do not require the presence of living cells. Bone in the body that has lost its living tissue may continue to generate potentials if it is intermittently deformed; thus it may escape destruction by osteoclasts.

If osteoclasts appear in regions where the electrical signal is diminished or absent, it should be possible to find a common electrical link between the factors known to cause bone destruction. For example, although it has been said that bone destruction requires a local increase in the number of blood vessels, it is not clear whether the increase occurs before the destruction or after it. If, as one investigator believes, the increase in the volume and rate of blood flow called active hyperemia causes

ELECTRICITY GENERATED BY DEFORMATION of bone is graphed by plotting increase of electrical output in percent (*vertical axis*) against the increase in deformation in percent (*horizontal axis*) for bone strips of several widths. The straight line represents an ideal linear, or one-to-one, relation. Broken lines indicate that bone strips have been deformed to the plastic range, that is, the point beyond which the strips will not spring back to normal. In this range there occurs a diminution in the rate of increase of electrical output.

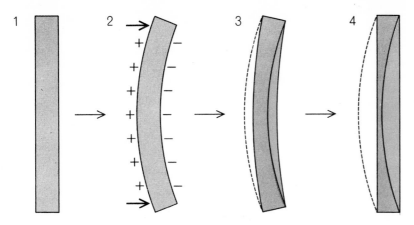
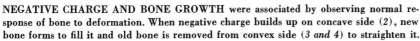
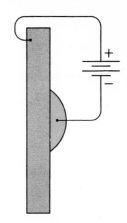

NEGATIVE CHARGE AND BONE GROWTH were associated by observing normal response of bone to deformation. When negative charge builds up on concave side (*2*), new bone forms to fill it and old bone is removed from convex side (*3 and 4*) to straighten it.

ELECTRIC CURRENT applied to undeformed bone caused growth in area of negative charge, no loss in area of positive.

bone destruction, it might do so by providing more oxygen molecules to act as electron "sinks." Furthermore, arteries are positively charged on the outside and negatively charged on the inside. It is therefore conceivable that the erosion of bone by the abnormal enlargement of an artery may be electrically mediated, because the larger vessel could conduct away more electrons. Finally, a recent observation that the hormone of the parathyroid glands influences the electrical conductivity of cell membranes lends support to the idea that bone destruction is controlled by electrical effects.

It appears more than likely, then, that changes in the orientation and mass of bone are controlled by stress-generated electric potentials, even

though it is far from clear exactly how these potentials achieve their effects. If this is true, electrical effects are obviously important not only in situations such as a broken bone but also in many other pathological conditions affecting the skeleton. Bone may function as an exquisitely sensitive piezoelectric gauge, responding to the slightest jar or deformation. There are several sources of normal mechanical input for the skeleton. The cardiovascular system provides a continual deforming force by means of hydrostatic pressures in the blood vessels, and possibly through the recoil of the heart. Gravity causes direct distortion of the skeleton, and it stimulates the tone of the muscles that must stabilize the body against gravity; the intermittent pull of these muscles also

deforms the bone. When a voluntary muscle action—such as a stride—is taken, additional mechanical stress is developed; with each step the shock from the impact is transmitted throughout the skeletal system. These sources of mechanical stress have some relevance to space travel. The astronaut who is subjected to prolonged periods of weightlessness loses the major portion of mechanical stimuli to bone, and must therefore expect his bones to lose mass at a more rapid rate than those of a person who must remain in bed or otherwise inactive for a protracted period. On the other hand, cardiovascular activity may suffice to provide the minimal stress that produces a threshold electric signal in bone—the signal that keeps the feedback system in operation.

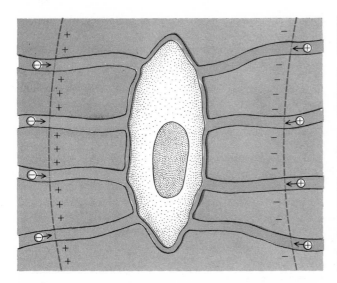
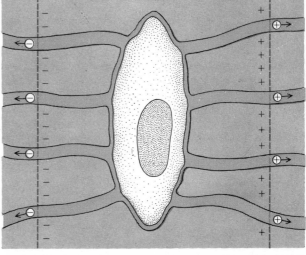

ELECTRICAL EFFECT ON BONE CELLS is outlined according to a hypothesis suggested by the author. A slight stress on bone (*left*) might generate an electric charge that attracts or repels electrically charged molecules and ions in the blood plasma bathing the osteocytes. Removal of stress (*right*) would cause reversal of charge and an opposite effect on charged particles. This electrical pumping system would explain how nutrients in the blood are passed through tiny canals to osteocytes deep within the bone.

11

The Antiquity of Human Walking

JOHN NAPIER
April 1967

Human walking is a unique activity during which the body, step by step, teeters on the edge of catastrophe. The fact that man has used this form of locomotion for more than a million years has only recently been demonstrated by fossil evidence. The antiquity of this human trait is particularly noteworthy because walking with a striding gait is probably the most significant of the many evolved capacities that separate men from more primitive hominids. The fossil evidence—the terminal bone of a right big toe discovered in 1961 in Olduvai Gorge in Tanzania—sets up a new signpost that not only clarifies the course of human evolution but also helps to guide those who speculate on the forces that converted predominantly quadrupedal animals into habitual bipeds.

Man's bipedal mode of walking seems potentially catastrophic because only the rhythmic forward movement of first one leg and then the other keeps him from falling flat on his face. Consider the sequence of events whenever a man sets out in pursuit of his center of gravity. A stride begins when the muscles of the calf relax and the walker's body sways forward (gravity supplying the energy needed to overcome the body's inertia). The sway places the center of body weight in front of the supporting pedestal normally formed by the two feet. As a result one or the other of the walker's legs must swing forward so that when his foot makes contact with the ground, the area of the supporting pedestal has been widened and the center of body weight once again rests safely within it. The pelvis plays an important role in this action: its degree of rotation determines the distance the swinging leg can move forward, and its muscles help to keep the body balanced while the leg is swinging.

At this point the "stance" leg—the leg still to the rear of the body's center of gravity—provides the propulsive force that drives the body forward. The walker applies this force by using muscular energy, pushing against the ground first with the ball of his foot and then with his big toe. The action constitutes the "push-off," which terminates the stance phase of the walking cycle. Once the stance foot leaves the ground, the walker's leg enters the starting, or "swing," phase of the cycle. As the leg swings forward it is able to clear the ground because it is bent at the hip, knee and ankle. This high-stepping action substantially reduces the leg's moment of inertia. Before making contact with the ground and ending the swing phase the leg straightens at the knee but remains bent at the ankle. As a result it is the

heel that strikes the ground first. The "heel strike" concludes the swing phase; as the body continues to move forward the leg once again enters the stance phase, during which the point of contact between foot and ground moves progressively nearer the toes. At the extreme end of the stance phase, as before, all the walker's propulsive thrust is delivered by the robust terminal bone of his big toe.

A complete walking cycle is considered to extend from the heel strike of one leg to the next heel strike of the same leg; it consists of the stance phase followed by the swing phase. The relative duration of the two phases depends on the cadence or speed of the walk. During normal walking the stance phase constitutes about 60 percent of the cycle and the swing phase 40 percent. Although

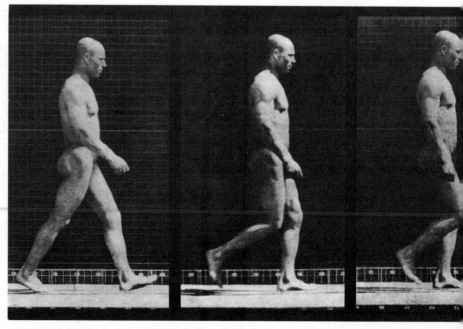

WALKING MAN, photographed by Eadweard Muybridge in 1884 during his studies of human and animal motion, exhibits the characteristic striding gait of the modern human.

the action of only one leg has been described in this account, the opposite leg obviously moves in a reciprocal fashion; when one leg is moving in the swing phase, the other leg is in its stance phase and keeps the body poised. Actually during normal walking the two phases overlap, so that both feet are on the ground at the same time for about 25 percent of the cycle. As walking speed increases, this period of double leg-support shortens.

Anyone who has watched other people walking and reflected a little on the process has noticed that the human stride demands both an up-and-down and a side-to-side displacement of the body. When two people walk side by side but out of step, the alternate bobbing of their heads makes it evident that the bodies undergo a vertical displacement with each stride. When two people walk in step but with opposite feet leading, they will sway first toward each other and then away in an equally graphic demonstration of the lateral displacement at each stride. When both displacements are plotted sequentially, a pair of low-amplitude sinusoidal curves appear, one in the vertical plane and the other in the horizontal [*see illustrations on next page*]. General observations of this kind were reduced to precise measurements during World War II when a group at the University of California at Berkeley led by H. D. Eberhart conducted a fundamental investigation of human walking in connection with requirements for the design of artificial legs. Eberhart and his colleagues found that a number of

functional determinants interacted to move the human body's center of gravity through space with a minimum expenditure of energy. In all they isolated six major elements related to hip, knee and foot movement that, working together, reduced both the amplitude of the two sine curves and the abruptness with which vertical and lateral changes in direction took place. If any one of these six elements was disturbed, an irregularity was injected into the normally smooth, undulating flow of walking, thereby producing a limp. What is more important, the irregularity brought about a measurable increase in the body's energy output during each step.

The Evidence of the Bones

What I have described in general and Eberhart's group studied in detail is the form of walking known as striding. It is characterized by the heel strike at the start of the stance phase and the push-off at its conclusion. Not all human walking is striding; when a man moves about slowly or walks on a slippery surface, he may take short steps in which both push-off and heel strike are absent. The foot is simply lifted from the ground at the end of the stance phase and set down flat at the end of the swing phase. The stride, however, is the essence of human bipedalism and the criterion by which the evolutionary status of a hominid walker must be judged. This being the case, it is illuminating to consider how the act of striding leaves its distinctive marks on the bones of the strider.

To take the pelvis first, there is a well-known clinical manifestation called Trendelenburg's sign that is regarded as evidence of hip disease in children. When a normal child stands on one leg, two muscles connecting that leg and the pelvis—the gluteus medius and the gluteus minimus—contract; this contraction, pulling on the pelvis, tilts it and holds it poised over the stance leg. When the hip is diseased, this mechanism fails to operate and the child shows a positive Trendelenburg's sign: the body tends to fall toward the unsupported side.

The same mechanism operates in walking, although not to the same degree. During the stance phase of the walking cycle, the same two gluteal muscles on the stance side brace the pelvis by cantilever action. Although actual tilting toward the stance side does not occur in normal walking, the action of the muscles in stabilizing the walker's hip is an essential component of the striding gait. Without this action the stride would become a slow, ungainly shuffle.

At the same time that the pelvis is stabilized in relation to the stance leg it also rotates to the unsupported side. This rotation, although small, has the effect of increasing the length of the stride. A familiar feature of the way women walk arises from this bit of anatomical mechanics. The difference in the proportions of the male and the female pelvis has the effect of slightly diminishing the range through which the female hip can move forward and back. Thus for a given length of stride women are obliged to rotate the pelvis through a greater

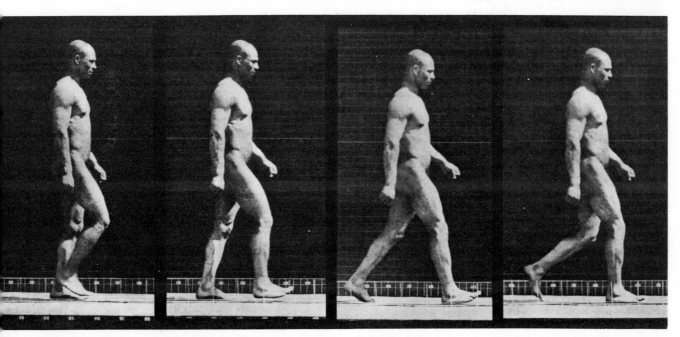

The free foot strikes the ground heel first and the body's weight is gradually transferred from heel to ball of foot as the opposite leg lifts and swings forward. Finally the heel of the stance foot rises and the leg's last contact with the ground is made with the big toe.

WALKING CYCLE extends from the heel strike of one leg to the next heel strike by the same leg. In the photograph, made by Gjon Mili in the course of a study aimed at improvement of artificial legs that he conducted for the U.S. Army, multiple exposures trace the progress of the right leg in the course of two strides. The ribbons of light allow analysis of the movement (*see illustration below*).

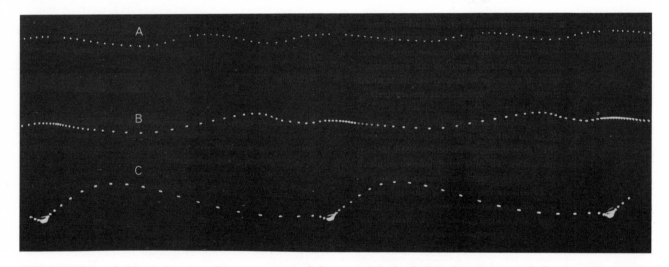

SINE CURVE described by the hip of a walking man was recorded on film by means of the experimental system illustrated above. An interrupter blade, passing in front of the camera lens at constant speed, broke the light from lamps attached to the walker into the three rows of dots. The speed of hip (*a*), knee (*b*) or ankle (*c*) during the stride is determined by measuring between the dots.

angle than men do. This secondary sexual characteristic has not lacked exploitation; at least in our culture female pelvic rotation has considerable erotogenic significance. What is more to the point in terms of human evolution is that both the rotation and the balancing of the pelvis leave unmistakable signs on the pelvic bone and on the femur: the leg bone that is joined to it. It is by a study of such signs that the walking capability of a fossil hominid can be judged.

Similar considerations apply to the foot. One way the role of the foot in walking can be studied is to record the vertical forces acting on each part of the foot while it is in contact with the ground during the stance phase of the walking cycle. Many devices have been built for this purpose; one of them is the plastic pedograph. When the subject walks across the surface of the pedograph, a motion-picture camera simultaneously records the exact position of the foot in profile and the pattern of pressures on the surface. Pedograph analyses show that the initial contact between the striding leg and the ground is the heel strike. Because the foot is normally turned out slightly at the end of the swing phase of the walking cycle, the outer side of the back of the heel takes the brunt of the initial contact [*see illustration on opposite page*]. The outer side of the foot contin- ues to support most of the pressure of the stance until a point about three-fifths of the way along the sole is reached. The weight of the body is then transferred to the ball of the foot and then to the big toe. In the penultimate stage of push-off the brunt of the pressure is under the toes, particularly the big toe. Finally, at the end of the stance phase, only the big toe is involved; it progressively loses contact with the ground and the final push-off is applied through its broad terminal bone.

The use of pedographs and similar apparatus provides precise evidence about the function of the foot in walking, but every physician knows that much the same information is recorded on the soles of everyone's shoes. Assuming that the shoes fit, their pattern of wear is a true record of the individual's habitual gait. The wear pattern will reveal a limp that one man is trying to hide, or unmask one that another man is trying to feign, perhaps to provide evidence for an insurance claim. In any case, just as the form of the pelvis and the femur can disclose the presence or absence of a striding gait, so can the form of the foot bones, particularly the form and proportions of the big-toe bones.

The Origins of Primate Bipedalism

Almost all primates can stand on their hind limbs, and many occasionally walk in this way. But our primate relatives are all, in a manner of speaking, amateurs; only man has taken up the business of bipedalism intensively. This raises two major questions. First, how did the basic postural adaptations that permit walking—occasional or habitual—arise among the primates? Second, what advantages did habitual bipedalism bestow on early man?

With regard to the first question, I have been concerned for some time with the anatomical proportions of all primates, not only man and the apes but also the monkeys and lower primate forms. Such consideration makes it possible to place the primates in natural groups according to their mode of locomotion. Not long ago I suggested a new group, and it is the only one that will concern us here. The group comprises primates with very long hind limbs and very short forelimbs. At about the same time my colleague Alan C. Walker, now at Makerere University College in Uganda, had begun a special study of the locomotion of living and fossil lemurs. Lemurs are among the most primitive offshoots of the basic primate stock. Early in Walker's studies he was struck by the frequency with which a posture best described as "vertical clinging" appeared in the day-to-day behavior of living lemurs. All the animals whose propensity for vertical clinging had been observed by Walker showed the same proportions—that is, long hind limbs and short forelimbs—I had proposed as forming a distinct locomotor group.

When Walker and I compared notes, we decided to define a hitherto unrecognized locomotor category among the primates that we named "vertical clinging and leaping," a term that includes both the animal's typical resting posture and the essential leaping component

in its locomotion. Since proposing this category a most interesting and important extension of the hypothesis has become apparent to us. Some of the earliest primate fossils known, preserved in sediments laid down during Eocene times and therefore as much as 50 million years old, are represented not only by skulls and jaws but also by a few limb bones. In their proportions and details most of these limb bones show the same characteristics that are displayed by the living members of our vertical-clinging-and-leaping group today. Not long ago Elwyn L. Simons of Yale University presented a reconstruction of the lemur-

like North American Eocene primate *Smilodectes* walking along a tree branch in a quadrupedal position [see "The Early Relatives of Man," by Elwyn L. Simons, Part IV, page 272, in this book]. Walker and I would prefer to see *Smilodectes* portrayed in the vertical clinging posture its anatomy unequivocally indicates. The fossil evidence, as far as it goes, suggests to us that vertical clinging and leaping was a major primate locomotor adaptation that took place some 50 million years ago. It may even have been the initial dynamic adaptation to tree life from which the subsequent locomotor patterns of all the living pri-

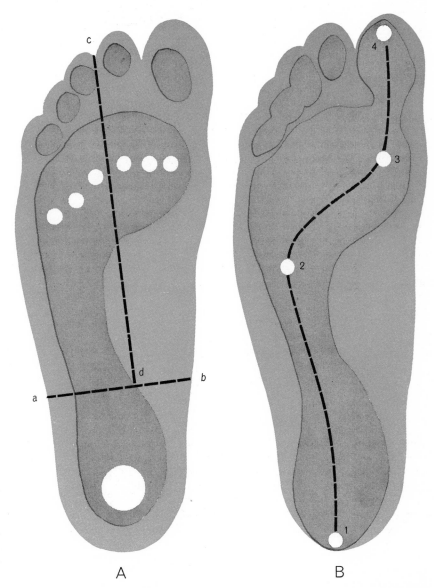

A   B

DISTRIBUTION OF WEIGHT in the human foot alters radically as action takes the place of rest. When motionless (A), the foot divides its static load (half of the body's total weight) between its heel and its ball along the axis a–b. The load on the ball of the foot is further divided equally on each side of the axis c–d. When striding (B), the load (all of the body's weight during part of each stride) is distributed dynamically from the first point of contact (1, heel strike) in a smooth flow via the first and fifth metatarsal bones (2, 3) that ends with a propulsive thrust (4, push-off) delivered by the terminal bone of the big toe.

mates, including man, have stemmed. Walker and I are not alone in this view. In 1962 W. L. Straus, Jr., of Johns Hopkins University declared: "It can safely be assumed that primates early developed the mechanisms permitting maintenance of the trunk in the upright position.... Indeed, this tendency toward truncal erectness can be regarded as an essentially basic primate character." The central adaptations for erectness of the body, which have been retained in the majority of living primates, seem to have provided the necessary anatomical basis for the occasional bipedal behavior exhibited by today's monkeys and apes.

What we are concerned with here is the transition from a distant, hypothetical vertical-clinging ancestor to modern, bipedal man. The transition was almost

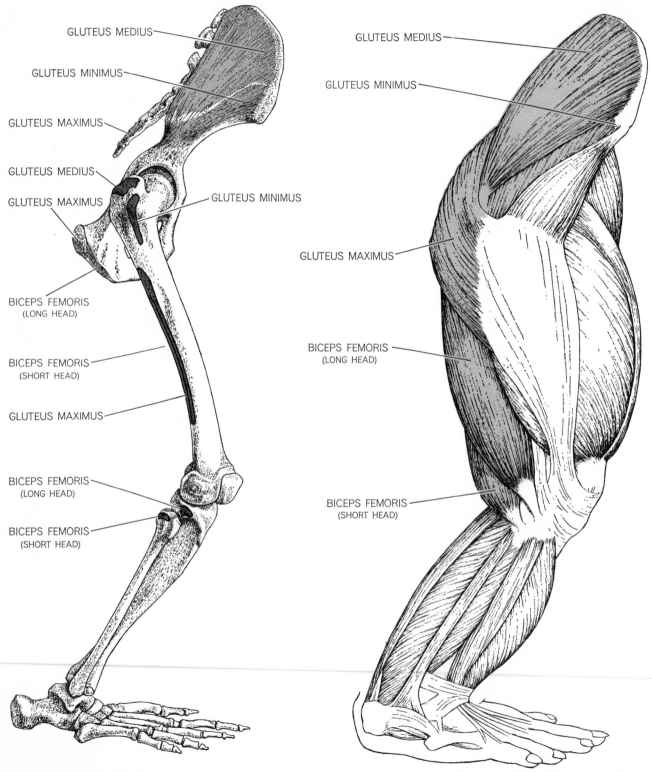

QUADRUPEDAL POSTURE needs two sets of muscles to act as the principal extensors of the hip. These are the gluteal group (the gluteus medius and minimus in particular), which connects the pelvis to the upper part of the femur, and the hamstring group. which connects the femur and the lower leg bones. Of these only the biceps femoris is shown in the gorilla musculature at right. The skeletal regions to which these muscles attach are shown in color at left. In most primates the gluteus maximus is quite small.

certainly marked by an intermediate quadrupedal stage. Possibly such Miocene fossil forms as *Proconsul*, a chimpanzee-like early primate from East Africa, represent such a stage. The structural adaptations necessary to convert a quadrupedal ape into a bipedal hom-

inid are centered on the pelvis, the femur, the foot and the musculature associated with these bones. Among the nonhuman primates living today the pelvis and femur are adapted for four-footed walking; the functional relations between hipbones and thigh muscles are

such that, when the animal attempts to assume a bipedal stance, the hip joint is subjected to a stress and the hip must be bent. To compensate for the resulting forward shift of the center of gravity, the knees must also be bent. In order to alter a bent-hip, bent-knee gait into

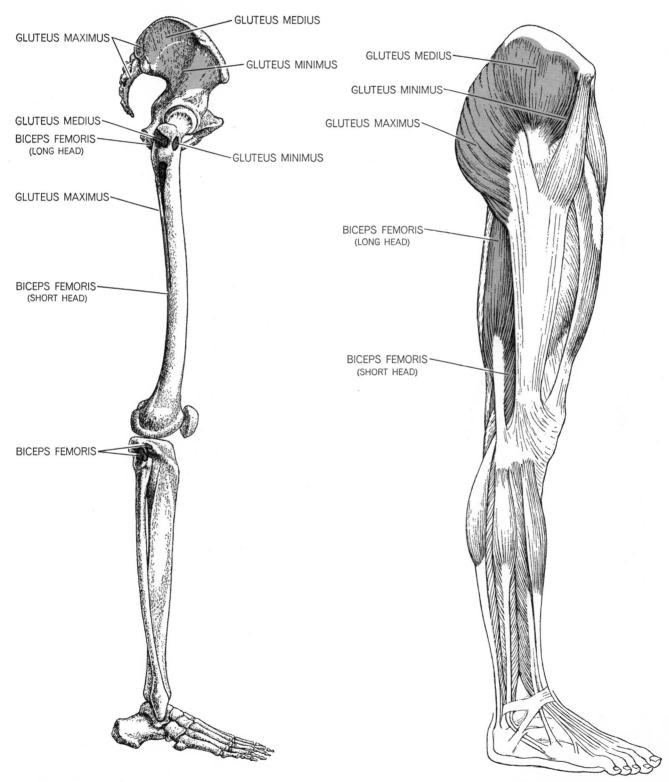

BIPEDAL POSTURE brings a reversal in the roles played by the same pelvic and femoral muscles. Gluteus medius and gluteus minimus have changed from extensors to abductors and the function of extending the trunk, required when a biped runs or climbs, has been assumed by the gluteus maximus. The hamstring muscles, in turn, now act mainly as stabilizers and extensors of the hip. At right are the muscles as they appear in man; the skeletal regions to which their upper and lower ends attach are shown in color at left.

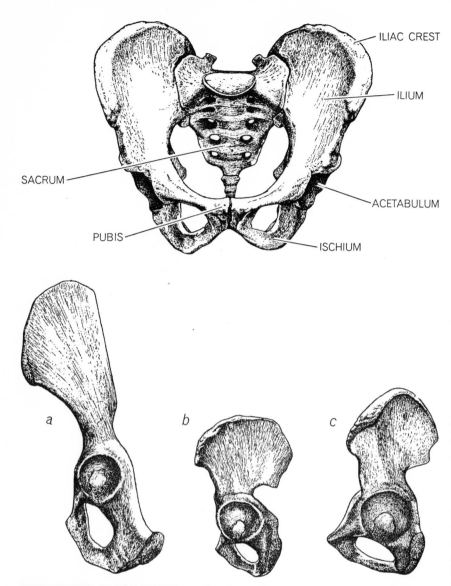

COMPONENTS OF THE PELVIS are identified at top; the bones are those of the human pelvis. Below, ilium and ischium of a gorilla (*a*), of *Australopithecus* (*b*) and of modern man (*c*) are seen from the side (the front is to the left in each instance). The ischium of *Australopithecus* is longer than man's; this almost certainly kept the early hominid from striding in the manner of *Homo sapiens*. Instead the gait was probably a kind of jog trot.

prisingly unimportant role in man's ability to stand, or even to walk on a level surface. In standing, for example, the principal stabilizing and extending agents are the muscles of the hamstring group. In walking on the level the gluteus maximus is so little involved that even when it is paralyzed a man's stride is virtually unimpaired. The gluteus maximus comes into its own in man when power is needed to give the hip joint more play for such activities as running, walking up a steep slope or climbing stairs [*see illustration on page 124*]. Its chief function in these circumstances is to correct any tendency for the human trunk to jackknife on the legs.

Because the gluteus maximus has such a specialized role I believe, in contrast to Washburn's view, that it did not assume its present form until late in the evolution of the striding gait. Rather than being the initial adaptation, this muscle's enlargement and present function appear to me far more likely to have been one of the ultimate refinements of human walking. I am in agreement with Washburn, however, when he states that changes in the ilium, or upper pelvis, would have preceded changes in the ischium, or lower pelvis [see the article "Tools and Human Evolution," by Sherwood L. Washburn, on page 169 in this book]. The primary adaptation would probably have involved a forward curvature of the vertebral column in the lumbar region. Accompanying this change would have been a broadening and a forward rotation of the iliac portions of the pelvis. Together these early adaptations provide the structural basis for improving the posture of the trunk.

Assuming that we have now given at least a tentative answer to the question of how man's bipedal posture evolved, there remains to be answered the question of why. What were the advantages of habitual bipedalism? Noting the comparative energy demands of various gaits, Washburn points out that human walking is primarily an adaptation for covering long distances economically. To go a long way with a minimum of effort is an asset to a hunter; it seems plausible that evolutionary selection for hunting behavior in man was responsible for the rapid development of striding anatomy. Gordon W. Hewes of the University of Colorado suggests a possible incentive that, acting as an agent of natural selection, could have prompted the quadrupedal ancestors of man to adopt a two-footed gait. In Hewes's view the principal advantage of bipedalism over quadrupedalism would be the free-

man's erect, striding walk, a number of anatomical changes must occur. These include an elongation of the hind limbs with respect to the forelimbs, a shortening and broadening of the pelvis, adjustments of the musculature of the hip (in order to stabilize the trunk during the act of walking upright), a straightening of both hip and knee and considerable reshaping of the foot.

Which of these changes can be considered to be primary and which secondary is still a matter that needs elucidation. Sherwood L. Washburn of the University of California at Berkeley has expressed the view that the change from four-footed to two-footed posture was initiated by a modification in the form and function of the gluteus maximus, a thigh muscle that is powerfully

developed in man but weakly developed in monkeys and apes [*see illustrations on preceding two pages*]. In a quadrupedal primate the principal extensors of the trunk are the "hamstring" muscles and the two upper-leg muscles I have already mentioned: the gluteus medius and gluteus minimus. In man these two muscles bear a different relation to the pelvis, in terms of both position and function. In technical terms they have become abductor muscles of the trunk rather than extensor muscles of the leg. It is this that enables them to play a critical part in stabilizing the pelvis in the course of striding. In man the extensor function of these two gluteal muscles has been taken over by a third, the gluteus maximus. This muscle, insignificant in other primates, plays a sur-

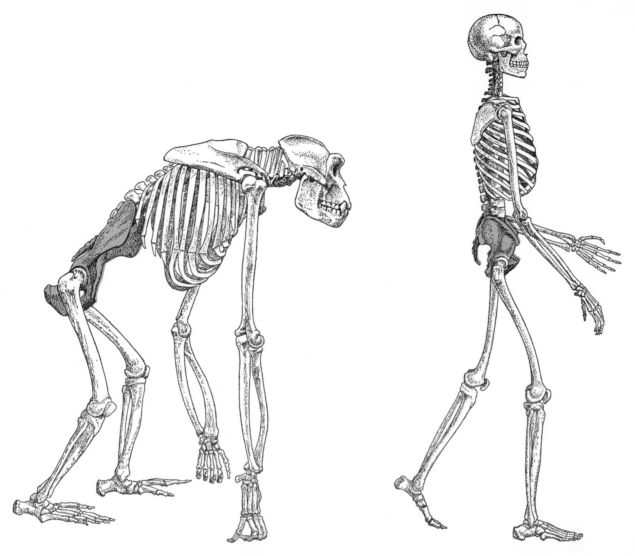

SHAPE AND ORIENTATION of the pelvis in the gorilla and in man reflect the postural differences between quadrupedal and bipedal locomotion. The ischium in the gorilla is long, the ilium extends to the side and the whole pelvis is tilted toward the horizontal (*see illustration on opposite page*). In man the ischium is much shorter, the broad ilium extends forward and the pelvis is vertical.

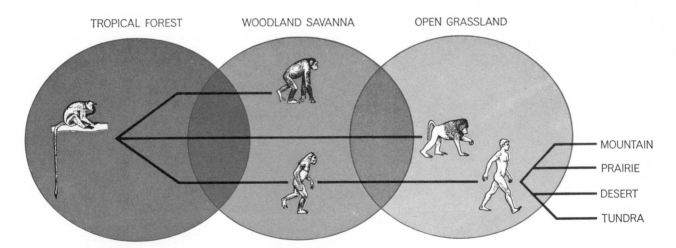

ECOLOGICAL PATHWAY to man's eventual mastery of all environments begins (*left*) with a quadrupedal primate ancestor living in tropical forest more than 20 million years ago. During Miocene times mountain-building produced new environments. One, a transition zone between forest and grassland, has been exploited by three groups of primates. Some, for example the chimpanzees, have only recently entered this woodland savanna. Both the newly bipedal hominids and some ground-living quadrupedal monkeys, however, moved beyond the transition zone into open grassland. The quadrupeds, for example the baboons, remained there. On the other hand, the forces of natural selection in the new setting favored the bipedal hominid hunters' adaptation of the striding gait typical of man. Once this adaptation developed, man went on to conquer most of the earth's environments.

ing of the hands, so that food could be carried readily from one place to another for later consumption. To assess the significance of such factors as survival mechanisms it behooves us to review briefly the ecological situation in which our prehuman ancestors found themselves in Miocene times, between 15 and 25 million years ago.

The Miocene Environment

During the Miocene epoch the worldwide mountain-building activity of middle Tertiary times was in full swing. Many parts of the earth, including the region of East Africa where primates of the genus *Proconsul* were living, were being faulted and uplifted to form such mountain zones as the Alps, the Himalayas, the Andes and the Rockies. Massive faulting in Africa gave rise to one of the earth's major geological features: the Rift Valley, which extends 5,000 miles from Tanzania across East Africa to Israel and the Dead Sea. A string of lakes lies along the floor of the Rift Valley like giant stepping-stones. On their shores in Miocene times lived a fantastically rich fauna, inhabitants of the forest and of a new ecological niche—the grassy savanna.

These grasslands of the Miocene were the domain of new forms of vegetation that in many parts of the world had taken the place of rain forest, the dominant form of vegetation in the Eocene and the Oligocene. The savanna offered new evolutionary opportunities to a variety of mammals, including the expanding population of primates in the rapidly shrinking forest. A few primates—the ancestors of man and probably also the ancestors of the living baboons—evidently reacted to the challenge of the new environment.

The savanna, however, was no Eldorado. The problems facing the early hominids in the open grassland were immense. The forest foods to which they were accustomed were hard to come by; the danger of attack by predators was immeasurably increased. If, on top of everything else, the ancestral hominids of Miocene times were in the process of converting from quadrupedalism to bipedalism, it is difficult to conceive of any advantage in bipedalism that could have compensated for the added hazards of life in the open grassland. Consideration of the drawbacks of savanna living has led me to a conclusion contrary to the one generally accepted: I doubt that the advent of bipedalism took place in this environment. An environment neglected by scholars but one far better

suited for the origin of man is the woodland-savanna, which is neither high forest nor open grassland. Today this halfway-house niche is occupied by many primates, for example the vervet monkey and some chimpanzees. It has enough trees to provide forest foods and ready escape from predators. At the same time its open grassy spaces are arenas in which new locomotor adaptations can be practiced and new foods can be sampled. In short, the woodland-savanna provides an ideal nursery for evolving hominids, combining the challenge and incentive of the open grassland with much of the security of the forest. It was probably in this transitional environment that man's ancestors learned to walk on two legs. In all likelihood, however, they only learned to stride when they later moved into the open savanna.

Moving forward many millions of years from Miocene to Pleistocene times, we come to man's most immediate hominid precursor: *Australopithecus*. A large consortium of authorities agrees that the shape of the pelvis in *Australopithecus* fossils indicates that these hominids were habitually bipedal, although not to the degree of perfection exhibited by modern man. A few anatomists, fighting a rearguard action, contend that on the contrary the pelvis of *Australopithecus*

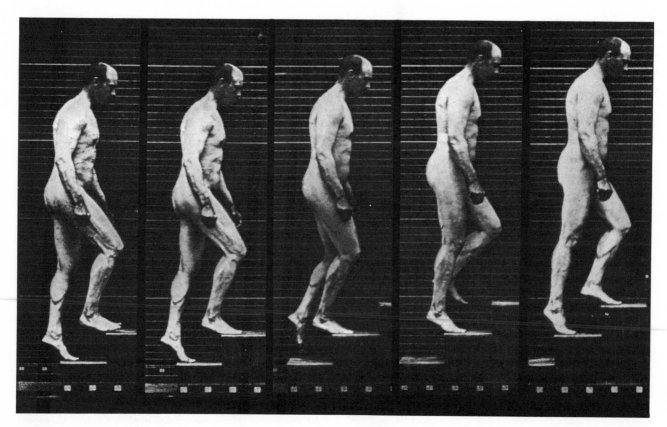

STAIR-CLIMBING, like running, is a movement that brings the human gluteus maximus into play. Acting as an extensor of the trunk, the muscle counteracts any tendency for the body to jackknife over the legs. Photographs are from Muybridge's collection.

shows that these hominids were predominantly quadrupedal. I belong to the first school but, as I have been at some pains to emphasize in the past, the kind of upright walking practiced by *Australopithecus* should not be equated with man's heel-and-toe, striding gait.

From Bipedalist to Strider

The stride, although it was not necessarily habitual among the earliest true men, is nevertheless the quintessence of the human locomotor achievement. Among other things, striding involves extension of the leg to a position behind the vertical axis of the spinal column. The degree of extension needed can only be achieved if the ischium of the pelvis is short. But the ischium of *Australopithecus* is long, almost as long as the ischium of an ape [see illustration on page 122]. Moreover, it has been shown that in man the gluteus medius and the gluteus minimus are prime movers in stabilizing the pelvis during each stride; in *Australopithecus* this stabilizing mechanism is imperfectly evolved. The combination of both deficiencies almost entirely precludes the possibility that these hominids possessed a striding gait. For *Australopithecus* walking was something of a jog trot. These hominids must have covered the ground with quick, rather short steps, with their knees and hips slightly bent; the prolonged stance phase of the fully human gait must surely have been absent.

Compared with man's stride, therefore, the gait of *Australopithecus* is physiologically inefficient. It calls for a disproportionately high output of energy; indeed, *Australopithecus* probably found long-distance bipedal travel impossible. A natural question arises in this connection. Could the greater energy requirement have led these early representatives of the human family to alter their diet in the direction of an increased reliance on high-energy foodstuffs, such as the flesh of other animals?

The pelvis of *Australopithecus* bears evidence that this hominid walker could scarcely have been a strider. Let us now turn to the foot of what many of us believe is a more advanced hominid. In 1960 L. S. B. Leakey and his wife Mary unearthed most of the bones of this foot in the lower strata at Olduvai Gorge known collectively as Bed I, which are about 1.75 million years old. The bones formed part of a fossil assemblage that has been designated by the Leakeys, by Philip Tobias of the University of the Witwatersrand and by me as possibly the earliest-known species of man: *Homo*

habilis. The foot was complete except for the back of the heel and the terminal bones of the toes; its surviving components were assembled and studied by me and Michael Day, one of my colleagues at the Unit of Primatology and Human Evolution of the Royal Free Hospital School of Medicine in London. On the basis of functional analysis the resem-

blance to the foot of modern man is close, although differing in a few minor particulars. Perhaps the most significant point of resemblance is that the stout basal bone of the big toe lies alongside the other toes [see upper illustration on next page]. This is an essentially human characteristic; in apes and monkeys the big toe is not exceptionally robust and

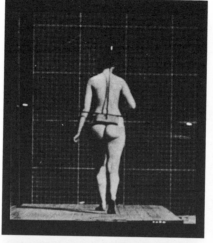
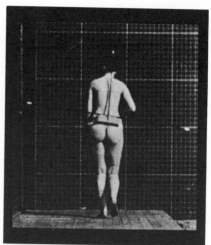
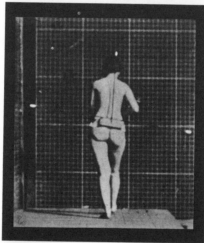
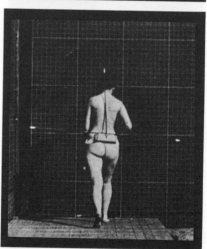
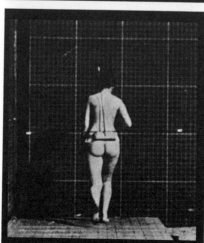
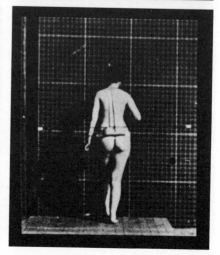

PELVIC ROTATION of the human female is exaggerated compared with that of a male taking a stride of equal length because the two sexes differ in pelvic anatomy. Muybridge noted the phenomenon, using a pole with whitened ends to record the pelvic oscillations.

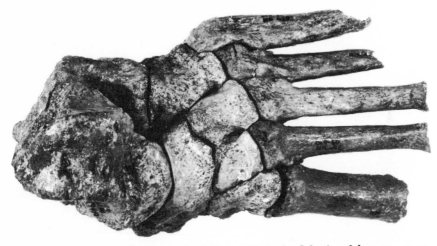

PRIMITIVE FOOT, complete except for the back of the heel and the tips of the toes, was unearthed from the lower level at Olduvai Gorge in Tanzania. Attributed to a very early hominid, *Homo habilis*, by its discoverer, L. S. B. Leakey, it is about 1.75 million years old. Its appearance suggests that the possessor was a habitual biped. Absence of the terminal bones of the toes, however, leaves open the question of whether the possessor walked with a stride.

BIG-TOE BONE, also discovered at Olduvai Gorge, is considerably younger than the foot bones in the top illustration but still probably more than a million years old. It is the toe's terminal bone (*bottom view at left, top view at right*) and bore the thrust of its possessor's push-off with each swing of the right leg. The tilting and twisting of the head of the bone in relation to the shaft is unequivocal evidence that its possessor walked with a modern stride.

diverges widely from the other toes. The foot bones, therefore, give evidence that this early hominid species was habitually bipedal. In the absence of the terminal bones of the toes, however, there was no certainty that *Homo habilis* walked with a striding gait.

Then in 1961, in a somewhat higher stratum at Olduvai Gorge (and thus in a slightly younger geological formation), a single bone came to light in an area otherwise barren of human bones. This fossil is the big-toe bone I mentioned at the beginning of this article [*see the illustration below*]. Its head is both tilted and twisted with respect to its shaft, characteristics that are found only in modern man and that can with assurance be correlated with a striding gait. Day has recently completed a dimensional analysis of the bone, using a multivariate statistical technique. He is able to show that the fossil is unquestionably human in form.

There is no evidence to link the big-toe bone specifically to either of the two recognized hominids whose fossil remains have been recovered from Bed I at Olduvai: *Homo habilis* and *Zinjanthropus boisei*. Thus the owner of the toe remains unknown, at least for the present. Nonetheless, one thing is made certain by the discovery. We now know that in East Africa more than a million years ago there existed a creature whose mode of locomotion was essentially human.

12

Human Growth

GEORGE W. GRAY

April 1967

Among the 160 children of various ages whose development is being followed in the remarkable study of human growth by the Child Research Council in Denver, Col., is a boy whom we shall call Tommy Smith. In nursery school he was a top member of his class—a happy, normal, healthy, highly intelligent youngster. But as he approached the age of five, the records began to show a flattening of his growth curve: he lost weight and stopped gaining in height. The staff nutritionist, calling at his home for a check-up, found that the boy's appetite had fallen off sharply. He was not eating enough, particularly not enough milk, and the result was a shortage in his intake of proteins and minerals. Actually, the whole staff for some time had been noticing symptoms of retardation in this apparently healthy boy. The psychologists had reported that Tommy had regressed in mind as well as in body. His I.Q. rating had dropped. He seemed tense, anxious, uncertain. His inner strains were reflected in his responses to the Rorschach inkspot test, the thematic apperception test and other psychological techniques.

A clue to his trouble was disclosed by one of these techniques: doll play. Three dolls, representing a man, a woman and a small boy, were placed on the floor, together with an assortment of doll furniture and other household accessories. Tommy proceeded to "play house," and in his play he sent the mother doll off "to the office," put the father doll in the kitchen getting the next meal and wondered aloud whether the little boy doll would grow up into a man. Maybe, he speculated, the boy would become a woman and go off to the office "like mamma."

Here was the anxiety that underlay Tommy's loss of interest in food, his interrupted growth and his lapses in I.Q. It turned out that the doll drama re-

enacted his actual home situation. Tommy's mother had a job which kept her away from home from early morning until late afternoon. The father, whose business hours were not exacting, did many of the housekeeping chores, fed and dressed the boy and took him to and from school. Because the mother frequently came home exhausted, the father often put the child to bed. It was all very confusing to Tommy. He was at the stage in which a normal boy wants to identify himself with a male figure, but his family setup was such that he was not certain what the figure stood for—and anyway, he was not sure that he wanted to be that kind of man.

The Child Research Council is not a clinic: it does not treat diseases or disorders. But when symptoms come to light in the course of its research, it calls them to the attention of the parents and their family physician. In this case the

parents finally recognized that their son's disturbance stemmed from themselves, and they immediately made adjustments to correct the situation. The mother went on half time at her business and made it her main job to love and care for Tommy. The father relinquished many of his mothering services. Within a few months after this realignment of the parental roles, Tommy was a much happier and better adjusted boy. He was eating so voraciously that the family doctor had to advise cutting down on his carbohydrates; his height and weight resumed their growth, and again he stood head and shoulders above his classmates in intelligence tests.

"This is not an unusual case," says Alfred H. Washburn, director of the Child Research Council. "I'm quite sure that other people working in guidance centers with play techniques could tell similar stories. But the episode does illustrate

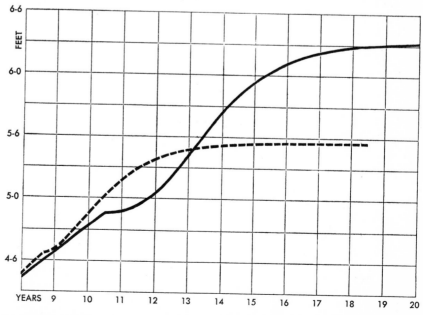

RATES OF GROWTH of a boy (solid line) and a girl (broken line) are contrasted by these curves. Girls enter and complete the adolescent phase of rapid growth earlier than boys.

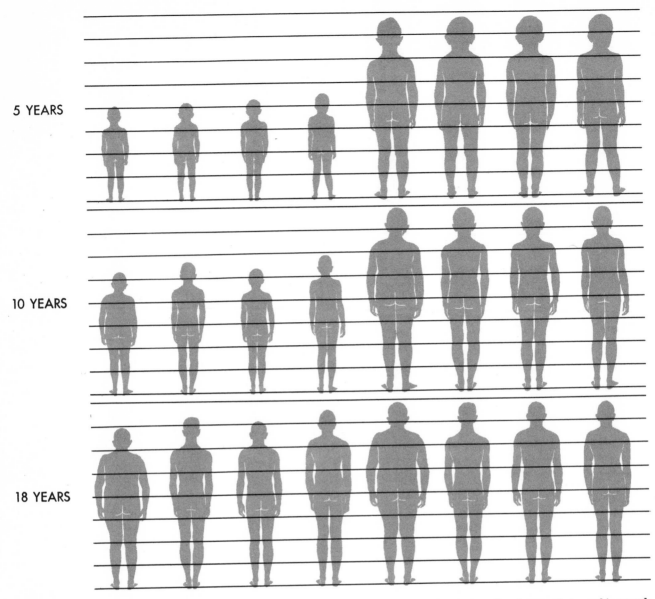

5 YEARS

10 YEARS

18 YEARS

CHANGES IN PROPORTIONS OF THE BODY that come with growth are illustrated by profiles of changing figures of four boys and four girls. The drawings are based upon photographic records kept by Child Research Council. In each panel, four figures are pic-

the three-fold nature of growth, and the interdependence of the growth factors. Human growth is a sensitively balanced complex of processes in which body structure, physiological function and emotion each plays its indispensable part—and a disturbance or deficiency of one factor can seriously affect the others. Here in Denver we are endeavoring to follow the course of each of these factors through the entire life spans of our children. We are keeping records of each individual from infancy into childhood and from childhood into adulthood. We intend to continue the study of each life until accident or old age eventually writes its finis."

Washburn, a tall, rangy man now in his late fifties, is a native of Boston who was graduated from Amherst College in

1916 and from the Harvard Medical School in 1921. Classmates recall that as a student he was not bashful about challenging medical dogma. During his internship something that he read in a book prompted Washburn to scribble this query in the margin: *Why hasn't medicine been more concerned with the problem of understanding the whole life cycle of a human being during healthy growth?*

Why not, indeed? There was a vast file of assorted information on the anatomy, physiology, psychology, behavior and diseases of the human system. There were multitudinous tomes on man-in-the-abstract. But never had a satisfactory study been made of the life cycle of even *one* human individual. "We know more about how a garden pea or a hog or a

laboratory rat grows and adapts to varying environmental conditions," reflected Washburn, "than we do about how a person grows up and becomes the kind of adult he is."

With such ideas stewing in his brain, the young medical graduate went West to start the private practice of pediatrics in Portland, Ore. While there he held an instructorship at the University of Oregon. The following year the University of California called him to Berkeley, and soon Washburn was the gadfly of its faculty with his persistent questions about the life cycle, about what is normal in human growth and about the importance of making a beginning toward a science of man.

Meanwhile an interest in these same questions was fermenting among physi-

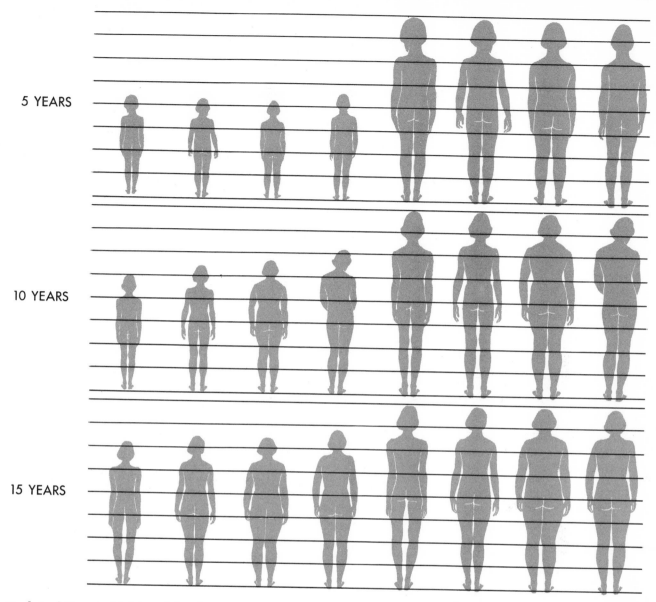

5 YEARS

10 YEARS

15 YEARS

tured at relative actual height at left and, at right, all of the figures are blown up to the same arbitrary height to bring out contrasts in proportion. Major change in both sexes is relative
increase of height to breadth of body as long bones achieve growth.

cians and public-spirited citizens in
Colorado. In the early 1920s a group in
Denver had set up a project in preven-
tive medicine to examine children periodically for early signs of tuberculosis
and respiratory disease. But after five
years of operation its financial support
had failed, and the project would have
lapsed but for the intervention of a few
local physicians and scientists. They had
caught the vision of a larger objective.
Instead of limiting the examinations to
tests for disease, they asked, why not
consider the child as a whole, study each
as an individual and follow his pattern
of growth and adaptation continuously?

The proponents of this idea enlisted
the interest of the president of the University of Colorado, and the project had
a new birth. It was incorporated by the

State as the Child Research Council.
The University of Colorado School of
Medicine offered laboratory and admin-
istrative quarters in its building, and the
Council agreed to make its findings
available to the school. But a leader was
needed, and at this stage the Council
discovered Washburn, then an associate
professor at California. It invited the
transplanted New Englander to Denver,
bombarded him with questions on his
favorite theme, and hired him on the
spot to become director of its research.
That was in 1930. Washburn gathered
an extraordinary team of investigators
which has now been working together
closely for more than two decades.

The oldest of the 160 persons whose
life cycles are being followed by Dr.
Washburn and his 26 associates is now

32 years of age, and the youngest was
born last month. Occasionally the group
loses a subject: a family moves to another city, a girl grows up and marries
an outsider, a boy goes away to a distant
job. But such losses are kept at a minimum by selecting the subjects from
stable families. By adding three to five
new babies annually, the Council has
steadily increased its roster. The current
enrollment is about as large as the present staff can keep track of, but the staff
may eventually be increased to where it
can enroll a maximum of 200 subjects.

"We have to realize that most of the
children we are studying now will out-
live every member of our present staff,"
Washburn observes. "Other investigators will complete the observations that
we begin, and reap the harvest of what

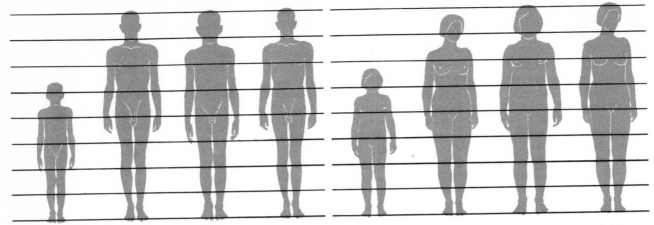

HOW BOY AND GIRL CHANGE in build between the age of five and completion of growth (boy at 18, girl at 15) is shown here. In each panel the figures are paired at the same relative age. The figures at right in each panel are blown up to same height.

we have sown. All the more important, then, is our obligation to plan the program on an adequate scale, to start each study with a full realization of what it may mean for the future and to record the findings with thoroughness and a scrupulous care for accuracy and relevance.

"Our effort is based on the theory that the adult is what he is, and behaves as he does, as a result of his total transactions of living—and that means the sum of his experiences from conception on to his present age. We proceed on the hypothesis that this continual interplay between the individual and his environment is susceptible of observation, measurement and interpretation at three levels of organization—physical, physiological and psychological. Those three categories define our study: *physical* growth and adaptation as shown by structure, *physiological* growth and adaptation as shown by functioning, and *psychological* growth and adaptation as shown by mental ability, emotional attitudes, social behavior and other ingredients of personality.

"We have tackled this many-sided, long-range and difficult research on the assumption that, from learning how people succeed or fail in adjusting to their world, we can obtain information which will guide children toward becoming happier, healthier and more useful members of society."

Physical Growth

Photography is an indispensable tool for studying growth. With X-ray photography the Council measures the

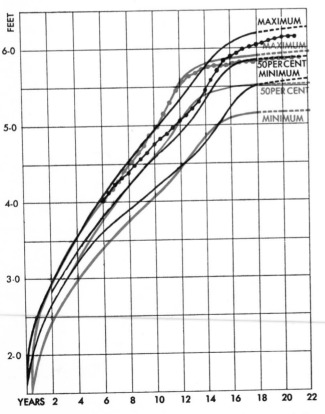

■■■ BOY CONTRASTING GROWTH PATTERNS of the
GIRL boy and girl whose figures are profiled above are

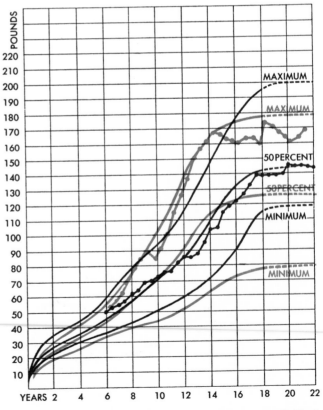

shown in charts which compare the curves of these individuals (beaded lines) with maximum, minimum and median curves for

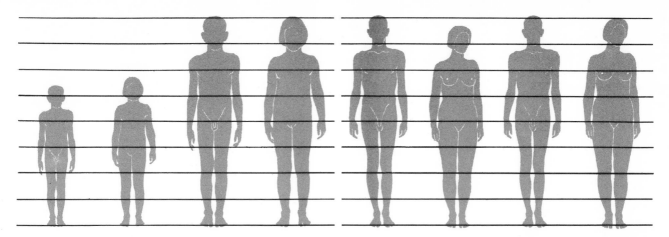

HOW BOY AND GIRL CONTRAST at the same stages of growth is shown in these two panels. In panel at left their figures are com- pared at the age of five; at right, at the completion of growth, with the figures blown up to same height at right in each panel.

growth of leg bones, arm bones, the head, chest, spine, heart, lungs, teeth and other internal organs and tissues; with direct photography it records the shape of bodily development. Nothing shows so plainly where and at what rate physical growth is taking place as a series of photographs of the same individual, taken at regular intervals over a period of years.

Edith Boyd, a pediatrician who specializes in anatomy, devised a simple technique which has enormously increased the value of the photographic

records. "I took an enlarger," explained Dr. Boyd, "and projected all the photographs of a subject at various ages to the same height; for example, using the height of the subject at his current age, say 16, the images of the child at one year, at five years, at 10 and at 12 were all blown up to this height. Then I could see at a glance what changes had taken place in his body form.

"One of the biggest differences among people is their distribution of mass—whether they are long-legged or short-legged, how wide they are for their

height, whether the hips or the shoulders are wider. In the series of pictures blown up to the same height, I found that I could measure how much of the child's mass was made up of his foot, how much of his leg, his thigh and so on up the body. I could follow and trace changes in the relative masses of these structural features. In a baby or small child, the shoulders may be wide compared to the hips; as a boy approaches school age, his shoulders and hips may come about even; as he goes into his puberty growth, his hips broaden out. While the boy's

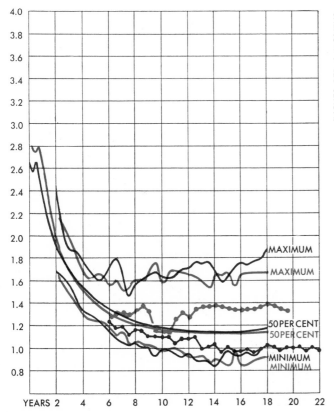

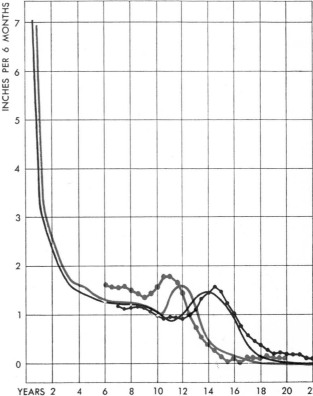

healthy children of the Denver group. Charts from left to right are height, weight, ratio of increase in height and weight, and rate of

growth. The girl is shown to be relatively heavy for her height, the boy relatively light. Girl's rate of growth peaks earlier than boy's.

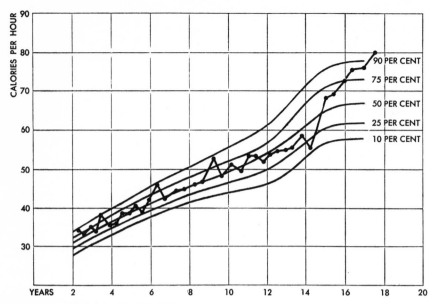

BASAL METABOLISM is a sensitive indicator of the demands of growth. X-ray pictures at the bottom of spread explain why this boy's metabolism ascends so sharply at 15 years.

hip mass is growing, the shoulder mass is standing still, so the ratio changes."

Dr. Boyd showed a series of photographs of a girl from infancy to her eleventh year. "Her shoulders will broaden, but her hips will grow still wider," she commented. "For a boy the probability is that as he grows into adolescence, his hips will not grow proportionately wider, but his shoulders will—and that, of course, is one of the major sex differences in physique.

"When a person reaches adulthood, growth is completed only in the sense that the body has reached its maximum stature. There will be further changes in the structure, but they will be more gradual, and a photograph every five years instead of every year should be sufficient. The oldest photograph in our present file was taken at age 28. I don't see why we shouldn't attempt to trace the structural changes of aging just as we trace the structural changes of growing up. Every period of life is significant in a life-cycle study. And so I hope my successor will follow these subjects through to the end."

Another pediatrician on the staff, Jean Deming, specializes in biometrics. Dr. Deming has subjected the growth data collected by Dr. Boyd to mathematical analysis and plotted the results in a curve for each individual. Actually two curves are necessary: one, known as the Rachel Jens curve, represents growth from birth to the beginning of adolescence; the other, an elongated S called the Gompertz curve, covers the period of adolescence. The Rachel Jens curve is fairly uniform for both boys and girls. But the Gompertz curve of adolescent growth is markedly different for the two sexes. In girls, the curve begins to bend upward into the first arm of the S at an earlier age and at a more rapid rate of ascent than in boys. But while the typical boy's curve starts later, and turns upward more slowly, it keeps ascending long after the typical girl's curve has leveled off.

"Plotting the growth of children brings out at a glance facts which, though obvious and well known, are apt to be ignored until they are shown graphically," said Dr. Deming. "One of these differences is the earlier maturing of the girl. You can see it dramatized in these two curves," and she picked up a sheet comparing a boy's and a girl's growth in height. "Note how almost parallel the two curves are up to the start of the girl's adolescence, which in this case occurred at 8½ years. The boy's adolescent growth spurt did not begin until he was 10½, when the girl's height was far above his, and she kept above him until about 13. Thereafter the boy kept on growing at a rapid rate, while the girl leveled off.

"We are all familiar with the fact that in junior high school the typical girl is much larger and more grown up than the typical boy of the same age. She's not interested in dates with these small boys; she wants to go with older boys. It is interesting also to see how the curve follows the personality pattern. The growth curve of a feminine type of boy—with a soft rounded body and a greater interest in dolls than in baseball, for example—usually follows the typical girl's

pattern. Similarly girls of the tomboy type usually have a growth pattern conforming to that of boys."

Internal Structure

The staff member primarily responsible for measuring the growth of the internal structure of the body is Marian Maresh. She also is a pediatrician with a specialty: X-ray. Some of the most exciting discoveries of physical growth have come through roentgenology. Dr. Maresh works in close collaboration with Dr. Deming and Dr. Boyd in interpreting the X-ray pictures. The Council's collection of X-ray photographs of the chest is the largest on healthy children in the world.

"This collection of films," said Dr. Maresh, "has helped us to define the range of normality and to understand the variations that an individual child may have and still remain healthy. We had been taught in medical school that a child's chest film must look a certain way. Now we know that each child has his own standard and carries it through life, as far as we have gone. As he grows up, he may have a severe pneumonia or any of a number of other acute infections, but as soon as he has recovered, he will swing back to his own pattern of normality. He will not carry with him the so-called scars of repeated infections, unless he is chronically ill.

"As for sinuses, we have found that their appearance in a child has very little relation to his health. He may have small

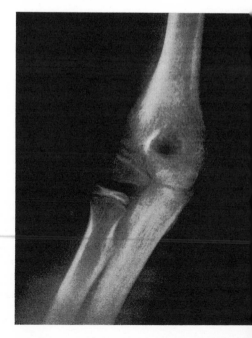

ELBOW JOINT is site of one of the principal mile stones in the process of growth. This is the fusion o

sinuses or large sinuses, occasionally cloudy sinuses, and still be a healthy child. This, of course, is quite contrary to what one finds in grown-ups. An adult with a cloudy sinus is apt to be sick."

The Council's chest X-rays have shown that the range of variability in the size and shape of the normal heart is greater than anatomists had believed. "Heart size is related to body size," declared Dr. Maresh. "A child who has been growing fast and is overweight is going to have a large heart. A child of medium body build, whose height-weight relationship is about average, will usually have a heart of average size. He will seldom have a small heart such as we find in the thin child. When it comes to shape, the hearts of healthy children have differences so great that some of them suggest textbook pictures of congenital heart disease—and yet nothing is wrong. The shape of a child's heart is his own business. After he gets that shape, he is going to keep it, barring affliction with a serious disease."

The growth spurt that marks the entrance to adolescence is revealed with a wealth of minutiae by the X-ray photographs. Within a few months the bones, lungs, heart and other organs may grow at a speed double or even treble the previous rate. As the general growth of the body slows down after adolescence, the heart actually decreases in size. This is not strange when you remember that the heart is a muscle. Muscles grow with use and diminish as the use grows less—and the heart is no exception.

Every child is an individual. Each has a unique structural pattern, which may or may not conform to what has been regarded as normal. In her X-ray study of the growth of bones, for example, Dr. Maresh has found a wide variation in the age at which the junctions between the long bones mature. Most boys are born with no wrist bones, only a soft cartilage, and girls rarely have more than one bone in the wrist at birth. The cartilage progressively calcifies into eight small bones. The rate at which they form has been taken as an index to bone development. But the Denver records show that at the age of five a healthy child may have anywhere from two to seven bony centers in the wrist; only 20 per cent of the children have the number heretofore regarded as normal for that age.

"The bone studies are my absorbing interest just now," went on Dr. Maresh. "We X-ray the left arm and leg at two-month intervals during the first six months of life, at six-month intervals from then on through adolescence and yearly thereafter. So I build up a serial picture of the growth of the upper arm, lower arm, upper leg, lower leg, and the relation of each to the growth of the body as a whole. The major difference between boys and girls is in the relative length of the forearm, which is longer in boys. That partly explains why women can't wear men's coats. My shoulders are as broad as my husband's, but his coat sleeves come down to the middle of my hand. This is a sex difference I did not

expect to find. There is no difference between the male and female in the relative length of the upper arm bone or in the length of the legs in relation to body height.

Five of the children in the Denver study group are cousins; their five fathers are all brothers. These children present a wide range in size; one, a boy, is among the smallest for his age in the entire group, and another, a girl, is one of the largest girls of her age. Despite the size variation, all five children have the same structural pattern. Their pattern of relative bone length is somewhat unusual—yet it is the same for all. "We believe," remarked Dr. Maresh, "that eventually we're going to learn how people are put together, and where they inherit the bits that make up the differences. It seems clear that what a child inherits is not his body as a whole, but segments of it, or functions of it, or perhaps patterns of development."

Physiological Growth

As the body grows toward its adult form, new functions are developed and old ones are extended. The production of blood, the input of food, the output of energy, the reaction of nerve and muscle to stimuli—each plays a part in this business of growing up. And so the Child Research Council has a team of biochemists, nutritionists, hematologists and others who concentrate their talents on the physiological aspects of growth, under the general supervision of Robert

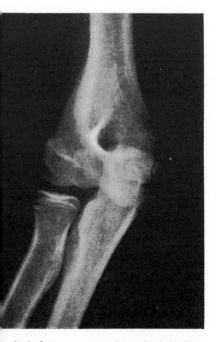 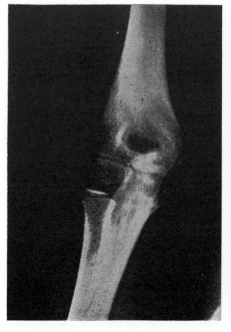 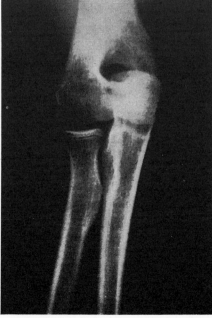

...e little bony center at the end of the long ...one in the upper arm with that bone. These two pairs of pictures show a boy's elbow (left) and a girl's before and after fusion. The boy's metabolism (see chart on opposite page) showed steep increase when this fusion was occurring.

McCammon, the assistant director of the council.

Fundamental to life is metabolism—the two-way process by which nutrients are built into new tissue and, inversely, broken down to release energy. Basal metabolism, the minimum expenditure of energy required by the body at rest, is a base-line for the study of all physiological phenomena. One of the first routines established by the Council was the periodic measurement of the basal metabolism of its children. As data from these studies accumulated, staff members were appalled to discover how little was available in the way of standards for comparison. Actually the Council's own measurements of metabolic rates, published in 1940, were the first reliable tables for the ages from infancy to adolescence. Today those rates recorded in Denver are the norms for medical practice in many parts of the world.

In the same way the Council instituted studies to determine the level of red cells, white cells and other cellular components of the blood at various stages of growth. A similar inquiry measured the proportions of albumin, globulins and other proteins in the blood. Many of these blood determinations have been widely accepted by pediatricians as the most comprehensive data on blood-cell and blood-protein levels in early life.

An infant's blood differs from that of older children in its proportions of both cells and proteins, and differs still more from that of adults. There are also striking sex differences. For example, girls tend to have fewer white cells than boys, but a larger proportion of their white cells are of the specialized infection-fighting kind known as lymphocytes. At certain age levels the girls have fewer red cells per unit of blood than the boys have. Carotene, a substance the body uses to make vitamin A, is found in greater abundance in infant girls than in infant boys. But when the children reach 12 or thereabouts, the situation reverses: then the boy's blood has the greater proportion of carotene. "This finding has fascinating implications," said Dr. Washburn, "for it indicates an inverse relationship between growth and a food factor. In infancy males tend to grow more rapidly than females, but at age 12 most girls are moving into their adolescent growth spurt, while the boys' growth is still on the slow side. And note that in each sex it is only at the period of accelerated growth that the carotene level falls to a low point. I don't know what it means yet, but here we

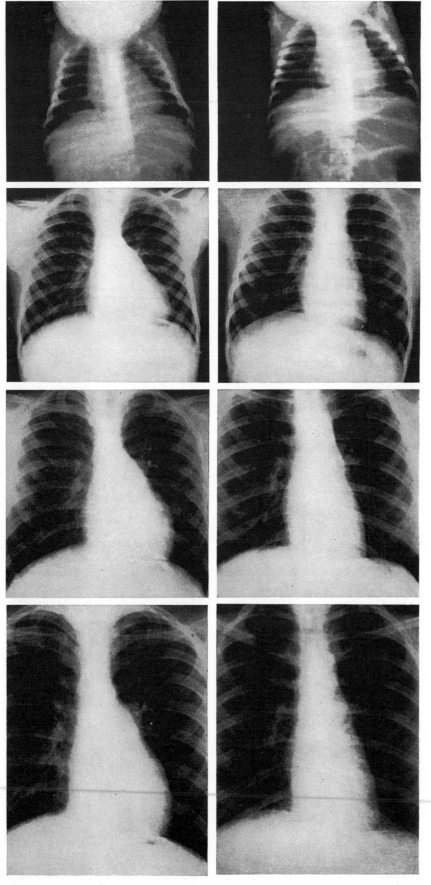

CHANGES IN HEART SIZE in response to the demands of growth found in this study have upset accepted notions of what "normal" heart size is in children. Here the heart of a boy (left) and a girl are shown at comparable stages of growth from infancy to adolescence.

have what seems to be a relationship between the intake of a food substance, the sex of the individual and the pattern of growth."

The record of each child's food intake begins even before the baby is born. In the third month of the mother's pregnancy, Virginia Beal, the nutritionist, visits the home, examines the menus and checks on the variety and quantities of food consumed. After the infant's arrival, these periodic check-ups record exactly what the child is eating. In several cases Miss Beal has been able to spot deficiencies and predict nutritional disorders.

"On one occasion," related Washburn, "Miss Beal came in and said: 'This baby is not getting enough protein, minerals or vitamin D—she's headed for rickets.' The other staff members were highly skeptical. We had never seen a case of rickets in our entire series of children and we couldn't believe that any nutritional measurement could be so accurate. But three months later Dr. Maresh brought me an X-ray film of that child, and there it unmistakably was in the photograph. The case was mild, to be sure, but the bone structure showed evidence of rickets."

The primary purpose of these nutritional studies is to see how the child's growth correlates with its food intake. "Quantitative, as well as qualitative, changes in the blood, bones and teeth have long been recognized as related to the composition of the diet," said Washburn. "But no one yet has done a good job of determining exactly how they are related. We have found evidence that the dietary standards recommended by the National Research Council may need correcting. Our data show that the NRC stated requirements for certain nutrients during the first five years of life are too high. Not even our healthiest children are living up to them. For certain other nutrients the NRC standards are probably too low. We have found that some of our children are getting more vitamins than they need or can use. In the case of vitamins A and D, an overdose can be damaging, and this whole field of accessory food factors needs appraising to determine how much of each vitamin is the optimum ration for a growing child."

It is fascinating to watch the correlations between physical and physiological growth. One of the milestones in physical growth is the joining of the first little bony center in the elbow with the long bone of the upper arm. While this fusion is taking place, the basal metabolic rate rapidly rises to a higher level. It is as though the two processes had to be syn-chronized as the body's whole system poises for the tremendous adolescent growth spurt.

Dr. McCammon and the group of biochemists and physiologists recently discovered a correlation between the levels of the blood proteins beta and gamma globulin and the development of lymph tissue in the body. When a child's blood contains high levels of these globulins, he is apt to have larger tonsils, larger adenoids and more lymph nodes of every kind. The observations suggest that such children are more resistant to colds and other respiratory diseases than children with a smaller endowment of globulins.

The protein content of the blood is related to the functioning of the heart. Over the years the Child Research Council has accumulated thousands of electrocardiograms of its children, and these are now in process of being analyzed. The results so far indicate that the difference in timing between the peaks and valleys of a child's electrically-recorded heart waves are correlated in some way with the levels of globulins and other plasma proteins in its blood.

"We might theorize," said Washburn, "that the same circumstance which leads the child to build up resistance to infections—namely, his stock of plasma proteins—is also concerned with keeping his heart functioning efficiently. This opens an interesting possibility. It suggests that here we may have a means of evaluating a child's ability to adapt to environmental handicaps."

Globulin relationships seem to pop up everywhere. Recently Washburn, in collaboration with the staff biochemist, Virginia Trevorrow, and the staff hematologist, Adula Meyers, completed a study of red cell sedimentation. Physicians have long used this test to diagnose certain diseases: they take a sample of blood from the patient and record the time it takes for the red cells to settle in a test tube. Fast sedimentation is taken to be a sign of an active infection, such as acute rheumatic fever or active tuberculosis. But Washburn and his associates have found that the blood of perfectly healthy children sometimes has a fast sedimentation rate, while that of rheumatic fever patients sometimes is slow. From many years of study they have concluded that there is no necessary relationship between an infection and the speed of sedimentation. They believe the sedimentation rate is influenced in part by the relative amount of certain proteins in the blood. And one of these proteins is gamma globulin! Some of the proteins are found in connection with infections,

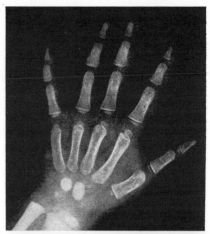

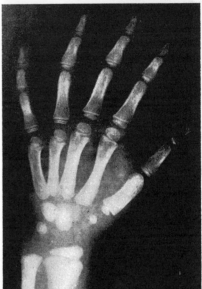

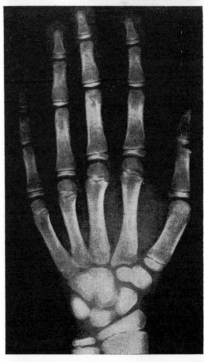

BONES OF WRIST are index of growth. Calcification of seven bones in child's wrist is shown at two, four and eight years.

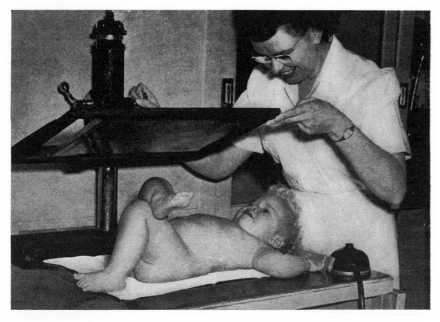

INFANT SUBJECT of study is here in midst of one of her first complete physical examinations at Denver Child Research Council which may record growth throughout her entire life.

others not; some increases in a protein represent good resistance, others not—and so the speed of sedimentation alone can no longer be accepted as a signal or measure of disease.

Psychological Growth

The Denver children vary widely in Intelligence Quotient. Moreover, the I.Q. is not constant; not only do individuals fluctuate but the group as a whole goes down at certain age levels. Studies conducted by Arnold Hilden indicate that a majority of the children are unable to function at their best in intelligence tests in the period from about age five to eight, and there is another dip at adolescence, when many youngsters fall back from 5 to 15 points.

There is a close correlation between a child's anxiety level and his performance in an intelligence test. It was found, for example, that a boy who suddenly dropped from a consistently high I.Q. to a low one was seething with resentment against his new step-mother—although she doted on him and never dreamed that the "honey-sweet" boy was other than an obedient, loving son. In instance after instance, when the I.Q. took a sudden tumble examination revealed that there was some home conflict or other development, real or imaginary, which was a source of emotional strain. It is significant that the drop in I.Q. between the fifth and eighth years coincides with the period when the child is preparing for or just entering school—a time of trial, uneasiness and uncertainty for most children. Similarly the slowing down at

adolescence synchronizes with a characteristically unsettled period in the teen-ager's emotional life.

Recognizing the critical role of the emotions, the Council gives particular attention to the dynamic aspects of psychology. John Benjamin, an M.D. who has had broad experience in psychiatry, is in charge of these studies. They begin before the child is born, when Dr. Benjamin or one of his associates calls at the home to get acquainted with the parents. This prenatal visit affords an opportunity to appraise the home, the attitude of the parents toward the expected baby and the emotional and cultural climate in which it will receive its first impressions of the world—the initial environmental stimuli to growth and adaptation.

The child's early impressions are important and at about six months they become enormously so. The second half of its first year is a period of acute sensitivity. Any attitude on the part of the mother that suggests withdrawal or denial of her love, any prolonged separation of the baby from the mother, any quarreling or other chronic conflicts in the home, can have serious repercussions. The anxieties which result from such situations can adversely affect the baby's intake of food, retard its growth and build up an emotional pattern which is reflected years later in its attitudes and behavior. Just how long the effect persists is not yet known, for the Council's studies of anxiety in infants extend back less than a decade. The Council has cases in which emotional traumas inflicted in the first year or two of life have shown specific outcroppings in the per-

sonalities of children four or five years later. Some of the resulting symptoms are enough to send the shivers down your back.

There are mothers to whom breast feeding is repugnant but who dutifully nurse their babies because they have been told, or have the impression, that it is best for the baby. No matter how conscientious such a mother may be, it is very difficult for her to give the breast feedings with the full sense of pleasure and satisfaction that the child craves. Actually a mother who feeds her infant from a bottle and at the same time lovingly cuddles it against her will do a better job of child raising. She will be rearing hers with much less of the uncertainty, doubt and anxiety that inevitably beset an infant whose mother dislikes the nursing process heartily and goes about it with a coldness and matter-of-factness that cannot be disguised.

The baby's reaction may express itself in the rejection of food or in bowel disturbances such as minor diarrhea and minor constipation. The Council psychologists have observed many cases in which an emotional upset was followed by disturbances in intake of food, in handling of food and in growth.

An experiment with animals made by a graduate student of the University of Colorado last year under Dr. Benjamin's supervision brings at least a suggestion of corroborative evidence. Twenty laboratory rats were divided into two groups. Each group was supplied with exactly the same kinds and amounts of food and was provided with the same living conditions. But the rats of one group were caressed and cuddled by the investigator, while the other group was treated coldly. "It sounds silly," said Washburn, "but the petted rats learned faster and grew faster." The experiment is now being repeated, with biochemical extensions, to find out if possible how the cuddled group could grow faster on the same food intake.

Besides the usual psychological and personality tests, the Council psychologists make use of many informal techniques to study their children from the second year on. These include doll play, free play, painting, drawing and clay modeling.

In free play all the toys are displayed, and the child is free to pick up anything and play with whatever strikes its fancy. Sometimes the child will take out the toys indiscriminately, scatter them around the room, and do nothing constructive. "This is harder to interpret than direct play," said Washburn, "but the child who merely throws things about is usually disturbed, though he doesn't know how to express his anxiety."

I was given an opportunity to listen in on a free play experience of a 4½-year-old boy observed by Katherine Tennes, one of the psychologists. The child ran quickly to the open cupboard of toys and took out two pistols. "I want a gun," he said. Handing a gun to Mrs. Tennes, he added: "Here's one for you." Then he said: "I'm Roy Rogers, and you're an Indian." He told her to sit in a chair, climbed to the top of the cupboard and shouted: "I'm going to shoot you!" After shooting, he remarked: "My father's name is Roy Rogers." Then, noticing a dish of candy on the cupboard, he asked: "Can I have a piece of candy?" When Mrs. Tennes nodded, he took a piece and ate it.

"Now that is a very simple episode," explained Mrs. Tennes, "but it conveyed a lot of meaning. This boy has aggressive feelings toward people, but he is usually quiet and polite. He expresses in play the feelings which in the ordinary circumstances of his life he is not permitted to show directly. He identified himself with Roy Rogers because Roy Rogers is someone who can't be hurt. The fact that he then called his father Roy Rogers showed that he has made a very positive identification with his father. That is one of the things we are interested in finding out about a child—whether he identifies more with his father or with his mother. It will make a difference in the smoothness of his adjustments as he grows up. The candy incident illustrated the usual polite, subdued behavior to which he returns when he is confronted with a reality situation."

Sometimes the free play becomes highly dramatic, and even violent, with the starkest sort of symbolism reminiscent of Freudian theory. What comes out in the play is checked by other procedures. In the finger painting, for example, an aggressive child will almost invariably select violent colors, such as red or purple, and lay them on in vertical strokes with broad lines, whereas one who is mild-mannered and placid usually paints with horizontal lines and soft colors.

These techniques are useful not only for unmasking the anxieties which are troubling the growing child, but also as instruments for testing, validating, and expanding personality theory. After all, the subject of the process of growing up is a person, and the final objective of all these studies—physical, physiological and psychological—is to understand how an infant person, starting at scratch, becomes the kind of adult that he does.

PART III
INTRAPOPULATION
VARIATION

*Introduction: Genetic mechanisms
and evolutionary adaptations*

Mutations changes in the amino acid sequence of DNA (see the article "The Genetic Code" by F. H. C. Crick in Part II) constitute the basis of all genetic variation, and thereby underlie all the complexity and variety of the living world. These mutations provide the raw material—the potential for the adaptation of living material to the constant expansion and elaboration of new ecosystems—brought about by the changing physical and chemical properties of the earth and atmosphere through the course of time, and by the diversification and evolution of living organisms themselves.

The directional force in the evolution of life, from simple forms to those as complex as man, has been and continues to be natural selection. Those organisms best adapted to each new and evolving environment or ecosystem at any point in time are those that leave the largest number of reproductively successful progeny in the succeeding generation. Individual organisms die, and life continues by the replacement of one generation of organisms by another (Wallace and Srb, 1964). Therefore, reproductive performance provides the only measure of adaptation, and populations rather than individuals constitute the units of evolution. Because environments and entire ecosystems are constantly fluctuating and changing, adaptation to any particular set of conditions must be accompanied by a retention in the population gene pool of genetic variability, a potential for adaptation to future environments. The most effective organisms in a given environment will eventually become extinct if this potential for adaptation to the ever changing environment is not retained. In all probability, this was the fate of the great reptiles, and the genus *Homo* stands in marked contrast. Its descendants have survived periods of radical environmantal changes, and now occupy a greater variety of ecological niches than any other organism.

The manner in which mutation and natural selection have cooperated in evolution and in the maintenance of genetic variability was introduced in the first article in Part I, "The Genetic Basis of Evolution," by Dobzhansky, and is further elaborated in this section in "Ionizing Radiation and Evolution" by James F. Crow. The article "The Evolution of the Hand," by John Napier, describes some of the adaptive and directional changes that have taken place in the course of man's evolutionary history. In "Adaptations to Cold," Laurence Irving presents an example of man's adaptation to one element of the physical environment. The success of this adaptation to cold has depended in great part upon man's abilities as a cultural animal.

It is surprising, but unfortunately true, that even when accepting the principles of Darwinian and genetic theory, social scientists tend to emphasize the word "natural" in natural selection, thereby thinking only of the physical environment and failing to recognize what an important selective force culture has exerted in the course of a large part of man's evolution. Many ethnologists consider culture to be above and completely separate from biological characteristics of the responsible organism. The fallacy of this thinking is illustrated by Sherwood L. Washburn in "Tools and Human Evolution," and is implied by Charles F. Hockett in "The Origin of Speech." Communication is fundamental to the adaptation of practically all forms of life (Wallace and Srb, 1964) and becomes particularly critical for bisexual organisms, in which successful reproduction (the basis of natural selection) may be dependent upon elaborate methods of communication. Culture, and the development of social systems, are totally dependent upon communication.

Related to man's elaborate systems of communication is his most unique characteristic—his mental capacities, afforded by his highly evolved central nervous system. The understanding of this constitutes the greatest challenge to modern biology, and at present, is the area in which the least is known. The article "Learning to Think," by Harry F. Harlow and Margaret Kuenne Harlow, introduces this problem area. There are, however, a number of ramifications, or consequences, of man's mental abilities that bear importantly upon genetic mechanisms as they operate in human populations, and they deserve notice here.

1. Because of the significance of culture as a selective force in human evolution and because of man's conscious control of critical behavioral patterns, one should refrain from too readily applying to man genetic models that have been derived from studies of infrahuman species. Man's cultural control and modification of his physical environment throughout much of his evolutionary history has probably subjected him, more than any other animal, to diversifying and disruptive types of selection pressures. Most theoretical formulations concerning natural selection are constructed for infrahuman species in which classic directional or stabilizing forms of selection have predominated. Diversifying and disruptive selection increases the variance within a species, whereas directional or stabilizing selection decreases variance.

2. Because of man's conscious control of population movements and mating patterns—based upon learned responses to complex cultural conditioning, such as responsibility or subservience to various types of extended family units, property ownership, trade specializations, and so on—neither the human species as a whole nor any sizeable subgroup of it has probably ever constituted a panmictic population.

3. Man, with his consciously controlled behavior and his participation in

various forms of problem-solving, made possible by his intellectual development, has engaged in almost constant population movements, expansions, and contractions throughout his evolutionary history. As a result, changes in human population size and composition have been relatively rapid, whereas those of other organisms, which have been stimulated primarily by the relatively slow fluctuations of the biotic and physical environment, have been gradual.

Total isolation of any human population has probably always been confined to small groups of people, and in general for only limited periods of time. More commonplace have been partial isolations, with some mixture or hybridization occurring at almost every generation level, sufficient, as evidenced by the unity of the diverse forms of the polytypic human species, to maintain coadaptive gene systems.

The importance of these unique features of man's evolutionary history has been overlooked by some students in their eagerness to apply to humans the more simple and ready-made formulations used for infrahuman species, and there has also been a not uncommon misinterpretation of certain basic principles of population genetics.

Selection or drift

One of the more important misconceptions is the dichotomization of selection and genetic drift, based on the assumption that changes in gene frequencies of evolutionary significance must be due either to variations in selection or to accidents of sampling (genetic drift). This point of view has probably been responsible for the fact that anthropological thought has been through a "drift" phase and is now in a largely "selection" phase. When Wright first proposed the drift theory to explain certain variances between populations, most differences between human populations were immediately assumed to be due to drift. Little was known at that time about man's possible adaptive mechanisms. Assumptions had been arrived at on the basis of Lamarckian concepts and it was convenient to think that all good "marker" genes, such as those that were responsible for the red cell antigens, were selectively neutral. The selection phase, which now prevails, resulted in part from increased sophistication in the identification of selection mechanisms. A classic example is presented in Anthony C. Allison's "Sickle Cells and Evolution." Although this represents important progress the tendency has been to disregard almost completely drift as a cause of frequency change in any important evolutionary genes, and, whenever a selection factor has been identified, to attempt to explain any difference between populations as the result of this single phenomenon.

It was pointed out by Sewall Wright, first in 1931 and again in 1948, that selection and drift are not mutually exclusive: the fluctuations of some genes are undoubtedly due to shifting conditions of selection; other genes in the same population may have a deviant frequency caused by drift; still others may be influenced by both selection and drift, therefore showing joint effects (Wright, 1931, 1948).

Dobzhansky and Povlovsky (1957) demonstrated in an experiment the manner in which genetic drift and selection can show joint effects. Twenty replicate experimental populations of *Drosophila pseudo-obscura* were kept in a uniform environment for eighteen months. Ten of the populations were established with 4,000 individuals each. The other ten populations each consisted of descendants from only twenty individuals. The parental generation in each of these twenty populations showed a 50-50 frequency for two different gene arrangements in the third chromosome. Heterozygotes for these two gene combinations are adaptively superior to the two homozygotes. At the end of the experiment, the frequencies of one of the arrangements varied, from 20–35 percent in the ten populations descended from large numbers, and from 16–47 percent in those descended from small numbers. Selection was operating but drift was also having an effect, causing significant heterogeneity in the replicate populations, and much greater heterogeneity in the populations descended from small numbers.

In the experiment of Dobzhansky and Povlovsky, the combined effects of selection and drift and the importance of population size were demonstrated. In populations derived from small numbers, succeeding generations will also be relatively small, with an increased likelihood that chance deviations in the sampling of genes will occur from one generation to the next. Had the small populations been established by a random drawing of the twenty founders from the parental stock, instead of by an intentional selection for a 50-50 frequency of the two gene arrangements, an additional random effect might have occurred. This is known as founder's effect, and is the chance deviation in sampling from the parental stock, and it is identical in both principle and effect with drift—the chance deviations which may occur during reproduction—in each succeeding generation. In this classic form, founder's effect is the mathematical equivalent of drift. In man, however, and possibly in many other animals as well, founder's effect is further complicated by the fact that the founders of a new colony or population are biologically related. This complication will be considered subsequently with the discussion of the consequences of small population size.

Effective population size

The general rejection in recent years of drift as an important factor in human evolution, and as an explanation of differences in gene frequencies between populations has been based, at least partly, on an exaggerated idea of the size of effective populations. This rejection may be one of the prices we have had to pay for the otherwise encouraging acceptance of the unity of the human species. To some anthropologists, unity of the human species means that, in the study of genetic problems, man can be considered as one great big panmictic family. This is not true, and probably has never been. However, because few if any ethnographies include quantitative information about the size and age structure of a population (Osborne, 1957), there is little empirical evidence with which to challenge this comfortable assumption.

Total population size has no actual genetic meaning. Only the effective population number, which is the number of breeding individuals who contribute to the succeeding generation (Kimura and Crow, 1963) is of any importance, and this may be a mere 30–50 percent of the total population. In populations having any unequal sex distribution at breeding age, the effective size is closer to the lower percentage. In populations that fluctuate in size from generation to generation—probably an almost universal characteristic of human populations throughout human evolution—the effective number is closer to the population low points than to the high points (Wright, 1931). The actual effective population number cannot be easily inferred from total population size at any one period of time. In studies on reproductive performance, it has been demonstrated that the complex of factors affecting reproduction also reduces the effective number. In one study, it was found that 25 percent of the women produced one-half of the progeny.

Centuries after the beginnings of agriculture, most communities numbered only a few hundred people, and even if several such communities had constituted the breeding unit the effective population size would be small enough for drift to be a factor. That drift and founder's effect are important influences in human populations is illustrated by H. Bentley Glass in "The Genetics of The Dunkers."

Founder's effect in human population

For a colonizing species, which man has been throughout his evolutionary history, founder's effect can be very important. Most colonies are formed by small numbers of individuals; repetitive colonization of small numbers would substantially increase drift effects, and would contribute importantly to the difference between groups and consequently to the development of a polytypic species.

Founder's effect can have an additional influence upon the genetic structure of a population. Because of man's conscious control of his behavior, colonization will rarely if ever result in a random sampling of a parent population. Brothers will follow brothers, and many members of one extended family group will participate in migration, while other families stay at home.

This tendency will enhance the genetic consequence of founder's effect. It assures a biased sampling of the parental gene pool and may contribute to a second correlate of population size, inbreeding effect.

In small populations, even if random mating were to pertain, common ancestors are less remote than in large populations. Every individual must have two parents, four grandparents, eight great grandparents, and so on. Ten generations removed, there are 1,024 such ancestors. If the effective breeding population has never exceeded more than a few hundred individuals, any two members of a mated pair have a number of common ancestors in the course of very few ancestral generations. This causes inbreeding effects, a correlation in the gene content of uniting gametes, or autozygosity (Kimura and Crow, 1963b). If a small number of founders giving rise to a population are already genetically related, the likelihood of inbreeding effects increases. Inbreeding results in a redistribution of variance. The consequence of preferred mating of cross cousins, which occurs in some cultures, is not a change in gene frequencies, but a change in the relative proportions of homozygotes to heterozygotes. Even with constant coefficients of selection, this will increase the efficiency of selection and thereby the speed of genetic change or evolution. In small populations, inbreeding increases the differences between breeding isolates and decreases the genetic variance within the breeding groups.

The history of the human species has been characterized by population movement and colonization, the latter occurring under conditions that have maximized both founder's effect and inbreeding effect. In the study of the human population problem, attention must be given to Sewall Wright's principle: "that in any large population divided and sub-divided into partially isolated local groups of small size, there is a continually shifting differentiation in and among these groups, intensified by local differences and selection, which inevitably brings about an infinitely continuing and irreversible adaptive and much more rapid evolution of the species" (Wright, 1931).

Migration and hybridization

The emphasis that Wright places upon "partially isolated groups of small size" constitutes a vital point missed by many anthropologists, who assume that only total isolation is important.

As stated previously, man's almost constant population movements, consequent upon his cultural control of the physical environment and his intellect, have resulted for the most part in frequent but only partial and short-term isolation of small groups. Although massive migration may swamp the effects of drift and selection, small migrations occurring under the conditions of partial isolation will not cancel the effects of either drift or selection (Wright, 1931). Differences in gene frequencies between groups will still accumulate. The small migrations will maintain genetic continuity between populations. As few as one migrant per generation may be sufficient to keep a common gene from going to fixation. Perhaps the greatest importance of migration as it most typically occurs, from large central populations into small marginal partial isolates, is that it necessitates the maintenance of coadaptive gene systems, and thereby assures the unity of the human species.

Literature cited

Dobzhansky, Theodosius, and O. Povlovsky. 1957. An Experimental Study of Interaction Between Genetic Drift and Natural Selection. *Evolut.*, Vol. 2, pp. 311–319.

Kimura, M., and J. F. Crow. 1963a. On the Measurement of Effective Population. *Evolut.*, Vol. 17, pp. 279–288.

——— — ———. 1963b. On the Maximum Avoidance of Inbreeding. *Genet. Res.*, Vol. 4, pp. 399–415.

Osborne, R. H. 1957. The Anthropologist and Population Genetics: A Discussion of of Ethnographic Method. *Davidson J. Anthro.*, Vol. 3, pp. 25–34.

Wallace, B., and A. M. Srb. 1964. *Adaptation*. 2nd ed., Englewood, New Jersey, Prentice-Hall.

Wright, Sewall. 1931. Evolution in Mendelian Populations. *Genet.*, Vol. 16, pp. 97–159.

———. 1948. On the Roles of Directed and Random Changes in Gene Frequency in the Genetics of Populations. *Evol.*, Vol. 2, pp. 279–295.

13

Ionizing Radiation and Evolution

JAMES F. CROW
September 1959

The mutant gene—a fundamental unit in the mechanism of heredity that has been altered by some cause, thereby changing some characteristic of its bearers—is the raw material of evolution. Ionizing radiation produces mutation. Ergo, ionizing radiation is an important cause of evolution.

At first this seems like a compelling argument. But is it really? To what extent is the natural rate at which mutations occur dependent upon radiation? Would evolution have been much the same without radiation? Is it possible that increased exposure to radiation, rising from human activities, has a significant effect upon the future course of human evolution?

Radiation has been of tremendous value for genetic research, and therefore for research in evolution. To clarify the issue at the outset, however, it is likely that ionizing radiation has played only a minor role in the recent evolutionary history of most organisms. As for the earliest stages of evolution, starting with the origin of life, it is problematical whether ionizing radiation played a significant role even then. Laboratory experiments show that organic compounds, including the amino acid units of the protein molecule, may be formed from simple nitrogen and carbon compounds upon exposure to ionizing radiation or an electric discharge. But ultraviolet radiation serves as well in these demonstrations, and was probably present in large amounts at the earliest ages of life. In the subsequent history of life the development of photosynthesis in plants and of vision in animals indicates the much greater importance of nonionizing radiation in the terrestrial environment.

Nonetheless, as will be seen, man presents an important special case in any discussion of the mutation-inducing effects of ionizing radiation. The mutation rate affects not only the evolution of the human species but also the life of the individual. Almost every mutation is harmful, and it is the individual who pays the price. Any human activity that tends to increase the mutation rate must therefore raise serious health and moral problems for man.

H. J. Muller's great discovery that radiation induces mutations in the fruit fly *Drosophila*, and its independent confirmation in plants by L. J. Stadler, was made more than 30 years ago. One of the first things to be noticed by the Drosophila workers was that most of the radiation-induced changes in the characteristics of their flies were familiar, the same changes having occurred repeatedly as a result of natural mutation. Not only were the external appearances of the mutant flies recognizable (white eyes, yellow body, forked bristles, missing wing-veins); it could also be shown that the mutant genes were located at the same sites on the chromosomes as their naturally occurring predecessors. Thus it seems that radiation-induced mutants are not unique; they are the same types that occur anyhow at a lower rate and that we call spontaneous because we do not know their causes.

The prevailing hypothesis is that the hereditary information is encoded in various permutations in the arrangement of subunits of the molecule of deoxyribonucleic acid (DNA) in the chromosomes. A mutation occurs when this molecule fails, for some reason, to replicate itself exactly. The mutated gene is thereafter reproduced until its bearer dies without reproducing, or until, by chance, the altered gene mutates again.

A variety of treatments other than radiation will induce mutation. Most agents, including radiation, seem to affect the genes indiscriminately, increasing the mutation rate for all genes in the same proportion. But some chemical mutagens are fairly selective in the genes they affect. It is even conceivable that investigators may find a chemical that will regularly mutate a particular gene and no other. This will probably be very difficult to achieve: A mutagen capable of affecting a specific gene would probably have to have the same order of informational complexity as the gene itself in order to recognize the gene and influence it.

Moreover, different mutant genes known to be at different locations on the chromosome frequently produce effects that mimic each other. Geneticists who work with fruit flies are familiar with several different genes that result in indistinguishable eye colors. This is not surprising when we consider the complexity of the relationship between genes and the characteristics that they produce. There are many different paths by which any particular end-point may be reached; it is to be expected that many different gene changes can lead to the same result, though the chemical pathways by which this is accomplished may be greatly different.

To consider another kind of example, many insects have come to survive insecticides. They do so by such diverse means as behavior patterns that enable them to avoid the insecticide, mechanisms that interfere with the entrance of the insecticide into the body, enzymes that detoxify the insecticide, and by somehow becoming able to tolerate more of the insecticide. All these modes of survival develop by selection of mutant genes that are already present in low frequency in the population. This is one of the characteristic features of evolution: its opportunism. It makes use of the raw materials—that is, the mutant genes—that happen to be available.

As a first conclusion it appears that radiation-induced mutations do not play any unique role in evolution. The same gene mutations would probably occur anyhow. Even if they did not, the same end result could be achieved with other mutants.

One might still suspect that spontaneous mutations are caused by natural radiations. This was quickly ruled out as a possibility in Drosophila. For one thing, the spontaneous-mutation rate is strongly dependent upon temperature, which would be surprising if mutation were a simple and direct consequence of radiation. But much more decisive evidence comes from the fact that the amount of natural radiation is entirely inadequate to account for the rate of spontaneous mutation. The natural-mutation rate in Drosophila, if it were caused solely by radiation, would require 50 or more r. Yet the amount of radiation received by a fly in the 12-day interval between egg and mature adult is about .004 r. Natural radiation would have to be increased more than 10,000 times to account for the natural Drosophila mutation rate! Thus, in Drosophila at least, radiation accounts for only a trivial part of the spontaneous rate. The same is true for mice. Although the fraction of spontaneous mutations that owe their origin to radiation is higher than that in Drosophila, it is still less than .1 per cent.

It is clear that natural-mutation rates, if they are measured in absolute time-units, cannot be the same in all organisms. One example will demonstrate this decisively. The spontaneous-mutation rate in Drosophila is such that about one embryo in 50 carries a lethal mutation (a mutation harmful enough to cause death) that occurred during the preceding generation. Most such mutations are recessive, that is, they have a lethal effect only when they are in a double dose, but this does not prevent the death; it only postpones it. The reproductive life-cycle in man is approximately 1,000 times as long as that of a fly: some 30 years as compared with 12 days. If the absolute mutation-rate in man were the same as that in Drosophila, each human embryo would bear an average of 20

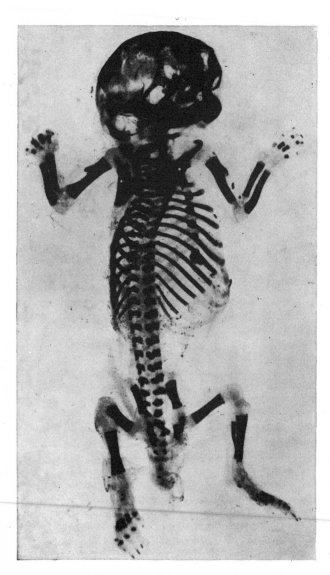

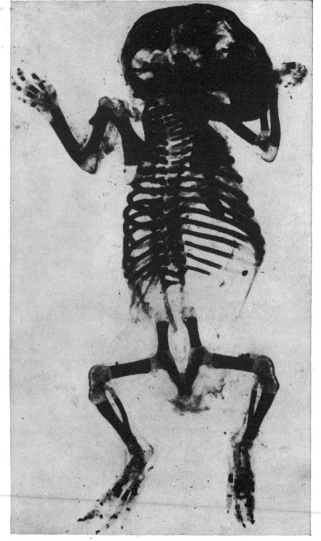

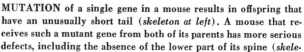

MUTATION of a single gene in a mouse results in offspring that have an unusually short tail (*skeleton at left*). A mouse that receives such a mutant gene from both of its parents has more serious defects, including the absence of the lower part of its spine (*skele-* *ton at right*); it dies soon after birth. These specimens were prepared in the laboratory of L. C. Dunn of Columbia University. The soft tissues were treated with strong alkali and glycerin to make them transparent; the bones were stained with a red dye.

new lethal mutations; man would quickly become extinct.

Actually, if the rate is measured in mutations per generation, the spontaneous-mutation rate of those few human genes whose mutation rates can be effectively measured is roughly the same as that of Drosophila genes. The rule seems to be that the absolute mutation-rate divided by the generation period is much more nearly constant from one species to another than the rate itself. The implication of this is exciting. It can only mean that the mutation rate itself is capable of modification; that it, too, is changed by natural selection. By being brought into adjustment with the life cycle, the underlying mechanism of evolution itself is undergoing evolution!

It appears, however, that the rates of radiation-induced mutations are not as readily modified. If these rates were being adjusted along with the rates of mutations from other causes, we would expect that mice would show a lesser response to radiation than do fruit flies because their life cycle is longer. The facts are otherwise; mouse genes average some 15 times as many mutations per unit of radiation as Drosophila genes.

This strongly suggests that the process whereby mutations are produced by radiation is less capable of evolutionary adjustment than other mutation-producing processes. The implication is that organisms with a long life-cycle—Sequoia trees, elephants, men—have a larger fraction of mutations due to natural radiations. It may be that the majority of mutations in a very long-lived organism are due to radiations. Possibly this sets an upper limit on the length of the life cycle.

Unfortunately the rate of radiation-induced mutations is not known for any organism with a long life-cycle. If we assume that the susceptibility of human genes to mutation by radiation is the same as that of mouse genes, we would conclude that less than 10 per cent of human mutations are due to natural radiations. But the exact fraction is quite uncertain, because of inaccurate knowledge of the rate of spontaneous human mutations. So it cannot be ruled out that even a majority of human mutations owe their origin to radiation.

Thus the over-all mutation rate is not determined by radiation to any significant extent, except possibly in some very long-lived organisms. In general, radiation does not seem to play an important role in evolution, either by supplying qualitatively unique types of mutations or by supplying quantitatively significant numbers of mutations.

There is another question: To what extent is the rate of evolution dependent on the mutation rate? Will an organism with a high mutation-rate have a correspondingly higher rate of evolution? In general, the answer is probably no.

The measurement of evolutionary rates is fraught with difficulty and doubt. There is always some uncertainty about the time-scale, despite steady improvements in paleontology and new techniques of dating by means of the decay of radioactive isotopes. In addition there is the difficulty of determining what a comparable rate of advance in different species is. Is the difference between a leopard and a tiger more or less than that between a field mouse and a house mouse? Or has man changed more in developing his brain than the elephant has by growing a trunk? How is it possible for one to devise a suitable scale by which such different things can be compared?

Despite these difficulties, the differences in rates of evolution in various lines of descent are so enormous as to be clear by any standard. One criterion is size. Some animals have changed greatly. The horse has grown from a fox-sized ancestor to its present size while many other animals have not changed appreciably. (The British biologist J. B. S. Haldane has suggested that the word "darwin" be used as a unit for rate of size change. One darwin is taken to be an increase by a factor e per million years. By this criterion the rate of evolution of tooth size in the ancestors of the horse was about 40 millidarwins.)

More difficult to quantify, but more significant, are changes in structure. Some animals have changed very little in enormous lengths of time. There are several examples of "living fossils," some of which are depicted on the preceding two pages. During the time the coelacanth remained practically unchanged whole new classes appeared: the birds and mammals, with such innovations as feathers, hair, hoofs, beaks, mammary glands, internal temperature-regulation and the ability to think conceptually. What accounts for such differences in rate?

The general picture of how evolution works is now clear. The basic raw material is the mutant gene. Among these mutants most will be deleterious, but a minority will be beneficial. These few will be retained by what Muller has called the sieve of natural selection. As the British statistician R. A. Fisher has said, natural selection is a "mechanism for generating an exceedingly high level of improbability." It is Maxwell's famous demon superimposed on the random process of mutation.

Despite the clarity and simplicity of the general idea, the details are difficult and obscure. Selection operates at many levels—between cells, between individual organisms, between families, between species. What is advantageous in the short run may be ruinous in the long run. What may be good in one environment may be bad in another. What is good this year may be bad next year. What is good for an individual may be bad for the species.

A certain amount of variability is necessary for evolution to occur. But the comparison of fossils reveals no consistent correlation between the measured variability at any one time and the rate of evolutionary change. George Gaylord Simpson, now at Harvard University, has measured contemporary representatives of low-rate groups (crocodiles, tapirs, armadillos, opossums) and high-rate ones (lizards, horses, kangaroos) and has found no tendency for the latter to be more variable. Additional evidence comes from domesticated animals and plants. G. Ledyard Stebbins, Jr., of the University of California has noted that domesticated representatives of slowly evolving plant groups produce new horticultural varieties just as readily as those from more rapidly evolving groups. Finally, the rates of "evolutionary" change in domestic animals and plants under artificial selection by man are tremendous compared with even the more rapidly evolving natural forms—perhaps thousands of times as fast. This can only mean that the genetic variability available for selection to work on is available in much greater abundance than the variability actually utilized in nature. The reasons why evolution is so slow in some groups must lie elsewhere than in insufficient genetic variability.

Instances of rapid evolution are probably the result of the opening-up of a new, unfilled ecological niche or environmental opportunity. This may be because of a change in the organism itself, as when the birds developed the power of flight with all the new possibilities this offered. It may also be due to opening-up of a new area, as when a few fortunate colonists land on a new continent.

One of the best-known examples of rapid change is to be found in the finches of the Galápagos Islands that Charles Darwin noted during his voyage on the *Beagle*. Darwin's finches are all descendants of what must have been a small number of chance migrants. They are a

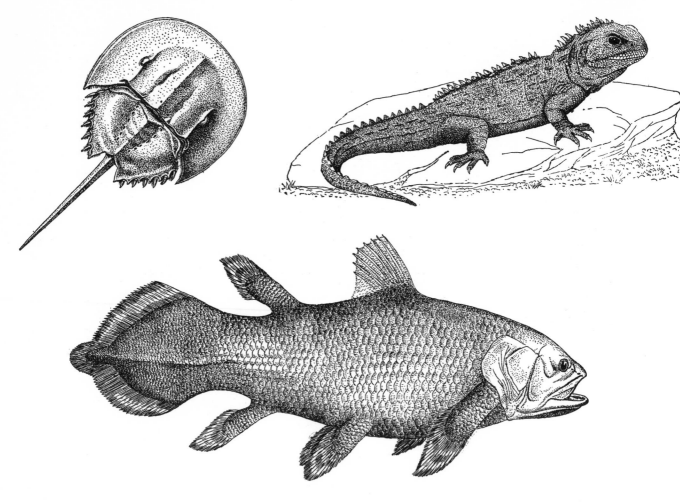

RATE OF EVOLUTION in certain organisms is extremely slow. Depicted in these drawings are four animals that have not changed appreciably over a period of millions or even hundreds of millions of years. At top left is the horseshoe crab; at top center, the tuatara;

particularly striking group, especially in their adaptations to different feeding habits. Some have sparrow-like beaks for seed feeding; others have slender beaks and eat insects; some resemble the woodpeckers and feed on insect larvae in wood; still others feed with parrot-like beaks on fruits. The woodpecker type is of special interest. Lacking the woodpecker's long tongue it has evolved the habit of using a cactus spine or a twig as a substitute—it is the only example of a tool-using bird. In the rest of the world the finches are a relatively homogeneous group. Their tremendous diversity on these islands must be due to their isolation and the availability of new, unexploited ecological opportunities. A similar example of multiple adaptations is found in the honey creepers of the Hawaiian Islands [see Illustration on page 150].

When paleontologists look into the ancestry of present-day animals,

they find that only a minute fraction of the species present 100 million years ago is represented by descendants now. It is estimated that 98 per cent of the living vertebrate families trace their ancestry to eight of the species present in the Mesozoic Era, and that only two dozen of the tens of thousands of vertebrate species that were then present have left any descendants at all. The overwhelmingly probable future of any species is extinction. The history of evolution is a succession of extinctions along with a tremendous expansion of a few fortunate types.

The causes of extinctions must be many. A change of environment—due to a flood, a volcanic eruption or a succession of less dramatic instances—may alter the ecological niche into which the species formerly fitted. Other animals and plants are probably the most important environmental variables: one species is part of the environment of another. There may be a more efficient predator, or a species that competes for shelter or

food supply, or a new disease vector or parasite. As Theodosius Dobzhansky of Columbia University has said, "Extinction occurs either because the ecological niche disappears, or because it is wrested away by competitors."

Extinction may also arise from natural selection itself. Natural selection is a short-sighted, opportunistic process. All that matters is Darwinian fitness, that is, survival ability and reproductive capacity. A population is always in danger of becoming extinct through "criminal" genes—genes that perpetuate themselves at the expense of the rest of the population. An interesting example is the so-called SD gene, found in a wild Drosophila population near the University of Wisconsin by Yuichiro Hiraizumi. Ordinarily the segregation ratio—the ratio of two alternative genes in the progeny of any individual that carries these genes—is 1:1. In this strain the segregation is grossly distorted to something like 10:1 in favor of the SD gene; hence its name, SD, for segregation distorter. The SD

at bottom center, the recently discovered coelacanth; at the far right, the opossum.

gene somehow causes the chromosome opposite its own chromosome to break just prior to the formation of sperm cells. As a result the cells containing the broken chromosome usually fail to develop into functional sperm. The SD-bearing chromosome thus tends to increase itself rapidly in the population by effectively killing off its normal counterpart. Such a gene is obviously harmful to the population. But it cannot be eliminated except by the extinction of the population, or by the occurrence of a gene that is immune to the SD effect.

A similar gene exists in many mouse populations. Causing tail abnormalities, it is transmitted to much more than the usual fraction of the offspring, though in this case the detailed mechanism is not known. L. C. Dunn of Columbia University has found this gene in many wild-mouse populations. Most of these genes are highly deleterious to the mouse (a mouse needs a tail!), and some are lethal when they are borne in a double dose, so that the gene never complete-

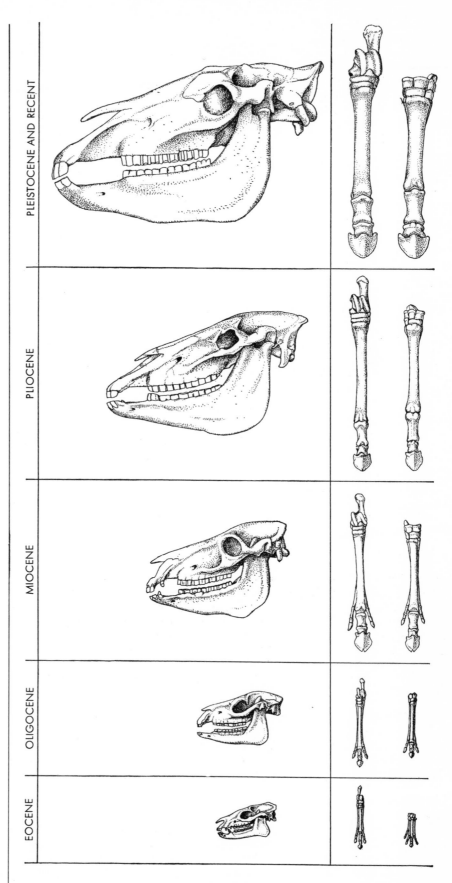

RAPID RATE OF EVOLUTION is illustrated by the horse. Comparisons of the skulls, hindfeet and forefeet of animals of successive periods indicate the changes which led from a fox-sized ancestor in the Eocene period, 60 million years ago, to the modern horse (top).

ly takes over despite its segregational advantage. The result is an equilibrium frequency determined by the magnitude of the two opposing selective forces: the harmfulness of the gene and its segregational advantage. The population as a whole suffers, a striking illustration of the fact that natural selection does not necessarily improve the fitness of the species.

A gene causing extremely selfish, antisocial behavior—for example genes for cannibalism or social parasitism—could have similar effects in the human population. Any species must be in constant danger from the short-sightedness of the process of natural selection. Those that are still here are presumably the descendants of those that were able to avoid such pitfalls.

Aside from mutation itself, the most important evolutionary invention is sexual reproduction, which makes possible Mendelian heredity. The fact that such an elaborate mechanism exists throughout the whole living world—in viruses and bacteria, and in every major group of plants and animals—attests to its significance.

In a nonsexual population, if two potentially beneficial mutations arise in separate individuals, these individuals and their descendants can only compete with each other until one or the other type is eliminated, or until a second mutation occurs in one or the other

HONEY CREEPERS of Hawaii are a striking example of rapid evolution. Dozens of varieties, adapted to different diets, arose from a common ancestor. The long bills of *Hemignathus lucidus affinis* (1), *Hemignathus wilsoni* (4) and *Hemignathus o. obscurus* (7) are used to seek insects as woodpeckers do or to suck nectar. The beaks of *Psittirostra kona* (2), *Psittirostra cantans* (3), and *Psittirostra psittacea* (6) are adapted to a diet of berries and seeds. *Loxops v. virens* (5) sucks nectar and probes for insects with its sharp bill. *Pseudonestor xanthrophrys* (8) wrenches at hard wood to get at burrowing insects. Some of these species are presently extinct.

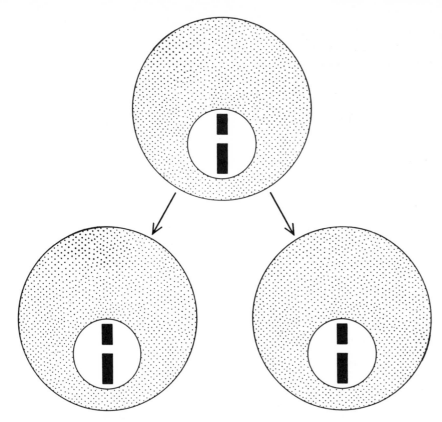

ASEXUAL REPRODUCTION permits little variability in a population; the evolution of asexual organisms depends entirely on mutation. At top is a schematic diagram of an asexual cell. Within its nucleus (*open circle*) are chromosomes (*rectangles*). When the cell divides (*bottom*), its two daughter cells have replicas of the original chromosomes and are exactly like the parent. To simplify the diagram only two of the chromosomes of a cell are shown.

direct observational evidence for this. Probably many asexual forms have become extinct because they were unable to adapt to changes. Other forms have become overspecialized, developing structures that fit them for only a particular habitat; when the habitat disappears, they are lost. The population size and structure are also important. To be successful in evolution, by the criterion of having left descendants many generations later, a species has the best chance if it has an optimum genetic system. But among a number of potentially successful candidates, only a few will succeed, and probably the main reason is simply the good luck of having been at the right place at the right time.

Of all the natural selection that occurs, only a small fraction leads to any progressive or directional change. Most selection is devoted to maintaining the status quo, to eliminating recurrent harmful mutations, or to adjusting to transitory changes in the environment. Thus much of the theory of natural selection must be a theory of statics rather than dynamics.

The processes that are necessary for evolution demand a certain price from the population in the form of reduced fitness. This might be said to be the price that a species pays for the privilege of evolving. The process of sexual reproduction, with its Mendelian gene-shuffling in each generation, produces a number of ill-adapted gene combinations, and therefore a reduction in average fitness. This can be avoided by a nonsexual system, but at the expense of genetic variability for evolutionary change in a changing environment.

The plant breeder knows that it is easy to maintain high-yielding varieties of the potato or sugar cane because they can be propagated asexually. But then his potential improvement is limited to the varieties that he has on hand. Only by combining various germ plasms sexually can he obtain varieties better than the existing best. But the potato and cane breeder can have his cake and eat it. He gets his new variants by sexual crosses; when he gets a superior combination of genes, he carries this strain on by an asexual process so that the combination is not broken up by Mendelian assortment.

Many species appear to have sacrificed long-term survival for immediate fitness. Some are highly successful. A familiar example is the dandelion; any lawn-keeper can testify to its survival value. In dandelion reproduction, although seeds are produced by what looks superficially like the usual method, the

group. A Mendelian species, with its biparental reproduction and consequent gene-scrambling, permits both mutants to be combined in the same individual. An asexual species must depend upon newly occurring mutations to provide it with variability. Sexual reproduction permits the combination and recombination of a whole series of mutants from the common pool of the species. Before they enter the pool the mutants have been to some extent pretested and the most harmful ones have already been eliminated.

Suppose that a population has 50 pairs of genes: Aa, Bb, Cc, etc. Suppose that each large-letter gene adds one unit of size. The difference between the smallest possible individual in this population (aa bb cc . . .) and the largest possible (AA BB CC . . .) is 100 units. Yet if all the genes are equally frequent, the size of 99.7 per cent of the population will be between 35 and 65 units. Only one individual in 2^{100} (roughly 1 followed by 30 zeros) would have 100 size units. Yet if the population is sexual, this type can be produced by selection utilizing only the genes already in the population.

This example illustrates the evolutionary power of a system that permits Mendelian gene-assortment. In an asexual system the organism would have to wait for new mutations. Most of the size-increasing mutations would probably have deleterious side effects. If the asexual organism had a mutation rate sufficient to give it the potential variability of a sexual population, it would probably become extinct from harmful mutations.

The very existence of sexual reproduction throughout the animal and plant kingdoms argues strongly for the necessity of an optimum genetic variability. This is plain, even though there is no consistent correlation between evolution rates as observed in the fossil record and the variability of the animals observed. It must be that a certain level of genetic variability is a necessary, but by no means sufficient, condition for progressive evolution.

Evolution is an exceedingly complex process, and it is obviously impossible, even in particular cases, to assign relative magnitudes to the various causal factors. Perhaps species have become extinct through mutation rates that are too high or too low, though there is no

chromosome-assorting features of the sexual process are bypassed and the seed contains exactly the same combination of genes as the plant that produced it. In the long run the dandelion will probably become extinct, but in the present environment it is highly successful.

The process of mutation also produces ill-adapted types. The result is a lowering of the average fitness of the population, the price that asexual, as well as sexual, species pay for the privilege of evolution. Intuition tells us that the effect of mutation on fitness should be proportional to the mutation rate; Haldane has shown that the reduction in fitness is, in fact, exactly equal to the mutation rate.

The environment is never constant, so any species must find itself continually having to adjust to transitory or permanent changes in the environment. The most rapid environmental changes are usually brought about by the continuing evolution of other species. A simple example was given by Darwin himself. He noted that a certain number of rabbits in every generation are killed by wolves, and that in general these will be the rabbits that run the slowest. Thus by gradual selection the running speed of rabbits would increase. At the same time the slower wolves would starve, so that this species too has a selective premium on speed. As a result both improve, but the position of one with respect to the other does not change. It is like the treadmill situation in Lewis Carroll's famous story: "It takes all the running *you* can do, to keep in the same place."

A change in the environment will cause some genes that were previously favored to become harmful, and some that were harmful to become beneficial. At first it might seem that this does not make any net difference to the species. However, when the change occurs, the previously favored genes will be common as a result of natural selection in the past. The ones that were previously deleterious will be rare. The population will not return to its original fitness until the gene numbers are adjusted by natural selection, and this has its costs.

Just how much does it cost to exchange genes in this way? Let us ask the question for a single gene-pair. If we start with a rare dominant gene present in .01 per cent of the population, it requires the equivalent of about 10 selective "genetic deaths" (*i.e.*, failure to survive or reproduce) per surviving individual in the population to substitute this gene for its predecessor. This means

that if the population is to share an average of one gene substitution per generation, it must have a sufficient reproductive capacity to survive even though nine out of 10 individuals can die without offspring in each generation. The cost is considerably greater if the gene is recessive. The surprising part of this result is that the number does not depend on the selective value of the gene. As long as the difference between two alternative genes is small, the cost of replacing one by the other depends only on the initial

frequency and dominance of the gene and not at all on its fitness.

If the gene is less rare, the cost is lowered. Thus the species can lower the price of keeping up with the environment by having a higher frequency of deleterious genes that are potentially favorable. One way to accomplish this is to have a higher mutation rate, but this, too, has its price. Once again there is the conflict between the short-term objective of high fitness and the longer-term objective of ability to change with

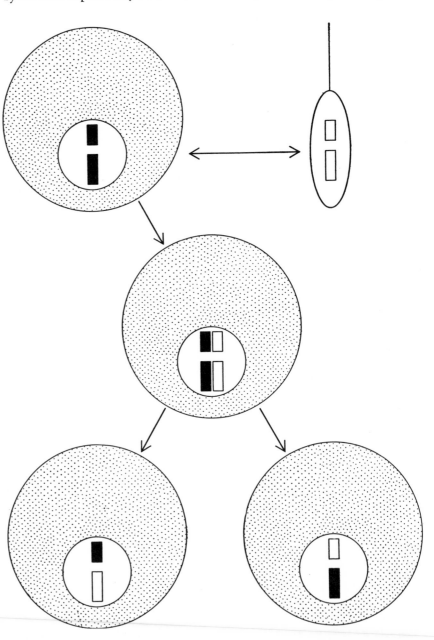

SEXUAL REPRODUCTION, also depicted in highly schematic form, depends on the union of two cells that may be from different lines of descent. At top left is an egg cell; at top right, a sperm cell. Each contains one set of chromosomes (*rectangles*). They join to form a new individual with two sets of chromosomes in its body cells (*center*). When this organism produces its own sperm or egg cells (*bottom*), each receives a full set of chromosomes. Some, however, may be from the father and some from the mother. Evolution in sexual organisms thus does not depend entirely on new mutations, because the genes already present in the population may be combined in different ways leading to improvements in the species.

the environment.

There are known to be genes that affect the mutation rate. Some of them are quite specific and affect only the mutation rate of a particular gene; others seem to enhance or depress the over-all rate. A gene whose effect is to lower the mutation rate certainly has selective advantage: it will cause an increase in fitness. This means that in most populations there should be a steady decrease in the mutation rate, possibly so far as to reduce the evolutionary adaptability of the organism. This is offset by selection for ability to cope with fluctuating environments.

How does man fare in this respect? From the standpoint of his biological evolution, is his mutation rate too high, is it too low or is it just right? It is not possible to say.

In general one would expect the evolutionary processes to work so that the mutation rate would usually be below the optimum from the standpoint of long-term evolutionary progress, because selection to reduce the mutation load has an immediate beneficial effect. Yet selection for a mutation-rate-adjusting gene is secondary to selection for whatever direct effects this gene has on the organism, such as an effect on size or metabolic rate. So we do not have much idea about how rapidly such selection would work.

Our early simian ancestors matured much more rapidly than we do now. This means that the mutation rate would have to be lowered in order to be brought into adjustment with the lengthening of our life cycle. To whatever extent the adjustment is behind the times, the mutation rate is too high. Furthermore, if it is true (as it appears to be) that radiation-induced mutation rates are less susceptible to evolutionary adjustment than those due to other causes, then an animal with a life cycle so long that it receives considerable radiation per generation may have too many from this cause.

I think it is impossible, however, to say whether man has a mutation rate that is too high or too low from the viewpoint of evolutionary advantage. It is worth noting that man, like any sexually reproducing organism, already has a tremendous store of genetic variability available for recombination. If all mutation were to stop, the possibilities for evolution would not be appreciably altered for a tremendous length of time —perhaps thousands of generations. Consider the immense range of human variability now found, for example the difference between Mozart, Newton, da Vinci and some of our best athletes, in contrast to a moron or the genetically impaired. Haldane once said: "A selector of sufficient knowledge and power might perhaps obtain from the genes at present available in the human species a race combining an average intellect equal to that of Shakespeare with the stature of Carnera." He goes on to say: "He could not produce a race of angels. For the moral character or for the wings he would have to await or produce suitable mutations." Surely the most hopefully naive eugenist would settle for considerably less!

I would argue that from any practical standpoint the question of whether

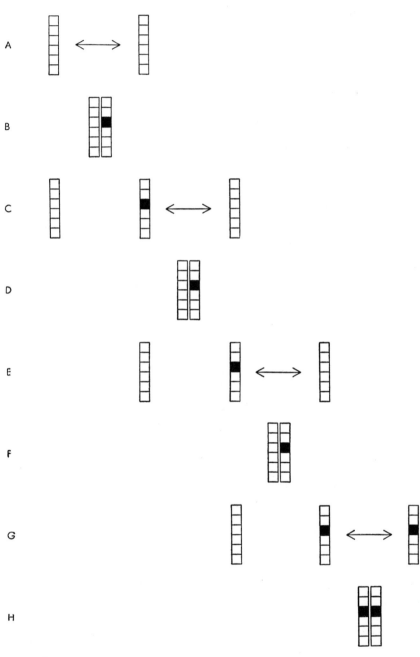

RECESSIVE MUTATION cannot be expressed in a sexual organism unless the corresponding gene of the paired chromosome has the same defect. Thus a harmful mutation can remain latent for generations. In this diagram the bars representing chromosomes are divided into squares, each symbolizing the gene for a different character. In row A the chromosomes of normal parents are paired (arrows). In row B a gene of their offspring mutates (black). In row C the mutant gene has been transmitted to the next generation but is still latent because the other parent has supplied a normal gene. This continues (rows E and F) until two individuals harboring the mutant gene mate (row G). The full effect of the mutation, harmful or otherwise, is expressed in offspring receiving a pair of mutant genes (row H).

man's mutation-rate is too high or too low for long-term evolution is irrelevant. From any other standpoint the present mutation rate is certainly too high. I suspect that man's expectations for future progress depend much more on what he does to his environment than on how he changes his genes. His practice has been to change the environment to suit his genes rather than vice versa. If he should someday decide on a program of conscious selection for genetic improvement, the store of genes already in the population will probably be adequate. If by some remote chance it is not, there will be plenty of ways to increase the number of mutations at that time.

There can be little doubt that man would be better off if he had a lower mutation-rate. I would argue, in our present ignorance, that the ideal rate for the foreseeable future would be zero. The effects produced by mutations are of all sorts, and are mostly harmful. Some cause embryonic death, some severe disease, some physical abnormalities, and probably many more cause minor impairments of body function that bring an increased susceptibility to the various vicissitudes of life. Some have an immediate effect; others lie hidden to cause their harm many generations later. All in all, mutations must be responsible for a substantial fraction of human premature death, illness and misery in general.

At the present time there is not much that can be done to lower the spontaneous-mutation rate. But at least we can do everything possible to keep the rate from getting any higher as the result of human activities. This is especially true for radiation-induced mutations; if anything they are probably more deleterious and less likely to be potentially useful than those from other causes. It is also important to remember that there are very possibly things in the environment other than radiation that increase the mutation rate. Among all the new compounds to which man is exposed as a result of our complex chemical technology there may well be a number of mutagenic substances. It is important that these be discovered and treated with caution.

The general conclusion, then, is that ionizing radiation is probably not an important factor in animal and plant evolution. If it is important anywhere it is probably in those species, such as man, that have a long life span, and at least for man it is a harmful rather than a potentially beneficial factor.

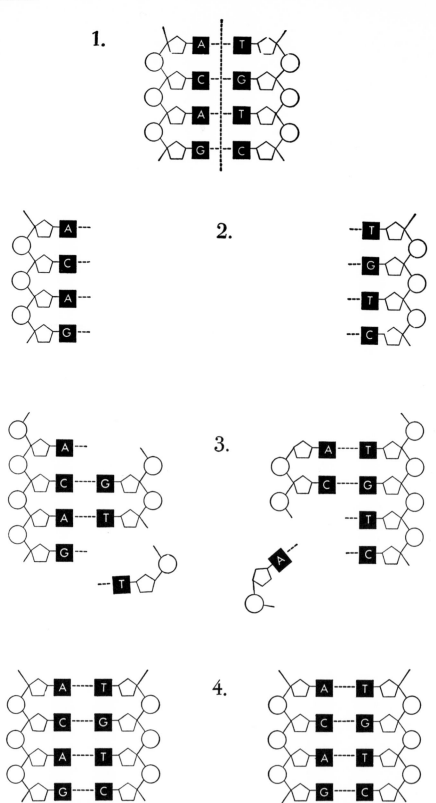

THE GENETIC MATERIAL, deoxyribonucleic acid (DNA), consists of a chain of sugar units (*pentagons*) and phosphate groups (*circles*) with side chains of bases: adenine (A), cytosine (C), thymine (T) and guanine (G). One possible mechanism for replication postulates that DNA normally contains two complementary strands, linked A—T and C—G (1). The chains then separate (2), and separate precursor units assemble along each chain (3). When they are completed, the double strands are identical to the original (4).

14

The Evolution of the Hand

JOHN NAPIER
December 1962

At Olduvai Gorge in Tanganyika two years ago L. S. B. Leakey and his wife Mary unearthed 15 bones from the hand of an early hominid. They found the bones on a well-defined living floor a few feet below the site at which in the summer of 1959 they had excavated the skull of a million-year-old man-ape to which they gave the name *Zinjanthropus*. The discovery of *Zinjanthropus* has necessitated a complete revision of previous views about the cultural and biological evolution of man. The skull was found in association with stone tools and waste flakes indicating that at this ancient horizon toolmakers were already in existence. The floor on which the hand bones were discovered has also yielded stone tools and a genuine bone "lissoir," or leather working

tool. Hence this even older living site carries the origins of toolmaking still further back, both in time and evolution, and it is now possible for the first time to reconstruct the hand of the earliest toolmakers.

Research and speculation on the course of human evolution have hitherto paid scant attention to the part played by the hand. Only last year I wrote: "It is a matter of considerable surprise to many to learn that the human hand, which can achieve so much in the field of creative art, communicate such subtle shades of meaning, and upon which the pre-eminence of *Homo sapiens* in the world of animals so largely depends, should constitute, in a structural sense, one of the most primitive and generalized parts of the human body." The im-

plication of this statement, which expresses an almost traditional view, is that the primate forebears of man were equipped with a hand of essentially human form long before the cerebral capacity necessary to exploit its potential had appeared. The corollary to this view is that the difference between the human hand and the monkey hand, as the late Frederic Wood Jones of the Royal College of Surgeons used to insist, is largely one of function rather than structure. Although broadly speaking it is true that the human hand has an extraordinarily generalized structure, the discovery of the Olduvai hand indicates that in a number of minor but nevertheless highly significant features the hand is more specialized than we had supposed.

Tool-using—in the sense of improvisa-

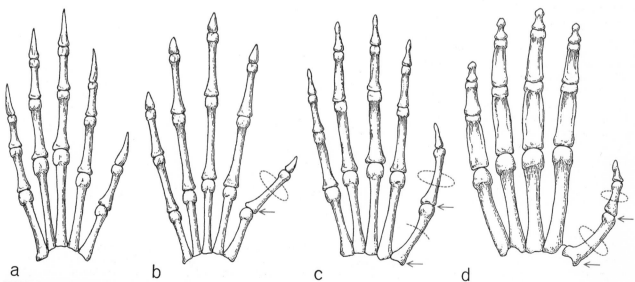

a b c d

HANDS OF LIVING PRIMATES, all drawn same size, show evolutionary changes in structure related to increasing manual dexterity. Tree shrew (*a*) shows beginnings of unique primate possession, specialized thumb (*digit at right*). In tarsier (*b*) thumb is distinct and can rotate around joint between digit and palm. In capuchin monkey (*c*), a typical New World species, angle between thumb and finger is wider and movement can be initiated at joint at base of palm. Gorilla (*d*), like other Old World species, has saddle joint at base of palm. This allows full rotation of thumb, which is set at a wide angle. Only palm and hand bones are shown here.

tion with naturally occurring objects such as sticks and stones—by the higher apes has often been observed both in the laboratory and in the wild and has even been reported in monkeys. The making of tools, on the other hand, has been regarded as the major breakthrough in human evolution, a sort of status symbol that could be employed to distinguish the genus *Homo* from the rest of the primates. Prior to the discovery of *Zinjanthropus*, the South African man-apes (Australopithecines) had been associated at least indirectly with fabri-

cated tools. Observers were reluctant to credit the man-apes with being tool-makers, however, on the ground that they lacked an adequate cranial capacity. Now that hands as well as skulls have been found at the same site with undoubted tools, one can begin to correlate the evolution of the hand with the stage of culture and the size of the brain. By the same token one must also consider whether the transition from tool-using to toolmaking and the subsequent improvement in toolmaking techniques can be explained purely in

terms of cerebral expansion and the refinement of peripheral neuromuscular mechanisms, or whether a peripheral factor—the changing form of the hand—has played an equally important part in the evolution of the human species. And to understand the significance of the specializations of the human hand, it must be compared in action—as well as in dissection—with the hands of lower primates.

In the hand at rest—with the fingers slightly curled, the thumb lying in the plane of the index finger, the poise of the

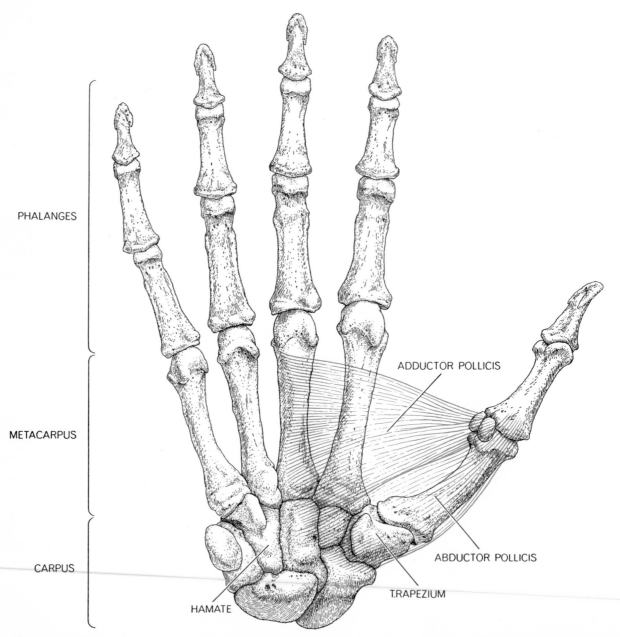

PHALANGES

METACARPUS

CARPUS

ADDUCTOR POLLICIS

ABDUCTOR POLLICIS

TRAPEZIUM

HAMATE

HAND OF MODERN MAN, drawn here actual size, is capable of precise movements available to no other species. Breadth of terminal phalanges (end bones of digits) guarantees secure thumb-to-finger grip. Thumb is long in proportion to index finger and is set at very wide angle. Strong muscles (*adductor pollicis* and *abductor pollicis*) implement movement of thumb toward and away from palm. Saddle joint at articulation of thumb metacarpal (a bone of the palm) and trapezium (a bone of the carpus, or wrist) enables thumb to rotate through 45 degrees around its own longitudinal axis and so be placed in opposition to all the other digits.

whole reflecting the balanced tension of opposing groups of muscles—one can see something of its potential capacity. From the position of rest, with a minimum of physical effort, the hand can assume either of its two prehensile working postures. The two postures are demonstrated in sequence by the employment of a screw driver to remove a screw solidly embedded in a block of wood [*see illustration below*]. The hand first grips the tool between the flexed fingers and the palm with the thumb reinforcing the pressure of the fingers; this is the "power grip." As the screw comes loose, the hand grasps the tool between one or more fingers and the thumb, with the pulps, or inner surfaces, of the finger and thumb tips fully opposed to one another; this is the "precision grip." Invariably it is the nature of the task to be performed, and not the shape of the tool or object grasped, that dictates which posture is employed. The power grip is the grip of choice when the full strength of the hand must be applied and the need for precision is subordinate; the precision grip comes into play when the need for power is secondary to the demand for fine control.

The significance of this analysis becomes apparent when the two activities are correlated with anatomical structure. The presence or absence of these structural features in the hands of a lower primate or early hominid can then be

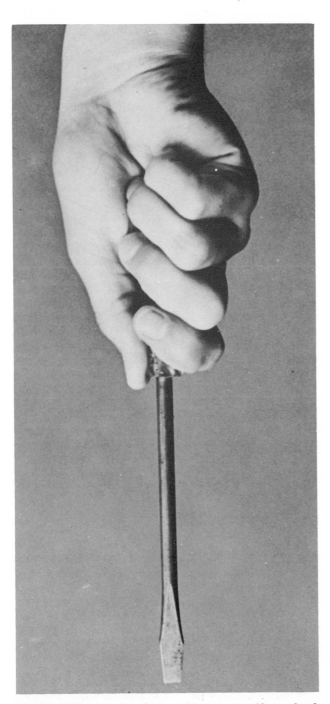

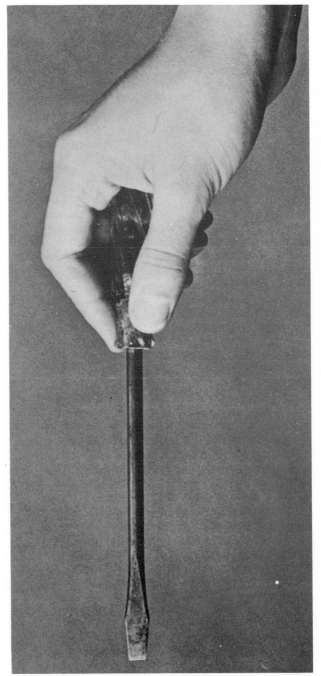

POWER GRIP is one of two basic working postures of human hand. Used when strength is needed, it involves holding object between flexed fingers and palm while the thumb applies counterpressure.

PRECISION GRIP is second basic working posture and is used when accuracy and delicacy of touch are required. Object is held between tips of one or more fingers and the fully opposed thumb.

taken to indicate, within limits, the capabilities of those hands in the cultural realm of tool-using and toolmaking. In the case of the hand, at least, evolution has been incremental. Although the precision grip represents the ultimate refinement in prehensility, this does not mean that more primitive capacities have been lost. The human hand remains capable of the postures and movements of the primate foot-hand and even of the paw of the fully quadrupedal mammal, and it retains many of the anatomical structures that go with them. From one stage in evolution to the next the later capability is added to the earlier.

The study of primate evolution is facilitated by the fact that the primates now living constitute a graded series representative of some of its principal chapters. It is possible, at least, to accept a study series composed of tree shrews, tarsiers, New World monkeys, Old World monkeys and man as conforming to the evolutionary sequence. In comparing the hands of these animals with one another and with man's, considerable care must be taken to recognize specializations of structure that do not form part of the sequence. Thus the extremely specialized form of the hand in the anthropoid apes can in no way be regarded as a stage in the sequence from tree shrew to man. The same objection does not apply, however, to certain fossil apes. The hand of the Miocene ancestral ape *Proconsul africanus* does not, for example, show the hand specializations of living apes and can legitimately be brought into the morphological sequence that branches off on the man-ape line toward man.

In the lowliest of the living primates —the tree shrew that inhabits the rain forests of the East Indies and the Malay Archipelago—the hand is little more than a paw. It exhibits in a primate sense only the most rudimentary manual capability. This is the movement of convergence that brings the tips of the digits together by a flexion of the paw at the metacarpophalangeal joints, which correspond in man to the knuckles at the juncture of the fingers and the rest of the hand. The opposite movement— divergence—fans the digits outward and is related to the pedal, or weight-bearing, function of the paw. With its paws thus limited the tree shrew is compelled to grasp objects, for example its insect prey, in two-handed fashion, two convergent paws being the functional equivalent of a prehensile hand. For purposes of locomotion in its arboreal

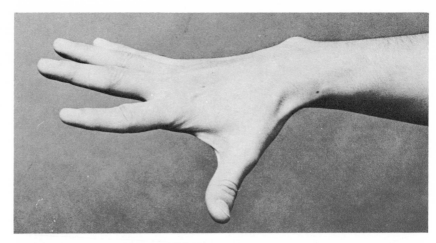

DIVERGENCE, generally associated with weight-bearing function of hand, is achieved by extension at the metacarpophalangeal joints. All mammalian paws are capable of this action.

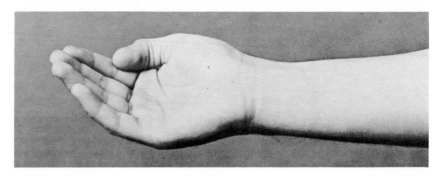

CONVERGENCE is achieved by flexion at metacarpophalangeal joints. Two convergent paws equal one prehensile hand; many mammals hold food in two convergent paws to eat.

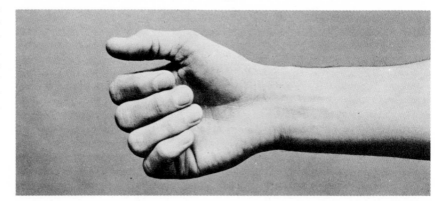

PREHENSILITY, the ability to wrap the fingers around an object, is a special primate characteristic, related to the emergence of the specialized thumb during evolutionary process.

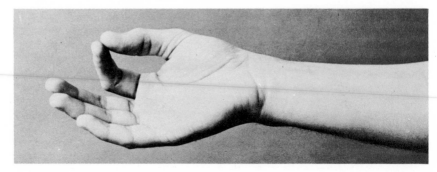

OPPOSABILITY is ability to sweep thumb across palm while rotating it around its longitudinal axis. Many primates can do this, but underlying structures are best developed in man.

STONE TOOLS to left of center are similar to those found at Olduvai Gorge, Tanganyika, in conjunction with the hand bones of an early hominid. Such crude tools can be made by using the power grip, of which the Olduvai hand was capable. Finely flaked Old Stone Age tools at right can be made only by using the precision grip, which may not have been well developed in Olduvai hand.

habitat, this animal does not require prehensility because, like the squirrel, it is small, it has claws on the tips of its digits and is a tree runner rather than a climber. Even in the tree shrew, however, the specialized thumb of the primate family has begun to take form in the specialized anatomy of this digit and its musculature. Occasionally tree shrews have been observed feeding with one hand.

The hand of the tarsier, another denizen of the rain forests of the East Indies, exhibits a more advanced degree of prehensility in being able to grasp objects by bending the digits toward the palm. The thumb digit also exhibits a degree of opposability to the other digits. This is a pseudo opposability in that the movement is restricted entirely to the meta-carpophalangeal joint and is therefore distinct from the true opposability of man's thumb. The movement is facilitated by the well-developed abductor and adductor muscles that persist in the hands of the higher primates. With this equipment the tarsier is able to support its body weight on vertical stems and to grasp small objects with one hand.

The tropical rain forests in which these animals live today are probably not very different from the closed-canopy forests of the Paleocene epoch of some 70 million years ago, during which the first primates appeared. In the wide variety of habitats that these forests provide, ecologists distinguish five major strata, superimposed like a block of apartments. From the top down these are the upper, middle and lower stories (the last being the main closed canopy), the shrub layer and the herb layer on the ground. To these can be added a sixth deck: the subterrain. In the emergence of prehensility in the primate line the three-dimensional arrangement of this system of habitats played a profound role. Prehensility is an adaptation to arboreal life and is related to climbing. In animals that are of small size with respect to the branches on which they live and travel, such as the tree shrew, mobility is not hampered by lack of prehensility. They can live at any level in the forest, from the forest floor to the tops of the tallest trees, their stability assured by the grip of sharp claws and the elaboration of visual and cerebellar mechanisms.

The tree-climbing as opposed to the tree-running phase of primate evolution may not have begun until the middle of the Eocene, perhaps 55 million years ago. What environmental pressure brought about this adaptation can only be guessed at. Thomas F. Barth of the University of Chicago has suggested that the advent of the widely successful order of rodents in the early Eocene may have led to the displacement of the primates from the shrub strata to the upper three strata of the forest canopy. In any case little is known about the form of the primates that made this transition.

In *Proconsul*, of the early to middle Miocene of 20 million years ago, the fossil record discloses a fully developed tree-climbing primate. His hand was clearly prehensile. His thumb, however, was imperfectly opposable. Functionally this hand is comparable to that of some of the living New World monkeys.

True opposability appears for the first time among the living primates in the Old World monkeys. In these animals the carpometacarpal joint shows a well-developed saddle configuration comparable to that in the corresponding joint of the human hand. This allows rotation of the thumb from its wrist articulation. Turning about its longitudinal axis through an angle of about 45 degrees, the thumb can be swept across the palm, and the pulp of the thumb can be directly opposed to the pulp surfaces of one of or all the other digits. This movement is not so expertly performed by the monkeys as by man. At the same time, again as in man, a fair range of movement is retained at the metacarpophalangeal joint, the site of pseudo opposability in the tarsier.

The hands of anthropoid apes display many of these anatomical structures but do not have the same degree of functional capability. This is because of certain specializations that arise from the fact that these apes swing from trees by their hands. Such specializations would seem to exclude the apes from the evolutionary sequence that leads to man. In comparing the hand of monkeys with the hand of man one must bear in mind an obvious fact that is all too often overlooked: monkeys are largely quadrupedal, whereas man is fully bipedal. Variations in the form of the hand from one species of monkey to the next are related to differences in their mode of locomotion. The typical monkey hand is rather long and narrow; the metacarpal, or "palm," bones are short compared with the digits (except in baboons); the terminal phalanges, or finger-tip bones, are slender and the tips of the fingers are consequently narrow from side to side. These are only the most obvious differences between the foot-hand of the Old World monkey and that of man. They serve nonetheless to show how too rigid an application of Frederic Wood Jones's criterion of morphological similarity can mislead one into assuming that the only important difference between the hands of men and monkeys lies in the elaboration of the central nervous system.

It seems likely that the terrestrial phase of human evolution followed on the heels of *Proconsul*. At that time, it is well known, the world's grasslands expanded enormously at the expense of the forests. By the end of the Miocene, 15 million years ago, most of the prototypes of the modern plains-living forms had appeared. During this period, apparently, the hominids also deserted their original forest habitats to take up life on the savanna, where the horizons were figuratively limitless. Bipedal locomotion, a process initiated by life in the trees and the ultimate mechanism for emancipation of the hands, rapidly followed the adoption of terrestrial life. The use of the hands for carrying infants, food and even weapons and tools could not have lagged far behind. As Sherwood L. Washburn of the University of California has suggested on the basis of observations of living higher primates,

tool-using must have appeared at an early stage in hominid evolution. It is a very short step from tool-using to tool-modifying, in the sense of stripping twigs and leaves from a branch in order to improve its effectiveness as a tool or weapon. It is an equally short further step to toolmaking, which at its most primitive is simply the application of the principle of modification to a stick, a stone or a bone. Animal bones are a convenient source of tools; Raymond A. Dart of the University of Witwatersrand in South Africa has advanced the hypothesis that such tools

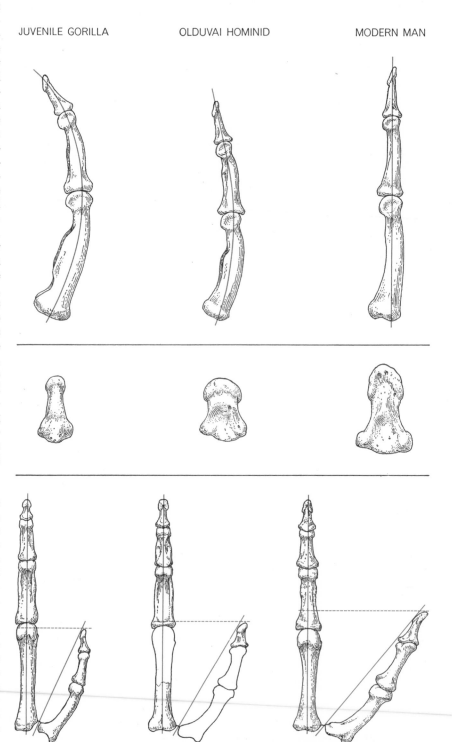

JUVENILE GORILLA   OLDUVAI HOMINID   MODERN MAN

HAND BONES of juvenile gorilla, Olduvai hominid and modern man are compared. Phalanges (*top row*) decrease in curvature from juvenile gorilla to modern man. Terminal thumb phalanx (*middle row*) increases in breadth and proportional length. Third row shows increase in length of thumb and angle between thumb and index finger. Olduvai bones in outline in third row are reconstructed from other evidence; they were not found.

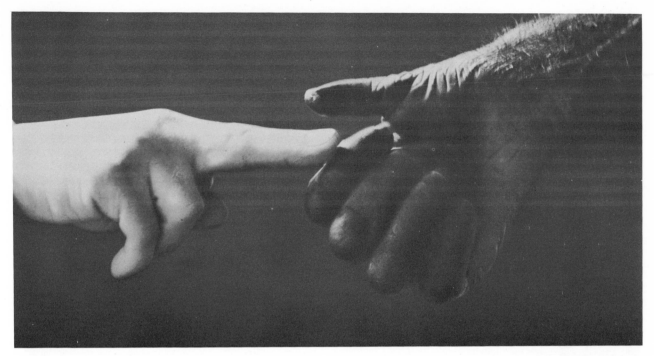

CHIMPANZEE, attempting to grasp experimenter's finger, uses an inefficient precision grip. Because animal's thumb is so short in pro-portion to the digits, it is compelled to bend the digits forward and grasp the object between the sides of index finger and thumb.

were used by early man-apes as part of an "osteodontokeratic" (bone-tooth-hair) culture.

The tools from the pre-*Zinjanthropus* stratum at Olduvai Gorge are little more than pebbles modified in the simplest way by striking off one or more flakes to produce a chopping edge. This technology could not have required either a particularly large brain or a hand of modern human proportions. The hand bones of the pre-*Zinjanthropus* individuals uncovered by the Leakeys in their more recent excavation of Olduvai Gorge are quite unlike those of modern *Homo sapiens*. But there seems to be no reason, on either geological or anthropological grounds, for doubting that the tools found with them are coeval. Modern man must recover from his surprise at the discovery that hands other than his own were capable of shaping tools.

At this point it may be useful to return to the analysis of the manual capability of modern man that distinguishes the power and the precision grip. When compared with the hand of modern man, the Olduvai hand appears to have been capable of a tremendously strong power grip. Although it was a smaller hand, the relative lengths of the metacarpals and phalanges indicate that the proportion of digits and palm was much the same as it is in man. In addition, the tips of the terminal bones of all the Olduvai fingers are quite wide and the finger tips themselves must therefore have been

broad—an essential feature of the human grip for both mechanical and neurological reasons. The curvature of the metacarpals and phalanges indicates that the fingers were somewhat curved throughout their length and were normally held in semiflexion. Unfortunately no hamate bone was found among the Olduvai remains. This wristbone, which articulates with the fifth metacarpal, meets at a saddle joint in modern man and lends great stability to his power grip.

It seems unlikely that the Olduvai hand was capable of the precision grip in its fullest expression. No thumb metacarpal was found in the Olduvai deposit; hence any inference as to the length of the thumb in relation to the other fingers must be derived from the evidence of the position of the wristbone with which the thumb articulates. This evidence suggests that the Olduvai thumb, like the thumb of the gorilla, was set at a narrower angle and was somewhat shorter than the thumb of modern man, reaching only a little beyond the metacarpophalangeal joint of the index finger. Thus, although the thumb was opposable, it can be deduced that the Olduvai hand could not perform actions as precise as those that can be undertaken by the hand of modern man.

Nonetheless, the Olduvai hand activated by a brain and a neuromuscular mechanism of commensurate development would have had little difficulty in making the tools that were found with it. I myself have made such pebble tools

employing only the power grip to hold and strike two stones together.

The inception of toolmaking has hitherto been regarded as the milestone that marked the emergence of the genus *Homo*. It has been assumed that this development was a sudden event, happening as it were almost overnight, and that its appearance was coincidental with the structural evolution of a hominid of essentially modern human form and proportions. It is now becoming clear that this important cultural phase in evolution had its inception at a much earlier stage in the biological evolution of man, that it existed for a much longer period of time and that it was set in motion by a much less advanced hominid and a much less specialized hand than has previously been believed.

For full understanding of the subsequent improvement in toolmaking over the next few hundred thousand years of the Paleolithic, it is necessary to document the transformation of the hand as well as of the brain. Attention can now also be directed toward evidence of the functional capabilities of the hands of early man that is provided by the tools they made. These studies may help to account for the radical changes in technique and direction that characterize the evolution of stone implements during the middle and late Pleistocene epoch. The present evidence suggests that the stone implements of early man were as good (or as bad) as the hands that made them.

15

Adaptations to Cold

LAURENCE IRVING
January 1966

All living organisms abhor cold. For many susceptible forms of life a temperature difference of a few degrees means the difference between life and death. Everyone knows how critical temperature is for the growth of plants. Insects and fishes are similarly sensitive; a drop of two degrees in temperature when the sun goes behind a cloud, for instance, can convert a fly from a swift flier to a slow walker. In view of the general hostility of cold to life and activity, the ability of mammals and birds to survive and flourish in all climates is altogether remarkable.

It is not that these animals are basically more tolerant of cold. We know from our own reactions how sensitive the human body is to chilling. A naked, inactive human being soon becomes miserable in air colder than 28 degrees centigrade (about 82 degrees Fahrenheit), only 10 degrees C. below his body temperature. Even in the Tropics the coolness of night can make a person uncomfortable. The discomfort of cold is one of the most vivid of experiences; it stands out as a persistent memory in a soldier's recollections of the unpleasantness of his episodes in the field. The coming of winter in temperate climates has a profound effect on human well-being and activity. Cold weather, or cold living quarters, compounds the misery of illness or poverty. Over the entire planet a large proportion of man's efforts, culture and economy is devoted to the simple necessity of protection against cold.

Yet strangely enough neither man nor other mammals have consistently avoided cold climates. Indeed, the venturesome human species often goes out of its way to seek a cold environment, for sport or for the adventure of living in a challenging situation. One of the marvels of man's history is the endurance and stability of the human settlements that have been established in arctic latitudes.

The Norse colonists who settled in Greenland 1,000 years ago found Eskimos already living there. Archaeologists today are finding many sites and relics of earlier ancestors of the Eskimos who occupied arctic North America as long as 6,000 years ago. In the middens left by these ancient inhabitants are bones and hunting implements that indicate man was accompanied in the cold north by many other warm-blooded animals: caribou, moose, bison, bears, hares, seals, walruses and whales. All the species, including man, seem to have been well adapted to arctic life for thousands of years.

It is therefore a matter of more than idle interest to look closely into how mammals adapt to cold. In all climates and everywhere on the earth mammals maintain a body temperature of about 38 degrees C. It looks as if evolution has settled on this temperature as an optimum for the mammalian class. (In birds the standard body temperature is a few degrees higher.) To keep their internal temperature at a viable level the mammals must be capable of adjusting to a wide range of environmental temperatures. In tropical air at 30 degrees C. (86 degrees F.), for example, the environment is only eight degrees cooler than the body temperature; in arctic air at −50 degrees C. it is 88 degrees colder. A man or other mammal in the Arctic must adjust to both extremes as seasons change.

The mechanisms available for making the adjustments are (1) the generation of body heat by the metabolic burning of food as fuel and (2) the use of insulation and other devices to retain body heat. The requirements can be expressed quantitatively in a Newtonian formula concerning the cooling of warm bodies. A calculation based on the formula shows that to maintain the necessary warmth of its body a mammal must generate 10 times more heat in the Arctic than in the Tropics or clothe itself in 10 times more effective insulation or employ some intermediate combination of the two mechanisms.

We need not dwell on the metabolic requirement; it is rarely a major factor. An animal can increase its food intake and generation of heat to only a very modest degree. Moreover, even if metabolic capacity and the food supply were unlimited, no animal could spend all its time eating. Like man, nearly all other mammals spend a great deal of time in curious exploration of their surroundings, in play and in family and social activities. In the arctic winter a herd of caribou often rests and ruminates while the young engage in aimless play. I have seen caribou resting calmly with wolves lying asleep in the snow in plain view only a few hundred yards away. There is a common impression that life in the cold climates is more active than in the Tropics, but the fact is that for the natural populations of mammals, including man, life goes on at the same leisurely pace in the Arctic as it does in warmer regions; in all climates there is the same requirement of rest and social activities.

The decisive difference in resisting cold, then, lies in the mechanisms for conserving body heat. In the Institute of Arctic Biology at the University of Alaska we are continuing studies that have been in progress there and elsewhere for 18 years to compare the

ARCTIC ZONE (20 TO −60 DEGREES C.)

TEMPERATE ZONE (20 TO −20 DEGREES C.)

TROPICAL ZONE (35 TO 25 DEGREES C.)

RANGE OF TEMPERATURES to which warm-blooded animals must adapt is indicated. All the animals shown have a body temperature close to 100 degrees Fahrenheit, yet they survive at outside temperatures that, for the arctic animals, can be more than 100 degrees cooler. Insulation by fur is a major means of adaptation to cold. Man is insulated by clothing; some other relatively hairless animals, by fat. Some animals have a mechanism for conserving heat internally so that it is not dissipated at the extremities.

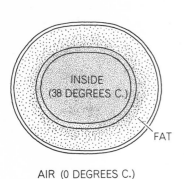

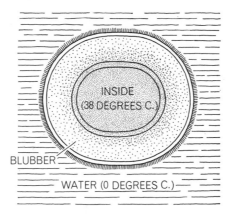

AIR (0 DEGREES C.)

WATER (0 DEGREES C.)

TEMPERATURE GRADIENTS in the outer parts of the body of a pig (*left*) and of a seal (*right*) result from two effects: the insulation provided by fat and the exchange of heat between arterial and venous blood, which produces lower temperatures near the surface.

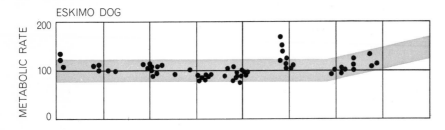

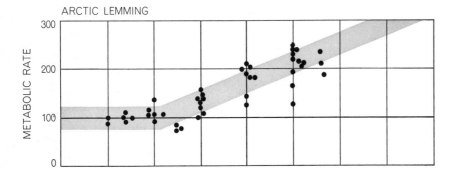

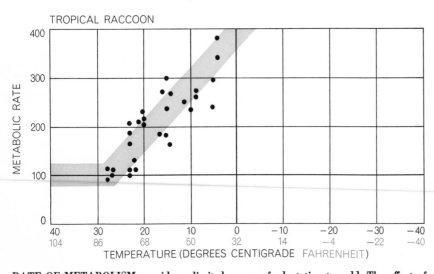

RATE OF METABOLISM provides a limited means of adaptation to cold. The effect of declining temperatures on the metabolic rate is shown for an Eskimo dog (*top*), an arctic lemming (*middle*) and a tropical raccoon (*bottom*). Animals in warmer climates tend to increase metabolism more rapidly than arctic animals do when the temperature declines.

mechanisms for conservation of heat in arctic and tropical animals. The investigations have covered a wide variety of mammals and birds and have yielded conclusions of general physiological interest.

The studies began with an examination of body insulation. The fur of arctic animals is considerably thicker, of course, than that of tropical animals. Actual measurements showed that its insulating power is many times greater. An arctic fox clothed in its winter fur can rest comfortably at a temperature of −50 degrees C. without increasing its resting rate of metabolism. On the other hand, a tropical animal of the same size (a coati, related to the raccoon) must increase its metabolic effort when the temperature drops to 20 degrees C. That is to say, the fox's insulation is so far superior that the animal can withstand air 88 degrees C. colder than its body at resting metabolism, whereas the coati can withstand a difference of only 18 degrees C. Naked man is less well protected by natural insulation than the coati; if unclothed, he begins shivering and raising his metabolic rate when the air temperature falls to 28 degrees C.

Obviously as animals decrease in size they become less able to carry a thick fur. The arctic hare is about the smallest mammal with enough fur to enable it to endure continual exposure to winter cold. The smaller animals take shelter under the snow in winter. Weasels, for example, venture out of their burrows only for short periods; mice spend the winter in nests and sheltered runways under the snow and rarely come to the surface.

No animal, large or small, can cover all of its body with insulating fur. Organs such as the feet, legs and nose must be left unencumbered if they are to be functional. Yet if these extremities allowed the escape of body heat, neither mammals nor birds could survive in cold climates. A gull or duck swimming in icy water would lose heat through its webbed feet faster than the bird could generate it. Warm feet standing on snow or ice would melt it and soon be frozen solidly to the place where they stood. For the unprotected extremities, therefore, nature has evolved a simple but effective mechanism to reduce the loss of heat: the warm outgoing blood in the arteries heats the cool blood returning in the veins from the extremities. This exchange occurs in the *rete mirabile* (wonderful net), a network of small arteries and veins near the junction between the trunk of the animal and the extremity [see "'The Wonderful Net,'" by P. F. Scholander; SCIENTIFIC AMERICAN, April, 1957]. Hence the extremities can become much colder than the body without either draining off body heat or losing their ability to function.

This mechanism serves a dual purpose. When necessary, the thickly furred animals can use their bare extremities to release excess heat from the body. A heavily insulated animal would soon be overheated by running or other active exercise were it not for these outlets. The generation of heat by exercise turns on the flow of blood to the extremities so that they radiate heat. The large, bare flippers of a resting fur seal are normally cold, but we have found that when these animals on the Pribilof Islands are driven overland at their laborious gait, the flippers become warm. In contrast to the warm flippers, the rest of the fur seal's body surface feels cold, because very little heat escapes through the animal's dense fur. Heat can also be dissipated by evaporation from the mouth and tongue. Thus a dog or a caribou begins to pant, as a means of evaporative cooling, as soon as it starts to run.

In the pig the adaptation to cold by means of a variable circulation of heat in the blood achieves a high degree of refinement. The pig, with its skin only thinly covered with bristles, is as naked as a man. Yet it does well in the Alaskan winter without clothing. We can read the animal's response to cold by its expressions of comfort or discomfort, and we have measured its physiological reactions. In cold air the circulation of heat in the blood of swine is shunted away from the entire body surface, so that the surface becomes an effective insulator against loss of body heat. The pig can withstand considerable cooling of its body surface. Although a man is highly uncomfortable when his skin is cooled to 7 degrees C. below the internal temperature, a pig can be comfortable with its skin 30 degrees C. colder than the interior, that is, at a temperature of 8 degrees C. (about 46 degrees F.). Not until the air temperature drops below the freezing point (0 degrees C.) does the pig increase its rate of metabolism; in contrast a man, as I have mentioned, must do so at an air temperature of 28 degrees C.

With thermocouples in the form of needles we have probed the tissues of pigs below the skin surface. (Some pigs, like some people, will accept a little

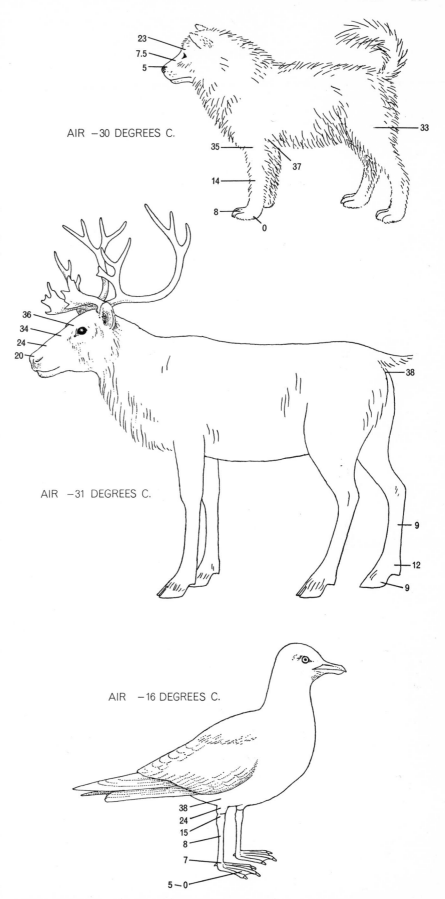

TEMPERATURES AT EXTREMITIES of arctic animals are far lower than the internal body temperature of about 38 degrees centigrade, as shown by measurements made on Eskimo dogs, caribou and sea gulls. Some extremities approach the outside temperature.

pain to win a reward.) We found that with the air temperature at −12 degrees C. the cooling of the pig's tissues extended as deep as 100 millimeters (about four inches) into its body. In warmer air the thermal gradient through the tissues was shorter and less steep. In short, the insulating mechanism of the hog involves a considerable depth of the animal's fatty mantle.

Even more striking examples of this kind of mechanism are to be found in whales, walruses and hair seals that dwell in the icy arctic seas. The whale

and the walrus are completely bare; the hair seal is covered only with thin, short hair that provides almost no insulation when it is sleeked down in the water. Yet these animals remain comfortable in water around the freezing point although water, with a much greater heat capacity than air, can extract a great deal more heat from a warm body.

Examining hair seals from cold waters of the North Atlantic, we found that even in ice water these animals did not raise their rate of metabolism. Their skin was only one degree or so warmer

than the water, and the cooling effect extended deep into the tissues—as much as a quarter of the distance through the thick part of the body. Hour after hour the animal's flippers all the way through would remain only a few degrees above freezing without the seals' showing any sign of discomfort. When the seals were moved into warmer water, their outer tissues rapidly warmed up. They would accept a transfer from warm water to ice water with equanimity and with no diminution of their characteristic liveliness.

How are the chilled tissues of all these animals able to function normally at temperatures close to freezing? There is first of all the puzzle of the response of fatty tissue. Animal fat usually becomes hard and brittle when it is cooled to low temperatures. This is true even of the land mammals of the Arctic, as far as their internal fats are concerned. If it were also true of extremities such as their feet, however, in cold weather their feet would become too inflexible to be useful. Actually it turns out that the fats in these organs behave differently from those in the warm internal tissues. Farmers have known for a long time that neat's-foot oil, extracted from the feet of cattle, can be used to keep leather boots and harness flexible in cold weather. By laboratory examination we have found that the fats in the bones of the lower leg and foot of the caribou remain soft even at 0 degrees C. The melting point of the fats in the leg steadily goes up in the higher portions of the leg. Eskimos have long been aware that fat from a caribou's foot will serve as a fluid lubricant in the cold, whereas the marrow fat from the upper leg is a solid food even at room temperature.

About the nonfatty substances in tissues we have little information; I have seen no reports by biochemists on the effects of temperature on their properties. It is known, however, that many of the organic substances of animal tissues are highly sensitive to temperature. We must therefore wonder how the tissues can maintain their serviceability over the very wide range of temperatures that the body surface experiences in the arctic climate.

We have approached this question by studies of the behavior of tissues at various temperatures. Nature offers many illustrations of the slowing of tissue functions by cold. Fishes, frogs and water insects are noticeably slowed down by cool water. Cooling by 10 degrees

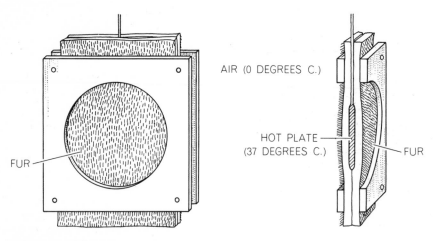

INSULATION BY FUR was tested in this apparatus, shown in a front view at left and a side view at right. The battery-operated heating unit provided the equivalent of body temperature on one side of the fur; outdoor temperatures were approximated on the other side.

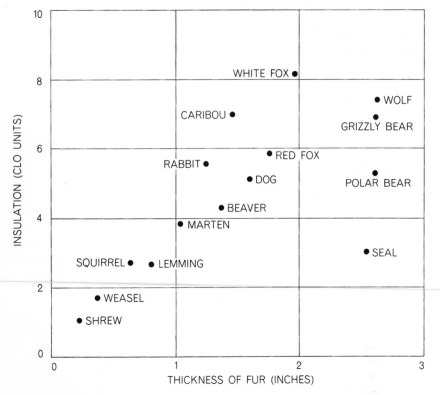

INSULATING CAPACITY of fur is compared for various animals. A "clo unit" equals the amount of insulation provided by the clothing a man usually wears at room temperature.

C. will immobilize most insects. A grasshopper in the warm noonday sun can be caught only by a swift bird, but in the chill of early morning it is so sluggish that anyone can seize it. I had a vivid demonstration of the temperature effect one summer day when I went hunting on the arctic tundra near Point Barrow for flies to use in experiments. When the sun was behind clouds, I had no trouble picking up the flies as they crawled about in the sparse vegetation, but as soon as the sun came out the flies took off and were uncatchable. Measuring the temperature of flies on the ground, I ascertained that the difference between the flying and the slow-crawling state was a matter of only 2 degrees C.

Sea gulls walking barefoot on the ice in the Arctic are just as nimble as gulls on the warm beaches of California. We know from our own sensations that our fingers and hands are numbed by cold. I have used a simple test to measure the amount of this desensitization. After cooling the skin on my fingertips to about 20 degrees C. (68 degrees F.) by keeping them on ice-filled bags, I tested their sensitivity by dropping a light ball (weighing about one milligram) on them from a measured height. The weight multiplied by the distance of fall gave me a measure of the impact on the skin. I found that the skin at a temperature of 20 degrees C. was only a sixth as sensitive as at 35 degrees C. (95 degrees F.); that is, the impact had to be six times greater to be felt.

We know that even the human body surface has some adaptability to cold. Men who make their living by fishing can handle their nets and fish with wet hands in cold that other people cannot endure. The hands of fishermen, Eskimos and Indians have been found to be capable of maintaining an exceptionally vigorous blood circulation in the cold. This is possible, however, only at the cost of a higher metabolic production of body heat, and the production in any case has a limit. What must arouse our wonder is the extraordinary adaptability of an animal such as the hair seal. It swims in icy waters with its flippers and the skin over its body at close to the freezing temperature, and yet under the ice in the dark arctic sea it remains sensitive enough to capture moving prey and find its way to breathing holes.

Here lies an inviting challenge for all biologists. By what devices is an animal able to preserve nervous sensitivity in tissues cooled to low temperatures? Beyond this is a more universal and more

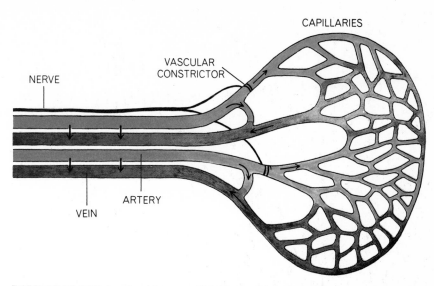

ROLE OF BLOOD in adaptation to cold is depicted schematically. One mechanism, indicated by the vertical arrows, is an exchange of heat between arterial and venous blood. The cold venous blood returning from an extremity acquires heat from an arterial network. The outgoing arterial blood is thus cooled. Hence the exchange helps to keep heat in the body and away from the extremities when the extremities are exposed to low temperatures. The effect is enhanced by the fact that blood vessels near the surface constrict in cold.

interesting question: How do the warm-blooded animals preserve their overall stability in the varying environments to which they are exposed? Adjustment to changes in temperature requires them to make a variety of adaptations in the various tissues of the body. Yet these changes must be harmonized to maintain the integration of the organism as a whole. I predict that further studies of the mechanisms involved in adaptation to cold will yield exciting new insights into the processes that sustain the integrity of warm-blooded animals.

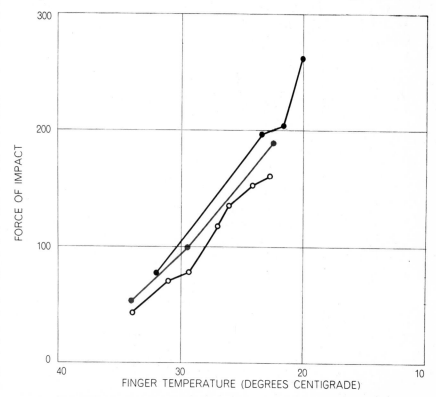

FINGER EXPERIMENT performed by the author showed that the more a finger was chilled, the farther a one-milligram ball had to be dropped for its impact to be felt on the finger. The vertical scale is arbitrary but reflects the relative increase in the force of impact.

16

Tools and Human Evolution

SHERWOOD L. WASHBURN

September 1960

A series of recent discoveries has linked prehuman primates of half a million years ago with stone tools. For some years investigators had been uncovering tools of the simplest kind from ancient deposits in Africa. At first they assumed that these tools constituted evidence of the existence of large-brained, fully bipedal men. Now the tools have been found in association with much more primitive creatures, the not-fully bipedal, small-brained near-men, or man-apes. Prior to these finds the prevailing view held that man evolved nearly to his present structural state and then discovered tools and the new ways of life that they made possible. Now it appears that man-apes—creatures able to run but not yet walk on two legs, and with brains no larger than those of apes now living—had already learned to make and to use tools. It follows that the structure of modern man must be the result of the change in the terms of natural selection that came with the tool-using way of life.

The earliest stone tools are chips or simple pebbles, usually from river gravels. Many of them have not been shaped at all, and they can be identified as tools only because they appear in concentrations, along with a few worked pieces, in caves or other locations where no such stones naturally occur. The huge advantage that a stone tool gives to its user must be tried to be appreciated. Held in the hand, it can be used for pounding, digging or scraping. Flesh and bone can be cut with a flaked chip, and what would be a mild blow with the fist becomes lethal with a rock in the hand. Stone tools can be employed, moreover, to make tools of other materials. Naturally occurring sticks are nearly all rotten, too large, or of inconvenient shape; some tool for fabrication is essential for the efficient use of wood. The utility of a mere pebble seems so limited to the user of modern tools that it is not easy to comprehend the vast difference that separates the tool-user from the ape which relies on hands and teeth alone. Ground-living monkeys dig out roots for food, and if they could use a stone or a stick, they might easily double their food supply. It was the success of the simplest tools that started the whole trend of human evolution and led to the civilizations of today.

From the short-term point of view, human structure makes human behavior possible. From the evolutionary point of view, behavior and structure form an interacting complex, with each change in one affecting the other. Man began when populations of apes, about a million years ago, started the bipedal, tool-using way of life that gave rise to the man-apes of the genus *Australopithecus*. Most of the obvious differences that distinguish man from ape came after the use of tools.

The primary evidence for the new view of human evolution is teeth, bones and tools. But our ancestors were not fossils; they were striving creatures, full of rage, dominance and the will to live. What evolved was the pattern of life of intelligent, exploratory, playful, vigorous primates; the evolving reality was a succession of social systems based upon the motor abilities, emotions and intelligence of their members. Selection produced new systems of child care, maturation and sex, just as it did alterations in the skull and the teeth. Tools, hunting, fire, complex social life, speech, the human way and the brain evolved together to produce ancient man of the genus *Homo* about half a million years ago. Then the brain evolved under the pressures of more complex social life until the species *Homo sapiens* appeared perhaps as recently as 50,000 years ago.

With the advent of *Homo sapiens* the tempo of technical-social evolution quickened. Some of the early types of tool had lasted for hundreds of thousands of years and were essentially the same throughout vast areas of the African and Eurasian land masses. Now the tool forms multiplied and became regionally diversified. Man invented the

STENCILED HANDS in the cave of Gargas in the Pyrenees date back to the Upper Paleolithic of perhaps 30,000 years ago. Aurignacian man made the images by placing hand against wall and spattering it with paint. Hands stenciled in black (*top*) are more distinct and apparently more recent than those done in other colors (*center*).

OLDUVAI GORGE in Tanganyika is the site where the skull of the largest known man-ape was discovered last summer by L. S. B. Leakey and his wife Mary. Stratigraphic evidence indicates that skull dates back to Lower Pleistocene, more than 500,000 years ago.

bow, boats, clothing; conquered the Arctic; invaded the New World; domesticated plants and animals; discovered metals, writing and civilization. Today, in the midst of the latest tool-making revolution, man has achieved the capacity to adapt his environment to his need and impulse, and his numbers have begun to crowd the planet.

Later events in the evolution of the human species are treated in other articles in this book [see, for example, "The Origin of Speech" by Hockett, page 183, and "The Distribution of Man" by Howells, page 215]. This article is concerned with the beginnings of the process by which biological evolution has transcended itself. From the rapidly accumulating evidence it is now possible to speculate with some confidence on the manner in which the way of life made possible by tools changed the pressures of natural selection and so changed the structure of man.

Tools have been found, along with the bones of their makers, at Sterkfontein, Swartkrans and Kromdraai in South Africa and at Olduvai in Tanganyika. Many of the tools from Sterkfontein are merely unworked river pebbles, but someone had to carry them from the gravels some miles away and bring them to the deposit in which they are found. Nothing like them occurs naturally in the local limestone caves. Of course the association of the stone tools with man-ape bones in one or two localities does not prove that these animals made the tools. It has been argued that a more advanced form of man, already present, was the toolmaker. This argument has a familiar ring to students of human evolution. Peking man was thought too primitive to be a toolmaker; when the first manlike pelvis was found with man-ape bones, some argued that it must have fallen into the deposit because it was too human to be associated with the skull. In every case, however, the repeated discovery of the same unanticipated association has ultimately settled the controversy.

This is why the discovery by L. S. B. and Mary Leakey in the summer of 1959 is so important. In Olduvai Gorge in Tanganyika they came upon traces of an old living site, and found stone tools in clear association with the largest man-ape skull known. With the stone tools were a hammer stone and waste flakes from the manufacture of the tools. The deposit also contained the bones of rats, mice, frogs and some bones of juvenile pig and antelope, showing that even the largest and latest of the

SKULL IS EXAMINED *in situ* by Mary Leakey, who first noticed fragments of it protruding from the cliff face at left. Pebble tools were found at the same level as the skull.

SKULL IS EXCAVATED from surrounding rock with dental picks. Although skull was badly fragmented, almost all of it was recovered. Fragment visible here is part of upper jaw.

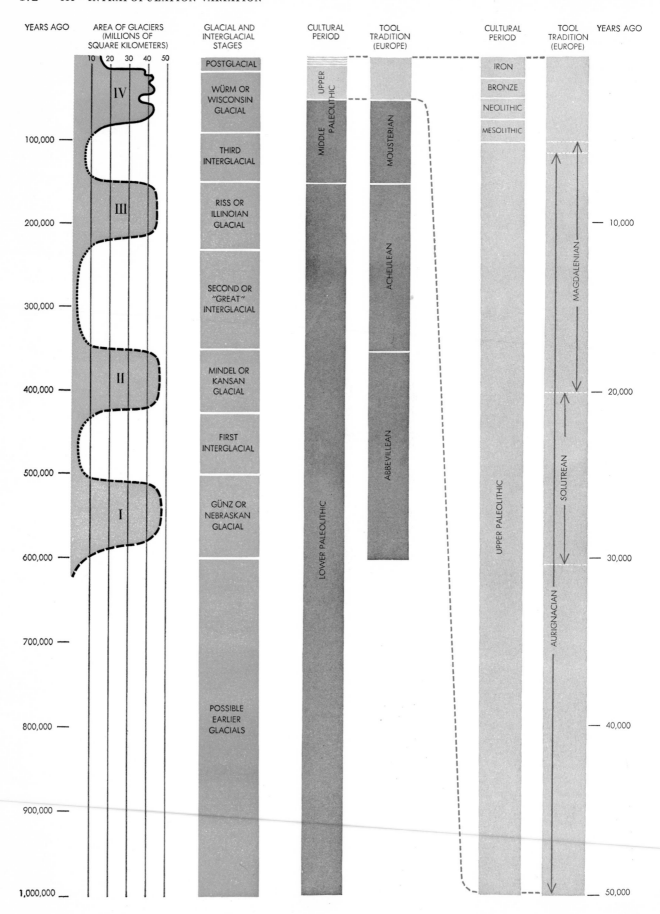

TIME-SCALE correlates cultural periods and tool traditions with the four great glaciations of the Pleistocene epoch. Glacial advances and retreats shown by solid black curve are accurately known; those shown by broken curve are less certain; those shown by dotted curve are uncertain. Light gray bars at far right show an expanded view of last 50,000 years on two darker bars at center. Scale was prepared with the assistance of William R. Farrand of the Lamont Geological Observatory of Columbia University.

man-apes could kill only the smallest animals and must have been largely vegetarian. The Leakeys' discovery confirms the association of the man-ape with pebble tools, and adds the evidence of manufacture to that of mere association. Moreover, the stratigraphic evidence at Olduvai now for the first time securely dates the man-apes, placing them in the lower Pleistocene, earlier than 500,000 years ago and earlier than the first skeletal and cultural evidence for the existence of the genus Homo [*see illustration on next two pages*]. Before the discovery at Olduvai these points had been in doubt.

The man-apes themselves are known from several skulls and a large number of teeth and jaws, but only fragments of the rest of the skeleton have been preserved. There were two kinds of man-ape, a small early one that may have weighed 50 or 60 pounds and a later and larger one that weighed at least twice as much. The differences in size and form between the two types are quite comparable to the differences between the contemporary pygmy chimpanzee and the common chimpanzee.

Pelvic remains from both forms of man-ape show that these animals were bipedal. From a comparison of the pelvis of ape, man-ape and man it can be seen that the upper part of the pelvis is much wider and shorter in man than in the ape, and that the pelvis of the man-ape corresponds closely, though not precisely, to that of modern man [*see top illustration on page 177*]. The long upper pelvis of the ape is characteristic of most mammals, and it is the highly specialized, short, wide bone in man that makes possible the human kind of bipedal locomotion. Although the man-ape pelvis is apelike in its lower part, it approaches that of man in just those features that distinguish man from all other animals. More work must be done before this combination of features is fully understood. My belief is that bipedal running, made possible by the changes in the upper pelvis, came before efficient bipedal walking, made possible by the changes in the lower pelvis. In the man-ape, therefore, the adaptation to bipedal locomotion is not yet complete. Here, then, is a phase of human evolution characterized by forms that are mostly bipedal, small-brained, plains-living, tool-making hunters of small animals.

The capacity for bipedal walking is primarily an adaptation for covering long distances. Even the arboreal chimpanzee can run faster than a man, and any monkey can easily outdistance him.

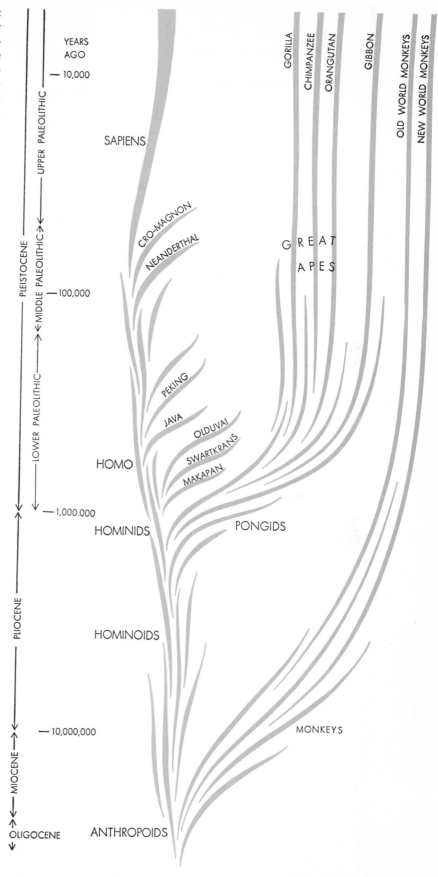

LINES OF DESCENT that lead to man and his closer living relatives are charted. The hominoid superfamily diverged from the anthropoid line in the Miocene period some 20 million years ago. From the hominoid line came the tool-using hominids at the beginning of the Pleistocene. The genus *Homo* appeared in the hominid line during the first interglacial (*see chart on opposite page*); the species *Homo sapiens*, around 50,000 years ago.

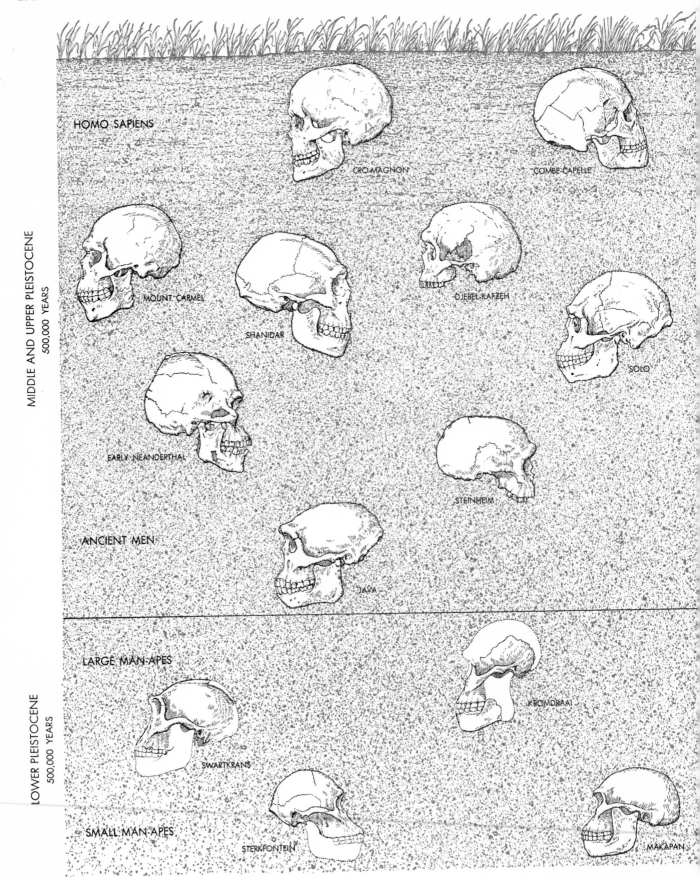

FOSSIL SKULLS of Pleistocene epoch reflect transition from man-apes (*below black line*) to *Homo sapiens* (*top*). Relative age of intermediate specimens is indicated schematically by their position on page. Java man (*middle left*) and Solo man (*upper center*) are members of the genus *Pithecanthropus*, and are related to Peking man (*middle right*). The Shanidar skull (*upper left*) be-

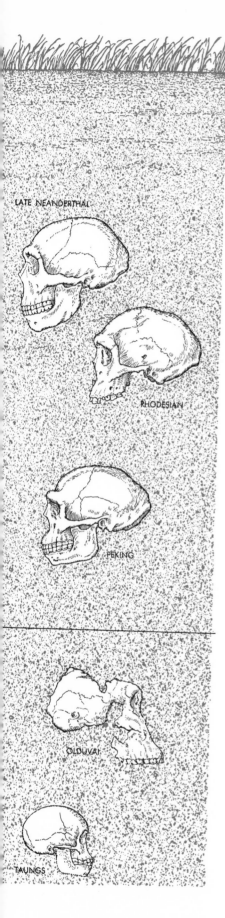

LATE NEANDERTHAL

RHODESIAN

PEKING

OLDUVAI

TAUNGS

longs to the Neanderthal family, while
Mount Carmel skull shows characteristics of Neanderthal and modern man.

A man, on the other hand, can walk for many miles, and this is essential for efficient hunting. According to skeletal evidence, fully developed walkers first appeared in the ancient men who inhabited the Old World from 500,000 years ago to the middle of the last glaciation. These men were competent hunters, as is shown by the bones of the large animals they killed. But they also used fire and made complicated tools according to clearly defined traditions. Along with the change in the structure of the pelvis, the brain had doubled in size since the time of the man-apes.

The fossil record thus substantiates the suggestion, first made by Charles Darwin, that tool use is both the cause and the effect of bipedal locomotion. Some very limited bipedalism left the hands sufficiently free from locomotor functions so that stones or sticks could be carried, played with and used. The advantage that these objects gave to their users led both to more bipedalism and to more efficient tool use. English lacks any neat expression for this sort of situation, forcing us to speak of cause and effect as if they were separated, whereas in natural selection cause and effect are interrelated. Selection is based on successful behavior, and in the man-apes the beginnings of the human way of life depended on both inherited locomotor capacity and on the learned skills of tool-using. The success of the new way of life based on the use of tools changed the selection pressures on many parts of the body, notably the teeth, hands and brain, as well as on the pelvis. But it must be remembered that selection was for the whole way of life.

In all the apes and monkeys the males have large canine teeth. The long upper canine cuts against the first lower premolar, and the lower canine passes in front of the upper canine. This is an efficient fighting mechanism, backed by very large jaw muscles. I have seen male baboons drive off cheetahs and dogs, and according to reliable reports male baboons have even put leopards to flight. The females have small canines, and they hurry away with the young under the very conditions in which the males turn to fight. All the evidence from living monkeys and apes suggests that the male's large canines are of the greatest importance to the survival of the group, and that they are particularly important in ground-living forms that may not be able to climb to safety in the trees. The small, early man-apes lived in open plains country, and yet

none of them had large canine teeth. It would appear that the protection of the group must have shifted from teeth to tools early in the evolution of the man-apes, and long before the appearance of the forms that have been found in association with stone tools. The tools of Sterkfontein and Olduvai represent not the beginnings of tool use, but a choice of material and knowledge in manufacture which, as is shown by the small canines of the man-apes that deposited them there, derived from a long history of tool use.

Reduction in the canine teeth is not a simple matter, but involves changes in the muscles, face, jaws and other parts of the skull. Selection builds powerful neck muscles in animals that fight with their canines, and adapts the skull to the action of these muscles. Fighting is not a matter of teeth alone, but also of seizing, shaking and hurling an enemy's body with the jaws, head and neck. Reduction in the canines is therefore accompanied by a shortening in the jaws, reduction in the ridges of bone over the eyes and a decrease in the shelf of bone in the neck area [see illustration on page 178]. The reason that the skulls of the females and young of the apes look more like man-apes than those of adult males is that, along with small canines, they have smaller muscles and all the numerous structural features that go along with them. The skull of the man-ape is that of an ape that has lost the structure for effective fighting with its teeth. Moreover, the man-ape has transferred to its hands the functions of seizing and pulling, and this has been attended by reduction of its incisors. Small canines and incisors are biological symbols of a changed way of life; their primitive functions are replaced by hand and tool.

The history of the grinding teeth—the molars—is different from that of the seizing and fighting teeth. Large size in any anatomical structure must be maintained by positive selection; the selection pressure changed first on the canine teeth and, much later, on the molars. In the man-apes the molars were very large, larger than in either ape or man. They were heavily worn, possibly because food dug from the ground with the aid of tools was very abrasive. With the men of the Middle Pleistocene, molars of human size appear along with complicated tools, hunting and fire.

The disappearance of brow ridges and the refinement of the human face may involve still another factor. One of the essential conditions for the organi-

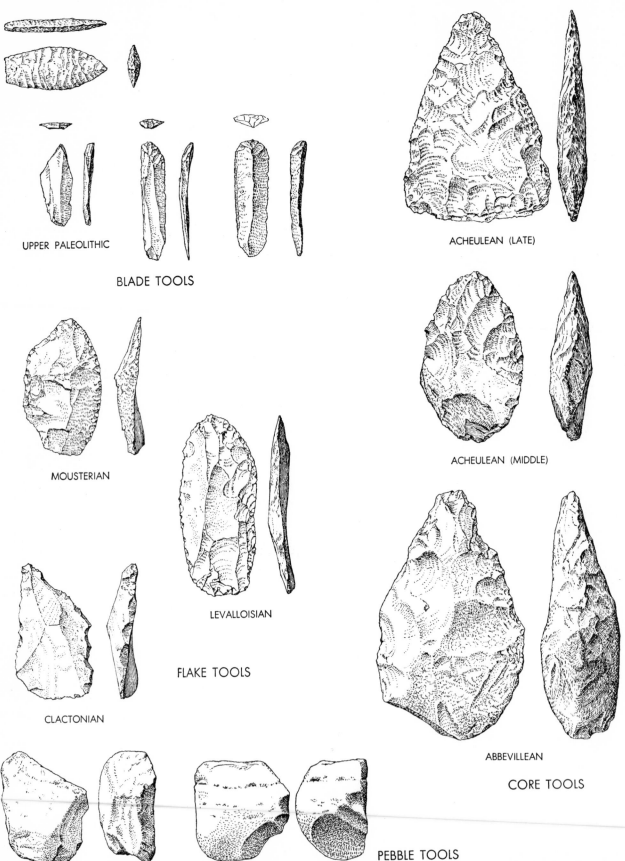

UPPER PALEOLITHIC

BLADE TOOLS

ACHEULEAN (LATE)

MOUSTERIAN

ACHEULEAN (MIDDLE)

LEVALLOISIAN

FLAKE TOOLS

CLACTONIAN

ABBEVILLEAN

CORE TOOLS

PEBBLE TOOLS

TOOL TRADITIONS of Europe are the main basis for classifying Paleolithic cultures. The earliest tools are shown at bottom of page; later ones, at top. The tools are shown from both the side and the edge, except for blade tools, which are shown in three views. Tools consisting of a piece of stone from which a few flakes have been chipped are called core tools (*right*). Other types of tool were made from flakes (*center and left*); blade tools were made from flakes with almost parallel sides. Tool traditions are named for site where tools of a given type were discovered; Acheulean tools, for example, are named for St. Acheul in France.

zation of men in co-operative societies was the suppression of rage and of the uncontrolled drive to first place in the hierarchy of dominance. Curt P. Richter of Johns Hopkins University has shown that domestic animals, chosen over the generations for willingness to adjust and for lack of rage, have relatively small adrenal glands. But the breeders who selected for this hormonal, physiological, temperamental type also picked, without realizing it, animals with small brow ridges and small faces. The skull structure of the wild rat bears the same relation to that of the tame rat as does the skull of Neanderthal man to that of *Homo sapiens*. The same is true for the cat, dog, pig, horse and cow; in each case the wild form has the larger face and muscular ridges. In the later stages of human evolution, it appears, the self-domestication of man has been exerting the same effects upon temperament, glands and skull that are seen in the domestic animals.

Of course from man-ape to man the brain-containing part of the skull has also increased greatly in size. This change is directly due to the increase in the size of the brain: as the brain grows, so grow the bones that cover it. Since there is this close correlation between brain size and bony brain-case, the brain size of the fossils can be estimated. On the scale of brain size the man-apes are scarcely distinguishable from the living apes, although their brains may have been larger with respect to body size. The brain seems to have evolved rapidly, doubling in size between man-ape and man. It then appears to have increased much more slowly; there is no substantial change in gross size during the last 100,000 years. One must remember, however, that size alone is a very crude indicator, and that brains of equal size may vary greatly in function. My belief is that although the brain of *Homo sapiens* is no larger than that of Neanderthal man, the indirect evidence strongly suggests that the first *Homo sapiens* was a much more intelligent creature.

The great increase in brain size is important because many functions of the brain seem to depend on the number of cells, and the number increases with volume. But certain parts of the brain have increased in size much more than others. As functional maps of the cortex of the brain show, the human sensory-motor cortex is not just an enlargement of that of an ape [*see illustrations on last three pages of this article*]. The areas

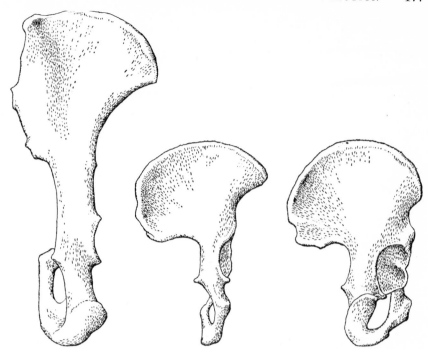

HIP BONES of ape (*left*), man-ape (*center*) and man (*right*) reflect differences between quadruped and biped. Upper part of human pelvis is wider and shorter than that of apes. Lower part of man-ape pelvis resembles that of ape; upper part resembles that of man.

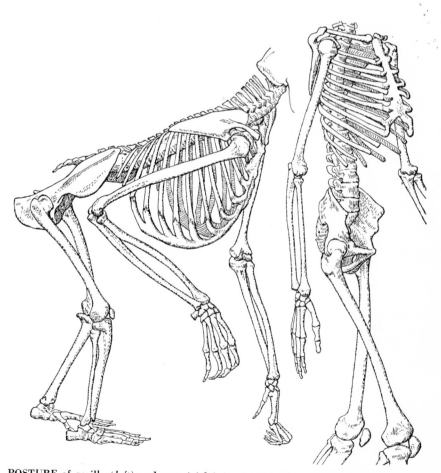

POSTURE of gorilla (*left*) and man (*right*) is related to size, shape and orientation of pelvis. Long, straight pelvis of ape provides support for quadrupedal locomotion; short, broad pelvis of man curves backward, carrying spine and torso in bipedal position.

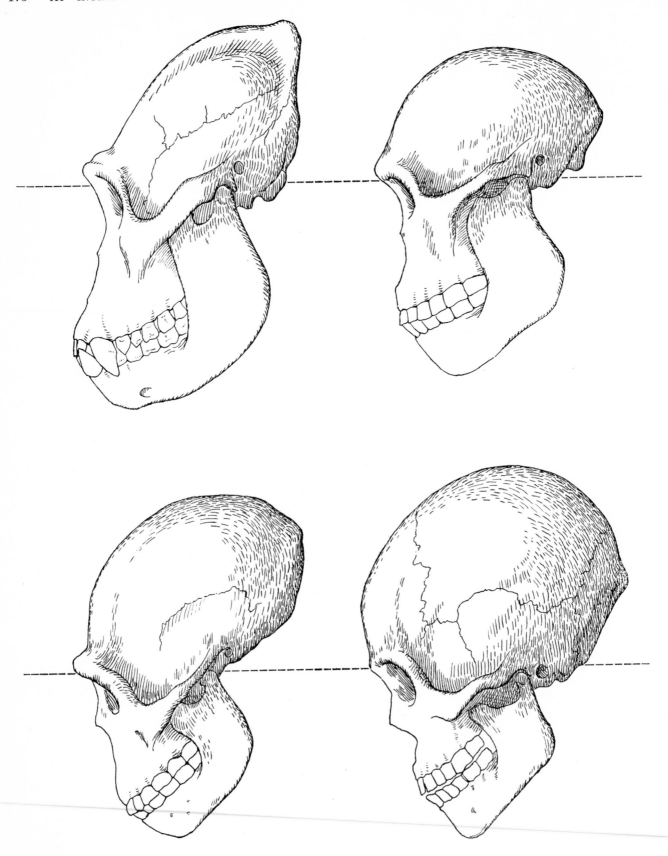

EVOLUTION OF SKULL from ape (*upper left*) to man-ape (*upper right*) to ancient man (*lower left*) to modern man (*lower right*) involves an increase in size of brain case (*part of skull above broken lines*) and a corresponding decrease in size of face (*part of skull below broken lines*). Apes also possess canine teeth that are much larger than those found in either man-apes or man.

for the hand, especially the thumb, in man are tremendously enlarged, and this is an integral part of the structural base that makes the skillful use of the hand possible. The selection pressures that favored a large thumb also favored a large cortical area to receive sensations from the thumb and to control its motor activity. Evolution favored the development of a sensitive, powerful, skillful thumb, and in all these ways —as well as in structure—a human thumb differs from that of an ape.

The same is true for other cortical areas. Much of the cortex in a monkey is still engaged in the motor and sensory functions. In man it is the areas adjacent to the primary centers that are most expanded. These areas are concerned with skills, memory, foresight and language; that is, with the mental faculties that make human social life possible. This is easiest to illustrate in the field of language. Many apes and monkeys can make a wide variety of sounds. These sounds do not, however, develop into language [see "The Origin of Speech," by C. F. Hockett, page 183]. Some workers have devoted great efforts, with minimum results, to trying to teach chimpanzees to talk. The reason is that there is little in the brain to teach. A human child learns to speak with the greatest ease, but the storage of thousands of words takes a great deal of cortex. Even the simplest language must have given great advantage to those first men who had it. One is tempted to think that language may have appeared together with the fine tools, fire and complex hunting of the large-brained men of the Middle Pleistocene, but there is no direct proof of this.

The main point is that the kind of animal that can learn to adjust to complex, human, technical society is a very different creature from a tree-living ape, and the differences between the two are rooted in the evolutionary process. The reason that the human brain makes the human way of life possible is that it is the result of that way of life. Great masses of the tissue in the human brain are devoted to memory, planning, language and skills, because these are the abilities favored by the human way of life.

The emergence of man's large brain occasioned a profound change in the plan of human reproduction. The human mother-child relationship is unique among the primates as is the use of tools. In all the apes and monkeys the baby clings to the mother; to be able to do so,

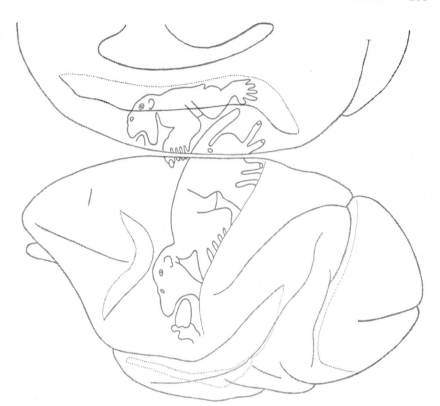

MOTOR CORTEX OF MONKEY controls the movements of the body parts outlined by the superimposed drawing of the animal (*color*). Gray lines trace the surface features of the left half of the brain (*bottom*) and part of the right half (*top*). Colored drawing is distorted in proportion to amount of cortex associated with functions of various parts of the body. Smaller animal in right half of brain indicates location of secondary motor cortex.

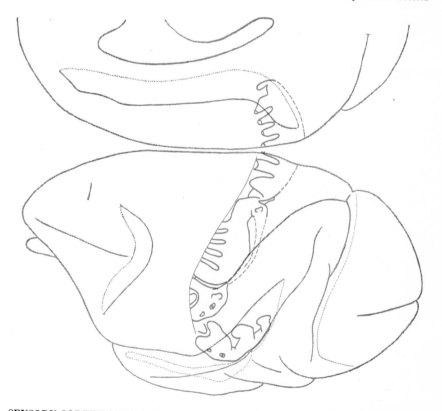

SENSORY CORTEX OF MONKEY is mapped in same way as motor cortex (*above*). As in motor cortex, a large area is associated with hands and feet. Smaller animal at bottom of left half of brain indicates location of secondary sensory cortex. Drawings are based on work of Clinton N. Woolsey and his colleagues at the University of Wisconsin Medical School.

the baby must be born with its central nervous system in an advanced state of development. But the brain of the fetus must be small enough so that birth may take place. In man adaptation to bipedal locomotion decreased the size of the bony birth-canal at the same time that the exigencies of tool use selected for larger brains. This obstetrical dilemma was solved by delivery of the fetus at a much earlier stage of development. But this was possible only because the mother, already bipedal and with hands free of locomotor necessities, could hold the helpless, immature infant. The small-brained man-ape probably developed in the uterus as much as the ape does; the human type of mother-child relation must have evolved by the time of the large-brained, fully bipedal humans of the Middle Pleistocene. Bipedalism, tool use and selection for large brains thus slowed human development and invoked far greater maternal responsibility. The slow-moving mother, carrying the baby, could not hunt, and the combination of the woman's obligation to care for slow-developing babies and the man's occupation of hunting imposed a fundamental pattern on the social organization of the human species.

As Marshall D. Sahlins suggests [see "The Origin of Society," Offprint #602], human society was heavily conditioned at the outset by still other significant aspects of man's sexual adaptation. In the monkeys and apes year-round sexual activity supplies the social bond that unites the primate horde. But sex in these species is still subject to physiological — especially glandular — controls. In man these controls are gone, and are replaced by a bewildering variety of social customs. In no other primate does

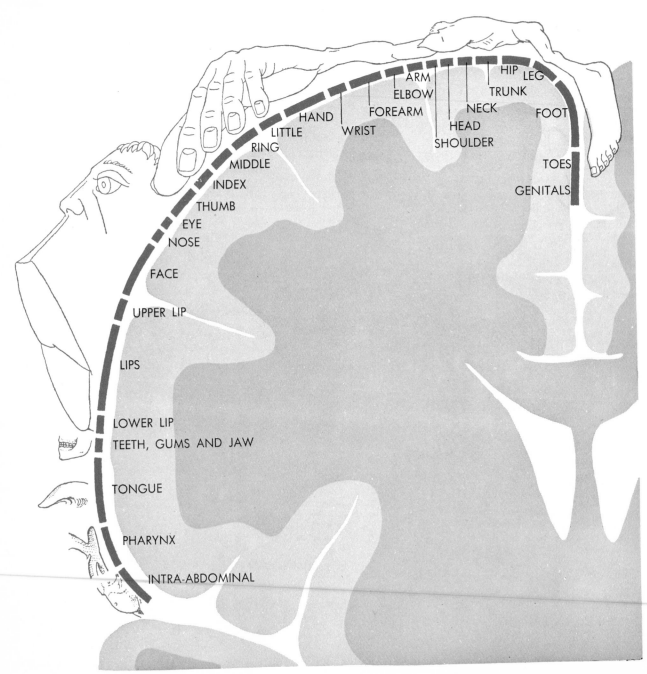

SENSORY HOMUNCULUS is a functional map of the sensory cortex of the human brain worked out by Wilder Penfield and his associates at the Montreal Neurological Institute. As in the map of the sensory cortex of the monkey that appears on the preceding page, the distorted anatomical drawing (*color*) indicates the areas of the sensory cortex associated with the various parts of the body.

a family exist that controls sexual activity by custom, that takes care of slow-growing young, and in which—as in the case of primitive human societies—the male and female provide different foods for the family members.

All these family functions are ultimately related to tools, hunting and the enlargement of the brain. Complex and technical society evolved from the sporadic tool-using of an ape, through the simple pebble tools of the man-ape and the complex toolmaking traditions of ancient men to the hugely complicated culture of modern man. Each behavioral stage was both cause and effect of biological change in bones and brain. These concomitant changes can be seen in the scanty fossil record and can be inferred from the study of the living forms.

Surely as more fossils are found these ideas will be tested. New techniques of investigation, from planned experiments in the behavior of lower primates to more refined methods of dating, will extract wholly new information from the past. It is my belief that, as these events come to pass, tool use will be found to have been a major factor, beginning with the initial differentiation of man and ape. In ourselves we see a structure, physiology and behavior that is the result of the fact that some populations of apes started to use tools a million years ago. The pebble tools constituted man's principal technical adaptation for a period at least 50 times as long as recorded history. As we contemplate man's present eminence, it is well to remember that, from the point of view of evolution, the events of the last 50,000 years occupy but a moment in time. Ancient man endured at least 10 times as long and the man-apes for an even longer time.

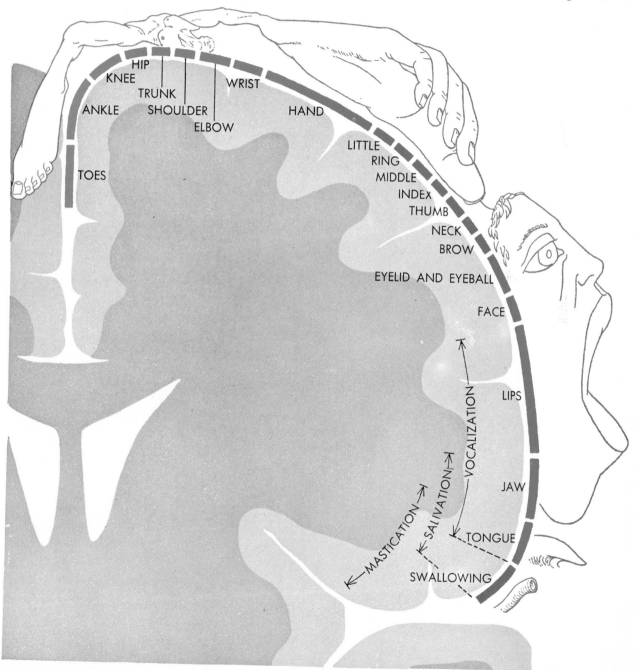

MOTOR HOMUNCULUS depicts parts of body and areas of motor cortex that control their functions. Human brain is shown here in coronal (ear-to-ear) cross section. Speech and hand areas of both motor and sensory cortex in man are proportionately much larger than corresponding areas in apes and monkeys, as can be seen by comparing homunculi with diagram of monkey cortex.

THREAT POSTURE of male stickleback is example of nonvocal communication in lower animals. In this picture, made by N. Tinbergen of the University of Oxford, the fish is responding to its mirror image by indicating readiness to fight "intruding" male.

17

The Origin of Speech

CHARLES F. HOCKETT

September 1960

About 50 years ago the Linguistic Society of Paris established a standing rule barring from its sessions papers on the origin of language. This action was a symptom of the times. Speculation about the origin of language had been common throughout the 19th century, but had reached no conclusive results. The whole enterprise in consequence had come to be frowned upon—as futile or crackpot—in respectable linguistic and philological circles. Yet amidst the speculations there were two well-reasoned empirical plans that deserve mention even though their results were negative.

A century ago there were still many corners of the world that had not been visited by European travelers. It was reasonable for the European scholar to suspect that beyond the farthest frontiers there might lurk half-men or man-apes who would be "living fossils" attesting to earlier stages of human evolution. The speech (or quasi-speech) of these men (or quasi-men) might then similarly attest to earlier stages in the evolution of language. The search was vain. Nowhere in the world has there been discovered a language that can validly and meaningfully be called "primitive." Edward Sapir wrote in 1921: "There is no more striking general fact about language than its universality. One may argue as to whether a particular tribe engages in activities that are worthy of the name of religion or of art, but we know of no people that is not possessed of a fully developed language. The lowliest South African Bushman speaks in the forms of a rich symbolic system that is in essence perfectly comparable to the speech of the cultivated Frenchman."

The other empirical hope in the 19th century rested on the comparative meth-od of historical linguistics, the discovery of which was one of the triumphs of the period. Between two languages the resemblances are sometimes so extensive and orderly that they cannot be attributed to chance or to parallel development. The alternative explanation is that the two are divergent descendants of a single earlier language. English, Dutch, German and the Scandinavian languages are related in just this way. The comparative method makes it possible to examine such a group of related languages and to construct, often in surprising detail, a portrayal of the common ancestor, in this case the proto-Germanic language. Direct documentary evidence of proto-Germanic does not exist, yet understanding of its workings exceeds that of many languages spoken today.

There was at first some hope that the comparative method might help determine the origin of language. This hope was rational in a day when it was thought that language might be only a few thousands or tens of thousands of years old, and when it was repeatedly being demonstrated that languages that had been thought to be unrelated were in fact related. By applying the comparative method to all the languages of the world, some earliest reconstructable horizon would be reached. This might not date back so early as the origin of language, but it might bear certain earmarks of primitiveness, and thus it would enable investigators to extrapolate toward the origin. This hope also proved vain. The earliest reconstructable stage for any language family shows all the complexities and flexibilities of the languages of today.

These points had become clear a half-century ago, by the time of the Paris ruling. Scholars cannot really approve of such a prohibition. But in this instance it had the useful result of channeling the energies of investigators toward the gathering of more and better information about languages as they are today. The subsequent progress in understanding the workings of language has been truly remarkable. Various related fields have also made vast strides in the last half-century: zoologists know more about the evolutionary process, anthropologists know more about the nature of culture, and so on. In the light of these developments there need be no apology for reopening the issue of the origins of human speech.

Although the comparative method of linguistics, as has been shown, throws no light on the origin of language, the investigation may be furthered by a comparative method modeled on that of the zoologist. The frame of reference must be such that all languages look alike when viewed through it, but such that within it human language as a whole can be compared with the communicative systems of other animals, especially the other hominoids, man's closest living relatives, the gibbons and great apes. The useful items for this sort of comparison cannot be things such as the word for "sky"; languages have such words, but gibbon calls do not involve words at all. Nor can they be even the signal for "danger," which gibbons do have. Rather, they must be the basic features of design that can be present or absent in any communicative system, whether it be a communicative system of humans, of animals or of machines.

With this sort of comparative method it may be possible to reconstruct the communicative habits of the remote ancestors of the hominoid line, which may be called the protohominoids. The task, then, is to work out the sequence by which that ancestral system became language as the hominids—the man-apes and ancient men—became man.

A set of 13 design-features is presented in the illustration on the opposite page. There is solid empirical justification for the belief that all the languages of the world share every one of them. At first sight some appear so trivial that no one looking just at language would bother to note them. They become worthy of mention only when it is realized that certain animal systems—and certain human systems other than language—lack them.

The first design-feature—the "vocal-auditory channel"—is perhaps the most obvious. There are systems of communication that use other channels; for example, gesture, the dancing of bees or the courtship ritual of the stickleback. The vocal-auditory channel has the advantage—at least for primates—that it leaves much of the body free for other activities that can be carried on at the same time.

The next two design-features—"rapid fading" and "broadcast transmission and directional reception," stemming from the physics of sound—are almost unavoidable consequences of the first. A linguistic signal can be heard by any auditory system within earshot, and the source can normally be localized by binaural direction-finding. The rapid fading of such a signal means that it does not linger for reception at the hearer's convenience. Animal tracks and spoors, on the other hand, persist for a while; so of course do written records, a product of man's extremely recent cultural evolution.

The significance of "interchangeability" and "total feedback" for language becomes clear upon comparison with other systems. In general a speaker of a language can reproduce any linguistic message he can understand, whereas the characteristic courtship motions of the male and female stickleback are different, and neither can act out those appropriate to the other. For that matter in the communication of a human mother and infant neither is apt to transmit the characteristic signals or to manifest the typical responses of the other. Again, the speaker of a language hears, by total feedback, everything of linguistic relevance in what he himself says. In contrast, the male stickleback does not see the colors of his own eye and belly that are crucial in stimulating the female. Feedback is important, since it makes possible the so-called internalization of communicative behavior that

constitutes at least a major portion of "thinking."

The sixth design-feature, "specialization," refers to the fact that the bodily effort and spreading sound waves of speech serve no function except as signals. A dog, panting with his tongue hanging out, is performing a biologically essential activity, since this is how dogs cool themselves off and maintain the proper body temperature. The panting dog incidentally produces sound, and thereby may inform other dogs (or humans) as to where he is and how he feels. But this transmission of information is strictly a side effect. Nor does the dog's panting exhibit the design-feature of "semanticity." It is not a signal meaning that the dog is hot; it is part of being hot. In language, however, a message triggers the particular result it does because there are relatively fixed associations between elements in messages (e.g., words) and recurrent features or situations of the world around us. For example, the English word "salt" means salt, not sugar or pepper. The calls of gibbons also possess semanticity. The gibbon has a danger call, for example, and it does not in principle matter that the meaning of the call is a great deal broader and more vague than, say, the cry of "Fire!"

In a semantic communicative system the ties between meaningful message-elements and their meanings can be arbitrary or nonarbitrary. In language the ties are arbitrary. The word "salt" is not salty nor granular; "dog" is not "canine"; "whale" is a small word for a large object; "microorganism" is the reverse. A picture, on the other hand, looks like what it is a picture of. A bee dances faster if the source of nectar she is reporting is closer, and slower if it is farther away. The design-feature of "arbitrariness" has the disadvantage of being arbitrary, but the great advantage that there is no limit to what can be communicated about.

Human vocal organs can produce a huge variety of sound. But in any one language only a relatively small set of ranges of sound is used, and the differences between these ranges are functionally absolute. The English words "pin" and "bin" are different to the ear only at one point. If a speaker produces a syllable that deviates from the normal pronunciation of "pin" in the direction of that of "bin," he is not producing still a third word, but just saying "pin" (or perhaps "bin") in a noisy way. The hearer compensates if he can, on the basis of context, or else fails to under-

stand. This feature of "discreteness" in the elementary signaling units of a language contrasts with the use of sound effects by way of vocal gesture. There is an effectively continuous scale of degrees to which one may raise his voice as in anger, or lower it to signal confidentiality. Bee-dancing also is continuous rather than discrete.

Man is apparently almost unique in being able to talk about things that are remote in space or time (or both) from where the talking goes on. This feature—"displacement"—seems to be definitely lacking in the vocal signaling of man's closest relatives, though it does occur in bee-dancing.

One of the most important design-features of language is "productivity"; that is, the capacity to say things that have never been said or heard before and yet to be understood by other speakers of the language. If a gibbon makes any vocal sound at all, it is one or another of a small finite repertory of familiar calls. The gibbon call system can be characterized as closed. Language is open, or "productive," in the sense that one can coin new utterances by putting together pieces familiar from old utterances, assembling them by patterns of arrangement also familiar in old utterances.

Human genes carry the capacity to acquire a language, and probably also a strong drive toward such acquisition, but the detailed conventions of any one language are transmitted extragenetically by learning and teaching. To what extent such "traditional transmission" plays a part in gibbon calls or for other mammalian systems of vocal signals is not known, though in some instances the uniformity of the sounds made by a species, wherever the species is found over the world, is so great that genetics must be responsible.

The meaningful elements in any language—"words" in everyday parlance, "morphemes" to the linguist—constitute an enormous stock. Yet they are represented by small arrangements of a relatively very small stock of distinguishable sounds which are in themselves wholly meaningless. This "duality of patterning" is illustrated by the English words

THIRTEEN DESIGN-FEATURES of animal communication, discussed in detail in the text of this article, are symbolized on opposite page. The patterns of the words "pin," "bin," "team" and "meat" were recorded at Bell Telephone Laboratories.

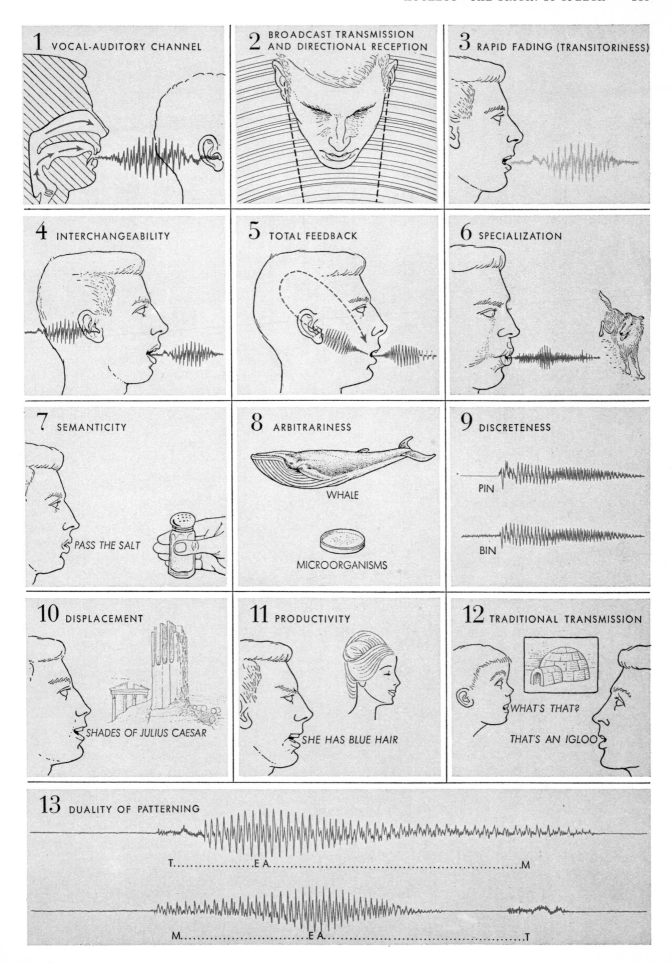

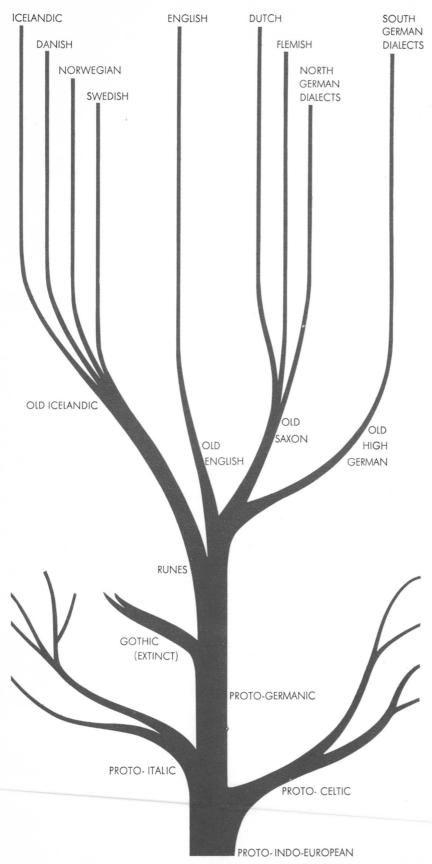

ICELANDIC

DANISH

NORWEGIAN

SWEDISH

ENGLISH

DUTCH

FLEMISH

NORTH
GERMAN
DIALECTS

SOUTH
GERMAN
DIALECTS

OLD ICELANDIC

OLD
ENGLISH

OLD
SAXON

OLD
HIGH
GERMAN

RUNES

GOTHIC
(EXTINCT)

PROTO-GERMANIC

PROTO- ITALIC

PROTO- CELTIC

PROTO- INDO-EUROPEAN

ORIGIN OF MODERN GERMANIC LANGUAGES, as indicated by this "family tree," was proto-Germanic, spoken some 2,700 years ago. Comparison of present-day languages has provided detailed knowledge of proto-Germanic, although no direct documentary evidence for the language exists. It grew, in turn, from the proto-Indo-European of 5000 B.C. Historical studies cannot, however, trace origins of language back much further in time.

"tack," "cat" and "act." They are totally distinct as to meaning, and yet are composed of just three basic meaningless sounds in different permutations. Few animal communicative systems share this design-feature of language—none among the other hominoids, and perhaps none at all.

It should be noted that some of these 13 design-features are not independent. In particular, a system cannot be either arbitrary or nonarbitrary unless it is semantic, and it cannot have duality of patterning unless it is semantic. It should also be noted that the listing does not attempt to include all the features that might be discovered in the communicative behavior of this or that species, but only those that are clearly important for language.

It is probably safe to assume that nine of the 13 features were already present in the vocal-auditory communication of the protohominoids—just the nine that are securely attested for the gibbons and humans of today. That is, there were a dozen or so distinct calls, each the appropriate vocal response (or vocal part of the whole response) to a recurrent and biologically important type of situation: the discovery of food, the detection of a predator, sexual interest, need for maternal care, and so on. The problem of the origin of human speech, then, is that of trying to determine how such a system could have developed the four additional properties of displacement, productivity and full-blown traditional transmission. Of course the full story involves a great deal more than communicative behavior alone. The development must be visualized as occurring in the context of the evolution of the primate horde into the primitive society of food-gatherers and hunters, an integral part, but a part, of the total evolution of behavior.

It is possible to imagine a closed system developing some degree of productivity, even in the absence of the other three features. Human speech exhibits a phenomenon that could have this effect, the phenomenon of "blending." Sometimes a speaker will hesitate between two words or phrases, both reasonably appropriate for the situation in which he is speaking, and actually say something that is neither wholly one nor wholly the other, but a combination of parts of each. Hesitating between "Don't shout so loud" and "Don't yell so loud," he might come out with "Don't shell so loud." Blending is almost always involved in slips of the tongue, but it may

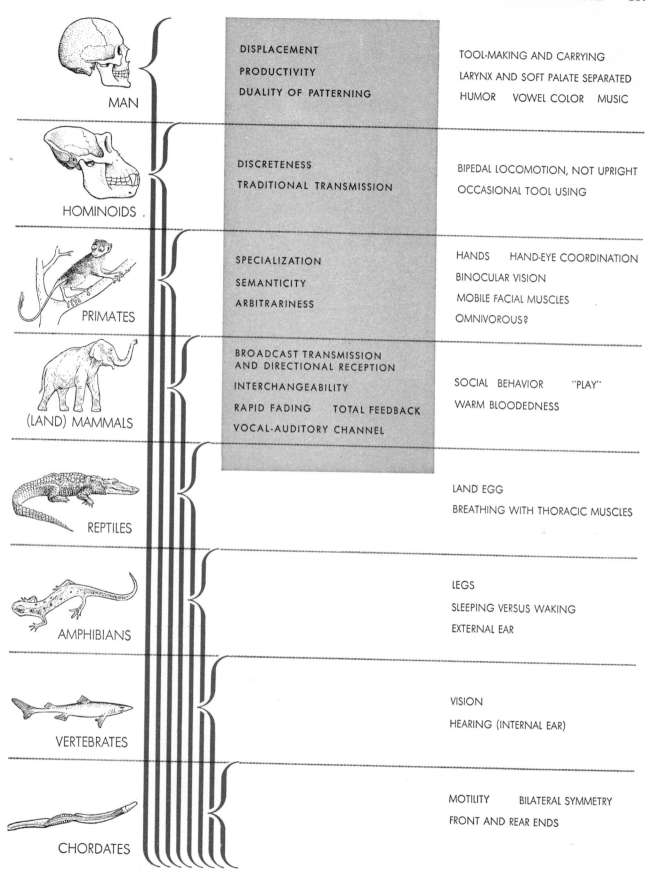

EVOLUTION OF LANGUAGE and some related characteristics are suggested by this classification of chordates. The lowest form of animal in each classification exhibits the features listed at the right of the class. Brackets indicate that each group possesses or has evolved beyond the characteristics exhibited by all the groups below. The 13 design-features of language appear in the colored rectangle. Some but by no means all of the characteristics associated with communication are presented in the column at right.

also be the regular mechanism by which a speaker of a language says something that he has not said before. Anything a speaker says must be either an exact repetition of an utterance he has heard before, or else some blended product of two or more such familiar utterances. Thus even such a smooth and normal sentence as "I tried to get there, but the car broke down" might be produced as a blend, say, of "I tried to get there but couldn't" and "While I was driving down Main Street the car broke down."

Children acquiring the language of their community pass through a stage that is closed in just the way gibbon calls

are. A child may have a repertory of several dozen sentences, each of which, in adult terms, has an internal structure, and yet for the child each may be an indivisible whole. He may also learn new whole utterances from surrounding adults. The child takes the crucial step, however, when he first says something that he has not learned from others. The only way in which the child can possibly do this is by blending two of the whole utterances that he already knows.

In the case of the closed call-system of the gibbons or the protohominoids, there is no source for the addition of new

unitary calls to the repertory except perhaps by occasional imitation of the calls and cries of other species. Even this would not render the system productive, but would merely enlarge it. But blending might occur. Let AB represent the food call and CD the danger call, each a fairly complex phonetic pattern. Suppose a protohominoid encountered food and caught sight of a predator at the same time. If the two stimuli were balanced just right, he might emit the calls ABCD or CDAB in quick sequence, or might even produce AD or CB. Any of these would be a blend. AD, for example, would mean "both food and danger." By

		A	B	C	D
		SOME GRYLLIDAE AND TETTIGONIIDAE	BEE DANCING	STICKLEBACK COURTSHIP	WESTERN MEADOWLARK SONG
1	THE VOCAL-AUDITORY CHANNEL	AUDITORY, NOT VOCAL	NO	NO	YES
2	BROADCAST TRANSMISSION AND DIRECTIONAL RECEPTION	YES	YES	YES	YES
3	RAPID FADING (TRANSITORINESS)	YES, REPEATED	?	?	YES
4	INTERCHANGEABILITY	LIMITED	LIMITED	NO	?
5	TOTAL FEEDBACK	YES	?	NO	YES
6	SPECIALIZATION	YES?	?	IN PART	YES?
7	SEMANTICITY	NO?	YES	NO	IN PART ?
8	ARBITRARINESS	?	NO		IF SEMANTIC, YES
9	DISCRETENESS	YES?	NO	?	?
10	DISPLACEMENT		YES, ALWAYS		?
11	PRODUCTIVITY	NO	YES	NO	?
12	TRADITIONAL TRANSMISSION	NO?	PROBABLY NOT	NO?	?
13	DUALITY OF PATTERNING	? (TRIVIAL)	NO		?

EIGHT SYSTEMS OF COMMUNICATION possess in varying degrees the 13 design-features of language. Column A refers to members of the cricket family. Column H concerns only Western music since the time of Bach. A question mark means that it is

virtue of this, AB and CD would acquire new meanings, respectively "food without danger" and "danger without food." And all three of these calls—AB, CD and AD—would now be composite rather than unitary, built out of smaller elements with their own individual meanings: A would mean "food"; B, "no danger"; C, "no food"; and D, "danger."

But this is only part of the story. The generation of a blend can have no effect unless it is understood. Human beings are so good at understanding blends that it is hard to tell a blend from a rote repetition, except in the case of slips of the tongue and some of the earliest and most tentative blends used by children. Such powers of understanding cannot be ascribed to man's prehuman ancestors. It must be supposed, therefore, that occasional blends occurred over many tens of thousands of years (perhaps, indeed, they still may occur from time to time among gibbons or the great apes), with rarely any appropriate communicative impact on hearers, before the understanding of blends became speedy enough to reinforce their production. However, once that did happen, the earlier closed system had become open and productive.

It is also possible to see how faint traces of displacement might develop in a call system even in the absence of productivity, duality and thoroughgoing traditional transmission. Suppose an early hominid, a man-ape say, caught sight of a predator without himself being seen. Suppose that for whatever reason—perhaps through fear—he sneaked silently back toward others of his band and only a bit later gave forth the danger call. This might give the whole band a better chance to escape the predator, thus bestowing at least slight survival value on whatever factor was responsible for the delay.

Something akin to communicative displacement is involved in lugging a stick or a stone around—it is like talking today about what one should do tomorrow. Of course it is not to be supposed that the first tool-carrying was purposeful, any more than that the first displaced communication was a discussion of plans. Caught in a *cul-de-sac* by a predator, however, the early hominid might strike out in terror with his stick or stone and by chance disable or drive off his enemy. In other words, the first tool-carrying had a consequence but not a purpose. Because the outcome was fortunate, it tended to reinforce whatever factor, genetic or traditional, prompted the behavior and made the outcome possible. In the end such events do lead to purposive behavior.

Although elements of displacement might arise in this fashion, on the whole it seems likely that some degree of productivity preceded any great proliferation of communicative displacement as well as any significant capacity for traditional transmission. A productive system requires the young to catch on to the ways in which whole signals are built out of smaller meaningful elements, some of which may never occur as whole signals in isolation. The young can do this only in the way that human children learn their language: by learning some utterances as whole units, in due time testing various blends based on that repertory, and finally adjusting their patterns of blending until the bulk of what they say matches what adults would say and is therefore understood. Part of this learning process is bound to take place away from the precise situations for which the responses are basically appropriate, and this means the promotion of displacement. Learning and teaching, moreover, call on any capacity for traditional transmission that the band may have. Insofar as the communicative system itself has survival value, all this bestows survival value also on the capacity

E	F	G	H
GIBBON CALLS	PARALINGUISTIC PHENOMENA	LANGUAGE	INSTRUMENTAL MUSIC
YES	YES	YES	AUDITORY, NOT VOCAL
YES	YES	YES	YES
YES, REPEATED	YES	YES	YES
YES	LARGELY YES	YES	?
YES	YES	YES	YES
YES	YES?	YES	YES
YES	YES?	YES	NO (IN GENERAL)
YES	IN PART	YES	
YES	LARGELY NO	YES	IN PART
NO	IN PART	YES, OFTEN	
NO	YES	YES	YES
?	YES	YES	YES
NO	NO	YES	

doubtful or not known if the system has the particular feature. A blank space indicates that feature cannot be determined because another feature is lacking or is indefinite.

for traditional transmission and for displacement. But these in turn increase the survival value of the communicative system. A child can be taught how to avoid certain dangers before he actually encounters them.

These developments are also necessarily related to the appearance of large and convoluted brains, which are better storage units for the conventions of a complex communicative system and for other traditionally transmitted skills and practices. Hence the adaptive value of the behavior serves to select genetically for the change in structure. A lengthened period of childhood helplessness is also a longer period of plasticity for learning. There is therefore selection for prolonged childhood and, with it, later maturity and longer life. With more for the young to learn, and with male as well as female tasks to be taught, fathers become more domesticated. The increase of displacement promotes re-

tention and foresight; a male can protect his mate and guard her jealously from other males even when he does not at the moment hunger for her.

There is excellent reason to believe that duality of patterning was the last property to be developed, because one can find little if any reason why a communicative system should have this property unless it is highly complicated. If a vocal-auditory system comes to have a larger and larger number of distinct meaningful elements, those elements inevitably come to be more and more similar to one another in sound. There is a practical limit, for any species or any machine, to the number of distinct stimuli that can be discriminated, especially when the discriminations typically have to be made in noisy conditions. Suppose that Samuel F. B. Morse, in devising his telegraph code, had proposed a signal .1 second long for "A," .2 second long for "B," and so on up to 2.6 seconds for "Z." Operators would have enormous

difficulty learning and using any such system. What Morse actually did was to incorporate the principle of duality of patterning. The telegraph operator has to learn to discriminate, in the first instance, only two lengths of pulse and about three lengths of pause. Each letter is coded into a different arrangement of these elementary meaningless units. The arrangements are easily kept apart because the few meaningless units are plainly distinguishable.

The analogy explains why it was advantageous for the forerunner of language, as it was becoming increasingly complex, to acquire duality of patterning. However it occurred, this was a major breakthrough; without it language could not possibly have achieved the efficiency and flexibility it has.

One of the basic principles of evolutionary theory holds that the initial survival value of any innovation is conservative in that it makes possible the maintenance of a largely traditional way of life in the face of changed circumstances. There was nothing in the makeup of the protohominoids that destined their descendants to become human. Some of them, indeed, did not. They made their way to ecological niches where food was plentiful and predators sufficiently avoidable, and where the development of primitive varieties of language and culture would have bestowed no advantage. They survive still, with various sorts of specialization, as the gibbons and the great apes.

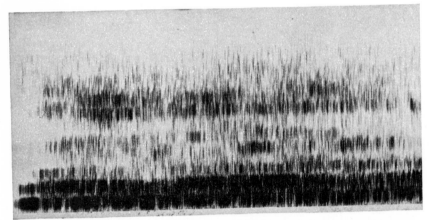
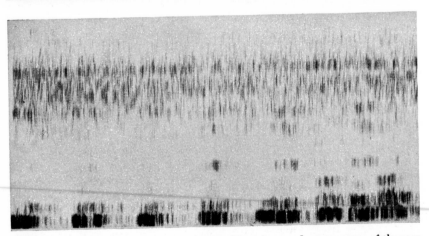

SUBHUMAN PRIMATE CALLS are represented here by sound spectrograms of the roar (*top*) and bark (*bottom*) of the howler monkey. Frequencies are shown vertically; time, horizontally. Roaring, the most prominent howler vocalization, regulates interactions and movements of groups of monkeys, and has both defensive and offensive functions. Barking has similar meanings but occurs when the monkeys are not quite so excited. Spectrograms were produced at Bell Telephone Laboratories from recordings made by Charles Southwick of the University of Southern Ohio during an expedition to Barro Colorado Island in the Canal Zone. The expedition was directed by C. R. Carpenter of Pennsylvania State University.

Man's own remote ancestors, then, must have come to live in circumstances where a slightly more flexible system of communication, the incipient carrying and shaping of tools, and a slight increase in the capacity for traditional transmission made just the difference between surviving—largely, be it noted, by the good old protohominoid way of life—and dying out. There are various possibilities. If predators become more numerous and dangerous, any nonce use of a tool as a weapon, any co-operative mode of escape or attack might restore the balance. If food became scarcer, any technique for cracking harder nuts, for foraging over a wider territory, for sharing food so gathered or storing it when it was plentiful might promote survival of the band. Only after a very long period of such small adjustments to tiny changes of living conditions could the factors involved —incipient language, incipient tool-carrying and toolmaking, incipient culture— have started leading the way to a new pattern of life, of the kind called human.

18

Learning to Think

HARRY F. HARLOW AND MARGARET KUENNE HARLOW
August 1949

HOW does an infant, born with only a few simple reactions, develop into an adult capable of rapid learning and the almost incredibly complex mental processes known as thinking? This is one of psychology's unsolved problems. Most modern explanations are not much more enlightening than those offered by 18th-century French and English philosophers, who suggested that the mind developed merely by the process of associating ideas or experiences with one another. Even the early philosophers realized that this was not a completely adequate explanation.

The speed and complexity of a human being's mental processes, and the intricacy of the nerve mechanisms that presumably underlie them, suggest that the brain is not simply a passive network of communications but develops some kind of organization that facilitates learning and thinking. Whether such organizing principles exist has been a matter of considerable dispute. At one extreme, some modern psychologists deny that they do and describe learning as a mere trial-and-error process—a blind fumbling about until a solution accidentally appears. At the other extreme, there are psychologists who hold that people learn through an innate insight that reveals relationships to them.

To investigate, and to reconcile if possible, these seemingly antagonistic positions, a series of studies of the learning process has been carried out at the University of Wisconsin. Some of these have been made with young children, but most of the research has been on monkeys.

For two basic reasons animals are particularly good subjects for the investigation of learning at a fundamental level. One is that it is possible to control their entire learning history: the psychologist knows the problems to which they have been exposed, the amount of training they have had on each, and the record of their performance. The other reason is that the animals' adaptive processes are more simple than those of human beings, especially during the first stages of the attack on a problem. Often the animal's reactions throw into clear relief certain mechanisms that operate more

obscurely in man. Of course this is only a relative simplicity. All the higher mammals possess intricate nervous systems and can solve complex problems. Indeed, it is doubtful that man possesses any fundamental intellectual process, except true language, that is not also present in his more lowly biological brethren.

Tests of animal learning of the trial-and-error type have been made in innumerable laboratories. In the special tests devised for our experiments, we set out to determine whether monkeys could progress from trial-and-error learning to the ability to solve a problem immediately by insight.

One of the first experiments was a simple discrimination test. The monkeys were confronted with a small board on which lay two objects different in color, size and shape. If a monkey picked up the correct object, it was rewarded by finding raisins or peanuts underneath. The position of the objects was shifted on the board in an irregular manner from trial to trial, and the trials were continued until the monkey learned to choose the correct object. The unusual feature of the experiment was that the test was repeated many times, with several hundred different pairs of objects. In other words, instead of training a monkey to solve a single problem, as had been done in most previous psychological work of this kind, we trained the animal on many problems, all of the same general type, but with varying kinds of objects.

When the monkeys first faced this test, they learned by the slow, laborious, fumble-and-find process. But as a monkey solved problem after problem of the same basic kind, its behavior changed in a most dramatic way. It learned each new problem with progressively greater efficiency, until eventually the monkey showed perfect insight when faced with this particular kind of situation—it solved the problem in one trial. If it chose the correct object on the first trial, it rarely made an error on subsequent trials. If it chose the incorrect object on the first trial, it immediately shifted to the correct object, and subsequently responded almost perfectly.

Thus the test appeared to demonstrate that trial-and-error and insight are but

two different phases of one long continuous process. They are not different capacities, but merely represent the orderly development of a learning and thinking process.

A LONG series of these discrimination problems was also run on a group of nursery-school children two to five years of age. Young children were chosen because they have a minimum of previous experience. The conditions in the children's tests were only slightly different from those for the monkeys: they were rewarded by finding brightly colored macaroni beads instead of raisins and peanuts. Most of the children, like the monkeys, made many errors in the early stages of the tests and only gradually learned to solve a problem in one trial. As a group the children learned more rapidly than the monkeys, but they made the same types of errors. And the "smartest" monkeys learned faster than the "dullest" children.

We have called this process of progressive learning the formation of a "learning set." The subject learns an organized set of habits that enables him to meet effectively each new problem of this particular kind. A single set would provide only limited aid in enabling an animal to adapt to an ever-changing environment. But a host of different learning sets may supply the raw material for human thinking.

We have trained monkeys and children to solve problems much more complex than the ones thus far described. For instance, a deliberate attempt is made to confuse the subjects by reversing the conditions of the discrimination test. The previously correct object is no longer rewarded, and the previously incorrect object is always rewarded. When monkeys and children face this switch-over for the first time, they make many errors, persistently choosing the objects they had previously been trained to choose. Gradually, from problem to problem, the number of such errors decreases until finally the first reversal trial is followed by perfect performance. A single failure becomes the cue to the subject to shift his choice from the object which has been rewarded many times to the object

MONKEY EXPERIMENTS at the University of Wisconsin illustrate the process of learning. In the drawing at the upper right a monkey is confronted with two different objects. Under one of them is always a raisin or a peanut. In the drawing at the right the monkey has learned consistently to pick the same object. In the drawing above the monkey has learned consistently to choose one object which differs from two others. In the two drawings below the monkey has learned a much more complicated process. In the drawing at the lower left it has learned that when the board is of a certain color it must choose the object that is odd in shape. In the drawing at the lower right it has learned that when the board is of another color it must choose the object that is odd in color. In all these problems the monkey first learned to solve the problem by trial and error. Later it solved them immediately by understanding.

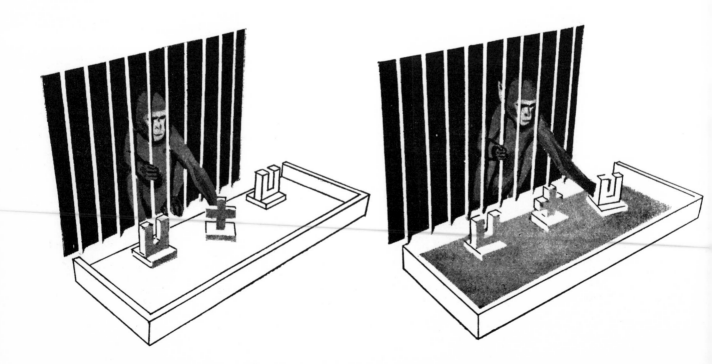

which has never been rewarded before. In this type of test children learn much more rapidly than monkeys.

A group of monkeys that had formed the discrimination-reversal learning set was later trained on a further refinement of the problem. This time the reward value of the objects was reversed for only one trial, and was then shifted back to the original relationship. After many problems, the monkeys learned to ignore the single reversal and treated it as if the experimenter had made an error!

The problem was made more complicated, in another test, by offering the subjects a choice among three objects instead of two. There is a tray containing three food wells. Two are covered by one kind of object, and the third is covered by another kind. The animal must choose the odd object. Suppose the objects are building blocks and funnels. In half the trials, there are two blocks and a funnel, and the correct object is the funnel. Then a switch is made to two funnels and one block. Now the correct object is the block. The animal must learn a subtle distinction here: it is not the shape of the object that is important, but its relation to the other two. The meaning of a specific object may change from trial to trial. This problem is something like the one a child faces in trying to learn to use the words "I," "you," and "he" properly. The meaning of the words changes according to the speaker. When the child is speaking, "I" refers to himself, "you" to the person addressed, and "he" to some third person. When the child is addressed, the child is no longer "I" but "you." And when others speak of him, the terms shift again.

Monkeys and children were trained on a series of these oddity problems, 24 trials being allowed for the solution of each problem. At first they floundered, but they improved from problem to problem until they learned to respond to each new problem with perfect or nearly perfect scores. And on this complex type of problem the monkeys did better than most of the children!

ONE of the most striking findings from these tests was that once the monkeys have formed these learning sets, they retain them for long periods and can use them appropriately as the occasion demands. After a lapse of a year or more, a monkey regains top efficiency, in a few minutes or hours of practice, on a problem that it may have taken many weeks to master originally.

All our studies indicate that the ability to solve problems without fumbling is not inborn but is acquired gradually. So we must re-examine the evidence offered in support of the theory that animals possess some innate insight that has nothing to do with learning.

The cornerstone of this theory is the work of the famous Gestalt psychologist Wolfgang Köhler on the behavior of chimpanzees. In a series of brilliant studies he clearly showed that these apes can use sticks to help them obtain bananas beyond their reach. They employed the sticks to knock the bananas down, to rake them in, to climb and to vault. The animals sometimes assembled short sticks to make a pole long enough to reach the food, and even used sticks in combination with stacked boxes to knock down high-dangling bait. That the chimpanzees frequently solved these problems suddenly, as if by a flash of insight, impressed Köhler as evidence of an ability to reason independently of learning. He even suggested that this ability might differentiate apes and men from other animals.

Unfortunately, since Köhler's animals had been captured in the jungle, he had no record of their previous learning. Recent studies on chimpanzees born in captivity at the Yerkes Laboratory of Primate Biology at Orange Park, Fla., throw doubt on the validity of Köhler's interpretations. Herbert Birch of the Yerkes Laboratory reported that when he gave sticks to four-year-old chimps in their cages, they showed little sign at first of ability to use them as tools. Gradually, in the course of three days, they learned to use the sticks to touch objects beyond their reach. Later the animals solved very simple stick problems fairly well, but they had difficulty with more complex problems.

Extending Birch's investigations, the late Paul Schiller presented a series of stick tasks to a group of chimpanzees from two to over eight years of age. The younger the animal, the more slowly it mastered the problems. Some young subjects took hundreds of trials to perform efficiently on even the simplest problems, while old, experienced animals solved them with little practice. None of the apes solved the tasks initially with sudden insight.

Even at the human level there is no evidence that children possess any innate endowment that enables them to solve tool problems with insight. Augusta Alpert of Columbia University tried some of Köhler's simple chimpanzee tests on bright nursery-school children. The younger children typically went through a trial-and-error process before solving the problems. Some of them failed to solve the easiest problem in the series in five experimental sessions.

Eunice Mathieson presented more difficult Köhler-type tasks to a group of University of Minnesota nursery-school children. The results were even more overwhelmingly against the notion that tool problems are solved by flashes of natural insight. The children rarely solved a problem without making many mistakes.

This research, then, supports our findings. In all clear-cut tests—that is, whenever the animals' entire learning history is known—monkeys, apes and children at first solve problems by trial and error. Only gradually does such behavior give way to immediate solutions.

WE began by pointing out that psychologists have sought to find in the higher mental processes some organizing mechanism or principle that would explain learning and thinking. We can now suggest such a mechanism: the learning set. Suppose we picture mental activity as a continuous structure built up, step by step, by the solution of increasingly difficult problems, from the simplest problem in learning to the most complex one in thinking. At each level the individual tries out various responses to solve each given task. At the lowest level he selects from unlearned responses or previously learned habits. As his experience increases, habits that do not help in the solution drop out and useful habits become established. After solving many problems of a certain kind, he develops organized patterns of responses that meet the demands of this type of situation. These patterns, or learning sets, can also be applied to the solution of still more complex problems. Eventually the individual may organize simple learning sets into more complex patterns of learning sets, which in turn are available for transfer as units to new situations.

Thus the individual learns to cope with more and more difficult problems. At the highest stage in this progression, the intelligent human adult selects from innumerable, previously acquired learning sets the raw material for thinking. His many years of education in school and outside have been devoted to building up these complex learning sets, and he comes to manipulate them with such ease that he and his observers may easily lose sight of their origin and development.

The fundamental role that language plays in the thinking process may be deduced easily from our experiments. They suggest that words are stimuli or signs that call forth the particular learning sets most appropriate for solving a given problem. If you listen to yourself "talk" while you are thinking, you will find that this is exactly what is happening. You review the different ways of solving a problem, and decide which is the best. When you ask a friend for advice, you are asking him to give you a word stimulus which will tell you the appropriate learning set or sets for the solution of your problem.

This principle is particularly well illustrated by some of our monkey experiments. Though monkeys do not talk, they can learn to identify symbols with appropriate learning sets. We have trained our monkeys to respond to signs in the form of differently colored trays

on which the test objects appear. In one test the monkeys were presented with three different objects—a red U-shaped block, a green U-shaped block and a red cross-shaped block. Thus two of the objects were alike in form and two alike in color. When the objects were shown on an orange tray, the monkeys had to choose the green block, that is, the object that was odd in color. When they were shown on a cream-colored tray, the animals had to choose the cross-shaped block, that is, the object odd in form. After the monkeys had formed these two learning sets, the color cue of the tray enabled them to make the proper choice, trial after trial, without error. In a sense, the animals responded to a simple sign language. The difficulty of this test may be judged by the fact that the German neurologist Kurt Goldstein, using similar tests for human beings, found that people with organic brain disorders could not solve such tasks efficiently.

At the Wisconsin laboratories, Benjamin Winsten devised an even more difficult test for the monkeys. This problem tested the animals' ability to recognize similarities and differences, a kind of task frequently used on children's intelligence tests. Nine objects were placed on a tray and the monkey was handed one of them as a sample. The animal's problem was to pick out all identical objects, leaving all the rest on the tray. In the most complicated form of this test the monkey was given a sample which was not identical with the objects to be selected but was only a symbol for them. The animal was handed an unpainted triangle as a sign to pick out all red objects, and an unpainted circle as a sign to select all blue objects. One monkey learned to respond almost perfectly. Given a triangle, he would pick every object with any red on it; given a circle, he selected only the objects with blue on them.

All these data indicate that animals, human and subhuman, must learn to think. Thinking does not develop spontaneously as an expression of innate abilities; it is the end result of a long learning process. Years ago the British biologist, Thomas Henry Huxley, suggested that "the brain secretes thought as the liver secretes bile." Nothing could be further from the truth. The brain is essential to thought, but the untutored brain is not enough, no matter how good a brain it may be. An untrained brain is sufficient for trial-and-error, fumble-through behavior, but only training enables an individual to think in terms of ideas and concepts.

MORE COMPLICATED TEST involves teaching a monkey to choose certain objects not by matching but by response to a symbol. In the pair of drawings at the top of this page the monkey is shown a triangular object and pushes forward all the red objects, here indicated by gray tone. In drawings at bottom the monkey, shown a round object, pushes forward blue objects.

19

Sickle Cells and Evolution

ANTHONY C. ALLISON

August 1956

Persevering study of small and seemingly insignificant phenomena sometimes yields surprising harvests of understanding. This article is an account of what has been learned from an oddly shaped red blood cell.

Forty-six years ago a Chicago physician named James B. Herrick, examining a Negro boy with a mysterious disease, found that many of his red blood cells were distorted into a crescent or sickle shape. After Herrick's report, doctors soon recognized many other cases of the same disease. They learned that it was hereditary and common in Negroes [see "Sickle-Cell Anemia," by George W. Gray; SCIENTIFIC AMERICAN, August, 1951]. The curious trait of the sickled blood cells gradually attracted the in-

terest of physiologists, biochemists, physical chemists, geneticists, anthropologists and others. And their varied investigations of this quirk of nature led to enlightenment on many unexpected subjects: the behavior of the blood's hemoglobin, inherited resistance to disease, the movements of populations over the world and the nature of some of the agencies that influence human evolution.

Let us review first what has been learned about the sickle cell phenomenon itself. As every student of biology knows, the principal active molecule in the red blood cells is hemoglobin, which serves as the carrier of oxygen. It appears that an unusual form of hemoglobin, pro-

duced under the influence of an abnormal gene, is responsible for the sickling of red cells. This hemoglobin molecule differs only slightly from the normal variety, and when there is an ample supply of oxygen it behaves normally: *i.e.*, it takes on oxygen and preserves its usual form in the red cells. But when the sickle cell hemoglobin (known as hemoglobin S) loses oxygen, as in the capillaries where oxygen is delivered to the tissues, it becomes susceptible to a peculiar kind of reaction. It can attach itself to other hemoglobin S molecules, and they form long rods, which in turn attract one another and line up in parallel. These formations are rigid enough to distort the red cells from their normal disk shape into the shape

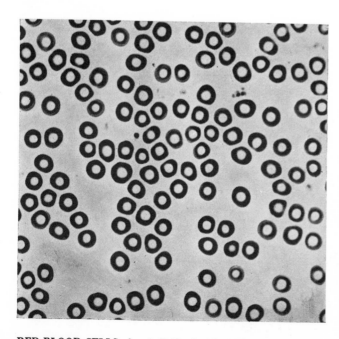

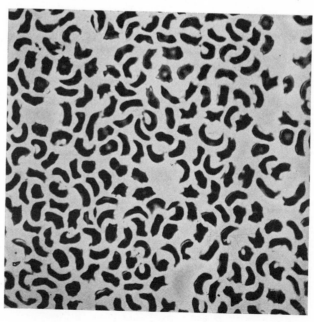

RED BLOOD CELLS of an individual with sickle cell trait, *i.e.*, a sickle cell gene from only one parent, are examined under the microscope. At the left are oxygenated red cells; they are disk-shaped. At the right are the same cells deoxygenated; they are sickle-shaped.

of a sickle [*see photomicrographs on page 3*]. Now the sickled cells may clog blood vessels; and they are soon destroyed by the body, so that the patient becomes anemic. The destruction of the hemoglobin converts it into bilirubin—the yellow pigment responsible for the jaundiced appearance often characteristic of anemic patients.

Most sufferers from sickle cell anemia die in childhood. Those who survive have a chronic disease punctuated by painful crises when blood supply is cut off from various body organs. There is no effective treatment for the disease.

From the first, a great deal of interest focused on the genetic aspects of this peculiarity. It was soon found that some Negroes carried a sickling tendency without showing symptoms of the disease. This was eventually discovered to mean that the carrier inherits the sickle cell gene from only one parent. A child who receives sickle cell genes from both parents produces only hemoglobin S and therefore is prone to sickling and anemia. On the other hand, in a person who has a normal hemoglobin gene from one parent and a hemoglobin S from the other sickling is much less likely; such persons, known as carriers of the "sickle cell trait," become ill only under exceptional conditions—for example, at high altitudes, when their blood does not receive enough oxygen.

The sickle cell trait is, of course, much more common than the disease. Among Negroes in the U. S. some 9 per cent carry the trait, but less than one fourth of 1 per cent show sickle cell anemia. In some Negro tribes in Africa the trait is present in as much as 40 per cent of the population, while 4 per cent have sickle cell genes from both parents and are subject to the disease.

The high incidence of the sickle cell gene in these tribes raised a most interesting question. Why does the harmful gene persist? A child who inherits two sickle cell genes (*i.e.*, is homozygous for this gene) has only about one fifth as much chance as other children of surviving to reproductive age. Because of this mortality, about 16 per cent of the sickle cell genes must be removed from the population in every generation. And yet the general level remains high without any sign of declining. What can be the explanation? Carriers of the sickle cell trait do not produce more children than those who lack it, and natural mutation could not possibly replace the lost sickle cell genes at any such rate.

The laws of evolution suggested a possible answer. Carriers of the sickle cell trait (a sickle cell gene from one parent and a normal one from the other) might have some advantage in survival over those who lacked the trait. If people with the trait had a lower mortality rate, counterbalancing the high mortality of sufferers from sickle cell anemia, then the frequency of sickle cell genes in the population would remain at a constant level.

What advantage could the sickle cell trait confer? Perhaps it protected its carriers against some other fatal disease—say malaria. The writer looked into the situation in malarious areas of Africa and found that children with the sickle cell trait were indeed relatively resistant to malarial infection. In some places they had as much as a 25 per cent better chance of survival than children without the trait. Children in most of Central Africa are exposed to malaria nearly all year round and have repeated infections during their early years. If they survive; they build up a considerable immunity to the disease. In some unknown way the sickle cell trait apparently protects young children against the malaria parasite during the dangerous years until they acquire an immunity to malaria.

On the African continent the sickle cell gene has a high frequency among people along the central belt, near the Equator, where malaria is common and is transmitted by mosquitoes through most

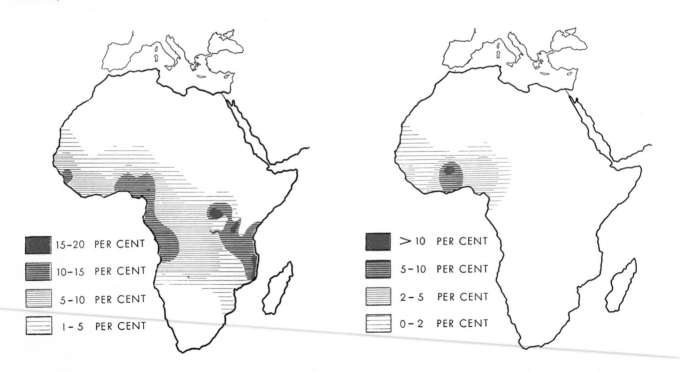

FREQUENCY OF THE SICKLE CELL GENE is plotted in per cent on the map of Africa. High frequencies are confined to a broad belt in which malignant tertian malaria is an important cause of death.

FREQUENCY OF THE HEMOGLOBIN C GENE is similarly plotted. Unlike the sickle cell gene, which has a widespread distribution, this gene is confined to a single focus in West Africa.

15-20 PER CENT
10-15 PER CENT
5-10 PER CENT
1-5 PER CENT

> 10 PER CENT
5-10 PER CENT
2-5 PER CENT
0-2 PER CENT

of the year. North and south of this belt, where malaria is less common and usually of the benign variety, the sickle cell gene is rare or absent. Moreover, even within the central belt, tribes in nonmalarious areas have few sickle cell genes.

Extension of the studies showed that similar situations exist in other areas of the world. In malarious parts of southern Italy and Sicily, Greece, Turkey and India, the sickle cell trait occurs in up to 30 per cent of the population. There is no reason to suppose that the peoples of all these areas have transmitted the gene to one another during recent times. The sickle cell gene may have originated independently in the several populations or may trace back to a few such genes passed along among them a thousand years ago. The high frequency of the gene in these populations today can be attributed mainly to the selective effect of malaria.

On the other hand, we should expect that when a population moves from a malarious region to one free of this disease, the frequency of the sickle cell gene will fall. The Negro population of the U. S. exemplifies such a development. When Negro slaves were first brought to North America from West Africa some 250 to 300 years ago, the frequency of the sickle cell trait among them was probably not less than 22 per cent. By mixed mating with Indian and white people this figure was probably reduced to about 15 per cent. In the absence of any appreciable mortality from malaria, the loss of sickle cell genes through deaths from anemia in 12 generations should have reduced the frequency of the sickle cell trait in the Negro population to about 9 per cent. This is, in fact, precisely the frequency found today.

Thus the Negroes of the U. S. show a clear case of evolutionary change. Within the space of a few hundred years this population, because of its transfer from Africa to North America, has undergone a definite alteration in genetic structure. This indicates how rapidly human evolution can take place under favorable circumstances.

Since the discovery of sickle cell hemoglobin (hemoglobin S), many other abnormal types of human hemoglobin have been found. (They are usually distinguished by electrophoresis, a separation method which depends on differences in the amount of the negative charge on the molecule.) One of the most

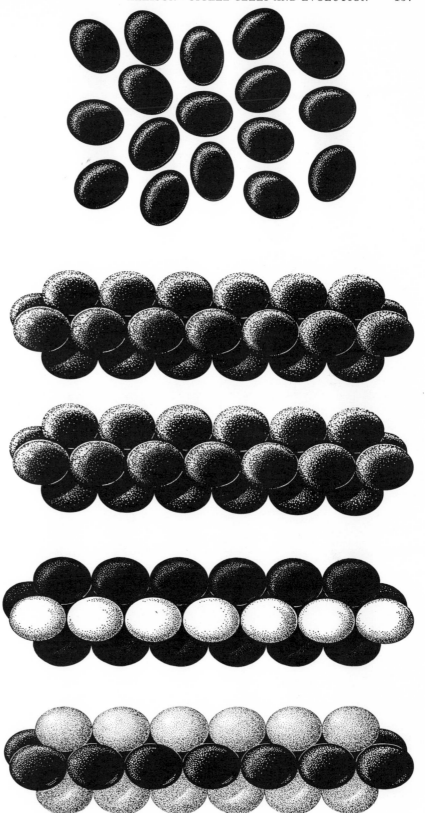

HEMOGLOBIN MOLECULES are represented as ellipsoids in these drawings. At the top are normal hemoglobin molecules, which are arranged almost at random in the red blood cell. Second and third from the top are sickle cell hemoglobin molecules, which form long helixes when they lose oxygen. Fourth is an aggregate of normal (*white*) and sickle cell molecules (*black*), in which every fourth molecule of the helix is normal. Fifth is an aggregate of hemoglobin C (*gray*) and sickle cell molecules; every other molecule is hemoglobin C.

common of these other varieties is called hemoglobin C. It, too, causes anemia in persons who have inherited the hemoglobin C gene from both parents. Moreover, the combination of hemoglobin S and hemoglobin C (one inherited from each parent) likewise leads to anemia. These two hemoglobins combine to form the rodlike structures that cause sickling of the red blood cells [*see drawings on* page 5].

The hemoglobin C gene is largely confined to West Africa, notably among people in the northern section of the Gold Coast, where the frequency of the trait runs as high as 27 per cent. Whether hemoglobin C, like hemoglobin S, protects against malaria is not known. But the C gene must give some advantage, else it would not persist. Obviously inheritance of both C and S is a disadvantage, since it leads to anemia. As a consequence we should expect to find that where the C gene is present, the spread of the S gene is retarded. This does seem to be the case: in the northern Gold Coast the frequency of the S gene goes no higher than 5 per cent.

Another gene producing abnormal hemoglobin, known as the thalassemia gene, is common in Greece, Italy, Cyprus, Turkey and Thailand. The trait is most prevalent in certain areas (*e.g.*, lowlands of Sardinia) where malaria used to be serious, but there have not yet been any direct observations as to whether its carriers are resistant to malaria. The trait almost certainly has some compensating advantage, for it persists in spite of the fact that even persons who have inherited the gene from only one parent have a tendency to anemia. The same is probably true of another deviant gene, known as the hemoglobin E gene, which is common in Thailand, Burma and among some populations in Ceylon and Indonesia.

By now the identified hemoglobin types form a considerable alphabet: besides S, C, thalassemia and E there are D, G, H, I, J, K and M. But the latter are relatively rare, from which it can be inferred that they provide little or no advantage.

For anyone interested in population genetics and human evolution, the sickle cell story presents a remarkably clear demonstration of some of the principles at play. It affords, for one thing, a simple illustration of the principle of hybrid vigor. Hybrid vigor has been investigated by many breeding experiments with fruit flies and plants, but in most cases the crossbreeding involves so many genes that it is impossible to say what gene combinations are responsible for the advantages of the hybrid. Here we can see a human cross involving only a single gene, and we can give a convincing explanation of just how the hybridization provides an advantage. In a population exposed to malaria the heterozygote (hybrid) possessing one normal hemoglobin gene and one sickle cell hemoglobin gene has an advantage over either homozygote (two normal genes or two sickle cell genes). And this selective advantage, as we can observe, maintains a high frequency of a gene which is deleterious in double dose but advantageous in single dose.

Secondly, we see a simple example of inherited resistance to disease. Resistance to infection (to say nothing of disorders such as cancer or heart disease) is generally complex and unexplainable, but in this case it is possible to identify a single gene (the sickle cell gene) which controls resistance to a specific disease (malaria). It is an unusually di-

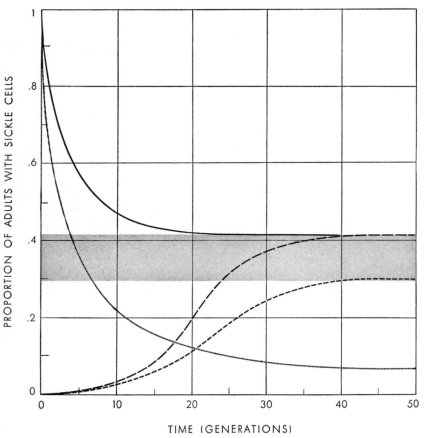

TIME (GENERATIONS)

RATE OF CHANGE IN FREQUENCY of adults with sickle cells under different conditions is shown in this chart. The horizontal gray band represents the equilibrium frequency in a region where individuals with the sickle cell trait have an evolutionary advantage of about 25 per cent over individuals without the sickle cell trait. If a population of individuals with a low sickle cell frequency enters the region, the frequency will increase to an equilibrium value (*long dashes*). If hemoglobin C is already established in the same population, the frequency will increase to a lower value (*short dashes*). If a population of individuals with a high sickle cell frequency enters the region, the frequency will decrease (*solid line*). If this population enters a nonmalarious region, the frequency will fall to a low value (*gray line*).

rect manifestation of the fact, now universally recognized but difficult to demonstrate, that inheritance plays a large role in controlling susceptibility or resistance to disease.

Thirdly, the sickle cell situation shows that mutation is not an unmixed bane to the human species. Most mutations are certainly disadvantageous, for our genetic constitution is so carefully balanced that any change is likely to be for the worse. To adapt an aphorism, all is best in this best of all possible bodies. Nonetheless, the sickle cell mutation, which at first sight looks altogether harmful, turns out to be a definite advantage in a malarious environment. Similarly other mutant genes that are bad in one situation may prove beneficial in another. Variability and mutation permit the human species, like other organisms, to adapt rapidly to new situations.

Finally, the sickle cell findings offer a cheering thought on the genetic future of civilized man. Eugenists often express alarm about the fact that civilized societies, through medical protection of the ill and weak, are accumulating harmful genes: *e.g.*, those responsible for diabetes and other hereditary diseases. The sickle cell history brings out the other side of the story: improving standards of hygiene may also *eliminate* harmful genes—not only the sickle cell but also others of which we are not yet aware.

PHENOTYPE	GENOTYPE	ELECTROPHORETIC PATTERN	HEMOGLOBIN TYPES
NORMAL	Hb^A ⊢⊣ Hb^A		A
SICKLE CELL TRAIT	Hb^S ⊢⊣ Hb^A		SA
SICKLE CELL ANEMIA	Hb^S ⊢⊣ Hb^S		SS
HEMOGLOBIN C SICKLE CELL ANEMIA	Hb^C ⊢⊣ Hb^S		CS
HEMOGLOBIN C DISEASE	Hb^C ⊢⊣ Hb^C		CC

HEMOGLOBIN SPECIMENS from various individuals are analyzed by electrophoresis. The phenotype is the outward expression of the genotype, which refers to the hereditary make-up of the individual. The H-shaped symbols in the genotype column are schematic representations of sections of human chromosomes, one from each parent. The horizontal line of the H represents a gene for hemoglobin type. Hb^A is normal hemoglobin; Hb^S, sickle cell hemoglobin; Hb^C, hemoglobin C. This kind of electrophoretic pattern is made on a strip of wet paper between a positive and a negative electrode. The specimen of hemoglobin is placed on the line at the left side of each strip. In this experiment hemoglobin A migrates faster toward the positive electrode than sickle cell hemoglobin, which migrates faster than hemoglobin C. Thus the pattern for individuals with two types of hemoglobin is double.

20

The Genetics of the Dunkers

H. BENTLEY GLASS

August 1953

THE DUNKERS, a small, sober religious sect that originally settled in eastern Pennsylvania, possess a characteristic of great interest to human geneticists. They are a group genetically isolated by strict marriage customs in the midst of a much larger community. Their beliefs have kept them distinct for more than two centuries. When Milton S. Sacks, director of the Baltimore Rh Typing Laboratory, and I were searching for a group in which to study how present blood-type and other hereditary differences arose in human populations, we turned to the Dunkers. Not only were they ideal for the study but also they opened up a larger area of inquiry. In them it is possible to perceive how racial differences which today distinguish millions of men first emerged and became set, so to speak, in small populations.

For 20 years anthropologists and geneticists have been increasingly aware of the importance in evolutionary processes of population size. In prehistoric times, when man was a hunter and gatherer, the world was sparsely inhabited. Hunting tribes are never large—1,000 people or so at most—and each tribe must range a rather large area to secure food and clothing. To keep this area inviolate and the tribe intact, primitive social customs include a simple avoidance of outsiders as well as active hostility, headhunting and cannibalism. Such customs tend to keep each tribe to itself and to make intermating between tribes quite rare. This was the period in human history when racial differences must have arisen and become set.

Such traits were probably established either by natural selection or by genetic drift, a term which may be explained as follows. In large populations chances in opposite directions tend to balance—*e.g.*, boy babies would generally equal girls in number—and the frequency of any genetic trait is expected to repeat itself generation after generation. But in small groups chance fluctuates more around the expected norm. No single family, for instance, is certain to have an equal number of boys and girls, and a predictable number of families will have all one or the other. If, in a small population, the initial proportion of brown eyes and blue were equal, the following generation might by chance have 45 per cent brown eyes and 55 per cent blue. This variation would then be expected to repeat itself by genetic law. However, the next generation might again by chance return to the 50-50 ratio or might shift to 40 per cent brown and 60 blue. If the latter were to happen, the expectation for the next generation would again be shifted, and this cumulative change by pure chance is what is meant by genetic drift. The phenomenon might continue until the whole population was either blue or brown eyed. Which ever way it went, once it had gone all the way it could not easily drift back. At that point it would be fixed in character until some mutation of the gene for eye color occurred. The chance of this in a small population is low, because the probability that a single gene will mutate is generally only one in 100,000 or even one in a million.

The actual operations of genetic drift are hard to pin down at this late date. Some present-day primitive peoples have been observed to have sharp divergences of inherited traits. The Eskimos of Thule in northern Greenland, where we are building a big air base, have a much higher frequency of the gene for blood group O (83.7 per cent) and a lower frequency of the gene for blood group A (9 per cent) than other Eskimos. They live far to the north and rarely mingle with the more populous Eskimo communities of the south. The Thule tribe numbers only 57. While its differences are probably due to genetic drift, we cannot rule out the possibility that some pressure of natural selection has operated more rigorously on blood-group genes in the far north than in the milder south.

A parallel case occurs in the aborigines of South Australia, whose traits have been studied for more than a decade by Joseph B. Birdsell of the University of California at Los Angeles. Among the South Australian desert tribes is the Pitjandjara, whose frequency of the gene for blood group A exceeds 45 per cent. To the west is a tribe of the same stock but having a much lower frequency of the group A gene (27.7 per cent); to the east is an apparently unrelated tribe with a frequency of this gene still lower (20 to 25 per cent). All three tribes are much more nearly alike in frequency of genes for the blood group MN. This is a situation to be expected from genetic drift, for it is not likely that in small populations chance will act on unrelated genes in the same way. But here again it is impossible to prove that genetic drift is the real agent. Each tribe has its own slightly different territory, customs and way of life: who is to say that it is not natural selection in a particular environment which has favored the marked increase of blood-group A in the Pitjandjara?

To get at the elusive drift in the frequencies of alternative kinds of genes, a small community of known origin is required, existing as nearly inviolate as possible in a larger civilization. After some discussion, it became apparent to Sacks and me that these requirements might happily be met right here among various German religious sects which immigrated to the U. S. in the 18th and 19th centuries. Not only are many of these sects still held together by strict rules regarding marriage, but also we have precise knowledge of their racial origins. This gives a starting point for comparison, since the present genetic composition of their homeland is also known. Moreover, they are now isolated in a much larger population, which provides an even more important basis for comparison. If natural selection or intermarriage were to influence their gene frequencies, these frequencies would shift from those of the homeland toward those characteristic of the large surrounding population. But if any sharp divergencies showed up, they would be attributable not to natural selection but to genetic drift.

After some exploration, a Dunker community in Pennsylvania's Franklin

DUNKERS of the study described in this article live in Franklin County, Pa. Although they seldom marry out-side the sect and their dress differs from that of their neighbors, their customs are not otherwise unusual.

GENETIC DRIFT is depicted by disembodied eyes. The group labeled 1 represents a small population in which 50 per cent of the people have brown eyes (*dark in drawing*) and 50 per cent have blue eyes (*light*). Group 2 shows a second generation in which 45 per cent of the people have brown eyes and 55 per cent have blue eyes. Group 3 indicates a third generation in which, if the proportion of brown eyes to blue did not return to that of the first generation, the percentages might be 40 for brown eyes and 60 for blue.

In all visible respects the Franklin County Dunkers live as their neighbors live. Most of them are farmers, though some have moved to the county's two medium-sized towns. They own cars and farm machinery; most have modest but comfortable frame houses; their food is typically American; the children attend public schools; medical care is good. Distinctions of dress are not conspicuous to the degree seen, for example, in the better-known Amish sect. Except for strict adherence to their religion, the Dunkers are typical rural and small-town Americans. In marriage pattern the community is not wholly self-contained. Over the last three generations about 13 per cent of their marriages were with members of other Old Order communities and about 24 per cent with converts, a factor taken into account in our study. Thus in each generation somewhat more than 12 per cent of the parents in the community came in from the general population. The equalizing force of this "gene flow" from outside would of course tend to make the Dunkers more like everyone else in hereditary makeup. The effects of genetic drift, if perceptible, would have to be large enough to overcome the equalizing tendency. Altogether the community now numbers 298 persons, or 350, if children who have left the church are included. For several generations the number of parents has been about 90. This, then, is exactly the type of small "isolate" in which the phenomenon of genetic drift might be expected to occur.

THE CHARACTERISTICS chosen for study in the Dunker group were limited to those in which inheritance is clearly established and in which alternative types are clear-cut, stable and, so far as is known, non-adaptive. The frequency records of these characteristics were available for both the West German and North American white populations, or at least the latter. Complete comparisons could be made for frequencies of the four ABO blood groups (O, A, B and AB) and the three MN types (M, MN and N). The Rh blood groups were almost as good. Although no Rh frequencies are available from West Germany, other European peoples have been studied, the English very extensively, and it is evident that all West Europeans are quite similar in this respect. Four other traits were examined in which the Dunkers could at least be compared with the surrounding American population. These were: (1) the presence or absence of hair on the middle segment of one or more fingers, known as "mid-digital hair"; (2) hitchhiker's thumb, technically called "distal hyperextensibility," the ability to bend the tip of the thumb back to form more than a 50-degree angle with the basal segment; (3) the nature of the ear lobes, which may be attached to the side of the

County was settled upon. No small part in influencing the choice was played by Charles Hess, a young medical student at the University of Maryland and a Dunker. He became interested in the project and gave invaluable help in collecting information and blood samples and in winning the cooperation of the Dunkers, without which the project could not have been carried out.

THE DUNKER sect, more formally known as the German Baptist Brethren, was founded in the province of Hesse in 1708, with a second center arising at Krefeld in the Rhineland. Between 1719 and 1729 some 20 families from the latter place and 30 from the former completely transplanted the sect to the New World, settling around Germantown, Pa. Over the next century the Dunkers doubled in number, and nearly all of them were descended from the original 50 families. To marry outside the church was a grave offense followed by either voluntary withdrawal or expulsion from the community. By 1882 the sect had grown to 58,000 and spread

to the Pacific Coast. Under this steady drain to the frontier the Pennsylvania groups remained fairly stationary in numbers. The Franklin County or Antietam Church community, the subject of this study, seems never to have grown larger than a few hundred persons up to 1882.

In that year a schism split the church and further contracted the size of this and other communities. For some time there had been trouble between those who wished to retain all the old tenets of the sect and those who wanted some relaxation of the more restrictive rules governing baptism, foot-washing, love feasts, head coverings for women, sober dress for men and the like. An open rupture finally separated the strict Old Order, as well as a Progressive group, from the main body, which went on to form the present-day Church of the Brethren. The Franklin County community studied by us remained in the Old Order, which from that day to this has numbered only about 3,000 people scattered in 55 communities over the country.

head or hang free; and (4) right- or left-handedness.

The findings were clear-cut. They show that in a majority of all these factors the Dunkers are neither like the West Germans nor like the Americans surrounding them, nor like anything in between. Instead, the frequencies of particular traits have deviated far to one extreme or the other. Whereas in the U. S. the frequency of blood group A is 40 per cent and in West Germany 45 per cent, among the Dunkers it has risen to nearly 60 per cent, instead of being intermediate as would be expected in the absence of genetic drift. On the other hand, frequencies of groups B and AB, which together amount to about 15 per cent in both major populations, have declined among the Dunkers to scarcely more than 5 per cent. These differences are statistically significant and unlike any ever found in a racial group of West European origin. One would have to go to the American Indians, Polynesians or Eskimos to find the like. The ancestry of all 12 persons with blood groups B and AB was checked to find out whether their B genes had been inherited from within the community. Only one had inherited this blood factor from a Dunker ancestor in the Franklin community; all the others had either been converts or married in from other Dunker groups. Evidently this gene was nearly extinct in the group before its recent reintroduction.

The three MN types showed even more unexpected trends. These have almost identical frequencies in West Germany and the U. S.: 30 per cent for type M, 50 for MN and 20 for N. In the Dunkers the MN percentage had diminished slightly, but frequencies for the other two types had deviated radically. M had jumped to 44.5 per cent and N had dropped to 13.5. One would have to go to the Near East or look in Finland, Russia or the Caucasus to find any whites with hereditary MN distributions like these. Only in the Rh blood groups do the Dunkers not differ greatly from their parent stock or adopted land. As against an average of close to 15 per cent for the Rh-negative type in both English and U. S. populations, the Dunkers show 11 per cent.

From the other traits in which comparisons were made almost equally striking conclusions can be drawn. Without going into details, the Dunkers had fewer persons with mid-digital hair or hitchhiker's thumb or an attached ear lobe than other U. S. communities. Only in right- and left-handedness, as in the Rh blood types, do the Dunkers agree well with the major populations used for comparison.

THERE SEEMS to be no explanation for these novel combinations of hereditary features except the supposition that genetic drift has been at work.

To clinch the matter, the Dunkers were divided into three age groups—3 to 27 years, 28 to 55 years and 56 years and older—roughly corresponding to three successive generations. When the ABO blood types were singled out, it was at once apparent that their frequencies were the same in all three generations. It follows that the unusual ABO distribution is of fairly long standing and antedates the birth of anyone still living. When the same analysis of MN blood types was made, however, a very different story emerged. In the oldest generation the M and N genes were exactly the same in frequency as in the surrounding population. In the second generation the frequency of M had risen to 66 per cent and N had dropped to 34. In the third generation this trend continued, M going to 74, N sinking to 26. While other genes remained unaltered in frequency, these genes were apparently caught in the act of drifting.

Let us consider the phenomenon a little more deeply. There can be no doubt from these instances that genetic drift does occur in small, reproductively isolated human groups in which the parents in any one generation number less than 100. Drift is probably somewhat effective, though slower, in populations two or three times that size. Such were the tribes of man before the dawn of agriculture. How inevitable it was, then, that numerous hereditary differences, perhaps of a quite noticeable but really unimportant kind, became established in different tribes. It is my opinion, no doubt open to dispute, that most inherited racial differences are of this kind and were not materially aided by natural selection.

Some traits, of course, must originally have been fixed by selection. Dark skin is probably a biological advantage in the

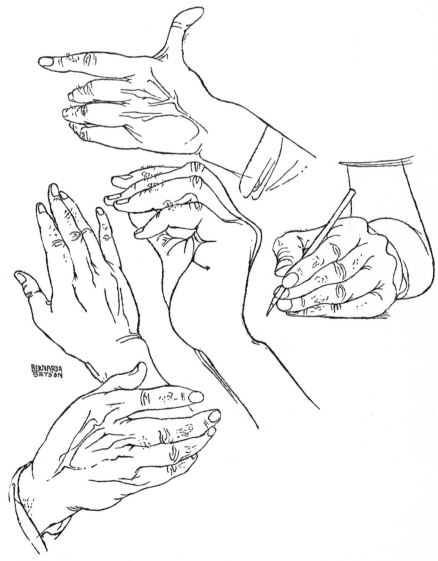

THREE OTHER CHARACTERISTICS were studied. One was "hitchhiker's thumb"·(*hand at top*), the ability to bend the end of the thumb backward at an angle of more than 50 degrees. The second was "mid-digital hair" (*hands at lower left*), or hair on the middle segments of the fingers. The third was right-handedness v. left-handedness (*hand at right*).

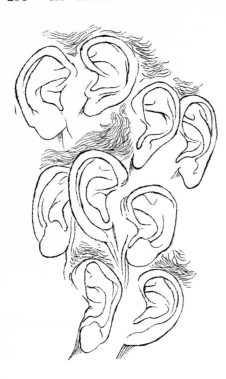

tropics, while pale skin may be an advantage in weaker northern light. The same may hold for kinky hair as against straight hair, for dark eyes as against light eyes, and the like. Many possibilities of this kind have been suggested in a recent book, *Races: A Study of the Problems of Race Formation in Man*, by Carleton S. Coon, Stanley M. Garn and Joseph B. Birdsell. I remain skeptical when I think of the prevailing hairlessness of man in many regions where more body hair would have helped to keep him warm. I am particularly skeptical of any selective advantage in blondness, "the most distinctive physical trait or group of traits shown by Europeans."

EAR LOBES either hang free or are attached to the head. Among Dunkers there are fewer attached lobes than among the U. S. population as a whole.

It seems more likely that these traits confer no advantage to speak of, in Europe or elsewhere. I would add that if blonds had been eliminated by selection in other parts of the world, and if a blond type happened by genetic drift to become established in Europe, then it could have persisted and spread in large populations and given rise to the present racial distribution of the blond caucasoid or "Nordic" man.

THE STUDY of the Dunker community confirms the suspicion of many anthropologists that genetic drift is responsible for not a few racial characteristics. Further studies along these lines, together with studies of mortality and fertility in contrasted hereditary types, may in time tell us which racial traits were established because of selective advantage and which owe their presence solely to chance and genetic drift.

PART IV
INTERPOPULATION
VARIATION

*Introduction: Population history
and human origins*

Modern races of mankind are very diverse although they belong to a single species. What mechanisms and conditions hold the human species together, in spite of great geographical distances and other diffusion barriers, is an inadequately explored objective of the study of human biology and evolution. The origins of human diversity, like the origin of the human species itself, is another. The similarities and the differences between populations, contemporary and extinct, provide a rich source of data for comparative studies.

Among the distinctive characteristics of the human species is a high degree of intergroup variation (Simpson, 1953, pp. 78–79). This diversity reflects the means by which man achieved his evolutionary success. Thus, racial differences reflect a statistical strategy of the species, a direct opposite of putting all our eggs in one basket. New variations are generated, by mutation and by recombination, in new populations as well as in the older, or parental, populations. Because human populations are only races, that is, subdivisions of the species, their variations can be captured or shared by other populations and thereby the species as a whole is enriched. The differences between groups reflect an old and successful system of evolution which has enable man to evolve at a rate faster than that of most animals, and to proliferate throughout the entire world without separating into new species. The fact that all the continents—

Africa, Europe, Asia, North and South America, and Australia—were occupied at least fifteen thousand years ago by primitive hunters and collectors, migrating solely on foot, demonstrates both the adaptive qualities of all the groups within the human species and the existence of several mechanisms that maintain the similarities existing between remote groups which have been separated for thousands of generations (Laughlin, 1967).

This intergroup diversity provides the necessary yardstick for interpreting differences between early forms of fossil man, and between fossil man and living races. We know that the differences—exhibited between living Bushmen (Tobias, 1966), Australian aborigines (Birdsell, 1953), and Eskimos (Laughlin, 1963)—are extensive. Each has some traits that the other two do not, and they differ in the frequencies of the traits they do share. Nevertheless, all three are contained within the human species, and they are fully capable of interbreeding with other populations and of generating all the necessary behavioral adaptations. The skulls of these diverse peoples can be sorted easily; they are as distinctive as the living representatives. If their skulls were found in geologically respectable deposits they might be identified as different species, because of the tendency of paleontologists to create new genera and species for each newly discovered fossil man. Thus, the names of fossil men are intended only to distinguish the different hominid forms from each other (Weidenriech, 1943, pp. 245–246), and they do not indicate the actual biological similarities and affinities between specimens. The student who is studying fossil forms must learn the various names that designate them, but he must carefully distinguish the name from the actual characteristics of a fossil form.

Population units and sampling aspects

Population units and the samples drawn from them are basic to the analysis of the human species, both past and present (Laughlin, 1966). Selection operates within populations, and populations are what actually evolve (Simpson, 1964, pp. 1535–1538). Populations, in all cases breeding populations, are internally structured (see Introduction, Part III). The breeding structure of individuals is nonrandom, and the gene pool is an integrated biological system. Breeding populations are part of a continuum or a reticulum of population systems, extending from the smallest local units (demes), through progressively inclusive units, to the entire species, which is the largest closed genetic system within which interbreeding between units can take place (Grant, 1963, p. 346). The two categories of species and race are inadequate to designate all the varying population systems unless the term "race" is used at several different levels of abstraction. The smallest population unit is commonly called a deme. Each deme belongs first to a small or local isolate, then to one or more larger, variously termed populations, sometimes to a geographic race, to one of the continental races (such as Negroes, Mongoloids, Europeans, American Indians, or Australian aborigines), and finally to the human species. The size limits of the various categories are not arbitrary, for the very good reason that these population units are dynamic variables, not watertight containers. For certain studies it is necessary to compare population units of unequal size and inclusiveness: for example, Lapps (30,000) with Chinese (300,000,000), or Polar Eskimos (300) with Bushmen (50,000). In fact one useful method of comparing groups is that of comparing each population unit under consideration with a mean value based on the entire species (Penrose, 1951, pp. 393–399). Although most population units cannot be contiguous with each other, there is gene exchange between all contiguous races and therefore between all races within the species.

Comparisons between groups (in all cases two or more breeding population units) can be of several kinds. Each breeding population may be compared to an average for the entire species. Clines or gradients may be composed to show the variation in value for a character, such as stature, or the frequency of blood group A, between groups within an area. Finally, groups may be formally classified: that is, using a combination of characters, one may statisti-

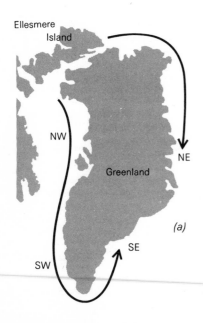

Figure 1. Geometric representations of similarities between populations. (a) Geographical distribution: Migration routes of Eskimos around Greenland; and position of four breeding isolates.

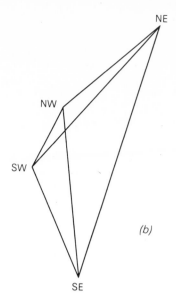

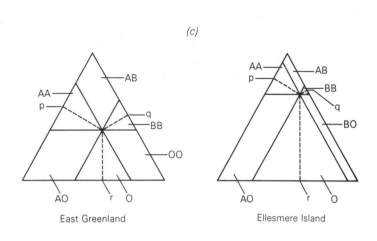

(c)

East Greenland   Ellesmere Island

Figure 1. (b) Geometric representation of the degree of physical similarity (generalized distance) between the four breeding isolates.

Figure 1. (c) Streng triangles: Geometric representation describing a population on the basis of its gene frequencies, in this case for ABO blood groups. Population as a whole is represented by the intersection of the three dotted lines, p, q, and r, whose lengths correspond to the relative gene frequencies of the blood groups A, B, and O. The proportion of homozygotes and heterozygotes is marked off by the solid lines parallel to the sides of the triangle.
Left: more A, more B; population as a whole represented by the intersection of lines.
Right: less A, much less B.

cally compute the relative biological distance or degree of similarity between three or more groups (Penrose, 1954). Technically, two groups can be compared but not classified in terms of relative biological distance. The resulting numerical values for relative degrees of similarity between populations can can also be represented geometrically (see the figure in this introduction). Classification is the arrangement of groups into a constellation, not simply the inventory or enumeration of the number of groups that an investigator intends to use. Thus, we will find that North American Indians are more similar to Eskimos than either group is to Icelanders. The characterization of a group (see the introduction to Part III)—a description and analysis—must always precede the classification. Never should the identification of a single individual or specimen be confused with classification. An individual is most accurately assigned to a breeding population by the noting of his parentage. A skeleton is most commonly assigned to a series by observing that a combination of characters fits it into a previously described series. For identification, or pigeon-holing, the pigeon holes must exist before the pigeon can be assigned to a hole. In classification, the arrangement of groups is unknown and is established on the basis of the relative degree of similarity between the groups being considered.

Continuity and discontinuity between the studies of the living and the dead

The study of the living differs from that of the dead in data, methods, and techniques, although there is, of course, a continuity of population history that extends back in time. This continuum exists by virtue of the fact that all persons must have two parents and that the line must be unbroken, from the beginning of life to the present. Microevolution (short term—present or recent) and macroevolution (long term—involving long periods of time) are two parts of the same spectrum. Nevertheless there are, on the basis of the available information, some natural dehiscences or actual breaks in this continuum.

In the study of skeletons, because there are no genealogies, pedigrees, or family lines, it is not possible to make a longitudinal study of growth (see the introduction to Part II), that is, to take measurements on the same individual at successive stages of growth. Other kinds of information are not ordinarily available. In most specimens, the cause of death is uncertain at best. Cardiac arrest or diseases like smallpox and diphtheria are not registered on the skeleton. In addition, since skeletons are not identifiable as siblings that can be identified with parents and distinguished from the offspring of others, it is not possible to study selection in the strict sense of demonstrating that particular matings produce more offspring than other matings and of relating this reproductive success to a particular trait. The demonstration of selection (as defined by a population geneticist) is not possible, or at least not conclusive, on skeletal specimens. However, the dearth of genetic information in human phylogeny (Harrison and Weiner, 1963, p. 83) does not mean that the student of paleontology will not benefit from an appreciation of the morphology of extinct populations, as well as the genetical basis of living populations. Rather, it means that appropriate methods of analysis must be learned for particular kinds of material.

Skeletal material provides an excellent source of information on living peoples—both individuals and populations—and it constitutes our real link with past populations. The study of skeletons is necessary for understanding evolution, past and present.

Bone tissue is sensitive to growth regulators, to mechanical stresses, to nutritional intake, and to many diseases (see the introduction to Part II). In addition, it is durable (especially the teeth) and thus remains preserved for a longer time than all other tissues. The following kinds of information about an individual can be obtained from the skeleton under favorable circumstances. These include (1) age at death; (2) sex; (3) race; (4) stature; (5) measurements of size and form; (6) handedness; (7) pathologies (including the effects of infectious diseases and of genetic anomalies); (8) nutritional deficiencies; (9) cultural deformations, such as cradle-board flattening of the cranium, and certain individual variations reflecting an event in the life history of that particular person. Each of these categories can be utilized for population studies, that is, for characterizing a population, and therefore they can be used for comparisons between populations. For example, the difference between populations in the overall pattern of diseases is substantial, and is not just in the frequencies of disease at a particular site, but in its patterning. Frequencies of diseases and other demographic characters as well as measures of central tendency and dispersion are valid only on populations or good samples of populations. Such series are available only for the past few thousand years of human history. Archaeologists have excavated large series of skeletons, occasionally as many as several hundred or even a few thousand, dating back as much as three or four thousand years and from several different places in the world. An information decrement sets in after only a few thousand years. The information secured on large series of many different varieties of living and recent races provides the best yardstick for the analysis of fossil man.

The readings in this section discuss living populations to fossil antecedents, in that order, thus proceeding from the area of maximum information to that of minimum information. Julian Huxley, in "World Population," calls attention to the increasing discrepancy between the numbers of people now living and their economic base, while William W. Howells, in "The Distribution of Man," discusses the kinds of peoples, the distribution of different races, and some of the genetic processes that may have led to their differentiation, and includes a sketch of the fossil lines leading to modern races. The article on the Pygmies ("The Lesson of the Pygmies," by Colin M. Turnbull) and that on the Dunkers (Glass; Part III) present two kinds of breeding isolates, for whom the conditions for life are substantially different although the genetic processes are the same for both. The Pygmies are a racial division of mankind that is of diminishing importance in human evolution and unfortunately is already doomed to extinction.

The transition to the study of fossil man is made by Richard S. MacNeish in "The Origins of New World Civilization" and by D. J. Mulvaney in "The Prehistory of the Australian Aborigine." The achievement of true civilization by American Indians, who evolved from primitive hunters, without outside influence from peoples of Europe or Asia, may be the most convincing illustration of internal genetic restructuring because tribes of Indians throughout the New World retained their similarity to one another in external traits (Ginsburg and Laughlin, 1966). The articles by William W. Howells and Elwyn L. Simons trace the different phases or grades of mankind and his antecedents further into the past, covering increasingly larger time periods and smaller sample sizes. More and more information that is directly applicable to human evolution as well as to primate evolution, generally, has been secured from the dentition. The Y-5 pattern, most clearly seen on the first lower molars of modern man, fossil man, and the related anthropoid apes, maintains its original form throughout, with the arms of the Y surrounding the middle outside cusp (called number three, or hypoconid). There are, however, different frequencies in different living populations for variations in both the fissural pattern and the numbers of cusps. Thus, of the teeth, this single tooth offers the most information on both living peoples and fossil men.

The subject of genetics, which is properly dependent upon data from interfertile crosses, is greatly removed from the study of fossils. Trying to determine which fossil skeletons belong within the same species, and which belong to the species that participated in the origin of man, is extremely difficult. Yet our knowledge of long-term trends, of the directions that human evolution has taken in its skeletal phenotypes, can be directly achieved only through the study of the available evidence, bones and teeth. For this reason, a thorough knowledge of both living populations and their fossil antecedents is desirable.

Selection of ancestors and precursors: Human origins

The study of fossil man is difficult and speculative, because whole skeletons are rarely found. Furthermore, the numbers of individuals represented from any one cave or living area are extremely small, so that the isolate sample is usually deficient. Because the number of populations represented is extremely small, little can be said about the range of characteristics of the species as a whole for any one time period. For the past half million years or so, we are dealing with indubitable human beings (see "Homo erectus," by William W. Howells).

It is sometimes assumed, somewhat dogmatically or even blithely, that *Australopithecus* gave rise to *Homo erectus*, and that *Homo erectus* gave rise to *Homo sapiens* with the European Neanderthal race serving as a midwife or at least standing by for the final delivery of our modern species. It should be observed that our knowledge of the progression from *Homo erectus* through a Neanderthal phase to modern man rests upon more secure evidence than does our knowledge of the immediate precursors of *Homo erectus*. In fact, enough is known of the progression to permit a tentative formulation of trends that are based upon at least three intercepts in time. These regularities permit an attempt at trend analysis that may supplement in certain respects the standard analytical techniques, which depend upon the direct comparison of morphological details, sometimes aggregated into complexes, of dimensions and indices, and the statistical manipulation of these.

The principal trends—extending from *Homo erectus* in his different forms, through the Neanderthal phase, to the various divisions of modern man—can be compacted into major trends each of which has many constituent items. Thus, our cranial evolution has involved (*a*) expansion of the brain, (*b*) flexing of the cranium, (*c*) reduction of the reinforcement system, (*d*) simplification of the tympanic plates, (*e*) formation of new features or enlargement of existing features (chin, suborbital fossa, nose, articular eminence, and so on), and (*g*) thinning of the vault bones. Excellent discussions of many of these are found in the writings of F. Weidenreich, of A. Hrdlicka, and of E. A. Hooton.

When these trends are extrapolated backward it becomes apparent either that major changes between *Australopithecus* and *Homo erectus* took place with unprecedented speed, or that the immediate precursors of *Homo erectus* have yet to be found. The crania of existing australopithecines are thin, whereas those of all fossil man are thick, becoming much thinner in recent man. The reinforcement system of *Homo erectus*—the brow ridges, sagittal elevation, occipital torus, suprameatal crest—is substantial and generally well delineated whereas, of the australopithecines only *Australopithecus robustus* has a major reinforcement system. The tympanic region of *Homo erectus* and of Neanderthal man is characterized by a division into an anterior labium and posterior labium, clearly separated by a vaginal crest, whereas in the tympanic region of modern man, the posterior labium has nearly disappeared, and the greatly enlarged anterior labium is commonly referred to as the tympanic plate. This region has not yet been studied in detail in the australopithecines, but it does appear to be somewhat pongid (apelike) in some respects and significantly different from that of *Homo erectus*.

The chronology of these forms then becomes critical. If *Homo erectus*, as represented by the Mauer mandible (Heidelberg man), is contemporaneous with *Australopithecus africanus*, or even close in time, then the likelihood that *Australopithecus africanus* is an immediate precursor is considerably reduced. The Mauer mandible may be 700,000 to 900,000 years old, and *Australopithecus africanus* may be as recent as 600,000 to 1,000,000 years (Grahmann and Müller-Beck, 1966; Hansjürgen Müller-Beck, personal communication, 1967).

The extensive degree of variation within the *Australopithecinae* is well attested (Clark, 1967), and we may consider the value of maintaining an open suspense account and of recognizing the possibility of another species of *Australopithecus*, or even a different genus, being more directly implicated in the immediate ancestry of *Homo erectus*.

The evolutionary relevance of various characters remains to be established. Specifically, their relevance for locomotion, for chewing, for maintaining balance, for the evolution of the brain, and for all the other functional changes subsumed under the grand rubric of evolution. Some features are parts of complexes and require a certain threshold, or combination of circumstances, to be manifested. For example, the upper attachments of the temporal muscles approach each other very closely in the skulls of Arctic Eskimos. The great size of the chewing muscles is compatible with the great size of the mandibles, the magnitude of the mandible being especially obvious in the ample breadth of its ascending ramus. The Eskimos have large cranial capacities and therefore cannot develop a sagittal crest; there is still enough room for these muscles on the walls of the cranial vault. However, in Aleut skulls and in those of subarctic Eskimos, who have very broad heads and very large mandibles, the temporal lines are separated by some 100 millimeters rather than by only 6 millimeters. Phrased in another way, if the Eskimo mandible were implanted on the small Bushman cranium, a sagittal crest for the accommodation of the temporal muscles would be necessary. The sagittal crest of *Australopithecus robustus* is not a unitary feature that has taxonomic relevance by itself, but it is part of a chewing complex and its appearance represents one end of a range of related features.

Although the significance of many osteological features of fossil forms is difficult to assess, they provide a rich source of comparative materials illustrating the variations which have actually occurred. As the significance of such variation in living races of man and in other primates is demonstrated by experimental, genetic, and comparative methods, our ability to interpret past forms is enhanced.

In discussing the origin of *Homo erectus*, Howells suggests that the remains from Olduvai Gorge seem to reflect a transition from an australopithecine level to an *erectus* level about a million years ago but that this date seems almost too late when one appreciates the age of *Homo erectus* from other places in the world. This possible discrepancy has been noted by P. Tobias in his analysis of the remains from Olduvai Gorge (Tobias, 1965). He refers to a gap between *Australopithecus* and *H. erectus* that is bigger than that between the apes and the australopithecines or between *H. erectus* and *H. sapiens*. He then suggests that *H. habilis* may be the most effective link between the australopithecines and *H. erectus* and may thus close this gap.

Another solution, based upon both dental and cranial trends, is indicated in the diagram (Figure 2), which has been prepared with special attention to long-term trends in the cranium and in the dentition. The distinctiveness of *Homo habilis* is recognized and a unique trend is based upon two intercepts in time. However, *Homo habilis* is depicted as another species that is in the related cluster of *Australopithecus robustus* and *africanus*, but not merged with *africanus*. Thus, the immediate precursor of man has not yet been found, and he, or they, must lie in the Pliocene, far earlier than any of the australopithecines so far discovered.

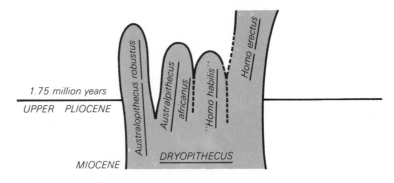

Figure 2. Diagram of human phylogeny based on dental and cranial trends from *Dryopithecus* to *Homo sapiens*.

In spite of the unique lower canine and the large posterior cheek teeth, the dentition of *Australopithecus africanus* is essentially human. However, occurring late as it does, it does not conform to a successional trend that is based upon modern races, upon the Neanderthal phase, and upon *Homo erectus*. In brief, we may expect that, if the dentitions are this similar in form and size pattern, they then represent hominids that are living at approximately the same time period or very close together in time. The complete hominid dental complex probably did not evolve separately in two different genera. More possibly, it is derived from the common ancestor that must be further back in morphological development and in chronology. This analysis tends to confirm the suggestion that a Dryopithecus or Ramapithecus form is an early ancestor of man, as discussed by Simons in "The Early Relatives of Man."

The intervening ancestor, the form or forms between Ramapithecus and the australopithecines and *Homo erectus*, may well have had a somewhat larger canine. We know that this tooth can develop independently into a typically human form because it did so in *Australopithecus robustus*. Size variations large enough to require a maxillary diastema may be expected because such a gap between the lateral incisor and canine appears in *Homo erectus* (in *Pithecanthropus robustus*; Verner Alexandersen, personal communication, 1967).

The problem of selecting human ancestors from the existing panel of contenders is especially illuminating in two ways, even though final and dogmatic answers are not possible. First, it requires a fundamental understanding of the range and patterning of variation in modern races and in other primates. This reinforces the study of contemporary variation. Secondly, it raises the question of what it is to be human, and this must include basic behavioral topics such as the faculty for language, a topic on which fossil remains are singularly inarticulate. Even for this question the amount of useful speculation is growing each year as investigations into the biological foundations of language are conducted, and each year a little more can be applied to the problem of the origins of humans. Owing to the paucity of human fossil remains, only a small amount of variation is available for description. This is in marked contrast to the abundant variation that may be observed within and between groups of living man and that is essential to the interpretation of the fossil record. Many more persons are needed to prepare for the investigation of human variation.

Literature cited

Birdsell, Joseph B. 1953. Some Environmental and Cultural Factors Influencing the Structuring of Australian Aboriginal Populations. *Am. Natural.,* Vol. 87, pp. 171–207.

Clark, Le Gros. 1967. *Man-Apes or Ape-Men?* New York, Holt, Rinehart and Winston.

Ginsburg, Benson E., and William S. Laughlin. 1966. The Multiple Bases of Human Adaptability and Achievement: A Species Point of View. *Eugen. Quart.,* Vol. 13, No. 3, pp. 240–257.

Grahmann, Rudoph, and Hansjürgen Müller-Beck. 1966. *Urgeschichte der Menschheit.* Stuttgart, W. Kohlhammer Verlag.

Grant, V. 1963. *The Origin of Adaptations.* New York, Columbia University Press.

Harrison, G. A., and J. S. Weiner. 1963. Some Considerations in the Formulation of Theories of Human Phylogeny. In Sherwood L. Washburn, ed., *Classification and Human Evolution.* Chicago, Aldine Publishing Company. pp. 75–84.

Howells, W. W. 1967. *Mankind in the Making.* Revised ed. New York, Doubleday.

Laughlin, William S. 1963. Eskimos and Aleuts: Their Origins and Evolution. *Science,* Vol. 142, No. 3593, pp. 633–645.

———. 1966. Race: A Population Concept. *Eugen. Quart.,* Vol. 13, No. 4, pp. 326–340.

———. 1967. Hunting: An Integrating Biobehavioral System and its Evolutionary Significance. In Irven DeVore and Richard B. Lee, eds., *Man the Hunter.* In press.

Penrose, L.S. 1951. Genetics of the Human Race. In L. C. Dunn, ed., *Genetics in the Twentieth Century.* New York, Macmillan.

———. 1954. Distance, Size and Shape. *Annals of Eugen.,* Vol. 18, Part 4, pp. 337–343.

Simpson, George Gaylord. 1953. *The Major Features of Evolution.* New York, Columbia University Press.

———. 1964. Organisms and Molecules in Evolution. *Science,* Vol. 146, No. 3651, pp. 1535–1538.

———. 1966. The Peoples of Africa South of the Sahara. In Paul T. Baker and J. S. Weiner, eds., *The Biology of Human Adaptability.* Oxford, England, Clarendon Press.

Weidenreich, Franz. 1943. The Skull of *Sinanthropus pekinensis,* A Comparative Study on a Primitive Hominid Skull. *Palaeon. Sinica* n.s.D., No. 10, whole ser. 127.

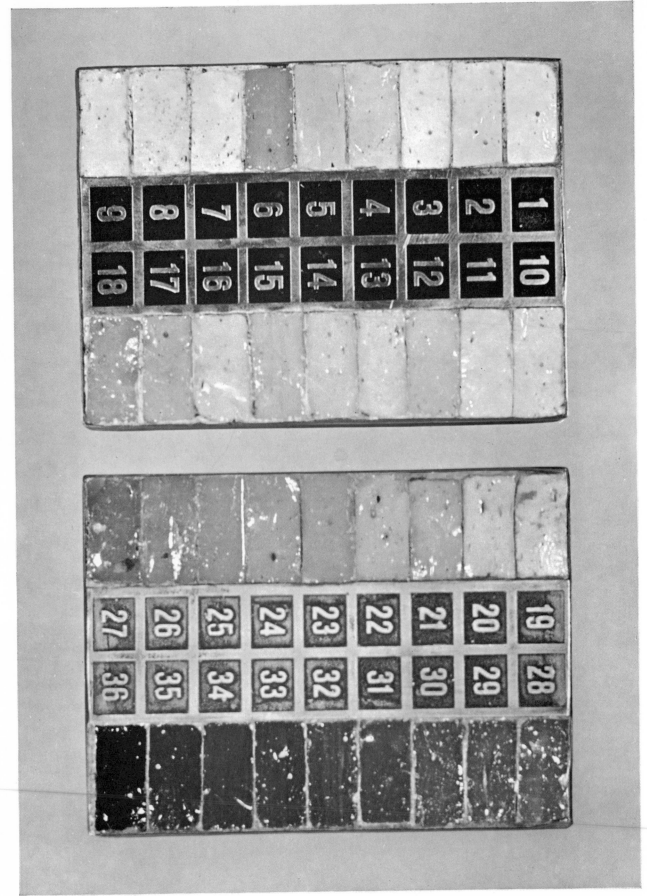

COLOR OF HUMAN SKIN is sometimes measured by physical anthropologists on the von Luschan scale. Reproduced here somewhat larger than natural size, the scale consists of numbered ceramic tiles which are compared visually to color of the underside of subject's forearm. Both sides of the scale are shown; colors range from almost pure white (*top right*) to black (*bottom left*).

21

The Distribution of Man

WILLIAM W. HOWELLS

September 1960

Men with chins, relatively small brow ridges and small facial skeletons, and with high, flat-sided skulls, probably appeared on earth in the period between the last two great continental glaciers, say from 150,000 to 50,000 years ago. If the time of their origin is blurred, the place is no less so. The new species doubtless emerged from a number of related populations distributed over a considerable part of the Old World. Thus *Homo sapiens* evolved as a species and began to differentiate into races at the same time.

In any case, our direct ancestor, like his older relatives, was at once product and master of the crude pebble tools that primitive human forms had learned to use hundreds of thousands of years earlier. His inheritance also included a social organization and some level of verbal communication.

Between these hazy beginnings and the agricultural revolution of about 10,000 years ago *Homo sapiens* radiated over most of the earth, and differentiated into clearly distinguishable races. The processes were intimately related. Like the forces that had created man, they reflected both the workings of man's environment and of his own invention. So much can be said with reasonable confidence. The details are another matter. The when, where and how of the origin of races puzzle us not much less than they puzzled Charles Darwin.

A little over a century ago a pleasingly simple explanation of races enjoyed some popularity. The races were separate species, created by God as they are today. The Biblical account of Adam and Eve was meant to apply only to Caucasians. Heretical as the idea might be, it was argued that the Negroes appearing in Egyptian monuments, and the skulls of the ancient Indian mound-

builders of Ohio, differed in no way from their living descendants, and so there could have been no important change in the only slightly longer time since the Creation itself, set by Archbishop Ussher at 4004 B.C.

With his *Origin of Species*, Darwin undid all this careful "science" at a stroke. Natural selection and the immense stretch of time provided by the geological time-scale made gradual evolution seem the obvious explanation of racial or species differences. But in his later book, *The Descent of Man,* Darwin turned his back on his own central notion of natural selection as the cause of races. He there preferred sexual selection, or the accentuation of racial features through long-established ideals of beauty in different segments of mankind. This proposition failed to impress anthropologists, and so Darwin's demolishing of the old views left something of a void that has never been satisfactorily filled.

Not for want of trying. Some students continued, until recent years, to insist that races are indeed separate species, or even separate genera, with Whites descended from chimpanzees, Negroes from gorillas and Mongoloids from orangutans. Darwin himself had already argued against such a possibility when a contemporary proposed that these same apes had in turn descended from three different monkey species. Darwin pointed out that so great a degree of convergence in evolution, producing thoroughgoing identities in detail (as opposed to, say, the superficial resemblance of whales and fishes) simply could not be expected. The same objection applies to a milder hypothesis, formulated by the late Franz Weidenreich during the 1940's. Races, he held, descended separately, not from such extremely divergent parents as the several

great apes, but from the less-separated lines of fossil men. For example, Peking man led to the Mongoloids, and Rhodesian man to the "Africans." But again there are more marked distinctions between those fossil men than between living races.

Actually the most reasonable—I should say the only reasonable—pattern suggested by animal evolution in general is that of racial divergence within a stock already possessing distinctive features of *Homo sapiens*. As I have indicated, such a stock had appeared at the latest by the beginning of the last glacial advance and almost certainly much earlier, perhaps by the end of the preceding glaciation, which is dated at some 150,000 years ago.

Even if fossil remains were more plentiful than they are, they might not in themselves decide the questions of time and place much more accurately. By the time *Homo sapiens* was common enough to provide a chance of our finding some of his fossil remains, he was probably already sufficiently widespread as to give only a general idea of his "place of origin." Moreover, bones and artifacts may concentrate in misleading places. (Consider the parallel case of the australopithecine "man-apes" known so well from the Lower Pleistocene of South Africa. This area is thought of as their home. In fact the region actually was a geographical *cul-de-sac,* and merely a good fossil trap at that time. It is now clear that such prehumans were widespread not only in Africa but also in Asia. We have no real idea of their first center of dispersion, and we should assume that our earliest knowledge of them is not from the actual dawn of their existence.)

In attempting to fix the emergence

of modern races of man somewhat more precisely we can apply something like the chronological reasoning of the pre-Darwinians. The Upper Paleolithic invaders of Europe (*e.g.*, the Cro-Magnons) mark the definite entrance of *Homo sapiens*, and these men were already stamped with a "White" racial nature at about 35,000 B.C. But a recently discovered skull from Liukiang in China, probably of the same order of age, is definitely not Caucasian, whatever else it may be. And the earliest American fossil men, perhaps 20,000 years old, are recognizable as Indians. No other remains are certainly so old; we cannot now say anything about the first Negroes. Thus racial differences are definitely older than 35,000 years. And yet—this is sheer guess—the more successful *Homo sapiens* would probably have overcome the other human types, such as Neanderthal and Rhodesian men, much earlier if he had reached his full development long before. But these types survived well into the last 50,000 years. So we might assume that *Homo sapiens*, and his earliest racial distinctions, is a product of the period between the last two glaciations, coming into his own early during the last glaciation.

When we try to envisage the causes of racial development, we think today of four factors: natural selection, genetic drift, mutation and mixture (interbreeding). With regard to basic divergence at the level of races, the first two are undoubtedly the chief determinants. If forces of any kind favor individuals of one genetic complexion over others, in the sense that they live and reproduce more successfully, the favored individuals will necessarily increase their bequest of genes to the next generation relative to the rest of the population. That is selection; a force with direction.

Genetic drift is a force without direction, an accidental change in the gene proportions of a population. Other things being equal, some parents just have more offspring than others. If such variations can build up, an originally homogeneous population may split into two different ones by chance. It is somewhat as though there were a sack containing 50 red and 50 white billiard balls, each periodically reproducing itself, say by doubling. Suppose you start a new population, drawing out 50 balls without looking. The most likely single result would be 25 of each color, but it is more likely that you would end up with some other combination, perhaps as extreme as 20 reds and 30 whites. After this population divides, you make a new drawing, and so on. Of course at each

subsequent step the departure from the then-prevailing proportion is as likely to favor red as white. Nevertheless, once the first drawing has been made with the above result, red has the better chance of vanishing. So it is with genes for hereditary traits.

Both drift and selection should have stronger effects the smaller and more isolated the population. It is easy to imagine them in action among bands of ancient men, living close to nature. (It would be a great mistake, however, to imagine that selection is not also effective in modern populations.) Hence we can look upon racial beginnings as part accident, part design, design meaning any pattern of minor change obedient to natural selection.

Darwin was probably right the first time, then, and natural selection is more important in racial adaptation than he himself later came to think. Curiously, however, it is extremely difficult to find demonstrable, or even logically appealing, adaptive advantages in racial features. The two leading examples of adaptation in human physique are not usually considered racial at all. One is the tendency among warm-blooded animals of the same species to be larger in colder parts of their territory. As an animal of a given shape gets larger, its inner bulk increases faster than its outer surface,

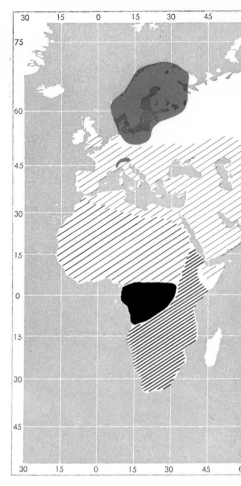

DISTRIBUTION OF MAN and his races in three epochs is depicted in the maps on these and the following two pages. Key to the races appears in legend below. Solid blue areas in map at top represent glaciers. According to available evidence, it is believed that by 8000 B.C. (*map at top*) early Mongoloids had already spread from the Old World to the New World, while late Mongoloids inhabited a large part of northern Asia. Distribution in A.D. 1000 (*map at bottom*) has late Mongoloids dominating Asia, northern Canada and southern Greenland, and early Mongoloids dominating the Americas. The Pygmies and Bushmen of Africa began a decline that has continued up to the present (*see map on next two pages*).

WHITE
EARLY MONGOLOID
LATE MONGOLOID
NEGRO
BUSHMAN
AUSTRALIAN
PYGMY

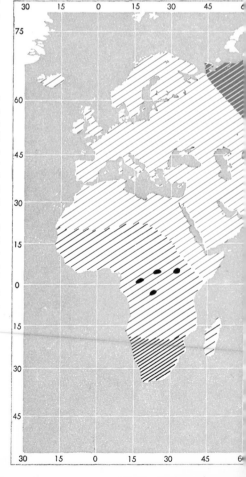

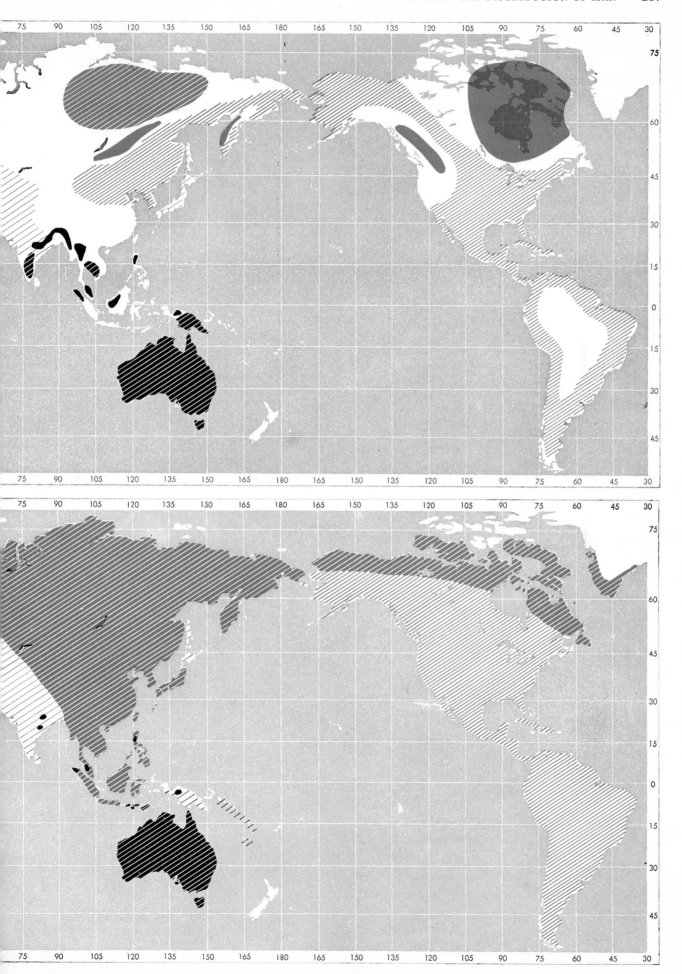

so the ratio of heat produced to heat dissipated is higher in larger individuals. It has, indeed, been shown that the average body weight of man goes up as annual mean temperature goes down, speaking very broadly, and considering those populations that have remained where they are a long time. The second example concerns the size of extremities (limbs, ears, muzzles). They are smaller in colder parts of the range and larger in warmer, for the same basic reason—heat conservation and dissipation. Man obeys this rule also, producing lanky, long-limbed populations in hot deserts and dumpy, short-limbed peoples in the Arctic.

This does not carry us far with the major, historic races as we know them. Perhaps the most striking of all racial features is the dark skin of Negroes. The color of Negro skin is due to a concentration of melanin, the universal human pigment that diffuses sunlight and screens out its damaging ultraviolet component. Does it not seem obvious that in the long course of time the Negroes, living astride the Equator in Africa and in the western Pacific, developed their dark skins as a direct response to a strong sun? It makes sense. It would be folly to deny that such an adaptation is present. But a great deal of the present Negro habitat is shade forest and not bright sun, which is in fact strongest in the deserts some distance north of the Equator. The Pygmies are decidedly forest dwellers, not only in Africa but in their several habitats in southeastern Asia as well.

At any rate there is enough doubt to have called forth other suggestions. One is that forest hunters needed protective coloration, both for stalking and for their protection from predators; dark skin would have lowest visibility in the patchy light and shade beneath the trees. Another is that densely pigmented skins may have other qualities—e.g., resistance to infection—of which we are unaware.

A more straightforward way out of the dilemma is to suppose that the Negroes are actually new to the Congo forest, and that they served their racial apprenticeship hunting and fishing in the sunny grasslands of the southern Sahara. If so, their Pygmy relatives might represent the first accommodation of the race to the forest, before agriculture but after dark skin had been acquired. Smaller size certainly makes a chase after game through the undergrowth less exhausting and faster. As for woolly hair, it is easy to see it (still without proof) as an excellent, nonmatting insulation against solar heat. Thick Negro lips? Every suggestion yet made has a zany sound. They may only be a side effect of some properties of heavily pigmented

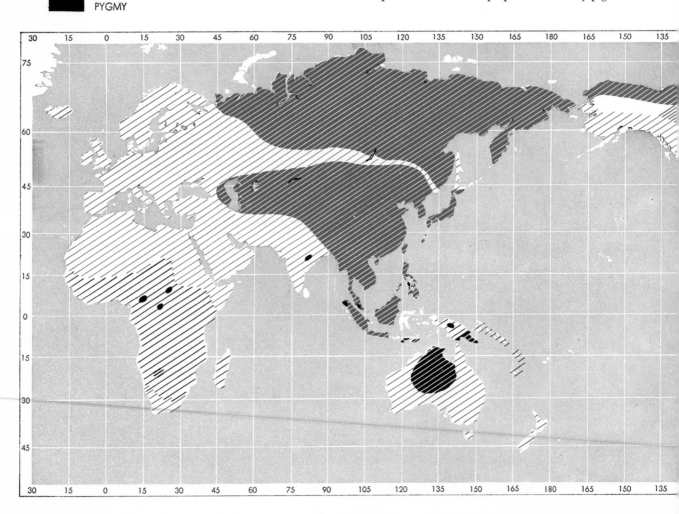

WHITE
EARLY MONGOLOID
LATE MONGOLOID
NEGRO
BUSHMAN
AUSTRALIAN
PYGMY

PRESENT DISTRIBUTION OF RACES OF MAN reflects dominance of White, late Mongoloid and Negro races. Diffusion of Whites has been attended by decline of early Mongoloids in America, Bushmen in Africa and indigenous population in Australia.

skin (ability to produce thick scar tissue, for example), even as blond hair is doubtless a side effect of the general depigmentation of men that has occurred in northern Europe.

At some remove racially from Negroes and Pygmies are the Bushmen and Hottentots of southern Africa. They are small, or at least lightly built, with distinctive wide, small, flat faces; they are rather infantile looking, and have a five-cornered skull outline that seems to be an ancient inheritance. Their skin is yellowish-brown, not dark. None of this has been clearly interpreted, although the small size is thought to be an accommodation to water and food economy in the arid environment. The light skin, in an open sunny country, contradicts the sun-pigment theory, and has in fact been used in favor of the protective-coloration hypothesis. Bushmen and background blend beautifully for color, at least as human beings see color.

Bushmen, and especially Hottentots, have another dramatic characteristic:

Narrow band of Whites in Asia represents Russian colonization of southern Siberia.

steatopygia. If they are well nourished, the adult women accumulate a surprising quantity of fat on their buttocks. This seems to be a simple storehouse mechanism reminiscent of the camel's hump; a storehouse that is not distributed like a blanket over the torso generally, where it would be disadvantageous in a hot climate. The characteristic nicely demonstrates adaptive selection working in a human racial population.

The Caucasians make the best argument for skin color as an ultraviolet screen. They extend from cloudy northern Europe, where the ultraviolet in the little available sunlight is not only acceptable but desirable, down to the fiercely sun-baked Sahara and peninsular India. All the way, the correspondence with skin color is good: blond around the Baltic, swarthy on the Mediterranean, brunet in Africa and Arabia, dark brown in India. Thus, given a long enough time of occupation, and doubtless some mixture to provide dark-skinned genes in the south, natural selection could well be held responsible.

On the other hand, the Caucasians' straight faces and often prominent noses lack any evident adaptive significance. It is the reverse with the Mongoloids, whose countenances form a coherent pattern that seems consistent with their racial history. From the standpoint of evolution it is Western man, not the Oriental, who is inscrutable. The "almond" eyes of the Mongoloid are deeply set in protective fat-lined lids, the nose and forehead are flattish and the cheeks are broad and fat-padded. In every way, it has been pointed out, this is an ideal mask to protect eyes, nose and sinuses against bitterly cold weather. Such a face is the pole toward which the peoples of eastern Asia point, and it reaches its most marked and uniform expression in the cold northeastern part of the continent, from Korea north.

Theoretically the Mongoloid face developed under intense natural selection some time during the last glacial advance among peoples trapped north of a ring of mountain glaciers and subjected to fierce cold, which would have weeded out the less adapted, in the most classic Darwinian fashion, through pneumonia and sinus infections. If the picture is accurate, this face type is the latest major human adaptation. It could not be very old. For one thing, the population would have had to reach a stage of advanced skill in hunting and living to survive at all in such cold, a stage probably not attained before the Upper Paleolithic (beginning about 35,000 B.C.). For an-

other, the adaptation must have occurred after the American Indians, who are Mongoloid but without the transformed face, migrated across the Bering Strait. (Only the Eskimos reflect the extension of full-fledged, recent Mongoloids into America.) All this suggests a process taking a relatively small number of generations (about 600) between 25,000 and 10,000 B. C.

The discussion so far has treated human beings as though they were any mammal under the influence of natural selection and the other forces of evolution. It says very little about why man invaded the various environments that have shaped him and how he got himself distributed in the way we find him now. For an understanding of these processes we must take into account man's own peculiar abilities. He has created culture, a milieu for action and development that must be added to the simplicities of sun, snow, forest or plain.

Let us go back to the beginning. Man started as an apelike creature, certainly vegetarian, certainly connected with wooded zones, limited like all other primates to tropical or near-tropical regions. In becoming a walker he had begun to extend his range. Tools, social rules and intelligence all progressed together; he learned to form efficient groups, armed with weapons not provided by nature. He started to eat meat, and later to cook it; the more concentrated diet widened his possibilities for using his time; the hunting of animals beckoned him still farther in various directions.

All this was probably accomplished during the small-brained australopithecine stage. It put man on a new plane, with the potential to reach all parts of the earth, and not only those in which he could find food ready to his hand, or be comfortable in his bare skin. He did not actually reach his limits until the end of the last glaciation, and in fact left large tracts empty for most of the period. By then he had become *Homo sapiens*, with a large brain. He had tools keen enough to give him clothes of animal skin. He had invented projectiles to widen the perimeter of his striking power: bolas, javelins with spear throwers, arrows with bows. He was using dogs to widen the perimeter of his senses in tracking. He had found what could be eaten from the sea and its shores. He could move only slowly, and was probably by no means adventurous. But hunting territory was precious, and the surplus of an expanding population had

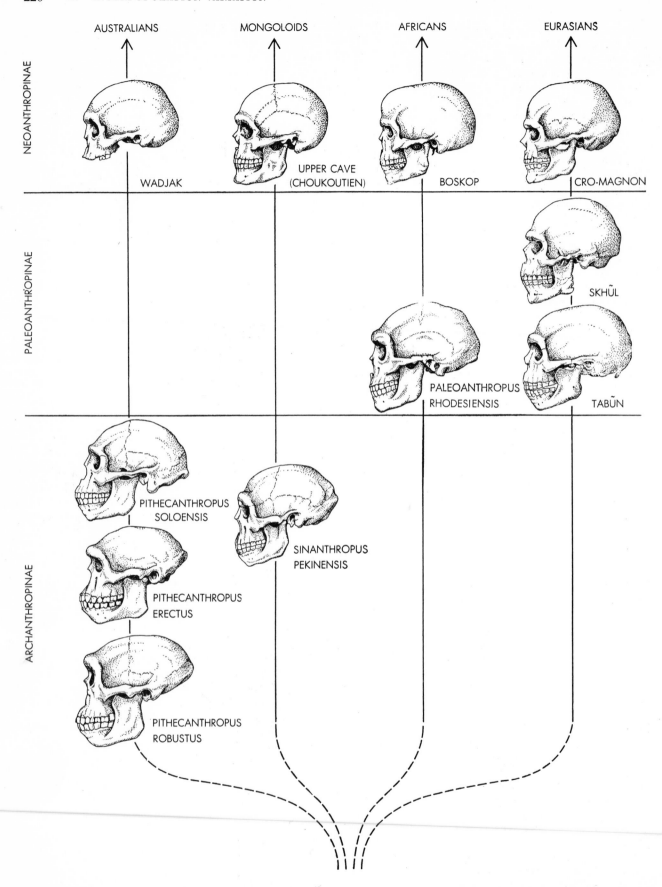

AUSTRALIANS   MONGOLOIDS   AFRICANS   EURASIANS

NEOANTHROPINAE

WADJAK   UPPER CAVE (CHOUKOUTIEN)   BOSKOP   CRO-MAGNON

PALEOANTHROPINAE

SKHŪL

PALEOANTHROPUS RHODESIENSIS   TABŪN

ARCHANTHROPINAE

PITHECANTHROPUS SOLOENSIS

SINANTHROPUS PEKINENSIS

PITHECANTHROPUS ERECTUS

PITHECANTHROPUS ROBUSTUS

POLYPHYLETIC SCHOOL of anthropology, chiefly identified with Franz Weidenreich, conceives modern races of man descending from four ancestral lines. According to this school, ancestors of Australians (*left*) include *Pithecanthropus soloensis* (Solo man) and *Pithecanthropus erectus* (Java man). Original ancestor of Mongoloids is *Sinanthropus pekinensis* (Peking man); of Africans, *Paleoanthropus rhodesiensis* (Rhodesian man). Four skulls at top are early *Homo sapiens*. Alternative theory is shown on next page.

to stake out new preserves wherever there was freedom ahead. So this pressure, and man's command of nature, primitive though it still was, sent the hunters of the end of the Ice Age throughout the Old World, out into Australia, up into the far north, over the Bering Strait and down the whole length of the Americas to Tierra del Fuego. At the beginning of this dispersion we have brutes barely able to shape a stone tool; at the end, the wily, self-reliant Eskimo, with his complicated traps, weapons and sledges and his clever hunting tricks.

The great racial radiation carried out by migratory hunters culminated in the world as it was about 10,000 years ago. The Whites occupied Europe, northern and eastern Africa and the Near East, and extended far to the east in Central Asia toward the Pacific shore. Negroes occupied the Sahara, better watered then, and Pygmies the African equatorial forest; south, in the open country, were Bushmen only. Other Pygmies, the Negritos, lived in the forests of much of India and southeastern Asia; while in the open country of these areas and in Australia were men like the present Australian aborigines: brown, beetle-browed and wavy-haired. Most of the Pacific was empty. People such as the American Indians stretched from China and Mongolia over Alaska to the Straits of Magellan; the more strongly Mongoloid peoples had not yet attained their domination of the Far East.

During the whole period the human population had depended on the supply of wild game for food, and the accent had been on relative isolation of peoples and groups. Still close to nature (as we think of nature), man was in a good position for rapid small-scale evolution, both through natural selection and through the operation of chance in causing differences among widely separated tribes even if selection was not strong.

Then opened the Neolithic period, the beginning of a great change. Agriculture was invented, at first inefficient and feeble, but in our day able to feed phenomenally large populations while freeing them from looking for food. The limit on local numbers of people was gradually removed, and with it the necessity for the isolation and spacing of groups and the careful observation of boundaries. Now, as there began to be surpluses available for trading, connections between communities became more useful. Later came a spreading of bonds from higher centers of trade and of authority. Isolation gave way to contact,

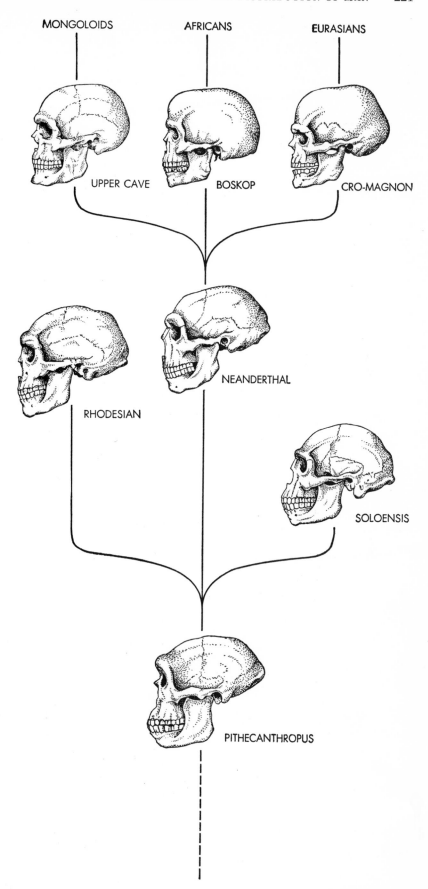

UNILINEAR OR "HAT-RACK" SCHOOL predicates three races descending from single ancestral line, as opposed to polyphyletic theory depicted at left. Rhodesian, Neanderthal and Solo man all descend from *Pithecanthropus*. Neanderthal is ancestor of early *Homo sapiens* (Upper Cave, Boskop and Cro-Magnon) from which modern races descended.

even when contact meant war.

The change was not speedy by our standards, though in comparison with the pace of the Stone Age it seems like a headlong rush. The new economy planted people much more solidly, of course. Farmers have been uprooting and displacing hunters from the time of the first planters to our own day, when Bushman survivors are still losing reservation land to agriculturalists in southwestern Africa. These Bushmen, a scattering of Australian aborigines, the Eskimos and a few other groups are the only representatives of their age still in place. On the other hand, primitive representatives of the Neolithic level of farming still live in many places after the thousands of years since they first became established there.

Nevertheless mobility increased and has increased ever since. Early woodland farmers were partly nomadic, moving every generation following exhaustion of the soil, however solidly fixed they may have been during each sojourn. The Danubians of 6,000 years ago can be traced archeologically as they made the same kind of periodic removes as central Africans, Iroquois Indians and pioneer Yankee farmers. Another side of farming—animal husbandry—gave rise to pastoral nomadism. Herders were much lighter of foot, and historically have tended to be warlike and domineering. With irrigation, villages could settle forever and evolve into the urban centers of high civilizations. Far from immobilizing man, however, these centers served

as fixed bases from which contact (and conflict) worked outward.

The rest of the story is written more clearly. New crops or new agricultural methods opened new territories, such as equatorial Africa, and the great plains of the U. S., never successfully farmed by the Indians. New materials such as copper and tin made places once hopeless for habitation desirable as sources of raw material or as way stations for trade. Thus an island like Crete rose from nothing to dominate the eastern Mediterranean for centuries. Well before the earliest historians had made records, big population shifts were taking place. Our mental picture of the aboriginal world is actually a recent one. The Bantu Negroes moved into central and

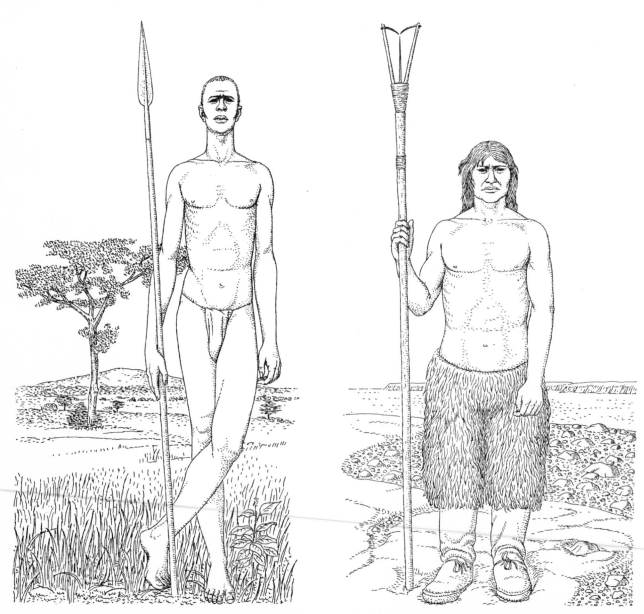

HUMAN ADAPTATION TO CLIMATE is typified by Nilotic Negro of the Sudan (*left*) and arctic Eskimo (*right*). Greater body surface of Negro facilitates dissipation of unneeded body heat; proportionately greater bulk of the Eskimo conserves body heat.

southern Africa, peoples of Mongoloid type went south through China and into Japan, and ancient folk of Negrito and Australoid racial nature were submerged by Caucasians in India. Various interesting but inconsequential trickles also ran hither and yon; for example, the migration of the Polynesians into the far Pacific.

The greatest movement came with the advent of ocean sailing in Europe. (The Polynesians had sailed the high seas earlier, of course, but they had no high culture, nor did Providence interpose a continent across their route at a feasible distance, as it did for Columbus.) The Europeans poured out on the world. From the 15th to the 19th centuries they compelled other civilized peoples to accept contact, and subjected or erased the uncivilized. So today, once again, we have a quite different distribution of mankind from that of 1492.

It seems obvious that we stand at the beginning of still another phase. Contact is immediate, borders are slamming shut and competition is fierce. Biological fitness in races is now hard to trace, and even reproduction is heavily controlled by medicine and by social values. The racial picture of the future will be determined less by natural selection and disease resistances than by success in government and in the adjustment of numbers. The end of direct European dominance in Africa and Asia seems to mean the end of any possibility of the infiltration and expansion of the European variety of man there, on the New World model. History as we know it has been largely the expansion of the European horizon and of European peoples. But the end in China of mere absorption of Occidental invention, and the passionate self-assertion of the African tribes, make it likely that racial lines and territories will again be more sharply drawn than they have been for centuries. What man will make of himself next is a question that lies in the province of prophets, not anthropologists.

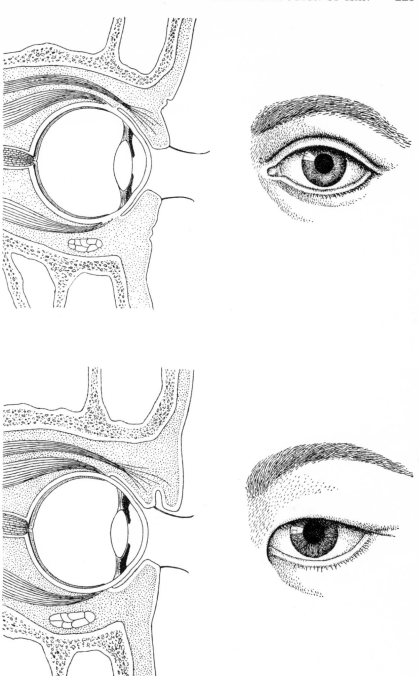

"ALMOND" EYE OF MONGOLOID RACES is among latest major human adaptations to environment. The Mongoloid fold, shown in lower drawings, protects the eye against the severe Asian winter. Drawings at top show the Caucasian eye with its single, fatty lid.

22

The Lesson of the Pygmies

COLIN M. TURNBULL

January 1963

In the welter of change and crisis confronting the lives of the peoples of Africa it would seem difficult to work up concern for the fate of the 40,000 Pygmies who inhabit the rain forests in the northeastern corner of the Congo. The very word "pygmy" is a term of derogation. According to early explorers and contemporary anthropologists, the Pygmies have no culture of their own—not even a language. They became submerged, it is said, in the village customs and beliefs of the Bantu and Sudanic herdsmen—cultivators who occupied the periphery of the forest and reduced them to a kind of serfdom some centuries ago. By the testimony of colonial administrators and tourists they are a scurvy lot: thievish, dirty and shrouded with an aura of impish deviltry. Such reports reflect in part the sentiments of the village tribes; in many villages the Pygmies are regarded as not quite people.

To argue that the Pygmies are people —even to show that they maintain to this day the integrity of an ancient culture— will not avert or temper the fate that is in prospect for them. The opening of the rain forests of Central Africa to exploitation threatens to extinguish them as a people. The Pygmies are, in truth, *bamiki nde ndura*: children of the forest. Away from the villages they are hunters and food gatherers. The forest provides them with everything they need, generally in abundance, and enables them to lead an egalitarian, co-operative and leisured existence to

which evil, in the sense of interpersonal malevolence, is so foreign that they have no word for it. After centuries of contact with the "more advanced" cultures of the villages and in spite of all appearances, their acculturation to any other mode of life remains almost nil. They have fooled the anthropologists as they have fooled the villagers. For this reason if for no other, the Pygmies deserve the concerned attention of the world outside. Their success should make us pause to reconsider the depth of acculturation that we have taken for granted as existing elsewhere, as industrial civilization has made its inexorable conquest of the earth.

The reason for the prevailing erroneous picture of the Pygmies is now clear. It has hitherto been generally impossible to have access to them except through the offices of the village headman, who would call the local Pygmies in from the forest to be interviewed. To all appearances they lived in some sort of symbiosis, if not serfdom, with the village people, subject to both the secular and the religious authority of the village. The fact that Pygmy boys undergo the village ritual of initiation in a relation of subservience to village boys was cited as evidence of ritual dependence, and it has been held that the Pygmies are economically dependent on the villages for metal and for plantation foods, presumably needed to supplement the meat they hunt in the forest. The few investigators who got away from the

villages did not manage to do so without an escort of villagers, acting as porters or guides. Even in the forest the presence of a single villager transforms the context as far as the Pygmies are concerned; therefore all such observations were still basically of Pygmies in the village, not in their natural habitat.

My own initial impression was just as erroneous. By good fortune my contact with the Pygmies circumvented the village and was established from the outset on a basis that identified me with the world of the forest. Seeing them almost exclusively in the context of the forest, I saw a picture diametrically opposed to the one generally drawn. Instead of dependence, I saw at first independence of the village, a complete lack of acculturation—in fact, little contact of any kind. It was only after two additional stays in the Ituri Forest, the home ground of the Congo Pygmies, that I was able to put the two contradictory pictures of their life together and to see the whole. It turned out that neither is wrong; each is right in its particular context. The relation of the Pygmies to the villagers is a stroke of adaptation that has served their survival and even their convenience without apparent compromise of the integrity of their forest-nurtured culture.

The BaMbuti, as the Pygmies of the Ituri Forest are known to themselves and to their neighbors, may be the original inhabitants of the great stretch of rain forest that reaches from the Atlantic

PYGMY WOMEN and children rest in the shade of the forest while the men collect honey from nearby trees. The women often accompany the men on honey-gathering and hunting expeditions, but they do not take part in the final stages of these activities.

PYGMY MEN remove from one of their vine nets a small forest antelope they have caught and killed. One edge of the net, which the men and older boys set up, can be seen at lower left center. The women served as beaters to drive the animal into the net.

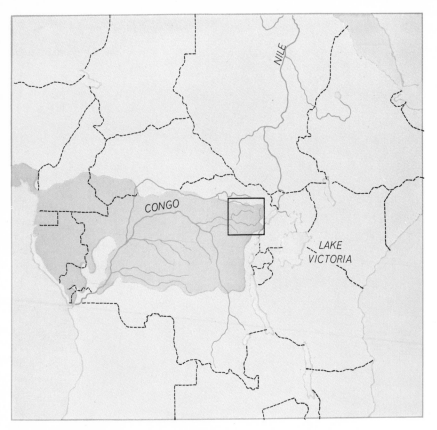

ITURI FOREST inhabited by the Pygmies occupies an area of roughly 50,000 square miles in the northeastern corner of the tropical rain forest of the Congo, in Central Africa.

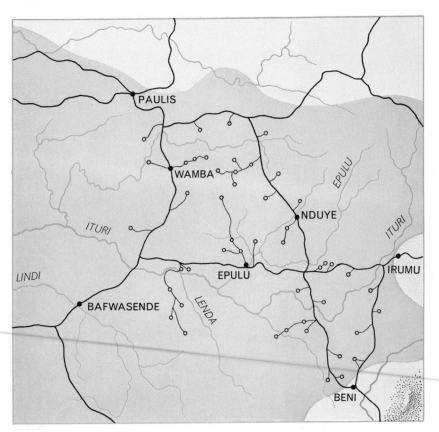

DETAIL MAP OF THE ITURI FOREST shows the Pygmy camps visited by the author (*small open circles*), villages (*black dots*) and various rivers (*blue lines*). The camps are connected by forest paths (*thin black lines*), the villages by roads (*heavy black lines*).

coast right across Central Africa to the open grassland country on the far side of the chain of great lakes that divides the Congo from East Africa. Their origin, along with that of Negrito peoples elsewhere in the world, is lost in the prehistoric past. Most Pygmies have unmistakable features other than height (they average less than four and a half feet) that distinguish them from Negroes. They are well muscled, usually sway-backed and have legs that are short in proportion to their torsos. Their faces, with wide-set eyes and flat, broad noses, have a characteristically alert expression, direct and unafraid, as keen as the attitude of the body, which is always poised to move with speed and agility at a moment's notice. They do not envy their neighbors, who jeer at them for their puny stature; in the enclosure of the forest, where life may depend on the ability to move swiftly and silently, the taller Negroes are as clumsy as elephants. For his part the Pygmy hunter wins his spurs by killing an elephant, which he does by running underneath the animal and piercing its bladder with a succession of quick jabs from a short-shafted spear.

A BaMbuti hunting band may consist of as many as 30 families, more than 100 men, women and children in all. On the move from one encampment to another they fill the surrounding forest with the sound of shouted chatter, laughter and song. Along with the venting of high spirits, this ensures that lurking leopards and buffaloes will be flushed into the forest well ahead of the band and not be accidentally cornered on the trail. The women, carrying or herding the infants, dart from the trail to gather food, and the men scout the forests for game on the flanks and in the van of the ragged procession. Arriving at the campsite in no particular order, all join in the task of building huts. The men usually cut the saplings to make the frames and sometimes also the giant Phrynium leaves to cover them; the women take charge of the actual building. The saplings are driven securely into the ground around a 10-foot circle, then deftly bent and intertwined to form a lattice dome; on this structure the leaves are hung like shingles, in overlapping tiers. Before nightfall, with the first arrivals helping the stragglers to complete their tasks, the camp is built and the smoke of cooking fires rises into the canopy of the forest. The entire enterprise serves to demonstrate a salient feature of BaMbuti life: everything gets done with no direction and with no apparent organization.

A morning is usually all that is needed to secure the supply of food. The women know just where to look for the wild fruits that grow in abundance in the forest, although they are hidden to outsiders. The women recognize the undistinguished *itaba* vine, which leads to a cache of nutritious, sweet-tasting roots; the kind of weather that brings mushrooms springing to the surface; the exact moment when termites swarm and must be harvested to provide an important delicacy. The men hunt with bows and poison-tipped arrows, with spears for larger game and with nets. The last involves the Pygmy genius for co-operation. Each family makes and maintains its own net, four feet high and many yards long. Together they string the nets across a strategically chosen stretch of ground. The hunters, often joined by the women and older children, beat the forest, driving the game into the nets.

By afternoon they have brought enough food into camp and sometimes a surplus that will enable them to stay in camp the next day. Time is then spent repairing the nets, making new bows and arrows, baskets and other gear and performing various other chores. This still leaves a fair amount of free time, which is spent, apart from eating and sleeping, either in playing with the children and teaching them adult activities or in gathering in impromptu groups for song and dance.

The BaMbuti have developed little talent in the graphic arts beyond the occasional daubing of a bark cloth with red or blue dye, smeared on with a finger or a twig. They do, however, have an intricate musical culture. Their music is essentially vocal and noninstrumental. It displays a relatively complex harmonic sense and a high degree of rhythmic virtuosity. With the harmony anchored in the dominant and therefore all in one chord, the singing is often in canon form, with as many parts as there are singers and with improvisations and elaborations contributed freely by each. A song may have some general meaning, but it may also be totally devoid of words and consist simply of a succession of vowel sounds. The real meaning of the song, its importance and power, is in the sound. In the crisis festival of the *molimo*, the closest approximation to a ritual in the unformalized life of the BaMbuti, the men of the band will sing, night after night, through the night until dawn. The function of the sound now is to "awaken the forest" so that it will learn the plight of its children or hear of their joy in its bounty.

The spirit of co-operation, seen in every activity from hunting to singing, takes the place of formal social organization in the BaMbuti hunting band. There is no headman, and individual authority and individual responsibility are shunned by all. Each member of the band can expect and demand the co-operation of others and must also give it. In essence the bonds that make two brothers hunt together and share their food are not much greater than those that obtain between a member of a band

HUT IN FOREST CAMP is larger than such huts usually are because a section has been added to accommodate a visiting relative. The average hut is the size of the section with an entrance. Camps are built in clearings like this one, found throughout the forest.

PYGMIES AND VILLAGERS dance together during the initial two-week period of the initiation rite described in the text. Of the 10 men in the immediate foreground, from left to right including the one with a white shirt at center, all are Pygmies except the fourth from left and the third from right. The villagers' legs are longer in proportion to their bodies.

VILLAGE CAMP on the outskirts of Epulu, formerly known as Camp Putnam, includes a village-style house built by a Pygmy, to the author's knowledge the only successful such attempt by a Pygmy in this section of the forest. Usually the villagers provide a house or the Pygmies construct leaf huts. Some of the village houses appear in the background.

and a visiting Pygmy, even if he is totally unrelated. Any adult male is a father to any child; any woman, a mother. They expect the same help and respect from all children and they owe the same responsibilities toward them.

When the Pygmies encamp for a while near a village, the character of the band and its activities undergo profound and complete transformation. This happens even when a lone villager pays a visit to a Pygmy camp. Not only do such activities as singing and dancing and even hunting change, but so also does the complex of interpersonal relations. The Pygmies then behave toward each other as they would if they were in a village. They are no longer a single, united hunting band, co-operating closely, but an aggregate of individual families, within which there may even be disunity. On periodic visits to the village with which their hunting band is associated, the Pygmies occupy their own semipermanent campsite between the village and the forest. Each family usually has a particular village family with which it maintains a loose and generally friendly exchange relation. At such times the Pygmies not only supply meat, they may also supply some labor. Their main function, as the villagers see it, is to provide such forest products as meat, honey and the leaves and saplings needed for the construction of village houses. The villagers do not like the forest and go into it as seldom as possible.

It is on these occasions that travelers have seen the Pygmies and decided that they are vassals to the villagers, with no cultural identity of their own. It is true that this is how the BaMbuti appear while they are in the villages, because in this foreign world their own code of behavior does not apply. In the village they behave with a shrewd sense of expediency. It in no way hurts them to foster the villagers' illusion of domination; it even helps to promote favorable economic relations. As far as the BaMbuti are concerned, people who are not of the forest are not people. The mixture of respect, friendship and cunning with which they treat their village neighbors corresponds to the way they treat the animals of the forest: they use them as a source of food and other goods, respecting them as such and treating them with tolerant affection when they are not needed. The Pygmies have a saying that echoes the proverb of the goose and the golden egg, to the effect that they never completely and absolutely eat the villagers, they just eat them.

In the mistaken interpretations of

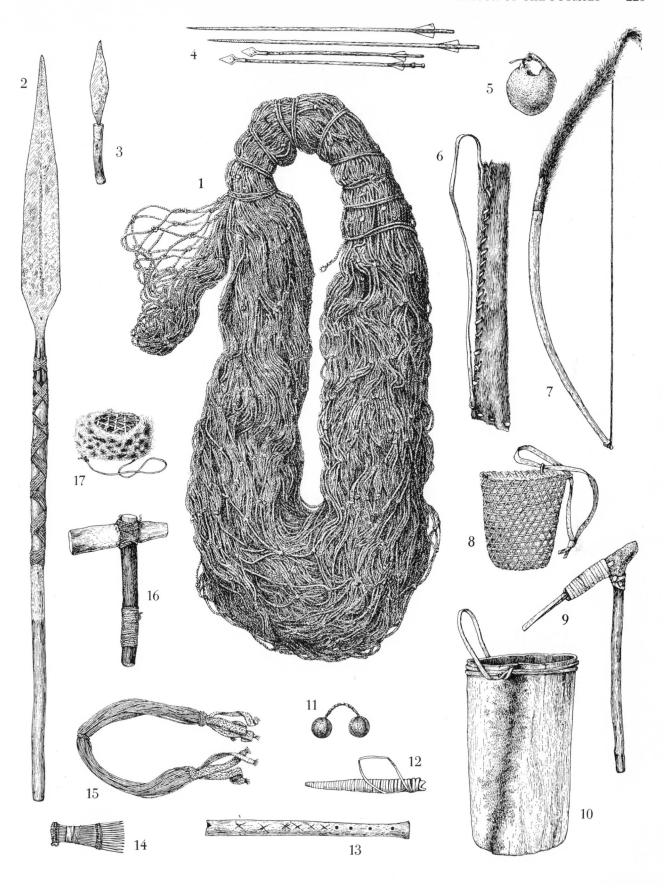

PYGMY ARTIFACTS are depicted at about a seventh of actual size: hunting net (1), metal-tipped spear (2), paring knife (3), pair of poison arrows and pair of metal-tipped nonpoisonous arrows (4), wrist guard made of monkey skin (5) for use with the bow (7), quiver made of antelope skin (6), child's basket (8), honey adz (9), bark pail for gathering honey (10), castanets (11), honey whistle (12), flute (13), comb (14), belt (15), hammer with a head of elephant tusk used in making bark cloth (16) and a hat (17).

AUGUST 1957

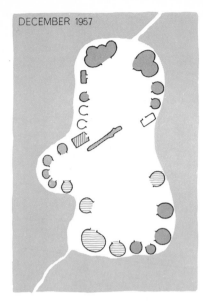

DECEMBER 1957

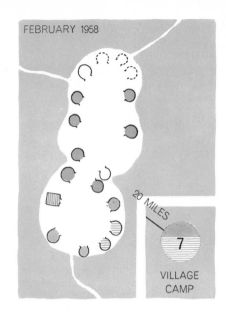

FEBRUARY 1958

MARCH 1958

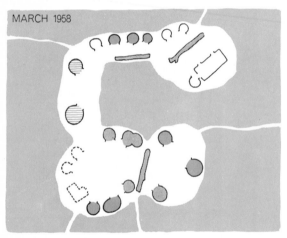

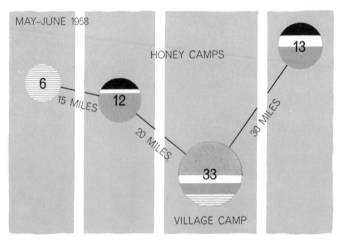

MAY–JUNE 1958

HONEY CAMPS

VILLAGE CAMP

JULY 1958

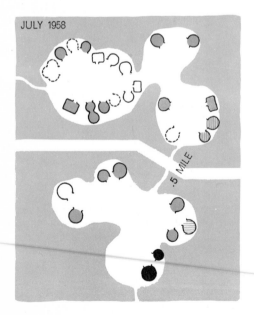

AUGUST 1958

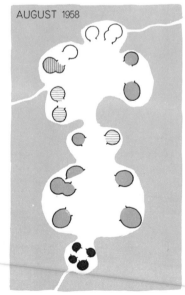

NOVEMBER 1958

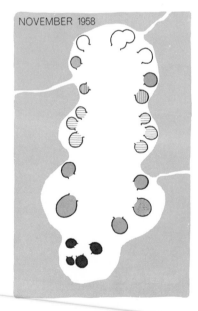

FOREST CAMPS change structure and constitution in cyclical fashion as Pygmies move from one campsite to another; they become increasingly fragmented at the approach of the honey season (May through June), break up during the season (*figures show number of families*) and re-form afterward. The disposition of huts, directions in which they face and their shapes are as shown; some were later abandoned (*broken lines*). Of the clans constituting the group with which the author stayed during this period, the main one was the Bapuemi (*solid-colored areas*). A quarrel resulted in a split camp (*lower left*), which gradually re-formed.

this peculiar relation the fact that the Pygmies seem to have lost their original language is often cited as evidence of their acculturation to the village. Linguists, on the other hand, see nothing surprising in this fact. Small, isolated hunting bands, caught up in the intertribal competition that must have attended the Bantu invasion that began half a millennium ago, could well have lost their own language in a couple of generations. It is by no means certain, however, that the Pygmy language is extinct. Certain words and usages appear to be unique to the Pygmies and do not occur in the languages and dialects of any of the numerous neighboring tribes. What is more, the Pygmies' intonation is so distinctive, no matter which of the languages they are speaking, as to render their speech almost unintelligible to the villager whose language it is supposed to be.

Some authorities maintain that the Pygmies rely on the villagers for food and metal. As for food, my own experience has shown that the BaMbuti hunting bands are perfectly capable of supporting themselves in the forest without any help from outside. The farther away from the villages they are, in fact, the better they find the hunting and gathering. If anything, it is the villagers who depend on the Pygmies, particularly for meat to supplement their protein-deficient diet.

It is more difficult to determine to what extent the BaMbuti are dependent on village metal. A few old men speak of hardening the points of their wooden spears in fire, and children's spears are still made in this way. Except for elephant hunting the spear is mostly a defensive weapon, and the loss of metal spear blades would not be serious. Knife and ax blades are more important; the word *machetti*—for the long, heavy-bladed brush-slashing knife—is well established in the Pygmy vocabulary. There are thorny vines, however, that can serve adequately as scrapers and others that when split give a sharp if temporary cutting edge, like that of split bamboo. When I have pressed the question, it has been stated to me that, in the absence of metal blades, "we would use stones." On the other hand, I have never succeeded in persuading a Pygmy to show me how. The answer to such a request was invariably: "Why should I go to all that trouble when it is so easy to get metal tools from the villagers?"

This is in fact the core of the Pygmies' economic relation with the villagers, and it renders the term "symbiosis" inapplicable. There is nothing they need badly enough to make them dependent on the villagers, although they use many artifacts acquired from them. Metal cooking utensils are a good example: the Pygmies can get along without these comfortably. They use them only for the cooking of village foods that require boiling, such as rice; forest foods call for no such utensils. The BaMbuti will exchange goods with the villagers and even work for them, but only as long as it suits their convenience and no longer. No amount of persuasion will hold them. If a villager attempts coercion, the Pygmy simply packs up and goes back to the forest, secure in the knowledge that he will not be followed. On the next occasion he will offer his goods in another village. Tribal records are full of disputes in which one villager has accused another of stealing "his" Pygmies.

In the absence of effective economic control the villagers attempt to assert political and religious authority. The villagers themselves are the source of the myth that they "own" the Pygmies in a form of hereditary serfdom. They appoint Pygmy headmen, each responsible for his band to the appropriate village headman. Because the bands not only shift territorially but also change as to their inner composition, however, a village headman can no more be sure which Pygmy families comprise "his" band than he can tell at any time where the band has wandered. In his appointed Pygmy headman he has a scapegoat he can blame for failure of the band to fulfill its side of some exchange transaction. But the Pygmy has no wealth with which to pay fines and can rarely be caught for the purpose of enforcing any other restitution.

The villagers nonetheless believe themselves to be the masters. They admit it is a hard battle and point out that the Pygmies are in league with the powerful and tricky spirits of the forest. The fear the villagers have of the forest goes beyond a fear of the animals; it is also a respect based on the knowledge that they are newcomers, if of several hundred years' standing. This respect is even extended to the Pygmies. Some villages make offering to the Pygmies of the first fruit, acknowledging that the Pygmies were there before them and so have certain rights over the land. This offering is also expected to placate the forest spirits. Ultimately, however, the villagers hope to subject the Pygmies to the village spirits and thereby to assume total domination.

In carrying the contest into the realm of the supernatural, the villagers invoke the full armory of witchcraft and sorcery. To the villagers these methods of social control are just as scientific and real as, say, political control through armed force. Moreover, although witchcraft and sorcery generally get their results by psychological pressure, they can sometimes be implemented by physiological poisons. There are strange tales of illness and of death due to sorcery, and no Pygmy wants to be cursed by a villager. On receiving threats of this kind the hunting band takes to the forest, secure in the belief that village magic is no more capable of following them into the forest than are the villagers themselves.

More subtly, the villagers engage the Pygmies in the various important rituals of the village culture. A Pygmy birth, marriage or death, occurring when the hunting band is bivouacked near a village, sets in motion the full village ceremonial appropriate to the occasion. The "owner" of the Pygmy in each case assumes the obligation of providing the child-protecting amulet, of negotiating the exchange of bride wealth or of paying the cost of the obsequies. Such intervention in a Pygmy marriage not only ensures that the union is regularized according to village ritual; it also gives the owners in question indissoluble rights, natural and supernatural, over the new family. The Pygmies willingly submit to the ritual because it means a three-day festival during which they will be fed by the villagers and at the end of which, with luck, they will be able to make off with a portion of the bride wealth. On returning to the forest the couple may decide that it was just a flirtation and separate, leaving the villagers to litigate the expense of the transaction and the wedding feast. Although they are economically the losers, the villagers nonetheless believe that by forcing or cajoling the Pygmies through the ritual they have subjected them, at least to some extent, to the control of the village supernatural.

The same considerations on both sides apply to a funeral. The ritual places certain obligations on the family of the deceased and lays supernatural sanctions on them; death also involves, almost invariably, allegations of witchcraft or sorcery. Once again, therefore, the villagers are eager to do what is necessary to bring the Pygmies within the thrall of the local spirit world. And once again the Pygmies are willing to co-operate, knowing that the village funerary ritual prescribes a funerary feast. Even though their custom calls

COLLECTING HONEY takes place during a season that lasts approximately two months. The Pygmy reaching into the tree with his left hand holds a honey adz in his right. This instrument is used whenever it becomes necessary to open the tree in order to get at the hive. The honey is usually found much higher up in a tree. All the photographs that appear in this article were made by the author.

for quick and unceremonious disposal of the dead, they are glad to let the villagers do the disposing and even to submit to head-shaving and ritual baths in return for a banquet.

By far the most elaborate ritual by which the villagers hope to bring the Pygmies under control is the initiation of the Pygmy boys into manhood through the ordeal of circumcision, called *nkumbi*. All village boys between the ages of nine and 12 are subject to this practice, which takes place every three years. Pygmy boys of the appropriate age who happen to be in the vicinity are put through the same ceremony with the village boys. A Pygmy boy is sent first "to clean the knife," as the villagers put it, and then he is followed by a village boy. These two boys are thereafter joined by the blood they shed together in the unbreakable bond of *kare,* or blood brotherhood. Any default, particularly on the part of the Pygmy, will invoke the wrath of the ancestors and bring all manner of curses on the offender. So once more the Pygmies are placed under the control of the village spirits and the putative bonds between the serfs and their owners are reinforced. Some villagers also see this practice as a means of securing for themselves an assured complement of Pygmy serfs to serve them in the afterworld.

As in all the other ritual relations, the BaMbuti have their own independent motivation and rationalization for submitting their sons to the pain and humiliation of *nkumbi*. For one thing, the Pygmy boys acquire the same secular adult status in the village world as their village blood brothers. The Pygmies, moreover, have the advantage of knowing that the bonds they do not consider unbreakable nonetheless tie their newly acquired village brothers; they made use of this knowledge by imposing on their *kare*. Finally, for the adult male relatives of the Pygmy initiates the ceremony means three months or so of continuous feasting at the expense of the villagers.

Once the *nkumbi* is over and the Pygmies have returned to the forest, it becomes clear that the ritual has no relevance to the inner life of the family and the hunting band. The boys who have gone to such trouble to become adults in the village sit on the laps of their mothers, signifying that they know they are really still children. In Pygmy society they will not become adults until they have proved themselves as hunters.

Back in the forest the Pygmies once again become forest people. Their counter to the villagers' efforts to bring them under domination is to keep the two worlds apart. This strategy finds formal expression in the festival of the *molimo*. The *molimo* songs are never sung when a band is making a visitation to a village or is encamped near it. Out in the forest, during the course of each night's singing, the trail leading off from the camp in the direction of the village is ceremonially blocked with branches and leaves, shutting out the profane world beyond.

The relation between the Pygmy and the village cultures thus resolves itself in a standoff. Motivated as it is by economics, the relation is inherently an adversary one. The villagers seek to win the contest by domination; the Pygmies seek to perpetuate it by a kind of indigenous apartheid. Because the relation is one of mutual convenience rather than necessity, it works with reasonable success in the economic realm. The villagers ascribe the success, however, to their spiritual domination; any breakdown they cannot correct they are content to leave to rectification by the supernatural, a formula that works within their own society. The Pygmies hold, on the other hand, that the forest looks after its own, a belief that is borne out by their

PESTLE AND MORTAR are used by a Pygmy woman to make plantains, such as those beside her, into a paste. Pestle, mortar, plantains and metal dish at left are village products.

DRYING MEAT OVER A FIRE preserves it against the time when it will be taken to the villages to be traded. Otherwise the meat would rot quickly. The Pygmies never store or preserve food for their own use.

daily experience. In the nature of the situation, each group is able to think it has succeeded, as indeed in its own eyes it has. The very separateness of the two worlds makes this dual solution possible. But it is a solution that can work only in the present context.

A breakdown began when the Belgians insisted that the villagers plant cotton and produce a food surplus. The villagers then needed the Pygmies even more as a source of manpower. At the same time, with roads being cut through the forest, the movement of game became restricted. If the process had continued, the Pygmies would have found it increasingly difficult to follow their hunting and food-gathering way of life and would indeed have become the economic dependents of the villagers. The present political turmoil in the Congo has given the Pygmies a temporary reprieve.

In some areas, however, the Belgians had decided to pre-empt the untapped Pygmy labor force for themselves and had already set about "liberating" the Pygmies from the mythical yoke of the villagers, persuading them to set up plantations of their own. The result was disastrous. Used to the constant shade of the forest, to the purity of forest water and to the absence of germ-carrying flies and mosquitoes, the Pygmies quickly succumbed to sunstroke and to various illnesses against which the villagers have some immunity. Worse yet, with the abandoning of hunting and food gathering the entire Pygmy social structure collapsed. Forest values were necessarily left behind in the forest, and there was nothing to take their place but a pathetic and unsuccessful imitation of the new world around them, the world of villagers and of Europeans.

This whole problem was much discussed among the Pygmies just prior to the independence of the Congo. In almost every case they reached the determination that as long as the forest existed they would try to go on living as they had always lived. More than once I was told, with no little insight, that "when the forest dies, we die." So for the Pygmies, in a sense, there is no problem. They have seen enough of the outside world to feel able to make their choice, and their choice is to preserve the sanctity of their own world up to the very end. Being what they are, they will doubtless continue to play a masterful game of hide-and-seek, but they will not easily sacrifice their integrity.

It is for future administrations of the Congo that the problem will be a real one, both moral and practical. Can the vast forest area justifiably be set aside as a reservation for some 40,000 Pygmies? And if the forest is to be exploited, what can one do with its inhabitants, who are physically, temperamentally and socially so unfitted for any other form of life? If the former assessment of the Pygmy-villager relation had been correct and the Pygmies had really been as acculturated as it seemed, the problem would have resolved itself into physiological terms only, serious enough but not insuperable. As it is, seeing that the Pygmies have for several hundred years successfully rejected almost every basic element of the foreign cultures surrounding them, the prospects of adaptation are fraught with hazards.

Traditional values die hard, it would seem, and continue to thrive even when they are considered long since dead and buried. In dealing with any African peoples, I suspect, we are in grave danger if we assume too readily that they are the creatures we like to think we have made them. If the Pygmies are any indication, and if we realize it in time, it may be as well for us and for Africa that they are not.

23

World Population

JULIAN HUXLEY

March 1956

The problem of population is the problem of our age. In the middle of the 20th century anyone who travels around the world, as I have recently done, cannot fail to be struck by the signs of growing pressure of population upon the resources of our planet. The traveler is impressed by the sheer numbers of people, as in China; by the crowding of the land, as in Java; by the desperate attempts to control population increase, as in Japan and India; and at the same time by the erosion, deforestation and destruction of wildlife almost everywhere. The experiences of travel merely highlight and illustrate a fact which for some time has been obtruding itself on the world's consciousness: that the increase of human numbers has initiated a new and critical phase in the history of our species.

This crisis was recognized by the holding of a Conference on World Population in Rome in 1954. Held under the aegis of the United Nations, the Conference was a milestone in history, for it was the first official international survey of the subject of human population as a whole. In 1949 the UN had convened a scientific conference on world resources at Lake Success. As Director General of UNESCO, invited to collaborate in this project, I had suggested that a survey of resources should be accompanied by a similar survey of the population which consumed the resources. I was told that there were technical, political and religious difficulties. Eventually these difficulties were smoothed over; censuses were taken; and a conference on population was duly held in 1954. During the five years it took to arrange for a look at the problem the world population had increased by more than 130 million.

Let me begin by setting forth some of the facts—often surprising and sometimes alarming—which justify our calling the present a new and decisive phase in the history of mankind. The first fact is that the total world population has been increasing relentlessly, with only occasional minor setbacks, since before the dawn of history. The second fact is the enormous present size of the population —more than 2.5 billion. The third is the great annual increase: some 34 million people per year, nearly 4,000 per hour, more than one every second. The human race is adding to its numbers the equivalent of a good-sized town, more than 90,000 people, every day of the year. The fourth and most formidable fact is that the rate of increase itself is increasing. Population, as Thomas Malthus pointed out in 1798, tends to grow not arithmetically but geometrically—it increases by compound interest. Until well into the present century the compound rate of increase remained below 1 per cent per annum, but it has now reached 1⅓ per cent per annum. What is more, this acceleration of increase shows no sign of slowing up, and it is safe to prophesy that it will continue to go up for at least several decades.

In short, the growth of human population on our planet has accelerated from a very slow beginning until it has now become an explosive process. Before the discovery of agriculture, about 6,000 B.C., the total world population was probably less than 20 million. It did not pass the 100 million mark until after the time of the Old Kingdom of Egypt, and did not reach 500 million until the latter part of the 17th century. By the mid-18th century it passed the billion mark, and in the 1920s it rose above two billion. That is to say, it doubled itself twice over in the period between 1650 and 1920. The first doubling took nearly two centuries, the second considerably less than one century. Now, at the present rate of acceleration, the population will have doubled itself again (from the 1920 figure) by the early 1980s—*i.e.*, in the amazingly short space of 60 years.

Each major upward step in numbers followed some major discovery or invention—agriculture, the initiation of urban life and trade, the harnessing of non-human power, the technological revolu-

HUGE CROWD of Indians was photographed in 1950 during the Kumbh-Mela, a

tion. During the present century the most decisive factor in increasing population has been of a different sort—the application of scientific medicine, or what we may call death control. In advanced countries death rates have been reduced from the traditional 35 or 40 per thousand to less than 10 per thousand. The average life span (life expectancy at birth) has been more than doubled in the Western world since the mid-19th century. It now stands at about 70 years in Europe and North America, and the process of lengthening life has begun to get under way in Asian countries: in India, for example, the life expectancy at birth has risen within three decades from 20 to 32 years.

Birth Rates *v.* Death Rates

Population growth appears to pass through a series of stages. In the first stage both the birth rate and the death rate are high, and the population increases only slowly. In the second stage the death rate falls sharply but the birth rate stays high; the population therefore expands more or less explosively. In the third, the birth rate also falls sharply, so that the increase of population is slowed. Finally both the birth and the death rates stabilize at a low figure; thereafter the population will grow only slowly unless it is spurred by some new development, such as access to new food sources or a change in ideas and values.

In the Western world the reduction of the death rate came gradually, and its effect on population growth was buffered by factors which tended at the same time to reduce the birth rate— namely, a rising standard of living and industrialization, which made children no longer an economic asset.

Matters have been very different in the still underdeveloped countries of Asia. There death control has been introduced with startling speed. Ancient diseases have been brought under control or totally abolished in the space of a few decades or even a few years. Let me give one example. In England malaria took three centuries to disappear; in Ceylon it was virtually wiped out in less than half a decade, thanks to DDT and a well-organized campaign. As a result of this and other health measures, the death rate in Ceylon was reduced from 22 to 12 per thousand in seven years—a fall which took exactly 10 times as long in England. But the Ceylon birth rate has not even begun to drop, and so the population is growing at the rate of 2.7 per cent per annum—about twice the highest rate ever experienced in Britain. If this rate of growth continues, the population of Ceylon will be doubled in 30 years.

Almost all the underdeveloped countries are now in this stage of explosive

religious festival during which Hindus bathe in the Ganges. At the Kumbh-Mela of 1954 the author witnessed a crowd estimated at four and a half million. This photograph was made by *Life* photographer David Douglas Duncan. Copyright 1950 by Time, Inc.

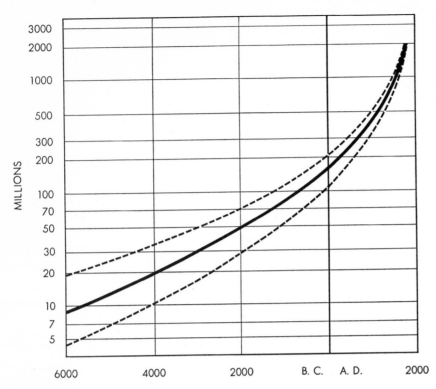

WORLD POPULATION GROWTH since 6000 B. C. is traced in this chart by the heavy curve. The curves above and below it represent upper and lower limits of the estimate.

position is made worse by the fact that the race isn't a straight one. Production starts far behind scratch: according to the latest estimates of the World Health Organization, at least two thirds of the world's people are undernourished. Production has to make good this huge deficiency as well as overtake the increase in human numbers.

A Population Policy

Is there then no remedy? Of course there is. The remedy is to stop thinking in terms of a race between population and food production and to begin thinking in terms of a balance. We need a population policy.

The most dangerous period lies in the next 30 or 40 years. If nothing is done to bring down the rate of human increase during that time, mankind will find itself living in a world exposed to disastrous miseries and charged with frustrations more explosive than any we can now envision.

Even primitive societies practice some form of population control—by infanticide or abortion or sexual abstinence or crude contraceptives. Since the invention of effective birth control methods in the 19th century, they have been very generally practiced in all Western countries. Their spread to other cultures has been retarded by various inhibitions—religious, ideological, economic, political. It is worth noting that one retarding factor in the past has been the reluctance of colonial powers to encourage birth control in their colonies, often out of fear that they might be considered to be seeking to use population control as a weapon against an "inferior" race.

Today the underdeveloped countries are making their own decisions; what is needed is a new and more rational view of the population problem everywhere. We must give up the false belief that mere increase in the number of human beings is necessarily desirable, and the despairing conclusion that rapid increase and its evils are inevitable. We must reject the idea that the quantity of human beings is of value apart from the quality of their lives.

Overpopulation—or, if you prefer, high population density—affects a great many other needs of mankind besides bread. Beyond his material requirements, man needs space and beauty, recreation and enjoyment. Excessive population can erode all these things. The rapid population increase has already created cities so big that they are beginning to defeat their own ends, pro-

expansion. When we recall that rates of expansion of this order (2 to 3 per cent) are at work among more than half of the world's 2.5 billion inhabitants, we cannot but feel alarmed. If nothing is done to control this increase, mankind will drown in its own flood, or, if you prefer a different metaphor, man will turn into the cancer of the planet.

Malthus, a century and a half ago, alarmed the world by pointing out that population increase was pressing more and more insistently on food supply, and if unchecked would result in widespread misery and even starvation. In recent times, even as late as the 1930s, it had become customary to pooh-pooh Malthusian fears. The opening up of new land, coupled with the introduction of better agricultural methods, had allowed food production to keep up with population increase and in some areas even to outdistance it. During the 19th century and the early part of the 20th food production increased in more than arithmetical progression, contrary to the Malthusian formula. We now realize, however, that this spurt in food production cannot be expected to continue indefinitely: there is an inevitable limit to the rate at which it can be increased. Although Malthus' particular formulation was incorrect, it remains true that there is a fundamental difference between the increase of population, which is based on

a geometrical or compound-interest growth mechanism, and the increase of food production, which is not.

There are still some optimists who proclaim that the situation will take care of itself, through industrialization and through the opening of new lands to cultivation, or that science will find a way out by improving food-production techniques, tapping the food resources of the oceans, and so on. These arguments seem plausible until we begin to look at matters quantitatively. To accelerate food production so that it can keep pace with human reproduction will take skill, great amounts of capital and, above all, time—time to clear tropical forests, construct huge dams and irrigation projects, drain swamps, start large-scale industrialization, give training in scientific methods, modernize systems of land tenure and, most difficult of all, change traditional habits and attitudes among the bulk of the people. And quite simply there is not enough skill or capital or time available. Population is always catching up with and outstripping increases in production. The fact is that an annual increase of 34 million mouths to be fed needs more food than can possibly go on being added to production year after year. The growth of population has reached such dimensions and speed that it cannot help winning in a straight race against production. The

ducing discomfort and nervous strain and cutting off millions of people from any real contact or sense of unity with nature. Even in the less densely inhabited regions of the world open spaces are shrinking and the despoiling of nature is going on at an appalling rate. Wildlife is being exterminated; forests are being cut down, mountains gashed by hydroelectric projects, wildernesses plastered with mine shafts and tourist camps, fields and meadows stripped away for roads and aerodromes. The pressure of population is also being translated into a flood of mass-produced goods which is washing over every corner of the globe, sapping native cultures and destroying traditional art and craftsmanship.

The space and the resources of our planet are limited. We must set aside some for our material needs and some for more ultimate satisfactions—the enjoyment of unspoiled nature and fine scenery, satisfying recreation, travel and the preservation of varieties of human culture and of monuments of past achievement and ancient grandeur. And in order to arrive at a wise and purposeful allocation of our living space we must have a population policy which will permit the greatest human fulfillment.

If science can be applied to increase the rate of food production and to satisfy our other needs, it can and should

also be applied to reduce the rate of people production. And for that, as for all scientific advance, we need both basic research and practical application. Basic research is needed not only on methods of birth control but also on attitudes toward family limitation and on population trends in different sections of the world. Once we have agreed on the need for a scientific population policy, the necessary studies and measures to be applied will surely follow. This does not mean that we should envisage a definite optimum population size for a given country or for the world as a whole. Indeed, to fix such a figure is probably impossible, and to use it as a definite target is certainly impracticable. For the time being our aim should be confined to reducing the over-rapid population growth which threatens to outstrip food supply. If we can do this, our descendants will be able to begin thinking of establishing a more or less stable level of population.

Japan and India

With these general observations as our guide, we can now get a clearer grasp of the population problems of individual countries. Since the end of World War II, we have seen a new phenomenon in the world's history. Two great and powerful nations, India and

Japan, have officially adopted the policy of population control.

Japan I was unable to visit, but its demographic plight is so extreme and so illuminating that I shall take it first. Japan's 90 million people are crowded into an area only one and one-half times as large as the small British Isles. The country is so mountainous that it affords only one seventh of an acre of cultivable land per head. And its population is increasing by more than 1 per cent per annum, so that within 10 years it will easily overshoot the 100-million mark.

The Japanese are not well nourished: the average daily calorie intake is only 2,000. About one fifth of this meager food supply must be imported, despite the fact that the Japanese have developed the highest rice yield per acre in Asia. Since the war lost them their empire, and the isolation of Communist China deprived them of their biggest market, the Japanese have been able to subsist only through aid given by the U. S. As a recent report on World Population and Resources by the Political and Economic Planning (P.E.P.) organization in Britain says: "Japan is undoubtedly the most overpopulated great country there has ever been."

Realizing that no expansion of its industry and trade could possibly take care of a major increase in its population, the Japanese Government has embarked on

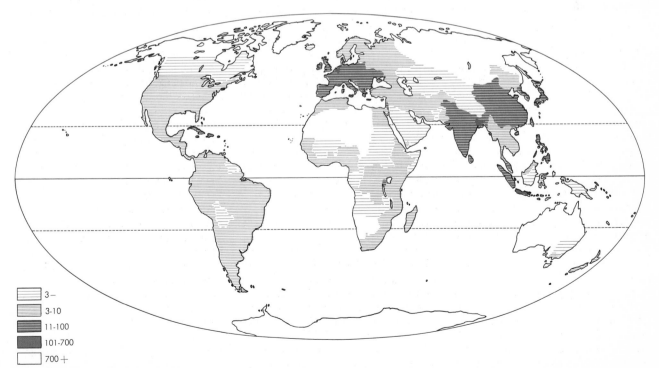

3 —
3-10
11-100
101-700
700 +

DENSITY OF POPULATION in various parts of the world is indicated in this map. The numbers beside the key at the left represent the number of people per square mile. In most cases the population density has been averaged within political boundaries.

a firm policy of population control. In Japan infanticide was widely practiced until some 80 years ago. As its first move after the recent war the Government turned to an almost equally desperate measure: it legalized and indeed encouraged abortion. The number of induced abortions rose from a quarter of a million in 1949 to well over a million in 1953. As was to be expected, the effects on the health of Japanese women were deplorable—and the annual percentage rate of population increase was still above the prewar level.

With these stark facts in mind, the Japanese Ministry of Health's Institute of Population Problems in 1954 passed a strong resolution urging government encouragement of contraception. It proposed that birth-control facilities be provided as part of the health services, that medical schools pursue research and include family planning in the curriculum, that doctors called upon to induce an abortion should be required to provide the woman with information about birth control for the future and that national wage and taxation policies should be such as to avoid "encouraging large families."

Drastic though these recommendations are, they or something very like them are necessary, and it is much to be hoped that they will be speedily and thoroughly implemented. If they are successfully put into practice, they will not only save Japan from disaster but

will provide valuable lessons for other countries.

India's problem is rather different. It is an immense country—the best part of a subcontinent—with large resources waiting to be developed. Its present rate of population increase is just under 1¼ per cent per annum—lower than that in the U. S. (which is 1.6 per cent, excluding immigration). Its immediate future is not quite as desperate as Japan's.

But India is still in the early expanding stage of the population cycle. Its death rate (now about 26 per thousand) has just begun to fall, and has a long way to go before it drops to that of advanced countries. Meanwhile its birth rate (about 40 per thousand according to the latest available figures) is well over double that in Western Europe, and shows no signs of dropping. If the death rate is cut to the extent that the Ministry of Health expects, and if the birth rate remains at its present level, within a few years India's annual increase of population will be some eight million—equivalent to adding a new London each year!

Moreover, India's population even now is not far from the borders of starvation; it must increase its food production drastically to achieve the barest minimum of decent living for its people. Their average daily diet is a mere 1,590 calories. At least two thirds of India's 380 million people are under-

nourished. Methods of cultivation and systems of land tenure are primitive and will need a painful and difficult process of improvement before they begin to satisfy modern requirements. Tradition, taboos, ignorance and illiteracy are grave obstacles to progress. Comparatively little more land could fruitfully be brought into cultivation, and deforestation compels the people to burn cow manure as fuel, thus robbing the soil of fertilizer.

Above all, the mere size of the problem is formidable. Even at the present rather modest rate of increase, five million people are added each year.

India's Masses

The size of India's human flood was forcibly brought home to me in 1954 when I visited the ill-fated Kumbh-Mela of that year. This religious festival is held at the junction of the two great rivers, the Jumna and the Ganges, at Allahabad. The assembled pilgrims acquire merit and salvation by bathing in the rivers' sacred waters. Every 12th year the festival is especially sacred, and the Kumbh-Mela of 1954 was uniquely important as being the first of these high points to occur after India's independence. One day of the festival is particularly auspicious and to bathe on that day is especially efficacious.

Pilgrims had converged from all over India—by train, by cart and by shanks'

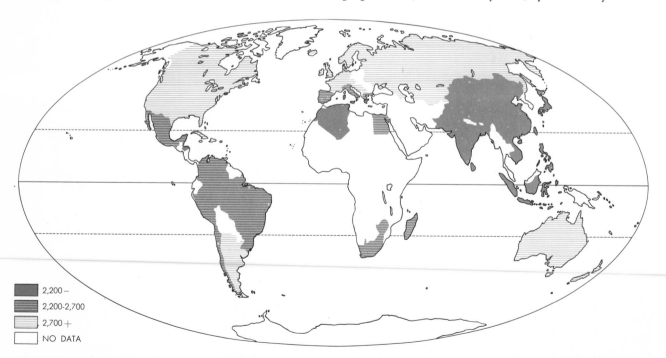

| 2,200 – |
| 2,200-2,700 |
| 2,700 + |
| NO DATA |

NUMBER OF CALORIES per person per day is plotted on the same projection. The minus sign in the key indicates less than 2,200 calories; the plus sign, more than 2,700 calories. The dotted lines are the Tropic of Cancer and the Tropic of Capricorn.

mare. On the day we arrived, two and a half million people were encamped on the flats by the river, and three days later, on the great day of the festival, the number had grown to four and a half million! I shall never forget the spectacle of this enormous human ant heap, with its local condensations of crowds converging onto the temporary pontoon bridges over the Jumna to reach the sacred bathing grounds. A crowd of this magnitude makes a frightening and elemental impression: it seems so impersonal and so uncontrollable. This impression was all too tragically borne out three days later, when the crowd got out of hand and trampled 400 of its helpless individual members to death.

Calcutta was another manifestation of India's mere bulk. The overgrowth of cities has been a constant accompaniment of the growth of population: the hypertrophy of Calcutta has been exceptionally rapid and severe. In 1941 the population of greater Calcutta was under three million; today it is nearly five million. Its appalling slums are crowded to the rooftops, and at night the pavements are strewn with an overflow of people who have nowhere else to sleep and are forced to share the streets with the miserable roaming cattle. This was impressed upon me on the evening of my first day in the city by a scene I shall never forget. In one of the busiest streets a man and a cow approached a traffic

island from opposite angles and composed themselves for the night on either side of the traffic policeman.

The Government of the new, independent India born in 1947 showed a refreshing courage in grasping the formidable nettle of overpopulation. Recognizing that superabundance of people was one of the major obstacles to Indian prosperity and Indian progress, they made the control of population one of the aims of their first Five-Year Plan. The Census Commissioner of India, in his report on the 1951 census, put the problem in quantitative terms. Efforts to keep pace with the growth of population by increasing food production were bound to fail, he said, when the population passed 450 million. If, however, India could "reduce the incidence of improvident maternity to about 5 per cent," an increase of 24 million tons per year in agricultural productivity would be sufficient to feed the population and bring a "visible reduction of human suffering and promotion of human happiness."

India's Efforts

The Indian Health Ministry has made grants for research on new contraceptives, for certain population studies, for training workers in the field of family planning and maternal and child welfare, for educating public opinion, and for assisting the family-planning ven-

tures of state governments and voluntary organizations.

It is heartening that a great country like India should make population control part of its national policy. But it must be confessed that the effects are as yet exceedingly small, and that to an outside observer the execution of the policy seems rather halfhearted.

Let me take an example. The one large-scale experiment initiated by the Government itself has been a pilot study of the so-called rhythm method of birth control, which is notoriously unreliable, owing to the great variation among individual women, and even in the same woman at different times, in the monthly period of infertility. I had the opportunity of visiting the chief center of the experiment in a village near Mysore, and of interviewing the capable and attractive woman in charge, a Negro social scientist from the U. S.

The results of the experiment were interesting. About three quarters of the married women in the village said they would like to learn some method of limiting their families. After their individual cycles were studied each woman was given a kind of rosary, with differently colored beads for "safe days" and "baby days." With this guidance a number of the women managed to avoid pregnancy during the 10 months of the experiment. The social scientist in charge thought that about 20 per cent of Indian village families might learn to

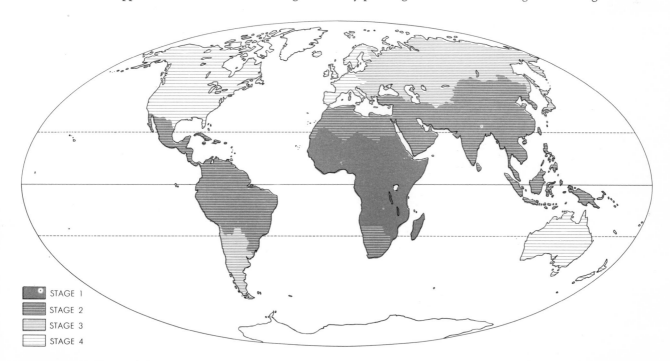

STAGES OF POPULATION CYCLE are also mapped. Stage 1 is characterized by high birth rates and high death rates; Stage 2, by high birth rates and falling death rates; Stage 3, by falling birth and falling death rates; Stage 4, by low birth and low death rates.

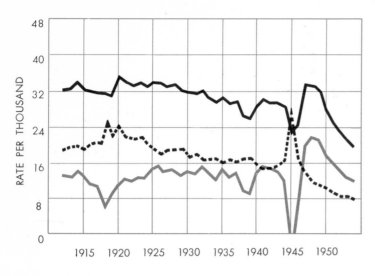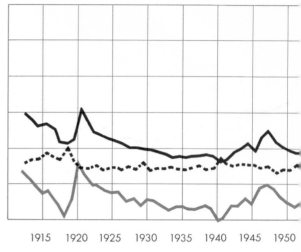

—— BIRTHS

----- DEATHS

—— NATURAL INCREASE

BIRTH AND DEATH RATES of four areas are plotted, together with the resulting natural increase of population. The first chart is for Japan; the second, for England and Wales; the third, for the U. S.;

practice the rhythm method successfully. This was a maximum; in any widespread campaign the figure is much more likely to be 15 or 10 per cent. Thus the method would be quite inadequate to control population growth to any significant degree.

Methods used in Western countries are difficult to apply in India, partly because of the cost, partly because of the lack of privacy and hygienic facilities in the vast majority of Indian homes. In addition, there is the persistent influence of Gandhi. As he narrated in his autobiography, Gandhi indulged excessively in sexual pleasure after his marriage. As a result of his disgust at his own indulgence, and his dislike of anything he considered to be scientific materialism, he pronounced against all mechanical or chemical methods of birth control and solemnly recommended abstinence as the cure for India's population problem!

The ideal solution would be the discovery of what laymen (much to the annoyance and distress of the experts) persist in calling "the pill"—a cheap and harmless substance taken by mouth which would temporarily prevent conception, either by preventing ovulation or by rendering the egg unfertilizable. A number of promising substances are being investigated, including some extracts of plants used by primitive peoples. So far nothing safe and reliable has emerged. But our knowledge of reproductive physiology and of biochemistry has been so enormously increased in the last few dec-

ades that I would be willing to bet that a solution can be found. A large-scale, concerted program of research is necessary, as it was for the atomic bomb. If we were willing to devote to the problem of controlling human reproduction a tenth of the money and scientific brain-power that we are devoting to the release of atomic energy, I would prophesy that we would have the answer within 10 years, certainly within a generation.

One of the facts that prompted the Indian Government to undertake the task of reducing population increase was the ghastly recurrence of famine in 1952, when a major tragedy was averted only by large-scale importations and gifts of wheat and other foodstuffs from other countries. Famine will continue to recur in India so long as population is not brought down into a reasonable balance with the production of food.

The Government has made heroic efforts to increase food production, and for the first time in modern history India has now a surplus of home-grown food—at the meager-diet level. But this has been made possible by two good seasons of abundant rain; when the climatic cycle brings the bad years around again, as it inevitably will, hunger once more will stalk the land. The long-term prospect is blacker: if population goes on increasing by five millions or more a year, food production cannot possibly continue catching up with the mouths to be fed.

The Government is also devoting more and more attention to industrializing the country, both by small-scale vil-

lage industries and by large-scale projects. However, while industrialization is highly desirable, it is chimerical to suppose that it alone can cope with India's food and population problem.

Indonesia

Indonesia, another country with an extraordinary population problem, contains the most densely populated large island in the world. Java has more than 50 million people on its 50,000 square miles—a density of population nearly twice that of highly industrialized Britain. Yet Java is almost entirely agricultural. Its cultivable land is very fertile, but there is less than two fifths of an acre per head. And much of the land is devoted to exportable products, so that rice has to be imported to feed the people, even at the insufficient level of about 2,000 calories per day.

Java's already overcrowded population is increasing at a compound interest rate of at least 1.5 per cent per year. A simple answer seems at hand: The excess should be transferred to the large nearby Indonesian islands of Sumatra and Borneo, which are far less thickly populated. But this facile suggestion has proved to be quite impracticable. With considerable difficulty the Indonesian authorities have persuaded some Javanese to move to Sumatra, but many of these have not been able to stand the hardships of pioneering agriculture and have either returned to Java or settled into a depressed urban life on the Sumatra coast. The fact is the material resources and the skills needed to convert the dense equatorial forest of Sumatra

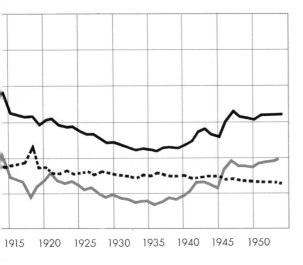

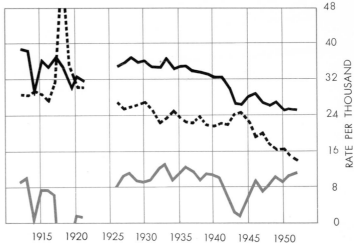

the fourth, for India. The peak in the death rate of all these areas between 1915 and 1920 is due to the influenza pandemic of 1918-1919. The peak in the Japanese death rate for 1945 is largely due to war casualties. The gap in the curves for India is due to lack of data.

and Borneo to agricultural production are not available. This is not to say that settlement should not be attempted. But resettlement of Java's population on the largest possible scale, plus other economic and political development, could not possibly cope with more than a part of Java's formidable annual surplus of people. Birth control also is necessary. Unfortunately there is no sign yet that the Indonesian Government recognizes this necessity.

Bali, whose population density (over 500 per square mile) is about half that of Java, grows just about enough rice to feed itself. However, if its population continues to grow at the present high rate it will seriously outstrip food production in two or at most three generations. Bali provides an extreme illustration of the erosion of a culture by world population pressure. The Balinese have a rich and vital cultural tradition, in which beauty is woven into everyday living. Every aspect of life is marked by some celebration or embellished with some form of decoration. Every Balinese participates in some form of creative activity—music, dance, drama, carving, painting or decoration. What is more, the tradition is not rigid, and the culture is a living and growing one, in which local and individual initiative are constantly introducing novelty and fresh variety. But the Balinese are afflicted with many preventable diseases; they are largely illiterate (though far from uncultured); their religion is now being undermined by the Christian missionaries who have at last been allowed to work in Bali; growing economic pressure forces them to take advantage of the

flood of cheap mass-produced goods from Western technology; their mounting population demands some adaptation to modern industrial life if living standards are to be raised or even maintained, and this in turn is imposing a Westernized system of compulsory education.

Most foreign residents prophesy that Bali's unique and vital culture is doomed, and will wither and die within 10 or 15 years. This may be overgloomy, but certainly it is in grave danger. We can only hope that the Indonesian Government will realize the value of this rich product of the centuries, and that UNESCO will justify the C in its name—C for Culture—and do all in its power to help. No one wants to keep the Balinese in a state of ill health and ignorance. Yet instead of being pushed by the well-meaning but ill-considered efforts of overzealous missionaries and "scientific" experts to believe that their traditional culture is a symbol of backwardness, they could be encouraged to retain faith in the essential validity of their indigenous arts and ceremonials, and helped in the task of adapting them to modern standards. A traditional culture, like a wild species of animal or plant, is a living thing. If it is destroyed the world is the poorer.

Thailand and Fiji

The situation of Siam, or Thailand as it is now officially called, is in some ways not dissimilar to that of Bali. It is in the fortunate position of producing enough rice not only to feed its own people but also to export a considerable amount to less favored countries. Its

people are well fed and look cheerful. Thailand is proud of its past, and especially of the fact that it alone of Southeast Asian countries has never lost its independence. There is a traditional culture in which the bulk of the people are content to find fulfillment, though there is not so much active participation or artistic creation as in Bali. At the same time, Thailand is crowded with organizations and agencies, international and national, which are giving advice and assistance on every possible subject: health, education, agriculture, democracy, scientific development, administration, industry, fish ponds and rural community life. As a result the traditional Siamese culture is being crushed or undercut.

Unless Thailand's birth rate falls along with the death rate, she will lose her proud distinction among Asian countries, and will become seriously overpopulated well before the end of the century. Thailand needs better coordination of her departments of government with the motley collection of foreign agencies, and an over-all plan which would take account of population and traditional culture as well as food production and industry, science and education.

Fiji is another island, with another problem. Its population of about a third of a million is made up of two separate populations, which at present are about equal in number—the indigenous Fijians and the immigrants from India (together with a handful of Europeans, Chinese and others).

The history of the two populations is instructive. The native Fijian population

CHILD BRIDE and her mother were photographed by the author near Mysore in India. It has been suggested that curtailing child marriage would help curb the population increase.

ness for Western education, and a definite dislike of regular agricultural work. Indians largely man Fiji's sugar plantation economy. They make excellent laborers and small farmers and traders, and have a notable thirst for education. They have even started secondary schools on their own initiative and at their own expense.

There is little intermarriage between the two groups, and indeed little liking. The Indians tend to regard the Fijians as barbaric, while the Fijians (who still take a sneaking pride in their warlike and cannibal past) find the Indians effeminate and affect to despise their laborious way of life. However, there are now signs of a rapprochement, and some of the younger Fijians are realizing that they must change their attitude toward work and education if the Fijian community is not to lapse into a sort of living fossil, cushioned by the protective measures of the Colonial Government. Once this new attitude is realized in practice, and the Fijians accept Western standards more wholeheartedly, their death rate is bound to fall and their numbers to jump. Since the Indian rate of increase shows no signs of falling, a demographic crisis looms ahead. Fiji will become overpopulated within the lifetime of its younger inhabitants, unless the Fijians and Indians alike are introduced to the necessity and desirability of family limitation. Unfortunately birth control is still taboo, or at least not publicly acceptable, in the British Colonial Office (and indeed in the governments of all other colonial powers). I can only hope that too much economic distress and social misery will not be required to force the action that present intelligent foresight could undertake—and could now undertake with much less difficulty than when the cohorts of the yet unborn have swelled the population to disastrous proportions.

Australia

Australia is a storm center of demographic controversy. She is a continent of close on three million square miles with only nine million human inhabitants. Yet she is committed to a "white Australia" policy, and admits no Asians or Africans as immigrants, though she is on Asia's back doorstep. The three great swarming countries of Asia—India, China and Japan—have for decades been casting longing eyes on Australian space as a possible outlet for their surplus people: if the Axis powers had won the war, the Japanese undoubtedly would have

numbered nearly 200,000 in 1850, had fallen to 150,000 when the islands were taken over by the British in 1874, and was steadily reduced by a succession of epidemics to a point well under 100,000 before health measures introduced by an alarmed administration reversed the decline. It is now around 140,000. Immigration from India started in 1879 and has continued to the present day. The Indian population outstripped the Fijian during World War II and has now

passed 150,000. Since its rate of increase is well above that of the Fijians, Indians will in the space of two or three generations constitute a large majority unless present trends change.

The two groups are very different in physique, cultural background, interests and work habits. The Fijians have the finest physique I have ever seen: they make good soldiers and wonderful athletes. But their athletic and warlike propensities have induced no great keen-

established settlements in Australia on a large scale.

However, Australia's open spaces are, from the point of view of human occupation, largely a mirage. For an indefinite time its uninhabited areas will remain blanks on the world's map. Three quarters of Australia is desert or semidesert. At the present time only 2.5 per cent of Australia's land is cultivated. It is true that big irrigation schemes are being planned, and that the discovery that much poor land could be enriched by adding trace elements is heartening the farmers and wine growers and herders. But heavy additions of fertilizers would also be needed, and these, like irrigation schemes, are expensive.

Never is a big word, but it looks as if much of the land can never be brought into cultivation. I was driven down from Darwin to Alice Springs—a thousand miles of increasingly sparse bush and increasingly stony and barren soil, miserable and for the most part intractable to human effort. The best estimates put 7.5 per cent as the maximum area of Australia's surface which can be brought into cultivation, and to achieve even this will demand great effort and great expenditures of capital.

Australia is underpopulated in the double sense that it could support a larger population and that a larger population would benefit its economy. How much larger is a question. Some say 50 million people, but this seems an overoptimistic estimate. A total of 25 or at most 30 millions seems more reasonable. And this would absorb less than one year's increase of Asia's population, less than five years of that of India alone. Furthermore, Australia already is hard put to it to keep up living standards in the face of its present rate of population growth, which is one of the highest in the world (about 2.5 per cent per annum), thanks to its policy of encouraging and assisting immigration from Europe. Thus the idea of Australia becoming an outlet for the spill-over of Asia is chimerical. The highest rate of human absorption possible without jeopardizing economic health could not take care of more than a small fraction of Asia's annual increase.

The white Australian policy remains as an affront to Asian sentiment. But this too has, in my opinion, strong arguments in its favor. Certainly it cannot and should not be justified on grounds of racial superiority or inferiority: there is no such thing. But it can be justified on cultural grounds. Cultural differences can create grave difficulties in national

OPEN-AIR BARBERSHOP beside a cow in Benares illustrates the conditions of sanitation which have traditionally kept the Indian death rate higher than that of Western countries.

ROW OF BEGGARS in Benares characterizes the narrow margin of subsistence in the large cities of India. All the photographs on pages 10 through 12 were made by the author.

FISH PONDS were photographed from the air along the coast of Java. In these shallow bodies of water the Javanese breed fish as part of the effort to solve their food problem.

RICE PADDIES on terraced hillsides in Bali indicate intensive use of the land. The Balinese grow all their own food, but within a relatively short time they may have to import it.

FISH TRAP is built by a fisherman in a Philippine stream. In their intensive fisheries the Filipinos also wade neck-deep to catch shrimp, and dip fish from water with ingenious nets.

development. They often do so when cultural and racial differences are combined. A large minority group which clings to its own standards and its own cultural and racial distinctiveness inevitably stands in the way of national unity and creates all sorts of frictions. And if the immigrant group multiplies faster than the rest of the population, the problem is aggravated, as we have seen in Fiji.

It should be put on record that there is little color prejudice in Australia. For its aborigines—the only nonwhite permanent inhabitants of the continent—the watchword now is assimilation: they are gradually to be incorporated into the country's social and economic life. Australia is also admitting a number of Asians as students or trainees, and giving them a very friendly welcome. What Australia seeks to guard against is the creation of permanent racial-cultural minorities.

Resources

Such are some of the population problems of individual countries as I saw them in my tour of Asia and the Far East. The obverse of the population problem is the problem of resources, and I must say a word about the alarming differentials in consumption between different regions and nations. Even in food these are serious enough. The average daily diet in India (1,590 calories) is less than half that in countries such as the U. S. or Ireland. And between the more privileged classes of favored countries and the poorer ones of the underdeveloped countries the difference of course is much greater—nearly fourfold instead of twofold. When we come to other resources, the contrasts are still more startling. In the field of energy, the U. S. per capita consumption is double that of Britain and more than 20 times that of India. The U. S. consumes 80 times more iron per capita than India and nearly two and one-half times more newsprint per capita than Britain. It uses about two thirds of all the world's production of oil.

As facts like these seep into the world's consciousness, they are bound to affect the world's conscience. Such inequalities appear intolerable. The privileged nations are beginning to experience a sense of shame. This guilty feeling finds a partial outlet in the various international schemes for technical and economic assistance to underdeveloped countries. But these schemes are not nearly bold or big enough. We need a world development plan on a scale at least 10 times as big as all existing schemes put together—a joint enterprise in which all nations would feel they were participating and working toward a common goal. To achieve even the roughest of justice for all peoples, the favored nations of the world will have not merely to cough up a fraction of their surpluses but voluntarily to sacrifice some of their high standard of living. For their part the underdeveloped countries, to qualify for membership in the international development club, must be willing not only to pledge themselves to hard and intelligent work but also to restrict their population growth.

As I have emphasized, the crux of the problem lies in establishing a satisfactory balance between the world's resources and the population which uses the resources. The Political and Economic Planning report to which I have referred surveys in some detail the prospects of the world's main resources for the next 25 years. It concludes that so far as energy, minerals and other inorganic raw materials are concerned, the total world requirements probably can be met during that period, and for energy the prospect continues reasonably bright up to the end of the 20th century. But when it comes to food, a world deficiency "of appalling magnitude" already exists, and "supplying the necessary foodstuffs to feed the expected newcomers and also to bring about substantial and lasting improvement in the position of the many millions now underfed is likely to prove exceedingly difficult and increasingly precarious."

This forecast, it must be emphasized, applies to global consumption; when we take the position of individual countries into account, the situation appears even more serious. The trend is toward a widening of the already grotesque differences in consumption between the well-nourished and the undernourished regions of the world. For one thing, a rise in living standards in food-exporting countries is reducing the amount of food they have available for export; for example, Argentina is exporting less meat because its people are consuming more of its production.

Everything points to one conclusion. While every effort must be made to increase food production, to facilitate distribution, to conserve all conservable resources and to shame the "have" nations into a fairer sharing of the good things of the world with the "have-nots," this alone cannot prevent disaster. Birth control also is necessary, on a world scale and·as soon as possible.

Though I may seem to have painted the picture in gloomy colors, I would like to end on a key of hope. Just as the portentous threat of atomic warfare has brought humanity to its senses and seems likely to lead to the abandonment of all-out war as an instrument of national policy, so I would predict that the threat of overpopulation will prompt a reconsideration of values and lead eventually to a new value system for human living. But time presses. This year will add more than 34 million people to humanity's total, and certainly for two or three decades to come each successive year will add more. If nothing is done soon, world overpopulation will be a fact well before the end of the century, bringing with it an explosive cargo of misery and selfish struggle, frustration and increasingly desperate problems.

It has taken just one decade from Hiroshima for the world to face up resolutely to the implications of atomic war. Can we hope that it will take no more than a decade from the 1954 World Population Conference in Rome for the world to face up equally resolutely to the implications of world overpopulation?

KAVA CEREMONY is conducted on the island of Fiji. The athletic and warlike Fijians are slow to accept education and agriculture. Their numbers have decreased since 1850.

INDIAN HIGH SCHOOL on Fiji was visited by the author (center). Immigration to Fiji from India began in 1879. Today the Indian population on the island outnumbers the Fijian.

24

The Origins of New World Civilization

RICHARD S. MacNEISH

November 1964

Perhaps the most significant single occurrence in human history was the development of agriculture and animal husbandry. It has been assumed that this transition from food-gathering to food production took place between 10,000 and 16,000 years ago at a number of places in the highlands of the Middle East. In point of fact the archaeological evidence for the transition, particularly the evidence for domesticated plants, is extremely meager. It is nonetheless widely accepted that the transition represented a "Neolithic Revolution," in which abundant food, a sedentary way of life and an expanding population provided the foundations on which today's high civilizations are built.

The shift from food-gathering to food production did not, however, happen only once. Until comparatively recent times the Old World was for the most part isolated from the New World. Significant contact was confined to a largely one-way migration of culturally primitive Asiatic hunting bands across the Bering Strait. In spite of this almost total absence of traffic between the hemispheres the European adventurers who reached the New World in the 16th century encountered a series of cultures almost as advanced (except in metallurgy and pyrotechnics) and quite as barbarous as their own. Indeed, some of the civilizations from Mexico to Peru possessed a larger variety of domesticated plants than did their European

conquerors and had made agricultural advances far beyond those of the Old World.

At some time, then, the transition from food-gathering to food production occurred in the New World as it had in the Old. In recent years one of the major problems for New World prehistorians has been to test the hypothesis of a Neolithic Revolution against native archaeological evidence and at the same time to document the American stage of man's initial domestication of plants (which remains almost unknown in both hemispheres).

The differences between the ways in which Old World and New World men achieved independence from the nomadic life of the hunter and gatherer are more striking than the similarities. The principal difference lies in the fact that the peoples of the Old World domesticated many animals and comparatively few plants, whereas in the New World the opposite was the case. The abundant and various herds that gave the peoples of Europe, Africa and Asia meat, milk, wool and beasts of burden were matched in the pre-Columbian New World only by a half-domesticated group of Andean cameloids: the llama, the alpaca and the vicuña. The Andean guinea pig can be considered an inferior equivalent of the Old World's domesticated rabbits and hares; elsewhere in the Americas the turkey was an equally inferior counterpart of the Eastern Hemisphere's many

varieties of barnyard fowl. In both the Old World and the New, dogs presumably predated all other domestic animals; in both beekeepers harvested honey and wax. Beyond this the New World list of domestic animals dwindles to nothing. All the cultures of the Americas, high and low alike, depended on their hunters' skill for most of their animal produce: meat and hides, furs and feathers, teeth and claws.

In contrast, the American Indian domesticated a remarkable number of plants. Except for cotton, the "water bottle" gourd, the yam and possibly the coconut (which may have been domesticated independently in each hemisphere), the kinds of crops grown in the Old World and the New were quite different. Both the white and the sweet potato, cultivated in a number of varieties, were unique to the New World. For seasoning, in place of the pepper and mustard of the Old World, the peoples of the New World raised vanilla and at least two kinds of chili. For edible seeds they grew amaranth, chive, panic grass, sunflower, quinoa, apazote, chocolate, the peanut, the common bean and four other kinds of beans: lima, summer, tepary and jack.

In addition to potatoes the Indians cultivated other root crops, including manioc, oca and more than a dozen other South American plants. In place of the Old World melons, the related plants brought to domestication in the New World were the pumpkin, the

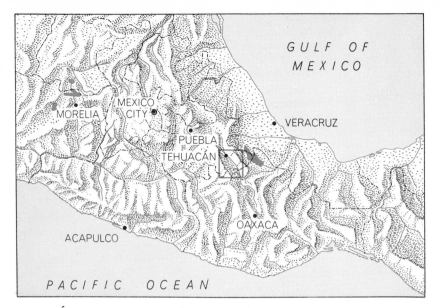

TEHUACÁN VALLEY is a narrow desert zone in the mountains on the boundary between the states of Puebla and Oaxaca. It is one of the three areas in southern Mexico selected during the search for early corn on the grounds of dryness (which helps to preserve ancient plant materials) and highland location (corn originally having been a wild highland grass).

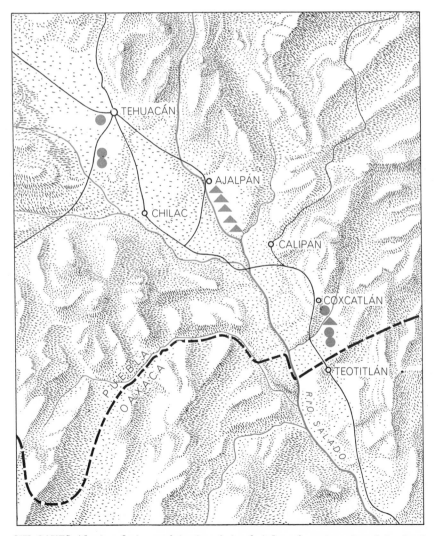

SIX CAVES (*dots*) and six open-air sites (*triangles*) have been investigated in detail by the author and his colleagues. Coxcatlán cave (*top dot at right*), where early corn was found in 1960, has the longest habitation record: from well before 7000 B.C. until A.D. 1500.

gourd, the chayote and three or four distinct species of what we call squash. Fruits brought under cultivation in the Americas included the tomato, avocado, pineapple, guava, elderberry and papaya. The pioneering use of tobacco—smoked in pipes, in the form of cigars and even in the form of cane cigarettes, some of which had one end stuffed with fibers to serve as a filter—must also be credited to the Indians.

Above all of these stood Indian corn, *Zea mays*, the only important wild grass in the New World to be transformed into a food grain as the peoples of the Old World had transformed their native grasses into wheat, barley, rye, oats and millet. From Chile to the valley of the St. Lawrence in Canada, one or another of 150 varieties of Indian corn was the staple diet of the pre-Columbian peoples. As a food grain or as fodder, corn remains the most important single crop in the Americas today (and the third largest in the world). Because of its dominant position in New World agriculture, prehistorians have long been confident that if they could find out when and where corn was first domesticated, they might also uncover the origins of New World civilization.

Until little more than a generation ago investigators of this question were beset by twin difficulties. First, research in both Central America and South America had failed to show that any New World high culture significantly predated the Christian era. Second, botanical studies of the varieties of corn and its wild relatives had led more to conflict than to clarity in regard to the domesticated plant's most probable wild predecessor [see "The Mystery of Corn," by Paul C. Mangelsdorf, SCIENTIFIC AMERICAN Offprint #26]. Today, thanks to close cooperation between botanists and archaeologists, both difficulties have almost vanished. At least one starting point for New World agricultural activity has been securely established as being between 5,000 and 9,000 years ago. At the same time botanical analysis of fossil corn ears, grains and pollen, together with plain dirt archaeology, have solved a number of the mysteries concerning the wild origin and domestic evolution of corn. What follows is a review of the recent developments that have done so much to increase our understanding of this key period in New World prehistory.

The interest of botanists in the history of corn is largely practical: they study the genetics of corn in order to produce improved hybrids. After the wild ancestors of corn had been sought for nearly a century the search had narrowed to two tassel-bearing New World grasses—teosinte and *Tripsacum*—that had features resembling the domesticated plant. On the basis of crossbreeding experiments and other genetic studies, however, Paul C. Mangelsdorf of Harvard University and other investigators concluded in the 1940's that neither of these plants could be the original ancestor of corn. Instead teosinte appeared to be the product of the accidental crossbreeding of true corn and *Tripsacum*. Mangelsdorf advanced the hypothesis that the wild progenitor of corn was none other than corn itself—probably a popcorn with its kernels encased in pods.

Between 1948 and 1960 a number of discoveries proved Mangelsdorf's contention to be correct. I shall present these discoveries not in their strict chronological order but rather in their order of importance. First in importance, then, were analyses of pollen found in "cores" obtained in 1953 by drilling into the lake beds on which Mexico City is built. At levels that were estimated to be about 80,000 years old—perhaps 50,000 years older than the earliest known human remains in the New World—were found grains of corn

pollen. There could be no doubt that the pollen was from wild corn, and thus two aspects of the ancestry of corn were clarified. First, a form of wild corn has been in existence for 80,000 years, so that corn can indeed be descended from itself. Second, wild corn had flourished in the highlands of Mexico. As related archaeological discoveries will make plain, this geographical fact helped to narrow the potential range—from the southwestern U.S. to Peru—within which corn was probably first domesticated.

The rest of the key discoveries, involving the close cooperation of archaeologist and botanist, all belong to the realm of paleobotany. In the summer of 1948, for example, Herbert Dick, a graduate student in anthropology who had been working with Mangelsdorf, explored a dry rock-shelter in New Mexico called Bat Cave. Digging down through six feet of accumulated deposits, he and his colleagues found numerous remains of ancient corn, culminating in some tiny corncobs at the lowest level. Carbon-14 dating indicated that these cobs were between 4,000 and 5,000 years old. A few months later, exploring the La Perra cave in the state of Tamaulipas far to the north of Mexico City, I found similar corncobs that proved to be about 4,500 years old. The oldest cobs at both sites came close

to fitting the description Mangelsdorf had given of a hypothetical ancestor of the pod-popcorn type. The cobs, however, were clearly those of domesticated corn.

These two finds provided the basis for intensified archaeological efforts to find sites where the first evidences of corn would be even older. The logic was simple: A site old enough should have a level of wild corn remains older than the most ancient domesticated cobs. I continued my explorations near the La Perra cave and excavated a number of other sites in northeastern Mexico. In them I found more samples of ancient corn, but they were no older than those that had already been discovered. Robert Lister, another of Mangelsdorf's coworkers, also found primitive corn in a cave called Swallow's Nest in the Mexican state of Chihuahua, northwest of where I was working, but his finds were no older than mine.

If nothing older than domesticated corn of about 3000 B.C. could be found to the north of Mexico City, it seemed logical to try to the south. In 1958 I went off to look for dry caves and early corn in Guatemala and Honduras. The 1958 diggings produced nothing useful, so in 1959 I moved northward into Chiapas, Mexico's southernmost state. There were no corncobs to be found,

EXCAVATION of Coxcatlán cave required the removal of one-meter squares of cave floor over an area 25 meters long by six meters wide until bedrock was reached at a depth of almost five meters. In this way 28 occupation levels, attributable to seven distinctive culture phases, were discovered. Inhabitants of the three lowest levels lived by hunting and by collecting wild-plant foods.

but one cave yielded corn pollen that also dated only to about 3000 B.C. The clues provided by paleobotany now appeared plain. Both to the north of Mexico City and in Mexico City itself (as indicated by the pollen of domesticated corn in the upper levels of the drill cores) the oldest evidence of domesticated corn was no more ancient than about 3000 B.C. Well to the south of Mexico City the oldest date was the same. The area that called for further search should therefore lie south of Mexico City but north of Chiapas.

Two additional considerations enabled me to narrow the area of search even more. First, experience had shown that dry locations offered the best chance of finding preserved specimens of corn. Second, the genetic studies of Mangelsdorf and other investigators indicated that wild corn was originally a highland grass, very possibly able to survive the rigorous climate of highland desert areas. Poring over the map of southern Mexico, I singled out three large highland desert areas: one in the southern part of the state of Oaxaca, one in Guerrero and one in southern Puebla.

Oaxaca yielded nothing of interest, so I moved on to Puebla to explore a dry highland valley known as Tehuacán. My local guides and I scrambled in and out of 38 caves and finally struck pay dirt in the 39th. This was a small rock-shelter near the village of Coxcatlán in the southern part of the valley of Tehuacán. On February 21, 1960, we dug up six corncobs, three of which looked more primitive and older than any I had seen before. Analysis in the carbon-14 laboratory at the University of Michigan confirmed my guess by dating these cobs as 5,600 years old—a good 500 years older than any yet found in the New World.

With this find the time seemed ripe for a large-scale, systematic search. If we had indeed arrived at a place where corn had been domesticated and New World civilization had first stirred, the closing stages of the search would require the special knowledge of many experts. Our primary need was to obtain the sponsorship of an institution interested and experienced in such research, and we were fortunate enough to enlist exactly the right sponsor: the Robert S. Peabody Foundation for Archaeology of Andover, Mass. Funds for the project were supplied by the National Science Foundation and by the agricultural branch of the Rockefeller

EVOLUTION OF CORN at Tehuacán starts (*far left*) with a fragmentary cob of wild corn of 5000 B.C. date. Next (*left to right*) are an early domesticated cob of 4000 B.C., an early hybrid variety of 3000 B.C. and an early variety of modern corn of 1000 B.C. Last (*far right*) is an entirely modern cob of the time of Christ. All are shown four-fifths of natural size.

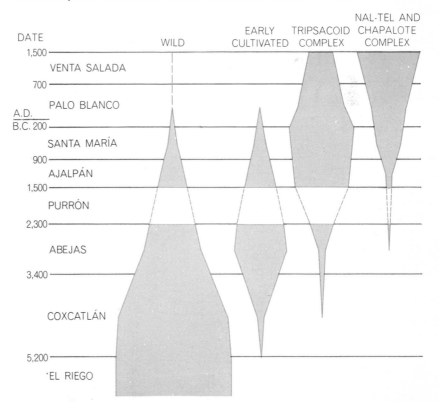

MAIN VARIETIES OF CORN changed in their relative abundance at Tehuacán between the time of initial cultivation during the Coxcatlán culture phase and the arrival of the conquistadors. Abundant at first, wild corn had become virtually extinct by the start of the Christian era, as had the early cultivated (but not hybridized) varieties. Thereafter the hybrids of the tripsacoid complex (produced by interbreeding wild corn with introduced varieties of corn-*Tripsacum* or corn-teosinte hybrids) were steadily replaced by two still extant types of corn, Nal-Tel and Chapalote. Minor varieties of late corn are not shown.

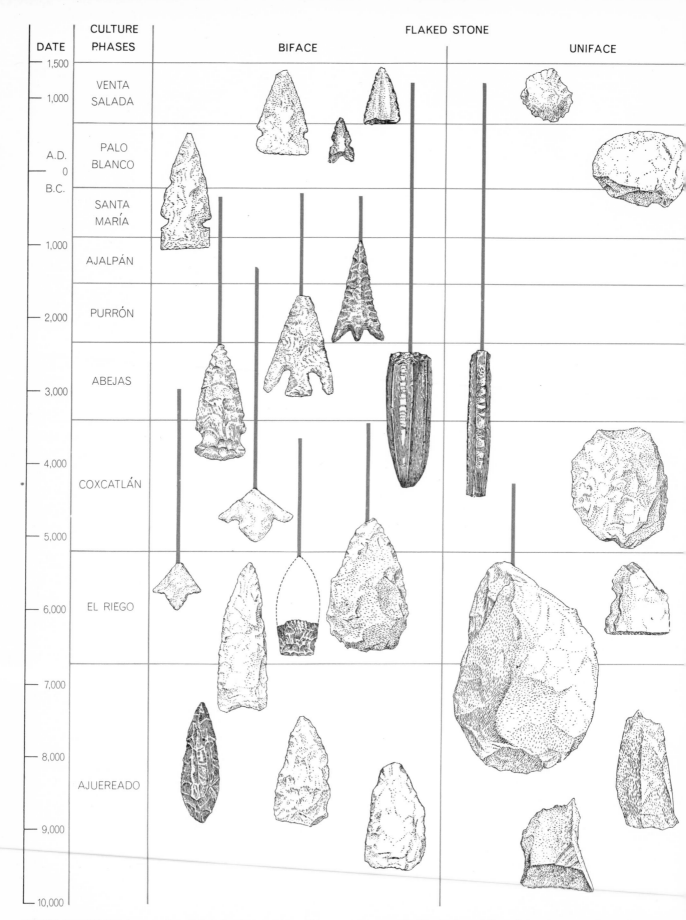

DATE	CULTURE PHASES	FLAKED STONE		
		BIFACE		UNIFACE
1,500				
1,000	VENTA SALADA			
A.D. 0	PALO BLANCO			
B.C.	SANTA MARÍA			
1,000	AJALPÁN			
2,000	PURRÓN			
3,000	ABEJAS			
4,000	COXCATLÁN			
5,000				
6,000	EL RIEGO			
7,000				
8,000	AJUEREADO			
9,000				
10,000				

STONE ARTIFACTS from various Tehuacán sites are arrayed in two major categories: those shaped by chipping and flaking (*left*) and those shaped by grinding and pecking (*right*). Implements that have been chipped on one face only are separated from those that show bifacial workmanship; both groups are reproduced at half their natural size. The ground stone objects are not drawn to a common scale. The horizontal lines define the nine culture phases thus far distinguished in the valley. Vertical lines (*color*) indicate the extent to which the related artifact is known in cultures other than the one in which it is placed. At Tehuacán the evolution of civilization failed to follow the classic pattern established by the Neolithic Revolution in the Old World. For instance, the mortars,

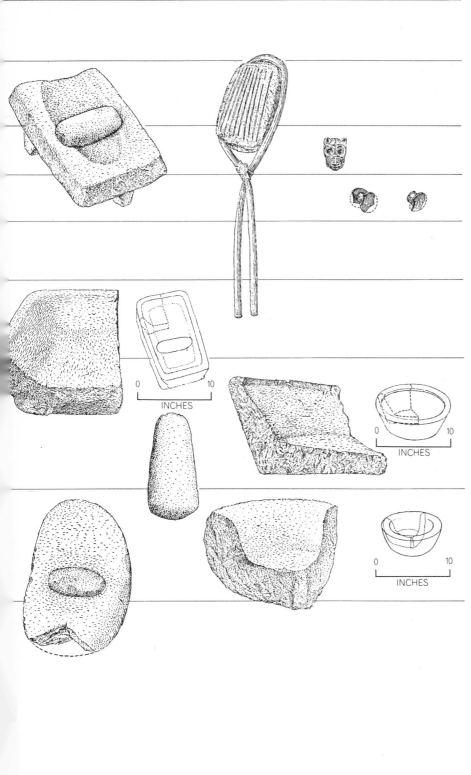

pestles and other ground stone implements that first appear in the El Riego culture phase antedate the first domestication of corn by 1,500 years or more. Not until the Abejas phase, nearly 2,000 years later (marked by sizable obsidian cores and blades and by grinding implements that closely resemble the modern mano and metate), do the earliest village sites appear. More than 1,000 years later, in the Ajalpán phase, earplugs for personal adornment occur. The grooved, withe-bound stone near the top is a pounder for making bark cloth.

Foundation in Mexico, which is particularly interested in the origins of corn. The project eventually engaged nearly 50 experts in many specialties, not only archaeology and botany (including experts on many plants other than corn) but also zoology, geography, geology, ecology, genetics, ethnology and other disciplines.

The Coxcatlán cave, where the intensive new hunt had begun, turned out to be our richest dig. Working downward, we found that the cave had 28 separate occupation levels, the earliest of which may date to about 10,000 B.C. This remarkably long sequence has one major interruption: the period between 2300 B.C. and 900 B.C. The time from 900 B.C. to A.D. 1500, however, is represented by seven occupation levels. In combination with our findings in the Purrón cave, which contains 25 floors that date from about 7000 B.C. to 500 B.C., we have an almost continuous record (the longest interruption is less than 500 years) of nearly 12,000 years of prehistory. This is by far the longest record for any New World area.

All together we undertook major excavations at 12 sites in the valley of Tehuacan [see bottom illustration on page 247]. Of these only five caves— Coxcatlán, Purrón, San Marcos, Tecorral and El Riego East—contained remains of ancient corn. But these and the other stratified sites gave us a wealth of additional information about the people who inhabited the valley over a span of 12,000 years. In four seasons of digging, from 1961 through 1964, we reaped a vast archaeological harvest. This includes nearly a million individual remains of human activity, more than 1,000 animal bones (including those of extinct antelopes and horses), 80,000 individual wild-plant remains and some 25,000 specimens of corn. The artifacts arrange themselves into significant sequences of stone tools, textiles and pottery. They provide an almost continuous picture of the rise of civilization in the valley of Tehuacán. From the valley's geology, from the shells of its land snails, from the pollen and other remains of its plants and from a variety of other relics our group of specialists has traced the changes in climate, physical environment and plant and animal life that took place during the 12,000 years. They have even been able to tell (from the kinds of plant remains in various occupation levels) at what seasons of the year many of the floors in the caves were occupied.

Outstanding among our many finds was a collection of minuscule corncobs that we tenderly extracted from the lowest of five occupation levels at the San Marcos cave. They were only about 20 millimeters long, no bigger than the filter tip of a cigarette [*see the top illustration on page 249*], but under a magnifying lens one could see that they were indeed miniature ears of corn, with sockets that had once contained kernels enclosed in pods. These cobs proved to be some 7,000 years old. Mangelsdorf is convinced that this must be wild corn—the original parent from which modern corn is descended.

Cultivated corn, of course, cannot survive without man's intervention; the dozens of seeds on each cob are enveloped by a tough, thick husk that prevents them from scattering. Mangelsdorf has concluded that corn's wild progenitor probably consisted of a single seed spike on the stalk, with a few pod-covered ovules arrayed on the spike and a pollen-bearing tassel attached to the spike's end [*see bottom illustration at right*]. The most primitive cobs we unearthed in the valley of Tehuacán fulfilled these specifications. Each had the stump of a tassel at the end, each had borne kernels of the pod-popcorn type and each had been covered with only a light husk consisting of two leaves. These characteristics would have allowed the plant to disperse its seeds at maturity; the pods would then have protected the seeds until conditions were appropriate for germination.

The people of the valley of Tehuacán lived for thousands of years as collectors of wild vegetable and animal foods before they made their first timid efforts as agriculturists. It would therefore be foolhardy to suggest that the inhabitants of this arid highland pocket of Mexico were the first or the only people in the Western Hemisphere to bring wild corn under cultivation. On the contrary, the New World's invention of agriculture will probably prove to be geographically fragmented. What can be said for the people of Tehuacán is that they are the first whose evolution from primitive food collectors to civilized agriculturists has been traced in detail. As yet we have no such complete story either for the Old World or for other parts of the New World. This story is as follows.

From a hazy beginning some 12,000 years ago until about 7000 B.C. the people of Tehuacán were few in number. They wandered the valley from season to season in search of jackrabbits, rats, birds, turtles and other small animals, as well as such plant foods as be-

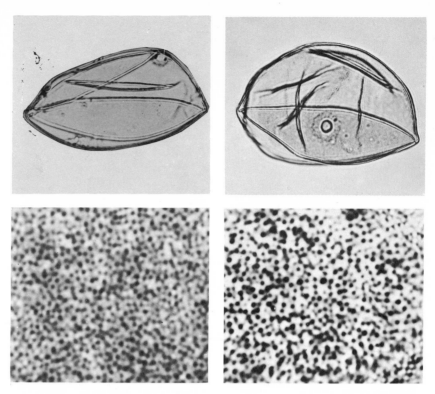

ANTIQUITY OF CORN in the New World was conclusively demonstrated when grains of pollen were found in drilling cores taken from Mexico City lake-bottom strata estimated to be 80,000 years old. Top two photographs (*magnification 435 diameters*) compare the ancient corn pollen (*left*) with modern pollen (*right*). Lower photographs (*magnification 4,500 diameters*) reveal similar ancient (*left*) and modern (*right*) pollen surface markings. The analysis and photographs are the work of Elso S. Barghoorn of Harvard University.

THREE NEW WORLD GRASSES are involved in the history of domesticated corn. Wild corn (*reconstruction at left*) was a pod-pop variety in which the male efflorescence grew from the end of the cob. Teosinte (*center*) and *Tripsacum* (*right*) are corn relatives that readily hybridized with wild and cultivated corn. Modern corn came from such crosses.

came available at different times of the year. Only occasionally did they manage to kill one of the now extinct species of horses and antelopes whose bones mark the lowest cave strata. These people used only a few simple implements of flaked stone: leaf-shaped projectile points, scrapers and engraving tools. We have named this earliest culture period the Ajuereado phase [*see illustration on pages 250 and 251*].

Around 6700 B.C. this simple pattern changed and a new phase—which we have named the El Riego culture from the cave where its first evidences appear—came into being. From then until about 5000 B.C. the people shifted from being predominantly trappers and hunters to being predominantly collectors of plant foods. Most of the plants they collected were wild, but they had domesticated squashes (starting with the species *Cucurbita mixta*) and avocados, and they also ate wild varieties of beans, amaranth and chili peppers. Among the flaked-stone implements, choppers appear. Entirely new kinds of stone tools—grinders, mortars, pestles and pounders of polished stone—are found in large numbers. During the growing season some families evidently gathered in temporary settlements, but these groups broke up into one-family bands during the leaner periods of the year. A number of burials dating from this culture phase hint at the possibility of part-time priests or witch doctors who directed the ceremonies involving the dead. The El Riego culture, however, had no corn.

By about 5000 B.C. a new phase, which we call the Coxcatlán culture,

had evolved. In this period only 10 percent of the valley's foodstuffs came from domestication rather than from collecting, hunting or trapping, but the list of domesticated plants is long. It includes corn, the water-bottle gourd, two species of squash, the amaranth, black and white zapotes, the tepary bean (*Phaseolus acutifolius*), the jack bean (*Canavalia ensiformis*), probably the common bean (*Phaseolus vulgaris*) and chili peppers.

Coxcatlán projectile points tend to be smaller than their predecessors; scrapers and choppers, however, remain much the same. The polished stone implements include forerunners of the classic New World roller-and-stone device for grinding grain: the mano and metate. There was evidently enough surplus energy among the people to allow the laborious hollowing out of stone water jugs and bowls.

It was in the phase following the Coxcatlán that the people of Tehuacán made the fundamental shift. By about 3400 B.C. the food provided by agriculture rose to about 30 percent of the total, domesticated animals (starting with the dog) made their appearance, and the people formed their first fixed settlements—small pit-house villages. By this stage (which we call the Abejas culture) they lived at a subsistence level that can be regarded as a foundation for the beginning of civilization. In about 2300 B.C. this gave way to the Purrón culture, marked by the cultivation of more hybridized types of corn and the manufacture of pottery.

Thereafter the pace of civilization in

the valley speeded up greatly. The descendants of the Purrón people developed a culture (called Ajalpán) that from about 1500 B.C. on involved a more complex village life, refinements of pottery and more elaborate ceremonialism, including the development of a figurine cult, perhaps representing family gods. This culture led in turn to an even more sophisticated one (which we call Santa María) that started about 850 B.C. Taking advantage of the valley's streams, the Santa María peoples of Tehuacán began to grow their hybrid corn in irrigated fields. Our surveys indicate a sharp rise in population. Temple mounds were built, and artifacts show signs of numerous contacts with cultures outside the valley. The Tehuacán culture in this period seems to have been strongly influenced by that of the Olmec people who lived to the southeast along the coast of Veracruz.

By about 200 B.C. the outside influence on Tehuacán affairs shifted from that of the Olmec of the east coast to that of Monte Alban to the south and west. The valley now had large irrigation projects and substantial hilltop ceremonial centers surrounded by villages. In this Palo Blanco phase some of the population proceeded to full-time specialization in various occupations, including the development of a salt industry. New domesticated food products appeared—the turkey, the tomato, the peanut and the guava. In the next period—Venta Salada, starting about A.D. 700—Monte Alban influences gave way to the influence of the Mixtecs. This period saw the rise of true

COXCATLÁN CAVE BURIAL, dating to about A.D. 100, contained the extended body of an adolescent American Indian, wrapped in a pair of cotton blankets with brightly colored stripes. This bundle in turn rested on sticks and the whole was wrapped in bark cloth.

SOPHISTICATED FIGURINE of painted pottery is one example of the artistic capacity of Tehuacán village craftsmen. This specimen, 2,900 years old, shows Olmec influences.

cities in the valley, of an agricultural system that provided some 85 percent of the total food supply, of trade and commerce, a standing army, large-scale irrigation projects and a complex religion. Finally, just before the Spanish Conquest, the Aztecs took over from the Mixtecs.

Our archaeological study of the valley of Tehuacán, carried forward in collaboration with workers in so many other disciplines, has been gratifyingly productive. Not only have we documented one example of the origin of domesticated corn but also comparative studies of other domesticated plants have indicated that there were multiple centers of plant domestication in the Americas. At least for the moment we have at Tehuacán not only evidence of the earliest village life in the New World but also the first (and worst) pottery in Mexico and a fairly large sample of skeletons of some of the earliest Indians yet known.

Even more important is the fact that we at last have one New World example of the development of a culture from savagery to civilization. Preliminary analysis of the Tehuacán materials indicate that the traditional hypothesis about the evolution of high cultures may have to be reexamined and modified. In southern Mexico many of the characteristic elements of the Old World's Neolithic Revolution fail to appear suddenly in the form of a new culture complex or a revolutionized way of life. For example, tools of ground (rather than chipped) stone first occur at Tehuacán about 6700 B.C., and plant domestication begins at least by 5000 B.C. The other classic elements of the Old World Neolithic, however, are slow to appear. Villages are not found until around 3000 B.C., nor pottery until around 2300 B.C., and a sudden increase in population is delayed until 500 B.C. Reviewing this record, I think more in terms of Neolithic "evolution" than "revolution."

Our preliminary researches at Tehuacán suggest rich fields for further exploration. There is need not only for detailed investigations of the domestication and development of other New World food plants but also for attempts to obtain similar data for the Old World. Then—perhaps most challenging of all —there is the need for comparative studies of the similarities and differences between evolving cultures in the Old World and the New to determine the hows and whys of the rise of civilization itself.

25

The Prehistory
of the Australian Aborigine

D. J. MULVANEY
March 1966

The prehistory of Australia ended in 1788, when the British landed at the site of modern Sydney. How many millenniums before that the continent's aboriginal inhabitants arrived has not been precisely established. Only a decade ago their prehistoric period was widely believed to have been no more than a brief prelude to the European colonization. Today it seems certain that the initial migration took place in Pleistocene times—no less than 16,000 years ago and probably much

earlier. Here I shall review the archaeological findings that shed some light on the prehistory of the aborigines and then describe recent field studies that, in my opinion, quite drastically alter earlier views.

Sundered from Asia before *Homo sapiens* evolved, Australia is a land mass almost the size of the U.S. It has 12,000 miles of coastline and extends from 43 degrees South latitude to within 11 degrees of the Equator. A third of its area lies north of the Tropic

of Capricorn. An equally extensive area annually receives less than 10 inches of rainfall. Only 7 percent of the land mass rises above 2,000 feet; indeed, the continent can be traversed from the Gulf of Carpentaria in the northeast to the southern coast without climbing higher than 600 feet. Australia's major mountain and river systems are restricted to its eastern and southeastern parts. These topographic realities must be reckoned with in considering prehistoric patterns of human settlement. Of equal significance are the usually dry watercourses and salt pans of the arid "outback," which testify to a more congenial climate in late Pleistocene or early postglacial times.

In 1788 Australia was inhabited by perhaps 500 aboriginal tribes; they probably mustered a total population of some 300,000. In coastal or river-valley environments, where the population density was comparatively high, there were one or two individuals per square mile. Elsewhere immense tracts supported no more than one person every 30 or 40 square miles. In so large an area one might expect considerable variety in the inhabitants' ecological and technological adaptations, and reports by early European observers and the scantier evidence of archaeology document such differences. For all its variety, however, the prehistoric period had an underlying unity. Over the entire continent the aborigines habitually hunted, fished and gathered wild plants; they had not learned agriculture. The extent of nomadism in each tribal area was largely determined by the local availability of food.

Regional variations in the Australian environment are actually more apparent than real. In other lands differences in topography, rainfall or latitude give

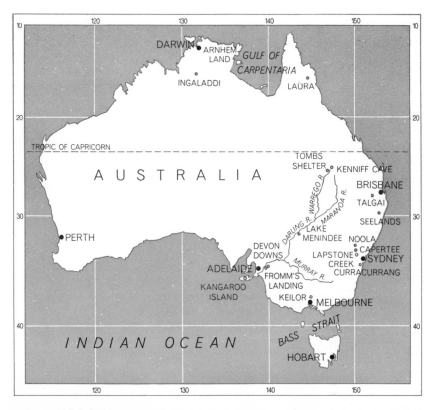

MAJOR PREHISTORIC SITES are located on a map of Australia. Devon Downs, in the Murray River valley, was the first stratified site to be found on the continent. Excavated in 1929, its lower levels are 4,500 years old. Kenniff Cave, a site the author found 1,000 miles north of Devon Downs in 1960, contains strata that span some 16,000 years of prehistory.

rise to diversity in plant and animal species; in Australia these factors may result merely in the substitution of one member of the same plant or animal family for another. The eucalyptus and the kangaroo are ubiquitous. Another phenomenon, universal in Australia and unique to it, is the absence in prehistoric times of formidable predatory animals competing with man for the same game. Such factors must have encouraged a degree of human standardization, both in the character of weapons and in the techniques of hunting and foraging. At the same time it can be postulated that these factors discouraged a dynamic experimental attitude within prehistoric Australian societies.

In terms of material culture few Paleolithic peoples were more impoverished than the aboriginal Australians. There were no horned, antlered or tusked species of animals to provide the raw material for the artifacts so valued in hunting societies elsewhere. Flint and similar fine-grained rocks were rare; instead the aborigines made most of their implements out of quartz or quartzite, materials from which even the most skilled knapper has difficulty producing elegant objects. As for the elements of culture beloved of so many writers on archaeology—dwellings, tombs, grave goods, ceramics, metals, precious stones, cultivated crops and domesticated animals (with the exception of the dog)—the aborigines had none.

Accordingly under the best of circumstances the investigator of Australian prehistory is faced with a paucity of archaeological evidence and a limited range of diagnostic cultural traits. To make matters worse, where bone artifacts might have survived, the high acidity of the soil has often eaten them away, and where desert dryness might have preserved wooden artifacts the voracious termite has destroyed them. These disadvantages are partly offset by the rich store of information on living aborigines, beginning with the first European descriptions and extending to the fieldwork of contemporary ethnographers. The prehistorian must guard against an anachronistic fallacy, however; he must not assume that customs and technologies recorded during the past 100 years constitute unambiguous evidence when it comes to interpreting prehistoric remains.

In 1929 a landmark in Pacific archaeology was established. In the valley of the Murray River east of Adelaide, Her-

BASE OF THE CLIFFS bordering the Murray River in South Australia was a popular prehistoric camping ground. Here, at Fromm's Landing rock-shelter No. 2, the excavation of a deep stratified deposit threw new light on earlier discoveries at nearby Devon Downs.

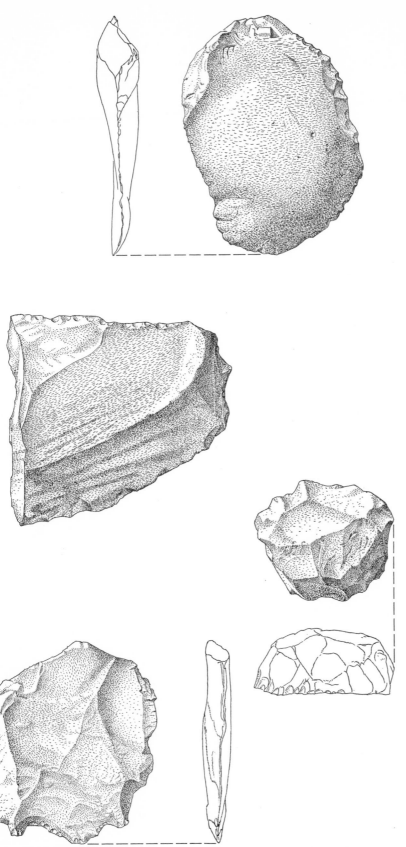

EARLIEST TOOLS found at Kenniff Cave were scrapers such as these, shown actual size. Made by trimming the edges of stone flakes, they were hand-held rather than hafted. They are (*top to bottom*) a quartzite side scraper, trimmed along its right edge; a scraper made from a broken quartzite flake, finely trimmed along its top edge; a round scraper, made from chert, that was trimmed very steeply (*see profile*), and a quartzite flake with trimmed projections and concavities on its bottom edge that suggest use in the manner of a spokeshave to work wood. Eleven thousand years passed before more elaborate tools were made.

bert M. Hale and Norman B. Tindale of the South Australian Museum excavated a rock-shelter site, known as Devon Downs, that contained 20 feet of stratified deposits of human occupation. Hale and Tindale divided the occupation layers into three successive cultural stages on the basis of the presence or absence of stone or bone implements they believed possessed diagnostic significance. They called the earliest culture Pirrian, because the *pirri*, a symmetrical stone projectile point flaked only on one side, was restricted to the lower layers of the site. Pirris are aesthetically perhaps the most pleasing of all the prehistoric aboriginal artifacts ["*c-1*" to "*c-3*" *in illustration on the next page*]. Many of them are found on the surface at sites in the interior of Australia, but it was at Devon Downs that they were first discovered in a stratigraphic context.

The excavators called the second culture Mudukian; *muduk* is the word used by the Murray River aborigines for a short length of bone, pointed at both ends, that resembles the simple kind of fishhook called a gorge ["*f*" *in illustration on the next page*]. At Devon Downs muduks were found in the occupation strata above those that contained pirris. Hale and Tindale gave the uppermost occupation layers the label Murundian; this was derived from the subtribal name of the local aborigines. The Murundian layers contain no distinctive objects of either stone or bone; in effect the archaeological definition of the culture is negative. Carbon-14 dating techniques were not available in those days, but charcoal from a sample of earth preserved in the South Australian Museum since 1929 was recently analyzed and yielded a date for one of the Pirrian strata of about the middle of the third millennium B.C.

Within the past decade I have excavated two rock-shelters at Fromm's Landing, a point only 10 miles downstream from Devon Downs. Carbon-14 dating indicates that the lowest levels in these deposits were occupied early in the third millennium B.C. Fromm's Landing and Devon Downs are thus very close, both geographically and temporally. The sequence of three cultures identified by Hale and Tindale at Devon Downs, however, was not evident at Fromm's Landing. This is a matter of more than casual importance because Tindale has asserted—and the assertion has received wide acceptance—that the three cultures are distributed

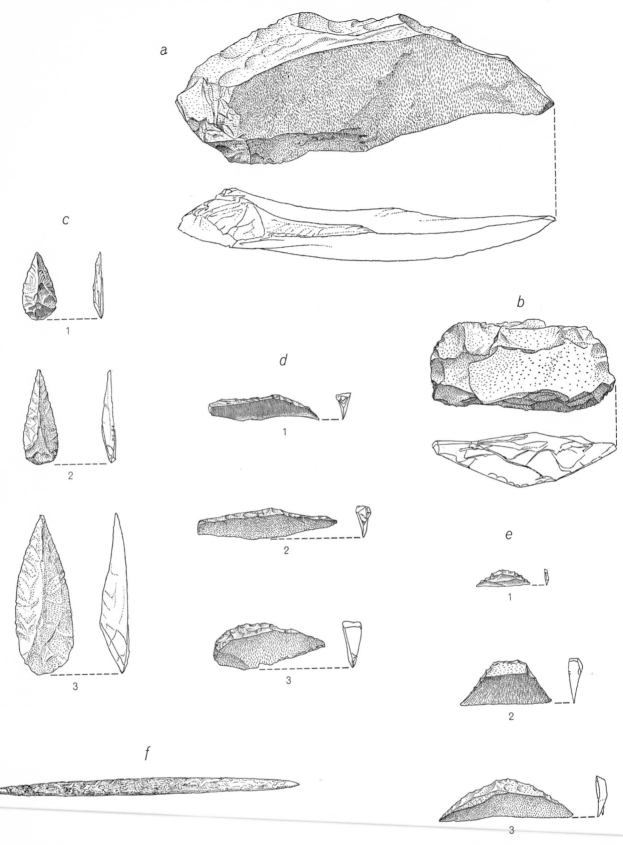

ARTIFACTS FOR HAFTING show a wide variety of forms. All are shown actual size. The knife *a* is from the topmost stratum at Kenniff Cave; stone blades like this, with resin or skin handgrips, were still used by Queensland aborigines early in the 19th century. The step-trimmed adze flake *b* was mounted on the end of a stick and served as a chisel or gouge. The neatly trimmed *pirri* points (*c-1 to c-3*) probably were projectile tips; *c-1* was excavated near Kenniff Cave and is 3,500 years old. The other two are surface finds from South Australia. The three blades (*d-1 to d-3*) are called Bondi points; their backs have been blunted by steep but delicate trimming. The three microliths (*e-1 to e-3*) show similar fine trimming on their backs. All presumably formed the working edges of various composite tools. The pointed bone (*f*) is a 400-year-old *muduk*; it may have served as a fishhook, a spear tip or even a nose ornament.

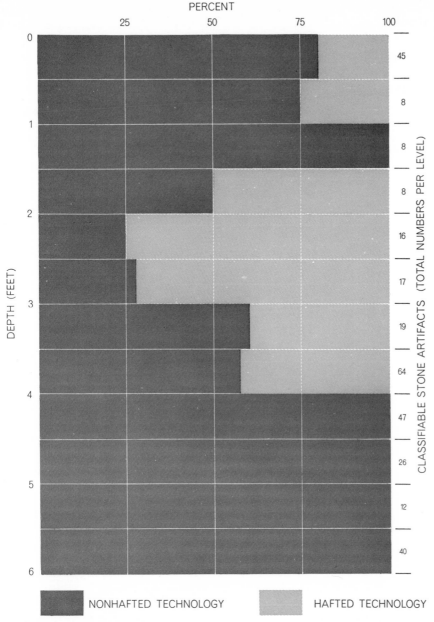

PERCENT

ADVANCE IN TECHNOLOGY at Kenniff Cave took place about 3000 B.C., when the concept of hafting was introduced. At four feet and deeper only hand-held scrapers (*gray*) were found; above that, entirely new kinds of stone artifact (*color*) appear among the scrapers (*see illustration on preceding page*). These artifacts are evidently parts of composite tools.

sources. Such an interpretation eliminates any need to imagine the successive arrival of separate culture groups, and all the elements of discontinuity that such a succession implies.

By the standards of archaeology in the Old World neither the Devon Downs nor the Fromm's Landing site is particularly ancient. Between 1960 and 1964, however, my associates and I excavated a rock-shelter in southern Queensland that contained 11 feet of stratified deposits; carbon-14 dating showed that the lowest levels at this site—Kenniff Cave on the Mount Moffatt cattle station—are at least 16,000 years old. Troweling and sieving 85 cubic yards of sand and ash, we recovered more than 21,000 stone flakes and waste fragments, most of them quartzite. Among them were some 850 deliberately shaped and retouched artifacts. About 60 percent of the artifacts were either broken or only lightly worked. As a result the total number of artifacts available for rigorous classification and measurement was little more than 350.

The sequence of stone artifacts at Kenniff Cave constitutes the point of departure for any current discussion of Australian prehistory. Two facts give the Kenniff Cave collection its special significance. First, it includes examples of most of the prehistoric implement types known in Australia, arranged in stratigraphic order. Second, the age of the collection ranges from the immediate past back to the late Pleistocene.

For those accustomed to the richness of Old World Paleolithic sites the Kenniff Cave assemblage will seem a small sample, but it is one of the largest Australian collections to be analyzed. Recent work in the vicinity of Sydney and in the Northern Territory (where one excavation has uncovered more than 2,000 worked projectile points) has been more productive, but the results have not yet been published. My experience elsewhere has often been daunting. An excavation in Victoria yielded 2,300 waste pieces and only eight artifacts; the strata of a South Australian site yielded an average of three artifacts per 1,000 years of occupation.

The Kenniff Cave assemblage includes 261 specimens of the generalized tool termed a scraper. Their distribution fluctuated with depth [*see illustration on this page*]. In the uppermost four feet of the deposit scrapers were

across the entire continent. I found the pirris at Fromm's Landing in association with microliths, tiny stone blades of the kind that in Old World cultures are sometimes set in a haft of bone or wood to form a composite tool. The association contradicts Tindale's belief that such microliths are artifacts typical not of the Pirrian but of the later Mudukian culture.

This finding and others at Fromm's Landing led me to question the basis of Tindale's cultural diagnosis at Devon Downs. It seemed more useful to consider the elements the three

Devon Downs assemblages had in common than to isolate discrete traits as Tindale did. Flakes of stone used as adzes, for example, were found in all three Devon Downs culture levels; there was no apparent break in the tradition of stoneworking from the earliest time to the latest. In reporting my findings at Fromm's Landing I suggested that the differences in the inventory of various Devon Downs strata might be attributable to changes in artifact preference on the part of an aboriginal population that was becoming increasingly adapted to life beside a river, with its varied and rich organic re-

relatively rare compared with other types of implement. Throughout the lower layers, however, they constituted 100 percent of all classifiable stone artifacts.

An implicit assumption underlies the use of a descriptive label such as "scraper." In this case the assumption is that scrapers were normally held in the user's hand. Scrapers are thus members of the family of nonhafted stone tools. They are technologically distinct from hafted, composite tools of the kind that presumably made use of the microliths unearthed at the Murray River sites in South Australia. Such tools possess handles or other extensions, together with fixatives such as resin or gum or lashings such as hair, vegetable fiber or sinew.

The sandy soil of Kenniff Cave is so acid that, if any such organic constituents of composite tools had once been present, no evidence of them now remains. The distinction between nonhafted and hafted artifacts at Kenniff Cave is therefore a subjective one. Nonetheless, the difference between the percentage of scrapers in the upper strata and in the lower led me to make a basic assumption about the place of nonhafted and hafted tools in Australian prehistory. I postulated that the apparent ignorance of hafting techniques on the part of the early inhabitants of Kenniff Cave was genuine ignorance, and that an extensive phase in the prehistory of the site occupied a period during which this advanced technology was literally unknown. Carbon-14 estimates indicate that this pre-hafting phase lasted for at least 11,000 years, or from about 14,000 to about 3000 B.C.

When the Kenniff Cave scrapers were set in their stratigraphic sequence and subjected to careful measurement and analysis, the results of the study confirmed that, as postulated, a continuity of tradition had existed during this period of 11 millenniums; the scrapers showed no significant change either in production technique or in size. Such technological stability—or lack of invention—may be relevant when one considers the social dynamics of a prehistoric culture.

In contrast to the long period of stability attested by the lower levels at Kenniff Cave, the upper levels told a sharply different story. Scrapers appear in diminishing percentages, and accompanying them are various types of small, delicately worked stone arti-

fact. Both the size and the shape of these objects—one specimen measuring only 1.7 centimeters by .5 by .1 centimeter is shown at *e-1* on page 5—imply their diverse functions as components of hafted implements. Such is certainly the case with the long stone knives and with the artifacts identifiable as adze flakes [*"a" and "b" in illustration on page 258*]. The latter objects, which have a characteristic stepped appearance, were the stone working edges of gouges or chisels, composite tools that are widely represented in Australian ethnographic collections. It is probably the case with the pirri points (which may have been mounted on projectile shafts) and geometric microliths (a type of artifact whose purpose is debated on other continents but that is everywhere assumed to be part of a hafted tool).

To judge from the level at which these tool types are first found in the stratigraphic sequence at Kenniff Cave, the technology of hafting materialized there about 5,000 years ago. The impact of the new technology was fundamental. During the 2,000 years that followed—until about 1000 B.C.—most of the characteristic types of stone implement that have been unearthed or collected on the surface by prehistorians in southern Australia were deposited in the upper strata of Kenniff Cave. It is of course conjectural that the acquired knowledge of hafting techniques was the factor that enabled the aboriginal populations of this period to develop greater flexibility in the design of tools, but it is unmistakable in the stratigraphic record at Kenniff Cave that the rate of technological advance accelerated during

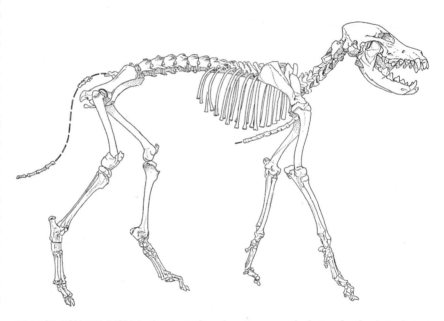

OLDEST KNOWN DINGO, the Australian dog, was unearthed at a depth of six feet at Fromm's Landing rock-shelter No. 6. Dating from 1000 B.C., the animal shows no morphological differences from the dingos of today. Man and the dingo were virtually the only predators in prehistoric Australia; they apparently killed off some species of marsupials.

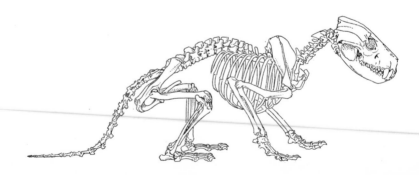

TASMANIAN DEVIL is one of two species of marsupials whose bones are found only in the lower strata at Fromm's Landing. Because no major climatic changes occurred during the 5,000 years the site was occupied, the disappearance of this animal and the Tasmanian wolf from the area in the second millennium B.C. may be attributable to man and the dingo.

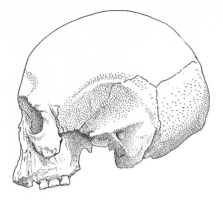
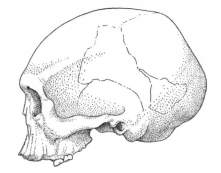
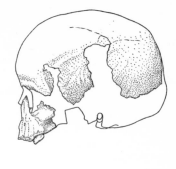

FOSSIL MAN in Australia may be most authentically represented by the skull unearthed at Keilor, near Melbourne, in 1940 (*left*); recent additional findings at Keilor suggest that the skull is as much as 18,000 years old. From the time of its discovery the Keilor skull has been considered nearly a twin of a fossil skull from Wad- jak in Java (*center*), discovered in 1890 and of unknown age. The discovery of an adolescent skull, possibly 40,000 years old (*right*), in the Niah Caves of Sarawak in 1959 has added another possible precursor to the aboriginal family tree. The scarcity of Australian fossil evidence, however, renders all these conclusions tentative.

the period from 3000 B.C. to 1000 B.C.

Bearing in mind the postulate that a long period of nonhafted-tool technology was followed by a briefer period of the more variable hafted-tool technology, it seems appropriate to review the findings of other archaeologists at a number of sites across the continent. Let us begin with the sites that seem, on the basis of established or assumed chronology, to belong to the nonhafted-tool phase. At the Tombs Shelter in Queensland, near Kenniff Cave, a few artifacts have been found that appear to date back to the eighth millennium B.C. They belong to the nonhafted tradition, and worked stones suitable for hafting are found in the strata above them. At Ingaladdi in the Northern Territory a stone-tool industry that consists of scrapers (and "cores" that were reworked as nonhafted scraping or chopping tools after flakes had been struck from them) yields a date in the fifth millennium B.C. Three sites in New South Wales—Seelands, Curracurrang and Capertee—cover a period from the sixth millennium to early in the second millennium B.C. All three evince non-hafted phases and all are overlain by layers containing artifacts suitable for hafting. These lower-level tool kits contain other nonhafted implements in addition to the ubiquitous scrapers; at least that is how I interpret saw-edged flakes at Capertee and core tools common to all three sites. The cores, flaked on one or both faces, suggest that they were held in the fist for some battering or chopping function. Specimens from Seelands have been measured by the prehistorian J. M. Matthews; he finds them comparable to the Southeast Asian pebble industry named Hoabhinian, after a Vietnamese site.

R. V. S. Wright of the University of Sydney has recently undertaken an important excavation at Laura, on Cape York in northeastern Queensland. The technological sequence he has uncovered may be comparable to that at Kenniff Cave. The same may be true of a ninth-millennium-B.C. occupation site Tindale has found at Noola, near Capertee in New South Wales. The Noola material has not yet been formally described, but Tindale's brief published note allows the relevant finds to be attributed to a nonhafted phase. Some years ago Tindale isolated a stone-tool industry on Kangaroo Island, off the coast of South Australia. No varieties of artifact associated with hafted implements were found there, but flaked pebbles, scrapers and massive core tools were numerous. Tindale postulated a Pleistocene date for the occupation; so far neither excavation nor carbon dating has been attempted. This is an intriguing field for further investigation.

Still another early date is proposed by Tindale and Richard Tedford of the University of California at Riverside for "nondescript" stone flakes found at a surface site at Lake Menindee in New South Wales. Charcoal samples at the site have yielded carbon-14 dates of 17,000 and 22,000 B.C., but detailed evidence for a direct association between the charcoal and the artifacts has not yet been published.

The reconstruction of the most recent 5,000 years of Australian prehistory is further along than the work on the earlier phases, although there is no better agreement on how the evidence from these five millenniums should be interpreted. It is nonetheless possible to relate my hypothesis concerning a significant technological change involv- ing hafting techniques during this period to the culturally oriented descriptions of findings by other workers. Much of this work is in progress, and since it would be improper to anticipate the results here the survey that follows— like those that have preceded it—draws primarily on published reports and my own experience.

The Kenniff Cave site in Queensland is more than 1,000 miles from the Devon Downs and Fromm's Landing sites in the Murray River valley of South Australia. In comparing the equivalent upper and later levels of the three sites, however, it is worth noting that Kenniff Cave lies in the same system of river valleys as Devon Downs and Fromm's Landing. The upper levels at Kenniff Cave, like those at the South Australian sites, contain pirri points, microliths, adze flakes and other stone artifacts representative of the hafted-tool tradition. There are no bone muduks at Kenniff Cave, but the acid sands of the site would have destroyed any that had been buried. Significantly there is considerable contrast between the size and finish of similar artifacts from the Queensland and the South Australian sites. This tends to confirm my view that artifacts of the same general type were subject to a process of differentiation.

Although many more excavations are needed to bridge existing gaps in knowledge and lay the foundation for valid generalizations, some hint of the rate at which the concept of hafting diffused among the aboriginal populations is provided by the following carbon-14 results. As I have noted, the Fromm's Landing site and the upper strata at Kenniff Cave belong to the early third millennium B.C., and a layer containing pirri points at Devon Downs dates from later in the same millennium. This parallels the age of the oldest hafted types of stone artifact found in New South Wales, those unearthed at Seelands. The Ingaladdi site in the Northern Territory has yielded pirris and other points, some finished on one side and some on both. These points appear with relative suddenness in a layer that has not been dated. A stratum a few inches below the points, however, contains an assemblage of nonhafted artifacts that has been dated to the latter part of the fifth millennium B.C. It begins to look as if the period centered on the fourth millennium B.C. will prove to be a crucial one in the reconstruction of Australian prehistory.

For many years a key figure in the documentation of the prehistory of New South Wales has been Frederick D. McCarthy, principal of the Australian Institute of Aboriginal Studies; his excavations at Lapstone Creek and Capertee have provided a working basis for systematizing evidence from elsewhere in the state. Recent investigations in the Sydney and New England areas of New South Wales have served to test and elaborate McCarthy's pioneering studies. Under the sponsorship of the institute Wright and J. V. S. Megaw of the University of Sydney have carried out important excavations, and Isabel McBryde of the University of New England has undertaken an all-inclusive field survey.

McCarthy believed he had isolated two cultures at Lapstone Creek. The earlier of these he called Bondaian; its characteristic tool is a small, asymmetric, pointed blade reminiscent of a penknife, with a sharp cutting edge and a blunt back edge ["d" in illustration on page 258]. The later culture he named Eloueran; the characteristic tool is a flake shaped like a segment of an orange, with its back heavily blunted and its cutting edge often polished by use. Also found in the Bondaian levels are geometric microliths. This is scarcely surprising when one considers that the skills needed to make microliths and small blades are essentially the same. Both require as their raw material thin blades, one edge of which is then artificially blunted.

Carbon-14 dates from Curracurrang, Capertee and Seelands place the characteristic artifacts of the Bondaian and the Eloueran cultures in the second and first millenniums B.C. Both could be assigned to my hafted phase. This emphasis on technology rather than on any cultural context accords with McCarthy's own observation that, in spite of fluctuations in the fortunes of specific traits, there is an underlying similarity in the stoneworking techniques of the two cultures.

The present rub in classifying Australian artifacts is how to decide where to draw boundaries and what degree of emphasis to give single culture traits. Within each group of artifacts there are variations in size, shape and trimming. What criteria, for example, distinguish a thin Eloueran flake from a large, crescent-shaped microlith? It is unsatisfactory to lump all the pirris together, and there is diversity even among the bone muduks. The truth is that early workers, myself included, selected an ideal type and then blurred the edges of distinction by treating deviations from this ideal as atypical, even though the deviations possessed inherent definable characteristics. Today, in common with the trend in archaeology around the world, the analysis of artifacts in Australia has shifted away from the subjective methods of the past toward laborious quantitative definition. Most assemblages that have been excavated recently are undergoing rigorous statistical investigation. The Bondaian-Eloueran problem should benefit from this objective approach.

I have presented evidence in support of the view that Australian prehistory can be divided into two phases, distinguishable by a change in technology from the exclusive use of nonhafted, hand-held stone artifacts to the employment of many specialized stone artifacts that were hafted to form composite implements. What of the people who used these nonhafted and hafted tools? Some of the most interesting evidence for the antiquity of man in Australia comes from gravel quarries at Keilor on the outskirts of Melbourne, where a creek has cut a series of terraces. A human skull was unearthed there in 1940, but its exact origin became a matter of dispute. In attempting to resolve the controversy, Edmund D. Gill of the National Museum of Victoria has obtained a series of carbon-14 dates for the Keilor quarries; his earliest date, centered around 16,000 B.C., is for charcoal taken from a point some feet below the 1940 level of the quarry floor. The crucial issue is whether this charcoal is from an aboriginal campfire or from some natural conflagration. The fact that a number of stone artifacts have been found in the creek bed and embedded in the banks of the terraces does not automatically mean that the charcoal is also the work of men. These objects lack the authority of artifacts excavated from undisturbed stratified de-

EXCAVATION AT KENNIFF CAVE revealed evidence of human occupation from about the 14th millennium B.C. until the present. The paler strata along the walls of the 11-foot pit represent periods when the shelter was virtually deserted by prehistoric hunters; the darker strata are rich in organic material. The outline paintings of human hands on the overhanging rock were made by aboriginal tribesmen who have used the shelter during recent years.

posits under well-controlled conditions.

In 1965 the evidence favoring the authentic antiquity of the Keilor skull suddenly multiplied. Two miles from the scene of the 1940 discovery earth-moving equipment exposed a human skeleton that was in a fair state of preservation. Preliminary indications are that the skeleton belongs to the same level of terrace as that proposed for the Keilor skull. Charcoal is plentiful at the site, although some of it—tree roots that were burned where they had grown—is clearly the work not of man but of nature. Artifacts are also present. Obviously men lived here during the period of terrace formation, and carbon-14 determinations should establish the age of the site. The National Museum of Victoria is coordinating the investigations now under way at Keilor.

Man may have arrived in Australia at the time of the continent's climatic climax, when inland rivers flowed, lakes brimmed and the giant herbivorous marsupials flourished. In any case he almost certainly played a role in altering the ecological character of the continent (and, less directly, the soil) through selective hunting activities and frequent burning of vegetation. One ecological effect resulted from man's introduction of the dog. Man and the dingo together represented a scourge to the prehistoric fauna; the two were virtually the sole predatory carnivores on the continent. What caused the extermination of numerous marsupial species: man and dog or climatic change? The findings at Fromm's Landing indicate that the two carnivores played their part. There is nothing in the evidence to imply that, during the 5,000 years spanned by the deposits at the site,

there were important fluctuations in climate that might have exerted an ecological influence. Mammal bones identified at Fromm's Landing represent 685 individuals of 31 species. In two cases—*Sarcophilus,* the Tasmanian devil, and *Thylacinus,* the Tasmanian wolf—there are indications that the species became extinct there during the second millennium B.C. It is relevant that a 3,000-year-old stratum at the site has yielded the skeleton of a dingo; this is the earliest authenticated occurrence of the dingo in Australia.

What were the racial origins of the prehistoric Australians? This question has been much debated, but the debate is conducted virtually in a vacuum because of the scarcity of early human fossils in Australia. Until the discovery of the Keilor skeleton there was not one such fossil whose authenticity was unchallengeable. Now the Keilor skull found in 1940—and perhaps a badly crushed skull from Talgai in Queensland—may gain a more respectable status. Still, two or three specimens make a small sample for determining the origin of a race. Two fossil skulls found at Wadjak in Java, to the northwest of Australia, have been proposed as a link in aboriginal evolution; these fossils, however, remain undated. A skull from the Niah Caves in Sarawak, to the north of Java, is possibly 40,000 years old and has also been compared with prehistoric Australian remains. Caution must be the keynote when there are such wide spatial gaps in the fieldwork and so few fossils.

The origin of the prehistoric inhabitants of Tasmania, the large island to the south of Australia, also remains

an open subject. The last Tasmanians (none survived the 19th century) were an ethnographic rarity: a society using stone tools without hafts of any kind. Studies of changes in the sea level during Pleistocene times have made it a tenable theory that the Tasmanians walked to Tasmania from Australia when the intervening strait was dry land; carbon-14 estimates have established their presence in Tasmania 8,000 years ago. During the past two years Rhys Jones of the University of Sydney has achieved striking success in fieldwork in northern Tasmania. When his carbon samples are dated and his human skeletal material is analyzed, Tasmanian archaeology will have entered an objective era.

Now that it seems certain that Australia was colonized in Pleistocene times, the inadequacy of evidence on this period not only in Australia but also in its northern neighbors such as New Guinea is painfully apparent. If we are to retrace the steps of Australia's first colonists, detailed studies of changes in the sea level are required. If we are to seek out their early patterns of settlement, we need far more precise dating of environmental changes in the continent's interior. With much of Australia archaeologically unexplored, with increasing numbers of investigators undertaking fieldwork and with carbon-14 chronologies providing new perspectives, these are exciting times for the study of the continent's prehistory. It is certain that during the next few years the nearly blank outline map of that prehistory will come to be filled with detail.

Homo Erectus

WILLIAM W. HOWELLS
November 1966

In 1891 Eugène Dubois, a young Dutch anatomist bent on discovering early man, was examining a fossil-rich layer of gravels beside the Solo River in Java. He found what he was after: an ancient human skull. The next year he discovered in the same formation a human thighbone. These two fossils, now known to be more than 700,000 years old, were the first remains to be found of the prehistoric human species known today as *Homo erectus*. It is appropriate on the 75th anniversary of Dubois's discovery to review how our understanding of this early man has been broadened and clarified by more recent discoveries of fossil men of similar antiquity and the same general characteristics, so that *Homo erectus* is now viewed as representing a major stage in the evolution of man. Also of interest, although of less consequence, is the way in which the name *Homo erectus*, now accepted by many scholars, has been chosen after a long period during which "scientific" names for human fossils were bestowed rather capriciously.

Man first received his formal name in 1758, when Carolus Linnaeus called him *Homo sapiens*. Linnaeus was trying simply to bring order to the world of living things by distinguishing each species of plant and animal from every other and by arranging them all in a hierarchical system. Considering living men, he recognized them quite correctly as one species in the system. The two centuries that followed Linnaeus saw first the establishment of evolutionary theory and then the realization of its genetic foundations; as a result ideas on the relations of species as units of plant and animal life have become considerably more complex. For example, a species can form two or more new species, which Linnaeus originally thought was impossible. By today's definition a species typically consists of a series of local or regional populations that may exhibit minor differences of form or color but that otherwise share a common genetic structure and pool of genes and are thus able to interbreed across population lines. Only when two such populations have gradually undergone so many different changes in their genetic makeup that the likelihood of their interbreeding falls below a critical point are they genetically cut off from each other and do they become separate species. Alternatively, over a great many generations an equivalent amount of change will take place in the same population, so that its later form will be recognized as a species different from the earlier. This kind of difference, of course, cannot be put to the test of interbreeding and can only be judged by the physical form of the fossils involved.

In the case of living man there is no reason to revise Linnaeus' assignment: *Homo sapiens* is a good, typical species. Evolution, however, was not in Linnaeus' ken. He never saw a human fossil, much less conceived of men different from living men. Between his time and ours the use of the Linnaean system of classification as applied to man and his relatives past and present became almost a game. On grasping the concept of evolution, scholars saw that modern man must have had ancestors. They were prepared to anticipate the actual discovery of these ancestral forms, and perhaps the greatest anticipator was the German biologist Ernst Haeckel. Working on the basis of fragmentary information in 1889, when the only well-known fossil human remains were the comparatively recent bones discovered 25 years earlier in the Neander Valley of Germany, Haeckel drew up a theoretical ancestral line for man. The line began among some postulated extinct apes of the Miocene epoch and reached *Homo sapiens* by way of an imagined group of "ape-men" (Pithecanthropi) and a group of more advanced but still speechless early men (Alali) whom he visualized as the worldwide stock from which modern men had evolved [*see illustration on page 266*]. A creature combining these various presapient attributes took form in the pooled imagination of Haeckel and his compatriots August Schleicher and Gabriel Max. Max produced a family portrait, and the still-to-be-discovered ancestor was given the respectable Linnaean name *Pithecanthropus alalus*.

Were he living today Haeckel would never do such a thing. It is now the requirement of the International Code of Zoological Nomenclature that the naming of any new genus or species be supported by publication of the specimen's particulars together with a description showing it to be recognizably different from any genus or species previously known. Haeckel was rescued from retroactive embarrassment, however, by Dubois, who gave Haeckel's genus name to Java man. The skull was too large to be an ape's and apparently too small to be a man's; the name *Pithecanthropus* seemed perfectly appropriate. On the other hand, the thighbone from the same formation was essentially modern; its possessor had evidently walked upright. Dubois therefore gave his discovery the species name *erectus*. Since Dubois's time the legitimacy of his finds has been confirmed by the discovery in Java (by G. H. R. von Koenigswald between 1936 and 1939 and by Indonesian workers within the past three years) of equally old and older fossils of the same population.

In the 50 years between Dubois's discovery and the beginning of World

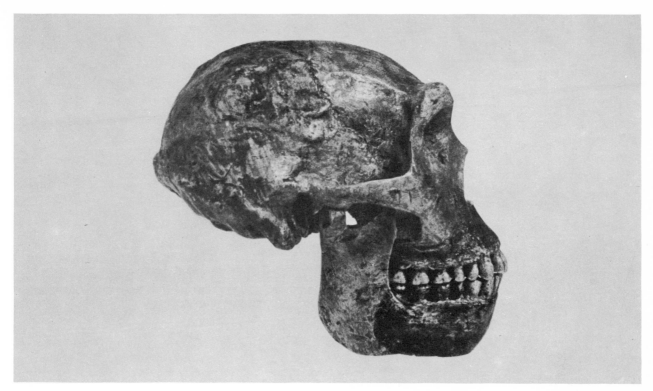

JAVA MAN, whose 700,000-year-old remains were unearthed in 1891 by Eugène Dubois, is representative of the earliest *Homo erectus* population so far discovered. This reconstruction was made recently by G. H. R. von Koenigswald and combines the features of the more primitive members of this species of man that he found in the lowest (Djetis) fossil strata at Sangiran in central Java during the 1930's. The characteristics that are typical of *Homo erectus* include the smallness and flatness of the cranium, the heavy browridge and both the sharp bend and the ridge for muscle attachment at the rear of the skull. The robustness of the jaws adds to the species' primitive appearance. In most respects except size, however, the teeth of *Homo erectus* resemble those of modern man.

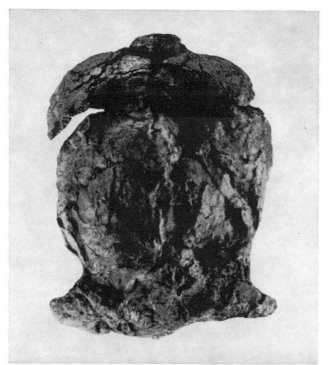

LANTIAN MAN is the most recently found *Homo erectus* fossil. The discovery consists of a jawbone and this skullcap (*top view, browridge at bottom*) from which the occipital bone (*top*) is partially detached. Woo Ju-kang of the Chinese Academy of Sciences in Peking provided the photograph; this fossil man from Shensi may be as old as the earliest specimens of *Homo erectus* from Java.

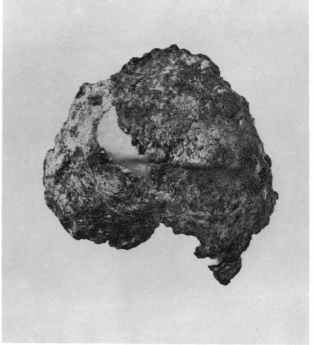

OCCIPITAL BONE found at Vértesszöllös in Hungary in 1965 is 500,000 or more years old. The only older human fossil in Europe is the Heidelberg jaw. The bone forms the rear of a skull; the ridge for muscle attachment (*horizontal line*) is readily apparent. In spite of this primitive feature and its great age, the skull fragment from Vértesszöllös has been assigned to the species *Homo sapiens*.

War II various other important new kinds of human fossil came into view. For our purposes the principal ones (with some of the Linnaean names thrust on them) were (1) the lower jaw found at Mauer in Germany in 1907 (*Homo heidelbergensis* or *Palaeanthropus*), (2) the nearly complete skull found at Broken Hill in Rhodesia in 1921 (*Homo rhodesiensis* or *Cyphanthropus*), (3) various remains uncovered near Peking in China, beginning with one tooth in 1923 and finally comprising a collection representing more than 40 men, women and children by the end of 1937 (*Sinanthropus pekinensis*), and (4) several skulls found in 1931 and 1932 near Ngandong on the Solo River not far from where Dubois had worked (*Homo soloensis* or *Javanthropus*). This is a fair number of fossils, but they were threatened with being outnumbered by the names assigned to them. The British student of early man Bernard G. Campbell has recorded the following variants in the case of the Mauer jawbone alone: *Palaeanthropus heidelbergensis*, *Pseudhomo heidelbergensis*, *Protanthropus heidelbergensis*, *Praehomo heidelbergensis*, *Praehomo europaeus*, *Anthropus heidelbergensis*, *Maueranthropus heidelbergensis*, *Europanthropus heidelbergensis* and *Euranthropus*.

Often the men responsible for these redundant christenings were guilty merely of innocent grandiloquence. They were not formally declaring their conviction that each fossil hominid belonged to a separate genus, distinct from *Homo*, which would imply an enormous diversity in the human stock. Nonetheless, the multiplicity of names has interfered with an understanding of the evolutionary significance of the fossils that bore them. Moreover, the human family trees drawn during this period showed a fundamental resemblance to Haeckel's original venture; the rather isolated specimens of early man were stuck on here and there like Christmas-tree ornaments. Although the arrangements evinced a vague consciousness of evolution, no scheme was presented that intelligibly interpreted the fossil record.

At last two questions came to the fore. First, to what degree did the fossils really differ? Second, what was the difference among them over a period of time? The fossil men of the most recent period—those who had lived between roughly 100,000 and 30,000 years ago—were Neanderthal man, Rhodesian man and Solo man. They have been known traditionally as *Homo neanderthalensis*, *Homo rhodesiensis* and *Homo soloensis*, names that declare each of the three to be a separate species, distinct from one another and from *Homo sapiens*. This in turn suggests that if Neanderthal and Rhodesian populations had come in contact, they would probably not have interbred. Such a conclusion is difficult to establish on the basis of fossils, particularly when they are few and tell very little about the geographical range of the species. Today's general view is a contrary one. These comparatively recent fossil men, it is now believed, did not constitute separate species. They were at most incipient species, that is, subspecies or variant populations that had developed in widely separated parts of the world but were still probably able to breed with one another or with *Homo sapiens*.

It was also soon recognized that the older Java and Peking fossils were not very different from one another. The suggestion followed that both populations be placed in a single genus (*Pithecanthropus*) and that the junior name (*Sinanthropus*) be dropped. Even this, however, was one genus too many for Ernst Mayr of Harvard University. Mayr, whose specialty is the evolutionary basis of biological classification, declared that ordinary zoological standards would not permit Java and Peking man to occupy

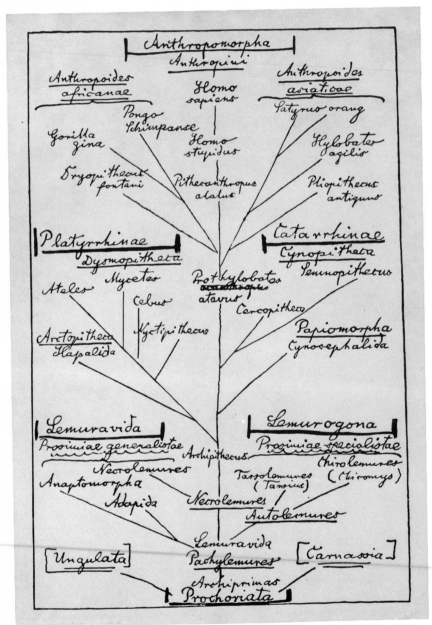

THE NAME "PITHECANTHROPUS," or ape-man, was coined by the German biologist Ernst Haeckel in 1889 for a postulated precursor of *Homo sapiens*. Haeckel placed the ape-man genus two steps below modern man on his "tree" of primate evolution, adding the species name *alalus*, or "speechless," because he deemed speech an exclusively human trait.

GRADE	EUROPE	NORTH AFRICA	EAST AFRICA	SOUTH AFRICA	EAST ASIA	SOUTHEAST ASIA
(5)	*HOMO SAPIENS (VÉRTESSZÖLLÖS)*					
(4)						*(HOMO ERECTUS SOLOENSIS)*
3	*HOMO ERECTUS HEIDELBERGENSIS*	*HOMO ERECTUS MAURITANICUS*	*HOMO ERECTUS LEAKEYI*		*HOMO ERECTUS PEKINENSIS*	
2						*HOMO ERECTUS ERECTUS*
1			*HOMO ERECTUS HABILIS*	*HOMO ERECTUS CAPENSIS*	*(HOMO ERECTUS LANTIANENSIS)*	*HOMO ERECTUS MODJOKERTENSIS*

EIGHT SUBSPECIES of *Homo erectus* that are generally accepted today have been given appropriate names and ranked in order of evolutionary progress by the British scholar Bernard G. Campbell. The author has added Lantian man to Campbell's lowest *Homo* *erectus* grade and provided a fourth grade to accommodate Solo man, a late but primitive survival. The author has also added a fifth grade for the *Homo sapiens* fossil from Vértesszöllös (*color*). Colored area suggests that Heidelberg man is its possible forebear.

a genus separate from modern man. In his opinion the amount of evolutionary progress that separates *Pithecanthropus* from ourselves is a step that allows the recognition only of a different species. After all, Java and Peking man apparently had bodies just like our own; that is to say, they were attacking the problem of survival with exactly the same adaptations, although with smaller brains. On this view Java man is placed in the genus *Homo* but according to the rules retains his original species name and so becomes *Homo erectus*. Under the circumstances Peking man can be distinguished from him only as a subspecies: *Homo erectus pekinensis*.

The simplification is something more than sweeping out a clutter of old names to please the International Commission on Zoological Nomenclature. The reduction of fossil hominids to not more than two species and the recognition of *Homo erectus* has become increasingly useful as a way of looking at a stage of human evolution. This has been increasingly evident in recent years, as human fossils have continued to come to light and as new and improved methods of dating them have been developed. It is now possible to place both the old discoveries and the new ones much more precisely in time, and that is basic to establishing the entire pattern of human evolution in the past few million years.

To consider dating first, the period during which *Homo erectus* flourished occupies the early middle part of the Pleistocene epoch. The evidence that now enables us to subdivide the Pleistocene with some degree of confidence is of several kinds. For example, the fossil animals found in association with fossil men often indicate whether the climate of the time was cold or warm. The comparison of animal communities is also helpful in correlating intervals of time on one continent with intervals on another. The ability to determine absolute dates, which makes possible the correlation of the relative dates derived from sequences of strata in widely separated localities, is another significant development. Foremost among the methods of absolute dating at the moment is one based on the rate of decay of radioactive potassium into argon. A second method showing much promise is the analysis of deep-sea sediments; changes in the forms of planktonic life embedded in samples of the bottom reflect worldwide temperature changes. When the absolute ages of key points in sediment sequences are determined by physical or chemical methods, it ought to be possible to assign dates to all the major events of the Pleistocene. Such methods have already suggested that the epoch began more than three million years ago and that its first major cold phase (corresponding to the Günz

glaciation of the Alps) may date back to as much as 1.5 million years ago. The period of time occupied by *Homo erectus* now appears to extend from about a million years ago to 500,000 years ago in terms of absolute dates, or from some time during the first interglacial period in the Northern Hemisphere to about the end of the second major cold phase (corresponding to the Mindel glaciation of the Alps).

On the basis of the fossils found before World War II, with the exception of the isolated and somewhat peculiar Heidelberg jaw, *Homo erectus* would have appeared to be a human population of the Far East. The Java skulls, particularly those that come from the lowest fossil strata (known as the Djetis beds), are unsurpassed within the entire group in primitiveness. Even the skulls from the strata above them (the Trinil beds), in which Dubois made his original discovery, have very thick walls and room for only a small brain. Their cranial capacity probably averages less than 900 cubic centimeters, compared with an average of 500 c.c. for gorillas and about 1,400 c.c. for modern man. The later representatives of Java man must be more than 710,000 years old, because potassium-argon analysis has shown that tektites (glassy stones formed by or from meteorites) in higher strata of the same formation are of that age.

The Peking fossils are younger, probably dating to the middle of the second Pleistocene cold phase, and are physically somewhat less crude than the Java ones. The braincase is higher, the face shorter and the cranial capacity approaches 1,100 c.c., but the general construction of skull and jaw is similar. The teeth of both Java man and Peking man are somewhat larger than modern man's and are distinguished by traces of an enamel collar, called a cingulum, around some of the crowns. The latter is an ancient and primitive trait in man and apes.

Discoveries of human fossils after World War II have added significantly to the picture of man's distribution at this period. The pertinent finds are the following:

1949: Swartkrans, South Africa. Jaw and facial fragments, originally given the name *Telanthropus capensis*. These were found among the copious remains at this site of the primitive subhumans known as australopithecines. The fossils were recognized at once by the late Robert Broom and his colleague John T. Robinson as more advanced than the australopithecines both in size and in traits of jaw and teeth. Robinson has now assigned *Telanthropus* to *Homo erectus,* since that is where he evidently belongs.

1955: Ternifine, Algeria. Three jaws and a parietal bone, given the name *Atlanthropus mauritanicus,* were found under a deep covering of sand on the clay floor of an ancient pond by Camille Arambourg. The teeth and jaws show a strong likeness to the Peking remains.

1961: Olduvai Gorge, Tanzania. A skullcap, not formally named but identified as the Bed II Hominid, was discovered by L. S. B. Leakey. Found in a context with a provisional potassium-argon date of 500,000 years ago, the skull's estimated cranial capacity is 1,000 c.c. Although differing somewhat in detail, it has the general characteristics of the two Far Eastern subspecies of *Homo erectus.* At lower levels in this same important site were found the remains of a number of individuals with small skulls, now collectively referred to as "Homo habilis."

1963–1964: Lantian district, Shensi, China. A lower jaw and a skullcap were found by Chinese workers at two separate localities in the district and given the name *Sinanthropus lantianensis.* Animal fossils indicate that the Lantian sites are older than the one that yielded Peking man and roughly as old as the lowest formation in Java. The form of the skull and jaw accords well with this

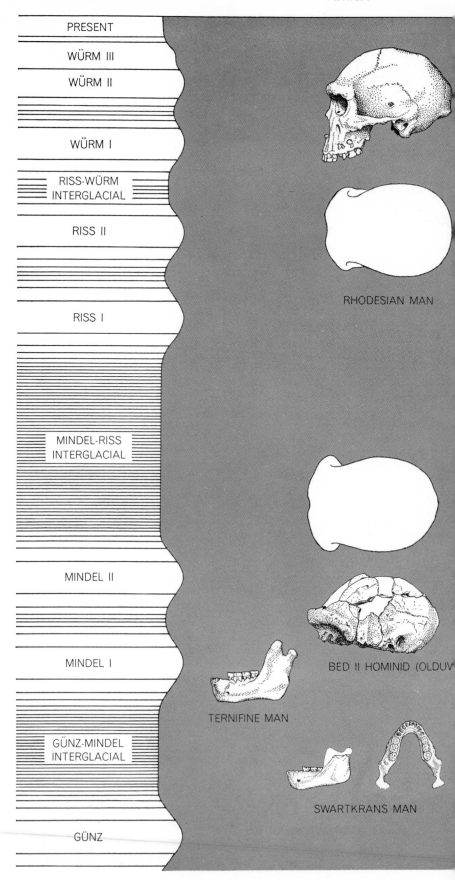

PRESENT

WÜRM III

WÜRM II

WÜRM I

RISS-WÜRM INTERGLACIAL

RISS II

RISS I

MINDEL-RISS INTERGLACIAL

MINDEL II

MINDEL I

GÜNZ-MINDEL INTERGLACIAL

GÜNZ

RHODESIAN MAN

BED II HOMINID (OLDUV

TERNIFINE MAN

SWARTKRANS MAN

FOSSIL EVIDENCE for the existence of a single species of early man instead of several species and genera of forerunners of *Homo sapiens* is presented in this array of individual remains whose age places them in the interval of approximately 500,000 years that separates the first Pleistocene interglacial period from the end of the second glacial period (*see scale at left*). The earliest *Homo erectus* fossils known, from Java and China, belong to the first interglacial period; the earliest *Homo erectus* remains from South Africa may be equally

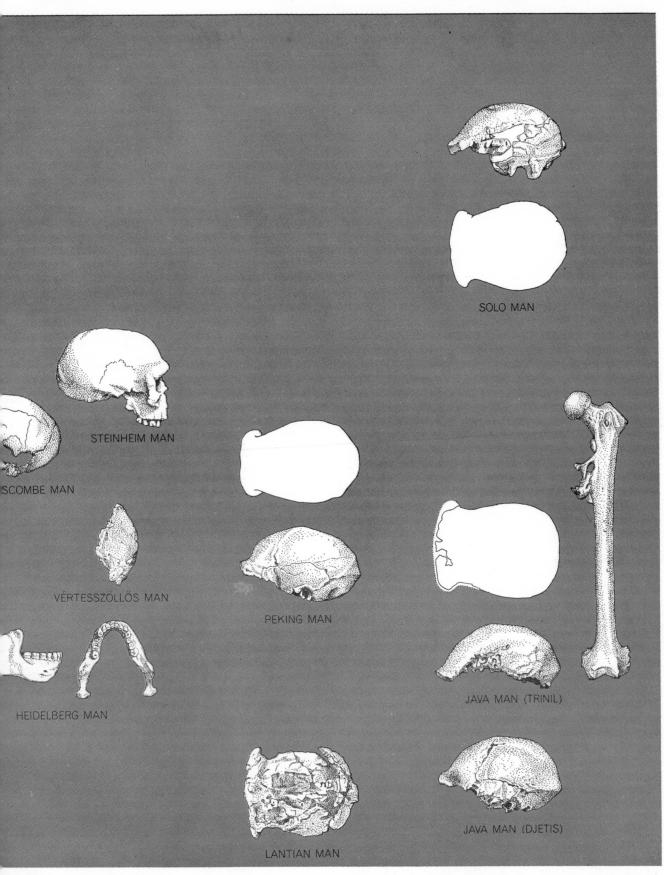

EUROPE   CHINA   JAVA

SOLO MAN

STEINHEIM MAN

SCOMBE MAN

VÉRTESSZÖLLÖS MAN

PEKING MAN

JAVA MAN (TRINIL)

HEIDELBERG MAN

LANTIAN MAN

JAVA MAN (DJETIS)

old. Half a million years later *Homo erectus* continued to be represented in China by the remains of Peking man and in Africa by the skull from Olduvai Gorge. In the intervening period this small-brained precursor of modern man was not the only human species inhabiting the earth, nor did *Homo erectus* become extinct when the 500,000-year period ended. One kind of man who had apparent-ly reached the grade of *Homo sapiens* in Europe by the middle or later part of the second Pleistocene glacial period was unearthed recently at Vértesszöllös in Hungary. In the following inter-glacial period *Homo sapiens* is represented by the Steinheim and Swanscombe females. Solo man's remains indicate that *Homo erectus* survived for several hundred thousand years after that.

dating; both are distinctly more primitive than the Peking fossils. Both differ somewhat in detail from the Java subspecies of *Homo erectus,* but the estimated capacity of this otherwise large skull (780 c.c.) is small and close to that of the earliest fossil cranium unearthed in Java.

1965: Vértesszöllös, Hungary. An isolated occipital bone (in the back of the skull) was found by L. Vértes. This skull fragment is the first human fossil from the early middle Pleistocene to be unearthed in Europe since the Heidelberg jaw. It evidently dates to the middle or later part of the Mindel glaciation and thus falls clearly within the *Homo erectus* time zone as defined here. The bone is moderately thick and shows a well-defined ridge for the attachment of neck muscles such as is seen in all the *erectus* skulls. It is unlike *erectus* occipital bones, however, in that it is both large and definitely less angled; these features indicate a more advanced skull.

In addition to these five discoveries, something else of considerable importance happened during this period. The Piltdown fraud, perpetrated sometime before 1912, was finally exposed in 1953. The detective work of J. S. Weiner, Sir Wilfrid Le Gros Clark and Kenneth Oakley removed from the fossil record a supposed hominid with a fully apelike jaw and manlike skull that could scarcely be fitted into any sensible evolutionary scheme.

From this accumulation of finds, many of them made so recently, there emerges a picture of men with skeletons like ours but with brains much smaller, skulls much thicker and flatter and furnished with protruding brows in front and a marked angle in the rear, and with teeth somewhat larger and exhibiting a few slightly more primitive traits. This picture suggests an evolutionary level, or grade, occupying half a million years of human history and now seen

to prevail all over the inhabited Old World. This is the meaning of *Homo erectus.* It gives us a new foundation for ideas as to the pace and the pattern of human evolution over a critical span of time.

Quite possibly this summary is too tidy; before the 100th anniversary of the resurrection of *Homo erectus* is celebrated complications may appear that we cannot perceive at present. Even today there are a number of fringe problems we cannot neglect. Here are some of them.

What was the amount of evolution taking place within the *erectus* grade? There is probably a good deal of accident of discovery involved in defining *Homo erectus.* Chance, in other words, may have isolated a segment of a continuum, since finds from the time immediately following this 500,000-year period are almost lacking. It seems likely, in fact practically certain, that real evolutionary progress was taking place,

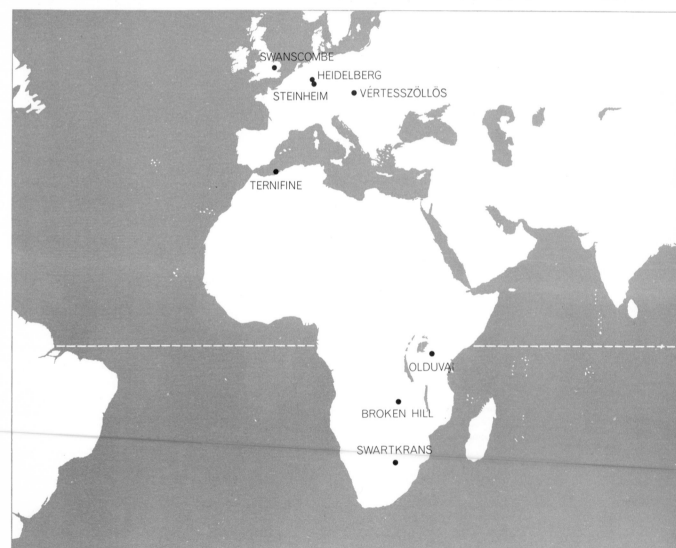

DISTRIBUTION of *Homo erectus* seemed to be confined mainly to the Far East and Southeast Asia on the basis of fossils unearthed before World War II; the sole exception was the Heidelberg jaw. Postwar findings in South, East and North Africa, as well as dis-

but the tools made by man during this period reveal little of it. As for the fossils themselves, the oldest skulls—from Java and Lantian—are the crudest and have the smallest brains. In Java, one region with some discernible stratigraphy, the later skulls show signs of evolutionary advance compared with the earlier ones. The Peking skulls, which are almost certainly later still, are even more progressive. Bernard Campbell, who has recently suggested that all the known forms of *Homo erectus* be formally recognized as named subspecies, has arranged the names in the order of their relative progressiveness. I have added some names to Campbell's list; they appear in parentheses in the illustration on page 267. As the illustration indicates, the advances in grade seem indeed to correspond fairly well with the passage of time.

What are the relations of *Homo erectus* to Rhodesian and Solo man? This is a point of particular importance, be-

covery of a new *Homo erectus* site in northern China, have extended the species' range.

cause both the African and the Javanese fossils are much younger than the date we have set as the general upward boundary for *Homo erectus*. Rhodesian man may have been alive as recently as 30,000 years ago and may have actually overlapped with modern man. Solo man probably existed during the last Pleistocene cold phase; this is still very recent compared with the time zone of the other *erectus* fossils described here. Carleton S. Coon of the University of Pennsylvania deems both late fossil men to be *Homo erectus* on the basis of tooth size and skull flatness. His placing of Rhodesian man is arguable, but Solo man is so primitive, so like Java man in many aspects of his skull form and so close to Peking man in brain size that his classification as *Homo erectus* seems almost inevitable. The meaning of his survival hundreds of thousands of years after the period I have suggested, and his relation to the modern men who succeeded him in Southeast Asia in recent times, are unanswered questions of considerable importance.

Where did *Homo erectus* come from? The Swartkrans discovery makes it clear that he arose before the last representatives of the australopithecines had died out at that site. The best present evidence of his origin is also from Africa; it consists of the series of fossils unearthed at Olduvai Gorge by Leakey and his wife and called Homo habilis. These remains seem to reflect a transition from an australopithecine level to an *erectus* level about a million years ago. This date seems almost too late, however, when one considers the age of *Homo erectus* finds elsewhere in the world, particularly in Java.

Where did *Homo erectus* go? The paths are simply untraced, both those that presumably lead to the Swanscombe and Steinheim people of Europe during the Pleistocene's second interglacial period and those leading to the much later Rhodesian and Neanderthal men. This is a period lacking useful evidence. Above all, the nature of the line leading to living man—*Homo sapiens* in the Linnaean sense—remains a matter of pure theory.

We may, however, have a clue. Here it is necessary to face a final problem. What was the real variation in physical type during the time period of *Homo erectus*? On the whole, considering the time and space involved, it does not appear to be very large; the similarity of the North African jaws to those of Peking man, for example, is striking in spite of the thousands of

miles that separated the two populations. The Heidelberg jaw, however, has always seemed to be somewhat different from all the others and a little closer to modern man in the nature of its teeth. The only other European fossil approaching the Heidelberg jaw in antiquity is the occipital bone recently found at Vértesszöllös. This piece of skull likewise appears to be progressive in form and may have belonged to the same general kind of man as the Heidelberg jaw, although it is somewhat more recent in date.

Andor Thoma of Hungary's Kossuth University at Debrecen in Hungary, who has kindly given me information concerning the Vértesszöllös fossil, will publish a formal description soon in the French journal *L'Anthropologie*. He estimates that the cranial capacity was about 1,400 c.c., close to the average for modern man and well above that of the known specimens of *Homo erectus*. Although the occipital bone is thick, it is larger and less sharply angled than the matching skull area of Rhodesian man. It is certainly more modern-looking than the Solo skulls. I see no reason at this point to dispute Thoma's estimate of brain volume. He concludes that Vértesszöllös man had in fact reached the *sapiens* grade in skull form and brain size and accordingly has named him a subspecies of *Homo sapiens*.

Thoma's finding therefore places a population of more progressive, *sapiens* humanity contemporary with the populations of *Homo erectus* 500,000 years ago or more. From the succeeding interglacial period in Europe have come the Swanscombe and Steinheim skulls, generally recognized as *sapiens* in grade. They are less heavy than the Hungarian fossil, more curved in occipital profile and smaller in size; they are also apparently both female, which would account for part of these differences.

The trail of evidence is of course faint, but there are no present signs of contradiction; what we may be seeing is a line that follows *Homo sapiens* back from Swanscombe and Steinheim to Vértesszöllös and finally to Heidelberg man at the root. This is something like the Solo case in reverse, a *Homo sapiens* population surprisingly early in time, in contrast to a possible *Homo erectus* population surprisingly late. In fact, we are seeing only the outlines of what we must still discover. It is easy to perceive how badly we need more fossils; for example, we cannot relate Heidelberg man to any later Europeans until we find some skull parts to add to his solitary jaw.

27

The Early Relatives of Man

ELWYN L. SIMONS

July 1964

A major feature of biological evolution during the past 70 million years has been the rapid rise to a position of dominance among the earth's land-dwelling vertebrates of the placental mammals (mammals other than marsupials such as the kangaroo and primitive egg-laying species such as the platypus). A major feature, in turn, of the evolution of the placental mammals has been the emergence of the primates: the mammalian order that includes man, the apes and monkeys. And a major event in the evolution of the primates was the appearance 12 million to 14 million years ago of animals, distinct from their ape contemporaries, that apparently gave rise to man.

Much of the evidence of the origin of man is new, but by no means all of it. For many years students of human evolution have broadly agreed that man's earliest ancestor would be found among the apelike primates that flourished during Miocene and early Pliocene times, roughly from 24 million to 12 million years ago [*see illustration on page 277*]. As long ago as the 1920's William K. Gregory of the American Museum of Natural History, after studying the limited number of jaw fragments and teeth then available, flatly pronounced man to be "a late Tertiary offshoot of the *Dryopithecus-Sivapithecus* group, or at least of apes that closely resembled those genera in the construction of jaw and dentition."

Until recently students of primate evolution have had little more evidence to work with than Gregory and his contemporaries did. Within the past 15 years, however, a number of significant new finds have been made—some of them in existing fossil collections. The early primates are now represented by many complete or nearly complete skulls, some nearly complete skeletons,

a number of limb bones and even the bones of hands and feet. In age these specimens extend across almost the entire Cenozoic era, from its beginning in the Paleocene epoch some 63 million years ago up to the Pliocene, which ended roughly two million years ago.

Sometimes a single jaw can tell a remarkably detailed evolutionary story, but there are no greater paleontological treasures than reasonably complete skulls and skeletons. Many such specimens have become available in recent years, but they do not lie in the exact line of man's ancestry. They are nonetheless important to the evolutionary history of all the primates. Both by their relative completeness and by their wide distribution in time they reveal new details concerning the main stages through which the primates probably passed during their evolutionary development.

To describe these stages is one of the two objectives of this article. The other objective is to summarize what is known about the relation of the early primates to the primate order's more advanced lineages, including man's own family: the Hominidae. The accomplishment of these objectives will show that the weight of today's knowledge fortifies Gregory's declaration of the 1920's.

Subdividing the Primates

Ideally zoological classification uses standard suffixes to guide the student through the maze of descending divisions: from class to order and thence —by way of suborders, infraorders, superfamilies, families, subfamilies and the like—to a particular genus and species. The grammar of primate taxonomy is not this simple. Two factors are responsible. First, there is no international agreement as to how the order of primates should be subdivided. Sec-

ond, generations of literary usage preceding man's first awareness of evolution have made all nouns derived from the Greek *anthropos* or the Latin *homo* virtually synonymous.

Nonetheless, an ability to read these taxonomic signposts is vital to an under

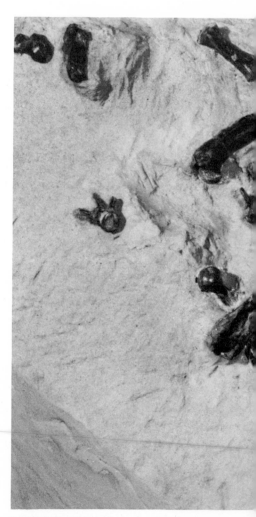

EARLY PRIMATE, about the size of a cat, was discovered in a Wyoming fossil deposit of middle Eocene age. One of the prosim-

standing not only of the relations among the 50-odd genera of living primates but also of the positions assigned to various extinct primates. This is because modern classification interrelates organisms in a pattern that reflects their evolutionary relations. In tracing the subdivisions that lead to man, for example, the first major branching divides the whole group of living primates into two suborders [*see illustration on the next two pages*]. The less advanced primates are assigned to the Prosimii; they are the various tree shrews, the many kinds of lemurs, the less abundant lorises and the solitary genus of tarsiers. The earliest known fossil primates belong exclusively to this suborder. The line to man, however, runs through successive divisions of the second primate suborder.

This suborder, consisting of the more advanced primates, is the Anthropoidea. It is divided into two infraorders. The less advanced anthropoids, including all the primates native to the New World, are the Platyrrhini. "Platyr-rhine," which literally means "broad-nosed," refers to the wide spacing of the nostrils that is characteristic of the New World anthropoids.

The more advanced anthropoids are the Catarrhini. They include all other living anthropoids: the Old World monkeys, the apes and man himself. "Catarrhine" is opposed to "platyrrhine"; it literally means "hooknosed" but refers to a close spacing of the nostrils. The catarrhine infraorder is in turn divided into two superfamilies: the Cercopithecoidea and the Hominoidea. The first of these means "apes with tails"; it embraces the two subfamilies and 13 genera of living Old World monkeys.

The second catarrhine superfamily, the Hominoidea, embraces the subdivisions that finally separate the genus *Homo* from the rest of the living primates. The hominoids are split three ways: the families Hylobatidae, Pongidae and Hominidae. The first of these takes its name from *Hylobates*, the gibbon of South Asia, and includes both this hominoid primate and the closely related siamang of Sumatra. The family Pongidae embraces the three genera of great apes: *Pongo,* the orangutan; *Pan,* the chimpanzee, and *Gorilla,* whose scientific name is the same as the common.

Of the family Hominidae, however complex its subfamilies and genera may or may not once have been, there survives today only the single genus *Homo* and its single species *Homo sapiens.* Man, then, is the sole living representative of the hominid family within the hominoid superfamily of the catarrhine infraorder of anthropoids. Or, to reverse the order of classification, among the 33 or so living genera of Anthropoidea whose names are accepted as valid there are only six genera of hominoids and a single hominid genus.

A Paleocene Tree-Dweller

The Age of Mammals was ushered in some 63 million years ago by a brief geological epoch: the Paleocene. Last-

ians, the less advanced of the two major divisions of the primate order, it is a member of the genus *Notharctus* and so belongs to a once abundant subfamily of tree-dwelling primates. Although primitive, the latter had many features in common with today's lemurs. They did not, however, give rise to any living prosimians and were extinct before the end of the Eocene, 36 million years ago.

ing perhaps five million years, the Paleocene was followed by the much longer Eocene epoch, which occupied roughly the next 22 million years. Both periods seem to have been characterized by warm temperatures that permitted tropical and subtropical forests to extend much farther north and south of the Equator than is the case today. These forests were inhabited by a diverse and abundant population of primates [*see illustration on page 277*]. The fossil record shows that species belonging to nearly 60 genera of prosimians, the bulk of them grouped in eight families, inhabited the Northern Hemisphere during Paleocene and Eocene times.

Three of these eight prosimian families are characterized by elongated front teeth, presumably adapted for chiseling and gnawing, as are the rather similar teeth of today's rodents and rabbits. It seems reasonable to suppose that these early primates started their evolutionary careers in competition for some kind of nibblers' and gnawers' niche in the warm forests. They were not successful; before the middle of the Eocene all three chisel-toothed prosimian families had become extinct. Perhaps they were put out of business by the rodents, which became abundant as these prosimians were dying out.

The skeletal remains of a member of one of these extinct families were recently found by D. E. Russell of the French national museum of natural history in late Paleocene strata near Cernay-lez-Reims in France. This early fossil primate belongs to the genus *Plesiadapis,* and the Cernay discovery includes a remarkably complete skull and a relatively complete series of limb and foot bones. An incomplete *Plesiadapis* skeleton is also known from Paleocene deposits in Colorado, and there are numerous jaws, jaw fragments and teeth from many other North American sites. These discoveries in opposite hemispheres, incidentally, make *Plesiadapis* the only genus of primate other than man's own that has inhabited both the Old and the New World.

Species of *Plesiadapis* varied in size from about the size of a squirrel to the size of a housecat. In life they probably looked as much like rodents as they did like primates [*see figure on page 278*]. The patterns of the crowns of *Plesiadapis'* cheek teeth, however, resemble such patterns in lemur-like fossil primates of the Eocene epoch, and the structure of its limb bones links it with such living prosimians as the lemurs of

the island of Madagascar (now the Malagasy Republic).

Plesiadapis is nonetheless distinctive. Its skull has a small braincase and a long snout. Its enlarged and forward-slanting incisors are widely separated from its cheek teeth. This arrangement is characteristic of the rodents, and although *Plesiadapis* appears too late to be an ancestor of the rodents, some workers have suggested that the order of rodents may be descended from animals not very different from it.

Plesiadapis exhibits two other traits that set the genus apart from almost all later primates. First, most if not all of its fingers and toes ended in long claws that were flattened at the sides. Among living primates only the tree shrews have a claw on each digit; all other species have either a combination of nails and claws or nails exclusively. Moreover, the claws of living primates are small compared with those of *Plesiadapis.* Regardless of their size, these claws probably served the same function as claws do among living tree shrews, helping this ancient arboreal primate to scramble up and down the trunks of trees.

The second peculiar trait, possibly one of lesser significance, is a resemblance between the structure of the middle ear of *Plesiadapis* and that of a nonprimate: the colugo, or "flying lemur," which still inhabits southeast Asia. The first thing to be said of the colugos, as George Gaylord Simpson has put it, is that they "are not lemurs and cannot fly." Colugos are so unusual that taxonomists have been obliged to place them in a mammalian order—the Dermoptera—all their own. The size of a squirrel or larger, with broad flaps of skin for gliding that run from its forelimbs to the tip of its tail, the colugo shows little outward resemblance to any other living mammal. It has been conjectured that the colugos are ultimately

TAXONOMY of the living primates ranks the order's 52 genera (*scientific and common names at far right*) according to divisions of higher grade. There is no universal agreement on how this should be done. For example, the two infraorders of anthropoids in this system are held by many investigators to be suborders and thus equal in rank with the Prosimii. It is generally agreed, however, that man belongs among the catarrhines and, within that group, is a member of the hominoid superfamily (as are all the apes) and the hominid family, in which he is the only living species of the genus *Homo.*

ORDER	SUBORDER	INFRAOR...
		LEMURIFO...
	PROSIMII	
		LORISIFO...
		TARSIIFO...
PRIMATES		PLATYRR...
	ANTHROPOIDEA	
		CATARR...

SUPERFAMILY	FAMILY	SUBFAMILY	GENUS	COMMON NAME
TUPAIOIDEA	TUPAIIDAE	TUPAIINAE	TUPAIA DENDROGALE UROGALE	COMMON TREE SHREW SMOOTH-TAILED TREE SHREW PHILIPPINE TREE SHREW
		PTILOCERCINAE	PTILOCERCUS	PEN-TAILED TREE SHREW
LEMUROIDEA	LEMURIDAE	LEMURINAE	LEMUR HAPALEMUR LEPILEMUR	COMMON LEMUR GENTLE LEMUR SPORTIVE LEMUR
		CHEIROGALEINAE	CHEIROGALEUS MICROCEBUS	MOUSE LEMUR DWARF LEMUR
	INDRIDAE		INDRI LICHANOTUS PROPITHECUS	INDRIS AVAHI SIFAKA
	DAUBENTONIIDAE		DAUBENTONIA	AYE-AYE
LORISOIDEA	LORISIDAE		LORIS NYCTICEBUS ARCTOCEBUS PERODICTICUS	SLENDER LORIS SLOW LORIS ANGWANTIBO POTTO
	GALAGIDAE		GALAGO	BUSH BABY
TARSIOIDEA	TARSIIDAE		TARSIUS	TARSIER
CEBOIDEA	CALLITHRICIDAE		CALLITHRIX LEONTOCEBUS	PLUMED AND PYGMY MARMOSETS TAMARIN
	CEBIDAE	CALLIMICONINAE	CALLIMICO	GOELDI'S MARMOSET
		AOTINAE	AOTES CALLICEBUS	DOUROUCOULI TITI
		PITHECINAE	PITHECIA CHIROPOTES CACAJAO	SAKI SAKI UAKARI
		ALOUATTINAE	ALOUATTA	HOWLER
		CEBINAE	CEBUS SAIMIRI	CAPUCHIN SQUIRREL MONKEY
		ATELINAE	ATELES BRACHYTELES LAGOTHRIX	SPIDER MONKEY WOOLLY SPIDER MONKEY WOOLLY MONKEY
ERCOPITHECOIDEA	CERCOPITHECIDAE	CERCOPITHECINAE	MACACA CYNOPITHECUS CERCOCEBUS PAPIO THEROPITHECUS CERCOPITHECUS ERYTHROCEBUS	MACAQUE BLACK APE MANGABEY BABOON DRILL GELADA GUENON PATAS MONKEY
		COLOBINAE	PRESBYTIS PYGATHRIX RHINOPITHECUS SIMIAS NASALIS COLOBUS	COMMON LANGUR DOUC LANGUR SNUB-NOSED LANGUR PAGI ISLAND LANGUR PROBOSCIS MONKEY GUERAZA
HOMINOIDEA	HYLOBATIDAE		HYLOBATES SYMPHALANGUS	GIBBON SIAMANG
	PONGIDAE		PONGO PAN GORILLA	ORANGUTAN CHIMPANZEE GORILLA
	HOMINIDAE		HOMO	MAN

related to both the primates and the bats. The resemblance in ear structure is not the only similarity between the living colugos and the long-extinct *Plesiadapis:* the colugo's digits also bear sizable claws. Both of these similarities, however, could have been acquired independently rather than from a common ancestor.

Although early in time and cosmopolitan in range, *Plesiadapis* is clearly too specialized a primate to be the ancestor of later prosimians. This sterile offshoot of the family tree is significant to primate history on other grounds. First, the relative completeness of its remains makes *Plesiadapis* the most thoroughly known primate of the Paleocene. Second, many details of its skeletal form serve to link its order with that of the even earlier placental mammals—the Insectivora, from which the primates arose.

Eocene Evolutionary Advances

The next fossil primates of which there are nearly complete remains come from North American strata of the middle Eocene. The best-known examples are species of two related lemur-like genera: *Notharctus* and *Smilodectes.* The degree to which these prosimians have advanced beyond *Plesiadapis* demonstrates the rapid evolution of primates as much as 50 million years ago. Many incomplete specimens of *Notharctus* were exhaustively studied in the 1920's by Gregory. Since then an even more complete skeleton of one species —probably *Notharctus tenebrosus*—has come to light in the paleontological research collection of Yale University. Although the skull is missing, the rest of the skeleton represents one of the two most complete individual primates yet recovered from fossil beds of such early date. C. Lewis Gazin of the Smithsonian Institution has recently recovered several complete skulls and many other bones of *Smilodectes gracilis* in southwestern Wyoming. The abundance of this new material has permitted the assembly of a skeleton and a restoration of *Smilodectes'* probable appearance [*see illustration on page 279*].

These New World primates resemble living lemurs both in their proportions and in their general structure. In contrast to the small-brained, snouty, side-eyed *Plesiadapis*, the skull of *Smilodectes* shows an enlargement of the front portion of the brain and a shifting of eye positions forward so that individual fields of vision can overlap in front. These features of the head, taken together with the animal's rather long hind limbs, suggest that in life *Smilodectes* looked rather like one of today's Malagasy lemurs, the sifaka.

It is most unlikely, however, that either *Smilodectes* or *Notharctus* contributed to the ancestry of living lemurs. This honor can more probably be conferred on some member of a European genus, such as *Protoadapis* or *Adapis*, of equal Eocene age, if indeed the ancestors of modern lemurs were not already in Africa by this time. *Adapis* has the distinction of being the first fossil primate genus ever described. The French paleontologist Baron Cuvier did so in 1822, although he originally thought *Adapis* was a hoofed mammal or a small pachyderm and not a primate at all. Unfortunately none of these possible Old World precursors of living lemurs is sufficiently represented by fossils to provide the kind of detailed skeletal information we possess for their New World contemporaries.

This is also the case for a roughly contemporary European prosimian: *Necrolemur,* known from skulls and limb bones found in the Quercy deposits of France and by extrapolation from parts of a related species recovered in Germany. In *Necrolemur* the evolutionary advances represented by *Notharctus* and *Smilodectes* have been extended. Enlargement of the forebrain and a further facial foreshortening are apparent. A forward shift of the eye position —with the consequent overlapping of visual fields and potential for depth perception—should have equipped *Necrolemur* for an active arboreal life in the Eocene forests. Actually this early primate, although it is probably not ancestral to any living prosimian, shows a much closer affinity for the comparatively advanced tarsier of southeast Asia than for the more primitive Malagasy lemurs.

The evolutionary progress made by prosimians during the Eocene, both in North America and in Europe, is obvious. Yet not a single fossil primate of the Eocene epoch from either continent appears to be an acceptable ancestor for the great infraorder of the catarrhines, embracing all the living higher Old World primates, man included. One cannot help wondering what developments may have been taking place in Africa and Asia during the Eocene's span of more than 22 million years. In both regions the record is almost mute. In Asia the only known primate fossils dating to this epoch are a few equivocal bits and pieces from China and some fragments from a late Eocene formation in Burma. From the Eocene of Africa there are not only no primates but also no small mammals of any kind.

One of the Burmese fragments is a section of lower jaw containing three premolar teeth and one molar, described in 1938 by Edwin H. Colbert of the American Museum of Natural History, who named the new species *Amphipithecus mogaungensis.* A brief lesson in primate teeth is necessary to understand its significance. The lesson is painless; it merely involves counting. The facts are these: Regardless of tooth size or shape all adult catarrhines—Old World monkeys, apes and man—have the same "dental formula." In each half of a jaw—upper and lower alike—are found from front to back two incisors, a single canine, two premolars and three molars. In anatomical shorthand the fact is written:

$$\frac{2:1:2:3}{2:1:2:3} \times 2 = 32\,.$$

Because of its three premolar teeth *Amphipithecus* is dentally more primitive than any catarrhine, fossil or living. It may have had such a dental formula as

$$\frac{2:1:3:3}{2:1:3:3} \times 2\,.$$

This is typical of some living lemurs and of many platyrrhines—the marmosets and monkeys of the New World. Yet in other characteristics the *Amphipithecus* jaw is advanced rather than primitive. The horizontal ramus—that portion of the jaw that holds the teeth— is deep and massive, as is also true in many fossil and living apes. The fossil premolars, and the molar as well, are

PHYLOGENY of all the primates traces the evolution of the order from its beginnings sometime before the middle of the Paleocene (*see time scale in illustration at right*). The first to appear were prosimian families that stemmed from a basic stock of small and sometimes arboreal mammals called Insectivora (whose living kin include the shrews and moles). The chart's broken lines show hypothetical evolutionary relations. In the interval between Eocene and Miocene times these relations are particularly uncertain. Solid lines (*color*) show the periods when species of the groups named (*black type*) are known to have flourished. The names of two prosimian and two anthropoid genera appear in color. Species of each are illustrated in detail on the four following pages.

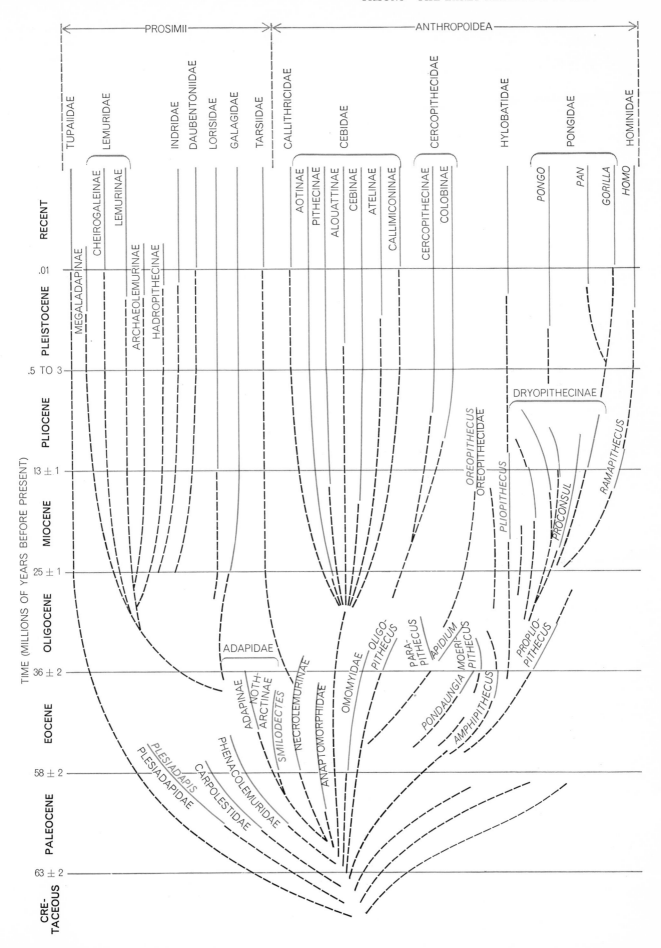

similar to the corresponding teeth in *Oligopithecus*, a newly discovered catarrhine from the Oligocene of Egypt.

The other Burmese fossil consists of both rear portions of a lower jaw, discovered together with a segment of upper jaw containing two molar teeth. G. E. Pilgrim of the Indian Geological Survey gave this find the name *Pondaungia cotteri* in 1927. The two molars almost equally resemble those of prosimians on the one hand and of some Old World higher primates on the other. The material is so fragmentary, however, that some scholars have even questioned *Pondaungia*'s inclusion in the primate order. If neither *Amphipithecus* nor *Pondaungia* were known, it would seem almost certain that the Old World anthropoids had arisen in Africa. Further collecting in the Burmese Eocene formation that contained both Pilgrim's and Colbert's fossils is required before final judgment of their significance can be made.

By the end of the Eocene the primates had been differentiating for almost 30 million years. This is a long time. Yet only one result is known with certainty: A number of primates, lemur-like and tarsier-like, had evolved in the Old World, some of which must have contributed to the ancestry of today's lower primates, the Prosimii. Not until the close of the Eocene do some puzzling fossil fragments from Burma offer a hint of what must have been a major, even though still undocumented, evolutionary development in the Old World Tropics. This development can be postulated with confidence, in spite of a paucity of evidence, because early in the following epoch—the Oligocene— fossil Anthropoidea appear in substantial numbers and varieties. It is highly improbable that these Oligocene primates could have evolved, in terms of geologic time, almost overnight. So

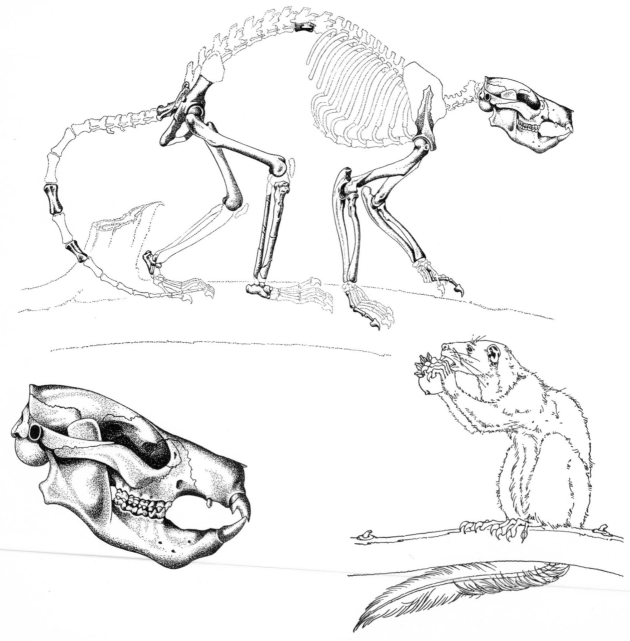

PALEOCENE PROSIMIAN *Plesiadapis* has been reconstructed (*skeleton at top*) on the basis of French and North American fossil finds and restored (*figure at bottom right*) by analogy with living tree shrews. Bones shown in outline are hypothetical. The charac- teristic wide gap between this rodent-like animal's cheek teeth and its slanting incisors is evident in the skull detail (*bottom left*). Species of *Plesiadapis* ranged from squirrel- to cat-size. They belong to an early primate family that died out 50 million years ago.

far our knowledge of their geographical distribution is exceedingly limited: all their remains discovered to date have come from a single formation in the desert badlands of the Egyptian province of the Fayum.

The Catarrhine Emergence

A hundred miles inland from the Mediterranean coast and some 60 miles southwest of Cairo a brackish lake stands at the edge of a series of escarpments and desert benches that are almost devoid of plant and animal life. At the end of the Eocene epoch the shore of the Mediterranean extended this far inland, and rivers flowed into the shallow sea through dense tropical forests. The rise and fall of sea and land is clearly revealed by alternating river-deposited strata and layers of marine limestone. In the middle of these escarpments, running from southwest to northeast between the lake and a lava-capped ridge called Gebel el Quatrani, is a fossil-rich stratum of sandy early Oligocene sediments that first yielded primate remains in the early 1900's.

Primates were not the only inhabitants of this forested Oligocene shoreline. Crocodiles and gavials swam in the sluggish streams. Tiny rodents and various relatives of today's hyrax lived in the underbrush, as did hog- and ox-sized cousins of the modern elephant. The largest animal of the fauna was a four-horned herbivore about the size and shape of today's white rhinoceros.

Until the recent Yale Paleontological Expedition the primate inventory from the Fayum totaled seven pieces of fossilized bone: one skull fragment (picked up by a professional collector in 1908 and sent to the American Museum of Natural History), one heel bone, three fragmentary portions of jawbone and two nearly complete lower jaws. This

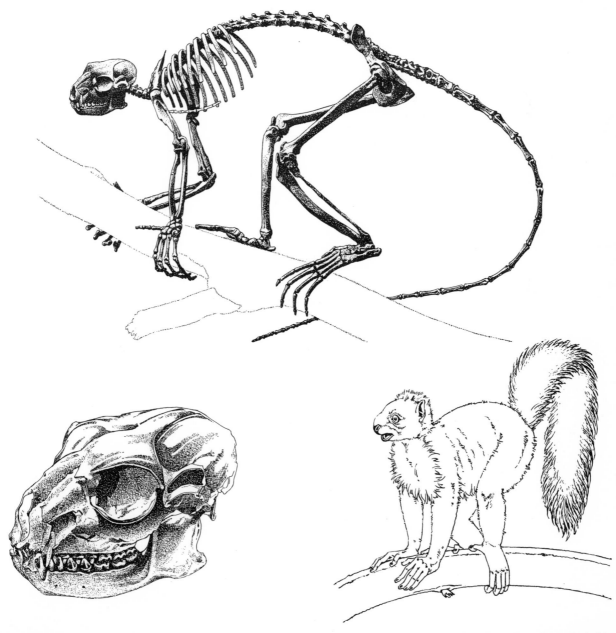

EOCENE PROSIMIAN *Smilodectes* is several million years junior to *Plesiadapis* and is a far more advanced animal. Its snout is shorter, the front portion of the brain is enlarged and its eyes are positioned on the skull in a manner that permits the visual fields to overlap. Although the notharctine subfamily to which this genus belongs was not ancestral to any of the living primates, its relatively long hind limbs give *Smilodectes* a remarkable resemblance to one modern prosimian, the sifaka, a Malagasy lemur.

may not seem a particularly rich haul, but studies over the years have shown that these seven fossils represent at least four distinct genera and species of Oligocene primates.

By the end of the Yale Expedition's fourth season this past winter more than 100 individual primate specimens had been added to the Fayum inventory. Although many of these finds consist of single teeth, there are also more than two dozen lower jaws, a skull fragment and some limb bones. Thus far the Fayum beds have not yielded any skulls or other skeletal remains of the kind that provide so much detailed informa-tion on Paleocene and Eocene prosimi-ans. What has been found, however, re-veals a great deal. As one example, an incomplete lower jaw was discovered in 1961 by a member of the expedition, Donald E. Savage of the University of California at Berkeley. This fragment permits the establishment of a new pri-mate genus, which I have named *Oligo-pithecus*. The molar teeth of the "type" species of the genus indicate that it may well be on or near the evolutionary line that gave rise to the superfamily of liv-ing Old World monkeys: the cercopith-ecoids.

The other Old World primate super-family—the hominoids—also appears to be well represented among the Fayum fossils. Possible ancestors for one family of living hominoids—the gibbons and siamangs—are present: the well-pre-served jaw of a gibbon-like animal, as yet undescribed, was turned up by the Yale Expedition in 1963. In this con-nection it should be noted that the study of all the Fayum fossils belong-ing to the genus *Propliopithecus*—for many years regarded as an ancestor of the gibbon—indicates that it probably represents a more generalized hominoid ancestor instead. This small Oligocene primate may well prove to be on or

MIOCENE ANTHROPOID *Pliopithecus* is reconstructed (*left*) on the basis of a fairly complete specimen discovered in 1957. Al-though it is as much as 20 million years old, its skull (*top right*) is very much like a modern gibbon's. These hominoids probably were ancestral to today's long-armed gibbons, but their anatomy is gen-eralized and their fore- and hind limbs are of almost equal length.

near the line of evolutionary development that led to the living pongids and to man.

The Miocene Hominoids

Throughout the entire 11-million-year span of the Oligocene the fossil fauna of Europe does not include a single primate. In the following epoch—the Miocene, which had its beginning some 24 to 26 million years ago—primates reappear in the European fossil record. A few years after Cuvier named *Adapis* the paleontologist-antiquarian Édouard Lartet reported a primate lower jaw from Miocene strata at Sansan in France. This fossil was the basis for establishing the genus *Pliopithecus*. Since then dozens of other *Pliopithecus* specimens have been uncovered in formations of Miocene and Pliocene age, in both Europe and Africa. The best of these *Pliopithecus* finds to date—a skull, including facial portions, and most of a skeleton—was made in a Miocene deposit near the Czechoslovakian town of Neudorf an der March in 1957. These remains provided the basis for the reconstruction shown on the opposite page.

Many millions of years younger than the gibbon-like hominoids of the Fayum, *Pliopithecus* presumably represents a further advance in the lineage that leads to the living gibbons. Yet this Miocene hominoid shows quite generalized characteristics. The arms of today's gibbons are considerably longer than their legs; *Pliopithecus*, in contrast, has hind limbs and forelimbs of nearly equal length. In fact, where comparisons are possible, *Pliopithecus* is not radically different from other roughly contemporary but not as fully preserved Miocene hominoids. Study of its skeleton tells us much about what the early hominoids were like.

A near contemporary of *Pliopithecus*

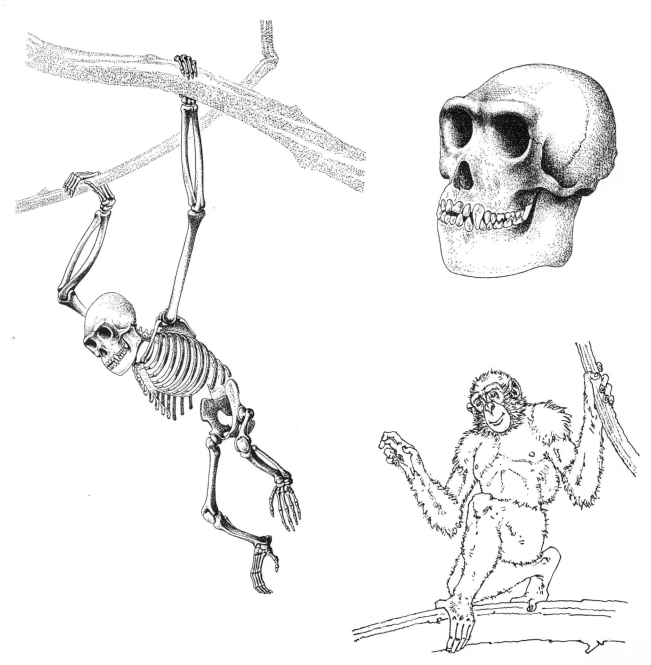

PLIOCENE ANTHROPOID *Oreopithecus* is not more than 14 million years old. Because most fossil anthropoids are small and their faces are snouty, the skeleton on which this reconstruction is based caused a sensation when first discovered. Its flat profile, four-foot height and also an apparent ability to walk erect brought *Oreopithecus* passing notoriety as a possible hominid "missing link."

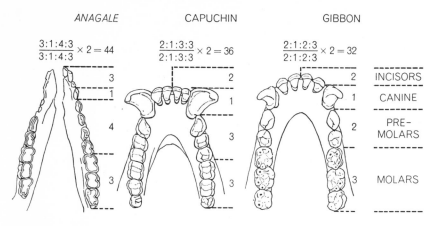

$$\frac{3:1:4:3}{3:1:4:3} \times 2 = 44$$ $$\frac{2:1:3:3}{2:1:3:3} \times 2 = 36$$ $$\frac{2:1:2:3}{2:1:2:3} \times 2 = 32$$

ANAGALE   CAPUCHIN   GIBBON

3 — INCISORS
1 — CANINE
4 / 3 / 2 — PRE-MOLARS
3 — MOLARS

HIGHER PRIMATES have fewer teeth than the original placental total of 44 (*see the lower jaw of* Anagale, *left*). The platyrrhine primates have lost an incisor and a premolar on each side of both jaws, and some have even lost molars. Thus the New World cebids have 36 teeth (*capuchin monkey, center*). All the catarrhines have lost one more premolar all around, so the Old World monkeys, apes and man have only 32 teeth (*gibbon, right*).

is *Dryopithecus,* the animal mentioned by Gregory as one candidate for a position ancestral to man. *Dryopithecus* was also named by Lartet; he described a lower jaw in 1856, almost 20 years after his discovery of *Pliopithecus.* Since that time many other fossil fragments of *Dryopithecus*—but no complete skulls or skeletons—have been found in strata of Miocene and even Pliocene age in Europe. In the late 1950's fossil teeth assignable to *Dryopithecus* were uncovered in brown coal deposits in southwestern China, indicating that the range of these hominoids extended across Europe to the Far East.

Because the fossil inventory for *Dryopithecus* consists mainly of individual teeth and teeth in incomplete jawbones, the reader will find useful some additional facts about primate dentition. These facts concern shape rather than number. First, although the crowns, or chewing surfaces, of any primate's molars may be ground flat by years of wear, each crown normally shows several bumps called cusps. Typically there are four cusps to a crown, one at each corner of the tooth. Second, all members of one of the two higher Old World primate superfamilies—the cercopithecoid monkeys—exhibit a unique cusp pattern. On the first and second upper and lower molars ridges of enamel project toward each other from the front pair of cusps; there are similar ridges between the back pair of cusps. Before the crown has been worn down there is often a gap in the middle of the ridge, but worn or unworn these molars are unmistakable.

The hominoids, on the other hand, have their own distinctive cusp pattern. The lower molars normally have five cusps rather than four, and the pattern of valleys that separate these bumps of enamel somewhat resembles the let-

ter Y, with the bottom of the Y facing inward. The pattern is called Y-5. The evolutionary significance of the pattern lies in the fact that the lower molars of *Dryopithecus* and of early men typically exhibit a Y-5 pattern. Thus Y-5 is a hereditary characteristic that has persisted among the hominoids for at least 24 million years.

Because the *Dryopithecus* fossil remains in Europe and the Far East are fragmentary, they reveal almost nothing about the skull and skeleton of this hominoid. Fortunately discoveries in Africa have altered the situation. There, thanks to the untiring efforts of L. S. B. Leakey and his colleagues, a substantial inventory of Miocene primate fossil remains has been accumulated, most of them from Rusinga Island in Lake Victoria and the nearby shores of the lake As a result several species of African proto-ape, apparently ranging from the size of a gibbon to that of a gorilla, have been described.

In spite of this variety in size, all these species are assigned to the single genus *Proconsul.* The name *Proconsul* is an "inside" British joke: the "pro" is simply "before" but "Consul" was the pet name of a chimpanzee that had long been a beloved resident of the London Zoo. All jokes apart, the name implies an evolutionary position for these African hominoids close to the ancestry of living chimpanzees and quite possibly to the ancestry of gorillas as well.

Among the *Proconsul* species the fossil remains that are most nearly complete belong to the gibbon-sized *Proconsul africanus.* They include parts of two skulls—almost complete in the facial portions—and some limb bones, including parts of a foot and a forelimb with a hand. The picture that emerges from the study of this material is that of an advanced catarrhine, showing some monkey-like traits of hand, skull and brain but hominoid and even partially hominid characteristics of face, jaws and dentition. The foot and forelimb are also more suggestive of some ape-like adaptations—including an incipient ability to swing by the arms from tree branch to tree branch—than they are of either arboreal or ground-dwelling Old World monkeys.

Recent taxonomic investigations show that species of the genus *Proconsul,* with their relative abundance of skeletal remains, should almost certainly be lumped together with the genus *Dryopithecus.* What such an assignment would mean, in effect, is that all these Miocene-Pliocene hominoids—not only Eurasian but African as well—belong to

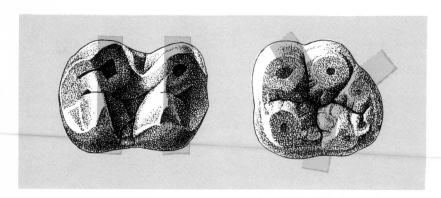

SHAPE OF MOLAR TEETH serves to split the catarrhines into two groups. The crowns of Old World monkeys' molars have a cusp at each corner (*baboon, left*): both front and rear pairs of cusps are connected by ridges (*color*). The crowns of apes' and man's lower molars normally have five cusps (*chimpanzee, right*), and the "valleys" between the cusps resemble the letter Y (*color*). This Y-5 pattern first appeared some 24 million years ago.

a single cosmopolitan genus. This might have been recognized 30 years ago except for a series of mischances. A. T. Hopwood of the British Museum (Natural History), who named *Proconsul* in 1933, stated that the lower jaws and teeth of *Proconsul* and *Dryopithecus* could not be distinguished as belonging to separate genera. He found the opposite to be true of the upper teeth, but it happens that the particular specimen of *Dryopithecus* upper teeth he chose for comparison was not of that genus at all: it belonged to another primate, *Ramapithecus*. When W. E. Le Gros Clark of the University of Oxford and Leakey later enlarged the definition of *Proconsul*, they still drew the primary upper-dental distinctions from the same specimen, which was not recognized as *Ramapithecus* until 1963. *Proconsul* and *Ramapithecus* are not the same genus. *Proconsul* and *Dryopithecus*, in all probability, are.

The Puzzle of the Coal Man

In any listing of the more complete early primates the Italian species *Oreopithecus bambolii*, sometimes irreverently known as the Abominable Coal Man, cannot be omitted. Its first bits and pieces were discovered almost 100 years ago. Since then *Oreopithecus* remains have been found in abundance in the brown-coal beds of central Italy, a formation that is variously assigned

to late Miocene or early Pliocene times. In 1956 Johannes Hürzeler of the natural history museum in Basel assembled a number of new *Oreopithecus* specimens, and in 1958 Hürzeler was instrumental in the recovery of a nearly complete skeleton from a coal mine at Grosseto in Italy. This superb fossil is still being examined by specialists from various nations.

Evidently these Miocene-Pliocene primates were of substantial size—some four feet tall and probably weighing more than 80 pounds. Among the living primates the closest in size would be a female chimpanzee. Because its face is short and flat instead of showing an elongated snout, and because studies of its pelvis and limb bones suggest the possibility of an erect walking posture, *Oreopithecus* has received some notoriety as a possible direct precursor of the hominid family. Intensive study of the 1958 specimen, however, has led a number of workers to rather different conclusions.

One of the surprising things about *Oreopithecus* was first noted by Gregory in the 1920's: the cheek teeth of its lower jaw strongly resemble the corresponding teeth of *Apidium*, one of the four primates named from the original Fayum finds of the early 1900's. The surprise is that *Apidium* dates to the Oligocene, some 20 to 25 million years earlier than *Oreopithecus*. This remarkable dental coincidence might easily

have remained no more than a curiosity if the Yale Expedition had not recovered a number of additional *Apidium* teeth—this time the cheek teeth from upper jaws. The study of these teeth is not yet complete, but it is already evident that the newfound *Apidium* uppers correspond as well to the equivalent *Oreopithecus* uppers as the lowers do to the lowers. Such a similarity strongly suggests that, in spite of their separation in time, the ancient *Apidium* and the comparatively modern *Oreopithecus* are representatives of a single group of now extinct Old World higher primates. *Apidium* cannot be directly ancestral to *Oreopithecus*, however, because it lacks one pair of incisors that are still present in *Oreopithecus*. Although in the evolutionary sense this group is not far removed from the pongid-hominid stem, it seems to have developed its own distinctive characteristics by early Oligocene times.

A Dryopithecine from India

Having come to the end of Miocene times, with a scant 12 million to 14 million years remaining in which to discover a human forebear, we must reexamine Gregory's declaration. One of his candidates, *Dryopithecus*, has now been shown to be a long-lived and cosmopolitan genus, one of an abundant dryopithecine group to which in all probability the African species of *Pro-*

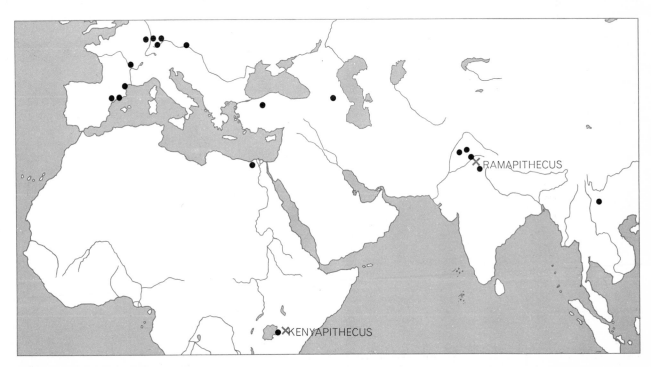

RANGE OF THE DRYOPITHECINES during Miocene and early Pliocene times extended across Eurasia from France to western China and also included East Africa and northwest India. No other hominoid primates of that time were so widespread. Crosses (*color*) show where the advanced hominoid genus, *Ramapithecus*, and the apparently identical *Kenyapithecus* have been found.

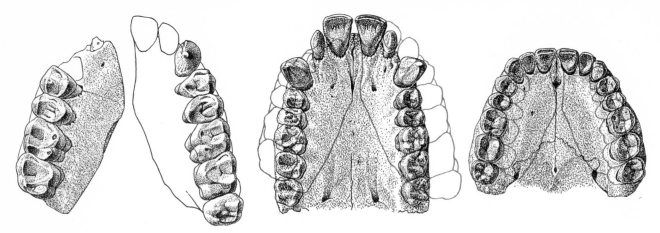

UPPER JAW OF RAMAPITHECUS, in a life-sized reconstruction at left, is compared with that of an orangutan (*center*) and a
man (*right*). In each comparison the jaws have been made the same
size. The U-shaped arc formed by the ape's teeth contrasts sharply
with the curved arc in *Ramapithecus*, which is closer to the human
curve. This, as well as the manlike ratio in comparative size of
front and cheek teeth and the modest canine, are grounds for
considering *Ramapithecus* man's earliest known hominid ancestor.

consul belong. What about *Sivapithecus*, Gregory's other nominee for a position as a hominid ancestor?

The Siwalik Hills of northwestern
India and adjacent Pakistan have been
known to paleontologists since the first
half of the 19th century for their fossil-
rich deposits of Miocene and Pliocene
age. It was from these strata that Pilgrim, who described the Burmese bor-
derline primate *Pondaungia*, uncovered
and named *Sivapithecus* in 1910. Later,
in the 1930's, G. Edward Lewis collected fossils for the Yale-Cambridge
North India Expedition from these
same beds and discovered a number of
primate jaw fragments and teeth. In
due course they were assigned to several separate primate genera, including
some additional examples of Pilgrim's
Sivapithecus.

Recent reexamination of *Sivapithecus*
species suggests that they are not markedly different from *Dryopithecus*. Like
Proconsul, they may well deserve nothing more than subgeneric status among
the cosmopolitan dryopithecines. This
would mean that not only Africa and
Eurasia but also India supported separate populations of a single hominoid
genus during Miocene and the earliest
of Pliocene times—a span of at least 15
million years. However confused and
confusing dryopithecine taxonomy and
evolutionary relations are at present,
the inescapable fact remains that
throughout this entire span of time
this is the only group of primates known
in any Old World continent that can be
considered close to the source of the
hominid family line.

Because of the dryopithecines' very
broad distribution throughout the Old
World, the precise time and location
of the primates' evolutionary advance
from hominoid animals to specifically
hominid ones may always remain uncertain. Yet a tentative guess is possible.

Another of the fossil primates Lewis
collected in the Siwalik Hills was *Ramapithecus*. The type species of *Ramapithecus* is founded on a portion of a
right upper jaw and is named *Ramapithecus brevirostris*. The fossil includes
the first two molars, both premolars, the
socket of the canine tooth, the root of the
lateral incisor and the socket of the central incisor. When it and other fossils of
Ramapithecus are used to reconstruct
an entire upper jaw, complete with
palate, the result is surprisingly human
in appearance [*see illustration above*].
The proportions of the jaw indicate a
foreshortened face. The size ratio between front teeth and cheek teeth is
about the same as it is in man. (The front
teeth of living apes are relatively large.)
Estimating from the size of its socket,
the canine tooth was not much larger
than the first premolar—another hominid
characteristic, opposed to the enlarged
canines of the pongids. The arc formed
by the teeth is curved as in man, rather
than being parabolic, or U-shaped, as
in the apes.

From Relative to Ancestor

Just such traits as these, intermediate
between the dryopithecines and hominids, had led Lewis in 1934 to suggest
that *Ramapithecus* might well belong
to the Hominidae. This suggestion was
challenged in the years immediately following. In my opinion, however, both
the reexamination of the type species
and the identification of new material reinforce Lewis' original conclusion.

Taxonomic decisions of this sort are not
made lightly, and to draw a large conclusion from limited fossil evidence is
always uncomfortable. Thus it was particularly gratifying to learn of Leakey's
recovery, in 1962, of the jaws of a similar hominid near Fort Ternan in southwestern Kenya.

Leakey has assigned this fossil to
the species *Kenyapithecus wickeri*. Like
the remains of Lewis' *Ramapithecus
brevirostris*, it preserves much of the
upper dentition. Included are the first
two molars on both sides, an intact second premolar and the stub of a first premolar. The socket for one canine is intact; a canine tooth and a central incisor
were found separately. Potassium-argon
dating of the specimen yields an absolute age of about 14 million years, a
time near the boundary between the
Miocene and the Pliocene.

The significance of the Fort Ternan
find lies in the fact that *Kenyapithecus*
not only has an abundance of close anatomical links with *Ramapithecus* but
also exhibits no pertinent differences. In
this new specimen, a continent removed
in space from *Ramapithecus*, are found
the same foreshortened face, dental
curve and small canine tooth—each a
hominid trait. The conclusion is now
almost inescapable: in late Miocene to
early Pliocene times both in Africa and
India an advanced hominoid species
was differentiating from more conservative pongid stock and developing important hominid characteristics in the
process. Pending additional discoveries
it may be wiser not to insist that the
transition from ape to man is now being
documented from the fossil record, but
this certainly seems to be a strong
possibility.

Biographical Notes
and Bibliographies

GENERAL REFERENCES

Barnicott, N. A. The Development and Scope of Human Biology. In G. A. Harrison, ed., *Teaching and Research in Human Biology* (Symposia of the Society for the Study of Human Biology, Vol. 6). Oxford, Pergamon Press, 1964, pp. 1-11.

Harrison, G. Ainsworth. The Professional Training of Human Biologists. *Ibid.*, pp. 115-131.

Howells, W. W. Some Present Aspects of Physical Anthropology. *Ann. Am. Acad. Pol. and Soc. Sci.*, Vol. 137 (1965), pp. 127-133.

Lasker, Gabriel. Recent Advances in Physical Anthropology. In Bernard J. Siegel, ed., *Biennial Review of Anthropology*. Stanford University Press, 1959, pp. 1-36.

Laughlin, William S. Aspects of Current Physical Anthropology: Method and Theory. *Southwest. J. Anthro.*, Vol. 16, No. 1 (1960), pp. 75-92.

Laughlin, W. S. The Teaching of Physical Anthropology: Concepts and Problems. In D. G. Mandelbaum, Gabriel W. Lasker and Ethel M. Albert, eds., *The Teaching of Anthro-*
pology. (American Anthropological Association, Memoir 94). New York, The Association; Berkeley, University of California Press, 1963, pp. 81-97.

Osborne, Richard H. The Anthropologist and Population Genetics: A Discussion of Ethnographic Method. *Davidson J. Anthro.*, Vol. 3, No. 2 (1957), pp. 25-34.

Roberts, D. F. and J. S. Weiner, Eds. *The Scope of Physical Anthropology and Its Place in Academic Studies.* (Symposia of the Society for the Study of Human Biology, Vol 1.) Oxford, Pergamon Press, 1958.

Spuhler, J. N. and F. B. Livingstone. The Relations of Physical Anthropology with the Biological Sciences. *The Teaching of Anthropology*, edited by D. G. Mandelbau, Gabriel W. Lasker, and Ethel M. Albert. *American Anthropological Association, Memoir 94*, 1963, pp. 475-484.

Washburn, S. L. The Strategy of Physical Anthropology. In A. L. Kroeber, ed., *Anthropology Today*. Chicago, University of Chicago Press, 1958, pp. 714-727.

PART I: PROCESSES AND HISTORY

1. The Genetic Basis of Evolution

The Author

THEODOSIUS DOBZHANSKY, professor of zoology at Columbia University, has spent much of his career unraveling the genetics of fruit flies. Born and educated in Russia, he "got excited" about biology at the age of ten, and dates his decision to specialize in genetics and evolution from his reading of *Origin of Species* when he was fifteen. After teaching at the University of Leningrad for a number of years, he came to the United States as a Rockefeller Foundation Research Fellow to study with Thomas Hunt Morgan. At the end of his fellowship Morgan invited him to stay permanently. Biology in America has been enriched in consequence, not only by Dobzhansky's own significant researches but by the many fruitful careers his teaching has inspired.

Bibliography

Genetics and the Origin of Species. Th. Dobzhansky. Columbia University Press, 1937.

2. Charles Lyell

The Author

LOREN C. EISELEY heads the department of anthropology at the University of Pennsylvania. His eight previous contributions to SCIENTIFIC AMERICAN include articles on Charles Darwin and Alfred Russel Wallace, reflecting his great interest in the theory of evolution and its history. His book *Darwin's Century* received the Athenaeum of Philadelphia Literary Award for nonfiction in 1958. Eiseley was born in Nebraska in 1907, and took degrees at the universities of Nebraska and Pennsylvania.

Bibliography

Charles Darwin, Edward Blyth and The Theory of Natural Selection. Loren C. Eiseley in *Proceedings of the American Philosophical Society*, Vol. 103, No. 1, pages 94-158; February 28, 1959.

Charles Lyell and Modern Geology. T. G. Bonney. Macmillan & Co., 1895.

Darwin's Century. Loren C. Eiseley. Doubleday & Co., Inc., 1958.

Life, Letters and Journals of Sir Charles Lyell, Bart. Edited by his sister-in-law, Mrs. Lyell. John Murray, 1881.

Principles of Geology. Charles Lyell. John Murray, 1830.

3. Charles Darwin

The Author

See biographical note under "Charles Lyell" above.

Bibliography

The Foundations of the Origin of Species. Charles Darwin. Cambridge University Press, 1909.

The Life and Letters of Charles Darwin. Edited by Francis Darwin. D. Appleton and Company, 1888.

4. Crises in the History of Life

The Author

NORMAN D. NEWELL has since 1945 been curator of the Department of Fossil Invertebrates at the American Museum of Natural History in New York and professor of invertebrate paleontology at Columbia University. Newell acquired his B.S. and M.A. from the University of Kansas and in 1933 received a Ph.D. in geology from Yale University. After a year as a Sterling Fellow at Yale, Newell taught at the University of Kansas·until 1937, when he left to serve as a U.S. delegate to the 17th International Geological Congress held in Moscow. He returned to the U.S. and became associate professor of geology at the University of Wisconsin, remaining there until he joined the museum and Columbia. Since 1950 Newell has been involved in extensive research on the paleontology and ecology of the coral reefs of the Bahama Islands in the West Indies. This work has included expeditions to Andros Island and to Raroia (the Pacific atoll reached by the *Kon-Tiki*). He made a fossil-collecting tour of Mexico and Guatemala in 1956 and did field work in Greece and Turkey in 1960. The present article was originally given as the Ermine Cowles Case Memorial Lecture at the University of Michigan in 1962.

Bibliography

Biotic Associations and Extinction. David Nicol in *Systematic Zoology,* Vol. 10, No. 1, pages 35–41; March, 1961.

Evolution of Late Paleozoic Invertebrates in Response to Major Oscillations of Shallow Seas. Raymond C. Moore in *Bulletin of the Museum of Comparative Zoology at Harvard College,* Vol. 112, No. 3, pages 259–286; October, 1954.

Paleontological Gaps and Geochronology. Norman D. Newell in *Journal of Paleontology,* Vol. 36, No. 3, pages 592–610; May, 1962.

Tetrapod Extinctions at the End of the Triassic Period. Edwin H. Colbert in *Proceedings of the National Academy of Sciences of the U.S.A.,* Vol. 44, No. 9, pages 973–977; September, 1958.

Further Readings for Part I

Count, Earl W. *This is Race.* New York, Henry Schuman, 1950.

Greene, John C. Some Early Speculations on the Origin of Human Races. *Am. Anthropologist,* Vol. 56 (1954), pp. 31–41.

––––, *The Death of Adam.* Ames, Iowa. Iowa State University Press (1959).

Howells, W. H. Some Present Aspects of Physical Anthropology. *Ann. Am. Acad. Pol. and Soc. Sci.,* Vol. 137 (1965), pp. 127–133.

Huxley, Thomas H. *Man's Place in Nature.* (Ann Arbor Paperbacks.) Ann Arbor, University of Michigan Press, 1959. [First published in 1863.]

Meggers, Betty J., ed. *Evolution and Anthropology: A Centennial Appraisal.* Washington, D.C., The Anthropological Society of Washington, 1959.

Penniman, T. K. *A Hundred Years of Anthropology.* 2nd ed., London, 1952.

II. INTRAINDIVIDUAL VARIATION

5. The Living Cell

The Author

JEAN BRACHET is professor of general biology at the Free University of Brussels, of which his father, the anatomist and embryologist Albert Brachet, had been the rector. As a medical student at the Free University, Brachet did research under the direction of Albert M. Dalcq, acquired an M.D. degree in 1934 and joined the faculty as an instructor in anatomy the same year. Brachet writes that he "preferred the satisfaction of doing original and independent research in biology to the responsibilities of medical practice…and decided to study the elementary forms of life, *i.e.,* cells and embryos. Such studies ultimately will lead to a better understanding of the origin of cancer and to a more logical therapeutic approach to disease." Brachet has held visiting professorships at the University of Pennsylvania, the Rockefeller Institute, the Pasteur Institute in Paris and the Indian Cancer Research Centre in Bombay.

Bibliography

The Cell: Biochemistry, Physiology, Morphology. Vol. I: Methods; Problems of Cell Biology. Vol. II: Cells and Their Component Parts. Edited by Jean Brachet and Alfred E. Mirsky. Academic Press Inc., 1959; 1961.

Cell Growth and Cell Function. Torbjörn O. Caspersson. W. W. Norton & Company, Inc., 1950.

The Ultrastructure of Cells. Marcel Bessis. Sandoz Monographs, 1960.

6. Mammalian Eggs in the Laboratory

The Author

R. G. EDWARDS is a research fellow in the physiological laboratory at the University of Cambridge. After graduation from the University College of North Wales he obtained a Ph.D. at the University of Edinburgh, where he began research on embryological and endocrinological genetics in mammals. He left Edinburgh in 1957 to work for a year at the California Institute of Technology, spent five years at the National Institute for Medical Research in London and went to the University of Cambridge in 1963. At intervals he has also worked at the University of Glasgow and at Johns Hopkins University. He recently conducted research activities at the University of North Carolina School of Medicine.

Bibliography

The Comparative Behavior of Mammalian Eggs in Vivo and in Vitro, I: The Activation of Ovarian Eggs. Gregory Pincus and E. V. Enzmann in *The Journal of Experimental Medicine*, Vol. 62, No. 5, pages 665–675; November 1, 1935.

The Growth, Maturation and Atresia of Ovarian Eggs in the Rabbit. G. Pincus and E. V. Enzmann in *Journal of Morphology*, Vol. 61, No. 2, pages 351–376; September, 1937.

The Mammalian Egg. Colin R. Austin. Blackwell Scientific Publications, 1961.

Preliminary Attempts to Fertilize Human Oocytes Matured in Vitro. R. G. Edwards, Roger P. Donahue, Theodore A. Baranki and Howard W. Jones, Jr., in *American Journal of Obstetrics and Gynecology*, in press.

The Maturation of Rabbit Oocytes in Culture and Their Maturation, Activation, Fertilization and Subsequent Development in the Fallopian Tubes. M. C. Chang in *The Journal of Experimental Zoology*, Vol. 128, No. 2, pages 379–405; March, 1955.

7. The Genetic Code

The Author

F. H. C. CRICK is, with James D. Watson and Maurice H. F. Wilkins, winner of the 1962 Nobel Prize in physiology and medicine for the discovery of the molecular structure of the genetic material deoxyribonucleic acid (DNA). Originally a physicist, Crick made significant contributions to the development of radar; after World War II he turned to basic research on the structure of viruses, collagen and nucleic acids. Working at Cambridge in the early 1950's, Crick and Watson conceived and built the now-classic double spiral model of the DNA molecule, confirming the results of earlier X-ray diffraction studies made by Wilkins at Kings College, London. Crick is carrying on his researches into the nature of the genetic code under the auspices of the Medical Research Council Laboratory of Molecular Biology at the University Postgraduate Medical School in Cambridge; in 1962 he was appointed a nonresident fellow of the newly founded Salk Institute of Biological Studies in San Diego, California.

Bibliography

The Fine Structure of the Gene. Seymour Benzer in *Scientific American*, Vol. 206, No. 1, pages 70–84; January, 1962.

General Nature of the Genetic Code for Proteins. F. H. C. Crick, Leslie Barnett, S. Brenner and R. J. Watts-Tobin in *Nature*, Vol. 192, No. 4809, pages 1227–1232; December 30, 1961.

Messenger RNA. Jerard Hurwitz and J. J. Furth in *Scientific American*, Vol. 206, No. 2, pages 41–49; February, 1962.

The Nucleic Acids: Vol. III. Edited by Erwin Chargaff and J. N. Davidson. Academic Press Inc., 1960.

8. How Do Cells Differentiate?

The Author

C. H. WADDINGTON, professor of animal genetics at the University of Edinburgh, Scotland, was a geologist before going into biology. Geology led him to an interest in evolution, he says, "and that led to genetics and that again to the mode of operation of genes in development and thus finally to embryology." Waddington was born in India in 1905 and spent the first few years of his life there. He was educated at Cambridge University, receiving a B.A. in geology in 1926 and an Sc.D. in biology in 1938. He taught at Cambridge until 1945, then took his present position at Edinburgh. During World War II he was in charge of the Operational Research Section of the Coastal Command of the Royal Air Force. In 1947 he was named a Fellow of the Royal Society. In addition to his technical books, Waddington has written *The Scientific Attitude* and *Science and Ethics*. His recreation is painting in oil. He confesses to a taste for "modern" but says his own productions "always turn out to be incompetent attempts at straight realism."

Bibliography

The Epigenetics of Birds. C. H. Waddington. Cambridge University Press, 1952.

Chemical Embryology. Jean Brachet. Interscience Publishers, Inc., 1950.

9. The Skin

The Author

WILLIAM MONTAGNA is director of the Oregon Regional Primate Research Center and also professor and chairman of the division of experimental biology at the University of Oregon Medical School. He is a native of Italy who came to the U.S. at the age of 14 and was graduated from Bethany College in 1936. He writes that "after abortive attempts to become first an ornithologist and then a forest ranger" he obtained a Ph.D. in zoology at Cornell University in 1944. Before assuming his present post he taught at Cornell, the Long Island College of Medicine and Brown University. In addition to the skin, about which he has written extensively, his chief interest is reproductive biology, which is one of several major research programs under way at the Oregon Regional Primate Research Center.

Bibliography

Advances in the Biology of Skin, Vol. V: Wound Healing. William Montagna and Rupert E. Billingham. Pergamon Press, 1964.

The Biology of Hair Growth. Edited by William Montagna and Richard A. Ellis, Academic Press, 1958.

Finger Prints, Palms and Soles: An Introduction to Dermatoglyphics. Harold Cummins and Charles Midlo. Dover Publications, Inc., 1961.

Human Perspiration. Yas. Kuno. Charles C. Thomas, Publisher, 1956.

Physiology and Biochemistry of the Skin. Stephen Rothman. The University of Chicago Press, 1954.

The Structure and Function of Skin. William Montagna. Academic Press, 1962.

10. Electrical Effects in Bone

The Author

C. ANDREW L. BASSETT is associate professor of orthopedic surgery at the Columbia University College of Physicians and Surgeons and attending orthopedic surgeon at Presbyterian Hospital in New York. Bassett, who was born in Maryland, took his medical training at Columbia-Presbyterian; he received an M.D. there in 1948 and a D.Sc. in medicine in 1955. His various professional activities outside his teaching and hospital work include service this year as chairman of the Committee on Scientific Investigation of the American Academy of Orthopedic Surgery. Bassett has been given awards for work in spinal-cord regeneration and in peripheral nerve-graft preservation and transplantation. Early in September he began a year's leave of absence, which he is spending at the Strangeways Laboratories in Cambridge, England, "probing some ultrastructural aspects of bone formation in tissue culture."

Bibliography

Generation of Electric Potentials by Bone in Response to Mechanical Stress. C. Andrew L. Bassett and Robert O. Becker in *Science*, Vol. 137, No. 3535, pages 1063–1064; September 28, 1962.

Muscle Action, Bone Rarefaction and Bone Formation: An Experimental Study. Max Geiser and Joseph Trueta in *The Journal of Bone and Joint Surgery*, Vol. 40-B, No. 2, pages 282–311; May, 1958.

Piezoelectric Effect in Bone. Morris H. Shamos, Leroy S. Lavine and Michael I. Shamos in *Nature*, Vol. 197, No. 4862, page 81; January 5, 1963.

11. The Antiquity of Human Walking

The Author

JOHN NAPIER is reader in anatomy at the Royal Free Hospital School of Medicine of the University of London and director of the school's Unit of Primate Biology and Human Evolution. Son of a former professor of tropical medicine at the University of Calcutta, Napier was educated in England, receiving a medical degree from St. Bartholomew's Hospital in London. In 1963 he obtained a D.Sc. from the University of London. Napier's principal interests are teaching and research in primate biology. With his wife he is about to publish a textbook on the primates. Napier has appeared on numerous television programs dealing with primates and human evolution.

Bibliography

The Ape-Men. Robert Broom in *Scientific American;* November, 1949.

The Foot and the Shoe. J. R. Napier in *Physiotherapy*, Vol. 43, No. 3, pages 65–74; March, 1957.

A Hominid Toe Bone from Bed 1, Olduvai Gorge, Tanzania. M. H. Day and J. R. Napier in *Nature*, Vol. 211, No. 5052, Pages 929–930; August 27, 1966.

12. Human Growth

The Author

GEORGE W. GRAY was on the staff of the Rockefeller Foundation until his death in 1962. Born in Texas, Gray entered the University of Texas and shortly found himself headed for a career in physiology. Within a year, however, he left the University because of illness. After his recovery he worked for the Houston *Post* and then went to Harvard University. He graduated in 1912 and joined the staff of the New York *World*. During the 1920s he turned freelance and began to concentrate on the natural sciences. In the years that followed he contributed many articles to magazines, as well as writing a number of books. One article, "The Great Ravelled Knot" (SCIENTIFIC AMERICAN, October, 1948), won him the A.A.A.S.-George Westinghouse Science Writing Award for the best magazine article of the year.

Bibliography

The Significance of Individual Variations. Alfred H. Washburn in *Journal of Pediatrics*, Vol. 8, No. 1, pp. 31-37; January, 1936.

Pediatric Potpourri. Alfred H. Washburn in *Pediatrics*, Vol. 8, No. 2, pp. 299-306; August, 1951.

Nutritional Intake of Children. I. Calories, Carbohydrate, Fat and Protein. Virginia. A. Beal in *Journal of Nutrition*, Vol. 50. No. 2, pp. 223-234; June, 1953.

Standards for the Basal Metabolism of Children from 2 to 15 Years of Age Inclusive. Robert C. Lewis, Anna Marie Duval and Alberta Iliff in *Journal of Pediatrics*, Vol. 23, No. 1, pp. 1-18; July, 1943.

Further Readings for Part II

Brothwell, D. R., *Digging Up Bones*. London, British Museum (Natural History), 1965.

Harrison, G. A., J. S. Weiner, J. M. Tanner, and N. A. Barnicot, *Human Biology: An Introduction to Human Evolution, Variation and Growth*. New York, Oxford University Press, 1964.

Hooton, Ernest Albert, *Up From the Ape*. New York, Macmillan Company, 1966.

Hulse, Frederick S., *The Human Species*. New York, Random House, 1963.

Krogman, Wilton Marion, *The Human Skeleton in Forensic Medicine*. Springfield, Illinois, Charles C. Thomas, 1962.

Kent, George C., *Comparative Anatomy of the Vertebrates*. Saint Louis, C. V. Mosby Company, 1965.

Roe, Anne, and George Gaylord Simpson, eds., *Behavior and Evolution*. New Haven, Yale University Press, 1958.

Tanner, J. M., *Education and Physical Growth*. London, University of London Press, Ltd., 1961.

Witkop, Carl J., Jr. *Genetics and Dental Health*. New York, McGraw-Hill, 1962.

III: INTRAPOPULATION VARIATION

13. Ionizing Radiation and Evolution

The Author

JAMES F. CROW is professor of genetics and chairman of the Department of Medical Genetics at the University of Wisconsin. He grew up in Kansas and attended Friends University at Wichita. "I started out to major in music, but discovered I wasn't talented enough, and shifted successively to physics, then to chemistry and finally to biology. I took a course in genetics . . . and decided that this was the most interesting of the biology courses and something that I would like to pursue." He took his Ph.D. in genetics at the University of Texas in 1941, and taught at Dartmouth College until he joined the Wisconsin faculty in 1948.

Bibliography

The Causes of Evolution. J. B. S. Haldane. Harper & Brothers, 1932.

The Darwinian and Modern Conceptions of Natural Selection. H. J. Muller in *Proceedings of the American Philosophical Society*, Vol. 93, No. 6, pages 459-479; December 29, 1949.

Evolution, Genetics and Man. Theodosius Dobzhansky. John Wiley & Sons, Inc., 1955.

Genetics, Paleontology and Evolution. Edited by Glenn L. Jepsen, Ernst Mayr and George Gaylord Simpson. Princeton University Press, 1949.

Radiation and the Origin of the Gene. Carl Sagan in *Evolution,* Vol. 11, No. 1, pages 40-55; March, 1957.

14. The Evolution of the Hand

The Author

JOHN NAPIER is reader in anatomy at the Royal Free Hospital School of Medicine of the University of London and director of the school's Unit of Primate Biology and Human Evolution. For further information, see biographical note 11, for "The Antiquity of Human Walking."

Bibliography

The Antecedents of Man: An Introduction to the Evolution of The Primates. W. E. Le Gros Clark. Edinburgh University Press, 1959.

Man the Tool-Maker. Kenneth P. Oakley. British Museum of Natural History, 1950.

The Prehensile Movements of the Human Hand. J. R. Napier in *The Journal of Bone and Joint Surgery,* Vol. 38-B, No. 4, pages 902-913; November, 1956.

Prehensility and Opposability in the Hands of Primates. J. R. Napier in *Symposia of the Zoological Society of London,* No. 5, pages 115-132; August, 1961.

The Tropical Rain Forest. P. W. Richards. Cambridge University Press, 1957.

15. Adaptations to Cold

The Author

LAURENCE IRVING is director of the Institute of Arctic Biology and professor of zoophysiology at the University of Alaska. A graduate of Bowdoin College, he received a master's degree at Harvard University in 1917 and a Ph.D. at Stanford University in 1924. He has worked in Alaska since 1947, going there after more than 20 years of teaching, mostly at Swarthmore College. "I have long been inclined to study the physiological adaptations that enable men and animals to succeed in extreme natural conditions," he writes. "It turned out that the natural physiological reactions of arctic animals to cold were of dimensions large enough to demonstrate general principles of adaptation to various temperatures that we had been unable to ascertain in mild climates and by the use of domesticated animals."

Bibliography

Body Insulation of Some Arctic and Tropical Mammals and Birds. P. F. Scholander, Vladimir Walters, Raymond Hock and Laurence Irving in *The Biological Bulletin,* Vol. 99, No. 2, pages 225-236; October, 1950.

Body Temperatures of Arctic and Subarctic Birds and Mammals. Laurence Irving and John Krog in *Journal of Applied Physiology,* Vol. 6, No. 11, pages 667-680; May, 1954.

Effect of Temperature on Sensitivity of the Finger. Laurence Irving in *Journal of Applied Physiology,* Vol. 18, No. 6, pages 1201-1205; November, 1963.

Metabolism and Insulation of Swine as Bare-skinned Mammals. Laurence Irving, Leonard J. Peyton and Mildred Monson in *Journal of Applied Physiology,* Vol. 9, No. 3, pages 421-426; November, 1956.

Physiological Insulation of Swine as Bare-skinned Mammals. Laurence Irving in *Journal of Applied Physiology,* Vol. 9, No. 3, pages 414-420; November, 1956.

Terrestrial Animals in Cold: Introduction. Laurence Irving in *Handbook of Physiology, Section 4: Adaptation to the Environment.* American Physiological Society, 1964.

16. Tools and Human Evolution

The Author

SHERWOOD L. WASHBURN is professor of anthropology at the University of California. He was born in Cambridge, Mass., in 1911, attended the Groton School and acquired his B.A. at Harvard University in 1935 and his Ph.D. in anthropology from the same institution in 1940. He taught anatomy at Columbia University from 1939 to 1942. He joined the department of anthropology at the University of Chicago in 1942, and the University of California faculty in 1959. He is a past president of the American Association of Physical Anthropologists, and since 1955 he has been editor of the Association's journal. He wishes to thank Raymond A. Dart, L. S. B. Leakey and J. T. Robinson for their kindness in allowing him to examine the man-ape fossils described in the present article.

Bibliography

Cerebral Cortex of Man. Wilder Penfield and Theodore Rasmussen. Macmillan Company, 1950.

The Evolution of Man, edited by Sol Tax. University of Chicago Press, 1960.

The Evolution of Man's Capacity for Culture. Arranged by J. N. Spuhler. Wayne State University Press, 1959.

Human Ecology during the Pleistocene and Later Times in Africa South of the Sahara. J. Desmond Clark in *Current Anthropology,* Vol. I, pages 307-324; 1960.

17. The Origin of Speech

The Author

CHARLES F. HOCKETT is professor of linguistics and anthropology at Cornell University. A native of Columbus, Ohio, he took his B.A. and M.A. in ancient history at Ohio State University in 1936 and his Ph.D. in anthropology at Yale University in 1939. After serving four years in the Army in World War II, during which time he traveled on every continent except Europe, he went to Cornell in 1946. Hockett's work on the origin of language described in the present article began in 1955, when he was at the Center for Advanced Study in the Behavioral Sciences at Stanford, Calif. There, he says, "I began to learn what zoologists, animal behavior students, ethologists and paleontologists had discovered."

Bibliography

A Course in Modern Linguistics. Charles F. Hockett. Macmillan Company, 1958.

Animal "Languages" and Human Language. C. F. Hockett in *The Evolution of Man's Capacity for Culture,* arrranged by J. N. Spuhler, pages 32-38. Wayne State University Press, 1959.

Bees: Their Vision, Chemical Senses, and Language. Karl von Frisch. Cornell University Press, 1950.

Language: An Introduction to the Study of Speech. Edward Sapir. Harcourt, Brace & Company. 1921.

18. Learning to Think

The Authors

HARRY F. HARLOW is George Cary Comstock Professor of Psychology and head of the Primate Laboratory at the University of Wisconsin. He received his A.B. from Stanford University in 1927 and his Ph.D. from the same institution in 1930, the year in which he joined the Wisconsin faculty. In 1958-59, he was president of the American Psychological Association. The Harlows, co-authors of this article, have four children.

Bibliography

The Nature of Learning Sets. H. F. Harlow in *Psychological Review*, Vol. 56, No. 1, pages 51-65; 1949.
The Mentality of Apes. W. Köhler. Harcourt, Brace & Co., 1925.

19. Sickle Cells and Evolution

The Author

ANTHONY C. ALLISON is a postgraduate fellow at the University of Oxford, where he is engaged in research on cell metabolism in the Medical Research Council Laboratories, directed by the famous biochemist H. A. Krebs. Allison was brought up on an estate in Kenya and was fluent in two African languages before he could speak English. "It was inevitable in these circumstances that I should become interested in anthropology and natural history. After qualifying in medicine at Oxford I turned to research in human genetics, which helped to satisfy these interests." His field work has taken him on expeditions to Lapland, Syria and most parts of Africa. In 1954 he was a research fellow at the California Institute of Technology.

Bibliography

Sickle-Cell Anemia. George W. Gray in *Scientific American*, Vol. 185, No. 2, pages 56-59; August, 1951.
Protection Afforded by Sickle-Cell Traits Against Subtertian Malarial Infection. A. C. Allison in *British Medical Journal*, Vol. 1, pages 290-301; February, 1954.

20. The Genetics of the Dunkers

The Author

H. BENTLEY GLASS is professor of biology at the State University of New York at Stony Brook. Previously, he has been a professor of biology at The Johns Hopkins University, associate editor of *The Quarterly Review of Biology*, and acting chairman of the editorial board of the American Association for the Advancement of Science, responsible for the publication of *Science* and *The Scientific Monthly*. Glass was born in China in 1906 and had his pre-college education in mission schools there. He took his undergraduate work at Baylor University and his Ph.D. at the University of Texas.

Bibliography

Genetic Drift in a Religious Isolate: An Analysis of the Causes of Variation in Blood Group and Other Gene Frequencies in a Small Population. Bentley Glass, Milton S. Sacks, Elsa F. Jahn and Charles Hess in *The American Naturalist*, Vol. 86, No. 828, pages 145-159; May-June, 1952.
Races: A Study of the Problems of Race Formation in Man. Carleton S. Coon, Stanley M. Garn and Joseph B. Birdsell. Charles C. Thomas, 1950.

Further Readings for Part III

Dobzhansky, Theodosius, *Evolution, Genetics and Man.* New York, John Wiley & Sons, Inc, 1955.
————, *Mankind Evolving.* New Haven, Yale University Press, 1962.
Harrison, G. A., J. S. Weiner, J. M. Tanner, and N. A. Barnicot. *Human Biology: An Introduction to Human Evolution, Variation and Growth.* New York, Oxford University Press, 1964.
Hulse, F. S. 1963. *The Human Species*, New York. Random House, 1963.
Wallace, B., and A. M. Srb. *Adaptation.* 2nd ed. Englewood, New Jersey, Prentice-Hall, 1964.

IV: INTERPOPULATION VARIATION

21. The Distribution of Man

The Author

WILLIAM W. HOWELLS, professor of anthropology at Harvard University is a grandson of the writer and critic William Dean Howells. He acquired his degrees at Harvard, receiving a Ph.D. in 1934. From 1939 to 1954 he taught at the University of Wisconsin, except for three years as a lieutenant in the Office of Naval Intelligence during World War II. He joined the faculty of Harvard in 1954. Howells is a past president of the American Anthropological Association and a past editor of the *American Journal of Physical Anthropology*. He is the author of *Mankind So Far*, and *Mankind in the Making*.

Bibliography

Human Ancestry from a Genetical Point of View. Reginald Ruggles Gates. Harvard University Press, 1948.
Mankind in the Making. William White Howells. Doubleday & Company, Inc., 1959.
Races: A Study of the Problems of Race Formation in Man. Carleton S. Coon, Stanley M. Garn and Joseph B. Birdsell. Charles C. Thomas, 1950.
The Story of Man. Carleton Stevens Coon. Alfred A. Knopf, Inc., 1954.

22. The Lesson of the Pygmies

The Author

COLIN M. TURNBULL is assistant curator of African ethnology at the American Museum of Natural History. Turnbull's entrance into anthropology resulted indirectly from his interest in philosophy and music. After taking a degree in philosophy and politics at the University of Oxford, Turnbull spent two years at the University of London studying Hindi and Sanskrit and another two years on a research fellowship at Banaras Hindu University in India. He returned to England by way of

Africa, spending most of his time in the Congo, where he stayed for several months in the home of Patrick Putnam, an American anthropologist who had settled there in the 1920's. It was through Putnam that Turnbull first gained access to the Pygmies of the Ituri Forest. Already aware of the importance of music in Indian society, Turnbull was particularly struck by the role of music among the Pygmies. On a second visit in 1954 and 1955 he concluded that any understanding of the music required a thorough understanding of the whole society. A grant from the Royal Anthropological Institute made possible a third visit in 1957 and 1958. Turnbull joined the Museum of Natural History in 1959, and in 1961 he published an account of his life among the Pygmies entitled *The Forest People*.

Bibliography

Die Bambuti-Pygmäen vom Ituri: Ergebnisse Zweier Forschungreisen zu den Zentralafrikanischen Pygmäen. Paul Schebesta. Libraire Folk Fils. George von Campenhout, Successeur, 1938.
The Elima: A Premarital Festival among the Bambuti Pygmies. Colin Turnbull in *Zaïre*, Vol. 14, No. 2-3, pages 175-192; 1960.
The Forest People. Colin Turnbull. Simon and Schuster, Inc., 1961.
Legends of the BaMbuti. Colin Turnbull in *The Journal of the Royal Anthropological Institute*, Vol. 89, Part 1, pages 45-60; January-June, 1959.
The Molimo: A Man's Religious Association among the Ituri Bambuti. Colin Turnbull in *Zaïre*, Vol. 14, No. 4, pages 307-340; 1960.

23. World Population

The Author

JULIAN HUXLEY, as a member of an illustrious family of scientists and writers, has done a good deal of writing himself. He is most widely known for his attempts to bring biological issues before the public, not only in his own books but also in volumes written in collaboration with J. B. S. Haldane and H. G. Wells. Huxley was Director General of UNESCO in 1947-1948. He is frequently in the U.S., and once taught at the Rice Institute in Texas (from 1912 to 1916). Much later, in 1943, he expressed his enthusiasm for an American experiment in *TVA: Adventure in Planning*. In *From an Antique Land*, which appeared in 1954, he told of impressions gathered in the Middle East.

Bibliography

Population and Planned Parenthood in India. S. Chandrasekhar. Allen & Unwin, 1955.
The Population Problem. A. M. Carr-Saunders. The Clarendon Press, 1922.
World Population and Resources. Allen & Unwin, 1955.

24. The Origins of New World Civilization

The Author

RICHARD S. MACNEISH is chairman of the department of archaeology at the University of Alberta. A native of New York City and a former Golden Gloves boxing champion, MacNeish was graduated from the University of Chicago in 1940. He went on to acquire an M.A. in anthropology and a Ph.D. in archaeology, physical anthropology and ethnology from Chicago in

1944 and 1949 respectively. Since 1936 MacNeish has participated in more than 40 archaeological field expeditions to various sites in the U.S., Canada and Mexico, and he has written more than 100 books, articles and reviews on New World archaeology. From 1949 to 1963 he was chief archaeologist for the national Museum of Canada. Between 1960 and 1964, he led four expeditions to the valley of Tehuacán in southern Mexico on behalf of the Robert S. Peabody Foundation for Archaeology; the results of these expeditions form the basis of the present article.

Bibliography

Ancient Mesoamerican Civilization. Richard S. MacNeish in *Science*, Vol. 143, No. 3606, pages 531-537; February, 1964.
Domestication of Corn. Paul C. Mangelsdorf, Richard S. MacNeish and Walton C. Galinat in *Science*, Vol. 143, No. 3606, pages 538-545; February, 1964.
First Annual Report of the Tehuacan Archaeological-Botanical Project. Richard Stockton MacNeish. Robert S. Peabody Foundation for Archaeology, 1961.
Mexico. Michael D. Coe. Frederick A. Praeger, 1962.
Second Annual Report of the Tehuacan Archaeological-Botanical Project. Richard Stockton MacNeish. Robert S. Peabody Foundation for Archaeology, 1962.

25. The Prehistory of the Australian Aborigine

The Author

D. J. MULVANEY is senior fellow in prehistory at the Australian National University. As an undergraduate at the University of Melbourne, concentrating on Greek and Roman history, he made a special study of Roman Britain and by that means became interested in archaeology. "I realized," he writes, "that archaeological methods could be applied in Australia, but no formal instruction in prehistoric archaeology was then offered in Australia." He went to the University of Cambridge to study prehistoric archaeology from 1951 to 1953. Thereafter for 10 years he lectured in ancient world history at the University of Melbourne "but spent much of my vacation time excavating aboriginal sites." In some of this work he had the sponsorship of the Nuffield Foundation. In 1965 he moved to the Australian National University in Canberra, where he devotes full time to research in prehistory.

Bibliography

Aboriginal Man in Australia. Edited by Ronald M. Berndt and Catherine H. Berndt. Angus and Robertson, 1965.
Australian Aboriginal Studies. Edited by H. Sheils. Oxford University Press, 1963.
Culture Succession in South Eastern Australia from Late Pleistocene to the Present. Norman B. Tindale in *Records of the South Australian Museum*, Vol. 13, No. 1, pages 1–49; April 30, 1957.
The Stone Age of Australia. D. J. Mulvaney in *Proceedings of the Prehistoric Society*, New Series, Vol. 27, pages 56–107; December, 1961.

26. Homo Erectus

The Author

WILLIAM W. HOWELLS is professor of anthropology at Harvard University. (For further information, see the biographical note 21, for "The Distribution of Man.") Howells wishes to acknowledge assistance in the preparation of his article from Andor Thoma, F. Fülep and L. Vértes of Hungary, who supplied him with information, a cast and a photograph of the Vértesszöllös find.

Bibliography

Mankind in the Making. William W. Howells. Doubleday & Company, Inc., revised edition in press.

The Nomenclature of the Hominidae. Bernard G. Campbell. Occasional Paper No. 22, Royal Anthropological Institute of Great Britain and Ireland, 1965.

The Taxonomic Evolution of Fossil Hominids. Ernst Mayr in *Classification and Human Evolution,* edited by Sherwood L. Washburn. Viking Fund Publications in Anthropology, No. 37, 1963.

27. The Early Relatives of Man

The Author

ELWYN L. SIMONS is associate professor of geology at Yale University and curator of vertebrate paleontology at Yale's Peabody Museum of Natural History. Simons received a B.A. in biology from Rice University in 1953 and a Ph.D. in vertebrate paleontology from Princeton University in 1956. He went to England in 1956 as a Marshall scholar to study with Joseph Weiner (the exposer of the Piltdown fraud) and Sir Wilfred Le Gros Clark at the University of Oxford, where he received a D.Phil. in 1959 for his dissertation on primate evolution. After short teaching stints at Princeton and the University of Pennsylvania, Simons joined the Yale faculty in 1960. He has since led six teaching and research expeditions for Yale, three to Wyoming and three to Egypt.

Bibliography

A Critical Reappraisal of Tertiary Primates. Elwyn L. Simons in *Evolutionary and Genetic Biology of Primates: Vol. I.* Academic Press, 1963.

The Miocene Hominoidea of East Africa. W. E. Le Gros Clark and L. S. B. Leakey in *Fossil Mammals of Africa; No. I, British Museum (Natural History),* pages 1–115; 1951.

A review of the Middle and Upper Eocene Primates of North America. C. Lewis Gazin in *Smithsonian Miscellaneous Collections,* Vol. 136, No. 1, pages 1–112; July, 1958.

Some Fallacies in the Study of Hominid Phylogeny. Elwyn L. Simons in *Science,* Vol. 141, No. 3584, pages 879–889; September, 1963.

Further Readings for Part IV

Baker, Paul T., and J. S. Weiner, eds. *The Biology of Human Adaptability.* Oxford, England, Clarendon Press, 1966.

Coon, Carleton S. *The Origin of Races.* New York, Alfred A. Knopf, 1963.

Goldschmidt, Elisabeth, ed. *The Genetics of Migrant and Isolate Populations.* New York, Williams & Wilkins Company, 1963.

Harrison, G. A. 1961. *Genetical Variation in Human Populations.* New York, Pergamon Press, 1961.

Hooton, E. A. *Up From the Ape.* New York, Macmillan Company, 1946.

Mayr, Ernst. 1963. *Animal Species and Evolution.* Cambridge, Harvard University Press, 1963.

Mourant, A. E. *The Distribution of the Human Blood Groups.* Springfield, Illinois, Charles C. Thomas, 1954.

Neel, J. V., M. W. Shaw, and W. J. Schull, eds. *Genetics and the Epidemiology of Chronic Diseases.* Public Health Service Publication No. 1163. Washington, D.C., 1965.

Index

National Research Council dietary standards, 135

A Naturalist's Voyage Around the World, 31

Natural selection: in ladybird beetle, 14; in *Drosophila,* 15; history of the term, 24; discussed by Blyth, 25; study of, in fossils, 208; in racial skin color, 218–219; in facial features, 218–219; operation in formation of races, 215–223 *passim;* in racial picture of future, 223; mentioned, 30, 33, 139, 140, 141–143 *passim,* 147, 150, 175, 200, 203, 204

Neanderthal man: brain compared to *Homo sapiens,* 177; link in evolution, 210; mentioned, 3, 4, 209, 216, 266, 271

Needham, A. E., 96

Needham, Joseph, 91

Negative-feedback system in bone repair, 108, 111, 115

Neolithic period, development of agriculture in, 221–222, 246

Neolithic revolution, 246, 254

Nirenberg, Marshall W., 82, 89

Nonprogressionism, 24

Notharctus, 276

Nucleoli, 67, 69, 79, 80

Nucleolus organizers, 79

Nucleotide, 82

Nucleus: central, 61, 62; membrane, 67; sap, 69; function, 69–70

Oakley, Kenneth, 270

Ochoa, Severo, 82, 89

Olduvai Gorge, 116, 125, 126, 155, 161, 171, 173, 175, 211, 268

Oligocene epoch, 5, 124

Oligopithecus, 278, 280

Oocyte, 73–81 *passim*

Ordovician period, mass extinction in, 39

Organelles, cellular, 61, 62, 66

Organizer of embryo, 91, 92. *See also* Blastopore; Differentiation

The Origin of Species, 16, 19, 22, 26, 32–33, 215

Oreopithecus, 283

Osteoblasts, 108, 113, 114

Osteoclasts, 108, 113, 114

Osteocytes, 114

Osteodontokeratic culture, 161

Osteogenesis, 108

Osteons: used in relative dating, 54; mentioned, 113

Owen, Richard, 24, 27

Pachytene stage, 74

Palade, George E., 67

Palaeanthropus, 266. *see also* Mauer mandible

Paleocene epoch, 159

Paleolithic period: entrance of *Homo sapiens* in, 216; cultural impoverishment of aboriginal Australians, 256; mentioned, 161

Paleontology, 147

Paleozoic era, geographic changes in, 50

Palo Blanco phase. *See* Tehuacán

Pearson, K., 52

Peking man, 171, 215, 266, 267, 268

Pelvis: role of, in striding, 116; importance of, in locomotion, 117–118; changes in iliac portions of, 122

Permian period, mass extinction in, 39, 49

Piezoelectric effect, 54, 108–115

Pilgrim, G. E., 278, 284

Piltdown fraud, 270

Pincus, Gregory, 77

Pirrian culture. *See* Devon Downs site

Pirri, 257, 259, 261, 267

Pithecanthropus, 3, 211, 264, 267

Pitjandjara tribe, gene frequency in, 200

Plasmagenes, 94

Plastic range, 111

Pleistocene epoch: date of, 4; Lyell names, 6; migrations in, 41, 255; mass extinction in, 42, 50; geographic changes in, 50; *Australopithecus* in, 124; man-apes in, 173; men of, 175, 179; evolution of mother-child relationship, 180; colonization of Australia in, 263; evidence for subdividing, 267; mentioned, 161, 215

Plesiadapis, 274–276

Pliocene epoch: Lyell names, 6; migrations in, 41; immediate precursor of man in, 211; mentioned, 5

Pliopithecus, 281–282

P-n junction in bone, 111

Polar body, 75, 78, 79, 81

Polge, Christopher, 78

Polymorphism: in *Drosophila,* 14; in ladybird beetle, 14

Polynucleotide chain, 82

Polypeptide chain, 82, 84, 87, 89

Pondaungia cotteri, 278, 284

Population: units of, 206; problems of, 234–245

Population gene pool of genetic variability, 139–140

Porter, K. R., 67

Povlovsky, O., 141, 142

Preoccupancy, principle of, 24

Principles of Geology, 21–26 *passim*

Proconsul africanus, 121, 124, 158, 282–283, 284

Progesterone, 75

Progression as an evolutional concept, 7, 19, 23, 24

Prophase, 73

Propliopithecus, 280

Prosimii, 273

Protein: regulation of synthesis, 62; synthesis of, 70; sequences of, 87

Protoadapis, 276

Puebla excavation, 249

Purrón culture. *See* Tehuacán

Pygmies, sociology of, 224–234

Queray deposits, 276

Quaternary period, 41

Race: genetic definition of, 15–16; effect of geographic isolation on, 16; formation of differences among, 200; levels of abstraction of term, 206; historical explanation of, 215; natural selection in formation of, 215–223 *passim;* causes of development of, 216; development of skin color differences, 218–219; development of facial feature differences, 218–219; radiation of, 221; later migrations of, 222–223

Races: A Study of the Problems of Race Formation in Man, 204

Rachel Jens curve, 132

Radiation, ionizing, 145–154 *passim*

Ramapithecus, 211, 283, 284

Recombination in T4 virus chromosomes, 82

Relative biological distance, 207

Reproduction, differential, 2

Reproductive variability. *See* Reproduction, differential

Rete mirabile, 164

Rhodesian Man: relations of *Homo erectus* to, 271; mentioned, 215, 216, 266

Ribosomes, 67, 70

Richter, Curt P., 177

Rift Valley, 124

RNA: and protein synthesis, 62, 67; synthesis of, 80; mentioned, 52, 79, 82, 95

RNA, messenger, 70, 80, 82, 87

Robinson, John T., 268

Russell, D. E., 274

Sacks, Milton S., 200

Sahlins, Marshall D., 180

Salmi, M. J., 49

San Marcos cave. *See* Tehuacán

Santa María culture. *See* Tehuacán

Sapir, Edward, 183

Savage, Donald E., 280

Schiller, Paul, 193

Schindewolf, Otto, 39, 41

Schleicher, August, 264

Schleiden, Matthias Jakob, 51, 52, 61

Schwann, Theodor, 51, 52, 61

Scrapers, 259–260

SD effect, 149

Sebum, 104

Sedgwick, Adam, 22

Seelands site, 261

Segregation ratio, 148

Shamos, Morris H., 111